Lecture Notes in Computer Science   8164

Commenced Publication in 1973
Founding and Former Series Editors:
Gerhard Goos, Juris Hartmanis, and Jan van Leeuwen

Editorial Board

Ernie Cohen   Andrey Rybalchenko (Eds.)

Verified Software: Theories, Tools, Experiments

5th International Conference, VSTTE 2013
Menlo Park, CA, USA, May 17-19, 2013
Revised Selected Papers

 Springer

Volume Editors

Ernie Cohen
107 Hewett Road, Wyncote, PA 19095, USA
E-mail: erniecohen1@gmail.com

Andrey Rybalchenko
Microsoft Research Cambridge
21 Station Road, CB1 2FB Cambridge, UK
E-mail: rybal@microsoft.com
and
Technical University Munich
Boltzmannstr. 3, 85748 Munich, Germany
E-mail: rybal@in.tum.de

ISSN 0302-9743   e-ISSN 1611-3349
ISBN 978-3-642-54107-0   e-ISBN 978-3-642-54108-7
DOI 10.1007/978-3-642-54108-7
Springer Heidelberg New York Dordrecht London

Library of Congress Control Number: 2013957812

CR Subject Classification (1998): D.2.4, D.2, F.3, D.3, D.1, C.2, F.4

LNCS Sublibrary: SL 2 – Programming and Software Engineering

Typesetting: Camera-ready by author, data conversion by Scientific Publishing Services, Chennai, India

Printed on acid-free paper

Springer is part of Springer Science+Business Media (www.springer.com)

Preface

This volume contains the papers presented at the 5th International Conference on Verified Software: Theories, Tool and Experiments (VSTTE), which was held in Menlo Park, USA, during May 17–19, 2013. Historically, the conference originated from the Verified Software Initiative (VSI), a cooperative, international initiative directed at the scientific challenges of large-scale software verification. The inaugral VSTTE conference was held at ETH Zurich in October 2005. Starting in 2008, the conference became a biennial event, VSTTE 2008 was held in Toronto, VSTTE 2010 was held in Edinburgh, and VSTTE 2012 was held in Philadelphia, which changed this year.

The goal of the VSTTE conference is to advance the state of the art through the interaction of theory development, tool evolution, and experimental validation.

VSTTE 2013 is especially interested in submissions describing large-scale verification efforts that involve collaboration, theory unification, tool integration, and formalized domain knowledge. We welcome papers describing novel experiments and case studies evaluating verification techniques and technologies. Topics of interest include education, requirements modeling, specification languages, specification/verification case-studies, formal calculi, software design methods, automatic code generation, refinement methodologies, compositional analysis, verification tools (e.g., static analysis, dynamic analysis, model checking, theorem proving, satisfiability), tool integration, benchmarks, challenge problems, and integrated verification environments.

There were 35 submissions. Each submission was reviewed by at least two, and on average 2.7, Program Committee members. The committee decided to accept 17 papers. The program also includes three invited talks, by Alex Aiken (Stanford University), Nikhil Swamy (Microsoft Research), and Andre Platzer (CMU), as well as an invited tutorial by Sandrine Blazy (University of Rennes 1).

We would like to thank the invited speakers, all submitting authors, the Steering Committee, the conference chair, the publicity chair, the external reviewers, and especially the Program Committee, who put a lot of hard work into reviewing and selecting the papers that appear in this volume.

We thank Andrei Voronkov for the access to EasyChair and Springer.

VSTTE 2013 was supported in part by NSF funding CISE award 1033105.

November 2013

Ernie Cohen
Andrey Rybalchenko

Organization

Program Committee

Josh Berdine	Microsoft Research
Ahmed Bouajjani	University of Paris 7, France
Marsha Chechik	Toronto University, Canada
Ernie Cohen	Microsoft
Jean-Christophe Filliatre	CNRS, LRI, Inria, France
Silvio Ghilardi	University of Milan, Italy
Aarti Gupta	NEC Labs
Arie Gurfinkel	CMU SEI
Jifeng He	East China Normal University, China
Andrew Ireland	Heriot-Watt University, UK
Ranjit Jhala	UC San Diego, USA
Cliff Jones	Newcastle University, UK
Rajeev Joshi	NASA JPL, USA
Gerwin Klein	NICTA, Australia
Daniel Kroening	Oxford University, UK
Gary Leavens	University of Central Florida, USA
Xavier Leroy	Inria, France
Zhiming Liu	UNI-IIST
Pete Manolios	Northeastern University
Tiziana Margaria	University of Potsdam, Germany
David Monniaux	VERIMAG, France
Peter Mueller	ETHZ
David Naumann	Stevens Institute of Technology, USA
Aditya Nori	Microsoft Research
Peter O'Hearn	UCL, UK
Matthew Parkinson	Microsoft Research
Wolfgang Paul	University of Saarland, Germany
Andreas Podelski	University of Freiburg, Germany
Andrey Rybalchenko	TUM
Natarajan Shankar	SRI International, Singapore
Zhong Shao	Yale University, USA
Willem Visser	University of Stellenbosch, South Africa
Thomas Wies	NYU
Jim Woodcock	University of York, UK
Kwangkeun Yi	Seoul National University, South Korea
Pamela Zave	AT&T Labs
Lenore Zuck	University of Illinois at Chicago, USA

Additional Reviewers

Chamarthi, Harsh Raju

Chen, Zhenbang

Christ, Jürgen

David, Cristina

Faber, Johannes

Joshi, Saurabh

Majumdar, Rupak

Nipkow, Tobias

Papavasileiou, Vasilis

Popeea, Corneliu

Qamar, Nafees

Tautschnig, Michael

Invited Talks

Using Learning Techniques in Invariant Inference

Alex Aiken

Stanford University

Abstract. Arguably the hardest problem in automatic program verification is designing appropriate techniques for discovering loop invariants (or, more generally, recursive procedures). Certainly, if invariants are known, the rest of the verification problem becomes easier. This talk presents a family of invariant inference techniques based on using test cases to generate an underapproximation of program behavior and then using learning algorithms to generalize the underapproximation to an invariant. These techniques are simpler, much more efficient, and appear to be more robust than previous approaches to the problem. If time permits, some open problems will also be discussed.

F*: Certified Correctness for Higher-Order Stateful Programs

Nikhil Swamy

Microsoft Research

Abstract. Abstract: F* is an ML-like programming language being developed at Microsoft Research. It has a type system based on dependent types and a typechecker that makes use of an SMT solver to discharge proof obligations. The type system is expressive enough to express functional correctness properties of typical, higher-order stateful programs.

We have used F* in a variety of settings, including in the verification of security protocol implementations; as a source language for secure web-browser extensions; as an intermediate verification language for JavaScript code; to verify the correctness of compilers; as a relational logic for probabilistic programs; and as a proof assistant in which to carry out programming language metatheory. We have also used F* to program the core typechecker of F* itself and have verified that it is correct. By bootstrapping this process using the Coq proof assistant, we obtain a theorem that guarantees the existence of a proof certificate for typechecked programs.

I will present a brief overview of the F* project, drawing on the examples just mentioned to illustrate the features of the F* language and certification system.

For more about F*, visit `http://research.microsoft.com/fstar`.

How to Explain Cyber-Physical Systems to Your Verifier

André Platzer

CMU

Abstract. Despite the theoretical undecidability of program verification, practical verification tools have made impressive advances. How can we take verification to the next level and use it to verify programs in cyber-physical systems (CPSs), which combine computer programs with the dynamics of physical processes. Cars, aircraft, and robots are prime examples where this matters, because they move physically in space in a way that is determined by discrete computerized control algorithms. Because of their direct impact on humans, verification for CPSs is even more important than it already is for programs.

This talk describes how formal verification can be lifted to one of the most prominent models of CPS called hybrid systems, i.e. systems with interacting discrete and continuous dynamics. It presents the theoretical and practical foundations of hybrid systems verification. The talk shows a systematic approach that is based on differential dynamic logic comes with a compositional proof technique for hybrid systems and differential equations. This approach is implemented in the verification tool KeYmaera and has been used successfully for verifying properties of aircraft, railway, car control, autonomous robotics, and surgical robotics applications.

A Tutorial on the CompCert Verified Compiler

Sandrine Blazy

University of Rennes 1

Abstract. Compilers are complicated pieces of software that sometimes contain bugs causing wrong executable code to be silently generated from correct source programs. In turn, this possibility of compiler-introduced bugs diminishes the assurance that can be obtained by applying formal methods to source code. This talk gives an overview of the CompCert project: an ongoing experiment in developing and formally proving correct a realistic, moderately-optimizing compiler from a large subset of C to popular assembly languages. The correctness proof, mechanized using the Coq proof assistant, establishes that the generated assembly code behaves exactly as prescribed by the semantic of the C source, eliminating all possibilities of compiler-introduced bugs and generating unprecedented confidence in this compiler. For more about CompCert, please visit `http://compcert.inria.fr`.

Table of Contents

Classifying and Solving Horn Clauses for Verification

Philipp Rümmer[1], Hossein Hojjat[2], and Viktor Kuncak[2]

[1] Uppsala University, Sweden
[2] Swiss Federal Institute of Technology Lausanne (EPFL)

Abstract. As a promising direction to overcome difficulties of verification, re-searchers have recently proposed the use of Horn constraints as intermediate representation. Horn constraints are related to Craig interpolation, which is one of the main techniques used to construct and refine abstractions in verification, and to synthesise inductive loop invariants. We give a classification of the different forms of Craig interpolation problems found in literature, and show that all of them correspond to natural fragments of (recursion-free) Horn constraints. For a logic that has the binary interpolation property, all of these problems are solvable, but have different complexity. In addition to presenting the theoretical classification and solvability results, we present a publicly available collection of benchmarks to evaluate solvers for Horn constraints, categorized according to our classification. The benchmarks are derived from real-world verification problems. The behavior with our tools as well as with Z3 prover indicates the importance of Horn clause solving as distinct from the general problem of solving quantified constraints by quantifier instantiation.

1 Introduction

Predicate abstraction [14] has emerged as a prominent and effective way for model checking software systems. A key ingredient in predicate abstraction is analyzing the spurious counter-examples to refine abstractions [4]. The refinement problem saw a significant progress when Craig interpolants extracted from unsatisfiability proofs were used as relevant predicates [20]. While interpolation has enjoyed a significant progress for various logical constraints [7–9, 24], there have been substantial proposals for more general forms of interpolation [1, 19, 24].

As a promising direction to extend the reach of automated verification methods to programs with procedures, and concurrent programs, among others, recently the use of Horn constraints as intermediate representation has been proposed [15, 16, 28]. This paper examines the relationship between various forms of Craig interpolation and syntactically defined fragments of recursion-free Horn clauses. We systematically examine binary interpolation, inductive interpolant sequences, tree interpolants, restricted DAG interpolants, and disjunctive interpolants, and show the recursion-free Horn clause problems to which they correspond. We present algorithms for solving each of these classes of problems by reduction to elementary interpolation problems. We also give a taxonomy of the various interpolation problems, and the corresponding systems of Horn clauses, in terms of their computational complexity.

E. Cohen and A. Rybalchenko (Eds.): VSTTE 2013, LNCS 8164, pp. 1–21, 2014.

The contributions of the paper are:

- a systematic study of relevant recursion-free Horn fragments, their relationship to forms of Craig interpolation, and their computational complexity;
- a library of recursion-free Horn problems, designed for benchmarking Horn solvers and interpolation engines;
- the generalisation of our results from recursion-free Horn clauses to general well-founded constraints, i.e., to constraints without infinite resolution proofs.

Organisation. Related work is surveyed in Sect. 2, following in Sect. 3 by an example of (recursive) Horn clauses. Sect. 4 formally introduces the concept of Horn clauses. Sect. 5 investigates the relationship between Horn fragments and Craig interpolation, and Sect. 6 their respective computational complexity. Sect. 7 presents our library of Horn benchmarks. Sect. 8 generalises from Horn clauses to well-founded clauses.

2   Related Work

Horn clauses have been used to represent analysis tasks in the context of constraint programming for a long time, for instance [29]. The authors of [16] propose Horn clauses for verification of multi-threaded programs. The underlying procedure for solving sets of recursion-free Horn clauses, over the combined theory of linear integer arithmetic and uninterpreted functions, was presented in [17], and a solver in [18]. A range of further applications of Horn clauses, including inter-procedural model checking, was given in [15]. Horn clauses are also proposed as intermediate/exchange format for verification problems in [6], and are natively supported by the SMT solver Z3 [11].

There is a long line of research on **Craig interpolation** methods, and generalised forms of interpolation, tailored to verification. For an overview of interpolation in the presence of theories, we refer the reader to [8, 9]. Binary Craig interpolation for implications $A \rightarrow C$ goes back to [10], was carried over to conjunctions $A \wedge B$ in [25], and generalised to inductive sequences of interpolants in [20, 27]. The concept of tree interpolation, strictly generalising inductive sequences of interpolants, is presented in the documentation of the interpolation engine iZ3 [24]; the computation of tree interpolants by computing a sequence of binary interpolants is also described in [19]. Restricted DAG interpolants [1] and disjunctive interpolants [30] are further generalisations of inductive sequences of interpolants, designed to enable the simultaneous analysis of multiple counterexamples or program paths.

The use of Craig interpolation for solving Horn clauses is discussed in [28], concentrating on the case of tree interpolation. Our paper extends this work by giving a systematic study of the relationship between different forms of Craig interpolation and Horn clauses, as well as general results about solvability and computational complexity, independent of any particular calculus used to perform interpolation.

Inter-procedural software model checking with interpolants has been an active area of research for the last decade. In the context of predicate abstraction, it has been discussed how well-scoped invariants can be inferred [20] in the presence of function calls. Based on the concept of Horn clauses, a predicate abstraction-based algorithm for bottom-up construction of function summaries was presented in [15]. Generalisations

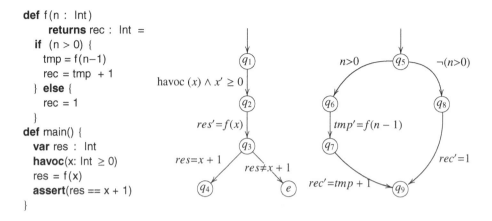

```
def f(n : Int)
    returns rec : Int =
    if (n > 0) {
        tmp = f(n−1)
        rec = tmp + 1
    } else {
        rec = 1
    }
def main() {
    var res : Int
    havoc(x: Int ≥ 0)
    res = f(x)
    assert(res == x + 1)
}
```

Fig. 1. A recursive program and its control flow graph (see Sect. 3)

(1)   r1(X, Res)   ← **true**
(2)   r2(X', Res)   ← r1(X, Res) ∧ X' ≥ 0
(3)   r3(X, Res')   ← r2(X, Res) ∧ rf(X, Res')
(4)   r4(X, Res)   ← r3(X, Res) ∧ Res = X + 1
(5)   **false**   ← r3(X, Res) ∧ Res ≠ X + 1

(6)   r5(N, Rec, Tmp)   ← **true**
(7)   r6(N, Rec, Tmp)   ← r5(N, Rec, Tmp) ∧ N > 0
(8)   r7(N, Rec, Tmp')   ← r6(N, Rec, Tmp) ∧ rf(N − 1, Tmp')
(9)   r8(N, Rec, Tmp)   ← r5(N, Rec, Tmp) ∧ N ≤ 0
(10) r9(N, Rec', Tmp)   ← r7(N, Rec, Tmp) ∧ Rec' = Tmp + 1
(11) r9(N, Rec', Tmp)   ← r8(N, Rec, Tmp) ∧ Rec' = 1
(12) rf (N, Rec)   ← r9(N, Rec, Tmp)

Fig. 2. The encoding of the program in Fig. 1 into a set of recursive Horn clauses

of the Impact algorithm [27] to programs with procedures are given in [19] (formulated using nested word automata) and [2]. Finally, function summaries generated using interpolants have also been used to speed up bounded model checking [31].

Several other tools handle procedures by increasingly inlining and performing under- and/or over-approximation [22, 32, 33], but without the use of interpolation techniques.

3   Example

We start with an example illustrating the use of Horn clauses to verify a recursive program. Fig. 1 shows an example of a recursive program, which is encoded as a set of (recursive) Horn constraints in Fig. 2. The encoding is done in such a way that the set of Horn constraints is satisfiable if and only if the program is safe, i.e., the assertion in function main cannot fail. We will use different subsets of the complete set of Horn constraints as examples throughout the paper.

$$r_1(x, res) \equiv true \qquad\qquad r_2(x, res) \equiv x \geq 0$$
$$r_3(x, res) \equiv res = x + 1 \qquad\qquad r_4(x, res) \equiv true$$
$$r_5(n, rec, tmp) \equiv true \qquad\qquad r_6(n, rec, tmp) \equiv n \geq 1$$
$$r_7(n, rec, tmp) \equiv n = tmp \qquad\qquad r_9(n, rec, tmp) \equiv rec = n + 1 \vee (n \leq 0 \wedge rec = 1)$$
$$r_8(n, rec, tmp) \equiv n \leq 0 \qquad\qquad r_f(n, rec) \equiv rec = n + 1 \vee (n \leq 0 \wedge rec = 1)$$

Fig. 3. Syntactic solution of the Horn clauses in Fig. 2

For translation to Horn clauses we assign an uninterpreted relation symbol ri to each state q_i of the control flow graph. The arguments of the relation symbol ri act as placeholders of the visible variables in the state q_i. The relation symbol rf corresponds to the summary of the function f. In the relation symbol rf we do not include the local variable tmp in the arguments since it is invisible from outside the function f. The first argument of rf is the input and the second one is the output. We do not dedicate any relation symbol to the error state e.

The initial states of the functions are not constrained at the beginning; they are just implied by *true*. The clause that has *false* as its head corresponds to the assertion in the program. In order to satisfy the assertion with the head *false*, the body of the clause should also be evaluated to *false*. We put the condition leading to error in the body of this clause to ensure the error condition is not happening. The rest of the clauses are one to one translation of the edges in the control flow graph.

For the edges with no function calls we merely relate the variables in the previous state to the variables in the next state using the transfer functions on the edges. For example, the clause (2) expresses that *res* is kept unchanged in the transition from q_1 to q_2 and the value of x is greater than or equal to 0 in q_2. For the edges with function call we should also take care of the passing arguments and the return values. For example, the clause (3) corresponds to the edge containing a function call from q_2 to q_3. This clause sets the value of res in the state q_3 to the return value of the function f. Note that the only clauses in this example that have more than one relation symbols in the body are the ones related to edges with function calls.

The solution of the obtained system of Horn clauses demonstrates the correctness of the program. In a solution each relation symbol is mapped to an expression over its arguments. If we replace the relation symbols in the clauses by the expressions in the solution we should obtain only valid clauses. In a system with a genuine path to error we cannot find any solution to the system since we have no way to satisfy the assertion clause. Fig. 3 gives one possible solution of the Horn clauses in terms of concrete formulae, found by our verification tool Eldarica.[1]

This paper discusses techniques to automatically construct solutions of Horn clauses. Although the Horn clauses encoding programs are typically recursive, it has been observed that the case of *recursion-free* Horn clauses is instrumental for constructing verification procedures operating on Horn clauses [15, 16, 28]. Sets of recursion-free

---

[1] http://lara.epfl.ch/w/eldarica

Horn clauses are usually extracted from recursive clauses by means of finite unwinding; examples are given in Sect. 5.3 and 5.5.

4 Formulae and Horn Clauses

Constraint languages. Throughout this paper, we assume that a first-order vocabulary of *interpreted symbols* has been fixed, consisting of a set $\mathcal{F}$ of fixed-arity function symbols, and a set $\mathcal{P}$ of fixed-arity predicate symbols. Interpretation of $\mathcal{F}$ and $\mathcal{P}$ is determined by a class S of structures (U, I) consisting of non-empty universe U, and a mapping I that assigns to each function in $\mathcal{F}$ a set-theoretic function over U, and to each predicate in $\mathcal{P}$ a set-theoretic relation over U. As a convention, we assume the presence of an equation symbol "=" in $\mathcal{P}$, with the usual interpretation. Given a countably infinite set X of variables, a *constraint language* is a set *Constr* of first-order formulae over $\mathcal{F}, \mathcal{P}, X$ For example, the language of quantifier-free Presburger arithmetic has $\mathcal{F} = \{+, -, 0, 1, 2, \ldots\}$ and $\mathcal{P} = \{=, \leq, |\})$.

A constraint is called *satisfiable* if it holds for some structure in S and some assignment of the variables X, otherwise *unsatisfiable*. We say that a set $\Gamma \subseteq Constr$ of constraints *entails* a constraint $\phi \in Constr$ if every structure and variable assignment that satisfies all constraints in Γ also satisfies ϕ; this is denoted by $\Gamma \models \phi$.

$fv(\phi)$ denotes the set of free variables in constraint ϕ. We write $\phi[x_1, \ldots, x_n]$ to state that a constraint contains (only) the free variables $x_1, \ldots, x_n$, and $\phi[t_1, \ldots, t_n]$ for the result of substituting the terms $t_1, \ldots, t_n$ for $x_1, \ldots, x_n$. Given a constraint ϕ containing the free variables $x_1, \ldots, x_n$, we write $Cl_\forall(\phi)$ for the *universal closure* $\forall x_1, \ldots, x_n.\phi$.

Craig interpolation is the main technique used to construct and refine abstractions in software model checking. A binary interpolation problem is a conjunction $A \wedge B$ of constraints. A *Craig interpolant* is a constraint I such that $A \models I$ and $B \models \neg I$, and such that $fv(I) \subseteq fv(A) \cap fv(B)$. The existence of an interpolant implies that $A \wedge B$ is unsatisfiable. We say that a constraint language has the *interpolation property* if also the opposite holds: whenever $A \wedge B$ is unsatisfiable, there is an interpolant I.

4.1 Horn Clauses

To define the concept of Horn clauses, we fix a set $\mathcal{R}$ of uninterpreted fixed-arity *relation symbols*, disjoint from $\mathcal{P}$ and $\mathcal{F}$. A *Horn clause* is a formula $C \wedge B_1 \wedge \cdots \wedge B_n \rightarrow H$ where

- C is a constraint over $\mathcal{F}, \mathcal{P}, X$;
- each B_i is an application $p(t_1, \ldots, t_k)$ of a relation symbol $p \in \mathcal{R}$ to first-order terms over $\mathcal{F}, X$;
- H is similarly either an application $p(t_1, \ldots, t_k)$ of $p \in \mathcal{R}$ to first-order terms, or is the constraint *false*.

H is called the *head* of the clause, $C \wedge B_1 \wedge \cdots \wedge B_n$ the *body*. In case $C = true$, we usually leave out C and just write $B_1 \wedge \cdots \wedge B_n \rightarrow H$. First-order variables (from X) in a clause are considered implicitly universally quantified; relation symbols represent set-theoretic relations over the universe U of a structure $(U, I) \in S$. Notions like (un)satisfiability and entailment generalise straightforwardly to formulae with relation symbols.

A *relation symbol assignment* is a mapping $sol : \mathcal{R} \to Constr$ that maps each n-ary relation symbol $p \in \mathcal{R}$ to a constraint $sol(p) = C_p[x_1, \ldots, x_n]$ with n free variables. The *instantiation* $sol(h)$ of a Horn clause h is defined by:

$$sol(C \wedge p_1(\bar{t}_1) \wedge \cdots \wedge p_n(\bar{t}_n) \to p(\bar{t})) = C \wedge sol(p_1)[\bar{t}_1] \wedge \cdots \wedge sol(p_n)[\bar{t}_n] \to sol(p)[\bar{t}]$$
$$sol(C \wedge p_1(\bar{t}_1) \wedge \cdots \wedge p_n(\bar{t}_n) \to false) = C \wedge sol(p_1)[\bar{t}_1] \wedge \cdots \wedge sol(p_n)[\bar{t}_n] \to false$$

Definition 1 (Solvability). *Let $\mathcal{HC}$ be a set of Horn clauses over relation symbols $\mathcal{R}$.*

1. *$\mathcal{HC}$ is called semantically solvable if for every structure $(U, I) \in S$ there is an interpretation of the relation symbols $\mathcal{R}$ as set-theoretic relations over U such the universally quantified closure $Cl_\forall(h)$ of every clause $h \in \mathcal{HC}$ holds in (U, I).*
2. *A $\mathcal{HC}$ is called syntactically solvable if there is a relation symbol assignment sol such that for every structure $(U, I) \in S$ and every clause $h \in \mathcal{HC}$ it is the case that $Cl_\forall(sol(h))$ is satisfied.*

Note that, in the special case when S contains only one structure, $S = \{(U, I)\}$, semantic solvability reduces to the existence of relations interpreting $\mathcal{R}$ that extend the structure (U, I) in such a way to make all clauses true. In other words, Horn clauses are solvable in a structure if and only if the extension of the theory of (U, I) by relation symbols $\mathcal{R}$ in the vocabulary and by given Horn clauses as axioms is consistent.

A set $\mathcal{HC}$ of Horn clauses induces a *dependence relation* $\to_{\mathcal{HC}}$ on $\mathcal{R}$, defining $p \to_{\mathcal{HC}} q$ if there is a Horn clause in $\mathcal{HC}$ that contains p in its head, and q in the body. The set $\mathcal{HC}$ is called *recursion-free* if $\to_{\mathcal{HC}}$ is acyclic, and *recursive* otherwise. In the next sections we study the solvability problem for recursion-free Horn clauses and then show how to use such results in general Horn clause verification systems.

Definition 2 (Normal Form). *A set $\mathcal{HC}$ of Horn clauses is in normal form [15] iff*

1. *every relation symbol has a unique, pairwise distinct vector of arguments,*
2. *every non-argument variable occurs in at most one clause.*

5   The Relationship between Craig Interpolation and Horn Clauses

It has become common to work with generalised forms of Craig interpolation, such as inductive sequences of interpolants, tree interpolants, and restricted DAG interpolants. We show that a variety of such interpolation approaches can be reduced to recursion-free Horn clauses. Recursion-free Horn clauses thus provide a general framework unifying and subsuming a number of earlier notions. As a side effect, we can formulate a general theorem about existence of the individual kinds of interpolants in Sect. 6, applicable to any constraint language with the (binary) interpolation property.

An overview of the relationship between specific forms of interpolation and specific fragments of recursions-free Horn clauses is given in Table 1, and will be explained in more detail in the rest of this section. Table 1 refers to the following fragments of recursion-free Horn clauses:

Table 1. Equivalence of interpolation problems and systems of Horn clauses

Form of interpolation	Fragment of Horn clauses
Binary interpolation [10, 25] $A \wedge B$	Pair of Horn clauses $A \rightarrow p(\bar{x})$, $B \wedge p(\bar{x}) \rightarrow false$ with $\{\bar{x}\} = fv(A) \cap fv(B)$
Inductive interpolant seq. [20, 27] $T_1 \wedge T_2 \wedge \cdots \wedge T_n$	Linear tree-like Horn clauses $T_1 \rightarrow p_1(\bar{x}_1)$, $p_1(\bar{x}_1) \wedge T_2 \rightarrow p_2(\bar{x}_2)$, ... with $\{\bar{x}_i\} = fv(T_1, \ldots, T_i) \cap fv(T_{i+1}, \ldots, T_n)$
Tree interpolants [19, 24]	Tree-like Horn clauses
Restricted DAG interpolants [1]	Linear Horn clauses
Disjunctive interpolants [30]	Body disjoint Horn clauses

Definition 3 (Horn clause fragments). *We say that a finite, recursion-free set $\mathcal{HC}$ of Horn clauses*

1. *is linear if the body of each Horn clause contains at most one relation symbol,*
2. *is body-disjoint if for each relation symbol p there is at most one clause containing p in its body; furthermore, every clause contains p at most once;*
3. *is head-disjoint if for each relation symbol p there is at most one clause containing p in its head;*
4. *is tree-like [17] if it is body-disjoint and head-disjoint.*

Theorem 1 (Interpolation and Horn clauses). *For each line of Table 1 it holds that:*

1. *an interpolation problem of the stated form can be polynomially reduced to (syntactically) solving a set of Horn clauses, in the stated fragment;*
2. *solving a set of Horn clauses (syntactically) in the stated fragment can be polynomially reduced to solving a sequence of interpolation problems of the stated form.*

5.1 Binary Craig Interpolants [10, 25]

The simplest form of Craig interpolation is the derivation of a constraint I such that $A \models I$ and $I \models \neg B$, and such that $fv(I) \subseteq fv(A) \cap fv(B)$. Such derivation is typically constructed by efficiently processing the proof of unsatisfiability of $A \wedge B$. To encode a binary interpolation problem into Horn clauses, we first determine the set $\bar{x} = fv(A) \cap fv(B)$ of variables that can possibly occur in the interpolant. We then pick a relation symbol p of arity $|\bar{x}|$, and define two Horn clauses expressing that $p(\bar{x})$ is an interpolant:

$$A \rightarrow p(\bar{x}), \qquad B \wedge p(\bar{x}) \rightarrow false$$

It is clear that every syntactic solution for the two Horn clauses corresponds to an interpolant of $A \wedge B$.

5.2 Inductive Sequences of Interpolants [20, 27]

Given an unsatisfiable conjunction $T_1 \wedge \ldots \wedge T_n$ (in practice, often corresponding to an infeasible path in a program), an *inductive sequence of interpolants* is a sequence $I_0, I_1, \ldots, I_n$ of formulae such that

1. $I_0 = true$, $I_n = false$,
2. for all $i \in \{1, \ldots, n\}$, the entailment $I_{i-1} \wedge T_i \models I_i$ holds, and
3. for all $i \in \{0, \ldots, n\}$, it is the case that $fv(I_i) \subseteq fv(T_1, \ldots, T_i) \cap fv(T_{i+1}, \ldots, T_n)$.

While inductive sequences can be computed by repeated computation of binary interpolants [20], more efficient solvers have been developed that derive a whole sequence of interpolants simultaneously [8, 9, 24].

Inductive Sequences as Linear Tree-Like Horn Clauses. An inductive sequence of interpolants can straightforwardly be encoded as a set of linear Horn clauses, by introducing a fresh relation symbol p_i for each interpolant I_i to be computed. The arguments of the relation symbols have to be chosen reflecting condition 3 of the definition of interpolant sequences: for each $i \in \{0, \ldots, n\}$, we assume that $\bar{x}_i = fv(T_1, \ldots, T_i) \cap fv(T_{i+1}, \ldots, T_n)$ is the vector of variables that can occur in I_i. Conditions 1 and 2 are then represented by the following Horn clauses:

$$p_0(\bar{x}_0), \quad p_0(\bar{x}_0) \wedge T_1 \rightarrow p_1(\bar{x}_1), \quad p_1(\bar{x}_1) \wedge T_2 \rightarrow p_2(\bar{x}_2), \quad \ldots, \quad p_n(\bar{x}_n) \rightarrow \mathit{false}$$

Linear Tree-Like Horn Clauses as Inductive Sequences. Suppose $\mathcal{HC}$ is a finite, recursion-free, linear, and tree-like set of Horn clauses. We can solve the system of Horn clauses by computing one inductive sequence of interpolants for every connected component of the $\rightarrow_{\mathcal{HC}}$-graph. Since $\mathcal{HC}$ is recursion-free and body-disjoint, it can be normalised according to Def. 2 by renaming variables. A connected component represents the following Horn clauses.

$$C_1 \rightarrow p_1(\bar{x}_1), \quad C_2 \wedge p_1(\bar{x}_1) \rightarrow p_2(\bar{x}_2), \quad C_3 \wedge p_2(\bar{x}_2) \rightarrow p_3(\bar{x}_3), \quad \ldots, \quad C_n \wedge p_n(\bar{x}_n) \rightarrow \mathit{false} \, .$$

(If the first or the last of the clauses is missing, we assume that its constraint is *false*.) Any inductive sequence of interpolants for $C_1 \wedge C_2 \wedge C_3 \wedge \cdots \wedge C_n$ solves the clauses.

5.3 Tree Interpolants [19, 24]

Tree interpolants strictly generalise inductive sequences of interpolants, and are designed with the application of inter-procedural verification in mind: in this context, the tree structure of the interpolation problem corresponds to (a part of) the call graph of a program. Tree interpolation problems correspond to recursion-free tree-like sets of Horn clauses.

Suppose (V, E) is a finite directed tree, writing $E(v, w)$ to express that the node w is a direct child of v. Further, suppose $\phi : V \rightarrow \mathit{Constr}$ is a function that labels each node v of the tree with a formula $\phi(v)$. A labelling function $I : V \rightarrow \mathit{Constr}$ is called a *tree interpolant* (for (V, E) and ϕ) if the following properties hold:

1. for the root node $v_0 \in V$, it is the case that $I(v_0) = false$,
2. for any node $v \in V$, the following entailment holds:

$$\phi(v) \wedge \bigwedge_{(v,w) \in E} I(w) \models I(v),$$

3. for any node $v \in V$, every non-logical symbol (in our case: variable) in $I(v)$ occurs both in some formula $\phi(w)$ for w such that $E^*(v, w)$, and in some formula $\phi(w')$ for some w' such that $\neg E^*(v, w')$. (E^* is the reflexive transitive closure of E).

Since the case of tree interpolants is instructive for solving recursion-free sets of Horn clauses in general, we give a result about the existence of tree interpolants. The proof of the lemma computes tree interpolants by repeated derivation of binary interpolants; however, as for inductive sequences of interpolants, there are solvers that can compute all formulae of a tree interpolant simultaneously [16, 17, 24].

Lemma 1. *Suppose the constraint language Constr that has the interpolation property. Then a tree (V, E) with labelling function $\phi : V \to Constr$ has a tree interpolant I if and only if $\bigwedge_{v \in V} \phi(v)$ is unsatisfiable.*

Proof. "$\Rightarrow$" follows from the observation that every interpolant $I(v)$ is a consequence of the conjunction $\bigwedge_{(v,w) \in E^+} \phi(w)$.
"$\Leftarrow$": let $v_1, v_2, \ldots, v_n$ be an inverse topological ordering of the nodes in (V, E), i.e., an ordering such that $\forall i, j. (E(v_i, v_j) \Rightarrow i > j)$. We inductively construct a sequence of formulae $I_1, I_2, \ldots, I_n$, such that for every $i \in \{1, \ldots, n\}$ the following properties hold:

1. the following conjunction is unsatisfiable:

$$\bigwedge \{I_k \mid k \leq i, \ \forall j. (E(v_j, v_k) \Rightarrow j > i)\} \wedge \left(\phi(v_{i+1}) \wedge \phi(v_{i+2}) \wedge \cdots \wedge \phi(v_n)\right) \quad (1)$$

2. the following entailment holds:

$$\phi(v_i) \wedge \bigwedge_{(v_i, v_j) \in E} I_j \models I_i$$

3. every non-logical symbol in I_i occurs both in a formula $\phi(w)$ with $E^*(v_i, w)$, and in a formula $\phi(w')$ with $\neg E^*(v_i, w')$.

Assume that the formulae $I_1, I_2, \ldots, I_i$ have been constructed, for $i \in \{0, \ldots, n-1\}$. We then derive the next interpolant I_{i+1} by solving the binary interpolation problem

$$\left(\phi(v_{i+1}) \wedge \bigwedge_{E(v_{i+1}, v_j)} I_j\right) \wedge$$

$$\left(\bigwedge \{I_k \mid k \leq i, \ \forall j. (E(v_j, v_k) \Rightarrow j > i+1)\} \wedge \phi(v_{i+2}) \wedge \cdots \wedge \phi(v_n)\right) \quad (2)$$

That is, we construct I_{i+1} so that the following entailments hold:

$$\phi(v_{i+1}) \wedge \bigwedge_{E(v_{i+1}, v_j)} I_j \models I_{i+1},$$

$$\bigwedge \{I_k \mid k \leq i, \ \forall j. (E(v_j, v_k) \Rightarrow j > i+1)\} \wedge \phi(v_{i+2}) \wedge \cdots \wedge \phi(v_n) \models \neg I_{i+1}$$

Furthermore, I_{i+1} only contains non-logical symbols that are common to the left and the right side of the conjunction.

Note that (2) is equivalent to (1), therefore unsatisfiable, and a well-formed interpolation problem. It is also easy to see that the properties 1–3 hold for I_{i+1}. Also, we can easily verify that the labelling function $I : v_i \mapsto I_i$ is a solution for the tree interpolation problem defined by (V, E) and ϕ. □

Tree Interpolation as Tree-Like Horn Clauses. The encoding of a tree interpolation problem as a tree-like set of Horn clauses is very similar to the encoding for inductive sequences of interpolants. We introduce a fresh relation symbol p_v for each node $v \in V$ of a tree interpolation problem $(V, E), \phi$, assuming that for each $v \in V$ the vector $\bar{x}_v = \bigcup_{E^*(v,w)} fv(\phi(w)) \cap \bigcup_{\neg E^*(v,w)} fv(\phi(w))$ represents the set of variables that can occur in the interpolant $I(v)$. The interpolation problem is then represented by the following clauses:

$$p_0(\bar{x}_0) \rightarrow false, \quad \left\{ \phi(v) \wedge \bigwedge_{(v,w) \in E} p_w(\bar{x}_w) \rightarrow p_v(\bar{x}_v) \right\}_{v \in V}$$

Tree-Like Horn Clauses as Tree Interpolation. Suppose $\mathcal{HC}$ is a finite, recursion-free, and tree-like set of Horn clauses. We can solve the system of Horn clauses by computing a tree interpolant for every connected component of the $\rightarrow_{\mathcal{HC}}$-graph. As before, we first normalise the Horn clauses according to Def. 2. The interpolation graph (V, E) is then defined by choosing the set $V = \mathcal{R} \cup \{false\}$ of relation symbols as nodes, and the child relation $E(p, q)$ to hold whenever p occurs as head, and q within the body of a clause. The labelling function ϕ is defined by $\phi(p) = C$ whenever there is a clause with head symbol p and constraint C, and $\phi(p) = false$ if p does not occur as head of any clause.

Example 1. We consider a subset of the Horn clauses given in Fig. 2:

(1) r1(X, Res)   ← **true**
(2) r2(X', Res)   ← r1(X, Res) ∧ X' ≥ 0
(3) r3(X, Res')   ← r2(X, Res) ∧ rf(X, Res')
(5) **false**   ← r3(X, Res) ∧ Res ≠ X + 1
(6) r5(N, Rec, Tmp) ← **true**
(9) r8(N, Rec, Tmp) ← r5(N, Rec, Tmp) ∧ N ≤ 0
(11) r9(N, Rec', Tmp) ← r8(N, Rec, Tmp) ∧ Rec' = 1
(12) rf (N, Rec)   ← r9(N, Rec, Tmp)

Note that this recursion-free subset of the clauses is body-disjoint and head-disjoint, and thus tree-like. Since the complete set of clauses in Fig. 2 is solvable, also any subset is; in order to compute a (syntactic) solution of the clauses, we set up the corresponding tree interpolation problem. Fig. 4 shows the tree with the labelling ϕ to be interpolated (in grey), as well as the head literals of the clauses generating the nodes of the tree. A tree interpolant solving the interpolation problem is given in Fig. 5. The tree interpolant can be mapped to a solution of the original tree-like Horn, for instance we set $r_8(n_8, rec_8, tmp_8) = (n_8 \leq 0)$ and $r_9(n_9, rec_9, tmp_9) = (n_9 \leq -1 \vee (rec_9 = 1 \wedge n_9 = 0))$.

Symmetric Interpolants. A special case of tree interpolants, *symmetric interpolants,* was introduced in [26]. Symmetric interpolants are equivalent to tree interpolants with

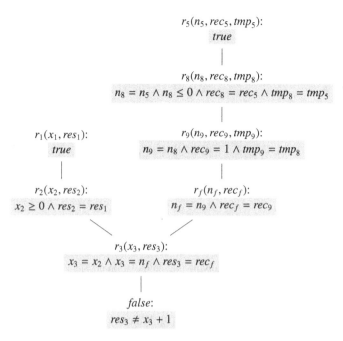

Fig. 4. Tree interpolation problem for the clauses in Example 1

a flat tree structure (V, E), i.e., $V = \{root, v_1, \ldots, v_n\}$, where the nodes $v_1, \ldots, v_n$ are the direct children of *root*.

5.4 Restricted (and Unrestricted) DAG Interpolants [1]

Restricted DAG interpolants are a further generalisation of inductive sequence of interpolants, introduced for the purpose of reasoning about multiple paths in a program simultaneously [1]. Suppose (V, E, en, ex) is a finite connected DAG with entry node $en \in V$ and exit node $ex \in V$, further $\mathcal{L}_E : E \to Constr$ a labelling of edges with constraints, and $\mathcal{L}_V : V \to Constr$ a labelling of vertices. A *restricted DAG interpolant* is a mapping $I : V \to Constr$ with

1. $I(en) = true$, $I(ex) = false$,
2. for all $(v, w) \in E$ the entailment $I(v) \wedge \mathcal{L}_V(v) \wedge \mathcal{L}_E(v, w) \models I(w) \wedge \mathcal{L}_V(w)$ holds, and
3. for all $v \in V$ it is the case that[2]

$$fv(I(v)) \subseteq \Big(\bigcup_{(a,v) \in E} fv(\mathcal{L}_E(a, v)) \Big) \cap \Big(\bigcup_{(v,a) \in E} fv(\mathcal{L}_E(v, a)) \Big).$$

---

[2] The definition of DAG interpolants in [1, Def. 4] implies that $fv(I(v)) = \emptyset$ for every interpolant $I(v), v \in V$, i.e., only trivial interpolants are allowed. We assume that this is a mistake in [1, Def. 4], and corrected the definition as shown here.

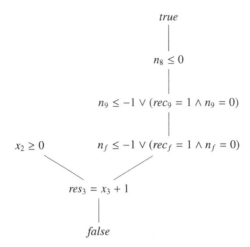

Fig. 5. Tree interpolant solving the interpolation problem in Fig. 4

The UFO verification system [3] is able to compute DAG interpolants, based on the interpolation functionality of MathSAT [9]. We can observe that DAG interpolants (despite their name) are incomparable in expressiveness to tree interpolation. This is because DAG interpolants correspond to *linear* Horn clauses, and might have shared relation symbol in bodies, while tree interpolants correspond to *possibly nonlinear tree-like* Horn clauses, but do not allow shared relation symbols in bodies.

Encoding of Restricted DAG Interpolants as Linear Horn Clauses. For every $v \in V$, let

$$\{\bar{x}_v\} = \left(\bigcup_{(a,v) \in E} fv(\mathcal{L}_E(a, v)) \right) \cap \left(\bigcup_{(v,a) \in E} fv(\mathcal{L}_E(v, a)) \right)$$

be the variables allowed in the interpolant to be computed for v, and p_v be a fresh relation symbol of arity $|\bar{x}_v|$. The interpolation problem is then defined by the following set of linear Horn clauses:

For each $(v, w) \in E$: $\mathcal{L}_V(v) \land \mathcal{L}_E(v, w) \land p_v(\bar{x}_v) \rightarrow p_w(\bar{x}_w)$,

$\mathcal{L}_V(v) \land \neg \mathcal{L}_V(w) \land \mathcal{L}_E(v, w) \land p_v(\bar{x}_v) \rightarrow false$,

For $en, ex \in V$: $true \rightarrow p_{en}(\bar{x}_{en})$, $p_{ex}(\bar{x}_{ex}) \rightarrow false$

Encoding of Linear Horn Clauses as DAG Interpolants. Suppose $\mathcal{HC}$ is a finite, recursion-free, and linear set of Horn clauses. We can solve the system of Horn clauses by computing a DAG interpolant for every connected component of the $\rightarrow_{\mathcal{HC}}$-graph. As in Sect. 5.2, we normalise Horn clauses according to Def. 2. We also assume that multiple clauses $C \land p(\bar{x}_p) \rightarrow q(\bar{x}_q)$ and $D \land p(\bar{x}_p) \rightarrow q(\bar{x}_q)$ with the same relation symbols are merged to $(C \lor D) \land p(\bar{x}_p) \rightarrow q(\bar{x}_q)$.

Let $\{p_1, \ldots, p_n\}$ be all relation symbols of one connected component. We then define the DAG interpolation problem $(V, E, en, ex), \mathcal{L}_E, \mathcal{L}_V$ by

- the vertices $V = \{p_1, \ldots, p_n\} \cup \{en, ex\}$, including two fresh nodes en, ex,
- the edge relation

$$
\begin{aligned}
E = \quad & \{(p, q) \mid \text{there is a clause } C \wedge p(\bar{x}_p) \rightarrow q(\bar{x}_q) \in \mathcal{HC}\} \\
& \cup \{(en, p) \mid \text{there is a clause } D \rightarrow p(\bar{x}_p) \in \mathcal{HC}\} \\
& \cup \{(p, ex) \mid \text{there is a clause } E \wedge p(\bar{x}_p) \rightarrow \textit{false} \in \mathcal{HC}\},
\end{aligned}
$$

- for each $(v, w) \in E$, the edge labelling

$$
\mathcal{L}_E(v, w) = \begin{cases}
C \wedge \bar{x}_v = \bar{x}_v \wedge \bar{x}_w = \bar{x}_w & \text{if } C \wedge v(\bar{x}_v) \rightarrow w(\bar{x}_w) \in \mathcal{HC} \\
D \wedge \bar{x}_w = \bar{x}_w & \text{if } v = en \text{ and } D \rightarrow w(\bar{x}_w) \in \mathcal{HC} \\
E \wedge \bar{x}_v = \bar{x}_v & \text{if } w = ex \text{ and } E \wedge v(\bar{x}_v) \rightarrow \textit{false} \in \mathcal{HC}
\end{cases}
$$

Note that the labels include equations like $\bar{x}_v = \bar{x}_v$ to ensure that the right variables are allowed to occur in interpolants.
- for each $v \in V$, the node labelling $\mathcal{L}_V(v) = \textit{true}$.

By checking the definition of DAG interpolants, it can be verified that every interpolant solving the problem $(V, E, en, ex), \mathcal{L}_E, \mathcal{L}_V$ is also a solution of the linear Horn clauses.

5.5   Disjunctive Interpolants [30]

Disjunctive interpolants were introduced in [30] as a generalisation of tree interpolants. Disjunctive interpolants resemble tree interpolants in the sense that the relationship of the components of an interpolant is defined by a tree; in contrast to tree interpolants, however, this tree is an and/or-tree: branching in the tree can represent either *conjunctions* or *disjunctions*. Disjunctive interpolants correspond to sets of body-disjoint Horn clauses; in this representation, and-branching is encoded by clauses with multiple body literals (like with tree interpolants), while or-branching is interpreted as multiple clauses sharing the same head symbol. For a detailed account on disjunctive interpolants, we refer the reader to [30].

The solution of body-disjoint Horn clauses can be computed by solving a sequence of tree-like sets of Horn clauses:

Lemma 2. *Let $\mathcal{HC}$ be a finite set of recursion-free body-disjoint Horn clauses. $\mathcal{HC}$ has a syntactic/semantic solution if and only if every maximum tree-like subset of $\mathcal{HC}$ has a syntactic/semantic solution.*

Proof. We outline direction "$\Leftarrow$" for syntactic solutions. Solving the tree-like subsets of $\mathcal{HC}$ yields, for each relation symbol $p \in \mathcal{R}$, a set SC_p of solution constraints. A global solution of $\mathcal{HC}$ can be constructed by forming a positive Boolean combination of the constraints in SC_p for each $p \in \mathcal{R}$.   □

Example 2. We consider a recursion-free unwinding of the Horn clauses in Fig. 2. To make the set of clauses body-disjoint, the clauses (6), (9), (11), (12) were duplicated, introducing primed copies of all relation symbols involved. The clauses are not head-disjoint, since (10) and (11) share the same head symbol:

(1)   r1(X, Res)   ← **true**
(2)   r2(X', Res)   ← r1(X, Res) ∧ X' ≥ 0
(3)   r3(X, Res')   ← r2(X, Res) ∧ rf(X, Res')
(5)   **false**   ← r3(X, Res) ∧ Res ≠ X + 1

(6)   r5(N, Rec, Tmp)   ← **true**
(7)   r6(N, Rec, Tmp)   ← r5'(N, Rec, Tmp) ∧ N > 0
(8)   r7(N, Rec, Tmp')   ← r6(N, Rec, Tmp) ∧ rf'(N − 1, Tmp')
(9)   r8(N, Rec, Tmp)   ← r5(N, Rec, Tmp) ∧ N ≤ 0
(10)   r9(N, Rec', Tmp)   ← r7(N, Rec, Tmp) ∧ Rec' = Tmp + 1
(11)   r9(N, Rec', Tmp)   ← r8(N, Rec, Tmp) ∧ Rec' = 1
(12)   rf (N, Rec)   ← r9(N, Rec, Tmp)

(6')   r5'(N, Rec, Tmp)   ← **true**
(6")   r5"(N, Rec, Tmp)   ← **true**
(9')   r8'(N, Rec, Tmp)   ← r5"(N, Rec, Tmp) ∧ N ≤ 0
(11')   r9'(N, Rec', Tmp)   ← r8'(N, Rec, Tmp) ∧ Rec' = 1
(12')   rf '(N, Rec)   ← r9'(N, Rec, Tmp)

There are two maximum tree-like subsets: T_1 = {(1), (2), (3), (5), (6), (9), (11), (12)}, and T_2 = {(1), (2), (3), (5), (7), (8), (10), (12), (6'), (6"), (9'), (11'), (12')}. The subset T_1 has been discussed in Example 1. In the same way, it is possible to construct a solution for T_2 by solving a tree interpolation problem. The two solutions can be combined to construct a solution of $T_1 \cup T_2$:

	T_1	T_2	$T_1 \cup T_2$
$r_1(x, r)$	true	true	true
$r_2(x, r)$	$x \geq 0$	true	$x \geq 0$
$r_3(x, r)$	$r = x + 1$	$r = x + 1$	$r = x + 1$
$r_5(n, c, t)$	true	true	true
$r_6(n, c, t)$	−	$n \geq 1$	$n \geq 1$
$r_7(n, c, t)$	−	$t = n$	$t = n$
$r_8(n, c, t)$	$n \leq 0$	−	$n \leq 0$
$r_9(n, c, t)$	$n \leq -1 \vee (c = 1 \wedge n = 0)$	$c = n + 1$	$n \leq -1 \vee c = n + 1$
$r_f(n, c)$	$n \leq -1 \vee (c = 1 \wedge n = 0)$	$c = n + 1$	$n \leq -1 \vee c = n + 1$
$r_5'(n, c, t)$	−	true	true
$r_5''(n, c, t)$	−	true	true
$r_8'(n, c, t)$	−	$n \leq 0$	$n \leq 0$
$r_9'(n, c, t)$	−	$n \leq -1 \vee (c = 1 \wedge n = 0)$	$n \leq -1 \vee (c = 1 \wedge n = 0)$
$r_f'(n, c, t)$	−	$n \leq -1 \vee (c = 1 \wedge n = 0)$	$n \leq -1 \vee (c = 1 \wedge n = 0)$

In particular, the disjunction of the two interpretations of $r_9(n, c, t)$ has to be used, in order to satisfy both (10) and (11) (similarly for $r_f(n, c)$). In contrast, the conjunction of the interpretations of $r_2(x, r)$ is needed to satisfy (3).

6   The Complexity of Recursion-Free Horn Clauses over Quantifier-Free Presburger Arithmetic

We give an overview of the considered fragments of recursion-free Horn clauses, and the corresponding interpolation problem, in Fig. 6. The diagram also shows the complexity of deciding (semantic or syntactic) solvability of a set of Horn clauses, for Horn clauses over the constraint language of quantifier-free Presburger arithmetic. Most of the complexity results occur in [30], but in addition we use the following two observations:

Lemma 3. *Semantic solvability of recursion-free linear Horn clauses over the constraint language of quantifier-free Presburger arithmetic is in co-NP.*

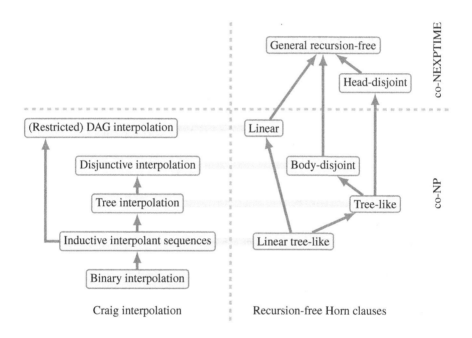

Fig. 6. Relationship between different forms of Craig interpolation, and different fragments of recursion-free Horn clauses. An arrow from A to B expresses that problem A is (strictly) subsumed by B. The complexity classes "co-NP" and "co-NEXPTIME" refer to the problem of checking solvability of Horn clauses over quantifier-free Presburger arithmetic.

Proof. A set $\mathcal{HC}$ of recursion-free linear Horn clauses is solvable if and only if the expansion $exp(\mathcal{HC})$ is unsatisfiable [30]. For linear clauses, $exp(\mathcal{HC})$ is a disjunction of (possibly) exponentially many formulae, each of which is linear in the size of $exp(\mathcal{HC})$. Consequently, satisfiability of $exp(\mathcal{HC})$ is in NP, and unsatisfiability in co-NP.   □

Lemma 4. *Semantic solvability of recursion-free head-disjoint Horn clauses over the constraint language of quantifier-free Presburger arithmetic is co-NEXPTIME-hard.*

Proof. The proof given in [30] for co-NEXPTIME-hardness of recursion-free Horn clauses over quantifier-free Presburger arithmetic can be adapted to only require head-disjoint clauses. This is because a single execution step of a non-deterministic Turing machine can be expressed as quantifier-free Presburger formula.   □

7 Towards a Library of Interpolation Benchmarks

In order to support the development of interpolation engines, Horn solvers, and verification systems, we have started to collect relevant benchmarks of recursion-free Horn clauses, categorised according to the classes determined in the previous sections.[3] The benchmarks have been extracted from runs of the model checker Eldarica [30], which processes systems of (usually recursive) Horn clauses by iteratively solving recursion-free unwindings, as outlined in Sect. 3. For each recursive verification problem, in this way a set of recursion-free systems of Horn clauses (of varying size) can be synthesised. The benchmarks can be used to evaluate both Horn solvers and interpolation engines, according to the correspondence in Fig. 6.

At the moment, our benchmarks are extracted from the verification problems in [30], and formulated over the constraint language of linear integer arithmetic; in the future, it is planned to also include other constraint languages, including rational arithmetic and the theory of arrays. The benchmarks are stored in SMT-LIB 2 format [5]. All of the benchmarks can be solved by Eldarica, and by the Horn solving engine in Z3 [21].

8 From Recursion-Free Horn Clauses to Well-Founded Clauses

It is natural to ask whether the considerations of the last sections also apply to clauses that are not Horn clauses (i.e., clauses that can contain multiple positive literals), provided the clauses are "recursion-free." Is it possible, like for Horn clauses, to derive solutions of recursion-free clauses by computing Craig interpolants?

To investigate the situation for clauses that are not Horn, we first have to generalise the concept of clauses being recursion-free: the definition provided in Sect. 4, formulated with the help of the dependence relation $\to_{\mathcal{HC}}$, only applies to Horn clauses. For non-Horn clauses, we instead choose to reason about the absence of infinite propositional resolution derivations. Because the proposed algorithms [30] for solving recursion-free sets of Horn clauses all make use of *exhaustive expansion* or *inlining,* i.e., the construction of all derivations for a given set of clauses, the requirement that no infinite derivations exist is fundamental.[4]

---

[3] http://lara.epfl.ch/w/horn-nonrec-benchmarks
  https://svn.sosy-lab.org/software/sv-benchmarks/
  trunk/clauses/LIA/Eldarica/

[4] We do not take subsumption between clauses, or loops in derivations into account. This means that a set of clauses might give rise to infinite derivations even if the set of derived clauses is finite. It is conceivable that notions of subsumption, or more generally the application of terminating saturation strategies [13], can be used to identify more general fragments of clauses for which syntactic solutions can effectively be computed. This line of research is future work.

Somewhat surprisingly, we observe that all sets of clauses without infinite derivations have the shape of Horn clauses, up to renaming of relation symbols. This means that procedures handling Horn clauses cover all situations in which we can hope to compute solutions with the help of Craig interpolation.

Since constraints and relation symbol arguments are irrelevant for this observation, the following results are entirely formulated on the level of propositional logic:

- a propositional *literal* is either a Boolean variable p, q, r (positive literals), or the negation $\neg p, \neg q, \neg r$ of a Boolean variable (negative literals).
- a propositional *clause* is a disjunction $p \lor \neg q \lor p$ of literals. The multiplicity of a literal is important, i.e., clauses could alternatively be represented as multi-sets of literals.
- a *Horn clause* is a clause that contains at most one positive literal.
- given a set $\mathcal{HC}$ of Horn clauses, we define the dependence relation $\to_{\mathcal{HC}}$ on Boolean variables by setting $p \to_{\mathcal{HC}} q$ if and only if there is a clause in $\mathcal{HC}$ in which p occurs positively, and q negatively (like in Sect. 4). The set $\mathcal{HC}$ is called *recursion-free* if $\to_{\mathcal{HC}}$ is acyclic.

We can now generalise the notion of a set of clauses being "recursion-free" to non-Horn clauses:

Definition 4. *A set C of propositional clauses is well-founded if there is no infinite sequence $c_0, c_1, c_2, c_3, \ldots$ of clauses with the property that*

- $c_0 \in C$ *is an input clause, and*
- *for each $i \geq 1$, the clause c_i is derived by means of binary resolution from c_{i-1} and an input clause, using the rule*

$$\frac{C \lor p \qquad D \lor \neg p}{C \lor D}.$$

Lemma 5. *A finite set $\mathcal{HC}$ of Horn clauses is well-founded if and only if it is recursion-free.*

Proof. "$\Leftarrow$" The acyclic dependence relation $\to_{\mathcal{HC}}$ induces a strict well-founded order $<$ on Boolean variables: $q \to_{\mathcal{HC}} p$ implies $p < q$. The order $<$ induces a well-founded order $\ll$ on Horn clauses:

$$(p \lor C) \ll (q \lor D) \quad \Leftrightarrow \quad p > q \text{ or } (p = q \text{ and } C <_{ms} D)$$
$$C \ll (q \lor D) \quad \Leftrightarrow \quad true$$
$$C \ll D \quad \Leftrightarrow \quad C <_{ms} D$$

where C, D only contain negative literals, and $<_{ms}$ is the (well-founded) multi-set extension of $<$ [12].

It is easy to see that a clause $C \vee D$ derived from two Horn clauses $C \vee p$ and $D \vee \neg p$ using the resolution rule is again Horn, and $(C \vee D) \ll (C \vee p)$ and $(C \vee D) \ll (D \vee \neg p)$. The well-foundedness of $\ll$ implies that any sequence of clauses as in Def. 4 is finite.

"$\Rightarrow$" If the dependence relation $\rightarrow_{HC}$ has a cycle, we can directly construct a non-terminating sequence $c_0, c_1, c_2, \ldots$ of clauses.   □

Definition 5 (Renamable-Horn [23]). *If A is a set of Boolean variables, and C is a set of clauses, then $r_A(C)$ is the result of replacing in C every literal whose Boolean variable is in A with its complement. C is called renamable-Horn if there is some set A of Boolean variables such that $r_A(C)$ is Horn.*

Theorem 2. *If a finite set C of clauses is well-founded, then it is renamable-Horn.*

Proof. Suppose C is formulated over the (finite) set $p_1, p_2, \ldots, p_n$ of Boolean variables. We construct a graph (V, E), with $V = \{p_1, p_2, \ldots, p_n, \neg p_1, \neg p_2, \ldots, \neg p_n\}$ being the set of all possible literals, and $(l, l') \in E$ if and only if there is a clause $\neg l \vee l' \vee C \in C$ (that means, a clause containing the literal l', and the literal l with reversed sign).[5]

The graph (V, E) is acyclic. To see this, suppose there is a cycle $l_1, l_2, \ldots, l_m, l_{m+1} = l_1$ in (V, E). Then there are clauses $c_1, c_2, \ldots, c_m \in C$ such that each c_i contains the literals $\neg l_i$ and l_{i+1}. We can then construct an infinite sequence $c_1 = d_0, d_1, d_2, \ldots$ of clauses, where each d_i (for $i > 1$) is obtained by resolving d_{i-1} with $c_{(i \bmod m)+1}$, contradicting the assumption that C is well-founded.

Since (V, E) is acyclic, there is a strict total order $<$ on V that is consistent with E, i.e., $(l, l') \in E$ implies $l < l'$.

Claim: if $p < \neg p$ for every Boolean variable $p \in \{p_1, p_2, \ldots, p_n\}$, then C is Horn.

Proof of the claim: suppose a non-Horn clause $p_i \vee p_j \vee C \in C$ exists (with $i \neq j$). Then $(\neg p_i, p_j) \in E$ and $(\neg p_j, p_i) \in E$, and therefore $\neg p_i < p_j$ and $\neg p_j < p_i$. Then also $\neg p_i < p_i$ or $\neg p_j < p_j$, contradicting the assumption that $p < \neg p$ for every Boolean variable p.

In general, choose $A = \{p_i \mid i \in \{1, \ldots, n\}, \neg p_i < p_i\}$, and consider the set $r_A(C)$ of clauses. The set $r_A(C)$ is Horn, since changing the sign of a Boolean variable $p \in A$ has the effect of swapping the nodes $p, \neg p$ in the graph (V, E). Therefore, the new graph (V, E') has to be compatible with a strict total order $<$ such that $p < \neg p$ for every Boolean variable p, satisfying the assumption of the claim above.   □

Example 3. We consider the following set of clauses:

$$C = \{\neg a \vee s,\ a \vee \neg p,\ p \vee \neg b,\ b \vee p \vee r,\ \neg p \vee q\}$$

By constructing all possible derivations, it can be shown that the set is well-founded. The graph (V, E), as constructed in the proof, is:

---

[5] This graph could equivalently be defined as the implication graph of the 2-sat problem introduced in [23], as a way of characterising whether a set of clauses is Horn.

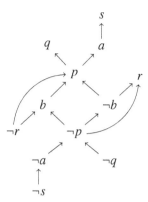

A strict total order that is compatible with the graph is:

$$\neg s < \neg q < \neg r < \neg a < \neg p < b < \neg b < r < p < q < a < s$$

From the order we can read off that we need to rename the variables $A = \{s, q, r, a, p\}$ in order to obtain a set of Horn clauses:

$$r_A(C) = \{a \vee \neg s,\ \neg a \vee p,\ \neg p \vee \neg b,\ b \vee \neg p \vee \neg r,\ p \vee \neg q\}$$

9   Conclusion

In recent years there has been a growing interest in more general forms of interpolation, organising formulae in non-linear structures such as trees, hyper-trees or directed acyclic graphs. In this paper we showed that many forms of interpolation can be defined as subclasses of recursion-free Horn clauses, provided a taxonomy of the various fragments, and investigated computational complexity. We believe that the results are valuable for application domains of Horn constraints, in particular in program verification and model checking.

References

1. Albarghouthi, A., Gurfinkel, A., Chechik, M.: Craig interpretation. In: Miné, A., Schmidt, D. (eds.) SAS 2012. LNCS, vol. 7460, pp. 300–316. Springer, Heidelberg (2012)
2. Albarghouthi, A., Gurfinkel, A., Chechik, M.: Whale: An interpolation-based algorithm for inter-procedural verification. In: Kuncak, V., Rybalchenko, A. (eds.) VMCAI 2012. LNCS, vol. 7148, pp. 39–55. Springer, Heidelberg (2012)
3. Albarghouthi, A., Li, Y., Gurfinkel, A., Chechik, M.: Ufo: A framework for abstraction- and interpolation-based software verification. In: Madhusudan, P., Seshia, S.A. (eds.) CAV 2012. LNCS, vol. 7358, pp. 672–678. Springer, Heidelberg (2012)
4. Ball, T., Podelski, A., Rajamani, S.K.: Relative completeness of abstraction refinement for software model checking. In: Katoen, J.-P., Stevens, P. (eds.) TACAS 2002. LNCS, vol. 2280, pp. 158–172. Springer, Heidelberg (2002)
5. Barrett, C., Stump, A., Tinelli, C.: The smt-lib standard: Version 2.0. Technical report (2010)
6. Bjørner, N., McMillan, K., Rybalchenko, A.: Program verification as satisfiability modulo theories. In: SMT Workshop at IJCAR (2012)

7. Bonacina, M.P., Johansson, M.: On interpolation in automated theorem proving (2012) (submitted)
8. Brillout, A., Kroening, D., Rümmer, P., Wahl, T.: An interpolating sequent calculus for quantifier-free Presburger arithmetic. Journal of Automated Reasoning 47, 341–367 (2011)
9. Cimatti, A., Griggio, A., Sebastiani, R.: Efficient generation of Craig interpolants in satisfiability modulo theories. ACM Trans. Comput. Log. 12(1), 7 (2010)
10. Craig, W.: Linear reasoning. A new form of the Herbrand-Gentzen theorem. The Journal of Symbolic Logic 22(3), 250–268 (1957)
11. de Moura, L., Bjørner, N.: Z3: An efficient SMT solver. In: Ramakrishnan, C.R., Rehof, J. (eds.) TACAS 2008. LNCS, vol. 4963, pp. 337–340. Springer, Heidelberg (2008)
12. Dershowitz, N., Manna, Z.: Proving termination with multiset orderings. Commun. ACM 22(8), 465–476 (1979)
13. Fermüller, C., Leitsch, A., Hustadt, U., Tammet, T.: Resolution decision procedures. In: Robinson, A., Voronkov, A. (eds.) Handbook of Automated Reasoning, ch. 25, pp. 1791–1850. Elsevier (2001)
14. Graf, S., Saïdi, H.: Construction of abstract state graphs with PVS. In: CAV 1997, pp. 72–83 (1997)
15. Grebenshchikov, S., Lopes, N.P., Popeea, C., Rybalchenko, A.: Synthesizing software verifiers from proof rules. In: PLDI (2012)
16. Gupta, A., Popeea, C., Rybalchenko, A.: Predicate abstraction and refinement for verifying multi-threaded programs. In: POPL (2011)
17. Gupta, A., Popeea, C., Rybalchenko, A.: Solving recursion-free Horn clauses over LI+UIF. In: Yang, H. (ed.) APLAS 2011. LNCS, vol. 7078, pp. 188–203. Springer, Heidelberg (2011)
18. Gupta, A., Popeea, C., Rybalchenko, A.: Generalised interpolation by solving recursion-free horn clauses. CoRR, abs/1303.7378 (2013)
19. Heizmann, M., Hoenicke, J., Podelski, A.: Nested interpolants. In: POPL (2010)
20. Henzinger, T.A., Jhala, R., Majumdar, R., McMillan, K.L.: Abstractions from proofs. In: POPL, pp. 232–244. ACM (2004)
21. Hoder, K., Bjørner, N.: Generalized property directed reachability. In: Cimatti, A., Sebastiani, R. (eds.) SAT 2012. LNCS, vol. 7317, pp. 157–171. Springer, Heidelberg (2012)
22. Lal, A., Qadeer, S., Lahiri, S.K.: A solver for reachability modulo theories. In: Madhusudan, P., Seshia, S.A. (eds.) CAV 2012. LNCS, vol. 7358, pp. 427–443. Springer, Heidelberg (2012)
23. Lewis, H.R.: Renaming a set of clauses as a Horn set. J. ACM 25(1), 134–135 (1978)
24. McMillan, K.L.: iZ3 documentation,
http://research.microsoft.com/en-us/um/
redmond/projects/z3/iz3documentation.html
25. McMillan, K.L.: Interpolation and SAT-based model checking. In: Hunt Jr., W.A., Somenzi, F. (eds.) CAV 2003. LNCS, vol. 2725, pp. 1–13. Springer, Heidelberg (2003)
26. McMillan, K.L.: Applications of craig interpolants in model checking. In: Halbwachs, N., Zuck, L.D. (eds.) TACAS 2005. LNCS, vol. 3440, pp. 1–12. Springer, Heidelberg (2005)
27. McMillan, K.L.: Lazy abstraction with interpolants. In: Ball, T., Jones, R.B. (eds.) CAV 2006. LNCS, vol. 4144, pp. 123–136. Springer, Heidelberg (2006)
28. McMillan, K.L., Rybalchenko, A.: Solving constrained Horn clauses using interpolation. Technical Report MSR-TR-2013-6 (January 2013),
http://research.microsoft.com/apps/pubs/default.aspx?id=180055
29. Méndez-Lojo, M., Navas, J.A., Hermenegildo, M.V.: A flexible (c)lp-based approach to the analysis of object-oriented programs. In: King, A. (ed.) LOPSTR 2007. LNCS, vol. 4915, pp. 154–168. Springer, Heidelberg (2008)

30. Rümmer, P., Hojjat, H., Kuncak, V.: Disjunctive Interpolants for Horn-Clause Verification (Extended Technical Report). ArXiv e-prints (January 2013), http://arxiv.org/abs/1301.4973

31. Sery, O., Fedyukovich, G., Sharygina, N.: Interpolation-based function summaries in bounded model checking. In: Eder, K., Lourenço, J., Shehory, O. (eds.) HVC 2011. LNCS, vol. 7261, pp. 160–175. Springer, Heidelberg (2012)

32. Suter, P., Köksal, A.S., Kuncak, V.: Satisfiability modulo recursive programs. In: Yahav, E. (ed.) Static Analysis. LNCS, vol. 6887, pp. 298–315. Springer, Heidelberg (2011)

33. Taghdiri, M., Jackson, D.: Inferring specifications to detect errors in code. Autom. Softw. Eng. 14(1), 87–121 (2007)

Static Analysis of Programs with Imprecise Probabilistic Inputs

Assale Adje[2], Olivier Bouissou[1], Jean Goubault-Larrecq[2],
Eric Goubault[1], and Sylvie Putot[1]

[1] CEA LIST
CEA Saclay, 91191 Gif-sur-Yvette CEDEX, France
`firstname.lastname@cea.fr`
[2] LSV, ENS Cachan
61 avenue du président Wilson, 94230 Cachan, France
`lastname@lsv.ens-cachan.fr`

Abstract. Having a precise yet sound abstraction of the inputs of numerical programs is important to analyze their behavior. For many programs, these inputs are probabilistic, but the actual distribution used is only partially known. We present a static analysis framework for reasoning about programs with inputs given as imprecise probabilities: we define a collecting semantics based on the notion of previsions and an abstract semantics based on an extension of Dempster-Shafer structures. We prove the correctness of our approach and show on some realistic examples the kind of invariants we are able to infer.

1 Introduction

Static analysis of embedded softwares faces the difficulty of correctly and precisely handling the program inputs. These inputs are usually given by sensors that measure a physical value continuously evolving with time. The classical abstraction of such inputs is to assign them with the range of values that the sensor may measure: in this way, we obtain a non-deterministic over-approximation of the values of the inputs which is then propagated through the program.

However, in addition to this non-deterministic abstraction of the values, we often have a probabilistic information on where the inputs lie in the range of possible values. This probabilistic information may be given by some knowledge on the physical environment with which the program interacts, or may be introduced as noise by the sensor. This noise can be very often modeled as a random variable with a Gaussian law; the value of the inputs is then given by $V + \varepsilon$ where V is a non-deterministically chosen value and ε is the probabilistic noise.

In this article, we present a framework to analyse *deterministic* programs with both probabilistic and non-deterministic inputs. In Section 2, we motivate our use of previsions and Probability-boxes. In Section 3, we define our concrete semantics based on previsions and in Section 4, we present our abstract semantics based on probabilistic affine forms. We prove its correctness in Section 5 and show in Section 6 the kind of invariants we are able to compute on realistic examples. Let us remark that to ease the understanding of this article, we have omitted

E. Cohen and A. Rybalchenko (Eds.): VSTTE 2013, LNCS 8164, pp. 22–47, 2014.

various technical details such as the use of floating-point numbers or the impact of run-time errors on the semantics. We discuss these points in the course of the exposition.

Running Example. In this article, we use a linear, order 2 filter to illustrate both our concrete and abstract semantics. This filter is given by the loop:

```
while(1) {
    y = 0.7*x - 1.3*x0 + 1.1*x1 + 1.4*y0 - 0.7*y1;
    x1 = x0; x0 = x; y1 = y0; y0 = y;
    x = input();
}
```

Numerical filters are very important for the analysis of embedded softwares as they are present in (almost) every software that must handle data coming from sensors. Computing the range of values reachable by the output variable y is a challenge adressed by many techniques [15]. However, all these methods assume that the inputs x (given by the function input() in the program) are bounded within a certain range and do not assume any distribution of the values within this range. Here, we assume that the input variables follow some probability distribution but we do not know which: we assume that x follows a uniform law on the range $[-A, A]$ for some $A \in [0, 0.2]$. Moreover, we assume that the distribution of the inputs may change during the execution of the filter, i.e. the distribution of input x read at iterate n (represented in the program by x) is not the same as the one of x read at iterate n-1 (represented in the program by x1). We however know that both are uniform distribution on some range $[-A, A]$. We ran 10 simulations of this filter and show below the 10 distributions in cumulative form (CDF) for the output variable y. Our goal is to compute guaranteed yet precise bounds on this set of distributions.

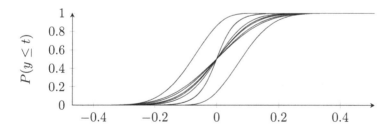

Contribution. In this paper, we present three main results. First, we define a semantics for imperative programs with inputs defined as imprecise probabilities. We define an operational and denotational semantics based on previsions and show their equivalence. Next, we define a new abstract domain based on probabilistic affine forms and especially new join and meet operators. Finally, we prove the correctness of the abstract semantics w.r.t the concrete ones and give some hints on how to adapt it to the analysis of hybrid systems by showing on one example how we can solve ODEs with our domain.

2   Related Work

One of our goals is to give a concrete semantics to an imperative language with access to imprecise inputs. Typically, these inputs will be numerical values given by physical sensors. Imagine a signal processing software that filters out thermal noise [29] from images given by a digital camera, for example with non-linear filtering techniques such as median filters [1]. Thermal noise is such that each pixel has an independent Gaussian noise, with zero mean and a standard deviation varying according to Nyquist law [29]. In particular, the standard deviation depends on the temperature, but not on pixels' values. In order to characterize the bounds on the noise after filtering, in all standard operational conditions (say, between -20 and 40 degrees Celsius), one has to consider all potential inputs, sum of a non-deterministic and bounded value (the range of the pixels, which is known) with a Gaussian noise of variance in a given interval, as computed by Nyquist law.

As exemplified above, one of our concerns will be to reason with so-called *imprecise probabilities*. There is a vast literature on the subject, and there are several mathematical notions that model imprecise probabilities, among which those based on *capacities* [8], and those based on *previsions* [41]. Capacities are simply monotone functions that map each measurable subset to its measure, such that the measure of the empty set is 0; but the measure of the disjoint union of two sets A and B does not necessarily coincide with the sum of their measures.

Previsions [41], on the other hand, are more abstract objects, but are better suited to giving semantics to programs [24], in a style akin to continuation-passing. Capacity-based semantics fail because we cannot even define sequential composition there [24]; sequential composition is defined by complex formulas in other models, such as convex powercones [40], where this involves unique extensions of maps to sets of non-empty closed convex subsets.

There are variations in what a prevision on a space X of values is. To us, a *prevision* on X will be any map $F \colon \langle X \to [0,1] \rangle \to [0,1]$ such that $F(ah) = aF(h)$ for all $a \in [0,1]$, where $\langle X \to [0,1] \rangle$ is the set of all measurable maps from X to $[0,1]$. We say that F is ω-*continuous* if and only if $F(\sup_{n \in \mathbb{N}} h_n) = \sup_{n \in \mathbb{N}} F(h_n)$ for every countable chain $(h_n)_{n \in \mathbb{N}}$, and F is ω-*cocontinuous* iff $F(\inf_{n \in \mathbb{N}} h_n) = \inf_{n \in \mathbb{N}} F(h_n)$, where the sups and infs are taken pointwise. Compared to [24], h is allowed to range over measurable maps, not just the bounded continuous maps, we drop the requirement of Scott-continuity, and the target space is $[0,1]$, not $\mathbb{R}^+$.

In this form, previsions are *generalized integrals*: we write $F(h)$ for the integral of h. Ordinary integrals $F(h) = \int_{x \in X} h(x)d\mu$ along an (additive) measure μ define particular cases of previsions F; distinctively, such previsions are linear, in the sense that $F(h + h') = F(h) + F(h')$, and are ω-continuous and ω-cocontinuous. Previsions do not demand linearity. Dropping linearity allows us to encode imprecise probabilities. For one, every capacity ν gives rise to a prevision, by the formula $F(h) = \int_{x \in X} h(x)d\nu$, where the integral with respect to the non-additive measure ν is the so-called Choquet integral [8]. E.g., if $\nu = \frac{1}{3}\mathfrak{e}_{A_1} + \frac{2}{3}\mathfrak{e}_{A_2}$ (the *example capacity* $\mathfrak{e}_A$ gives measure 1 to any set that meets A, and 0 to the others), then $F(h) = \int_{x \in X} h(x)d\nu = \frac{1}{3}\sup_{x \in A_1} h(x) + \frac{2}{3}\sup_{x \in A_2} h(x)$. Not all previsions are obtained as integrals from capacities, and this is the key ingredient used in [24] to provide a monad-based semantics to languages with non-deterministic and probabilistic choice. The basic intuition is that while capacities encode measures over sets, previsions encode sets of measures. Precisely, an *upper* prevision F (i.e. $\forall h, h'$, $F(h) + F(h') \geq F(h+h')$, and F is ω-cocontinuous), encodes the set of all linear previsions G that are pointwise below F. The single functional F therefore encodes the set of all those measures μ such that $\int_{x \in X} h(x) d\mu \leq F(h)$ for every h. There is also a dual notion of *lower* prevision F (namely, $F(h) + F(h') \leq F(h + h')$, and F is ω-continuous), which encodes the set of all the measures μ such that $\int_{x \in X} h(x) d\mu \geq F(h)$ for every h.

Implementations of Imprecise Probabilities. P-boxes [17] and Dempster-Shafer structures [36], which are both related to capacities, are used to propagate both probabilistic and non-deterministic information in numerical simulation for instance. Arithmetic rules on P-boxes were defined in e.g. [42], and implementations are available, for instance the DSI Toolbox [2] based on Matlab and INTLAB [34], Statool [4] implementing the arithmetic of [3] and RiskCalc [16]. They were not designed to be used for static analysis of programs (there is no consideration on semantics of programs nor join operators defined, typically) as we do in this paper but are rather designed for making numerical simulations or optimizations [19] for instance for risk assessment [18]. Several recent papers proposed extensions of these arithmetics that either increase the precision or the efficiency of this arithmetic, as in e.g. [7], [37], [38] and [5]. Let us mention as well Neumaier's clouds [33] as another way to formalize imprecise probabilities (used in [19]). A unification of the different uncertainty representations was proposed in [11,12] with comparisons between P-boxes and clouds.

The domain theoretic foundations of imprecise probabilities were studied by several authors, among which one of the authors of this paper [24,23,26,25]. In particular, the *convex powerdomains* of spaces of measures on X was studied by Mislove [31], by Tix *et al.* [39,40], and by Morgan and McIver [30].

Static Analysis of Probabilistic Systems. There is a large literature in static analysis of probabilistic systems, some in abstract interpretation but most notably in model-checking. Our work is orthogonal to the one in probabilistic model-checking (as implemented in e.g. PRISM [27]) where probability distributions (but not imprecise probabilities) are considered on transitions of a transition model (and not on data, as we do here). The models used are mostly based on discrete time Markov chains [14].

In static analysis of programs by abstract interpretation, which is the subject of this paper, several abstract semantics have been considered. Monniaux [32] automatically constructs a probabilistic abstract domain as a collection of abstract elements with an associated weight. This is very similar to Dempster-Shafer structures where focal elements are elements of the underlying abstract domain. Our main advantage with respect to Monniaux' framework is that our arithmetic is efficient, precise and keeps some dependencies between variables, while the construction in [32] is not optimized for a specific abstract domain.

Another choice that has been sometimes made in abstract interpretation is to model imprecise probabilistic choice by *random variables* instead of probability distributions. The distinction is tenuous but real. Instead of giving a probability distribution over the intended value, one defines a probability distribution π on another, fixed space Ω (of so-called events), and describe the probability over the intended value v as the image measure of π by some measurable map f from Ω to the space of values. This is the approach taken by Cousot and Monereau [10], where Ω is the space of infinite sequences of coin flips, each coin flip being independent and unbiased. A probability distribution on a space X is then encoded by a measurable map $f \colon \Omega \to X$, and the (image) measure of $A \subseteq X$ is $\pi(f^{-1}(A))$. One can then encode imprecise probabilities as well, as sets of measurable maps f.

The difficulty with this approach is that every probability law has to be described through some measurable map $f \colon \Omega \to X$, and must be implemented by a program $[f]$ for the analysis to proceed. E.g., to describe the Gaussian distribution on $X = \mathbb{R}$ with mean μ and standard deviation σ, one would implement a function $[f]$ that takes a sequence of independent, unbiased random booleans, and returns a (μ, σ)-normal random real. This is certainly possible, but the static analyzer will have to be sufficiently precise to derive meaningful, precise semantic invariants from the code of $[f]$. Our approach, based on P-box approximants to actual sets of distribution laws, is more direct.

Another approach, which is very promising, is taken in [35] that presents an approach for finding interval bounds on the probability of assertions over program variables by examining finitely many paths and performing a standard symbolic execution along each path. The goal of this approach is to use polyhedral volume bounding techniques for summing up the probability of assertion being satisfied along each path. The probability of unexplored paths is computed and added to the overall interval bound. Unlike our work, Sankaranarayanan et al. deal with precisely specified probability distributions whereas our work can handle imprecise probabilities. Furthermore, our approach here can represent the joint distributions of program variables at intermittent program points to potentially answer a larger set of questions about the program behavior. Whereas, their work focuses on queries posed at the end of the program execution. Since their work is unpublished at the time of writing, we provide an indirect comparison by demonstrating our technique on some of the benchmarks used in their paper.

3   Concrete Semantics

We consider the toy imperative language shown in Figure 1 as the core of languages such as C, to which we add a specific assignment instruction $x_1, \ldots, x_k :=$ input, which we explain below, and program points $\ell \colon$, where ℓ is taken from a countably infinite set $\mathcal{L}$ of so-called *labels*. The latter are used to name program points, not as targets of goto statements.

All instructions except one are standard. The input construction is meant to read the value of some sensors. Semantically, theses values will be probability

$$e ::= v \mid c \mid e_1 + e_2 \mid e_1 - e_2 \mid e_1 \times e_2 \mid e_1 \div e_2$$
$$b ::= \mathtt{true} \mid \mathtt{false} \mid x \le c \mid x < c \mid x \ge c \mid x > c \mid \neg b$$

$$
\begin{aligned}
s ::= \; & x := e & & \text{assignment} \\
\mid \; & \ell: & & \text{program point} \\
\mid \; & x_1, \ldots, x_k := \mathtt{input} & & \text{sensor input} \\
\mid \; & s_1; s_2 & & \text{sequence} \\
\mid \; & \mathtt{if}\ (b)\ \{\, s_1 \,\}\ \mathtt{else}\ \{\, s_2 \,\} & & \text{conditional} \\
\mid \; & \mathtt{while}(b)\ \{\, s_1 \,\} & & \text{loop}
\end{aligned}
$$

Fig. 1. Syntax

distributions, so it may be helpful to visualize them as returning some actual value plus some random noise. We assume k noisy sensors, which may be correlated. If they were uncorrelated, i.e., independently distributed, then a language with k sensor-reading expressions $\mathtt{input}_i$, each one returning the distribution of sensor number i, would have been sufficient. Instead, we use one $\mathtt{input}$ construction that returns a *joint* distribution $\nu_{\mathtt{inp}}$ over all the values of the k sensors. To make the semantics simpler, we reserve k variables x_1, ..., x_k as destinations of the $\mathtt{input}$ instruction, and call them the *sensor variables*. If one wishes to read, say, the first and the fourth sensor variables only, and in variables x and z instead of the fixed variables x_1 and x_4, one should write $x := x_1; z := x_4$ after the instruction $x_1, \ldots, x_k := \mathtt{input}$. Our concrete semantics is parameterized by the joint sensor distribution $\nu_{\mathtt{inp}}$, which we do not necessarily know. Our abstract semantics will abstract the latter by so-called Dempster-Shafer structures.

The variable x in assignments $x := e$ denotes any non-sensor variable; these form a finite set Var. We shall write Var^+ for $Var \cup \{x_1, \ldots, x_k\}$. The set Σ of environments is $\mathbb{R}^{Var^+}$, the set of all maps, denoted ρ, from Var^+ to $\mathbb{R}$. Expressions e and boolean tests b have deterministic semantics $[\![e]\!]\rho \in \mathbb{R}$ and $[\![b]\!]\rho \in \mathbb{B}$. We shall not describe it in detail, as it is mostly obvious, e.g., $[\![e_1 + e_2]\!]\rho = [\![e_1]\!]\rho + [\![e_2]\!]\rho$. The maps $\lambda\rho \cdot [\![b]\!]\rho$ and $\lambda\rho \cdot [\![e]\!]\rho$ are measurable maps of $\rho \in \Sigma$, where Σ is equated with $\mathbb{R}^{|Var^+|}$, equipped with its standard σ-algebra. We do not consider runtime errors here, and therefore assume division by 0 to return some arbitrary real number. We discuss this choice (and the choice of real numbers) at the end of this section.

We write a sequence of statements, i.e. a program, as Λ. We define an operational semantics of this language that infers judgments of the form $\ell \vdash (\Lambda, \rho) \downarrow_\kappa^\pm a$, for $\pm \in \{+, -\}$, where $\ell \in \mathcal{L}$, $a \in [0, 1]$ and $\kappa : \Sigma \to [0, 1]$ is a bounded measurable map. When κ is the indicator map χ_E of a measurable subset E of Σ, the intended meaning will be: starting from Λ in environment ρ, the probability of reaching label ℓ with some environment in E is at least (resp. at most) a if $\pm$ is $-$ (resp. $+$). In general, it is practical to use general measurable maps κ instead of indicator maps χ_E, and the meaning of $\ell \vdash (\Lambda, \rho) \downarrow_\kappa^- a$ will be: the average value of $\kappa(\rho')$ over all environments ρ' reached when at label ℓ is at least a (at most a for $\ell \vdash (\Lambda, \rho) \downarrow_\kappa^+ a$). For lack of space, we won't describe it here, but see Appendix A. We directly proceed to a prevision-based, denotational

$$[\![x := e]\!]_{\ell,\kappa}^{\pm} h\rho = h(\rho[x \mapsto [\![e]\!]\rho]) \qquad [\![s_1; s_2]\!]_{\ell,\kappa}^{\pm} h\rho = [\![s_1]\!]_{\ell,\kappa}^{\pm}\left([\![s_2]\!]_{\ell,\kappa}^{\pm}h\right)\rho$$

$$[\![\ell:\,]\!]_{\ell,\kappa}^{\pm} h\rho = \kappa(\rho) \vee^{\pm} h(\rho) \qquad [\![\ell':\,]\!]_{\ell,\kappa}^{\pm} h\rho = h(\rho) \text{ if } \ell' \neq \ell$$

$$[\![^{\ell}x_1,\ldots,x_k := \mathtt{input}]\!]_{\ell,\kappa}^{\pm} h\rho = F_{\mathtt{inp}}^{\pm}(\lambda v_1,\ldots,v_k \cdot h(\rho[x_1 \mapsto v_1,\ldots,x_k \mapsto v_k]))$$

$$[\![\mathtt{if}\ (b)\ \{\,s_1\,\}\ \mathtt{else}\ \{\,s_2\,\}]\!]_{\ell,\kappa}^{\pm} h\rho = \begin{cases} [\![s_1]\!]_{\ell,\kappa}^{\pm}h\rho & \text{if } [\![b]\!]\rho = 1 \\ [\![s_2]\!]_{\ell,\kappa}^{\pm}h\rho & \text{if } [\![b]\!]\rho = 0 \end{cases}$$

$$[\![\mathtt{while}(b)\ \{\,s_1\,\}]\!]_{\ell,\kappa}^{\pm} = \bigvee_{i\in\mathbb{N}}^{\pm} H_{b,s_1}^{i}(\bot^{\pm})$$
$$\text{where } H_{b,s_1} = \lambda\varphi\colon \langle \Sigma \to [0,1]\rangle \to \langle \Sigma \to [0,1]\rangle\cdot$$
$$\lambda h \in \langle \Sigma \to [0,1]\rangle, \rho \in \Sigma \cdot \begin{cases} [\![s_1]\!]_{\ell,\kappa}^{\pm}(\varphi(h))\rho & \text{if } [\![b]\!]\rho = 1 \\ h(\rho) & \text{if} [\![b]\!]\rho = 0 \end{cases}$$

Fig. 2. Concrete semantics

semantics that will play a role similar to collecting semantics in non-probabilistic settings, and will get us closer to an abstract semantics. For a proof that the prevision-based semantics matches the operational semantics, see Appendix B.

Our prevision-based denotational semantics is in the spirit of [24], except for the use of measure theory in place of domain theory. This is given in Figure 2: $[\![s]\!]_{\ell,\kappa}^{\pm} h\rho$ is meant to give the sup (if $\pm$ is $+$), resp. the inf (if $\pm$ is $-$) over all possible non-deterministic choices (when to stop and observe κ, which probability distribution $\nu_{\mathtt{inp}}$ satisfying (6) to choose) of the average values that κ takes when we reach ℓ, running statement s starting from environment ρ. It is helpful to think of h as a continuation, as in [24], and of κ as another continuation, triggered at certain times where we reach label ℓ: . Write $a \vee^{\pm} b$ for $\min(a,b)$ if $\pm$ is $-$, $\max(a,b)$ if $\pm$ is $+$. We define $[\![\ell':\,]\!]_{\ell,\kappa}^{\pm} h\rho$, when $\ell' = \ell$, as the result of a non-deterministic choice ($\vee^{\pm}$, i.e., max or min) of what happens if we choose to end computation right here (giving an expected value of $\kappa(\rho)$), and of what happens ($h(\rho)$) if we decide to proceed. The semantics is defined for continuations h that are measurable maps from Σ to $[0,1]$, just like for κ, and produces functionals $[\![s]\!]_{\ell,\kappa}^{\pm}$ mapping continuations h and environments $\rho \in \Sigma$ to elements of $[0,1]$. The *bottom* functional $\bot^{-}$ maps all h, ρ to 0, and the *top* functional $\bot^{+}$ maps all h, ρ to 1. This is used in the rule for while loops, where we also agree to write $\bigvee^{+}$ for sup and $\bigvee^{-}$ for inf.

The semantics of Figure 2 is only defined provided the integral used in the case of noisy (random) inputs is defined. This is ensured by checking that the semantics of any program is measurable. In the case of while loops, this follows from the fact that the pointwise sup of a countable chain of measurable maps is measurable. To prove this in the case of sequential composition, we need to prove the following more general result.

Theorem 1. *For every measurable maps $\kappa, h\colon \Sigma \to [0,1]$, $[\![s]\!]_{\ell,\kappa}^{\pm} h\rho$ is a well-defined number in $[0,1]$. For fixed κ, h, $[\![s]\!]_{\ell,\kappa}^{\pm} h\colon \Sigma \to [0,1]$ is a measurable map. For fixed κ, the map $\lambda h \cdot [\![s]\!]_{\ell,\kappa}^{\pm} h\rho$ is a prevision, which is upper if $\pm$ is $+$, lower* *if $\pm$ is $-$. For fixed h, the map $\lambda\kappa \cdot [\![s]\!]^+_{\ell,\kappa} h\rho$ is ω-continuous, and $\lambda\kappa \cdot [\![s]\!]^-_{\ell,\kappa} h\rho$ is ω-cocontinuous.*

Proof. (Sketch.) By structural induction on s. For assignments $x := e$, the measurability of $[\![x := e]\!]^{\pm}_{\ell,\kappa} h = \lambda\rho \cdot h(\rho[x \mapsto [\![e]\!]\rho])$ follows from the fact that $\lambda\rho \cdot [\![e]\!]\rho$ is measurable, and that h is measurable. For sequences $s_1; s_2$, we use the fact that composition preserves measurability, monotonicity, being upper, being lower, ω-continuity, and ω-cocontinuity. In the case of while loops, we use the fact that the sup of a countable chain of measurable, resp., ω-continuous maps, is again measurable, resp., ω-continuous. Dually, the inf of a countable chain of measurable, resp., ω-cocontinuous maps, is again measurable, resp., ω-cocontinuous.   □

We extend the denotational semantics to lists Λ by $[\![\epsilon]\!]^{\pm}_{\ell,\kappa} = \mathrm{id}$ (i.e., $[\![\epsilon]\!]^{\pm}_{\ell,\kappa} h\rho = h(\rho)$), and $[\![s \bullet \Lambda]\!]^{\pm}_{\ell,\kappa} = [\![s]\!]^{\pm}_{\ell,\kappa} \circ [\![\Lambda]\!]^{\pm}_{\ell,\kappa}$; so the semantics of $\Lambda = s_1 \bullet s_2 \bullet \ldots \bullet s_n$ coincides with that of the sequence $s_1; s_2; \ldots; s_n$. Now, given a program Λ, an intial state ρ, a label ℓ and a measurable map κ, the denotational semantics computes two values $[\![\Lambda]\!]^-_{\ell,\kappa} h_1\rho$ and $[\![\Lambda]\!]^+_{\ell,\kappa} h_0\rho$ that enclose the possible value of κ on the program variables when we reach ℓ. Here, h_0 (resp. h_1) is the constant map associating to each environment ρ h_0 (resp. h_1).

We finish this section with a remark on real vs. floating-point numbers. This semantics is what we shall call the *ideal semantics* of expressions and tests. Actual programs will handle floating-point numbers, not real numbers. At the level of the concrete semantics, that would be easily repaired, as follows. First, there is a finite subset $\mathbb{F} \subseteq \mathbb{R}$ of so-called floating-point numbers, and a rounding function $\pi_{\mathbb{F}} \colon \mathbb{R} \to \mathbb{F}$. Mathematically, $\pi_{\mathbb{F}}$ is a projection, namely $\pi_{\mathbb{F}}(v) = v$ for every $v \in \mathbb{F}$. The floating-point semantics $[\![e]\!]'\rho$ is obtained by rounding back results, as in, e.g., $[\![e_1 + e_2]\!]'\rho = \pi_{\mathbb{F}}([\![e_1]\!]'\rho + [\![e_2]\!]'\rho)$. Considering a floating-point semantics instead of the ideal semantics would make the statement of our semantics complicated. We would have to take rounding modes into account, and the fact that they can change over the course of a program running; we would need to extend $\mathbb{R}$ and $\mathbb{F}$ to include non-numerical values such as infinites and NaNs; and we would have to make several cases to define the results of tests such as $e_1 < e_2$ whenever $[\![e_1]\!]'\rho$ or $[\![e_2]\!]'\rho$ is non-numerical. Errors would also handle the case of division by zero, which we mentioned earlier.

We consider these issues orthogonal to the present paper, whose main purpose is to give a semantics to numerical programs *with uncertain probabilities*. Errors incurred by the fact that actual programs use floating-point values instead of real numbers can be handled at the level of the abstract semantics. One can extend probabilistic affine forms to handle rounding errors, as quickly described in [5], in the same way as for affine forms [22], and we intend to invest in that direction in the future.

4   Abstract Semantics

We now formally define our abstract semantics. It is based on an abstract domain that extends the probability affine forms of [5] as it introduces a join operator and an order relation. We first recall the notion of Dempster-Shafer structures.

4.1   Dempster-Shafer Structures

An interval based Dempster-Shafer structure [36] (DSI in short) is a finite set of closed intervals (named focal elements), each associated with a weight (in a more general setting [36], focal elements are not necessarily closed intervals). DSI structures thus represent real variables whose value can be obtained by first probabilistically picking up an interval, and then non-deterministically picking up a value within this interval. In this article, we write a DSI structure d as $d = \{\langle x_1, w_1 \rangle, \langle x_2, w_2 \rangle, \ldots, \langle x_n, w_n \rangle\}$, where $x_i \in \mathbb{I}$ is a closed interval and $w_i \in (0, 1]$ is the associated probability. For example, the DSI

$$d_1 = \big\{\langle [-1, 0.25], 0.3 \rangle \,;\, \langle [-0.5, 0.5], 0.2 \rangle \,;\, \langle [0.25, 1], 0.5 \rangle\big\}$$

represents a real-valued random variable X whose value is in $[-1, 0.25]$ with probability 0.3, in $[-0.5, 0.5]$ with probability 0.2, and in $[0.25, 1]$ with probability 0.5. We require that all intervals are non-empty, and that $\sum_{k=1}^{n} w_k \leq 1$: when the inequality is strict, this means that the variable X is with probability $1 - \sum_{k=1}^{n} w_k > 0$ in $\mathbb{R} \backslash \bigcup_{k=1}^{n} x_k$. We write $\mathbb{DS}$ for the set of all DSI structures over closed intervals.

Remark that there exists another popular model for imprecise probabilities, namely Probability-boxes [17] (P-box in short). We already showed in [5] that finite DSI structures and discrete P-box are equivalent. Intuitively, a P-box is a couple of two increasing functions $[\underline{P}, \overline{P}]$ that pointwise enclose a set of cumulative distribution functions. From a DSI d, we define the P-box $[\underline{P_d}, \overline{P_d}]$ by $\underline{P_d}(u) = \sum_{\overline{x_i} < u} w_i$ and $\overline{P_d}(u) = \sum_{\underline{x_i} \leq u} w_i$. We then graphically represent d by the graphs of the two functions $[\underline{P_d}, \overline{P_d}]$.

Example 1. Let $d_1 = \{\langle [-1, 0.25], 0.1 \rangle \,;\, \langle [-0.5, 0.5], 0.2 \rangle \,;\, \langle [0.25, 1], 0.3 \rangle \,;\, \langle [0.5, 1], 0.1 \rangle \,;\, \langle [0.5, 2], 0.1 \rangle \,;\, \langle [1, 2], 0.2 \rangle\}$. Then $[\underline{P_2}, \overline{P_2}] = \zeta(d_1)$ is plotted on the graph below.

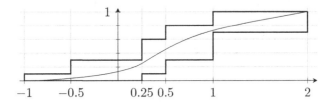

Join and Meet on DS Structures. The *join* of two DSI d_X and d_Y is defined as the union of all focal elements from d_X and d_Y, with the same probabilities, followed potentially by a normalization if the sum of all probabilities is greater than 1. For example, the join of the DSI $d_x = \{\langle [-1, 0], 0.5 \rangle \,;\, \langle [0, 1], 0.4 \rangle\}$ and $d_y = \{\langle [0.5, 1.5], 0.2 \rangle\}$ is $\{\langle [-1, 0], 0.46 \rangle \,;\, \langle [0, 1], 0.36 \rangle \,;\, \langle [0.5, 1.5], 0.18 \rangle\}$.

We do not define a *meet* operator on DSI but rather we define the operator $\mathrm{lt}_d(d_x, d_y)$ that reduces a DSI on a variable X to enforce the constraint $X \leq Y$. Intuitively, the resulting DSI contains all the focal elements of the form $\mathrm{lt}_{\mathbb{I}}(x_i, y_j)$, when $\langle x_i, a_i \rangle$ is a focal element of d_x and $\langle y_j, b_j \rangle$ is a focal element of d_y, with:

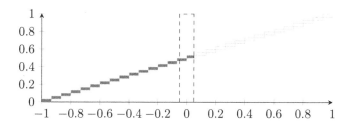

Fig. 3. Intersection between two DSI structures d_1 (in gray) and d_2 (dotted). The result is the filled DSI.

$$\mathtt{lt}_\mathbb{I}([a,b],[c,d]) = \begin{cases} \emptyset & \text{if } a > d \\ [a, \min(b,d)] & \text{otherwise} \end{cases}$$

and the associated probability is then $w_i \times w_j$. For example, if d_x is a DSI over-approximating a uniform distribution on $[-1, 1]$ and d_y is the DSI with one focal element $[-0.05, 0.05]$ (i.e. mimicking a Dirac at 0), then $\mathtt{lt}_d(d_x, d_y)$ is depicted on Figure 3. Remark that even if d_x and d_y are normalized (with the sum of probabilities equal to 1), $\mathtt{lt}_d(d_x, d_y)$ may be denormalized. We use this operator to give the semantics of conditional statements of the form `if (X<=Y) s1 else s2`, and define equivalently a $\mathtt{gt}_d(d_x, d_y)$ operator that enforces that $X \geq Y$.

4.2   Abstract Domain: Probabilistic Affine Forms

Clearly, P-boxes or DSI could be chosen as an abstraction of a set of probability distributions, arithmetic rules and an order relation can also be easily defined. However, P-boxes alone cannot be used efficiently for the analysis of programs as the arithmetic between them must differentiate the case when variables are independent or not [3]. And in the case when two variables x and y are not independent, the interpretation of arithmetic operations creates a large over-approximation as any dependency relation between x and y must be assumed. To increase the precision, we present the abstract domain of probabilistic affine forms, for which arithmetic operations were defined in [5].

Intuitively, a probabilistic affine form encodes both the linear dependency between every program variable and the input (as with classical affine forms, see [21]), and an abstraction of the inputs as a DSI. We can thus compute the DSI associated with each variable (it is a linear transformation of the inputs), and we use the linear correlations between variables to compute the arithmetic operations. The potential non-linear relations (due to non-linear operations in the program) are over-approximated by an additional linear term.

More formally, perturbed affine forms [20,21] are an extension of affine forms [9] in which each variable x is over-approximated by an expression of the form $\hat{x} = \alpha_0^x + \sum_{i=1}^{n} \alpha_i^x \varepsilon_i + \sum_{j=1}^{m} \beta_j^x \eta_j$ where the noise symbols ε_i or η_j are formal variables ranging over $[-1, 1]$ just as in affine forms, but where we differenciate the symbols ε_i that are directly related to an (uncertain) input value or parameter, and the symbols η_j that express an uncertainty in the analysis (loss of relation due to non linear computations for instance). For probabilistic affine forms, we will also use two kind of symbols, which will be random variables: the ε_i that are considered independent from one another, the η_j have unknown dependencies to the others.

Affine forms are closed under affine transformations: for $\lambda \in \mathbb{R}$,

$$\hat{x} + \lambda\hat{y} = \alpha_0^x + \lambda\alpha_0^y + \sum_{i=1}^{n}(\alpha_i^x + \lambda\alpha_i^y)\varepsilon_i + \sum_{j=1}^{m}(\beta_j^x + \beta_j^y)\eta_j \ .$$

Multiplication creates a new symbol η_{m+1} associated with the non-linear part:

$$\hat{x} \times \hat{y} = \alpha_0^x\alpha_0^y + \frac{R}{2} + \sum_{i=1}^{n}(\alpha_0^x\alpha_i^y + \alpha_i^x\alpha_0^y)\varepsilon_i + \sum_{j=1}^{m}(\alpha_0^x\beta_j^y + \beta_j^x\alpha_0^y)\eta_j + T\eta_{m+1}$$

with $R = \sum_{i=1}^{n}|\alpha_i^x\alpha_i^y| + \sum_{j=1}^{m}|\beta_j^x\beta_j^y|$ and

$$T = \sum_{i=1}^{n}\sum_{j=1}^{m}|\alpha_i^x\beta_j^y + \beta_j^x\alpha_i^y| + \sum_{i=1}^{n}\sum_{j>i}^{n}|\alpha_i^x\alpha_j^y + \alpha_j^x\alpha_i^y| + \sum_{i=1}^{m}\sum_{j>1}^{m}|\beta_i^x\beta_j^y + \beta_j^x\beta_i^y| + \frac{1}{2}R \ .$$

We next define probabilistic affine forms, an extension of affine forms, and formally define our abstract semantics.

Definition 1 (Probabilistic affine form). *We define a probabilistic affine form for variable x, on n independent noise symbols $(\varepsilon_1, \ldots, \varepsilon_n)$ and m noise symbols $(\eta_1, \ldots, \eta_m)$ with unknown dependency to the others, by a form*

$$\hat{x} = \alpha_0^x + \sum_{i=1}^{n}\alpha_i^x\varepsilon_i + \sum_{j=1}^{m}\beta_j^x\eta_j$$

together with n DSI $(d_{\varepsilon_1}, \ldots, d_{\varepsilon_n})$ and m DSI $(d_{\eta_1}, \ldots, d_{\eta_m})$ describing the possible random variables (of support $[-1, 1]$) for the noise symbols.

The interest of affine forms is to be able to represent affine relations that hold between uncertain quantities. We still have this representation, except only *imprecise* affine relations hold, as can be shown in the example below.

Example 2. Let $\hat{x}_1 = 1 + \varepsilon_1 - \eta_1$, $\hat{x}_2 = -\frac{1}{2}\varepsilon_1 + \frac{1}{4}\eta_1$, $d_{\varepsilon_1} = \{\langle[-1,0], \frac{1}{2}\rangle, \langle[0,1], \frac{1}{2}\rangle\}$, $d_{\eta_1} = \{\langle[-\frac{1}{10}, 0], \frac{1}{2}\rangle, \langle[0, \frac{1}{10}], \frac{1}{2}\rangle\}$, Then $\hat{x}_1 + 2\hat{x}_2 = 1 - \frac{1}{2}\eta_1$, with $d = d_{x_1+2x_2} = \{\langle[\frac{19}{20}, 1], \frac{1}{2}\rangle, \langle[1, \frac{21}{20}], \frac{1}{2}\rangle\}$. Thus the lower probability that $x_1 + 2x_2 \leq \frac{21}{20}$ is 1; and the upper probability that $x_1 + 2x_2 < \frac{19}{20}$ is 0. But for instance, $x_2 + 2x_2 \leq 1$ has upper probability $\frac{1}{2}$ and lower probability 0 and is thus an imprecise relation.

Given a probabilistic affine form $\hat{x}$, we define its enclosing DS structure, denoted $\gamma_d(\hat{x})$, by: $\gamma_d(\hat{x}) = \alpha_0^x + \Sigma_{i=1}^{n}\alpha_i^x d_{\varepsilon_i} \oplus \bigoplus_{j=1}^{m}\beta_j^x d_{\eta_j}$, where $+$ and Σ represents the sum of DSI using the independent arithmetic, and $\oplus$ is the sum of DSI using the unknown dependency arithmetic [5]. In other worlds, $\gamma_d(\hat{x})$ computes a DSI by summing the DSI associated with each noise symbol of $\hat{x}$.

Definition 2 (Abstract environment). *Given variables Var^+, an abstract environment $\rho^\sharp$ is a function mapping each variable $x \in Var^+$ to a probabilistic affine form over the same set of noise symbols. Let $\Sigma^\sharp$ be the set of all abstract environments. For $x \in Var^+$, we shall write:*

$$\rho^\sharp(x) = \alpha_0^x + \sum_{i=1}^n \alpha_i^x \varepsilon_i + \sum_{j=1}^m \beta_j^x \eta_j \ .$$

Our abstract semantics is a classical collecting operational semantics on abstract environments. Given a program, equivalently a statement list Λ, and an initial environment ρ_0, the abstract semantics associates an abstract environment with each label ℓ such that ℓ : is in Λ. We thus define a function $[\![\Lambda]\!]_\ell^\sharp : \Sigma \to \Sigma^\sharp$. Its value on a variable x is an affine P-box which encodes an upper set of probability distributions on the value that x can take at control point ℓ. They are potentially denormalized since this is not describing the conditional probability distributions of x knowing that we are in ℓ but rather the probability distributions of reaching ℓ with certain values. We will prove in Section 5 that $[\![\Lambda]\!]_\ell^\sharp(\rho_0)$ is a correct abstraction of $[\![\Lambda]\!]_{\ell,\kappa}^\pm \rho_0$. The abstract semantics depends on various elementary operations on abstract environnments: input, join, meet and expression evaluation. We present them in the rest of this section.

Inputs. The concrete semantics is parametrized by probability distribution $\nu_{\texttt{inp}}$ for the possible values of the input variables. Equivalently, our abstract semantics is parametrized by a set of DSI $d_1, \ldots, d_k$ such that all marginal distributions of $\nu_{\texttt{inp}}$ for x_i are contained in d_i, for $i \in [1, k]$. Then, the abstract semantics $[\![x_1, \ldots, x_k := \texttt{input}]\!]^\sharp$ assigns each input variable x_i to a new noise symbol (either ε_k or η_k depending on the assumed dependency between inputs and other variables) and we associate the DSI d_i with this noise symbol. For example, if we assume we have one input variable x_1 independent from other variables and uniformly distributed on $[a, b]$, the probabilistic affine form $\hat{x}_1$ after the instruction $x_1 := \texttt{input}$ will be $\hat{x}_1 = \frac{a+b}{2} + \frac{b-a}{2} \varepsilon_k$ where ε_k is a fresh noise symbol associated with a DSI enclosing the uniform distribution on $[-1, 1]$.

Join. Let $\rho_1^\sharp$ and $\rho_2^\sharp$ be two abstract environments. We define the join $\rho_1^\sharp \sqcup \rho_2^\sharp$ pointwise, i.e. $\forall x \in Var$, $\rho_1^\sharp \sqcup \rho_2^\sharp(x) = \rho_1^\sharp(x) \sqcup \rho_2^\sharp(x)$ where $\sqcup$ is the join operator between two affine forms defined below.

Let now $x \in Var$ and let us write $\rho_1^\sharp(x) = \alpha_0^1 + \sum_{i=1}^n \alpha_i^1 \varepsilon_i + \sum_{j=1}^m \beta_j^1 \eta_j$ and $\rho_2^\sharp(x) = \alpha_0^2 + \sum_{i=1}^n \alpha_i^2 \varepsilon_i + \sum_{j=1}^m \beta_j^2 \eta_j$. As in [21], the join $\hat{x} = \rho_1^\sharp(x) \sqcup \rho_2^\sharp(x)$ is computed as an affine transformation of the existing noise symbols plus a new noise symbol η_{m+1} that is used to over-approximate the error made by the linearization, i.e. $\hat{x} = \hat{x}_l + \eta_{m+1}$ with $\hat{x}_l = \alpha^0 + \sum_{i=1}^n \alpha^i \varepsilon_i + \sum_{j=1}^m \beta^j \eta_j$ where the values of the coefficients are given by Equations (1) to (3).

$$\alpha^0 = m\big(\gamma_d(\alpha_1^0) \curlyvee \gamma_d(\alpha_1^0)\big) \tag{1}$$

$$\forall i \in [1, n], \ \alpha^i = \operatorname{argmin}(\alpha_1^i, \alpha_2^i) \tag{2}$$

$$\forall j \in [1, m], \ \beta^j = \operatorname{argmin}(\beta_1^j, \beta_2^j) \tag{3}$$

Intuitively, the central term of $\hat{x}$ is the middle of the support of the DSI concretization of both affine forms (we note this $m(d)$ for a DSI d). The argmin function, defined by $\mathrm{argmin}(x, y) = z$ with $z \in [\min(x, y), \max(x, y)]$ and $|z|$ is minimal, keeps the best possible relation between on each noise symbol between the affine forms $\rho_1^\sharp(x)$ and $\rho_2^\sharp(x)$.

The new noise symbol η_{m+1} is defined to compensate this linearization. So, we define the DSI associated with η_{m+1} by $d_{\eta_{m+1}} = \gamma_d(\hat{x}_l - x) \curlyvee \gamma_d(\hat{x}_l - y)$. Recall that $\curlyvee$ is the join operator on DSI.

Meet. As for DSI, we do not define formally the meet over probabilistic affine forms but rather give an operator $\mathtt{lt}_d(\hat{x}, \hat{y})$ that reduces the DSI of each symbol in $\hat{x}$ to enforce that the variables x and y verify $x \leq y$. It will be used in our abstract semantics to handle boolean expressions of the form $X \leq Y$. We here use an approach equivalent to the one over deterministic affine forms as introduced in [20], in which the meet was interpreted in an abstract domain over noise symbols. To simplify the presentation, let us consider two probabilistic affine forms $\hat{x}$ and $\hat{y}$ over two noise symbols ε_1 and ε_2. The generalization to arbitrary many noise symbols is straightforward. Intuitively, we want to enforce that $\alpha_0^x + \alpha_1^x d_{\varepsilon_1} + \alpha_2^x d_{\varepsilon_2} \leq \alpha_0^y + \alpha_1^y d_{\varepsilon_1^y} + \alpha_2^y d_{\varepsilon_2^y}$, which leads to the following reduction:

$$d_{\varepsilon_1} = \mathtt{lt}_d\left(d_{\varepsilon_1}, \frac{\alpha_0^x - \alpha_0^y + (\alpha_2^x - \alpha_2^y)d_{\varepsilon_2}}{\alpha_1^x - \alpha_1^y}\right)$$

$$d_{\varepsilon_2} = \mathtt{lt}_d\left(d_{\varepsilon_2}, \frac{\alpha_0^x - \alpha_0^y + (\alpha_1^x - \alpha_1^y)d_{\varepsilon_1}}{\alpha_2^x - \alpha_2^y}\right)$$

These equations can be iterated to reduce the DSI associated with ε_1 and ε_2, and we define $\mathtt{lt}(\hat{x}, \hat{y})$ as the greatest fixpoint of the iteration of these two equations.

Arithmetic Operations. We defined the arithmetic operations on probabilistic affine forms in [5]. For affine arithmetic operations, there is nothing new compared to the deterministic case and the DSI structures attached to symbols are not modified. For non-linear operations, we can rely on the affine form calculus, but instead of only bounding the non-linear part of the multiplication of the affine forms, we use the available calculus on DSI to form a correct DSI representing this non-linear part. This makes the calculus correct even for denormalized DSI. We carefully alternate between the independent and unknown dependency arithmetic on DSI to have a sound over-approximation.

5   Correctness Proofs

In this section, we relate our notion of probabilistic affine forms with the semantics defined in Section 3. Intuitively, for each label ℓ that appears in the program, both semantics compute a set of probability distributions on the program variables when the program reaches ℓ. The concrete semantics computes bounds on the probability distributions at each label ℓ, they are denoted $[\![A]\!]_{\ell,\kappa}^{-}\rho$ and $[\![A]\!]_{\ell,\kappa}^{+}\rho$. Our abstract semantics associates a probabilistic affine form with each label of the program, from which we can define a set $\mathcal{P}$ of *compatible* probability distributions, see Section 5.1. We will prove that the bounds one can infer on the probabilities over program variables using $\mathcal{P}$ over-approximate the bounds computed by the concrete semantics. We first define the concretization function and then state and prove our soundness theorem.

5.1 Concretization

We assume that we have k variables $x_1, \ldots, x_k$, to each of them being attached an affine form $\hat{x}_i$ on n central and m perturbed noise symbols:

$$\hat{x}_i = \alpha_0^{x_i} + \sum_{i=1}^{n} \alpha_i^{x_i} \varepsilon_i + \sum_{j=1}^{m} \beta_j^{x_i} \eta_j .$$

Each noise symbol is associated with a DS structure denoted d_{ε_i} or d_{η_j}. We may represent this abstract element as a matrix $M \in \mathcal{M}^{d \times n + m}$ defined by $M_{i,j} = \alpha_j^{x_i}$ if $j \leq n$ and $M_{i,j} = \beta_j^{x_i}$ for $n < j \leq n + m$ and a $\mathbb{R}^d$-vector A where $A_i = \alpha_0^{x_i}$. In the purely non-deterministic case, i.e. when the DS structures are the interval $[-1, 1]$, the concretization of such an affine form is the set of points obtained by the linear transformation M of some point in $[-1, 1]^{m+n}$. In the case of probabilistic affine forms, we proceed in a similar way: the concretization of the abstract element is the set of all probabilities on $\mathbb{R}^d$ that are obtained as the image under the linear transformation M of some probability on $[-1, 1]^{n+m}$ which is *compatible* with the DS structures on the noise symbols. In the rest of the section, we formally define these notions of compatibility for probabilities.

We say that a probability P on $[-1, 1]$ is compatible with a DS structure d, denoted $P \frown d$, if and only if, for all $u \in [-1, 1]$, $\underline{P_d}(u) \leq \int_{[-1,u]} dP \leq \overline{P_d}(u)$. This means that the cumulative distribution function (CDF, [14]) associated with the probability P belongs to the P-box constructed from the DSI d.

The collecting semantics that we use relies on sets of probability distributions P on $\mathbb{R}^d$. Up to a linear transformation, we must ensure that all probabilities marginals P_i are compatible with the DSI d_{ε_i} (or d_{η_i}). We recall that the marginal probability $P_{1,\ldots,k}$ on $[-1, 1]^k$ of a probability distribution P on $[-1, 1]^{n+m}$ is defined as follows, for all Borel sets B on $[-1, 1]^k$:

$$P_{1,\ldots,k}(B) = \int_{\{x=(y,z)\in[-1,1]^k \times [-1,1]^{n+m-k} | y \in B\}} dP(x)$$

When $k = 1$, we get the probability marginal on a fixed coordinate. We can thus define the CDF marginal by the simple formula, for all $u \in [-1, 1]$:

$$F_i(u) = \int_{\{x \in [-1,1]^{n+m} | x_i \in [-1,u]\}} dP_i(x)$$

Given a probability P on $[-1,1]^{n+m}$ and $n + m$ DSI on $[-1,1]$ denoted $ds_1, \ldots, ds_{n+m}$, we denote by $P \simeq (ds_1, \ldots, ds_{n+m})$ if and only if $\forall i \in [1, n + m]$, $P_i \frown ds_i$.

Finally, we need to recall how we construct a probability distribution $[-1,1]^k$ from a probability on $[-1,1]^i$ and a probability on $[-1,1]^j$ where $i + j = k$. This will be needed as we will construct i marginal probabilities compatible with the DSI of the ε symbols and j compatible with the DSI of the η symbols, and then construct the probability on $[-1,1]^k$.

Let P_i and P_j two probability measures on respectively $[-1,1]^i$ and $[-1,1]^j$. We define the probability measure $P_i \otimes P_j$ as the unique probability measure on $[-1,1]^k$ such that, for all $A \in [-1,1]^i$ and $B \in [-1,1]^j$,

$$P_i \otimes P_j(A \times B) = P_i(A) \times P_j(B)$$

Now, given n central noise symbols ε_i and m perturbation symbols η_j, we define the probabilities on $[-1,1]^{n+m}$ compatible with them as the set of probabilities compatible with the DS structures attached to noise symbols and that are coherent with the independency of the noise symbol ε_i. Thus the ε-marginal probability is the product of the i-th marginal probabilities for $1 \leq i \leq n$. This is formally stated in Definition 3.

Definition 3 (Compatible probabilities). *Let $\varepsilon_1, \ldots, \varepsilon_n$ and $\eta_1, \ldots, \eta_m$ be noise symbols with attached DS structures d_{ε_i} and d_{η_j}. We define the set of compatible probabilities, denoted $P_{\varepsilon, \eta}$, as:*

$$P_{\varepsilon,\eta} = \left\{ \begin{array}{ll} & P \text{ probabilities on } \mathbb{R}^{n+m} \text{ such that:} \\ (1) & P \simeq (d_{\varepsilon_1}, \ldots, d_{\varepsilon_n}, d_{\eta_1}, \ldots, d_{\eta_m}) \\ (2) & P_\epsilon = P_{\varepsilon_1, \ldots, \varepsilon_n} = \otimes_{i=1}^n P_{\epsilon_i} \end{array} \right\}.$$

As stated before, the concretization of a probabilistic affine form is the set of all previsions that are expressed as the image via the affine transformation of a prevision compatible with the DS structures of the noise symbols. We thus need to define the notion of image prevision (see Definition 4), then we can formally define the concretization function (see Definition 5).

Definition 4 (Probability image). *Let P be a probability on $[-1,1]^{n+m}$ and $M : [-1,1]^{n+m} \to \mathbb{R}^d$ be a measurable map. We define the probability image of P by M, denoted $M(P)$, as the probability on $\mathbb{R}^d$ given by $M(P)(B) = \lambda B.P(M^{-1}(B))$.*

Definition 5 (Concretization function). *Let $\rho^\sharp$ be a probabilistic affine form over d variables $x_1, \ldots, x_d$ and with n independent noise symbols ε_i and m perturbation noise symbols η_j. For each $k \in [1, d]$, let*

$$\rho^\sharp(x_k) = \alpha_0^k + \sum_{i=1}^n \alpha_i^k \varepsilon_i + \sum_{j=1}^m \beta_j^k \eta_j$$

and let $M_{\rho^\sharp} \in \mathcal{M}^{k \times m + n}$ be the matrix as defined above. We define the concretization of $\rho^\sharp$, denoted $\gamma(\rho^\sharp)$ as:

$$\gamma(\rho^\sharp) = \left\{ P \mid \exists P' \in P_{\varepsilon,\eta}, \ P = M(P') \right\} .$$

In other words, $\gamma(\rho^\sharp)$ is the image by the affine transformation $M_{\rho^\sharp}$ of the set of compatible probabilities $P_{\varepsilon,\eta}$.

5.2   Correctness Results

Theorem 2 (Correctness of the abstraction). *Let Λ be a program and ℓ a label appearing in Λ. Let ρ be an initial environment for program variables and let $\rho^\sharp = [\![\Lambda]\!]_\ell^\sharp(\rho)$, then we have:*

$$\forall \kappa : \Sigma \to [0,1], \quad \begin{cases} [\![\Lambda]\!]_{\ell,\kappa}^- 1\rho \geq \inf\left\{ \int_{y \in \mathbb{R}^n} \kappa(y) dP \mid P \in \gamma(\rho^\sharp) \right\} \\ [\![\Lambda]\!]_{\ell,\kappa}^+ 0\rho \leq \sup\left\{ \int_{y \in \mathbb{R}^n} \kappa(y) dP \mid P \in \gamma(\rho^\sharp) \right\} \end{cases} . \quad (4)$$

As usual, we prove this theorem by proving the correctness of each syntactic construction of the language. Due to the lack of space, we do not give all the proofs but give the main lemmas that are useful to prove this result. In particular, we show how the composition of programs impact the probabilistic semantics.

Lemma 1. *We have:* $[\![s_1; \ell' :; s_2; \ell :]\!]_{\ell,\kappa}^\pm h\rho = [\![s_1]\!]_{\ell', [\![s_2]\!]_{\ell,\kappa}^\pm h}^\pm h\rho.$

Proof (Proof sketch). We prove it for $\pm = +$ and $h = 0$, the same proof runs easily for $\pm = -$ and $h = 1$. By the rules for $;$ and $l' :$ of Figure 2 we deduce:

$$[\![s_1; \ell' :; s_2; \ell :]\!]_{\ell,\kappa}^+ h\rho = [\![s_1; \ell' :]\!]_{\ell,\kappa}^+ \left(\lambda\rho'.[\![s_2; \ell :]\!]_{\ell,\kappa}^+ h\rho' \right)\rho$$

$$= [\![s_1; \ell' :]\!]_{\ell,\kappa}^+ \left(\lambda\rho'.[\![s_2]\!]_{\ell,\kappa}^+ (\lambda\rho''.[\![\ell :]\!]_{\ell,\kappa}^+ h\rho'')\rho' \right)\rho$$

$$= [\![s_1; \ell' :]\!]_{\ell,\kappa}^+ \left(\lambda\rho'[\![s_2]\!]_{\ell,\kappa}^+ (\lambda\rho''.\kappa(\rho''))\rho' \right)\rho$$

$$= [\![s_1; \ell' :]\!]_{\ell,\kappa}^+ \left(\lambda\rho'[\![s_2]\!]_{\ell,\kappa}^+ \kappa\rho' \right)\rho$$

$$= [\![s_1]\!]_{\ell,\kappa}^+ \left(\lambda\rho''.[\![\ell' :]\!]_{\ell,\kappa}^+ (\lambda\rho'.[\![s_2]\!]_{\ell,\kappa}^+ \kappa\rho')\rho'' \right)\rho$$

$$= [\![s_1]\!]_{\ell,\kappa}^+ \left(\lambda\rho''.[\![s_1]\!]_{\ell,\kappa}^+ \kappa\rho'' \right)\rho$$

And we also have, for all $\kappa : \Sigma \to [0,1]$: $[\![s_1; \ell' :]\!]_{\ell',\kappa}^+ 0\rho = [\![s_1]\!]_{\ell',\kappa}^+ (\kappa)\rho$, which ends the proof using the correct κ. $\square$

We use Lemma 1 to prove that the abstract semantics is correct for Λ of the form $s_1; \ell' :; x := e; \ell :$. Let thus $\rho \in \Sigma$ be the initial environment and let $\kappa : \Sigma \to [0,1]$ be a measurable map. Let $\rho_1^\sharp = [\![s_1]\!]_{\ell'}^\sharp(\rho)$ and $\rho^\sharp = [\![\Lambda]\!]_\ell^\sharp(\rho)$. We have: $\rho^\sharp = [\![x := e]\!]^\sharp(\rho_1^\sharp)$, i.e. $\rho^\sharp$ is obtained by evaluating the assignment $x := e$ using probabilistic affine forms. We assume that Equation (4) is true for $\rho_1^\sharp$ and show that it remains true for $\rho^\sharp$. We thus have (for $+$ and 0) $[\![s_1]\!]_{\ell',\kappa}^+ 0\rho \leq \sup_{P \in \gamma(\rho_1^\sharp)} \int_{y \in \mathbb{R}^n} \kappa(y) dP$. Now, using Lemma 1, we have $[\![A]\!]_{\ell,\kappa}^+ 0h \leq \sup_{P \in \gamma(\rho_1^\sharp)} \int_{y \in \mathbb{R}^n} [\![x := e; l :]\!]_{\ell,\kappa}^+ 0y dP$ and $\int_{y \in \mathbb{R}^n} [\![x := e; l :]\!]_{\ell,\kappa}^+ 0y dP = \int_{y \in \mathbb{R}^n} \kappa(y[x \mapsto [\![e]\!]y]) dP$. Using the image-measure property, we get $\int_{y \in \mathbb{R}^n} [\![x := e; l :]\!]_{\ell,\kappa}^+ 0y dP = \int_{y \in \mathbb{R}^n} \kappa(y) df(P)$ where $f : \mathbb{R}^n \to \mathbb{R}^n$ is the function $f(y)$ is y except for the dimension of x which is changed to $[\![e]\!]y$. According to the rules of our abstract semantics, we know that $\{f(P) \mid P \in \gamma(\rho_1^\sharp)\} \subseteq \gamma(\rho^\sharp)$, so we get:

$$[\![A]\!]_{\ell,\kappa}^+ 0h \leq \sup_{P \in \gamma(\rho^\sharp)} \int_{y \in \mathbb{R}^n} \kappa(y) dP$$

which ends the proof. The proofs for other statements are similar.

6 Experimentations

6.1 Running Example

In this section, we describe on our running example the results of our analyzer which implements the abstract semantics we defined in Section 4. To assert the precision of our analysis, we compare these results with simulations of the same example with as inputs probability distributions within the set of possible inputs. Recall that our running example computes the iterations of the filter:

$$y_n = S = 0.7 * x_n - 1.3 * x_{n-1} + 1.1 * x_{n-2} + 1.4 * y_{n-1} - 0.7 * y_{n-2}$$

where the inputs (x_n) are random variables following a uniform distribution between $-x$ and x, for any $x \in [0, 0.2]$. In other words, the inputs of the filter are the sets of all uniform distribution with support $[-x, x]$. For our analysis, we use as inputs a DSI that contains all these distributions; its is shown on Figure 4(a).

We first show the precision of our abstract domain by computing the 100th iterate of the filter, without computing the union, i.e. we completely unfold the loop. The result is shown on Figure 4(b) on which we depict both the simulations and the P-box obtained by our abstract semantics. We can see that we obtain a correct over-approximation of all the distributions computed by the simulations. This over-approximation however is large because the input P-box we chose contains many more distributions than just the uniform ones on $[-x, x]$. We made some other simulations with such distributions (for example, distributions that follow closely the upper and lower functions of the P-box) and obtained the dotted curves of Figure 4(b) which are much closer to the P-box we computed. We get a distance between the lower and upper probabilities, in the abstract which is about twice as much as in our simulations, which is still quite precise.

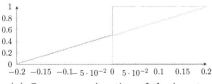

(a) Over-approximation of the input.

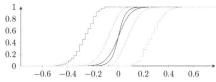

(b) P-box of the output (red-green) and simulations (black).

Fig. 4. Analysis on the running example

6.2 Ferson Polynomial

We now use an example from [13] to test the precision and performance of our abstract domain on arithmetic operations. The problem is to compute bounds on the solution of the differential equations

$$\dot{x}_1 = \theta_1 x_1 (1 - x_2) \quad \dot{x}_2 = \theta_2 x_2 (x_1 - 1) \tag{5}$$

under the assumption that the initial values are $x_1(0) = 1.2$ and $x_2(0) = 1.1$ but the parameters θ_1 and θ_2 are uncertain: they are given by a normal distribution with mean 3 and 1, resp., but with an unknown standard deviation in the range $[-0.01, 0.01]$. As in [13], we used VSPODE [28] to obtain a Taylor model polynomial that expresses the solution at $t_f = 20$ as an order 5 polynomial of θ_1 and θ_2. We then used the probabilistic affine forms to evaluate the Horner form of this polynomial. Figure 5 shows both the input DSI for θ_1 and the output DSI for x_1 at the final time. Our abstract domain is precise enough to correctly bound the output variables and the figure shows that we can also, with high probability, discard some values in the resulting interval. For example, we could show that $P(x_1 \leq 1.13) \leq 0.0552$, which is an even more precise enclosure than the one obtained by RiskCALC [13]. Our analysis took 104s on a 1.6Ghz laptop.

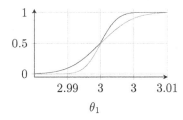

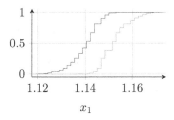

Fig. 5. DSI of the uncertain parameter and the output of problem (5)

6.3 Tank Filling

Our final example is a simple modification of the tank filling program of [35] that can be found at https://sites.google.com/site/probabilisticanalysis/. It consists of a tank of volume V that is filled with water: at each time instant, water is added into the tank but an error is attached to the added volume of water and the measured volume is also equiped with a probabilistic error. The filling stops when the measured volume v_m is greater than V, and we are interested in knowing how long the filling process takes. The error on the inputs is as follows: the input volume at each time instant is given by a uniform law with support $[0.07, 0.13]$ and the error on the sensor that measures the volume is also a normal law but with support $[-0.03, 0.03]$, i.e. the sensor is very noisy.

We compute the affine form attached to the measured volume $v_m(i)$ at each time instant i and can thus bound the probability of the program ending in i time instants: we compute the upper and lower bound of the probability $P(v_m(i) < V)$ at each time instant. Then, we can prove that the program stops in less than 26 steps (with $V = 2$) as $P(v_m(26) \leq V) = 0$. We can also prove that the program ends in more than 20 steps with probability less than 0.63, which seems to be a rather precise estimate. Note that we can still slightly improve the precision of our analysis and decrease the bound 0.63 by increasing the maximal number of focal elements in DSI. This impact the performances (the computations are quadratic in the number of focal elements) but greatly increases precision. With 300 focal elements per DSI, we could prove that the program ends in more than 20 steps with probability less than 0.595.

We also made some experimentations on the EGFR example from [35] which computes the *Estimated Globular Filtration Rate* and studies the impact of noise on the computed value. Our model of probabilistic affine forms can efficiently handle such a problem as it tracks down the dependency between a variable (the EGFR) and its noisy version.

7   Conclusion

We have presented a framework for the verification of embedded programs with both probabilistic and non-deterministic inputs. In particular, we have defined a concrete collecting semantics using (higher and lower) previsions to enclose a set of probability distributions and an abstract semantics using probabilistic affine forms to efficiently compute an over-approximation of this set.

Note that our analysis is an extension of the purely non-deterministic case: if we have no information about the probability distribution associated to each noise symbol, we shall use DS structures with only one focal element and a weight of 1 and then get the same results as standard affine forms analysis.

In this work, we focused on numerical programs that usually appear in embedded systems and only treated them as open-loop programs, i.e. we ignored the feedback from the program to its plant. In the future, we shall extend this work to treat hybrid systems as in [6]. This will require to be able to handle ODEs with initial values given as probabilistic affine forms. As shown by our second benchmark, we think that we can extend guaranteed ODE solvers to make them compute with imprecise probabilities.

References

1. Arce, G.: Nonlinear Signal Processing: A Statistical Approach. Wiley (2005)
2. Auer, E., Luther, W., Rebner, G., Limbourg, P.: A verified matlab toolbox for the dempster-shafer theory. In: Workshop on the Theory of Belief Functions (2010)
3. Berleant, D., Goodman-Strauss, C.: Bounding the results of arithmetic operations on random variables of unknown dependency using intervals. Reliable Computing 4(2), 147–165 (1998)
4. Berleant, D., Xie, L., Zhang, J.: Statool: A tool for distribution envelope determination (denv), an interval-based algorithm for arithmetic on random variables. Reliable Computing 9, 91–108 (2003)
5. Bouissou, O., Goubault, E., Goubault-Larrecq, J., Putot, S.: A generalization of p-boxes to affine arithmetic. Computing, 1–13 (2011), 10.1007/s00607-011-0182-8
6. Bouissou, O., Goubault, E., Putot, S., Tekkal, K., Vedrine, F.: Hybridfluctuat: A static analyzer of numerical programs within a continuous environment. In: Bouajjani, A., Maler, O. (eds.) CAV 2009. LNCS, vol. 5643, pp. 620–626. Springer, Heidelberg (2009)
7. Busaba, J., Suwan, S., Kosheleva, O.: A faster algorithm for computing the sum of p-boxes. Journal of Uncertain Systems 4(4) (2010)
8. Choquet, G.: Theory of capacities. Annales de l'Institut Fourier 5, 131–295 (1953)
9. Comba, J.L.D., Stolfi, J.: Affine arithmetic and its applications to computer graphics. In: SEBGRAPI 1993 (1993)
10. Cousot, P., Monerau, M.: Probabilistic abstract interpretation. In: Seidl, H. (ed.) ESOP 2012. LNCS, vol. 7211, pp. 169–193. Springer, Heidelberg (2012)
11. Destercke, S., Dubois, D., Chojnacki, E.: Unifying practical uncertainty representations - I: Generalized p-boxes. J. of Approximate Reasoning 49(3) (2008)
12. Destercke, S., Dubois, D., Chojnacki, E.: Unifying practical uncertainty representations. II: Clouds. Intl. J. of Approximate Reasoning 49(3) (2008)
13. Enszer, J.A., Lin, Y., Ferson, S., Corliss, G.F., Stadtherr, M.A.: Probability bounds analysis for nonlinear dynamic process models. AIChE Journal 57(2) (2011)
14. Feller, W.: An Introduction to Probability Theory and Its Applications. Wiley (1968)
15. Feret, J.: Static analysis of digital filters. In: Schmidt, D. (ed.) ESOP 2004. LNCS, vol. 2986, pp. 33–48. Springer, Heidelberg (2004)
16. Ferson, S.: RAMAS Risk Calc 4.0 Software: Risk Assessment with Uncertain Numbers. Lewis Publishers (2002)
17. Ferson, S., Kreinovich, V., Ginzburg, L., Myers, D., Sentz, K.: Constructing probability boxes and Dempster-Shafer structures. Tech. Rep. SAND2002-4015, Sandia National Laboratories (2003)
18. Ferson, S.: What Monte-Carlo methods cannot do. Human and Ecological Risk Assessment 2, 990–1007 (1996)
19. Fuchs, M., Neumaier, A.: Potential based clouds in robust design optimization. J. Stat. Theory Practice 3, 225–238 (2009)
20. Ghorbal, K., Goubault, E., Putot, S.: A logical product approach to zonotope intersection. In: Touili, T., Cook, B., Jackson, P. (eds.) CAV 2010. LNCS, vol. 6174, pp. 212–226. Springer, Heidelberg (2010)
21. Goubault, E., Putot, S.: A zonotopic framework for functional abstractions. CoRR abs/0910.1763 (2009)
22. Goubault, E., Putot, S.: Static analysis of finite precision computations. In: Jhala, R., Schmidt, D. (eds.) VMCAI 2011. LNCS, vol. 6538, pp. 232–247. Springer, Heidelberg (2011)

23. Goubault-Larrecq, J.: Continuous capacities on continuous state spaces. In: Arge, L., Cachin, C., Jurdziński, T., Tarlecki, A. (eds.) ICALP 2007. LNCS, vol. 4596, pp. 764–776. Springer, Heidelberg (2007)

24. Goubault-Larrecq, J.: Continuous previsions. In: Duparc, J., Henzinger, T.A. (eds.) CSL 2007. LNCS, vol. 4646, pp. 542–557. Springer, Heidelberg (2007)

25. Goubault-Larrecq, J.: Prevision domains and convex powercones. In: Amadio, R.M. (ed.) FOSSACS 2008. LNCS, vol. 4962, pp. 318–333. Springer, Heidelberg (2008)

26. Goubault-Larrecq, J., Keimel, K.: Choquet-Kendall-Matheron theorems for non-Hausdorff spaces. MSCS 21(3), 511–561 (2011)

27. Kwiatkowska, M., Norman, G., Parker, D.: Prism 4.0: Verification of probabilistic real-time systems. In: Gopalakrishnan, G., Qadeer, S. (eds.) CAV 2011. LNCS, vol. 6806, pp. 585–591. Springer, Heidelberg (2011)

28. Lin, Y., Stadtherr, M.A.: Validated solution of initial value problems for odes with interval parameters. In: NSF Workshop on Reliable Engineering Computing (2006)

29. Mancini, R., Carter, B.: Op Amps for Everyone. Electronics & Electrical (2009)

30. McIver, A., Morgan, C.: Demonic, angelic and unbounded probabilistic choices in sequential programs. Acta Informatica 37(4/5), 329–354 (2001)

31. Mislove, M.W.: Nondeterminism and probabilistic choice: Obeying the laws. In: Palamidessi, C. (ed.) CONCUR 2000. LNCS, vol. 1877, pp. 350–364. Springer, Heidelberg (2000)

32. Monniaux, D.: Abstract interpretation of probabilistic semantics. In: Palsberg, J. (ed.) SAS 2000. LNCS, vol. 1824, pp. 322–340. Springer, Heidelberg (2000)

33. Neumaier, A.: Clouds, fuzzy sets and probability intervals. Reliable Computing (2004)

34. Rump, S.: INTLAB - INTerval LABoratory. In: Csendes, T. (ed.) Developments in Reliable Computing, pp. 77–104. Kluwer Academic Publishers (1999)

35. Sankaranarayanan, S., Chakarov, A., Gulwani, S.: Static analysis for probabilistic programs: inferring whole program properties from finitely many paths. In: Boehm, H.J., Flanagan, C. (eds.) PLDI, pp. 447–458. ACM (2013)

36. Shafer, G.: A Mathematical Theory of Evidence. Princeton University Press (1976)

37. Sun, J., Huang, Y., Li, J., Wang, J.M.: Chebyshev affine arithmetic based parametric yield prediction under limited descriptions of uncertainty. In: ASP-DAC 2008, pp. 531–536. IEEE Computer Society Press (2008)

38. Terejanu, G., Singla, P., Singh, T., Scott, P.D.: Approximate interval method for epistemic uncertainty propagation using polynomial chaos and evidence theory. In: 2010 American Control Conference, Baltimore, Maryland (2010)

39. Tix, R.: Continuous D-Cones: Convexity and Powerdomain Constructions. Ph.D. thesis, Technische Universität Darmstadt (1999)

40. Tix, R., Keimel, K., Plotkin, G.: Semantic domains for combining probability and non-determinism. ENTCS 129, 1–104 (2005)

41. Walley, P.: Statistical Reasoning with Imprecise Probabilities. Chapman Hall (1991)

42. Williamson, R.C., Downs, T.: Probabilistic arithmetic I: Numerical methods for calculating convolutions and dependency bounds. J. Approximate Reasoning (1990)

A   Operational Semantics

We start with a small-step operational semantics, given in Figure 6. Its states are pairs (Λ, ρ), where Λ is a finite list of statements, to be executed sequentially. The grammar for such lists is: $\Lambda ::= \epsilon \mid s \bullet \Lambda$. The states (ϵ, ρ) are final. The $\longrightarrow$ relation defined in Figure 6 form the deterministic part of the semantics, and should be clear. We write $\rho[x \mapsto v]$ for the environment that maps x to v, and every $y \neq x$ to $\rho(y)$.

To define the rest of the semantics, and in particular the semantics of the inputs $x_1, \ldots, x_k := \mathtt{input}$, we use judgments of the form $\ell \vdash (\Lambda, \rho) \downarrow_\kappa^\pm a$, for $\pm \in \{+, -\}$, where $\ell \in \mathcal{L}$, $a \in [0, 1]$ and $\kappa \colon \Sigma \to [0, 1]$ is a bounded measurable map[1]. When κ is the indicator map χ_E of a measurable subset E of Σ, the intended meaning will be: starting from Λ in environment ρ, the probability of reaching label ℓ with some environment in E is at least (resp. at most) a if $\pm$ is $-$ (resp. $+$). In general, it is practical to use general measurable maps κ instead of indicator maps χ_E, and the meaning of $\ell \vdash (\Lambda, \rho) \downarrow_\kappa^- a$ will be: the average value of $\kappa(\rho')$ over all environments ρ' reached when at label ℓ is at least a (at most a for $\ell \vdash (\Lambda, \rho) \downarrow_\kappa^+ a$).

We should mention that our intuition here fails to capture an essential point. Consider a simple loop, say $\mathtt{while}(b) \{ \ell \colon s_1 \}$, where s_1 may do some readings of the random inputs. There is no such thing as the probability of reaching program point ℓ. Instead, there is a probability of reaching ℓ in one turn of the loop, another probability of reaching ℓ in two turns of the loop, and so on. In general, for each $n \in \mathbb{N}$, there is a probability of reaching ℓ in exactly n turns. What we shall be interested in is the sup, resp. the inf, over all n, of these probabilities—and, more generally, the sup/inf over all n of the average value of κ over all runs that reach ℓ for the nth time. The judgment $\ell \vdash (\Lambda, \rho) \downarrow_\kappa^+ a$ will state that whatever n is, the average value of κ over all runs reaching ℓ for the nth time is at most a, while $\ell \vdash (\Lambda, \rho) \downarrow_\kappa^+ a$ will state that whatever n is, the average value of h over all reaching ℓ for the nth time is at least a.

A note to the expert: in effect, we are implementing a semantics with mixed non-deterministic and probabilistic choice. While inputs account for probabilistic choice, the statement $\ell \colon$ (for the given label at the left of $\vdash$) chooses non-deterministically whether it should stop right here and evaluate κ, or proceed. So our semantics is already not purely probabilistic, as in Kozen[2] and Panangaden[3]. One may also observe that the latter semantics are unsuited to our purposes, as they only observe the probability of reaching final states. As such, they are probabilistic analogues of *big-step* semantics. In abstract interpretation, we need to evaluate probabilities (largest, smallest) of reaching states that may not be final, such as those at label ℓ in our example above.

---

[1] We equate Σ with $\mathbb{R}^{|Var^+|}$ with its standard σ-algebra.

[2] Kozen, D.: Semantics of probabilistic programs. Journal of Computer and Systems Sciences 30(2), 162–178 (1985)

[3] Panangaden, P.: Probabilistic relations. In: Baier, C., Huth, M., Kwiatkowska, M., Ryan, M. (eds.) Proceedings of PROBMIV'98. pp. 59–74 (1998)

Since this is equally easy, and is needed later, we allow the distribution ν_{inp} to vary in some set of probability measures over $\mathbb{R}^k$. For our purposes, it is practical to merely give a pair of a lower prevision F_{inp}^- and of an upper prevision F_{inp}^+ on $\mathbb{R}^k$, and to consider those distributions ν_{inp} that lie between them:

$$F_{\text{inp}}^-(f) \leq \int_{(v_1,\ldots,v_k)\in\mathbb{R}^k} f(v_1,\ldots,v_k)d\nu_{\text{inp}} \leq F_{\text{inp}}^+(f) \tag{6}$$

for every bounded measurable map $f\colon \mathbb{R}^k \to [0,1]$. ($F_{\text{inp}}^-$ and F_{inp}^+ will be described through Dempster-Shafer structures.)

$$\left(x := e \bullet \Lambda, \rho\right) \longrightarrow \left(\Lambda, \rho[x \mapsto [\![e]\!]\rho]\right) \qquad \left((s_1; s_2) \bullet \Lambda, \rho\right) \longrightarrow \left(s_1 \bullet s_2 \bullet \Lambda, \rho\right)$$

$$\left((\texttt{if } (b) \ \{s_1\} \ \texttt{else } \{s_2\}) \bullet \Lambda, \rho\right) \longrightarrow \begin{cases} \left(s_1 \bullet \Lambda, \rho\right) & \text{if } [\![b]\!]\rho = 1 \\ \left(s_2 \bullet \Lambda, \rho\right) & \text{if } [\![b]\!]\rho = 0 \end{cases}$$

$$\left((\texttt{while}(b) \ \{s_1\}) \bullet \Lambda, \rho\right) \longrightarrow \begin{cases} \left(s_1 \bullet (\texttt{while}(b) \ \{s_1\}) \bullet \Lambda, \rho\right) & \text{if } [\![b]\!]\rho = 1 \\ \left(\Lambda, \rho\right) & \text{if } [\![b]\!]\rho = 0 \end{cases}$$

$$\frac{\ell \vdash \left(\Lambda', \rho'\right) \downarrow_\kappa^\pm a \quad (\Lambda, \rho) \longrightarrow (\Lambda', \rho')}{\ell \vdash (\Lambda, \rho) \downarrow_\kappa^\pm a} \ (Det^\pm)$$

$$\frac{\ell \vdash (\Lambda, \rho) \downarrow_\kappa^\pm a \quad \ell' \neq \ell}{\ell \vdash (\ell' : \bullet \Lambda, \rho) \downarrow_\kappa^\pm a} \ (\mathcal{L}_{\neq}^\pm) \qquad \frac{\ell \vdash (\Lambda, \rho) \downarrow^\pm a \quad \kappa(\rho) \bowtie_\kappa^\pm a}{\ell \vdash (\ell : \bullet \Lambda, \rho) \downarrow_\kappa^\pm a} \ (\mathcal{L}_{=}^\pm)$$

$$\frac{}{\ell \vdash (\epsilon, \rho) \downarrow_\kappa^\pm a} \ (Fin^\pm) \qquad \frac{}{\ell \vdash (\Lambda, \rho) \downarrow_\kappa^+ 1} \ (\perp^+) \qquad \frac{}{\ell \vdash (\Lambda, \rho) \downarrow_\kappa^- 0} \ (\perp^-)$$

$$\frac{\overset{(v_1,\ldots,v_k)\in\mathbb{R}^k}{\ell \vdash \left(\Lambda, \rho[x_1 \mapsto v_1, \ldots, x_k \mapsto v_k]\right) \downarrow_\kappa^\pm f(v_1,\ldots,v_k))} \quad F_{\text{inp}}^\pm(f) \bowtie^\pm a}{\ell \vdash \left(x_1,\ldots,x_k := \texttt{input} \bullet \Lambda, \rho\right) \downarrow_\kappa^\pm a} \ (Inp^\pm)$$

Fig. 6. Operational semantics

The result is given by the derivation rules at the bottom of Figure 6, which are in a style inspired by[4]. We write $\bowtie^\pm$ for $\geq$ if $\pm$ is $-$, or for $\leq$ if $\pm$ is $+$. The $(Det^\pm)$ rule is simple: if $(\Lambda, \rho) \longrightarrow (\Lambda', \rho')$, then this is a deterministic computation step, and there is no label to observe κ on when in state (Λ, ρ), so the average of κ must be taken on the rest of the execution, starting from (Λ', ρ'). If this is above a (or below a; see premise), then the average of κ starting from (Λ, ρ) (conclusion) must also be above/below a. $(\mathcal{L}_{\neq}^\pm)$ is explained similarly: we

[4] Goubault-Larrecq, J.: Full abstraction for non-deterministic and probabilistic extensions of PCF I: the angelic cases. Journal of Logic and Algebraic Programming (2012), submitted. Presented at the Domains X Workshop, Swansea, UK, 2011.

do not observe κ at ℓ', since $\ell' \neq \ell$, and additionally the effect of ℓ': is a no-op. $(\mathcal{L}^{\pm}_{\equiv})$ is more interesting, and is the only place where κ is really used. Let us investigate $(\mathcal{L}^{-}_{\equiv})$, the other case being similar. The possible averages of κ at each time we reach label ℓ are exactly the current value $\kappa(\rho)$ of κ (since we *are* at label ℓ), and those obtained when we reach ℓ later. The first premise states that the latter averages are above a, while the second premise states that $\kappa(\rho) \geq a$. In any case, the possible averages of κ must be above a, and this is the conclusion of the rule.

The $(Fin^{\pm})$ rules state what happens on termination. Since ℓ is never reached in a terminated run (of length *zero*), the possible averages of κ on this run form an empty set: all such averages are below every $a \in [0,1]$ (rule (Fin^{+})) and above every $a \in [0,1]$ (rule (Fin^{-})). The $(\perp^{\pm})$ rules express the trivial facts that the average of a map κ with values in $[0,1]$ must be between 0 and 1.

The $(Inp^{\pm})$ rule is a bit intimidating, since it has infinitely many premises—at least as many as there are tuples $(v_1, \ldots, v_k)$ in $\mathbb{R}^k$—and is parameterized by a bounded measurable map $f \colon \mathbb{R}^k \to [0,1]$. This is mandated by the fact that ν_{inp} may be an arbitrary, not discrete, measure. We should be reassured by looking at (Inp^{-}) in a simple case, say when $k = 1$, and ν_{inp} implements a discrete random choice between $v_1 = 1.2$ with probability $1/6$ ($= f(1.2)$), $v_1 = 1.3$ with probability $1/2$, and $v_1 = 1.4$ with probability $1/3$. (Let us also take the $\leq$ signs in (6) to be equalities.) Then (Inp^{-}) specializes to the following rule (up to irrelevant premises):

$$\frac{\ell \vdash \left(\Lambda, \rho[x_1 \mapsto 1.2]\right) \downarrow^{-}_{\kappa} a_1 \quad \ell \vdash \left(\Lambda, \rho[x_1 \mapsto 1.3]\right) \downarrow^{-}_{\kappa} a_2 \quad \ell \vdash \left(\Lambda, \rho[x_1 \mapsto 1.4]\right) \downarrow^{-}_{\kappa} a_3}{\ell \vdash \left(x_1, \ldots, x_k := \mathtt{input} \bullet \Lambda, \rho\right) \downarrow^{-}_{\kappa} a.} \quad 1/6\, a_1 + 1/2\, a_2 + 1/3\, a_3 \geq a$$

In particular, if you think of a_1 as the (minimal) average value of κ when x_1 is set to 1.2, and similarly for a_2 and a_3, this states that the values a below the (minimal) average value that κ takes when running $x_1, \ldots, x_k := \mathtt{input} \bullet \Lambda$ are exactly those below the average $1/6\, a_1 + 1/2\, a_2 + 1/3\, a_3$ that one should expect.

B   Adequacy Theorem

We here prove that the operational and denotational semantics are equivalent. On the operational side, note that whenever $\ell \vdash (\Lambda, \rho) \downarrow^{-}_{\kappa} a$ is derivable and $a \geq b$, then $\ell \vdash (\Lambda, \rho) \downarrow^{-}_{\kappa} b$ is also derivable. So the set of values a such that $\ell \vdash (\Lambda, \rho) \downarrow^{-}_{\kappa} a$ is derivable is a downward-closed interval $[0, c]$ or $[0, c)$: let us write $[\Lambda]^{-}_{\ell,\kappa}\rho$ for c, the sup of these values a. Similarly, we write $[\Lambda]^{+}_{\ell,\kappa}\rho$ for the inf of the values a such that $\ell \vdash (\Lambda, \rho) \downarrow^{+}_{\kappa} a$ is derivable. Write 0 for the constant 0 map, and similarly for 1.

Theorem 3 (Adequacy). $[\Lambda]^{-}_{\ell,\kappa}1\rho = [\Lambda]^{-}_{\ell,\kappa}\rho$, and $[\Lambda]^{+}_{\ell,\kappa}0\rho = [\Lambda]^{+}_{\ell,\kappa}\rho$.

Proof. We deal with the $-$ case, as the $+$ case is similar.

($\geq$) We first show that $[\Lambda]^{-}_{\ell,\kappa}1\rho \geq [\Lambda]^{-}_{\ell,\kappa}\rho$. Equivalently, we show that for every $a \in [0,1]$ such that $\ell \vdash (\Lambda, \rho) \downarrow^{-}_{\kappa} a$ is derivable, then $[\Lambda]^{-}_{\ell,\kappa}1\rho \geq a$. This is by structural induction on the given derivation. We look at each rule in turn.

(Fin^-). We must show that $[\![\epsilon]\!]^-_{\ell,\kappa} 1\rho \geq a$, which is obvious since $[\![\epsilon]\!]^-_{\ell,\kappa} 1\rho = 1$.

$(\bot^-)$. $[\![\Lambda]\!]^-_{\ell,\kappa} 1\rho \geq 0$, by Theorem 1, first part.

(Det^-). For each rule $(\Lambda, \rho) \longrightarrow (\Lambda', \rho')$, one checks easily that $[\![\Lambda]\!]^-_{\ell,\kappa} 1\rho = [\![\Lambda']\!]^-_{\ell,\kappa} 1\rho$. By the induction hypothesis, the right-hand side is $\geq a$, so this is also the case of the left-hand side.

$(\mathcal{L}^-_{\neq})$. We must show that $[\![\ell': \bullet \Lambda]\!]^-_{\ell,\kappa} 1\rho \geq a$, where the induction hypothesis gives us $[\![\Lambda]\!]^-_{\ell,\kappa} 1\rho \geq a$. This is again clear, since $[\![\ell': \bullet \Lambda]\!]^-_{\ell,\kappa} 1\rho = [\![\Lambda]\!]^-_{\ell,\kappa} 1\rho$.

$(\mathcal{L}^-_{=})$. The induction hypothesis now gives us that not only $[\![\Lambda]\!]^-_{\ell,\kappa} 1\rho \geq a$, but also $\kappa(\rho) \geq a$. So $[\![\ell: \bullet \Lambda]\!]^-_{\ell,\kappa} 1\rho = [\![\ell:]\!]^-_{\ell\kappa} ([\![\Lambda]\!]^-_{\ell,\kappa} 1)\rho = \min(\kappa(\rho), [\![\Lambda]\!]^-_{\ell,\kappa} 1\rho) \geq a$.

(Inp^-). The induction hypothesis gives us a measurable map $f: \mathbb{R}^k \to [0,1]$, with the property that, for every $(v_1, \ldots, v_k) \in \mathbb{R}^k$, $[\![\Lambda]\!]^-_{\ell,\kappa} 1(\rho[x_1 \mapsto v_1, \ldots, x_k \mapsto v_k]) \geq f(v_1, \ldots, v_k)$, and $F^-_{inp}(f) \geq a$. Since F^-_{inp} is monotonic, $F^-_{inp}(\lambda v_1, \ldots, v_k \cdot [\![\Lambda]\!]^-_{\ell,\kappa} 1(\rho[x_1 \mapsto v_1, \ldots, x_k \mapsto v_k])) \geq F^-_{inp}(f) \geq a$. But the left hand side is exactly $[\![x_1, \ldots, x_k := \mathtt{input}]\!]^-_{\ell,\kappa} ([\![\Lambda]\!]^-_{\ell,\kappa} 1)\rho = [\![x_1, \ldots, x_k := \mathtt{input} \bullet \Lambda]\!]^-_{\ell,\kappa} 1\rho$.

($\leq$) The converse inequality is harder. We shall show that for every $a \ll [\![\Lambda]\!]^-_{\ell,\kappa} 1\rho$ (implicitly, with $a \geq 0$), there is a derivation of $\ell \vdash (\Lambda, \rho) \downarrow^-_\kappa a$. (The $\ll$ relation is the so-called way-below relation on $[0,1]$, and is defined by $a \ll b$ iff $a < b$ or $a = 0$. Note that every $b \in [0,1]$ is the sup of the values a such that $a \ll b$. Moreover, if $a \ll b$, then for every sequence $b_0 \leq b_1 \leq \ldots \leq b_n \leq \ldots$ whose sup is at least b, then $a \leq b_n$ for n large enough, a property that we shall the Fundamental Property of $\ll$.) This is proved by double induction on the number of statements in Λ first, and when non-empty, by induction on the structure of the first statement in Λ.

Base case, $\Lambda = \epsilon$. We simply apply rule (Fin^-), since $a \in [0,1]$, which follows from the first part of Theorem 1.

In the inductive case, we consider a non-empty list, say of the form $s \bullet \Lambda$, and some $a \ll [\![s \bullet \Lambda]\!]^-_{\ell,\kappa} 1\rho = [\![s]\!]^-_{\ell,\kappa} ([\![\Lambda]\!]^-_{\ell,\kappa} 1)\rho$. We must exhibit a derivation of $\ell \vdash (s \bullet \Lambda, \rho) \downarrow^-_\kappa a$, under the following two induction hypotheses, which we name for future reference:

(H_1) for every $\rho' \in \Sigma$, for every $a' \ll [\![\Lambda]\!]^-_{\ell,\kappa} 1\rho'$, there is a derivation of $\ell \vdash (\Lambda, \rho') \downarrow^-_\kappa a'$;

(H_2) for every proper substatement s' of s, for every list Λ', for every $\rho' \in \Sigma$, for every $a' \ll [\![s']\!]^-_{\ell,\kappa} ([\![\Lambda']\!]^-_{\ell,\kappa} 1)\rho'$, there is a derivation of $\ell \vdash (s' \bullet \Lambda', \rho') \downarrow^-_\kappa a'$.

Assignment. $s = (x := e)$. By assumption, $a \ll [\![x := e \bullet \Lambda]\!]^-_{\ell,\kappa} 1\rho = [\![x := e]\!]^-_{\ell,\kappa} ([\![\Lambda]\!]^-_{\ell,\kappa} 1)\rho = [\![\Lambda]\!]^-_{\ell,\kappa} 1(\rho[x \mapsto [\![e]\!]\rho])$. Now use (H_1) with $\rho' = \rho[x \mapsto [\![e]\!]\rho]$ and $a' = a$. We obtain a derivation of $\ell \vdash (\Lambda, (\rho[x \mapsto [\![e]\!]\rho])) \downarrow^-_\kappa a$. Now use (Det^-) on the latter, and we obtain a derivation of $\ell \vdash (x := e \bullet \Lambda, \rho) \downarrow^-_\kappa a$.

The case of labels ℓ': (with $\ell' = \ell$, or with $\ell' \neq \ell$) is similar.

Sequences. $s = (s_1; s_2)$. By assumption, $a \ll [\![s_1; s_2 \bullet \Lambda]\!]^-_{\ell,\kappa} 1\rho$, namely, $a \ll [\![s_1]\!]^-_{\ell,\kappa} ([\![s_2]\!]^-_{\ell,\kappa} ([\![\Lambda]\!]^-_{\ell,\kappa} 1))\rho$. Use (H_2) with $s' = s_1$, $\Lambda' = s_2 \bullet \Lambda$, $\rho' = \rho$, $a' = a$ and obtain a derivation of $\ell \vdash (s_1 \bullet s_2 \bullet \Lambda, \rho) \downarrow^-_\kappa a$. Add an instance of (Det^-) to obtain a derivation of $\ell \vdash ((s_1; s_2) \bullet \Lambda, \rho) \downarrow^-_\kappa a$, and we are done.

Tests $\texttt{if } (b) \{ s_1 \} \texttt{ else } \{ s_2 \}$ are dealt with similar, using (H_2) with $s' = s_1$ if $[\![b]\!]\rho = 1$, with $s' = s_2$ if $[\![b]\!]\rho = 0$.

Inputs. $s = x_1, \ldots, x_k := \texttt{input}$. Define $f(v_1, \ldots, v_k) = [\![\Lambda]\!]^-_{\ell, \kappa} 1(\rho[x_1 \mapsto v_1, \ldots, x_k \mapsto v_k])$. This is a measurable map from $\mathbb{R}^k$ to $[0, 1]$. For every $\epsilon > 0$, let $f_\epsilon(v_1, \ldots, v_k) = \max(f(v_1, \ldots, v_k) - \epsilon, 0)$. Note that this is way below $f(v_1, \ldots, v_k)$. By (H_1) with $\rho' = \rho[x_1 \mapsto v_1, \ldots, x_k \mapsto v_k]$, $a' = f_\epsilon(v_1, \ldots, v_k)$, there is a derivation of $\ell \vdash (\Lambda, ()\rho[x_1 \mapsto v_1, \ldots, x_k \mapsto v_k]) \downarrow^-_\kappa f_\epsilon(v_1, \ldots, v_k)$, one for each tuple $(v_1, \ldots, v_k) \in \mathbb{R}^k$. Since $F^-_{\texttt{inp}}$ is monotonic and ω-continuous, $(F^-_{\texttt{inp}}(f_{1/n}))_{n \in \mathbb{N}}$ is a monotone sequence whose sup is $F^-_{\texttt{inp}}(f)$. But $F^-_{\texttt{inp}}(f) = [\![x_1, \ldots, x_k := \texttt{input} \bullet \Lambda]\!]^-_{\ell, \kappa} 1\rho$, by definition of the right-hand side, and a is way below the latter. So $a \ll \sup_{n \in \mathbb{N}} F^-_{\texttt{inp}}(f_{1/n})$, which implies that $a \leq F^-_{\texttt{inp}}(f_{1/n})$ for n large enough, by the Fundamental Property of $\ll$. We can now apply rule (Inp^-) (with f replaced by $f_{1/n}$) and the result is a derivation of $\ell \vdash (x_1, \ldots, x_k := \texttt{input} \bullet \Lambda, \rho) \downarrow^-_\kappa a$.

While loops. $s = (\texttt{while}(b) \{ s_1 \})$. Since $a \ll [\![s]\!]^-_{\ell, \kappa}([\![\Lambda]\!]^-_{\ell, \kappa} 1)\rho$, it is plain to see that there is a $b \in [0, 1]$ such that $a \ll b \ll [\![s]\!]^-_{\ell, \kappa}([\![\Lambda]\!]^-_{\ell, \kappa} 1)\rho$. Since $[\![s]\!]^-_{\ell, \kappa} = [\![\texttt{while}(b) \{ s_1 \}]\!]^-_{\ell, \kappa}$ is defined as the sup of a monotone chain, the Fundamental Property of $\ll$ applies to conclude that $a \ll b \leq H^i_{b, s_1}(\perp^-)([\![\Lambda]\!]^-_{\ell, \kappa} 1)\rho = H^i_{b, s_1}(0)([\![\Lambda]\!]^-_{\ell, \kappa} 1)\rho$, for some $i \in \mathbb{N}$, using the notations of Figure 2. It now suffices to show that there is a derivation of $\ell \vdash ((\texttt{while}(b) \{ s_1 \}) \bullet \Lambda, \rho) \downarrow^-_\kappa a$, and we do this by an auxiliary induction on i.

If $i = 0$, then $a \ll H^i_{b, s_1}(0)([\![\Lambda]\!]^-_{\ell, \kappa} 1)\rho = 0$ implies $a = 0$, and we apply rule $(\perp^-)$. (This is the only purpose of this rule: to be able to derive $\ell \vdash ((\texttt{while}(b) \{ s_1 \}) \bullet \Lambda, \rho) \downarrow^-_\kappa 0$ when the while loop does not terminate; without it, we would simply have no derivation at all.) If $i \geq 1$, then we have two cases.

If $[\![b]\!]\rho = 0$, then $H^i_{b, s_1}(0)([\![\Lambda]\!]^-_{\ell, \kappa} 1)\rho = H_{b, s_1}(H^{i-1}_{b, s_1}(0))([\![\Lambda]\!]^-_{\ell, \kappa} 1)\rho = [\![\Lambda]\!]^-_{\ell, \kappa} 1\rho$. By (H_1) with $a' = a$ and $\rho' = \rho$, there is a derivation of $\ell \vdash (\Lambda, \rho) \downarrow^-_\kappa a$. Now we apply (Det^-) with the rule $((\texttt{while}(b) \{ s_1 \}) \bullet \Lambda, \rho) \longrightarrow (\Lambda, \rho)$ to obtain a derivation of $\ell \vdash ((\texttt{while}(b) \{ s_1 \}) \bullet \Lambda, \rho) \downarrow^-_\kappa a$.

If $[\![b]\!]\rho = 1$, then $H^i_{b, s_1}(0)([\![\Lambda]\!]^-_{\ell, \kappa} 1)\rho = H_{b, s_1}(H^{i-1}_{b, s_1}(0))([\![\Lambda]\!]^-_{\ell, \kappa} 1)\rho$, which is equal to $[\![s_1]\!]^-_{\ell, \kappa}(H^{i-1}_{b, s_1}(0)([\![\Lambda]\!]^-_{\ell, \kappa} 1))\rho$. By the definition of the semantics of $\texttt{while}$ as a sup, $H^{i-1}_{b, s_1}(0)([\![\Lambda]\!]^-_{\ell, \kappa} 1) \leq [\![\texttt{while}(b) \{ s_1 \}]\!]^-_{\ell, \kappa}([\![\Lambda]\!]^-_{\ell, \kappa} 1) = [\![\texttt{while}(b) \{ s_1 \} \bullet \Lambda]\!]^-_{\ell, \kappa} 1$. Since $\lambda h \cdot [\![s_1]\!]^-_{\ell \kappa} h\rho$ is monotonic (as a prevision, see Theorem 1), we obtain $a \ll [\![s_1]\!]^-_{\ell, \kappa}([\![\texttt{while}(b) \{ s_1 \} \bullet \Lambda]\!]^-_{\ell, \kappa} 1)\rho$. By (H_2), we obtain a derivation of $\ell \vdash s_1, [\![\texttt{while}(b) \{ s_1 \} \bullet \Lambda]\!]^\rho \downarrow^-_\kappa a$. Apply (Det^-) with the rule

$$((\texttt{while}(b) \{ s_1 \}) \bullet \Lambda, \rho) \longrightarrow (s_1, (\texttt{while}(b) \{ s_1 \}) \bullet \Lambda, \rho)$$

this yields the desired derivation of $\ell \vdash (\texttt{while}(b) \{ s_1 \} \bullet \Lambda, \rho) \downarrow^-_\kappa a$. $\square$

Effect Analysis for Programs with Callbacks

Etienne Kneuss[1], Viktor Kuncak[1,*], and Philippe Suter[1,2]

[1] École Polytechnique Fédérale de Lausanne (EPFL), Switzerland
[2] IBM T.J. Watson Research Center, Yorktown Heights, NY, USA
{firstname.lastname}@epfl.ch, psuter@us.ibm.com

Abstract. We introduce a precise interprocedural effect analysis for programs with mutable state, dynamic object allocation, and dynamic dispatch. Our analysis is precise even in the presence of dynamic dispatch where the context-insensitive estimate on the number of targets is very large. This feature makes our analysis appropriate for programs that manipulate first-class functions (callbacks). We present a framework in which programs are enriched with special effect statements, and define the semantics of both program and effect statements as relations on states. Our framework defines a program composition operator that is sound with respect to relation composition. Computing the summary of a procedure then consists of composing all its program statements to produce a single effect statement. We propose a strategy for applying the composition operator in a way that balances precision and efficiency.

We instantiate this framework with a domain for tracking read and write effects, where relations on program states are abstracted as graphs. We implemented the analysis as a plugin for the Scala compiler. We analyzed the Scala standard library containing 58000 methods and classified them into several categories according to their effects. Our analysis proves that over one half of all methods are pure, identifies a number of conditionally pure methods, and computes summary graphs and regular expressions describing the side effects of non-pure methods.

1 Introduction

An appealing programming style uses predominantly functional computation steps, including higher-order functions, with a disciplined use of side effects. An opportunity for parallel execution further increases the potential of this style. Whereas higher-order functions have always been recognized as a pillar of functional programming, they have also become a standard feature of object-oriented languages such as C# (in the form of *delegates*), the 2011 standard of C++, and Java 8.[1] Moreover, design patterns popular in the object-oriented programming community also rely on callbacks, for instance the *strategy pattern* and the *visitor pattern* [13].

---

[*] This research was supported in part by the European Research Council Project "Implicit Programming".

[1] See JSR 335 "Project Lambda" http://www.jcp.org/en/jsr/detail?id=335

Precise analysis of side effects is essential for automated as well as manual reasoning about such programs. The combination of callbacks and mutation makes it difficult to design an analysis that is both scalable enough to handle realistic code bases, and precise enough to handle common patterns such as local side effects and initialization, which arise both from manual programming practice and compilation of higher-level concepts. Among key challenges are flow-sensitivity and precise handling of aliases, as well as precise and scalable handling of method calls.

Our aim is to support not only automated program analyses and transformations that rely on effect information, but also program understanding tasks. We therefore seek to generate readable effect summaries that developers can compare to their intuition of what methods should and should not affect in program heap. Such summaries must go beyond a pure/impure dichotomy, and should ideally capture the exact frame condition of the analyzed code fragment — or at least an acceptable over-approximation. We expect our results in this direction will help in bootstrapping annotations for Scala effect type systems [26], as well as lead to the design of more precise versions of such systems.

This paper presents the design, implementation, and evaluation of a new static analysis for method side effects, which is precise and scalable even in the presence of callbacks, including higher-order functions. Key design aspects of our analysis include:

- a relational analysis domain that computes summaries of code blocks and methods by flow-sensitively tracking side effects and performing strong updates;
- a framework for relational analyses to compute higher-order relational summaries of method calls, which are parameterized by the effects of the methods being called;
- an automated effect classification and presentation of effect abstractions in terms of regular expressions, facilitating their understanding by developers.

Our static analyzer, called Insane (INterprocedural Static ANalysis of Effects) is publicly available from

```
https://github.com/epfl-lara/insane
```

We have evaluated Insane on the full Scala standard library, which is widely used by all Scala programs, and is also publicly available. Our analysis works on a relatively low-level intermediate representation that is close to Java bytecodes. Despite this low-level representation, we were able to classify most method calls as not having any observational side effects. Moreover, our analysis also detects conditionally pure methods, for which purity is guaranteed provided that a specified set of subcalls are pure. We also demonstrate the precision of our analysis on a number of examples that use higher-order functions as control structures. We are not aware of any other fully automated static analyzer that achieves this precision while maintaining reasonable performance.

2   Overview of Challenges and Solutions

In this section, we present some of the challenges that arise when analyzing programs written in a higher-order style, and how Insane can tackle them.

Effect Attribution. Specific to higher-order programs is the problem of correctly attributing heap effects. Consider a simple class and a (first-order) function:

class Cell(**var** visited : Boolean)

def toggle(c : Cell) = {
  c.visited = !c.visited
}

Any reasonable analysis for effects would detect that toggle potentially alters the heap, as it contains a statement that writes to a field of an allocated object. That effect could informally be summarized as "*toggle may modify the .value field of its first argument*". That information could in turn be retrieved whenever toggle is used. Consider now the function

def apply(c : Cell, f : Cell⇒Unit) = {
  f(c)
}

where Cell⇒Unit denotes the type of a function that takes a Cell as argument and returns no value. What is the effect of apply on the heap? Surely, apply potentially has all the effects that toggle has, since the call apply(c, toggle) is equivalent to toggle(c). It can also potentially have no effect on the heap at all, e.g. if invoked as apply(c, (cell ⇒ ())). The situation can also be much worse, for instance in the presence of global objects that may be modified by f. In fact, in the absence of a dedicated technique, the only sound approximation of the effect of apply is to state that it can have any effect. This approximation is of course useless, both from the perspective of a programmer, who doesn't gain any insight on the behaviour of apply, and in the context of a broader program analysis, where the effect cannot be reused modularly.

The solution we propose in this paper is, intuitively, to define the effect of apply to be "*exactly the effect of calling its second argument with its first as a parameter*". To support this, we extend the notion of effect to be expressive enough to represent *control-flow graphs* where edges can themselves be effects. In the context of Insane we have applied this idea to a domain designed for tracking heap effects (described in Section 3), although the technique applies to any relational analysis, as we show in Section 4.

Equipped with this extended notion of effects, we can classify methods as *pure*, *impure*, and *conditionally pure*. The apply function falls in this last category: it is pure as long as the methods called from within it are pure as well (in this case, the invocation of f). Notable examples of conditionally pure functions include many of the standard higher-order operations on structures which are used extensively in functional programs (map, fold, foreach, etc.). As an example, a typical implementation of foreach on linked lists is the following:

```
class LinkedList[T](var hd : T, var tl : LinkedList[T]) {
  def foreach(f : T ⇒ Unit) : Unit = {
    var p = this
    do {
      f(p.hd)
      p = p.tl
    } while(p != null)
  }
}
```

Correctly characterizing the effects of such functions is essential to analyzing programs written in a language such as Scala.

Making Sense of Effects. Another challenge we address in this paper is one of presentation: when a function is provably pure, this can be reported straightforwardly to the programmer. When however it can have effects on the heap, the pure/impure dichotomy falls short. Consider a function that updates all (mutable) elements stored in a linked list:

```
def update(es : LinkedList[Cell]) = {
  es.foreach(c ⇒ c.visited = true)
}
```

Because the closure passed to foreach has an effect, so does the overall function. A summary stating only that it is impure would be highly unsatisfactory, though: crucially, it would not give any indication to the programmer that the structure of the list itself cannot be affected by the writes. As we will see, the precise internal representation of effects, while suited to a compositional analysis, is impractical for humans, not the least because it is non-textual. We propose to bridge this representation gap by using an additional abstraction of effects in the form of regular expressions that describe sets of fields potentially affected by effects (see Section 5). This abstraction captures less information than the internal representation but can readily represent complex effect scenarios. For the example given above, the following regular expression is reported to the programmer:

$$es(.tl)^*.hd.visited$$

It shows that the fields affected are those *reachable* through the list (by following chains of .tl), but belonging to elements only, thus conveying the desired information. In Section 6.2, we further demonstrate this generation of human-readable effect summaries on a set of examples that use the standard Scala collections library.

3   Effect Analysis for Mutable Shared Structures

The starting point for our analysis is the effect analysis [28,32]. We here present an adaptation to our setting, with the support for strong updates, which take into account statement ordering for mutable heap operations. In the next section we lift this analysis to the case of programs with callbacks (higher-order programs), for which most existing analyses are imprecise. We thus obtain a unique combination of precision, both for field updates and for higher-order procedure invocations.

We start by describing a target language that is expressive enough to encode most of the intermediate representation of Scala programs that we analyze.

3.1   Intermediate Language Used for the Analysis

The language we target is a typical object oriented language with dynamic dispatch. A program is made of a set of classes $\mathcal{C}$ which implement methods. We identify methods uniquely by using the method name prefixed with its declaring class as in $C.m$ and denote the set of methods in a program $\mathcal{M}$. Our intermediate language has no ad-hoc method overloading because the affected methods can always be renamed after type checking. We assume that, for each method, a standard control-flow graph is available, where edges are labeled with simple program statements. Each of these graphs contains a source node *entry*, and a sink node *exit*. Figure 1 lists the statements in our intermediate language, along with their meaning.

Statement	Meaning
v = w	assign w to v
v = o.f	read field o.f into v
o.f = v	update field o.f with v
v = **new** C	allocate an object of class C and store the reference to it in v
v = o.m(a1, ..., an)	call method m of object o and store the result in v

Fig. 1. Program statements $\mathcal{P}$ considered in the target language

Because of dynamic dispatch, a call statement can target multiple methods, depending on the runtime type of the receiver object. For each method call $o.m()$, we can compute a superset of targets $\text{targets}(o.m) \subseteq \mathcal{M} \cup \{?\}$ using the static type of the receiver. If the hierarchy is not bounded through **final** classes or methods, we also include the special "?" target to represent the arbitrary methods that could be defined in unknown extensions of the program. Thus, we do not always assume access to the entire program: this assumption is defined as a parameter of the analysis, and we will see later how it affects it.

3.2   Effects as Graph Transformers

We next outline our graph-based representation of compositional effects. Our approach is related to the representation originally used for escape analysis [27,28]. The meaning of such an effect is a relation on program heaps which over-approximates the behavior of a fragments of code (e.g. methods). Section 4

```
class List(var elem: Int,
           var nxt: List = null)

def prepend(lst: List, v: Int) {
  lst.nxt = new List(lst.elem, lst.nxt)
  lst.elem = v
}
```

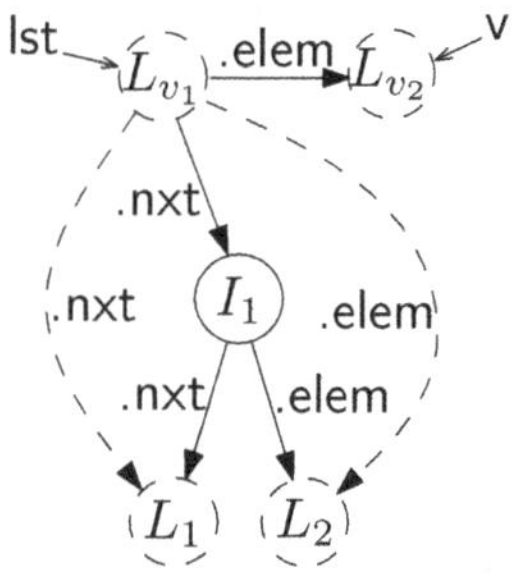

Fig. 2. Example of a graph representing the effects of prepend. Read edges lead to load nodes that represent unknown values, and solid edges represent field assignments.

lifts this representation to a more general, higher-order settings, which gives our final analysis.

Figure 2 shows an example of a simple function and its resulting graph-based effect. In this graph, L_{v_1} and L_{v_2} represent unknown local variables, here the parameters of the function. I_1 is an inside node corresponding to an object allocation. L_1 and L_2 are two load nodes that reference values for fields of L_{v_1} which are unknown at this time. While read (dashed) edges do not strictly represent effects, they are necessary to resolve the meaning of nodes when composing this effect at call-sites.

In general, our effect graphs are composed of nodes representing memory locations. We distinguish three kinds of nodes: *inside* nodes are allocated objects. Because we use the allocation-site abstraction for these, we associate with them a flag indicating whether the node is a singleton or a summary node. *Load* nodes represent unknown fields. Load nodes represent accesses to unknown parts of the heap; supporting them is a crucial requirement for modular effect analyses. Finally, graphs may contain special nodes for unresolved *local variables*, such as parameters.

We also define two types of edges labeled with fields. *Write* edges, represented by a plain (solid) edge in the graphical representation, and *read* edges, represented by dashed edges in the graph. Read edges provide an access paths to past or intermediate values of fields, and are used to resolve *load* nodes. *Write* edges represent *must-write* modifications. Along with the graph, we also keep a mapping from local variables to sets of nodes.

Our analysis directly defines rules to compute the composition of any effect graph with a statement that makes an individual heap modification. It is also possible to represent the meaning of each individual statement as an effect graph itself; the result of executing statement on a current effect graph then corresponds to *composing* two effect graphs. However, the main need for composition arises in modular analysis of function calls.

3.3   Composing Effects

Composition is a key component of most modular analyses. It is typically required for interprocedural reasoning. In our setting, it also plays an important role as a building block in our analysis framework for programs with callbacks, which we describe in Section 4. We now describe how composition applies to effect graphs. This operation is done in a specific direction: we say that an *inner* effect graph is applied to an *outer* effect graph. Merging graphs works by first constructing a map from inner nodes to equivalent outer nodes. This map, initially incomplete, expands during the merging process.

Importing Inside Nodes. The first step of the merging process is to import inside nodes from the inner graph to the outer graph. We specialize the labels representing their allocation sites to include the label corresponding to the point at which we compose the graphs. This property is crucial for our analysis as case-classes, an ubiquitous feature of Scala, rewrite to factory methods. Once the refined label is determined, we check whether we import a singleton node in an environment in which it already exists. In such case, the node is imported as a summary node.

Resolving Load Nodes. The next important operation when merging two graphs is the resolution of load nodes from the inner graph to nodes in the outer graph. The procedure works as follows: for each inner load node we look at all its source nodes, by following read edges in the opposite direction. Note that the source node of a load node might be a load node itself, in which case we recursively invoke the resolution operation. We then compute using the map all the nodes in the outer graph corresponding to the source nodes.

The resolution follows by performing a read operation from the corresponding source nodes in the outer graph. Once a load node is resolved to a set of nodes in the outer graph, the equivalence map is updated to reflect this.

Applying Write Effects. Given the map obtained by resolving load nodes, we apply write edges found in the inner graph to corresponding edges in the outer graph. We need to make sure that a strong update in the inner graph can remain strong, given the outer graph and the map.

The composition not only executes the last two steps, but repeats them until convergence of the outer graph. Once a fix-point is reached, we have successfully applied full meaning of the inner graph to the outer graph. Such application until fix-point is crucial for correctness in the presence of unknown aliasing and strong updates. We illustrate this merging operation in Figure 3.

4   Compositional Analysis of Higher-Order Code

The composition operator on effect graphs presented in the previous section allows us to analyze programs without dynamic dispatch. Standard approaches to extend it to dynamic dispatch are either imprecise or lose modularity.

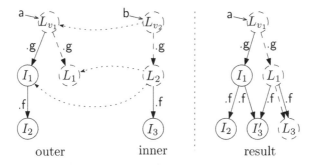

Fig. 3. Merging a graph with load nodes and strong updates in a context that does not permit a strong update. Inside nodes are imported after refining their label.

In this section, we therefore extend the basic analysis to support dynamic dispatch (including higher-order functions and callbacks) in both precise and a rather modular way. The methodology by which we extend the core analysis to the higher-order case is independent of the particular domain of effect graphs, so we present it in terms of a framework for precise interprocedural analysis of functions with callbacks.

Our framework works on top of any abstract interpretation-based analysis whose abstract domain R represents relations between program states. The abstract domain described in the previous section matches these requirements. Along with a set of control-flow graphs over statements $\mathcal{P}$ previously discussed, we assume the existence of other usual components of such analyses: a concretization function $\gamma : R \to (2^S)^S$ and a transfer function $T_f : (\mathcal{P} \times R) \to R$.

We now define a *composition operator* $\diamond : R \times R \to R$ for elements of the abstract domain, with the following property:

$$\forall e, f \in R \ . \ (\gamma(e) \circ \gamma(f)) \subseteq \gamma(e \diamond f)$$

that is

$$\forall s_0, s_1, s_2 \ . \ s_1 \in \gamma(e)(s_0) \wedge s_2 \in \gamma(f)(s_1) \implies s_2 \in \gamma(e \diamond f)(s_0)$$

In other words, $\diamond$ must compose abstract relations in such a way that the result is a valid approximation of the corresponding composition in the concrete domain.

4.1 Control-Flow Graph Summarization

Summarization consists of replacing a part of the control-flow graph by a statement that over-approximates its effects. Concretely, we first augment the language with a special summary statement, characterized by a single abstract value:

$$\mathcal{P}_{ext} = \mathcal{P} \cup \{\mathsf{Smr}(a \in R)\}$$

Consequently, we define $T_{f_{ext}}$ over $\mathcal{P}_{ext}$:

$$T_{f_{ext}}(s)(r) = \begin{cases} T_f(s)(r) \text{ if } s \in \mathcal{P} \\ r \diamond a \qquad \text{if } s = \mathsf{Smr}(a) \end{cases}$$

Let c be the control-flow graph of some procedure over $\mathcal{P}_{ext}$, and a and b two nodes of c such that a strictly dominates b and b post-dominates a. In such a situation, all paths from entry to b go through a and all paths from a to exit go through b. Let us consider the sub-graph between a and b, which we denote by $a \circlearrowright b$. This graph can be viewed as a control-flow graph with a as its source and b as its sink. The summarization consists of replacing $a \circlearrowright b$ by a single edge labelled with a summary statement obtained by analyzing the control-flow graph $a \circlearrowright b$ in isolation.

We observe that while composition over the concrete domain is associative, it is generally not the case for $\diamond$. Moreover, different orders of applications yield incomparable results. In fact, the order in which the summarizations are performed plays an important role in the overall result. When possible, left-associativity is preferred as it better encapsulates a forward, top-down analysis and can leverage past information.

4.2   Partial Unfolding

Control-flow graph summarization presented above is one of the building blocks of our compositional framework. The other one is a mechanism for replacing method calls by summaries, or *unfolding*, which we present here.

When faced with a call statement $o.m(\overline{args})$, the analysis will extract information about o from the data-flow facts and compute the set of its potential static targets $T_{o.m} \subseteq \mathcal{M}$. The control-flow graphs corresponding to the targets are then included after a non-deterministic split. It is worth noting that the set of targets $T_{o.m}$ is generally not complete. Indeed, this process is performed during the fix-point computation, facts about o might still grow in the lattice during future iterations. The original call is therefore kept and annotated to exclude targets already unfolded as pictured in Figure 4. In certain situations, we can conclude that all targets have been covered, rendering the alternative call edge infeasible and thus removable.

4.3   Combining Unfolding and Summarization

We distinguish two main kinds of summaries. A summary that contains unanalyzed method calls is said to be *conditional*. In contrast, a *definite* summary is fully reduced down to a single edge with a summary statement.

We now illustrate the flexibility provided by our framework through a simple example displayed in Figure 5. There are in general multiple ways to generate a definite summary from a control-flow graph, depending on the interleaving of summarization and unfolding operations.

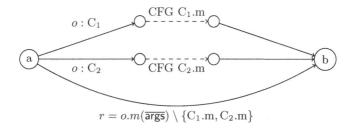

$$r = o.m(\overline{\text{args}}) \setminus \{C_1.m, C_2.m\}$$

Fig. 4. Example of unfolding with $T_{call} = \{C_1.m, C_2.m\}$

```
sealed class A {                          // .. continuing class A
  def m1() {
    val o = new A;                          def m3() { }
    this.m2(o)
  }                                         def f() { }
                                          }
  def m2(o: A) {
    this.m3()                             class B extends A {
    o.f()                                   override def f() { .. }
  }                                       }
```

Fig. 5. Example of a chain of method calls

For instance, one way to generate a summary for $A.m1$ would consist of the following steps: first, we fully summarize $A.m3$, $A.f$ and $B.f$. We unfold their call in $A.m2$, summarize the result, unfold it in $A.m1$ and finally summarize it. This would represent a completely modular approach, where summaries are reused as much as possible. While being perhaps the most efficient way to compute a summary (since intermediate summaries for $A.m2$, $A.m3$, $A.f$ and $B.f$ are small, definite effects) it is also the least precise. Indeed, in this order, we have no precise information on o at the time of analyzing o.f() and thus we have to consider every static targets— here $A.f$ and $B.f$, leading to an imprecise summary. We note that this approach, while generally used by traditional compositional analyses, falls short in the presence of callbacks where the number of static targets is typically large (>1'000 for the Scala library). In contrast, we could have waited to analyze o.f() by generating a conditional summary for $A.m2$ where **this**.m3() is unfolded but o.f() remains unanalyzed. We refer to the decision of not analyzing a method call as *delaying*.

4.4   Controlled Delaying

We have seen through the examples above that choosing when to unfold a method call can have a important impact in terms of performance and precision. In our framework, we delegate this decision to a function $D(call, ctx)$. The precision and performance of the analysis are thus parametrized in D. Fixing $D(\ldots) = $ false ensures that every method is analyzed modularly, in a top-down fashion, leading to an imprecise analysis. On the other hand, having $D(\ldots) = $ true forces the analysis to delay every method call, leading to the analysis of the complete control-flow graph at the entry point. While it ensures a precise result, it will produce the largest intermediate graphs, which will slow the analysis considerably. Another problem we can identify is with respect to recursion, which we discuss specifically in the following section.

We also note that the analysis must be able to conservatively reason about delayed method calls in order to proceed past them. A conservative approach is to assume that facts flowing through such method calls get reset to the identity relation.

4.5   Handling Recursion

Assuming the underlying abstract interpretation-based analysis does terminate (which we do ensure for effect graphs), we still need to ensure that the control-flow graph does not keep changing due to unfoldings. For this reason, we need to take special measures for cycles in the call-graph.

Detecting recursion statically is non-trivial, especially in the presence of callbacks. An attempt using a refined version of a standard class analysis proved to be overly imprecise: it would flag every higher-order functions as recursive. Therefore, Insane discovers recursive methods lazily during the analysis when closing a loop in the progressively constructed call-graph. It then rewinds the analysis until the beginning of the loop in the lasso-shaped call-graph in order to handle the cycle safely. We handle recursion by ensuring that only definite summaries are generated for methods within the cycle. We in fact enforce termination by requiring that $D(c, ctx)$ returns *false* for any call c within the call-graph cycle.

It is worth noting that $D(\ldots)$ is only constrained for calls within the call-graph cycle: we are free to decide to delay when located at the boundaries of a cycle. It is in general critical for precision purposes to delay the analysis of the entire cycle as much as possible. When analyzing a set of mutually recursive functions, we start by assuming that all have a definite summary of identity, indicating no effect. The process then uses a standard fix-point iterative process and builds up summaries until convergence.

4.6   Instantiation for Effect Graphs

We now discuss the instantiation of this framework in the context of effect graphs presented in Section 3. We can quickly identify that our abstract domain is relational and thus candidate for use in this framework. The original statements are thus extended with a summary statement characterized by an effect graph:

$$\mathcal{P}_{ext} := \mathcal{P} \cup \{\mathsf{Smr}(G)\}$$

We can also notice that the graph merging operation acts as composition operator $\diamond$:

$$G_1 \diamond G_2 := \text{merge } G_2 \text{ in } G_1$$

For the delaying decision function D, we base our decision on a combination of multiple factors. One important factor is of course the number of targets a method currently has. We also check whether the receiver escapes the current function, indicating that delaying might improve its precision. As expected, experiments indicate that this decision function dictates the trade-off between performance and precision of the overall analysis.

In case the call at hand is recursive, we conservatively prevent its delaying. However, we also check whether the number of targets is not too big. In practice, we consider this upper limit to be 50. We argue that effects would become overly imprecise anyway once we exceeds this many targets for a single call, without the ability to delay. In such cases, the analysis gives up and assigns $\top$ as definite summary to all concerned functions.

Compositional summaries already give us a powerful form of context sensitivity but it is not always sufficient in practice, namely in the presence of recursive methods relying on callbacks. We thus had to introduce another form of context-sensitivity, which specializes the analysis of the same method for multiple call signatures. We compute these signatures combining the type-estimates for each argument.

5 Producing Readable Effect Summaries

We have demonstrated that summaries based on control-flow graphs are a flexible and expressive representation of heap modifications. However, such graph-based summaries are often not directly usable as feedback to programmers, for several reasons. First, they capture both read and write effects, whereas users are likely interested primarily in write effects. Next, they can refer to internal memory cells that are allocated within a method and do not participate directly in an effect. Last, but not the least they are not in textual form and can be difficult to interpret by developers used to textual representations.

To improve the usefulness of the analysis for program understanding purposes, we aim to describe effect summaries of methods in a more concise and textual form. For this purpose we adopt regular expressions because they are a common representation for infinite sets of strings, and can therefore characterize access paths [10]. They also have a notable tradition of use for representing heap effects [17]. We adopt the general idea of representing graphs using sets of paths to generate an approximate textual representation of graph-based summaries for our analysis.

We first show how we construct a regular expression for a *definite* summary. For definite summaries, a graph-based effect is available that summarizes the method. The graph not only describes which fields can been modified, but also to which value they can be assigned. On the other hand, the corresponding regular expression only describes which fields could be written to. The task therefore reduces to generating a conservative set of paths to fields that may be modified. We construct the following non-deterministic finite state automaton $(Q, \Sigma, \delta, q_0, \{q_f\})$ based on a graph effect G:

$$Q := G.V \cup \{q_f, q_0\}$$
$$\Sigma := \{f \mid v_1 \overset{f}{\to} v_2 \in G.E\}$$
$$\delta := G.E \cup \{q_0 \overset{n}{\to} n \mid n \in G.V \wedge \text{connecting}(n)\}$$
$$\cup \{v_1 \overset{f}{\to} q_f \mid v_1 \overset{f}{\to} v_2 \in G.IE \wedge v_1 \text{ is not an inside node}\}$$

The automaton accepts strings of words where "letters" are names of the method arguments and field accesses. Given an access path, $o.f_1.f_2.\cdots.f_{n-1}.f_n$, the automaton accepts it if f_n might be modified on the set of objects reached via $o.f_1.f_2.\cdots.f_{n-1}$. We exclude writes on inside nodes, as they represent writes that are not be observable from outside, since the node represents objects allocated within the function. From the non-deterministic automaton, we produce a regular expression by first determinizing it, then minimizing the obtained deterministic automaton, and finally applying a standard transformation into a regular expression by successive state elimination. Figure 6 shows the effect graph and the corresponding automata (non-minimized and minimized) for the example from the end of Section 2. In general, we found the passage through determinization and minimization to have a significant positive impact on the conciseness of the final expression.

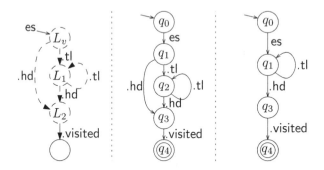

Fig. 6. Transformation steps from an effect graph to a minimized DFA. The graph on the left is the *definite* effect of an impure list traversal. The center graph is the corresponding NFA whose accepting language represents paths to modified fields. The last graph is the minimized DFA to be translated to a regular expression.

For a *conditional* summary, we extract the set of unanalyzed method calls, then compute a (definite) effect assuming that they are all pure, and present the corresponding regular expression along with the set of calls. The natural interpretation is that the regular expression captures all possible writes under the assumption that no function in the set has a side effect.

Section 6.2 and in particular Figure 8 below show some of the regular expressions that were built from our analysis of collections in the standard Scala library.

6   Evaluation on Scala Library

We implemented the analysis described in the previous sections as part of a tool called Insane. Insane is a plugin for the official Scala compiler.

6.1   Overall Results

To evaluate the precision of our analysis, we ran it on the entire Scala library, composed of approximately 58000 methods at our stage of compilation. We believe this is a relevant benchmark: due to the functional paradigm encouraged in Scala, several methods are of higher-order nature. For instance, collection classes typically define traversal methods that take functions as arguments, such as filter, fold, exists, or foreach . It is worth noting that we assumed a closed-world in order to analyze the library. Indeed, since most classes of the library are fully extensible, analyzing it without this assumption would not yield interesting results. Given that even getters and setters can in general be extended, most of effects would depend on future extensions, resulting in almost no definite summary.

We proceeded as follows: for each method, we analyzed it using its declaration context and classified the resulting summary as a member of one of four categories: if the summary is definite, we look for observable effects. Depending on the presence of observable effects, the method is flagged either as *pure* or *impure*. If the summary is conditional, we check if the effect would be pure under the assumption that every remaining (delayed) method call is pure. In such cases, the effect is said to be *conditionally pure*. Otherwise, the effect is said to be *impure*. Lastly, an effect can be *top* if either the analysis timed out, or if more than 50 targets were to be unrolled in a situation where delaying was not available (e.g. recursive methods). We used a timeout of 2 minutes per function. We note that while these parameters are to some extent arbitrary, we estimate that they correspond to reasonable expectations for the analysis to be useful. The different categories of effects form a lattice:

$$\text{pure} \sqsubseteq \text{conditionally pure} \sqsubseteq \text{impure} \sqsubseteq \top$$

Figure 7 displays the number of summaries per category and per package. Observe that most methods are either *pure* or *conditionally pure*, which is what one would expect in a library that encourages functional programming.

Overall, the entire library takes short of twenty hours to be fully processed. This is mostly due to the fact that in this scenario, we compute a summary for each method. Thanks to its modularity though, this analysis could be used in an incremental fashion, reanalyzing only modified code and new dependencies while reusing past, unchanged results. Depending on the level of context-sensitivity, past results can be efficiently reused in an incremental fashion and allow the analysis to scale well to large applications.

Package	Methods	Pure	Cond. Pure	Impure	⊤
`scala`	5721	79%	11%	10%	1%
`scala.annotation`	41	93%	2%	2%	2%
`scala.beans`	25	64%	8%	28%	0%
`scala.collection`	34810	46%	17%	29%	8%
`scala.compat`	9	22%	33%	44%	0%
`scala.io`	546	47%	11%	40%	2%
`scala.math`	1847	67%	28%	5%	0%
`scala.parallel`	39	77%	23%	0%	0%
`scala.ref`	113	58%	3%	39%	0%
`scala.reflect`	5862	50%	9%	40%	1%
`scala.runtime`	1620	61%	25%	14%	1%
`scala.sys`	767	44%	22%	30%	4%
`scala.testing`	44	52%	2%	43%	2%
`scala.text`	115	87%	0%	11%	2%
`scala.util`	1786	51%	11%	32%	6%
`scala.util.parsing`	2206	56%	12%	27%	5%
`scala.xml`	2860	56%	11%	30%	3%
Total:	58410	52%	15%	27%	6%

Fig. 7. Decomposition of resulting summaries per package

`immutable.TreeSet`:	Generic trav.	Any
	Pure trav.	Pure
	Impure trav.	`es.tree(.right` | `.left)`*`.key.visited`
	Grow	Pure
`immutable.List`:	Generic trav.	Pure (conditionally on the closure)
	Pure trav.	Pure
	Impure trav.	`es.tl`*`.hd.visited`
	Grow	Pure
`mutable.HashSet`:	Generic trav.	Pure (conditionally on the closure)
	Pure trav.	Pure
	Impure trav.	`es.table.store.visited`
	Grow	`es.tableSize` | `es.table.store` | `es.sizemap.store` | `es.sizemap` | `es.table`
`mutable.LinkedList`:	Generic trav.	Pure (conditionally on the closure)
	Pure trav.	Pure
	Impure trav.	`es.next`*`.elem.visited`
	Grow	`es.next.next`*
`mutable.ArrayBuffer`:	Generic trav.	Any
	Pure trav.	Pure
	Impure trav.	`es.array.store.visited`
	Grow	`es.size0` | `es.array.store` | `es.array`

Fig. 8. Readable effect descriptions obtained from graph summaries from four operations performed on five kinds of collections

6.2 Selected Examples

To demonstrate the precision of the analysis, we take a closer look at several methods relying on the library, for which the pre-computed summaries can be reused in order to efficiently produce precise results. We targeted five collections, two immutable ones: TreeSet and List, and three mutable ones: HashSet, LinkedList and ArrayBuffer. For each of these collections, we analyze code performing four operations, shown in Figure 9. Figure 10 shows functions corresponding to these four operations when applied to the TreeSet collection, and summarizes the general classes of operations.

1. Generic Traversal: call foreach with an arbitrary closure,
2. Pure Traversal: call foreach with a pure closure,
3. Impure Traversal: call foreach with a closure modifying the collection elements,
4. Growing: build a larger collection, by copying and extending it for immutable ones, or modifying it in place for mutable ones. The method used for growing depends on what is available in the public interface of the collection, e.g. add, append or prepend.

Fig. 9. Operations on containers used to evaluate analysis results

```
class Elem(val i: Int) { var visited = false }
def genTrav(es: TreeSet[Elem], f: Elem ⇒ Unit) = es.foreach(f)
def pureTrav(es: TreeSet[Elem]) = es.foreach { e ⇒ () }
def impureTrav(es: TreeSet[Elem]) = es.foreach { _.visited = true }
def grow(es: TreeSet[Elem], e: Elem) = es + e
```

Fig. 10. The particular four operations applied on the TreeSet collection

The resulting effects are converted into a readable format, as described in Section 5 and displayed in Figure 8. We note that producing these regular expressions takes in each case under 5 seconds. First of all, we can see that all pure traversals are indeed proved pure and have no effect on the internal representation of the collections. Also, we are often able to report that a generic traversal has no effect on the collection assuming the closure passed is pure. The exceptions are the generic traversals of TreeSet and ArrayBuffer. In these two cases, the computed effect is ⊤, due to the fact that their respective traversal routines are implemented using a recursive function with highly dynamic dispatch within its body. We can see however that thanks to context sensitivity, we are able to obtain precise results when the closure is determined. For impure traversal of TreeSet, the analysis had to generate and combine no less than 27 method summaries. The fact that the resulting effect remains precise despite the fundamental complexity of the library shows that the analysis achieves its goal of combining precision and modularity through summaries, even in the case of higher-order programs.

In the cases of impure traversals, the effects correctly report that all elements of the collections may be modified. Additionally, they uncover the underlying implementation structures. For example, we can see that the HashSet class is implemented using a flat hash table (using open addressing) instead of the usual array of chained buckets. It is worth noting that TreeSet is implemented using red-black trees. For mutable collections, growing the collection indeed has an effect on the underlying implementation. Growing immutable collections remains pure since the modifications are applied to the returned copy only.

Overall, we believe such summaries are extremely useful, as they qualify the impurity. In almost all cases, the programmer can rely on the result produced by Insane to conclude that the functions have the intended effects.

7   Related Work

Our goals stand at the intersection of two long-standing fundamental problems:

1. effect and alias analysis for mutable linked structures; [8,6,16,21,31,25];
2. control-flow analysis [29] for higher-order functional programs.

Because we have considered the heap analysis to be the first-order challenge, we have focused on adapting the ideas from the first category to higher-order settings. In the future we will also consider the dual methodology, incorporating recent insights from the second line of approaches [20].

The analysis domain presented in this paper builds on the work [27,28], who used graphs to encode method effect summaries independently from aliasing relations. The elements of this abstract domain are best understood as state transformers, rather than sets of heaps. This observation, which is key to the applicability of the generic relational framework described in Section 4, was also made by Madhavan, Ramalingam, and Vaswani [18], who have formalized their analysis and applied it to C# code. The same authors very recently extended their analysis to provide special support for higher-order procedures [19]. An important difference with our work is that [19] summarizes higher-order functions using only CFGs or a particular, fixed, normal form: a loop around the un-analyzed invocations. Because our analysis supports arbitrary conditional summaries, it is a strict generalization in terms of precision of summaries. Another distinctive feature of our analysis is its support for strong updates, which is crucial to obtain a good approximation of many patterns commonly found in Scala code. In fact, the reduction of CFGs to normal form in [19] relies on graph transformers being monotonic, a property that is incompatible with strong updates. Finally, our tool also produces regular expression summaries, delivering results that can be immediately useful to programmers.

The idea of delaying parts of the analysis has been explored before in interprocedural analyses to improve context-sensitivity [9,33] or to speed up bottom-up whole-program analyses [14]. Our work shows that this approach also brings benefits to the analysis of programs with callbacks, and is in fact critical to its applicability.

Our analysis masks only effects that can be proved to be performed on fresh objects in given procedure call contexts. A more ambitious agenda is to mask effects across method calls of an abstract data types, which resulted in a spectrum of techniques with different flexibility and annotation burden [15,24,5,7,4,12,2,1]. What differentiates our analysis is that it is fully automated, but we do hope to benefit in the future from user hints expressing encapsulation, information hiding, or representation independence.

Separation logic [11,3] and implicit dynamic frames [30,23] are two popular paradigms for controlling modifications to heap regions. Nordio et al. describe an adaptation of dynamic frames [22] for the automated verification of programs with higher-order functions. We note that effect analysis is a separate analysis, whereas separation logic analyses need to perform shape and effect analyses at the same time. This coupling of shape and effect, through the notion of footprint, makes it harder to deploy separation logic-based analyses as lightweight components that are separate from subsequent analysis phases. Moreover, the state of the art in separation logic analyses is such that primarily linked list structures can be analyzed in a scalable way, whereas our analysis handles general graphs and is less sensitive to aliasing relationships.

The importance of conditional effects expressed as a function of arguments has been identified in an effect system [26] for Scala, which requires some type annotations and is higher-level, but provides more control over encapsulation and elegantly balances the expressive power with the simplicity of annotations. The resulting system is fully modular and supports, e.g. separate compilation. In the future, we will consider using a system such as Insane as an automated annotation engine for the effect system, alleviating the bootstrapping problems that come with the annotation requirements.

8 Conclusion

Knowing the effects of program procedures is a fundamental activity for any reasoning task involving imperative code. We have presented an algorithm, a tool, and experiments showing that this task is feasible for programs written in Scala, a modern functional and object-oriented language. Our solution involves a general framework for relational effect analyses designed to support different automated reasoning strategies and allowing analysis designers to experiment with trade-offs between precision and time. Building on this framework we have introduced an abstract domain designed to track read and write effects on the heap. Combining the framework with the abstract domain, we have obtained an effect analysis for Scala. We have implemented and evaluated the analysis on the entire Scala standard library, producing a detailed breakdown of its 58000 functions by purity status. Finally, we have developed and implemented a technique to produce human-readable summaries of the effects to make them immediately useful to programmers. We have shown that these summaries can concisely and naturally describe heap regions, thus producing feedback that conveys much more information than a simple pure/impure dichotomy. Insane works on unannotated code and can thus readily be applied to existing code bases, facilitating program understanding, as well as subsequent deeper analyses and verification tasks.

References

1. Banerjee, A., Naumann, D.A.: State based ownership, reentrance, and encapsulation. In: Gao, X.-X. (ed.) ECOOP 2005. LNCS, vol. 3586, pp. 387–411. Springer, Heidelberg (2005)
2. Barnett, M., DeLine, R., Fähndrich, M., Leino, K.R.M., Schulte, W.: Verification of object-oriented programs with invariants. J. Object Technology 3(6), 27–56 (2004)
3. Berdine, J., Cook, B., Ishtiaq, S.: SLAyer: Memory safety for systems-level code. In: Gopalakrishnan, G., Qadeer, S. (eds.) CAV 2011. LNCS, vol. 6806, pp. 178–183. Springer, Heidelberg (2011)
4. Boyapati, C., Liskov, B., Shrira, L.: Ownership types for object encapsulation. In: POPL, pp. 213–223 (2003)
5. Cavalcanti, A., Naumann, D.A.: Forward simulation for data refinement of classes. In: Eriksson, L.-H., Lindsay, P.A. (eds.) FME 2002. LNCS, vol. 2391, pp. 471–490. Springer, Heidelberg (2002)
6. Chase, D.R., Wegman, M.N., Zadeck, F.K.: Analysis of pointers and structures. In: PLDI, pp. 296–310 (1990)
7. Clarke, D., Drossopoulou, S.: Ownership, encapsulation and the disjointness of type and effect. In: OOPSLA (2002)
8. Cooper, K.D., Kennedy, K.: Interprocedural side-effect analysis in linear time. In: PLDI, pp. 57–66 (1988)
9. Cousot, P., Cousot, R.: Modular static program analysis. In: Nigel Horspool, R. (ed.) CC 2002. LNCS, vol. 2304, pp. 159–178. Springer, Heidelberg (2002)
10. Deutsch, A.: A storeless model of aliasing and its abstractions using finite representations of right-regular equivalence relations. In: Proc. Int. Conf. Computer Languages, Oakland, California, pp. 2–13 (1992)
11. Dinsdale-Young, T., Dodds, M., Gardner, P., Parkinson, M.J., Vafeiadis, V.: Concurrent abstract predicates. In: D'Hondt, T. (ed.) ECOOP 2010. LNCS, vol. 6183, pp. 504–528. Springer, Heidelberg (2010)
12. Fähndrich, M., Leino, K.R.M.: Heap monotonic typestates. In: Aliasing, Confinement and Ownership in object-oriented programming (IWACO) (2003)
13. Gamma, E., Helm, R., Johnson, R., Vlissides, J.: Design Patterns. Addison-Wesley, Reading (1994)
14. Jensen, S.H., Møller, A., Thiemann, P.: Interprocedural analysis with lazy propagation. In: Cousot, R., Martel, M. (eds.) SAS 2010. LNCS, vol. 6337, pp. 320–339. Springer, Heidelberg (2010)
15. Jifeng, H., Hoare, C.A.R., Sanders, J.W.: Data refinement refined. In: Robinet, B., Wilhelm, R. (eds.) ESOP 1986. LNCS, vol. 213, pp. 187–196. Springer, Heidelberg (1986)
16. Jouvelot, P., Gifford, D.K.: Algebraic reconstruction of types and effects. In: POPL, pp. 303–310 (1991)
17. Larus, J.R., Hilfinger, P.N.: Detecting conflicts between structure accesses. In: Proc. ACM PLDI, Atlanta, GA (June 1988)
18. Madhavan, R., Ramalingam, G., Vaswani, K.: Purity analysis: An abstract interpretation formulation. In: Yahav, E. (ed.) Static Analysis. LNCS, vol. 6887, pp. 7–24. Springer, Heidelberg (2011)
19. Madhavan, R., Ramalingam, G., Vaswani, K.: Modular heap analysis for higher-order programs. In: Miné, A., Schmidt, D. (eds.) SAS 2012. LNCS, vol. 7460, pp. 370–387. Springer, Heidelberg (2012)

20. Might, M., Smaragdakis, Y., Horn, D.V.: Resolving and exploiting the k-CFA paradox: illuminating functional vs. object-oriented program analysis. In: PLDI, pp. 305–315 (2010)
21. Milanova, A., Rountev, A., Ryder, B.G.: Parameterized object sensitivity for points-to and side-effect analyses for java. In: ISSTA, pp. 1–11 (2002)
22. Nordio, M., Calcagno, C., Meyer, B., Müller, P., Tschannen, J.: Reasoning about function objects. In: Vitek, J. (ed.) TOOLS 2010. LNCS, vol. 6141, pp. 79–96. Springer, Heidelberg (2010)
23. Parkinson, M.J., Summers, A.J.: The relationship between separation logic and implicit dynamic frames. In: Barthe, G. (ed.) ESOP 2011. LNCS, vol. 6602, pp. 439–458. Springer, Heidelberg (2011)
24. de Roever, W.P., Engelhardt, K.: Data Refinement: Model-oriented proof methods and their comparison. Cambridge University Press (1998)
25. Rountev, A.: Precise identification of side-effect-free methods in java. In: ICSM, pp. 82–91 (2004)
26. Rytz, L., Odersky, M., Haller, P.: Lightweight polymorphic effects. In: Noble, J. (ed.) ECOOP 2012. LNCS, vol. 7313, pp. 258–282. Springer, Heidelberg (2012)
27. Sălcianu, A., Rinard, M.: Purity and side effect analysis for Java programs. In: Cousot, R. (ed.) VMCAI 2005. LNCS, vol. 3385, pp. 199–215. Springer, Heidelberg (2005)
28. Salcianu, A.D.: Pointer Analysis for Java Programs: Novel Techniques and Applications. Ph.D. thesis, Massachusetts Institute of Technology (2006)
29. Shivers, O.: Control-flow analysis in scheme. In: PLDI, pp. 164–174 (1988)
30. Smans, J., Jacobs, B., Piessens, F.: Implicit dynamic frames: Combining dynamic frames and separation logic. In: Drossopoulou, S. (ed.) ECOOP 2009. LNCS, vol. 5653, pp. 148–172. Springer, Heidelberg (2009)
31. Tkachuk, O., Dwyer, M.B.: Adapting side effects analysis for modular program model checking. In: ESEC / SIGSOFT FSE, pp. 188–197 (2003)
32. Whaley, J., Rinard, M.: Compositional pointer and escape analysis for Java programs. In: Proc. 14th Annual ACM Conference on Object-Oriented Programming, Systems, Languages, and Applications, Denver (November 1999)
33. Yorsh, G., Yahav, E., Chandra, S.: Generating precise and concise procedure summaries. In: POPL, pp. 221–234. ACM (2008)

Compositional Network Mobility

Pamela Zave[1] and Jennifer Rexford[2]

[1] AT&T Laboratories—Research, Florham Park, New Jersey, USA
pamela@research.att.com
[2] Princeton University, Princeton, New Jersey, USA
jrex@cs.princeton.edu

Abstract. Mobility is a network capability with many forms and many uses. Because it is difficult to implement at Internet scale, there is a large and confusing landscape of mobility proposals which cannot easily be compared or composed. This paper presents formal models of two distinct patterns for implementing mobility, explaining their generality and applicability. We also employ formal verification to show that different instances of the patterns, used for different purposes in a network architecture, compose without alteration or interference. This result applies to all real implementations that are refinements of the patterns.

1 Introduction

By "mobility," people usually mean a network capability that enables all of a machine's communication services to continue working as the machine moves geographically. In fact, network mobility is much more general. Because it is the machine's *attachment* to the network that is moving, the machine might also be changing from one transmission medium to another (*e.g.*, cellular to WiFi) or from one service provider to another. Also, communication services can be provided by layers of middleware, supporting higher-level, application-oriented abstractions. With these abstractions a communicating entity could represent, *e.g.*, a person's bank account. The account could be attached to the network through a numbered account at a particular bank, and mobility would allow the person to change banks without disrupting automated banking transactions.

Mobility is tremendously important. Today, mobile services are the major area of growth for many network service providers. In the near future, "ubiquitous computing" will cause an explosion in the number and variety of networked mobile devices. Robust middleware for application-level mobility would be a valuable enhancement to service-oriented architectures.

Mobility is also complex, subtle, and notoriously difficult to implement at Internet scale. The classic Internet architecture [3] has a hierarchical address space in which the hierarchy reflects a combination of geographic, topological, and administrative relationships. Machines are assigned Internet Protocol (IP) addresses according to their locations in the hierarchy. Subtrees of the hierarchy are treated as address blocks, and routing works at Internet scale only because of block aggregation. A mobile machine breaks the rules of this scheme by carrying an individual IP address to a location where it does not belong.

E. Cohen and A. Rybalchenko (Eds.): VSTTE 2013, LNCS 8164, pp. 68–87, 2014.
© Springer-Verlag Berlin Heidelberg 2014

Because of these difficulties, the landscape of mobility implementations is a confusing picture. A recent survey [17] cites 22 mobility proposals, and we know of at least 10 others. With the exception of GTP (used by cellular networks) and Ethernet protocols for mobility within local area networks (LANs), none have been widely deployed. These proposals are extremely difficult to compare, so that network service providers struggle to make wise choices for future growth. Even though mobility obviously occurs at different levels of the protocol stack, for many different reasons, and with many different performance profiles, most of these proposals would be impossible to compose with each other, or to re-use in different contexts, with any confidence.

In short, mobility is too complex to understand and reason about without the aid of formal methods. The purpose of this paper is to give the study of mobility a firm foundation by modeling and analyzing abstract implementations of mobility. The abstractions are general enough to describe all proposed implementations, with some slight modifications to improve separation of concerns. Our major result, that implementations of mobility can be safely composed, applies to all implementations that are refinements of the abstract implementations.

We begin with a basic model of network architecture called the "geomorphic view" of networking (Section 2). This model provides consistent terminology and a global framework in which specific implementation mechanisms can be placed. It is precise enough so that proposed network architectures have unique descriptions within the framework, which is essential for purposes of comparison. This section introduces two new formal models of different aspects of the geomorphic view.

Because the geomorphic view is an abstraction of real implementations that hides detail and separates concerns, it makes it possible to see that there are two very distinct patterns for implementing mobility (Section 3). Although every well-known mobility proposal fits into these two patterns [16], these two patterns have never been observed before. Section 3 describes the patterns both informally and formally. It also contains brief discussions of the applicability constraints, design choices, and cost/performance trade-offs of each pattern. Although mobility is an enhancement to the implementation of a point-to-point communication channel, preserving the channel even while its endpoints move, we do not consider black-box specifications of channel or mobility behavior (*e.g.,* [1,2,5]).

Section 4 introduces the goal of a design space of mobility in which engineers could handle each instance of mobility with exactly the right implementation mechanism at exactly the right place in a layered network architecture. This goal requires, of course, that different instances of the mobility implementations compose—without alteration or interference. This section also includes an example of the benefits of a compositional design space.

Section 5 presents arguments, based on our formal models, that the two implementation patterns as described in the geomorphic view are indeed compositional. These arguments include analysis with the Alloy Analyzer [8] and the Spin model checker [6]. This automated verification is no mere exercise, as the

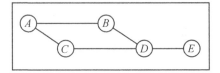

Fig. 1. Members and links of a layer

inherent subtlety of composed mobility mechanisms is too great for reliable informal reasoning. The implication of our result is that any real implementations that are refinements of our abstract implementations are also compositional.

2 The Geomorphic View of Networking

In the geomorphic view of networking, the architectural module is a *layer*. Each layer is a microcosm of networking—it has all of the basic ingredients of networking in some form. In a network architecture there are many layer instances; they appear at different levels, with different scopes, with different versions of the basic ingredients, and for different purposes.

2.1 Components of a Layer

A layer has *members*, each of which has a unique, persistent *name*. For example, Figure 1 is a snapshot of a layer with five members, each having a capital letter as a name. In general a member is a concurrent process, *i.e.*, a locus of state and control with the potential for autonomous action.

The members of a layer communicate with each other through *links*, shown by lines in Figure 1. A link is a communication channel. In general, a layer does not have a link between each pair of members.

One of the two primary functions of a layer is to enable members to send messages to each other. To do this, a layer needs *routes* indicating how one member can reach another through links and intermediate members. For example, (*A, B, D, E*) is a route from *A* to *E*. It also needs a *forwarding protocol* that runs in all members. The forwarding protocol enables members to send and receive messages. In addition, when a member receives a message on an incoming link that is not destined for itself, its forwarding protocol uses the route information to decide on which outgoing link or links it will forward the message.

A *channel* is an instance of a communication service. As mentioned above, a link is a channel. Sometimes a layer implements its own links internally. Most commonly, however, the links of a layer are implemented by other layers that this layer uses, placing the other layers lower in the *"uses" hierarchy*.

If an underlay (lower layer) is implementing a link for an overlay (higher layer), then the basic attributes of the channel must be stored in the states of both layers. In the overlay, the channel object is one of its *links*. In the underlay,

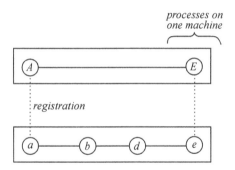

Fig. 2. Implementation of a link in an overlay by a session in an underlay

the channel object is one of its *sessions*. There must be two names for the sets of channels of interest to a layer, because a typical layer both uses *links* and implements *sessions*.

The second primary function of a layer is to implement enriched communication services on top of its bare message transmission. Typical enrichments for point-to-point services include reliability, FIFO delivery, and quality-of-service guarantees. This function is carried out by a *session protocol*. A layer can implement sessions on behalf of its own members, as well as or instead of as a service to overlays.

For a link in an overlay to be implemented by a session in an underlay, both endpoint *machines* must have members in both layers, as shown in Figure 2. A *machine* is delimited by an operating system that provides fast, reliable communication between members of different layers on the machine. This fast, reliable operating-system communication is the foundation on which networked communication is built.[1]

A *registration* is a record that relates an overlay member to an underlay member on the same machine. Registrations must be stored as data in both layers. In the overlay they are called *attachments*, because they indicate how a member is attached to the network through a lower layer. In the underlay they are called *locations*, because they indicate that a member is the location of a process in a higher layer.

The session protocol creates and maintains *sessions* data in its layer, and uses *locations* data. For example, in Figure 2, A sent a request to a for a session with E. To create this session, a learned from its layer's *locations* that E is currently located at e. Messages sent from A to E through the link in the overlay

---

[1] Although layer members have been described as concurrent processes, they are not usually "processes" as defined by the operating system; processes in an operating system have many more properties and associations. A virtual machine can be regarded as a *machine*, in which case communication through the hypervisor and soft switch of the physical machine is regarded as networked communication.

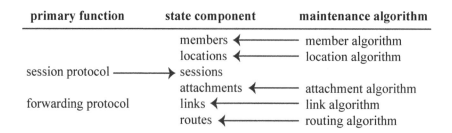

Fig. 3. Major components of a layer. Arrows show which protocol or algorithm writes a state component.

travel through *a, b, d,* and *e;* the first and last steps uses operating-system communication, while the middle three steps use networked communication.

The six major components of the state of a layer are listed in Figure 3. All can be dynamic. We have seen that the session protocol creates and maintains *sessions;* the other five are created and maintained by their own maintenance algorithms.

2.2 Layers Within a Network Architecture

The geomorphic view may seem familiar and obvious because both the classic Internet architecture [3] and the OSI reference model [7] also describe network architecture as a hierarchy of layers, but in fact there are several radical differences, which the name "geomorphic" has been chosen to emphasize.

In the Internet and OSI architectures, each layer has a specialized function that is viewed as different from the function of the other layers. In both architectures, there is a fixed number of global layers. In the geomorphic view, each layer is viewed as the same in containing all the basic functions of networking, and there can be as many layers as needed. Consequently, the network (IP) and transport (TCP/UDP) layers of the classic Internet architecture fit into one "Internet core" layer of the geomorphic view (see Figure 4). In this layer, IP is the forwarding protocol and TCP and UDP are variants of the session protocol offering variants of Internet communication service.

Because layers instantiated at different levels have different purposes, their functions take different forms. For one example, the best-known routing algorithms are in the Internet core, where their purpose is reachability. A higher-level middleware layer might offer security as part of its communication services. Implementing security might entail routing all messages to a particular destination through a particular filtering server, so that, in this layer, part of the purpose of routing is security. An application layer might have a link or potential link between any two members, implemented by communication services below, so that in this layer the routing algorithm is vestigial.

The *scope* of a layer is its set of potential members. In the Internet and OSI architectures scope is not precisely defined, so diagrams usually show exactly one

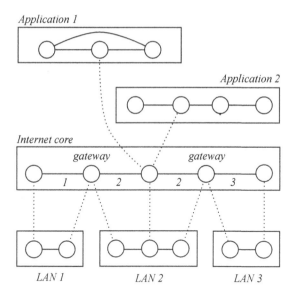

Fig. 4. Geomorphic view of the classic Internet architecture. Internet links are labeled with the LAN that implements them.

layer at each level of the hierarchy, each with global scope. In the geomorphic view, as shown in Figure 4, a layer can have a small scope, and there can be many layers at the same level of the hierarchy.

Figure 4 also shows that each application is a layer with its own members, name space, and communication services. These layers overlap geographically, while sharing the resources of the Internet core. The overlapping and abutting shapes in Figure 4 are common to both geological diagrams and networking.

Today's Internet is host to many customized architectures running simultaneously [14,15]. Middleware is an important part of the ecosystem, while cloud services and virtual private networks add extra layers to the classic Internet architecture. It is self-evident that fixed layer structures cannot describe these architectures adequately. The geomorphic view is intended not only to describe them, but also to generate a design space including many others not yet explored.

We will use two formal models of the geomorphic view for reasoning about mobility. One is a model of shared state written in Alloy [8]. Shared state is state of a layer that may be read or written by more than one layer member. The other is a Promela [6] model of an end-to-end channel protocol. The states model private control information of each endpoint, so they are complementary to the Alloy model. Both models are available at `http://www2.research.att.com/~pamela/ mobility.html`.[2]

---

[2] As a bonus, the Promela model is organized and documented as a tutorial on modular verification. Different properties require different forms of verification, so approximately 16 different verification techniques and Spin features are explained.

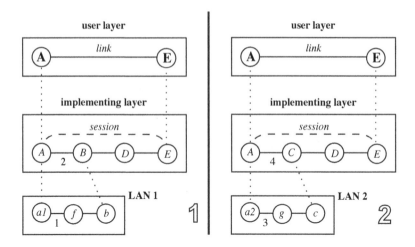

Fig. 5. Two stages in an instance of dynamic-routing mobility

3   Implementations of Mobility

In this section we show that there are two completely different patterns for implementing mobility. They differ in where the mobility appears with respect to the implementing layer, in which algorithms and protocols of the implementing layer are involved in implementing mobility, and in which parts of the shared state are altered. They also differ in their detailed design decisions, and in their cost, performance, and scalability issues. Although there are many examples of both kinds of mobility in the literature, it has never before been observed that there are two major and radically different approaches. This finding is a result of taking the geomorphic view of networking.

3.1   Dynamic-Routing Mobility

Figure 5 has two stages depicting the effect of mobility on an inter-layer channel. Recall that the channel is a *link* in the state of the layer that uses it, and a *session* in the state of the layer that implements it; its *higher endpoints* are in the user layer, while its *lower endpoints* are in the implementing layer.

The precise site of mobility here is the lower endpoint A. In Stage 1 A is *attached* to $a1$ in LAN 1. Recall that $a1$ is the *location* of A, and the association between them is a *registration*. $a1$ and A are connected to the rest of their layers through Links 1 and 2, respectively. Link 2 is implemented by LAN 1, which might be an Ethernet or wireless subnetwork.

Between Stage 1 and Stage 2 Link 1 stops working, possibly because the machine on which A and $a1$ reside has been unplugged from an Ethernet, or has moved out of range of a wireless subnetwork. In a cascading sequence of events, Link 1 is destroyed, Link 2 is destroyed, and the registration of A at $a1$ is destroyed. A is now disconnected from the rest of its layer.

Eventually the mobile machine may become plugged into another Ethernet or enter the range of another wireless subnetwork, as shown in Stage 2. In a cascading sequence of events, member $a2$ (which is the mobile machine's member in the new LAN 2) connects to the rest of its layer through Link 3, A becomes attached to new location $a2$, and new Link 4 is created in the mobility layer and implemented by LAN 2. Note that A is now linked to C rather than B; this change is necessary because C is attached to LAN 2 and B is not.

Between Stages 1 and 2 there may be an interval during which A has no connection with the rest of its layer. The hard problem to be solved in Figure 5 is that even after A is again reachable by other members of its layer such as D and E, they do not know how to find it because the routes to it are obsolete. *Dynamic-routing mobility* relies on the routing algorithm of the layer, which must learn about new links, recompute routes, and disseminate new routes. After this is accomplished, D will know that it can reach A by forwarding to C.

There are three ways in which actual dynamic-routing mobility can differ from the example in Figure 5. Fortunately, none of them affect what the implementation has to do, so none of them need be discussed separately. First, the new attachment $a2$ could be in the same layer as $a1$, rather than in a different layer. Because $a1$ and $a2$ are different locations, after the move A is probably linked to a different member of its own layer, even though the new link is implemented by the same lower layer as before.

Second, in Figure 5 the mobile member A has only one attachment and one necessary link. As shown in Figure 4, members such as gateways have multiple simultaneous attachments to different underlays. Because each such attachment is necessary for the gateway's purpose and supports its own link or links, the mobility of each attachment is a separate problem to be solved.

Third, occasionally a layer implements sessions for the benefit of its own members, rather than as a service to a higher user layer. In this case there is no **A** or **E**, and the beneficiaries of the mobility implementation are A and E.

Often the tasks of forwarding and executing the routing algorithm are delegated to specialized layer members called *routers*. The principal costs of dynamic-routing mobility are *update cost* (to compute new routes and disseminate them to all routers) and *storage cost* (to store routes to individual mobile nodes in all routers that need them). As mentioned in Section 1, these costs can be prohibitive in a large layer that requires aggregated routing to work at scale. Dynamic-routing mobility is most used in LANs, which have smaller scopes and can function without hierarchical name spaces and aggregated routing.

Another common design approach is to reduce update and storage costs by drastically reducing the number of routers that know the routes to mobile members. Because this approach introduces a separate set of routes and a separate routing algorithm, in the geomorphic view it must be described in two separate layers—even though it is usually described in one layer with *ad hoc* "tunneling." This is an example of a modified description of an implementation to improve separation of concerns, as was mentioned in Section 1.

The performance of this approach is sensitive to the number of mobile routers. If many routers know the route to a mobile member, then update and storage costs are higher. If few routers know the route to a mobile member, then update and storage costs are low, but there is *path stretch* because every message to a mobile member must pass through one of these routers, regardless of where the source, router, and mobile member are located. More details can be found in [16], where we compare 5 well-known proposals for dynamic-routing mobility.

3.2   Mobility in the Model of Shared State

Figure 6 shows the signatures of the Alloy model of shared state used to study mobility. With one exception (see below), all the state components in Figure 3 correspond to relations in the signature of a layer. In Alloy time and events are explicit, so that a layer has a member with name *m* at time *t* if and only if the pair *(m, t)* is in the *members* relation of the layer. Members of the basic type *name* play many roles in these relations, which the comments attempt to clarify.

In this model each *channel* is point-to-point, having *initiator* and *acceptor* endpoints that must be *hosted* on different machines. Each channel has a user layer and an implementing layer, which may be the same or different. If they are different, the channel is one of the *links* in the user layer, and one of the *sessions* in the implementing layer. If they are the same, the channel is either a link or a session of that layer (but not both).

The *overlays* and *underlays* of a layer determine the "uses" hierarchy. The *attachments* and *locations* are the *registrations* as presented in Section 2.1.

The *directoryServer, directory, initFarLoc,* and *accptFarLoc* relations will be explained in Section 3.3. Except for these relations, the model says nothing about how the shared state of a layer is distributed and replicated across the layer.

In the model, links are partitioned into inter-layer (*implemented*) links and intra-layer (primitive) links. Primitive links are further partitioned into *active* and *inactive* links; this partitioning is dynamic, as a primitive link's current partition represents its current state. There are *DeactivateLink* and *ActivateLink* events that make primitive links inactive and active, respectively. There are *DestroyLink* events that destroy links of any type. There are *CreateLink* events that create implemented or active primitive links.

For implemented links, there is a predicate *ImplementationActive* that determines whether the link is active or inactive, based on the state of its implementation. Among the necessary conditions in this predicate, both higher endpoints must be registered at lower endpoints in the implementing layer, and the lower endpoints must be mutually reachable in that layer.

The challenge of implementing mobility is to bring an inactive implemented link back to an active state, after occurrences such as those discussed in Section 3.1 cause it to be suspended. The two patterns for implementing mobility operate on attachments, locations, links, and sessions. Coordination among these changes has little to do with dynamic routing itself, which is a self-contained algorithm assuming no more than reachability. Taking advantage of this separation, the model does not contain *routes*, and simply assumes that a routing algorithm

```
sig Time { }
sig Event { pre: Time, post: Time }
sig Name { }
sig Channel {
   userLayer: Layer,
   implLayer: Layer,
   initiator: Name,                          -- name: member of userLayer
   acceptor: Name          }                 -- name: member of userLayer
sig Machine { hosted: Layer -> Name -> Time }   -- name: member of layer
sig Layer {
   overlays: set Layer,
   underlays: set Layer,

   members:  Name -> Time,                    -- name: member of layer
   directoryServer: Name,                     -- name: member of layer

   attachments: underlays -> Name -> Time,          -- name: attached
   locations: overlays -> Name -> Name -> Time, -- names: attached->location
   directory: overlays -> Name -> Name -> Time, -- names: attached->location

   sessions: Channel -> Time,
   initFarLoc: Channel -> Name -> Time,      -- name: endpoint's location
   accptFarLoc: Channel -> Name -> Time      --               of far endpoint

   links: Channel -> Time,
   activeLinks: Channel -> Time,                     -- self-implemented
   inactiveLinks: Channel -> Time,                   -- self-implemented
   implementedLinks: Channel -> Time,
   reachable: Name -> Name -> Time,                  -- names: from -> to
}
```

Fig. 6. Signatures of the Alloy model of shared state

is present in each layer and working correctly. Instead, each layer has a dynamic, binary, symmetric relation *reachable* on members. By definition, a pair *(m1, m2)* is in this relation if and only if there is a path between *m1* and *m2* consisting of active links, whether implemented or primitive. The model assumes that if such a path exists, the routing algorithm will find it and the forwarding protocol will be able to use it.

The basic model includes a large number of consistency constraints on the instantiation of these signatures. One example is that the *overlays* and *underlays* fields in layers are consistent and form a directed acyclic graph that is the "uses" hierarchy of layers. Another example is that if there is a *link* in layer *L1* naming *L2* as the implementing layer, then there is a corresponding *session* in *L2* naming *L1* as the user layer.

The model also includes *CreateRegistration* and *DestroyRegistration* events. A layer member can have at most one location in an underlay. Thus the model excludes mobility implementations that allow a higher endpoint to have multiple simultaneous locations (lower endpoints) during handoff.

How does Figure 5 correspond to the Alloy model? Assume that all links at the LAN level are primitive and active. In Stage 1 the link in the user layer is active. After Stage 1, Link 1, Link 2, and the registration between A and $a1$ are destroyed by modeled events. Between Stage 1 and Stage 2 the benefiting link in the user layer is inactive because its lower endpoints A and E are not mutually reachable. Before Stage 2, Link 3, Link 4, and the registration between A and $a2$ are created by modeled events. In Stage 2 the benefiting link is active again.

3.3   Session-Location Mobility

Figure 7 is similar to Figure 5. One difference is that **A**'s location in the implementing layer changes from $A1$ to $A2$, rather than staying the same. Another difference is that the LAN level is not shown. This is because the relevant change of attachment is now between the user layer and the implementing layer, not between the implementing layer and the LAN level, so what happens at the LAN level is irrelevant.[3]

This is a crucial difference from the perspective of the implementing layer, and requires a completely different mechanism for implementing mobility. The bulk of the work of implementing session-location mobility lies in ensuring that **A**'s correspondents know that it is now located at $A2$ rather than $A1$. The distributed version of the *locations* mapping that is used for lookup must be updated. Each lower endpoint that was participating in a session with $A1$ on behalf of **A** must be informed that it should now be corresponding with $A2$ instead.

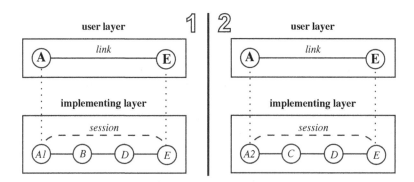

Fig. 7. Two stages in an instance of session-location mobility

The change of registration from $A1$ to $A2$ should be familiar from observing what happens when a laptop containing an application layer member **A** moves to a new subnetwork of the Internet, and gets a new IP address from DHCP. From the perspective of the Internet, the laptop has died as member $A1$ and

---

[3] Most often layer members $A1$ and $a1$ at the LAN level would be destroyed, and members $A2$ and $a2$ created. In this case there would be no mobility between their levels because each of the Aj is attached to the same aj throughout its lifetime.

become reborn as member *A2*. Fortunately it is easy to transfer session state from lower endpoint *A1* to lower endpoint *A2*, because *A1* and *A2* are on the same machine, and are actually the same process with different names.

It should be apparent that session-location mobility is a natural choice for implementing mobility in a hierarchical layer, because the lower endpoint of a session can change names when it moves with respect to the hierarchy. Strictly speaking some dynamic routing could be involved, because *A2* is a new member of the layer and there must be routes to it. In practice this is rarely an issue, because the name *A2* is part of some larger address block to which routes already exist.

The principal costs of implementing session-location mobility are the cost of a scalable distributed implementation of *locations*, the cost of updating it when there is a move, and the cost of updating the session states of correspondents. Some implementations have a new lower endpoint send updates to all its correspondent lower endpoints, while other endpoints have a lower endpoint poll for refreshed locations of its correspondent upper endpoints. More details can be found in [16], where we compare 5 well-known proposals for session-location mobility.

To capture the challenges of implementing this pattern, the Alloy model has a relation *directory* with the same type as *locations*. *Locations* is understood to represent the ground truth about which overlay members are attached to which locations in this layer. This ground truth is stored locally in the machines where the registrations are created, and cannot be accessed globally. *Directory* represents a public copy stored in a distinguished *directoryServer*, and part of the implementation work is to keep *directory* as faithful to *locations* as possible.

In addition, the shared state of each session is augmented with a dynamic *initFarLoc* name and *acceptFarLoc* name, storing the current location of the initiator's and acceptor's far ends. For example, suppose that the channel in Figure 7 is initiated by **A**. When the channel is set up, the *initFarLoc* of the session is *E* and the *acceptFarLoc* of the session is *A1*. After the move from Stage 1 to Stage 2, the *acceptFarLoc* of the session is *A2*. The predicate *ImplementationActive*, determining whether a link is active or inactive, also includes the necessary condition that both far locations are correct.

When there is a *CreateRegistration* event after a move, it should be followed by an *UpdateDirectory* event in which the *directory* relation is updated with the new location. The preconditions of this event include that the new location and the directory server are mutually reachable in the implementing layer.

Generally the fastest handoffs are achieved when a new lower endpoint sends updates directly to all its correspondent lower endpoints. This is modeled by the *UpdateFarLocFromEndpoint* event, which updates the *initFarLoc* or *acceptFarLoc* of a single channel from a single mobile endpoint. Its preconditions include that both higher endpoints of the channel are registered in the implementing layer, the two current lower endpoints are mutually reachable, and the endpoint sending the update has the correct *FarLoc* for the other endpoint, so that it can send a message to it.

Interesting behavior arises if both endpoints of a channel move concurrently. In this case the last precondition of *UpdateFarLocFromEndpoint* will be false at both ends of the channel, and neither endpoint will be able to update the other.

In this case a mobile endpoint, finding that it cannot reach a far endpoint to update it, knows that the far endpoint has moved also. The endpoint can update its own *FarLoc* from the directory by using *UpdateFarLocFromDirectory*. The preconditions of this event are that the far endpoint's directory entry is correct and the lower endpoint requesting the update can reach the directory server. After a double handoff these preconditions will eventually be true on both ends, and both ends can be updated successfully. The *UpdateFarLocFromDirectory* event also models the behavior of implementations that poll for fresh locations rather than sending updates to correspondents.

4   Composition of Mobility Implementations

4.1   The Design Space of Mobility

One of our goals is to give network architects the freedom to handle any instance of mobility with any mobility implementation. The first step was to identify the two possible implementation patterns and to provide sufficiently abstract versions of them. The next step, taken in this section, is to show that any instance of mobility can be implemented with either pattern at almost any level of the layer hierarchy. The final step, taken in Section 5, will be to show that multiple implementations can be freely composed.

In the left column of Figure 8, top half, we see a fundamental instance of mobility in which the old and new locations are in the same layer at Level 0. As noted, the channel at Level 1 can be preserved by session-location mobility (SLM) at Level 0. In the left column, bottom half, we see a fundamental instance of mobility in which the old and new locations are in different layers at Level 0. As noted, a channel at Level 2 can be preserved by dynamic routing mobility (DRM) at Level 1.

The middle column of the figure shows the effects of a "lifting" transformation in which each mobility implementation is moved up a level in the hierarchy. The purpose is to show that mobility can be implemented in many different places, if the current architecture allows it or the designer has control of the content and design of relevant layers. In each case member m at Level 1 is replaced by two members $m1$ and $m2$. Neither $m1$ nor $m2$ is mobile, as each has a stationary registration in Level 0 throughout its lifetime. Now member m' at Level 2 is mobile. As shown in the figure (top), a channel in Level 2 with m' as its higher endpoint can be preserved by SLM at Level 1. Or, as shown at the bottom, a channel in Level 3 with m'' as its higher endpoint and m' as its lower endpoint can be preserved by DRM at Level 2.

The right column of the figure shows where one implementation pattern can be replaced by the other. To replace SLM by DRM (top right), it is necessary to lift the channel up one level. To replace DRM by SLM (bottom right), the channel can stay at the same level, but the mobility must be lifted up a level.

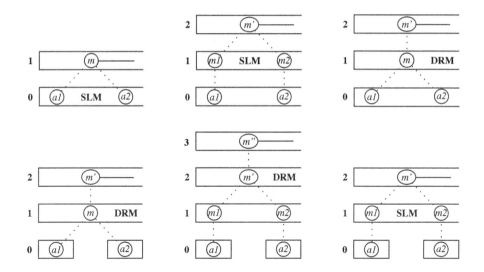

Fig. 8. Generating the design space

4.2   An Example of Composition

In this section we consider a user's laptop as a mobile endpoint. Sometimes the user gets on a bus. During the ride, the laptop is attached to a LAN (wired or wireless) on the bus, and the bus maintains its connection to the Internet by means of a series of roadside wireless networks. This mobility problem is interesting because there are two mobile machines, one of which is sometimes a router on the path to the other.

Figure 9 illustrates a possible solution. The top layer contains a member M representing the laptop, and a member S with an ongoing link to M. The middle layer, which has hierarchical naming and routing, implements session-location mobility for M. When M is on the bus, it is attached to a member bm in the name block of the bus LAN. When M is off the bus, it has some other attachment nm. Session-location mobility must be active when M moves with respect to the bus, but not when the bus moves.

The middle layer contains a member b representing the router on the bus. There is a link between b and bm implemented by the bus LAN. Attachments to the bus LAN have no mobility.

In the middle layer, b also needs a channel to bc, the bus company router, that is preserved as the bus moves and b changes its attachment from one roadside LAN to another. In this example the channel is an intra-layer session, and it is preserved by dynamic routing mobility in the middle layer. As explained in Section 3.1, this is the same as mobility preserving an inter-layer channel, except without the inter-layer interface. Dynamic routing mobility must be active when the bus moves, but not when M moves with respect to the bus. Note that when M is off the bus and attached to nm, it is reached by another route (not shown in the figure) that does not go through bc or b.

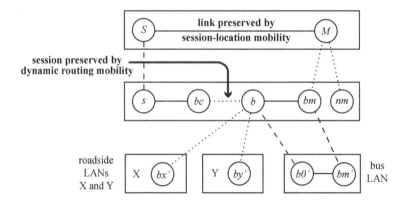

Fig. 9. One implementation of mobile laptops on a bus. Mobile attachments are drawn with dotted lines, while stationary attachments are drawn with dashed lines.

To our knowledge, this is the first solution to this problem in which bus mobility and laptop mobility are completely independent.

5   Verification of Compositional Properties

The purpose of this section is to show that instances of the abstract implementations of mobility presented in Section 3 can be used anywhere within a layer hierarchy, concurrently, without alteration or interference.

5.1   Composition of Control States

As we have seen, an inter-layer channel has both higher endpoints and lower endpoints. The channel is created and destroyed on the volition of the higher endpoints, and each of the four processes involved has its own private control state. Channel creation is independent of mobility, and is not considered here.

A higher endpoint of a channel can detect that the channel is not meeting its performance requirements, primarily by monitoring round-trip times. On detecting such a failure, the endpoint may respond by destroying the channel and initiating failure-recovery procedures such as retry or an attempt to create an alternative channel.

When a channel is not responsive at a higher endpoint because the lower endpoint is disconnected from its layer, the higher endpoint should know it. This information might prevent the higher endpoint from destroying a channel that will be restored to full utility by a mobility implementation. It should certainly prevent the higher endpoint's initiating replacement attempts, as these are doomed to failure. For these reasons the inter-layer interface should be augmented with *suspend* and *resume* events. A lower endpoint signals *suspend* to its higher endpoint when it becomes disconnected from its layer, and *resume* when it becomes connected again.

To verify this augmentation we wrote a Promela [6] model of a channel with suspension/resumption at either or both endpoints. The model includes higher and lower processes at each end, with buffered communication between them to be implemented by an operating system. The lower endpoints communicate with each other through network links, which can lose or re-order messages in transit. To make up for the unreliable network, the lower endpoints implement a simple protocol for reliable, FIFO, duplicate-free transmission. Model-checking with the Spin model-checker proves that the model has all the necessary properties. These include: (1) there are no safety violations such as deadlocks; (2) if the channel is not destroyed and both endpoints are eventually active, then all data sent is eventually received; (3) the control states of higher and lower endpoints are eventually consistent; (4) channels terminate cleanly in all cases.

For composition of the implementation patterns we need a different view, shown as a finite-state machine in Figure 10. The primary state labels (in bold-face type) indicate the states of a layer member implementing dynamic-routing mobility. (For simplicity, the model assumes that the member has at most one link at a time to the rest of its layer.) The transitions caused by the member are labeled in boldface type. The member should attempt to stay **linked**, so that it can do its job in its layer.

The states in the figure are oval when the member is attached to a member in an underlay, and half-oval when it is not. The oval states are compositions of the states of two processes, overlay member and underlay member (both on the same machine). States and transitions of the underlay member are shown in Italic type.

The overlay member is attempting to stay **linked**, but can only do so if it is attached and the underlay member is *active*. At any time the process can

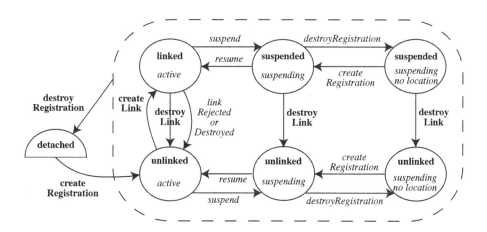

Fig. 10. A finite-state machine representing private control states of a layer member and the underlay member to which it is currently attached, if any. The dashed contour is a superstate.

abandon its attachment and eventually make another, but its links are attachment-dependent and cannot be preserved across this change.

Next we consider the states and transitions of the underlay member. It can *suspend* and *resume* according to its diagnosis of its own condition. This view is slightly more general than the description in the first part of this section, because it can *suspend* and *resume* with respect to the attachment, regardless of whether the attachment is currently being used to implement a link or not.

The underlay member can also implement session-location mobility. When it is already *suspending* because of poor performance, the underlay member can first destroy its registration with the overlay member. Now the overlay member has no official attachment/location, but the underlay member still exists as a software process and is maintaining session state. Eventually, while in this state, the underlay member changes identity within its layer as described in Section 3.3, effectively becoming a different member of its layer. It then creates a new registration with the overlay member, and eventually resumes activity.

Most interestingly, the same process can play both roles in Figure 10, being an underlay member and an overlay member at the same time. Consider what happens when such a member is not **linked** as an overlay member, and is therefore *suspending* as an underlay member. It can choose dynamic routing mobility, in which case it causes **destroyRegistration** as an overlay member, and seeks to find a better attachment below under its own current identity. Or it can choose session-location mobility, in which case its current identity and state as an overlay member are irrelevant, because they will disappear. It will take on a new identity as an overlay member, and get an initial attachment below under its new identity.

To behave correctly, a process playing both roles should seek to be **linked** as an overlay member whenever possible, so that it can be *active* as an underlay member. Whenever it is not **linked** as an overlay member, it should *suspend* as an underlay member. Whenever it becomes **linked** again, it should *resume* as an underlay member. The important observation is that the *suspend/resume* events are in a *different instance* of Figure 10 than the **linked** state, so the two are independent, and the process is always free to perform them.

5.2   Composition in the Model of Shared State

The Alloy model of shared state includes all the events required for implementations of mobility. Each event of the Alloy model has a set of preconditions with the following purposes: (1) They ensure that the arguments make sense. For example, if the argument list includes a name, it names a current member of the appropriate layer. (2) They ensure that two layer members associated by a registration are hosted on the same machine, and that two layer members associated by a channel are hosted on different machines. (3) They ensure that the event will change the state of the model. (There are no idempotent events.) Each event of the Alloy model also has a safety assertion stating that it preserves the overall consistency of the model state and makes the intended change.

Verifying these safety assertions shows that mobility implementations are compositional in the sense that each event is safe regardless of context. This means that events from many simultaneous instances of mobility can be safely interleaved. The limitation of this verification is that although the *effect* of each event is localized within a layer, its enabling preconditions are global.

All of the Alloy correctness assertions have been checked with the Alloy Analyzer, which means that they have been verified for models of bounded size (scope) by means of exhaustive enumeration of model instances. In debugging the Alloy model, all counterexamples to conjectures were found with a scope of 2 layers, 5 names, 5 machines, and 5 channels. Nevertheless, we have verified the properties in this paper for scopes of 5 layers, 6 names, 6 machines, and 12 channels.

The next step is to establish that progress is always possible, *i.e.*, that if any link is inactive, it can eventually become active. The proof is inductive, starting from the bottom of a layer hierarchy, at a layer in which all links are primitive rather than implemented. We verified with the Alloy Analyzer that in any state of such a layer, either each pair of members is mutually reachable, or the preconditions are satisfied to either (1) activate an inactive primitive link or (2) create a new active primitive link between previously disconnected members. After a finite number of such steps, all members must be mutually reachable.

Assuming that all members of an implementing layer can become mutually reachable, an inactive implemented link can always become active in three stages: (1) both its higher endpoints must become registered in the implementing layer; (2) in addition, both its higher endpoints must have correct directory entries in the implementing layer; (3) in addition, both its far locations in the session state in the implementing layer must be correct. For the first stage, we verified that in any state, either each higher endpoint is registered or the precondition for its *CreateRegistration* event is satisfied. Recall that all events change the model state, so that it is not possible for an event to occur without making progress. For the second stage, we verified that in any state, if both higher endpoints are registered, either each directory entry is correct or the precondition for its *UpdateDirectory* event is satisfied. For the third stage, we verified that in any state, if both higher endpoints have correct directory entries, either each far location is correct or the precondition for its *UpdateFarLocFromDirectory* event is satisfied.

If a bottom layer of a hierarchy is at Level 0, this shows that any implemented link at Level 1 can eventually become active. By informal reasoning, the "reachability progress" result now applies to a layer at Level 1, so that it can be substituted as the implementation layer in the reasoning above. By informal induction, an inactive implemented link at any level of the hierarchy can eventually become active.

6   Related and Future Work

For historical reasons, the discipline of networking suffers from a scarcity of abstractions [13]. This deficiency is becoming more obvious as the complexity of networking grows and the needs for common vocabulary, modularity, separation of concerns, compositional reasoning, and design principles become more acute.

Loo *et al.* show that it is feasible to generate network software from declarative programs [10]. In further work, Mao *et al.* generate new layers by composing multiple existing layers, described declaratively [11]. Both have the limitation of focusing exclusively on routing. Their abstractions are not generalizations over all implementations, but rather lead to implementations in which there is a logic-programming engine on each participating machine, serving as the runtime environment for declarative programs.

The geomorphic view of networking was inspired by the work of Day [4], although we have made many changes and additions in both content and presentation. Day points out that mobility is a change of registration, but assumes that all mobility is dynamic-routing mobility, and discusses it only briefly. Mysore and Bharghavan claim to explore the design space of mobility, but cover only dynamic-routing mobility [12]. Karsten *et al.* aim to "express precisely and abstractly the concepts of *naming* and *addressing*" as well as routing and forwarding [9]. Although they include many mobility examples, there is no recognition of session-location mobility.

There is a great deal of future work to do on mobility. The models should be enhanced to include distribution of shared state and localized evaluation of event preconditions. They should also be generalized to include process migration (in which a layer member's new attachment is on a different machine) and cases in which a layer member's old attachment overlaps in time with its new one. Furthermore, our understanding of mobility should be extended to include resource and performance measures, and our understanding of composition should be extended to include the quantitative effects of composition on these measures. Perhaps most importantly, we need to find ways to bridge any gaps that exist between real implementations and the slightly more modular, but composable, abstractions of them.

We have looked at many other aspects of networking through the lens of the geomorphic view, including multihoming, anycast, broadcast, failure recovery, middleboxes, and autonomous-domain boundaries. Although none of these aspects have been studied in the same detail as mobility yet, they appear to fit well into the geomorphic view. When we add them to the formal models, interesting challenges may arise if new structures introduce new dependencies that falsify previous verifications.

Despite these reservations, our work on network mobility reduces an extremely complex subject to concise and comprehensible formal models. It yields new insights into the design space of mobility, and enables us to reason rigorously about the composition of mobility mechanisms. This constitutes significant progress toward bringing the benefits of abstraction to the exceedingly important discipline of networking.

References

1. Bishop, S., Fairbairn, M., Norrish, M., Sewell, P., Smith, M., Wansbrough, K.: Rigorous specification and conformance testing techniques for network protocols, as applied to TCP, UDP and sockets. In: Proceedings of SIGCOMM 2005. ACM (August 2005)
2. Cardelli, L., Gordon, A.D.: Mobile ambients. Theoretical Computer Science 240(1), 177–213 (2000)
3. Clark, D.D.: The design philosophy of the DARPA Internet protocols. In: Proceedings of SIGCOMM. ACM (August 1988)
4. Day, J.: Patterns in Network Architecture: A Return to Fundamentals. Prentice Hall (2008)
5. Herzberg, D., Broy, M.: Modeling layered distributed communication systems. Formal Aspects of Computing 17(1), 1–18 (2005)
6. Holzmann, G.J.: The Spin Model Checker: Primer and Reference Manual. Addison-Wesley (2004)
7. ITU. Information Technology—Open Systems Interconnection—Basic Reference Model: The basic model. ITU-T Recommendation X.200 (1994)
8. Jackson, D.: Software Abstractions: Logic, Language, and Analysis. MIT Press (2006, 2012)
9. Karsten, M., Keshav, S., Prasad, S., Beg, M.: An axiomatic basis for communication. In: Proceedings of SIGCOMM, pp. 217–228. ACM (August 2007)
10. Loo, B.T., Condie, T., Hellerstein, J.M., Maniatis, P., Roscoe, T., Stoica, I.: Implementing declarative overlays. In: Proceedings of the 20th ACM Symposium on Operating System Principles, pp. 75–90. ACM (2005)
11. Mao, Y., Loo, B.T., Ives, Z., Smith, J.M.: MOSAIC: Unified declarative platform for dynamic overlay composition. In: Proceedings of the 4th Conference on Future Networking Technologies. ACM SIGCOMM (2008)
12. Mysore, J., Bharghavan, V.: A new multicasting-based architecture for Internet host mobility. In: Proceedings of the 3rd Annual ACM/IEEE International Conference on Mobile Computing and Networking. ACM (1997)
13. Rexford, J., Zave, P.: Report of the DIMACS Working Group on Abstractions for Network Services, Architecture, and Implementation. ACM SIGCOMM Computer Communication Review 43(1), 56–59 (2013)
14. Roscoe, T.: The end of Internet architecture. In: Proceedings of the 5th Workshop on Hot Topics in Networks (2006)
15. Spatscheck, O.: Layers of success. IEEE Internet Computing 17(1), 3–6 (2013)
16. Zave, P., Rexford, J.: The design space of network mobility. In: Bonaventure, O., Haddadi, H. (eds.) Recent Advances in Networking. ACM SIGCOMM (to appear, 2013)
17. Zhu, Z., Wakikawa, R., Zhang, L.: A survey of mobility support in the Internet. IETF Request for Comments 6301 (July 2011)

Parallel Bounded Verification of Alloy Models by TranScoping[*]

Nicolás Rosner[1], Carlos Gustavo López Pombo[1,2], Nazareno Aguirre[3,2],
Ali Jaoua[4], Ali Mili[5], and Marcelo F. Frias[6,2]

[1] Department of Computer Science, FCEyN, Universidad de Buenos Aires, Argentina
{nrosner,clpombo}@dc.uba.ar
[2] Consejo Nacional de Investigaciones Científicas y Técnicas (CONICET), Argentina
[3] Department of Computer Science, FCEFQyN,
Universidad Nacional de Río Cuarto, Argentina
naguirre@dc.exa.unrc.edu.ar
[4] Qatar University, Qatar
jaoua@qu.edu.qa
[5] New Jersey Institute of Technology, USA
ali.mili@njit.edu
[6] Department of Software Engineering,
Instituto Tecnológico de Buenos Aires (ITBA), Argentina
mfrias@itba.edu.ar

Abstract. Bounded verification is a technique associated with the Alloy specification language that allows one to analyze Alloy software models by looking for counterexamples of intended properties, under the assumption that data type domains are restricted in size by a provided bound (called the *scope* of the analysis). The absence of errors in the analyzed models is relative to the provided scope, so achieving verifiability in larger scopes is necessary in order to provide higher confidence in model correctness. Unfortunately, analysis time usually grows exponentially as the scope is increased. A technique that helps in scaling up bounded verification is *parallelization*. However, the performance of parallel bounded verification greatly depends on the particular strategy used for partitioning the original analysis problem, which in the context of Alloy is a boolean satisfiability problem. In this article we present a novel technique called *tranScoping*, which aims at improving the scalability of bounded exhaustive analysis by using information mined at smaller scopes to guide decision making at larger ones. In its application to parallel analysis, tranScoping compares different ways to split an Alloy-borne SAT problem at small scopes, and extrapolates this information to select an adequate partitioning criterion for larger scopes. As our experiments show, tranScoping allows us to find suitable criteria that extend the tractability barrier, and in particular leads to successful analysis of models on scopes that have been elusive for years.

---

[*] This publication was made possible by NPRP grant NPRP-4-1109-1-174 from the Qatar National Research Fund (a member of Qatar Foundation). The statements made herein are solely the responsibility of the authors.

E. Cohen and A. Rybalchenko (Eds.): VSTTE 2013, LNCS 8164, pp. 88–107, 2014.

Keywords: Alloy Analyzer, Parallel analysis, Bounded verification, Parallel SAT-solving.

1   Introduction

Software specification is a crucial activity for software development. It consists of describing software and its intended properties without the operational details of implementations. By specifying software, and especially if one does so prior to implementation, one is able to better understand the software to be developed, and even validate requirements, which would save time and development costs compared to finding flaws in them in later stages of development. The vehicle to specify software is the specification language. Some important characteristics of specification languages are declarativeness, expressiveness and analyzability. Declarativeness and expressiveness allow one to capture requirements more naturally and precisely, while analyzability allows one to better *exploit* specifications by more effectively finding flaws, inconsistencies, etc.

Due to their intrinsic well-defined formal semantics, formal approaches to specification are usually better suited for analysis. Representatives of formal specification languages are, for instance, B [1], Z [9], the Object Constraint Language (OCL), the Java Modeling Language (JML) [3], and Alloy [14]. Some of these languages, B and Alloy in particular, have been designed with *analysis* as a main concern. A main difference between these two languages is that the analysis underlying B's design is *heavyweight* (semi automated theorem proving, essentially), while Alloy favors fully automated analysis. The main analysis technique behind Alloy is *lightweight*, based on boolean satisfiability (SAT). This analysis turned out to be extremely useful in making subtle modeling errors visible, as is evidenced by approaches to the analysis of all the aforementioned specification languages (or, more precisely, fragments thereof) that translate to Alloy in order to profit from the latter's analysis mechanism.

The analysis mechanism implemented by the Alloy Analyzer, the tool associated with Alloy, is *bounded verification*. Bounded verification is a lightweight formal analysis technique that consists of looking for assertion violations of a *model*, under the assumption that the data domains in the model are bounded by a user provided bound (called the *scope* of the analysis). Thus, the absence of errors in the analyzed models is relative to the provided scope, and errors might be exposed in larger scopes. Consequently, confidence in the correctness of models depends on the scope: the larger the scope, the more confident we will be that the specification is correct. That is, achieving verifiability in larger scopes is necessary in order to provide higher confidence on model correctness. Unfortunately, analysis time usually grows exponentially as the scope increases, so approaches to increase the scalability of bounded verification are essential. A technique that helps to increase the scalability of bounded verification is *parallelization*. Essentially, this consists of partitioning the original SAT problem into a number of different independent smaller problems, which can be solved in parallel.

Typically, the speed up obtained by parallelization strongly depends on how the original problem is partitioned. Unfortunately, finding an adequate partition for a problem is difficult; for problems whose sequential analysis takes hundreds of hours, most partitions of the original problem often lead to parallel analyses that still exhaust the available resources (time or memory). In this article, we study the problem of choosing an appropriate partition of a SAT problem, in order to analyze it in parallel. We present a novel technique called *tranScoping*, which consists of examining alternative partitions for small scopes, and extrapolating this information to select an adequate partition for larger scopes. As the experiments presented in Section 5 show, tranScoping indeed allows us to find suitable partitions that make the parallel analysis feasible. Moreover, the experiments in Section 5 deal with problems whose sequential analyses take hundreds of hours, and whose parallel analyses most often timeout as well, but by extrapolating analysis information via tranScoping we can efficiently analyze them. In particular, tranScoping allows us to analyze models on scopes that have been elusive for years. In Section 6 we discuss related work, and finally, in Section 7 we conclude and present some ideas for further work.

2   Bounded Verification: Alloy and the Alloy Analyzer

Alloy is a formal language based on a simple notation, with a simple relational semantics, which resembles the modelling constructs of less formal object oriented notations, and therefore is easier to learn and use for developers without a strong mathematical background. In addition to being a relevant specification language, Alloy has also received attention as an *intermediate* language: there exist many translations from other languages into Alloy. For instance, a translation from JML (a formal language for behavioral specification of Java programs) to Alloy is implemented as part of the TACO tool [11]. A number of tools have also been developed for translating OCL-annotated UML models into Alloy (e.g., [2,15]). Alloy has also been the target of translations from Event-B [17] and Z [16].

There is a good reason for the existence of the above mentioned translations from other languages into Alloy: Alloy offers a completely automated SAT based analysis mechanism, implemented in the Alloy Analyzer [13]. Basically, given a system specification and a statement about it, the Alloy Analyzer exhaustively searches for a counterexample of this statement (under the assumptions of the system description), by reducing the problem to the satisfiability of a propositional formula. Since the Alloy language features quantifiers, the exhaustive search for counterexamples has to be performed up to certain bound in the number of elements in the universe of the interpretations, called the *scope* of the analysis. Thus, this analysis procedure cannot be used in general to guarantee the absence of counterexamples for a model. Nevertheless, it is very useful in practice, since it allows one to discover subtle counterexamples of intended properties, and when none is found, gain confidence in the validity of our specifications. The existence of the many translations from other languages into Alloy provides evidence of the usefulness of the Alloy Analyzer's analysis in practice.

```
module addressBook

abstract sig Target {}
sig Addr extends Target {}
sig Name extends Target {}
sig Book { addr: Name -> Target }

fact Acyclic { all b: Book | no n: Name | n in n.^(b.addr) }

pred add [b, b': Book, n: Name, t: Target] { b'.addr = b.addr + n -> t }

fun lookup [b: Book, n: Name]: set Addr { n.^(b.addr) & Addr }

assert addLocal { all b,b': Book, n,n': Name, t: Target |
                add [b,b',n,t] and n != n' => lookup [b,n'] = lookup [b',n'] }

// This command should produce a counterexample
check addLocal for 3
```

Fig. 1. An Alloy example: the addressBook sample model from [14, Fig. 5.1]

Let us introduce the Alloy language by means of an example, which will also serve the purpose of explaining how the Alloy Analyzer performs its analyses. Consider the address book example from [14, Fig. 5.1], presented in Fig. 1. In this example, an Alloy model of an address book, consisting of a set of known people and their corresponding addresses, is proposed. Let us go through the elements of an Alloy model. Alloy is a rich declarative language. It allows one to define data domains by means of *signatures*, using the keyword "sig". An abstract signature is one whose underlying data set contains those objects belonging to *extending* signatures. In the example, the data domain associated with signature Target is composed of the union of the (disjoint) domains Addr and Name. Signatures are, in some sense, similar to classes, and may have fields. For instance, signature Book has a field named addr, which represents the mapping from names to targets (other names or addresses) that constitutes an address book. According to Alloy semantics, fields are relations. In this case, since "->" stands for Cartesian product, addr $\subseteq$ Book $\times$ Name $\times$ Target. Axioms are provided in Alloy as *facts*, while predicates (defined using the keyword "pred") and functions (defined using the keyword "fun"), offer mechanisms for defining parameterized formulas and expressions, respectively. Formulas are defined using a Java-like notation for connectives. Alloy features quantifiers: "all" denotes universal quantification, while "some" is existential quantification. Terms are built from set-theoretic/relational operators. They include constants (like "univ", denoting the set of all objects in the model, or "none", which denotes the empty set). Unary relational operators include transposition (which flips tuples from relations) and is denoted by "~". Alloy also includes transitive closure (noted by "^") and reflexive-transitive closure (noted by "*"), which apply to binary relations. Relational union is noted by "+", intersection by "&", and composition by ".".

Fact Acyclic in the model specifies that there are no cyclic references in address books (formula "no n: Name | ..." is equivalent to "all n: Name | not ..."). Predicate add, on the other hand, is used to capture an *operation* of the model – the one corresponding to adding a new entry into an address book.

The formula corresponding to this predicate indicates which is the relationship between the pre- and post-states of the address book (referred to as b and b' in the predicate).

In addition to the described elements, an Alloy model may also have *assertions*. An assertion represents an intended property of a model, i.e., a model that is expected to hold as a consequence of the specification. Assertions can be analyzed, by checking their validity in all possible scenarios within a provided scope. The "check" command is used to instruct the Alloy Analyzer on how to analyze an assertion, in particular by specifying the corresponding scope. The Alloy Analyzer translates the model and the assertion of interest to a propositional formula. Notice that the model may include explicit facts (the model axioms), implicit facts (properties that follow from the typing of fields and "subtyping" between signatures), and the assertion to be analyzed. The Analyzer then produces a propositional formula representing the conjunction:

$$Explicit\ Facts\ \ \&\&\ \ Implicit\ Facts\ \ \&\&\ \ !Assert\ .$$

The translation is made possible due to the finitization information provided by the scopes in the check statement. Notice that if the resulting propositional formula is satisfiable, then the Alloy Analyzer can retrieve a valuation that satisfies the facts, yet violates the assertion (a counterexample showing that the property of interest does not hold in the model). Since the analysis is performed relative to the prescribed scope, a verdict of unsatisfiability only implies that counterexamples do not exist *within the scope*. The assertion under analysis may be false but larger domains may be necessary to exhibit counterexamples.

3   Parallel SAT-Solving

Parallel SAT solving corresponds to the problem of deciding the satisfiability of a propositional formula, by dividing the original problem into smaller instances, and then solving these independently. Parallelization approaches to SAT solving use a divide-and-conquer pattern: problems that are too hard to be tackled directly are split into several (hopefully easier) subproblems, by choosing n propositional variables, and splitting the problem into the 2^n disjoint smaller subproblems, where the chosen propositional variables are instantiated with all possible combinations of boolean values. As we will see, how many non trivial subproblems are obtained, whether they are in fact easier, or how much easier than the parent problem these turn out to be, all strongly depend on the branching variables chosen to partition the search space into disjoint subproblems.

In our case, the splitting process is achieved by means of a mechanism similar to guiding paths [25], with some differences that are worth noting. While one could simply choose n branching variables to split a problem into 2^n disjoint smaller ones, our experience working with CNF formulas arising from the translation of Alloy specifications suggests that the actual number of nontrivial subproblems is usually small compared to the number of subproblems, and often significantly smaller. It is worth it to try and filter out subproblems that can easily be shown to be trivially unsatisfiable during the splitting process, without ever producing or enqueueing them. For instance, if the n branching variables happen to be part of the same "row" within the representation of a functional Alloy relation, a quick round of boolean constraint propagation will easily discard most combinations, and only the $n + 1$ subproblems where at most one of the variables is true will "pass the filter" and become new subproblems. This is the approach we follow.

Two separate parameters control how problems are split. One of them is a *source* of branching variables, i.e., a criterion determining which sequence of decision variables should be considered (but not how many). The second one is a limit on the number of subproblems to be spawned, i.e., how many new tasks the system is willing to accept. The actual number of nontrivial subproblems may greatly vary depending on which variables are chosen. So, an *a priori* limit on the number of variables to branch is hard to determine. We therefore generate subproblems and solve the trivial ones as part of the same process. The following pseudocode illustrates our resulting approach to splitting a satisfiability problem into subproblems:

```
children = [[]]

while varSource.hasMore() and len(children) < children_limit:

    var = varSource.next()
    newchildren = []

    for litlist in children:
        for newlit in (-var, +var):
            newlitlist = litlist + [newlit]
            if not trivially UNSAT(newlitlist):
                newchildren.append(newlitlist)

    children = newchildren
```

The above described approach to parallel SAT solving is implemented in our prototype distributed solving tool ParAlloy. The parallel analysis experiments featured in this article were run using the latest prototype of ParAlloy, which runs on any cluster of independent commodity PCs. Its main system requirements are a working MPI [6] implementation, a C++ compiler and a Python interpreter. The latest version of the Minisat [5] solver is used at the core of each worker process. Python and mpi4py [7] are used to glue the dynamic aspects of the system together.

The implementation constantly monitors the subproblem solving rate, i.e., the average number of tasks that are proved UNSAT (thus closing a branch of the search space) per unit of time. At regular intervals, said rate is inspected and compared with a threshold, in order to take action if not enough progress is taking place. If the rate is below the threshold, the oldest worker process (whichever has been solving its subproblem for the longest amount of time) is instructed to split that subproblem. In order to keep efficiency rates high, this is also done if the UNSAT rate is above the threshold but there are idle workers (which implies that all pending task queues are empty). In the current version of the ParAlloy tool, inspection of the UNSAT rate (and possibly corrective action) takes place every 5 seconds, and the UNSAT rate threshold is set at 0.15 per second per worker. For the 68-worker setup used in the parallel analysis experiments shown in Section 5, this means that a progress threshold of 10.2 UNSATs per second is enforced.

4   TranScoping

In this section we present *tranScoping*, the main contribution of the article. *TranScoping* is a new technique for improving the scalability of bounded exhaustive analysis by using information mined at smaller scopes to guide decision making at larger ones. This exploits the regularity often observed across scopes during analysis of an Alloy model.

In this paper we focus on one particular application – that of parallelizing the analysis. For the problem of parallel bounded exhaustive analysis, transCoping compares the performance of different alternative ways of splitting a SAT problem for small scopes, and extrapolates this information to select an adequate splitting approach to be used with larger scopes.

Let us start by introducing the notion of *splitter*, corresponding to a criterion for selecting propositional variables to split a propositional satisfiability problem.

Definition 1. *Given an Alloy model A whose translation to conjunctive normal form (CNF) is a propositional formula P, and a bound b on the number of new subproblems, a splitter is an algorithm for selecting propositional variables from P in such a way that the number n of produced subproblems satisfies $n \leq b$.*

Not every variable-selecting algorithm is an appropriate splitter. We require a splitter S to satisfy the following properties:

- *tranScopability*: it must be possible for S to extrapolate how to partition a problem at a larger scope, based on how the problem was partitioned by S at a smaller scope.
- *predictability in a class C of splitters*: if S is the best splitter in C for scope k (the one yielding the partition that can be solved the fastest in parallel), then there exists a scope i $(i < k)$, such that S is the best splitter in C for all scopes j such that $i \leq j < k$.

While tranScopability is in general easy to guarantee (we will discuss this property later on, when the splitters are presented), predictability may, on the other hand, be more intricate. In order to understand why, consider, as an example, the model of the mark and sweep garbage collection algorithm provided as part of the Alloy Analyzer's distribution, and the assertion *Soundness2* in it. The sequential analysis times (in seconds) for this assertion are 1, 23, 217 and 2855, for scopes 7, 8, 9 and 10, respectively. Notice that for scope 7 the sequential analysis takes only 1 second. Therefore, all the splitters will generate partitions whose problems in general will have a very low analysis time, which prevents us from perceiving a clear order if one exists. So, we must consider larger scopes in which the differences between analysis times are easier to perceive. Unfortunately, the analysis time grows quite fast. Already for scope 10, applying all the available splitters (that will be presented in Section 4.1) and analyzing the generated subproblems in order to define an adequate ordering, is too costly. Therefore, we will be limited to the conclusions that we can reach by mining the data obtained for the smallest scopes that are large enough to allow us to differenciate splitters (e.g., for *Soundness2*, scopes 8 and 9). As we will show in Section 5, in the case of *Soundness2*, this is enough to arrive at valuable conclusions.

4.1   A Portfolio of Splitters

Let us now describe an initial collection of splitters, that we assume that satisfy tranScopability and predictability. We will present evidence to this effect when the tranScoping technique is evaluated, in Section 5.

The VSIDS Splitter. VSIDS is a particular decision heuristic that many modern SAT-solvers (including MiniSat) use in order to select the next variable to *decide*, i.e., to be used for splitting (by instantiating it with true and false). The heuristic keeps track of the number of occurrences of a given literal in the formula under analysis, a value that is incremented by a fixed amount whenever new clauses containing the literal are learnt. When a new variable is selected to be decided, the one with the largest VSIDS ranking is chosen. Given k, the maximum number of subproblems to be generated, the VSIDS splitter is defined as follows:

> *Once the underlying SAT-solver is interrupted, select branching variables by considering the ranking of the variable activity score in the solving process, until the number of nontrivial subproblems reaches k.*

For the evaluation in Section 5, in order to compute the VSIDS rank we will analyze the problem sequentially and use the ranking resulting at the end of the sequential analysis. This forces us to use small scopes during the mining phase (otherwise the complete sequential analysis becomes infeasible). Alternatively, we could use an intermediate ranking (for example, the ranking obtained after 10 seconds of analysis), but that would add another dimension to the evaluation, making it too complex for our purposes. For those scopes in which the complete sequential analysis is infeasible, we will use the ranking produced after 5 seconds of SAT-solving (this is the case when analyzing a problem for large scopes after the mining phase). As we will see in Section 5, this limitation does not affect the quality of the analysis of the presented examples (or any other example we used for assessment).

TranScopability is clearly satisfied by VSIDS, since lifting variables from the VSIDS ranking is algorithmic. Notice that there is no direct relationship between the variables selected using VSIDS in a small scope, and the variables selected in larger scopes. As the experiments in Section 5 show, predictability is achieved just by using the same technique.

The "Field" Family of Splitters. Alloy models include *signature fields*. During the process of translating a model to a propositional formula, fields are modeled as matrices of propositional variables. Matrix dimensions are determined by the field typing and the analysis scopes. As an example, consider an Alloy specification containing the following signature declaration:

```
sig Source {
    field : Target
}
```

Suppose we want to analyze the command `check assertion for k but 4 Source, 5 Target`. If the assertion has counterexamples, each counterexample must provide domains $S = \{S_0, S_1, S_2, S_3\}$ and $T = \{T_0, T_1, T_2, T_3, T_4\}$ for signatures `Source` and `Target`, respectively, as well as a binary relation $field \subseteq S \times T$, that make the formula corresponding to the assertion satisfiable. The relation *field* is characterized by the following matrix:

$$M_{field} := \begin{vmatrix} p_{S_0,T_0} & p_{S_0,T_1} & p_{S_0,T_2} & p_{S_0,T_3} & p_{S_0,T_4} \\ p_{S_1,T_0} & p_{S_1,T_1} & p_{S_1,T_2} & p_{S_1,T_3} & p_{S_1,T_4} \\ p_{S_2,T_0} & p_{S_2,T_1} & p_{S_2,T_2} & p_{S_2,T_3} & p_{S_2,T_4} \\ p_{S_3,T_0} & p_{S_3,T_1} & p_{S_3,T_2} & p_{S_3,T_3} & p_{S_3,T_4} \end{vmatrix}$$

whose entries are propositional variables, and where $p_{S_i,T_j} = true \iff \langle S_i, T_j \rangle \in field$. Different fields have different degrees of relevance on a satisfiability problem, depending on how the fields are involved in the model. So one may consider different fields, to choose variables from these fields' representations in order to partition the SAT problem. Each model field f gives rise to a different splitter. The "Field" family of splitters is defined as follows:

> select variables from those in matrix M_f, from the bottom-right entry, and towards the top-left, while the number of subproblems does not surpass the given bound k.

For the above matrix, the order in which variables would be selected is:

$$p_{S_3,T_4}, p_{S_3,T_3}, p_{S_3,T_2}, \ldots, p_{S_0,T_1}, p_{S_0,T_0}.$$

Other Candidate Splitters. Various other splitters have been devised. However, for the case studies assessed so far, the Field family and VSIDS are the most promising ones. The parallel SAT-solver PMSat [12] uses as its variable-selecting heuristic those variables that occur in more clauses. This could give origin to a new splitter by selecting those variables that are more frequently found in the formula. Similarly, one can determine, for a given variable, which are the variables whose decision propagate the value of more literals. A splitter is then defined by selecting those variables that propagate the most.

4.2 Selecting the Right Splitter

Given an Alloy model containing an assertion A to be checked, a splitter S and a bound b on the number of subproblems to generate, S provides an algorithm to select variables to be used in an initial splitting of the (CNF translation of the) model. The splitting produces CNF subproblems $sp_1, \ldots, sp_k$, with $k \leq b$, which can be SAT-solved sequentially ($sp_1; \cdots ; sp_k$), or in parallel ($sp_1 || \cdots || sp_k$).

Once all the splitters are run on scopes $i, i+1, \ldots, j$, we must decide which splitter is going to be used in scopes larger than j. In order to make an informed decision we will store, for each splitter S and scope l ($i \leq l \leq j$), the following information. Given a problem on scope l,

NUM$_{S,l}$ is the number of subproblems generated by splitter S.

MAX$_{S,l}$ is the maximum analysis time incurred by any of the subproblems generated by splitter S.

AVG$_{S,l}$ is the average time required by subproblems generated by S.

SUM$_{S,l}$ is the sum over the analysis times of the subproblems generated by S.

DEV$_{S,l}$ is the standard deviation of the analysis times of the subproblems generated by splitter S.

MED$_{S,l}$ is the median of the analysis times of subproblems generated by S.

Our goal is to convey our insight on how the information about how splitters behave for small scopes has to be interpreted in order to decide which splitter to use for larger scopes (as opposed to defining a *unique* mechanism for ranking splitters based on this information). As we will see in Section 5, based on this information it is often possible to choose a good splitter.

Of the above listed parameters, **MAX** is the most important. A high value of **MAX** (close to the time required to analyze the source problem before being splitted), shows that a child subproblem (the one that has **MAX** as its analysis time) is likely to be nearly as hard to be analyzed as its parent, deeming the splitting performed not useful. On occasion, **MAX** alone is not enough in order to appropriately comparing splitters. This can be observed in Table 1 (see Section 5), where splitters VSIDS and Domain2.dstBinding alternate their order with respect to **MAX**, as the scope is increased. By looking at the value of the **SUM** parameter in scope 8, one can see that VSIDS has a much lower value than Domain2.dstBinding (218.29" versus 1678.88"), allowing us to decide between these splitters. A high sum (compared to the other splitters) usually indicates a bad splitting, where subproblems share complex portions of the SAT-solving search space. Therefore, splitters with a high sum are usually demoted to lower positions in the ordering. The most appropriate ordering in this case would then be VSIDS < Domain2.dstBinding.

It is important to remark that the heuristics just presented allow us to predict the best splitter (within the available set) for each of the case studies to be discussed in Section 5. Moreover, computing the parameters **MAX, SUM**, etc. for each splitter in a small scope is inexpensive. We have both a sequential prototype and parallel prototype that can be used interchangeably depending on the availability of the cluster infrastructure, in order to compute these values.

An alternative to the use of the above heuristics for ordering the splitters is to carry out the actual parallel analysis in smaller scopes. This would allow us to rank the splitters according to the parallel analysis times they induce, yielding an ordering that is usually more precise. We will nevertheless stick to the heuristics presented, resorting to parallel analysis in small scopes only if required. Although the latter will not be necessary in this article for detecting the best splitter, we will show in Section 5.5 that performing the parallel analyses yields a better ordering on the whole set of splitters.

5   Experimental Results

In this section we evaluate the heuristics for choosing an appropriate splitter for larger scopes, by analyzing the performance of splitters for smaller scopes. Our evaluation is performed for a number of case studies. For each case study we discuss how the VSIDS and the Field splitters can be ordered, and show that by using the best splitter according to the defined ordering we achieve analyzability in larger scopes. In Section 5.1 we describe the computing infrastructure used in the evaluation; in Sections 5.2–5.5 we present our case studies, and in Section 5.6 we discuss some possible threats to the validity of our experimental results. Since the parallel analysis times depend on the actual scheduling of the queued jobs, we run each experiments 3 times and report the average analysis time. All the times are given in seconds. In all the experiments we set the maximum number of generated subproblems to 256. For each experiment we will report the time required for computing the tranScoping data. This time is almost negligible when compared to the analysis time in the largest scopes. In all the reported experiments we were able to analyze assertions in scopes that were infeasible (analysis would invariably diverge) without tranScoping.

5.1   The Computing Infrastructure

All experiments were run on the CeCAR [26] cluster, which consists of 17 identical quad-core PCs, each featuring two Intel Dual Core Xeon 2.67 GHz processors with 2 MB of L2 cache per core and 2 GB main memory per host. Parallel analyses were run as 17x4 jobs, i.e., 17 nodes running one process per core (1 master + 68 workers). Sequential analyses were run on a single dedicated CeCAR node.

5.2   A Model of Routing in Heterogeneous Networks

In [24], a model of routing in heterogeneous networks is presented. A companion Alloy model can be downloaded from the author's web page. This model is equipped with an assertion, shown in Fig. 2, that could not be checked for some relatively small scopes. As explained before, it is important to analyze model properties on larger scopes, since the larger the analyzed scope, the greater our confidence will be in the validity of the model. This model is very difficult to analyze; its sequential analysis time grows very steeply, from 308 seconds in scope 8

```
assert StructureSufficientForPairReturnability {
    all g: Agent, a1, a2: Address, d1, d2: Domain3 |
        StructuredDomain[d1] &&
        MobileAgentMove[g,a1,a2,d1,d2]
        => ReturnableDomainPair[d1,d2]
}
check StructureSufficientForPairReturnability for 2 but
    2 Domain, 2 Path, 4 Agent, 7 Identifier -- checked
check StructureSufficientForPairReturnability for 2 but
    2 Domain, 2 Path, 3 Agent, 8 Identifier -- checked
check StructureSufficientForPairReturnability for 2 but
    2 Domain, 2 Path, 3 Agent, 9 Identifier -- this one is too big also
check StructureSufficientForPairReturnability for 2 but
    2 Domain, 2 Path, 3 Agent, 11 Identifier
-- attempted but not completed at MIT; formula is not that large; results
-- suggest that the problem is very hard, and that the formula is almost
-- certain unsatisfiable [which means that the assertion holds]
```

Fig. 2. Assertion `StructureSufficientForPairReturnability` and its companion checks

to over 15 days in scope 10 (cf. Table 4). Problems like this one require strategies for scaling up bounded analysis, and parallelization could be a valuable tool for it. Still, the parallel analysis technique presented in Section 3 only allowed us to complete the analysis for scopes 1 to 10. In fact, before tranScoping, our repeated attempts to analyze this assertion for scope 11 were unsuccessful. As shown in Table 4, tranScoping allowed us to select splitter `Domain3.srcBinding`, and to analyze successfully the assertion using this splitter.

In order to evaluate which splitter to choose, we started by mining information about the performance of all splitters, for scopes 6 to 8, shown in Table 1. Using this information, we discarded for scope 9 those splitters that stand no chance of becoming best candidates. The possibility of separating viable from inviable splitters is a good quality of tranScoping, since it allows us to reduce the time invested in the data computing phase. It took 868.27 seconds to compute this table. We start by sorting splitters according to **MAX**, as shown in Table 1. This is insufficient to decide an adequate splitter. In particular, observe the ordering between splitters `Domain2.dstBinding` and VSIDS (the same applies to the ordering between splitters `Domain2.dstBinding` and `Domain.routing`). For scope 8, `Domain2.dstBinding` < VSIDS with respect to **MAX**, but by looking at value **SUM**, we see that `Domain2.dstBinding` has a **SUM** that is 7.7 times larger than VSIDS' **SUM**. The difference is large enough to justify promoting VSIDS above `Domain2.dstBinding`. This decision is backed up by Table 2, which shows the performance of each of the splitters in the parallel analysis of the assertion. A timeout (TO) was set at 600 seconds. Notice that the best two splitters (according to tranScoping) performed better than the others. At first sight the two best splitters seem to have performed similarly. In fact, `Domain3.srcBinding` performed better than `Domain3.BdstBinding`, as we expected. Not because the former took 1 second less to finish the analysis (that difference might even be reverted if more analyses were made before averaging the results), but because the number of subproblems that it had to generate (see the **UNSATs** column in Table 2) is definitely smaller than the number of subproblems generated by the latter. This has a direct correlation with the **MAX** value: a larger **MAX**

Table 1. Routing: mined tranScoping information, scopes 6 to 9, sorted by **MAX**

Scope	Splitter	NUM	MAX	AVG	SUM	DEV	MED
6	Domain3.srcBinding	77	0.08	0.02	1.45	0.02	0.01
	Domain3.BdstBinding	77	0.09	0.02	1.50	0.02	0.01
	Domain2.dstBinding	192	0.18	0.04	7.67	0.03	0.03
	Domain.routing	102	0.21	0.02	1.98	0.03	0.01
	VSIDS	228	0.49	0.01	3.55	0.05	0.00
	Domain3.AdstBinding	192	1.22	0.05	9.78	0.10	0.02
	Identifier_remainder	64	2.31	0.73	46.94	0.52	0.59
7	Domain3.BdstBinding	136	0.84	0.12	17.00	0.18	0.08
	Domain3.srcBinding	141	0.90	0.10	14.60	0.19	0.06
	VSIDS	140	3.39	0.13	19.18	0.38	0.01
	Domain2.dstBinding	192	3.71	0.49	94.74	0.42	0.32
	Domain.routing	192	4.46	0.14	27.51	0.40	0.04
	Domain3.AdstBinding	192	13.05	0.53	101.28	1.04	0.23
	Identifier_remainder	128	25.97	7.45	953.82	6.41	4.93
8	Domain3.srcBinding	136	8.09	1.13	154.17	1.37	0.51
	Domain3.BdstBinding	136	18.06	1.28	173.48	1.95	0.72
	Domain2.dstBinding	192	36.25	8.74	1678.88	7.45	5.78
	VSIDS	174	63.62	1.25	218.29	6.27	0.05
	Domain.routing	192	89.41	2.18	418.04	7.66	0.39
	Domain3.AdstBinding	192	288.79	10.18	1954.07	22.36	2.46
	Identifier_remainder	256	376.70	86.03	22024.53	81.98	56.98
9	Domain3.srcBinding	365	7.57	163.47	2764.89	15.53	3.68
	Domain3.BdstBinding	272	13.25	360.04	3603.38	27.38	5.89

Table 2. Routing: parallel analysis time, scope 9, all splitters. Timeout (TO) set to 600 seconds.

Splitter	Time	Pending	UNSATs
Domain3.srcBinding	171.30	0	1562
Domain3.BdstBinding	172.23	0	2117
VSIDS	350.39	0	5974
Domain.routing	562.74	0	4534
Domain2.dstBinding	TO	11709	735
Domain3.AdstBinding	TO	17268	475
Identifier_remainder	TO	7682	32

value implies that there are some subproblems that are more complex and have to be split more times (thus causing a larger number of UNSATs) in order to be tamed. In this case this is not reflected in the analysis times because the hardware available was able to cope with the number of subproblems generated by both splitters. Table 3 reports the parallel analysis times for these two splitters in scope 10, where the better performance of **Domain3.srcBinding** can be clearly appreciated.

By using tranScoping we are able to analyze the assertion for scopes 1 through 11, as Table 4 shows. We set a timeout (indicated as TO when reached) of 15 days. The sequential analysis for scope 10 did not finish in 15 days. Looking at the progression of sequential values, it is clear that the sequential analysis for scope 11 may take most probably over a year. Therefore, we use the notation $\gg$ to indicate that the actual speed-up is most probably much larger than the indicated speed up. We do not report parallel analysis times for scopes 6 and 7 because the sequential time is too small and the problem is solved before even being split.

Table 3. Routing: comparing splitters `Domain3.srcBinding` and `Domain3.BdstBinding` during parallel analysis, scope 10

Splitter	Time	Pending	UNSATs
Domain3.srcBinding	1053.48	0	10231
Domain3.BdstBinding	1129.49	0	10884

Table 4. Sequential versus parallel analysis time, and speed-up obtained by using the best tranScoped splitter: Domain3.srcBinding. Timeout (TO) = 15 days.

Scope	6	7	8	9	10	11
Sequential time	1.60	18.34	308.26	76168.16	TO	TO
Parallel time	-	-	26.55	171.30	1053.48	10949.72
Speed-up			11X	444X	>1230X	≫ 118X

5.3   A Model of the Mark and Sweep Garbage Collection Algorithm

Mark and Sweep is a garbage collection algorithm that, as its name conveys, traverses the memory marking those objects reachable from the memory heap, and then sweeping those objects that are no longer reachable. An Alloy model of the mark and sweep algorithm comes as a sample model with the Alloy Analyzer's distribution. Among the assertions to be checked we have Soundness2. Unlike assertion Soudness1 in the same model (whose analysis time grows slowly as the scope increases), assertion Soundness2 is hard to analyze (Table 7 shows a growth in the analysis time of at least 10 times from a scope to the next).

We also start with this case study by mining information about the performance of all splitters, for scopes 7 to 9, ordered by **MAX**, and reported in Table 5. It took 1007.41 seconds to compute this table. While splitter VSIDS appears to be the best option in scope 7, splitter HeapState.marked takes a clear lead in scopes 8 and 9. Moreover, as shown in Table 6, the information mined extrapolates to the parallel analysis: HeapState.marked is the best splitter and VSIDS comes in second place. Table 7 shows that, resorting to the tranScoped splitter HeapState.marked, we are able to analyze assertion Soundness2 for scopes 1 to 10, obtaining significant speed-ups.

5.4   A Model of the *Mondex* Electronic Purse

Mondex is a smart card electronic cash system owned by Master Card. A Mondex smart card allows its owner to perform secure commercial transactions and offers features similar to those provided by ATM machines (albeit with greater mobility). An Alloy model of the Mondex electronic purse is provided and analyzed in [19]. Among the many assertions to be verified, there is assertion Rab_archive. Table 8 displays the tranScoping information for this assertion. It took 1145.74 seconds to compute this table. The sequential time required to analyze the assertion in scope 4 is 3.62 seconds. Such short time compresses all the information for the different splitters, preventing us from ordering the splitters precisely. Still, we can at least separate those splitters whose application is bound to be

Table 5. Mark&Sweep: mined tranScoping information, scopes 7 to 9, sorted by **MAX**

Scope	Splitter	NUM	MAX	AVG	SUM	DEV	MED
7	VSIDS	154	0.12	0.03	4.14	0.02	0.02
	HeapState.marked	252	1.75	0.03	8.50	0.11	0.03
	HeapState.left	192	3.36	0.43	82.97	0.41	0.31
	HeapState.freeList	164	4.39	1.49	245.29	0.57	1.38
	HeapState.right	192	4.44	0.46	87.94	0.49	0.32
8	HeapState.marked	254	0.30	0.07	17.67	0.06	0.05
	VSIDS	200	2.32	0.19	38.90	0.25	0.12
	HeapState.right	162	34.54	5.65	914.84	7.13	2.78
	HeapState.left	162	45.38	5.42	877.34	7.17	2.73
	HeapState.freeList	146	50.06	24.45	3570.58	8.32	22.68
9	HeapState.marked	254	1.73	0.21	54.65	0.28	0.12
	VSIDS	181	7.78	0.85	154.07	1.06	0.41
	HeapState.freeList	182	260.93	131.26	23890.37	42.94	131.95
	HeapState.right	200	272.34	32.42	6483.97	42.99	14.96
	HeapState.left	200	301.02	31.43	6285.75	42.22	15.32

Table 6. Mark&Sweep: parallel analysis time, scope 9, all splitters. Timeout (TO) set to 600 seconds.

Splitter	Time	Pending	UNSATs
HeapState.marked	9.95	0	128
VSIDS	184.88	0	2472
HeapState.left	TO	16491	726
HeapState.right	TO	17064	699
HeapState.freeList	TO	7201	1575

expensive. For instance, out of the 16 splitters in Table 8, only 5 seem to have a chance of producing good parallel analyses. The tranScoping data collected for these 5 splitters in scopes 5 and 6, allows us to conclude that the best candidate to use in larger scopes is VSIDS. In effect, in scope 6 VSIDS has a substantially lower **SUM** than the other 4 splitters, while having a comparable (even smaller) **MAX** as well. The results in Table 9 confirm our prediction, by showing that for scope 6 VSIDS produces a better parallel analysis. Table 10 shows that, resorting to the tranScoped splitter VSIDS, we are able to analyze assertion Rab_archive for scopes 1 to 8. Notice that while the speed-up obtained is modest, it is the best speed-up that can be obtained with these splitters. Better analyses are perhaps possible, but they require to devise new splitters that perform better than VSIDS.

5.5   An Alloy Specification of the XPath Data Model

XPath [23] is a language for querying XML documents. In [22], an Alloy model for the XPath 1.0 data model is presented. Subelements inside an XML element cannot be duplicated. As part of the model, assertion nodup_injective, states the equivalence between two distinct ways of expressing this fact.

Table 11 reports the values computed for the different parameters in scopes 6 and 7, for the XPath case study. It took 609.02 seconds to compute this data. Based on the retrieved information, some of the splitters can be immediately

Table 7. Mark&Sweep: parallel analysis time and speed-up obtained by using the best tranScoped splitter, HeapState.marked

Scope	6	7	8	9	10
Sequential time	0.25	1.37	22.98	217.31	2855.30
Parallel time	-	-	10.13	9.95	28.35
Speed-up			2X	21X	100X

Table 8. Mondex: mined tranScoping information, scopes 4 to 6, sorted by **MAX**

Scope	Splitter	NUM	MAX	AVG	SUM	DEV	MED
4	common/TransferDetails.from	149	1.20	0.38	56.58	0.26	0.31
	common/TransferDetails.to	149	1.82	0.84	124.58	0.41	0.85
	a/AbPurse.abLost	256	2.80	0.35	88.82	0.27	0.29
	common/TransferDetails.value	256	2.84	1.86	475.69	0.41	1.92
	c/ConPurse.status	256	3.04	0.69	176.87	0.93	0.17
	cw/ConWorld.archive	256	3.19	0.12	30.81	0.31	0.02
	c/ConPurse.nextSeqNo	256	4.00	0.69	177.98	1.00	0.16
	cw/ConWorld.ether	128	4.21	0.91	117.11	1.00	0.52
	c/PayDetails.toSeqNo	149	4.39	1.44	215.03	1.08	1.33
	c/PayDetails.fromSeqNo	149	4.46	1.72	255.81	1.14	1.62
	c/ConPurse.pdAuth	256	4.55	2.15	549.94	0.38	2.08
	a/AbPurse.abBalance	256	4.61	0.56	144.19	0.61	0.42
	VSIDS	184	4.84	0.14	25.50	0.43	0.01
	cw/ConWorld.conAuthPurse	224	5.57	0.28	63.38	0.60	0.05
	c/ConPurse.exLog	256	6.16	0.80	204.89	1.02	0.35
	c/ConPurse.balance	256	9.92	1.34	342.87	1.06	1.18
5	common/TransferDetails.from	131	16.05	7.52	984.80	3.46	7.04
	VSIDS	138	28.08	1.77	244.26	4.44	0.09
	cw/ConWorld.conAuthPurse	200	36.92	1.94	388.25	5.46	0.12
	a/AbPurse.abLost	256	39.81	2.90	742.30	5.66	1.50
	cw/ConWorld.archive	256	49.69	2.72	696.12	5.39	0.79
6	VSIDS	176	202.18	2.83	498.34	21.12	0.048
	common/TransferDetails.from	151	206.73	89.23	13473.59	38.86	90.19
	a/AbPurse.abLost	256	423.67	20.37	5215.74	62.26	5.02
	cw/ConWorld.conAuthPurse	164	506.25	12.34	2024.09	51.73	0.35
	cw/ConWorld.archive	256	559.32	40.79	10442.80	66.75	16.36

ruled out as best candidates in larger scopes. This is the case for instance for splitters Name.NSName, Node.stringvalue, Name.Localname, PI.expanded_name and PI.target, whose **SUM** value is much larger than those for the other splitters. The remaining splitters (those that were not discarded) are listed in Table 12, and their parallel analysis times are reported along other useful information. In this table, splitters are listed in the order inferred from Table 11, following the heuristics discussed in Section 4.2. Notice that the ordering thus determined is flawed; splitter VSIDS appears in a better place than it should. At the end of Section 4.2 we proposed to perform the parallel analysis in a small scope in order to tranScope the ordering more accurately. We performed the corresponding analyses for scope 7, and VSIDS now falls behind splitter NodeWithChildren.chseq, which is consistent with the ordering expected from observing the results reported in Table 12. The results obtained with the selected splitter, and the corresponding speed-up with respect to sequential analysis, are reported in Table 13.

Table 9. Mondex: parallel analysis time, scope 6. Timeout (TO) = 600 seconds.

Splitter	Time	Pending	UNSATs
VSIDS	170.18	0	2185
cw/ConWorld.conAuthPurse	TO	5551	4385
common/TransferDetails.from	TO	5499	4619
cw/ConWorld.archive	TO	13160	2233
a/AbPurse.abLost	TO	9627	2576

Table 10. Mondex: parallel analysis time and speed-up obtained by using the best tranScoped splitter: VSIDS)

Scope	6	7	8
Sequential time	456.33	8111.65	149678.26
Parallel time	170.18	1643.91	78685.75
Speed-up	2X	5X	2X

5.6   Threats to Validity

TranScoping is a heuristic for deciding which splitter to use along the analysis of an assertion in a large scope. While we perceive the technique as a breakthrough that allowed us to analyze assertions in scopes in which the analysis (even the parallel one) was previously infeasible, tranScoping is so far only supported experimentally. As such, it requires more experiments. We tried tranScoping in the assertions packed within the sample problems distributed with the Alloy Analyzer as well as in selected interesting models downloaded from the Internet. For assertions whose analyses in large scopes are beyond the capabilities of the Alloy Analyzer, tranScoping gave us useful insights into how to choose a splitter, usually leading to parallel analyzability in larger scopes.

The information compiled in Tables 1, 5, 8 and 11 is based on splitting the root problem just once (with each splitter). Our hypothesis is that a good initial splitting propagates its advantages to the rest of the parallel analysis (or, conversely put, that a bad initial splitting will ruin the parallel analysis altogether). This is confirmed in our case studies, since we were always able to predict the best splitter amongst the ones available in each experiment. But, as discussed in Section 5.5, a more accurate ordering (one not just focusing on the best splitter) is obtained if the complete parallel analysis is performed on the smaller scopes.

The variables selected by the VSIDS splitter strongly depend on how long is the analysis allowed to run before observing the ranking. Therefore, different query times may produce quite distinct sequences of variables. This did not prevent tranScoping from predicting the best splitter in the case studies in this article and other examples we ran. Yet we noticed that the different runs of the VSIDS splitter (whose times are averaged when reported in the tables), yielded analysis times with significant variation.

Finally, we are presenting a very limited, albeit useful, set of general purpose splitters. Further research has to be conducted in order to identify other general purpose splitters, or new domain-specific ones.

Table 11. XPath: mined tranScoping information, scopes 6 and 7, sorted by **MAX**

Scope	Splitter	NUM	MAX	AVG	SUM	DEV	MED
6	Node.parent	150	0.56	0.18	26.42	0.09	0.17
	VSIDS	166	1.42	0.04	8.02	0.19	0.01
	NodeWithChildren.ch	144	2.99	0.13	18.94	0.28	0.06
	NodeWithChildren.chseq	129	4.12	0.05	6.75	0.36	0.01
	Attribute.name	98	4.51	0.12	11.51	0.48	0.01
	Element.nss	134	4.68	0.10	14.01	0.42	0.02
	PI.expanded_name	135	4.83	0.64	87.65	0.55	0.45
	Element.gi	133	5.24	4.12	548.67	0.83	4.28
	PI.target	135	5.44	0.69	93.61	0.56	0.51
	Name.Localname	150	5.84	2.77	416.77	2.20	4.19
	Node.stringvalue	150	5.88	4.72	708.71	1.03	4.95
	Name.NSName	147	6.22	5.01	735.98	0.38	4.94
7	Node.parent	155	8.51	1.43	222.15	1.38	1.11
	VSIDS	168	53.34	0.84	141.39	4.23	0.02
	NodeWithChildren.ch	192	67.32	0.95	182.98	5.00	0.15
	Attribute.name	99	92.43	1.38	136.37	9.33	0.05
	PI.target	178	109.93	7.40	1317.73	8.70	5.25
	NodeWithChildren.chseq	171	129.51	0.80	137.17	9.90	0.03
	PI.expanded_name	178	134.24	8.24	1466.69	10.21	6.36
	Element.nss	140	201.73	1.73	241.64	17.05	0.02
	Name.Localname	153	235.16	83.57	12786.90	65.44	110.10

Table 12. XPath: parallel analysis time, scope 8, only splitters that are viable candidates according to tranScoping. Timeout (TO) set to 600 seconds.

Splitter	Time	Pending	UNSATs
Node.parent	98.61	0	1231
VSIDS	TO	13160	5698
NodeWithChildren.ch	227.09	0	4456
Attribute.name	286.32	0	1384
NodeWithChildren.chseq	548.66	0	7947
Element.nss	419.45	0	1926

6   Related Work

Parallel bounded verification has been used mainly in the context of program static analysis. For example, [21] proposes to split the program control flow graph and use JForge [10] (a tool for program bounded verification) to analyze each slice. An approach to parallelizing scope-bounded program analysis based on data-flow analysis was presented in [20].

An alternative to tranScoping is the use of a large-scale parallel SAT-solver. Unfortunately, while multi-core tools are starting to take off, *distributed* parallel SAT-solvers are still scarce. CryptoMiniSat2 [8] is an award-winning open source solver with sequential and parallel operation modes. The author also mentions distributed solving among its long-term goals. No public release or other news about this have been announced. GrADSAT [4] reported experiments showing an average 3.27X and a maximum 19.9X speed-up using various numbers of workers ranging between 1 and 34. C-sat [18] is a SAT-solver for clusters. It reports linear speed-ups, but the tool is not available for experimentation. PMSat [12], an MPI-based, cluster-oriented SAT-solver is indeed available for experimentation, but reports generally small speed-ups.

Table 13. XPath: parallel analysis time and speed-up obtained by using the best tranScoped splitter: `Node.parent`

Scope	6	7	8	9
Sequential time	5.15	140.90	2560.17	19559.49
Parallel time	–	23.95	98.61	1473.32
Speed-up		6X	26X	13X

7   Conclusions and Further Work

We presented *TranScoping*, a technique for principled selection of splitting heuristics in parallel bounded verification. This approach exploits information from simple analyses in small scopes of a model under analysis, in order to give the user of the technique the insight necessary to infer an adequate splitter for larger scopes. We evaluated this approach on a number of case studies, showing that by tranScoping we are able to analyze assertions in scopes where we failed before many times. As these experiments show, for many problems the enormous growth of the analysis times causes them to have a bad initial splitting, resulting in diverging analysis. We believe tranScoping is a useful tool, that helps us make an informed decision about the most critical point in the parallel SAT solving analysis process.

TranScoping opens a new research line, namely, the search for new splitters that may produce better speed-ups than the general purpose splitters we presented in this article. Also, it may be possible to find splitters tailored to specific domains (SAT based program analysis, parallel test generation using SAT, etc.). We plan to work on defining and evaluatiing such new splitters.

References

1. Abrial, J.-R.: The B-Book: Assigning Programs to Meanings. Cambridge University Press (1996)
2. Anastasakis, K., Bordbar, B., Georg, G., Ray, I.: On challenges of model transformation from UML to Alloy. Software and Systems Modeling 9(1), 69–86 (2010)
3. Chalin, P., Kiniry, J.R., Leavens, G.T., Poll, E.: Beyond Assertions: Advanced Specification and Verification with JML and ESC/Java2. In: de Boer, F.S., Bonsangue, M.M., Graf, S., de Roever, W.-P. (eds.) FMCO 2005. LNCS, vol. 4111, pp. 342–363. Springer, Heidelberg (2006)
4. Chrabakh, W., Wolski, R.: GrADSAT: A Parallel SAT Solver for the Grid. In: UCSB Computer Science Technical Report Number 2003-05
5. Eén, N., Sörensson, N.: An Extensible SAT-solver. In: Giunchiglia, E., Tacchella, A. (eds.) SAT 2003. LNCS, vol. 2919, pp. 502–518. Springer, Heidelberg (2004)
6. MPI2: A Message Passing Interface Standard. Message Passing Interface Forum, High Performance Computing Applications 12, 1–2, 1–299 (1998)
7. Dalcin, L., Paz, R., Storti, M., D'Elia, J.: MPI for Python: Performance improvements and MPI-2 extensions. J. Parallel Distrib. Comput. 68(5), 655–662
8. http://www.msoos.org/cryptominisat2

9. Davies, J., Woodcock, J.: Using Z: Specification, Refinement and Proof. International Series in Computer Science. Prentice Hall (1996)

10. Dennis, G., Chang, F., Jackson, D.: Modular Verification of Code with SAT. In: ISSTA 2006, pp. 109–120 (2006)

11. Galeotti, J.P., Rosner, N., Pombo, C.L., Frias, M.F.: Analysis of invariants for efficient bounded verification. In: ISSTA 2010, pp. 25–36 (2010)

12. Gil, L., Flores, P., Silveira, L.M.: PMSat: a parallel version of MiniSAT. Journal on Satisfiability, Boolean Modeling and Computation 6, 71–98 (2008)

13. Jackson, D., Schechter, I., Shlyakhter, I.: Alcoa: the alloy constraint analyzer. In: Proceedings of ICSE 2000, Limerick, Ireland (2000)

14. Jackson, D.: Software Abstractions. MIT Press (2006)

15. Maoz, S., Ringert, J.O., Rumpe, B.: CD2Alloy: Class Diagrams Analysis Using Alloy Revisited. In: Whittle, J., Clark, T., Kühne, T. (eds.) MODELS 2011. LNCS, vol. 6981, pp. 592–607. Springer, Heidelberg (2011)

16. Malik, P., Groves, L., Lenihan, C.: Translating Z to Alloy. In: Frappier, M., Glässer, U., Khurshid, S., Laleau, R., Reeves, S. (eds.) ABZ 2010. LNCS, vol. 5977, pp. 377–390. Springer, Heidelberg (2010)

17. Matos, P.J., Marques-Silva, J.: Model Checking Event-B by Encoding into Alloy. In: Börger, E., Butler, M., Bowen, J.P., Boca, P. (eds.) ABZ 2008. LNCS, vol. 5238, pp. 346–346. Springer, Heidelberg (2008)

18. Ohmura, K., Ueda, K.: c-sat: A Parallel SAT Solver for Clusters. In: Kullmann, O. (ed.) SAT 2009. LNCS, vol. 5584, pp. 524–537. Springer, Heidelberg (2009)

19. Ramananandro, T.: Mondex, an electronic purse: specification and refinement checks with the Alloy model-finding method. Formal Aspects of Computing 20(1), 21–39 (2008)

20. Shao, D., Gopinath, D., Khurshid, S., Perry, D.: Optimizing Incremental Scope-Bounded Checking with Data-Flow Analysis. In: ISSRE 2010, pp. 408–417 (2010)

21. Shao, D., Khurshid, S., Perry, D.: An Incremental Approach to Scope-Bounded Checking Using a Lightweight Formal Method. In: Cavalcanti, A., Dams, D.R. (eds.) FM 2009. LNCS, vol. 5850, pp. 757–772. Springer, Heidelberg (2009)

22. Sperberg-McQueen, C.M.: Alloy version of XPath 1.0 data model, http://www.blackmesatech.com/2010/01/xpath10.als

23. World Wide Web Consortium (W3C), XML Path Language (XPath) Version 1.0, W3C Recommendation (November 16, 1999)

24. Zave, P.: Compositional binding in network domains. In: Misra, J., Nipkow, T., Sekerinski, E. (eds.) FM 2006. LNCS, vol. 4085, pp. 332–347. Springer, Heidelberg (2006)

25. Zhang, H., Bonacina, M.P., Hsiang, J.: PSATO: a distributed propositional prover and its application to quasigroup problems. J. Symb. Comput. 21, 4–6 (1996)

26. http://cecar.fcen.uba.ar/

Extending the Theory of Arrays: memset, memcpy, and Beyond

Stephan Falke, Florian Merz, and Carsten Sinz

Institute for Theoretical Computer Science
Karlsruhe Institute of Technology (KIT), Germany
{stephan.falke,florian.merz,carsten.sinz}@kit.edu

Abstract. The theory of arrays is widely used in program analysis, (deductive) software verification, bounded model checking, and symbolic execution to model arrays in programs or the computer's main memory. Nonetheless, the theory as introduced by McCarthy is not expressive enough in many cases since it only supports array updates at single locations. In programs, memory is often modified at multiple locations at once using functions such as memset or memcpy. Furthermore, initialization loops that store loop-counter-dependent values in an array are commonly used. This paper presents an extension of the theory of arrays with λ-terms which makes it possible to reason about such cases. We also discuss how loops can be automatically summarized using such λ-terms.

1 Introduction

The theory of arrays is widely used in formal methods such as program analysis, (deductive) software verification, bounded model checking, or symbolic execution. In the most simple case, the computer's main memory is modelled using a one-dimensional array, but the use of the theory of arrays goes beyond such flat memory models. Reasoning about arrays is thus an essential part of systems that are based on the aforementioned methods.

Since the theory of arrays is quite basic, it is insufficient (or at least inconvenient to use) in many application cases. While it supports storing and loading of data at specific locations, it does not support the functionality provided by C library functions such as memset or memcpy which operate on regions of locations. While these region-based operations can be broken down into operations on single locations in some cases (e.g., a memcpy operation of size 10 can be simulated using 10 read and 10 write operations), this approach does not scale if the involved regions are large. Even worse, the sizes of the affected regions might not be statically known, making it more complicated to break down region-based operation into operations on single locations.

Apart from library functions, a further construct that often occurs in real-life programs are initialization loops such as

```
1  for (i = 0; i < n; ++i) {
2      a[i] = 2 * i + 1;
3  }
```

E. Cohen and A. Rybalchenko (Eds.): VSTTE 2013, LNCS 8164, pp. 108–128, 2014.
© Springer-Verlag Berlin Heidelberg 2014

which sets the array entry $a[i]$ to the value $2 * i + 1$ for all indices between 0 and $n - 1$. Representing the array a after these initializations is not easily possible in the theory of arrays if n is a large constant or not statically known.

In software bounded model checking tools such as CBMC [9] or ESBMC [11], calls to memset and memcpy are handled by including an implementation of these methods and unrolling the loop contained in the implementations. Due to this unrolling, CBMC and ESBMC are incomplete in their treatment of memset and memcpy if the number of loop iterations cannot be bounded by a constant.[1] Our own software bounded model checking tool LLBMC [24] was equally incomplete since it relied on user-provided implementations of memset and memcpy until we implemented the approach discussed in the preliminary version of this work [14].

In this paper, we present an extension of the theory of arrays with λ-terms which makes it possible to reason about memset, memcpy, initialization loops as discussed above, etc. We show that satisfiability of quantifier-free formulas in this theory is decidable by presenting three reductions to decidable theories supported by SMT solvers. An evaluation shows that using this new theory in LLBMC outperforms the unrolling based approach as used in CBMC and ESBMC.

Example 1. Consider the following program fragment:

```
1  int i, j, n = ...;
2  int *a = malloc(2 * n * sizeof(int));
3  for (i = 0; i < n; ++i) {
4      a[i] = i + 1;
5  }
6  for (j = n; j < 2 * n; ++j) {
7      a[j] = 2 * j;
8  }
```

Using the theory of arrays with λ-terms, the array a after executing line 2 can be described using a fresh constant a_2 since nothing is known about the content of the array. The array a after executing the loop in lines 3–5 can be described using the λ-term $a_5 = \lambda i.\ \mathsf{ITE}(0 \leq i < n,\ i+1,\ \mathsf{read}(a_2, i))$ which represents the array containing as entry $a[i]$ the value $i+1$ whenever $0 \leq i < n$, and the original value of a at index i (i.e., $\mathsf{read}(a_2, i)$) otherwise. Here, ITE is the *if-then-else* operator. Similarly, the array a after executing the loop in lines 6–8 can be described using the λ-term $a_8 = \lambda j.\ \mathsf{ITE}(n \leq j < 2*n,\ 2*j,\ \mathsf{read}(a_5, j))$, which could be simplified to get $a_8' = \lambda j.\ \mathsf{ITE}(n \leq j < 2*n,\ 2*j,\ \mathsf{ITE}(0 \leq j < n,\ j+1,\ \mathsf{read}(a_2, j)))$.   ◊

A preliminary version of this work has appeared as an extended abstract in [14]. This paper extends that preliminary version in two important directions:

- The previous version was restricted to memset and memcpy and did not support any other extension of the theory of arrays. As shown in this paper, the use of λ-terms makes it possible to simulate memset and memcpy, as well as many kinds of initialization loops. Furthermore, we discuss how such loop can be summarized *automatically* using λ-terms.

---

[1] The situation is similar in symbolic execution tools such as EXE [8] or KLEE [7].

– While [14] discusses decidability of the extended theory of arrays, soundness and correctness proofs were missing. In contrast, the aforementioned reductions are formally shown to be sound and complete in this paper.

The present paper is structured as follows: Sect. 2 presents preliminaries and fixes notation. Sect. 3 first recalls the theory $\mathcal{T}_A$ of arrays and then introduces our generalization $\mathcal{T}_{\lambda A}$. Several uses of $\mathcal{T}_{\lambda A}$, including loop summarization, are discussed in Sect. 4. Reductions that establish the decidability of satisfiability for quantifier-free $\mathcal{T}_{\lambda A}$ formulas are presented in Sect. 5. Sect. 6 describes the implementation within LLBMC and contains the results of an evaluation of the different reductions. Related work is surveyed in Sect. 7, while Sect. 8 concludes.

2   Preliminaries

In many-sorted logic, a *signature* Σ is a triple $(\Sigma^S, \Sigma^F, \Sigma^P)$ where Σ^S is a set of sorts, Σ^F is a set of function symbols, and Σ^P is a set of predicate symbols. Σ-*terms*, Σ-*formulas*, and Σ-*sentences* are defined in the usual way.

We use the standard definition of a Σ-*structure* $\mathfrak{M}$. It contains non-empty, pairwise disjoint sets M_σ for every sort $\sigma \in \Sigma^S$ and an interpretation of the function symbols in Σ^F and the predicate symbols in Σ^P that respects sorts and arities. We use $\mathfrak{M}(f)$ to denote the interpretation of $f \in \Sigma^F$ in $\mathfrak{M}$ and $\mathfrak{M}(P)$ to denote the interpretation of $P \in \Sigma^P$ in $\mathfrak{M}$. The interpretation of an arbitrary term t in $\mathfrak{M}$ is denoted $[\![t]\!]^{\mathfrak{M}}$ and defined in the standard way. Similarly, $[\![\varphi]\!]^{\mathfrak{M}} \in \{\top, \bot\}$ denotes the truth value of a formula φ in $\mathfrak{M}$. Finally, a structure $\mathfrak{M}$ is a model of a formula φ if $[\![\varphi]\!]^{\mathfrak{M}} = \top$.

A (first-order) Σ-*theory* $\mathcal{T}$ is a set of Σ-sentences, its axioms. An *empty theory* is a theory not containing any axioms. A Σ-theory is *single-sorted* if $|\Sigma^S| = 1$. For a single-sorted theory $\mathcal{T}_i$, its only sort is usually denoted by σ_i.

Two signatures Σ_1 and Σ_2 are *disjoint* if $F_1 \cap F_2 = \varnothing$ and $P_1 \cap P_2 = \varnothing$. A Σ_1-theory $\mathcal{T}_1$ and a Σ_2-theory $\mathcal{T}_2$ are disjoint if Σ_1 and Σ_2 are disjoint. The *combined theory* $\mathcal{T}_1 \oplus \mathcal{T}_2$ of two disjoint theories $\mathcal{T}_1$ and $\mathcal{T}_2$ is the $(\Sigma_1 \cup \Sigma_2)$-theory containing the union of $\mathcal{T}_1$'s and $\mathcal{T}_2$'s axioms. Theory combination of a theory with itself is defined to be the same theory again: $\mathcal{T}_1 \oplus \mathcal{T}_1 = \mathcal{T}_1$.

The symbol $=_\sigma$ is implicitly defined for most sorts σ. It is not part of any signature Σ and is always interpreted as the identity relation over σ. For brevity, its subscript is usually omitted.

If x, t_1, t_2 are terms, then $t_1[x/t_2]$ stands for the term obtained from t_1 by substituting all occurrences of x by t_2. A substitution is applied to a formula by applying it to all terms in the formula.

For two terms t_1, t_2, writing $t_1 \hookrightarrow t_2$ indicates that the term t_1 can be *simulated* by the term t_2. This means that for any formula φ containing t_1, the formula $\varphi[t_1/t_2]$ is equivalent to φ. Thus, t_1 can be rewritten to t_2.

For any formula ψ and terms t_1, t_2 with the same sort σ, the meta-symbol $\mathsf{ITE}(\psi, t_1, t_2)$ stands for an *if-then-else* expression. Conceptually, for any formula φ containing the term $t \equiv \mathsf{ITE}(\psi, t_1, t_2)$, an equisatisfiable formula φ' not containing t can be constructed as follows. If the identity relation $=_\sigma$ is available, then φ' can be defined as

$$\varphi[t/t_3] \wedge (\psi \implies t_3 = t_1) \wedge (\neg\psi \implies t_3 = t_2)$$

where t_3 is a fresh constant. If $=_\sigma$ is not available, then φ' can be defined as

$$(\psi \wedge \varphi[t/t_1]) \vee (\neg\psi \wedge \varphi[t/t_2])$$

Note that most SMT solvers natively support the ITE construct, i.e., φ' does not need to be constructed up front.

3   The Theory $\mathcal{T}_{\lambda A}$

The theory $\mathcal{T}_{\lambda A}$ is an extension of the non-extensional theory of arrays $\mathcal{T}_A$ that was introduced by McCarthy in his seminal paper [23] in 1962. The theory $\mathcal{T}_A$ is parameterized by the *index theory* $\mathcal{T}_\mathcal{I}$ and the *element theory* $\mathcal{T}_\mathcal{E}$. Here, both $\mathcal{T}_\mathcal{I}$ and $\mathcal{T}_\mathcal{E}$ are single-sorted theories of sort $\sigma_\mathcal{I}$ and $\sigma_\mathcal{E}$, respectively. Note that $\mathcal{T}_\mathcal{I}$ and $\mathcal{T}_\mathcal{E}$ may coincide. In the most simple case, both $\sigma_\mathcal{I}$ and $\sigma_\mathcal{E}$ are uninterpreted sorts and $\mathcal{T}_\mathcal{E}$ and $\mathcal{T}_\mathcal{I}$ are both empty. In practice, $\mathcal{T}_\mathcal{I}$ and $\mathcal{T}_\mathcal{E}$ are often the theory of linear integer arithmetic ($\mathcal{T}_{\mathcal{LIA}}$) or the theory of bit-vectors ($\mathcal{T}_{\mathcal{BV}}$). $\mathcal{T}_A$ now adds the sort σ_A and function symbols read : $\sigma_A \times \sigma_\mathcal{I} \to \sigma_\mathcal{E}$ and write : $\sigma_A \times \sigma_\mathcal{I} \times \sigma_\mathcal{E} \to \sigma_A$ to the combination $\mathcal{T}_\mathcal{I} \oplus \mathcal{T}_\mathcal{E}$. Due to non-extensionality, $=_{\sigma_A}$ is not available. *Terms* in $\mathcal{T}_A$ are built according to the following grammar, where the detailed definitions of $t_\mathcal{I}$ and $t_\mathcal{E}$ depend on the theories $\mathcal{T}_\mathcal{I}$ and $\mathcal{T}_\mathcal{E}$:

index terms	$t_\mathcal{I} ::= \ldots$
element terms	$t_\mathcal{E} ::= \ldots \mid \text{read}(t_A, t_\mathcal{I})$
array terms	$t_A ::= a \mid \text{write}(t_A, t_\mathcal{I}, t_\mathcal{E})$

Here, a stands for a constant of sort σ_A.

Objects of sort σ_A denote arrays, i.e., maps from indices to elements. The write function is used to store an element in an array, and the read function is used to retrieve an element from an array. Formally, the semantics of these functions is given by the following read-*over*-write axioms:[2]

$$p = r \quad \implies \quad \text{read}(\text{write}(a, p, v), r) = v \tag{1}$$
$$\neg(p = r) \quad \implies \quad \text{read}(\text{write}(a, p, v), r) = \text{read}(a, r) \tag{2}$$

These axioms state that storing the value v into an array a at index p and subsequently reading a's value at index r results in the value v if the indices p and r are identical. Otherwise, the write operation does not influence the result of the read operation.

---

[2] Here and in the following, all variables in axioms are implicitly universally quantified. Also, variables a, b range over arrays, variables p, q, r, s range over indices, and the variable v ranges over elements.

In a simple implementation of a decision procedure for $\mathcal{T}_{\mathcal{A}}$ based on the *reduction approach* [20], the read-over-write axioms are applied from left to right using the *if-then-else* operator ITE, i.e., a term $\mathsf{read}(\mathsf{write}(a, p, v), q)$ is replaced by $\mathsf{ITE}(p = q, \ v, \ \mathsf{read}(a, q))$. After this transformation has been applied exhaustively, only read operations where the first argument is a constant remain. The read symbol can then be treated as an uninterpreted function, and a decision procedure for the combination $\mathcal{T}_{\mathcal{I}} \oplus \mathcal{T}_{\mathcal{E}} \oplus \mathcal{T}_{\mathcal{EUF}}$ can be used, where $\mathcal{T}_{\mathcal{EUF}}$ denotes the theory of equality with uninterpreted functions.

Instead of this eager approach, modern SMT solvers use abstraction refinement. For this, they apply techniques such as lazy axiom instantiation or lemmas-on-demand (see, e.g., [5,15]) to efficiently support the theory of arrays.

The theory $\mathcal{T}_{\lambda\mathcal{A}}$ extends the theory of arrays by anonymous arrays that are built using λ-expressions, i.e., the term formation rules are extended as follows:

index terms	$t_{\mathcal{I}} ::= \ldots$
element terms	$t_{\mathcal{E}} ::= \ldots \mid \mathsf{read}(t_{\mathcal{A}}, t_{\mathcal{I}})$
array terms	$t_{\mathcal{A}} ::= a \mid \mathsf{write}(t_{\mathcal{A}}, t_{\mathcal{I}}, t_{\mathcal{E}}) \mid \lambda i.\, t_{\mathcal{E}}$

Here, the "i" occurring in the λ-expression $\lambda i.\, t_{\mathcal{E}}$ is a bound variable of sort $\sigma_{\mathcal{I}}$. In $\mathcal{T}_{\lambda\mathcal{A}}$, the bound variable i may not occur below any further λ-binder (i.e., each occurrence of i has De Bruijn index 1).[3]

Intuitively, $\lambda i.\, s$ denotes the anonymous array that maps each index i to the element denoted by the term s. Formally, this is captured by the following read-*over*-λ axiom scheme:

$$\mathsf{read}(\lambda i.\, s, r) = s[i/r] \tag{3}$$

Here, variables bound by λ-terms within s are first suitably renamed in order to be different from i. This axiom scheme is essentially the well-known β-reduction from λ-calculus.

Note that array terms of the form $\mathsf{write}(a, p, v)$ can be simulated using λ-terms as follows:

$$\mathsf{write}(a, p, v) \quad \hookrightarrow \quad \lambda i.\, \mathsf{ITE}(i = p, \ v, \ \mathsf{read}(a, i))$$

It is, however, advantageous to keep the write operation since this makes it possible to reduce $\mathcal{T}_{\lambda\mathcal{A}}$ to $\mathcal{T}_{\mathcal{A}}$ instead of the combination $\mathcal{T}_{\mathcal{I}} \oplus \mathcal{T}_{\mathcal{E}} \oplus \mathcal{T}_{\mathcal{EUF}}$. Thus, the efficient techniques employed by modern SMT solvers for $\mathcal{T}_{\mathcal{A}}$ can be applied (see Sect. 5 for details).

In [14], we have presented the theory $\mathcal{T}_{\mathcal{ASC}}$, which generalizes $\mathcal{T}_{\mathcal{A}}$ by introducing set, set_∞, copy, and copy_∞ operations. In $\mathcal{T}_{\mathcal{ASC}}$, the term formation rules of $\mathcal{T}_{\mathcal{A}}$ are extended as follows:

index terms	$t_{\mathcal{I}} ::= \ldots$
element terms	$t_{\mathcal{E}} ::= \ldots \mid \mathsf{read}(t_{\mathcal{A}}, t_{\mathcal{I}})$
array terms	$t_{\mathcal{A}} ::= a \mid \mathsf{write}(t_{\mathcal{A}}, t_{\mathcal{I}}, t_{\mathcal{E}})$
	$\mid \mathsf{set}(t_{\mathcal{A}}, t_{\mathcal{I}}, t_{\mathcal{E}}, t_{\mathcal{I}}) \mid \mathsf{set}_\infty(t_{\mathcal{A}}, t_{\mathcal{I}}, t_{\mathcal{E}})$
	$\mid \mathsf{copy}(t_{\mathcal{A}}, t_{\mathcal{I}}, t_{\mathcal{A}}, t_{\mathcal{I}}, t_{\mathcal{I}}) \mid \mathsf{copy}_\infty(t_{\mathcal{A}}, t_{\mathcal{I}}, t_{\mathcal{A}}, t_{\mathcal{I}})$

---

[3] This is not a restriction when modeling programs where an array at a given point in the program does not depend on arrays at a *later* point in the program.

For $\mathcal{T}_{ASC}$, the index theory $\mathcal{T}_\mathcal{I}$ needs to be a linear arithmetical theory containing $+$, $-$, $\leq$, and $<$ (e.g., linear integer arithmetic or bit-vectors). Intuitively, $\mathsf{set}(a, p, v, s)$ denotes the array obtained from a by setting the entries in the range $[p, p+s)$ to v and $\mathsf{set}_\infty(a, p, v)$ denotes the array obtained from a by setting all entries starting from p to v. Furthermore, $\mathsf{copy}(a, p, b, q, s)$ denotes the array obtained from a by setting the entries in the range $[p, p+s)$ to the values contained in b in the range $[q, q+s)$ and $\mathsf{copy}_\infty(a, p, b, q)$ denotes the array obtained from a by setting the entries starting from p to the values contained in b starting from q. Formally, the semantics of the operations is given by the following axioms:[4]

$$
\begin{aligned}
p \leq r < p+s &\implies \mathsf{read}(\mathsf{set}(a,p,v,s),r) = v \\
\neg(p \leq r < p+s) &\implies \mathsf{read}(\mathsf{set}(a,p,v,s),r) = \mathsf{read}(a,r) \\
r \geq p &\implies \mathsf{read}(\mathsf{set}_\infty(a,p,v),r) = v \\
\neg(r \geq p) &\implies \mathsf{read}(\mathsf{set}_\infty(a,p,v),r) = \mathsf{read}(a,r) \\
p \leq r < p+s &\implies \mathsf{read}(\mathsf{copy}(a,p,b,q,s),r) = \mathsf{read}(b,q+(r-p)) \\
\neg(p \leq r < p+s) &\implies \mathsf{read}(\mathsf{copy}(a,p,b,q,s),r) = \mathsf{read}(a,r) \\
r \geq p &\implies \mathsf{read}(\mathsf{copy}_\infty(a,p,b,q),r) = \mathsf{read}(b,q+(r-p)) \\
\neg(r \geq p) &\implies \mathsf{read}(\mathsf{copy}_\infty(a,p,b,q),r) = \mathsf{read}(a,r)
\end{aligned}
$$

Now it is easy to see that $\mathcal{T}_{ASC}$ can be simulated within $\mathcal{T}_{\lambda\mathcal{A}}$:

$$
\begin{aligned}
\mathsf{set}(a,p,v,s) &\hookrightarrow \lambda i.\ \mathsf{ITE}(p \leq i < p+s,\ v,\ \mathsf{read}(a,i)) \\
\mathsf{set}_\infty(a,p,v) &\hookrightarrow \lambda i.\ \mathsf{ITE}(i \geq p,\ v,\ \mathsf{read}(a,i)) \\
\mathsf{copy}(a,p,b,q,s) &\hookrightarrow \lambda i.\ \mathsf{ITE}(p \leq i < p+s,\ \mathsf{read}(b,q+(i-p)),\ \mathsf{read}(a,i)) \\
\mathsf{copy}_\infty(a,p,b,q) &\hookrightarrow \lambda i.\ \mathsf{ITE}(i \geq p,\ \mathsf{read}(b,q+(i-p)),\ \mathsf{read}(a,i))
\end{aligned}
$$

4   Applications of $\mathcal{T}_{\lambda\mathcal{A}}$

As already noted in [14], the operations set and copy, and therefore also $\mathcal{T}_{\lambda\mathcal{A}}$'s λ-terms, can be used to model the C standard library functions memset and memcpy. Intuitively, this is done by summarizing the loops that implement these functions, thereby modelling a simultaneous execution of all loop iterations.[5]

But the theory $\mathcal{T}_{\lambda\mathcal{A}}$ goes beyond what is possible with $\mathcal{T}_{ASC}$ in that it can be used to summarize a wider range of loops than the particular loops in those specific library functions.

4.1   Loop Summarization Using $\mathcal{T}_{\lambda\mathcal{A}}$

Broadly speaking, $\mathcal{T}_{\lambda\mathcal{A}}$ can be used to summarize loops with data independent loop iterations where consecutive loop iterations only write to consecutive array positions. More precisely, loops need to satisfy the following requirements:

---

[4] Similar formulas could be used as postconditions for memset and memcpy in deductive verification tools such as VCC [10] and Frama-C [12].

[5] Because of this, copy's semantics is actually closer to memmove than to memcpy.

- The loop does not contain nested loops.
- The induction variable is incremented by one in each iteration.
- For an array a declared outside the loop, each iteration of the loop uncondi-
  tionally modifies only the ith element of a, where i is the induction variable.
- All other variables declared outside the loop are not modified by the loop.
- Any iteration of the loop may not use elements of a that have been modified
  in earlier iterations of the loop.

In many cases, these requirements can be fulfilled by applying code transformations that are similar to standard compiler optimizations.

Example 2. Consider the following program fragment implementing part of the
Sieve of Eratosthenes:

```
1   void filter_multiples(int p, int n)
2   {
3       for (int j = p*p; j <= n; j += p) {
4           a[j] = 0;
5       }
6   }
```

The loop can easily be transformed into functionally equivalent code that
increments the induction variable by one, thereby making it λ-summarizable:

```
1   void filter_multiples(int p, int n)
2   {
3       for (int j = p*p; j <= n; ++j) {
4           a[j] = ((j − p*p) % p == 0 ? 0 : a[j]);
5       }
6   }
```

Note that such transformations can be performed automatically.   ◊

4.2   Further Uses

While this is already useful by itself, applicability of $\mathcal{T}_{\lambda A}$ goes beyond summarization of loops and calls to `memset` and `memcpy`. Some applications that we
would like to explore in future work include the following:

- Zero-initialization of global variables (as required by the C standard) can be
  achieved using a λ-term corresponding to a **set** operation.
- Zero-initialization of new memory pages before the operating system hands
  them to a process can similarly be modelled using a λ-term.
- If certain memory locations should be set to unconstrained values (*havocked*),
  then this can be done using a λ-term $\lambda i.\ \mathsf{ITE}(\psi,\ \mathsf{read}(h, i),\ \mathsf{read}(a, i))$, where
  ψ describes the memory locations that are to be havocked and h is a fresh
  array constant. Similarly, memory-mapped I/O can be modelled.

– Tracking metadata for memory addresses. For instance, allocation information can be modeled using an array containing information on the allocation
state of the locations. Memory allocation and memory de-allocation can then
be modelled using λ-terms corresponding to a set operation. This makes it
possible to develop an alternative to the SMT theory of memory allocation
presented in [13] and to the memory model presented in [28].

5 Deciding $\mathcal{T}_{\lambda\mathcal{A}}$

In this section, we discuss several possibilities for deciding whether a quantifier-
free $\mathcal{T}_{\lambda\mathcal{A}}$ formula is satisfiable. All approaches work by a reduction to a theory
that is already supported by current SMT solvers.

In order to ease presentation, it is advantageous to represent formulas in
flattened form (similar to [27]). For this, a formula φ is represented using a pair
$(\Delta_\varphi, c_\varphi)$, where Δ_φ is a list of definitions of the form

$$v \equiv f(v_1, \ldots, v_n) \qquad\qquad c \equiv P(v_1, \ldots, v_n)$$
$$v \equiv \lambda i.\, s \qquad\qquad c \equiv c_1 \star c_2 \qquad \text{for } \star \in \{\wedge, \vee\}$$
$$v \equiv \mathsf{ITE}(c,\, v_1,\, v_2) \qquad\qquad c \equiv \neg c_1$$

and c_φ is one of the c's denoting the root proposition of the formula. Here, f is
a function symbol, P is a predicate symbol, $v, v_1, \ldots, v_n, s$ are constants, c, c_1, c_2
are propositions, and each v and c is defined *before* it is used (we assume in
the following that adding definitions to a formula ensures that this property is
preserved). Constants occurring in the left-hand side of a definition need to be
fresh, uninterpreted constants. Thus, the v's and c's should be seen as *names*
for terms and formulas, respectively. We use $v \prec w$ to denote that the definition
of w uses v (def-use-relation) and $v \prec_\mathcal{A} w$ to denote that $v \prec w$ and v is of sort
$\sigma_\mathcal{A}$. The transitive closures of $\prec$ and $\prec_\mathcal{A}$ are denoted $\prec^+$ and $\prec_\mathcal{A}^+$, respectively,
and $\prec^*$ denotes the reflexive-transitive closure of $\prec$. Note that a definition for
v such that $v \not\prec^* c_\varphi$ can be deleted from Δ_φ (*clean-up*) without affecting the
satisfiability status of the formula.

Example 3. Consider the following $\mathcal{T}_{\mathcal{ASC}}$ formula (with $\mathcal{T}_\mathcal{I} = \mathcal{T}_\mathcal{E} = \mathcal{T}_{\mathcal{LIA}}$):

$$\mathsf{read}(\mathsf{write}(\mathsf{copy}_\infty(\mathsf{copy}_\infty(a, 0, a, 1), 1, \mathsf{copy}_\infty(a, 0, a, 1), 0), 0, \mathsf{read}(a, 0)), k)$$
$$\neq$$
$$\mathsf{read}(a, k)$$

This formula states that the array obtained from a by first moving all array
elements at indices ≥ 1 down by one positions, then all elements at indices
≥ 0 up by one positions, and afterwards replacing the element at index 0 by
the original element $\mathsf{read}(a, 0)$ differs at index k from the initial array a. This
formula is clearly unsatisfiable.

The formula can be converted into the following $\mathcal{T}_{\lambda\mathcal{A}}$ formula φ:

$$\mathsf{read}(\mathsf{write}(\lambda j.\ \mathsf{ITE}(j \geq 1,\ \mathsf{read}(\lambda i.\ \mathsf{ITE}(i \geq 0,\ \mathsf{read}(a, i+1),\ \mathsf{read}(a, i)), j-1),$$
$$\mathsf{read}(\lambda i.\ \mathsf{ITE}(i \geq 0,\ \mathsf{read}(a, i+1),\ \mathsf{read}(a, i)), j)),$$
$$0, \mathsf{read}(a, 0)),$$
$$k)$$
$$\neq$$
$$\mathsf{read}(a, k)$$

The flattened form is then given as $(\Delta_\varphi, c_\varphi)$ where Δ_φ contains

$v_1 \equiv \mathsf{read}(a, 0)$	$a_1 \equiv \lambda i.\ s_1$	$a_2 \equiv \lambda j.\ s_2$
$c_1 \equiv i \geq 0$	$c_2 \equiv j \geq 1$	$a_3 \equiv \mathsf{write}(a_2, 0, v_1)$
$v_2 \equiv i + 1$	$v_5 \equiv j - 1$	$v_8 \equiv \mathsf{read}(a, k)$
$v_3 \equiv \mathsf{read}(a, v_2)$	$v_6 \equiv \mathsf{read}(a_1, v_5)$	$v_9 \equiv \mathsf{read}(a_3, k)$
$v_4 \equiv \mathsf{read}(a, i)$	$v_7 \equiv \mathsf{read}(a_1, j)$	$c_3 \equiv v_8 \neq v_9$
$s_1 \equiv \mathsf{ITE}(c_1,\ v_3,\ v_4)$	$s_2 \equiv \mathsf{ITE}(c_2,\ v_6,\ v_7)$	

and $c_\varphi = c_3$. Note that the subterm $\lambda i.\ \mathsf{ITE}(i \geq 0,\ \mathsf{read}(a, i+1),\ \mathsf{read}(a, i))$ is shared in the flattened form.   ◇

5.1   Eager Reduction

The first reduction reduces satisfiability of a quantifier-free $\mathcal{T}_{\lambda\mathcal{A}}$ formula to satisfiability of a quantifier-free $\mathcal{T}_\mathcal{I} \oplus \mathcal{T}_\mathcal{E} \oplus \mathcal{T}_{\mathcal{EUF}}$ formula. This reduction is based on exhaustively applying the read-over-write and read-over-λ axioms in order to eliminate all array terms except for constants. Note that this reduction establishes decidability of satisfiability for quantifier-free $\mathcal{T}_{\lambda\mathcal{A}}$ formulas in the case where satisfiability of quantifier-free $\mathcal{T}_\mathcal{I} \oplus \mathcal{T}_\mathcal{E} \oplus \mathcal{T}_{\mathcal{EUF}}$ formulas is decidable.

Theorem 1. *Each quantifier-free $\mathcal{T}_{\lambda\mathcal{A}}$ formula φ can effectively be converted into an equisatisfiable quantifier-free $\mathcal{T}_\mathcal{I} \oplus \mathcal{T}_\mathcal{E} \oplus \mathcal{T}_{\mathcal{EUF}}$ formula φ'.*

Proof. The reduction is similar to the reduction from $\mathcal{T}_\mathcal{A}$ to $\mathcal{T}_\mathcal{I} \oplus \mathcal{T}_\mathcal{E} \oplus \mathcal{T}_{\mathcal{EUF}}$ described in Sect. 3, i.e., the read-over-write axioms (1) and (2) and the read-over-λ axiom scheme (3) are applied exhaustively as rewrite rules using the innermost strategy.[6] Thus, if Δ_φ contains definitions $a_k \equiv \mathsf{write}(a_l, p_l, v_l)$ and $v_m \equiv \mathsf{read}(a_k, p_n)$, then v_m is replaced by v'_m with the definition $v'_m \equiv \mathsf{ITE}(c,\ v_l,\ v)$, where the new definitions $c \equiv p_l = p_n$ and $v \equiv \mathsf{read}(a_l, p_n)$ are added as well. Similarly, if Δ_φ contains definitions $a_k \equiv \lambda i.\ s$ and $v_m \equiv \mathsf{read}(a_k, p_n)$, then v_m is replaced by v'_m, where v'_m names the flattened form of $s[i/p_n]$ and all definitions needed for this flattened form are added as well.

---

[6] The innermost reduction strategy is obeyed if the list of definitions is processed from front to back and new definitions are added after the definition they replace.

In order to show that this rewrite process is terminating, recursively define the function ρ by letting

$$\rho(\text{write}(a, p, v)) = 1 + \rho(a) + \rho(p) + \rho(v)$$
$$\rho(f(v_1, \ldots, v_n)) = \rho(v_1) + \ldots + \rho(v_n) \qquad \text{if } f \neq \text{write}$$
$$\rho(\lambda i.\ s) = 1 + \rho(s)$$
$$\rho(\text{ITE}(c, v_1, v_2)) = \rho(c) + \rho(v_1) + \rho(v_2)$$
$$\rho(P(v_1, \ldots, v_n)) = \rho(v_1) + \ldots + \rho(v_n)$$
$$\rho(c_1 \star c_2) = \rho(c_1) + \rho(c_2) \qquad \text{for } \star \in \{\wedge, \vee\}$$
$$\rho(\neg c_1) = \rho(c_1)$$

Thus, ρ counts occurrences of write and λ, where multiple uses of the same definitions are counted multiple times. Since the rewriting process is triggered by read-definitions, it now suffices to show that each transformation step replaces a definition of the form $v_m \equiv \text{read}(a_k, p_k)$ by finitely many new definitions of the form $v' \equiv \text{read}(a', p')$ with $\rho(v_m) > \rho(v')$ and does not increase the ρ-number of any remaining read-definition. For both of these properties, it is sufficient to show that $\rho(v_m) > \rho(v'_m)$ when v_m is replaced by v'_m.

In the first case, $a_k \equiv \text{write}(a_l, p_l, v_l) \in \Delta_\varphi$ and the new definition $v \equiv \text{read}(a_l, p_n)$ is introduced. First, note that $\rho(p_l) = \rho(v_l) = \rho(p_n) = \rho(c) = 0$ due to the innermost reduction strategy since the rewrite rules suffice to eliminate all occurrences of write and λ in terms of sort $\sigma_\mathcal{I}$ or $\sigma_\mathcal{E}$ (and thus also in propositions since $\mathcal{T}_{\lambda\mathcal{A}}$ is non-extensional). Then the desired $\rho(v_m) > \rho(v'_m)$ easily follows since $\rho(v_m) = \rho(a_k) = 1 + \rho(a_l) > \rho(a_l) = \rho(v'_m)$.

In the second case, $a_k \equiv \lambda i.\ s \in \Delta_\varphi$ and new read-definitions are only introduced in the construction of $s[i/p_n]$. As in the first case, $\rho(p_n) = 0$ due to the innermost reduction strategy. Thus, $\rho(v'_m) = \rho(s)$ and therefore $\rho(v_m) = \rho(a_k) = 1 + \rho(s) > \rho(s) = \rho(v'_m)$.

After exhaustive application of the rewrite rules, a clean-up produces a quantifier-free $\mathcal{T}_\mathcal{I} \oplus \mathcal{T}_\mathcal{E} \oplus \mathcal{T}_{\mathcal{E}\mathcal{U}\mathcal{F}}$ formula φ'. Equisatisfiability of φ and φ' follows since the conversion only applies axioms of $\mathcal{T}_{\lambda\mathcal{A}}$. □

Example 4. Continuing Ex. 3, the definition of v_9 is first replaced, by an application of the read-over-write axioms (1) and (2), by the definitions

$$c_7 \equiv k = 0 \qquad\qquad v_{18} \equiv \text{read}(a_2, k) \qquad\qquad v'_9 \equiv \text{ITE}(c_7, v_1, v_{18})$$

Then, the definition of v_{18} is replaced, by an application of the read-over-λ axiom scheme (3), by the definitions

$$c_6 \equiv k \geq 1 \qquad\qquad v_{14} \equiv \text{read}(a_1, v_{10}) \qquad\qquad v'_{18} \equiv \text{ITE}(c_6, v_{14}, v_{17})$$
$$v_{10} \equiv k - 1 \qquad\qquad v_{17} \equiv \text{read}(a_1, k)$$

obtained from c_2, v_5, v_6, v_7, and s_2 when constructing $s_2[j/k]$.

Next, the definitions of v_{14} and v_{17} are replaced, again by applications of the read-over-λ axiom scheme (3), by the definitions

$$c_4 \equiv v_{10} \geq 0 \qquad v_{13} \equiv \mathsf{read}(a, v_{10}) \qquad v_{15} \equiv k + 1$$
$$v_{11} \equiv v_{10} + 1 \qquad v'_{14} \equiv \mathsf{ITE}(c_4,\ v_{12},\ v_{13}) \qquad v_{16} \equiv \mathsf{read}(a, v_{15})$$
$$v_{12} \equiv \mathsf{read}(a, v_{11}) \qquad c_5 \equiv k \geq 0 \qquad v'_{17} \equiv \mathsf{ITE}(c_5,\ v_{16},\ v_8)$$

obtained when constructing $s_1[i/v_{10}]$ and $s_1[i/k]$.

Similar replacements take place for v_7 and v_6. After a clean-up, the following definitions remain:

$$v_1 \equiv \mathsf{read}(a, 0) \qquad v_{13} \equiv \mathsf{read}(a, v_{10}) \qquad c_6 \equiv k \geq 1$$
$$v_8 \equiv \mathsf{read}(a, k) \qquad v'_{14} \equiv \mathsf{ITE}(c_4,\ v_{12},\ v_{13}) \qquad v'_{18} \equiv \mathsf{ITE}(c_6,\ v'_{14},\ v'_{17})$$
$$v_{10} \equiv k - 1 \qquad c_5 \equiv k \geq 0 \qquad c_7 \equiv k = 0$$
$$c_4 \equiv v_{10} \geq 0 \qquad v_{15} \equiv k + 1 \qquad v'_9 \equiv \mathsf{ITE}(c_7,\ v_1,\ v'_{18})$$
$$v_{11} \equiv v_{10} + 1 \qquad v_{16} \equiv \mathsf{read}(a, v_{15}) \qquad c_3 \equiv v_8 \neq v'_9$$
$$v_{12} \equiv \mathsf{read}(a, v_{11}) \qquad v'_{17} \equiv \mathsf{ITE}(c_5,\ v_{16},\ v_8)$$

Unsatisfiability of this formula can easily be established using an SMT solver for $\mathcal{T_I} \oplus \mathcal{T_E} \oplus \mathcal{T_{EUF}}$. $\Diamond$

5.2   Using Quantifiers

The next approach reduces satisfiability of a quantifier-free $\mathcal{T_{\lambda A}}$ formula to satisfiability of a $\mathcal{T_A}$ formula containing quantifiers that range over the sort $\sigma_\mathcal{I}$. The idea for the reduction is to replace a λ-term $\lambda i.\ s$ by a constant a_k while adding the constraint $\forall i.\ \mathsf{read}(a_k, i) = s$ that restricts the interpretation of this constant to agree with the λ-term for all indices. Note that due to the introduced quantifiers, this reduction *does not* establish decidability of satisfiability for quantifier-free $\mathcal{T_{\lambda A}}$ formulas even if satisfiability of quantifier-free $\mathcal{T_A}$ formulas is decidable. It is, however, illustrative for the approach in Sect. 5.3, which can be seen as a complete instantiation strategy for the introduced quantifiers.

First, the representation of formulas is extended to quantifiers by admitting definitions of the form $c \equiv \forall i.\ c_1$ for universal quantification (existential quantification could also be admitted, but this is not needed for our reduction).

Theorem 2. *Each quantifier-free $\mathcal{T_{\lambda A}}$ formula φ can effectively be converted into an equisatisfiable $\mathcal{T_A}$ formula φ' containing universal quantifiers that range over the sort $\sigma_\mathcal{I}$.*

Proof. The reduction proceeds by repeating the following step: Let (Δ_n, c_n) be the formula in the nth iteration (i.e., $(\Delta_1, c_1) = (\Delta_\varphi, c_\varphi)$). If Δ_n contains a definition of the form $a_k \equiv \lambda i.\ s$, then this definition is deleted from Δ_n (turning a_k into an uninterpreted constant) and the definitions $v_{a_k} \equiv \mathsf{read}(a_k, i)$, $c_{a_k} \equiv v_{a_k} = s$, and $c_{\forall_{a_k}} \equiv \forall i.\ c_{a_k}$ are added instead. Furthermore, add $c_{n+1} \equiv c_n \wedge c_{\forall_{a_k}}$, resulting in the formula (Δ_{n+1}, c_{n+1}) for the next iteration. Since φ contains only finitely many λ-terms and no new λ-terms are introduced in the reduction, this process eventually terminates. Furthermore, equisatisfiability of (Δ_n, c_n) and

(Δ_{n+1}, c_{n+1}) is easily seen for all $n \geq 1$ due to the restriction on the De Bruijn indices of the occurrences of i in s.   □

Example 5. Continuing Ex. 3, the reduction to a quantified $\mathcal{T}_A$ formula produces the following definitions:

$$
\begin{array}{lll}
v_1 \equiv \mathsf{read}(a, 0) & c_{\forall a_1} \equiv \forall i.\; c_{a_1} & c_{\forall a_2} \equiv \forall j.\; c_{a_2} \\
c_1 \equiv i \geq 0 & c_2 \equiv j \geq 1 & a_3 \equiv \mathsf{write}(a_2, 0, v_1) \\
v_2 \equiv i + 1 & v_5 \equiv j - 1 & v_8 \equiv \mathsf{read}(a, k) \\
v_3 \equiv \mathsf{read}(a, v_2) & v_6 \equiv \mathsf{read}(a_1, v_5) & v_9 \equiv \mathsf{read}(a_3, k) \\
v_4 \equiv \mathsf{read}(a, i) & v_7 \equiv \mathsf{read}(a_1, j) & c_3 \equiv v_8 \neq v_9 \\
s_1 \equiv \mathsf{ITE}(c_1,\; v_3,\; v_4) & s_2 \equiv \mathsf{ITE}(c_2,\; v_6,\; v_7) & c_4 \equiv c_3 \wedge c_{\forall a_1} \\
v_{a_1} \equiv \mathsf{read}(a_1, i) & v_{a_2} \equiv \mathsf{read}(a_2, j) & c_5 \equiv c_4 \wedge c_{\forall a_2} \\
c_{a_1} \equiv v_{a_1} = s_1 & c_{a_2} \equiv v_{a_2} = s_2 &
\end{array}
$$

The resulting formula (with $c_\varphi = c_5$) is unsatisfiable, as can be shown, e.g., using the SMT solvers Z3 [26] or CVC4 [2].   ◇

5.3   Instantiating Quantifiers

Since reasoning involving quantifiers is hard for current SMT solvers, the goal of this section is to develop a method that can be seen as a sound and complete instantiation strategy for the quantifiers introduced in Sect. 5.2. For this, the quantifier introduced for the constant a_k is instantiated for all indices that occur in read operations $v_l \equiv \mathsf{read}(a_j, p_j)$ such that $a_k \prec_\mathcal{A}^+ v_l$. Intuitively, these instantiations are sufficient since the elements at indices that are never read from a_k are not relevant for the satisfiability status of the formula. Note that this reduction establishes decidability of satisfiability for such quantifier-free $\mathcal{T}_{\lambda A}$ formulas in the case where satisfiability of quantifier-free $\mathcal{T}_A$ formulas is decidable.

While the approach introduced in this section can be seen as an instantiation strategy for the quantifiers, it is conceptually simpler to state it independent of these quantifiers and give a direct reduction.

Theorem 3. *Each quantifier-free $\mathcal{T}_{\lambda A}$ formula φ can effectively be converted into an equisatisfiable quantifier-free $\mathcal{T}_A$ formula φ'.*

Proof. The reduction proceeds by repeating the following step: Let (Δ_n, c_n) be the formula in the nth iteration (i.e., $(\Delta_1, c_1) = (\Delta_\varphi, c_\varphi)$). If Δ_n contains a definition of the form $a_k \equiv \lambda i.\; s$ such that $a_k \not\prec_\mathcal{A}^+ a_l$ for all $a_l \equiv \lambda i'.\; s'$ (the last definition of a λ-term in the list of definitions satisfies this requirement), then let $P = \{p_1, \ldots, p_n\}$ denote the set of all read indices occurring in a definition $v_l \equiv \mathsf{read}(a_j, p_j)$ with $a_k \prec_\mathcal{A}^+ v_l$ (see Ex. 7 below for an explanation why it does *not* suffice to only consider definitions of the form $v_l \equiv \mathsf{read}(a_k, p_j)$). For the transformation, the definition of a_k is deleted from Δ_n (turning a_k into an uninterpreted constant) and the definitions $v_{p_j} \equiv \mathsf{read}(a_k, p_j)$ and $c_{p_j} \equiv v_{p_j} = s_{p_j}$

are added for all $p_j \in P$. Here, s_{p_j} names the flattened form of $s[i/p_j]$ and all definitions needed for this flattened form are added as well. Furthermore, add the definition $c_{n+1} \equiv c_n \wedge c$, where c names the flattened form of $c_{p_1} \wedge \ldots \wedge c_{p_n}$ and all definitions needed for this flattened form are added as well. Finally, a clean-up is performed. The resulting formula for the next iteration is then (Δ_{n+1}, c_{n+1}).

This transformation process eventually terminates since φ contains only finitely many λ-terms and flattening $s[i/p_j]$ does not introduce any new λ-terms due to the restriction on the De Bruijn indices of the occurrences of i (this assumes that the construction of the flattened form of $s[i/p_j]$ maximally shares common definitions with s).

Equisatisfiability of (Δ_n, c_n) and (Δ_{n+1}, c_{n+1}) for all all $n \geq 1$ is shown as follows. First, assume that (Δ_n, c_n) is satisfiable and let $\mathfrak{M}$ be a model of this formula. Let $\mathfrak{M}'$ be obtained from $\mathfrak{M}$ by adding the interpretation $\mathfrak{M}'(a_k) = [\![a_k]\!]^{\mathfrak{M}}$. Then $\mathfrak{M}'$ is a model of (Δ_{n+1}, c_{n+1}) since the read-over-λ axiom (3) implies that $[\![\mathsf{read}(a_k, p_j)]\!]^{\mathfrak{M}'} = [\![s[i/p_j]]\!]^{\mathfrak{M}'}$ for all $p_j \in P$.

For the reverse direction, assume that (Δ_{n+1}, c_{n+1}) is satisfiable and consider the assignment $\mathfrak{M}(a_k)$ in a model $\mathfrak{M}$ of this formula (note that a_k is an uninterpreted constant in (Δ_{n+1}, c_{n+1})). Let $\mathfrak{M}'$ be the structure obtained from $\mathfrak{M}$ by "forgetting" the assignment $\mathfrak{M}(a_k)$. Then $\mathfrak{M}'$ is a model of (Δ_n, c_n) since an easy induction on the position in the list Δ_n shows that

1. $[\![v]\!]^{\mathfrak{M}'} = [\![v]\!]^{\mathfrak{M}}$ for all definitions $v \equiv \ldots \in \Delta_n$ of sort $\sigma_\mathcal{I}$ or $\sigma_\mathcal{E}$,
2. $[\![a]\!]^{\mathfrak{M}'} = [\![a]\!]^{\mathfrak{M}}$ for all definitions $a \equiv \ldots \in \Delta_n$ of sort $\sigma_\mathcal{A}$ with $a_k \not\prec_\mathcal{A}^* a$,
3. $[\![\mathsf{read}(a, p)]\!]^{\mathfrak{M}'} = [\![\mathsf{read}(a, p)]\!]^{\mathfrak{M}}$ for all definitions $a \equiv \ldots \in \Delta_n$ of sort $\sigma_\mathcal{A}$ with $a_k \prec_\mathcal{A}^* a$ and all $p \in P$, and
4. $[\![c]\!]^{\mathfrak{M}'} = [\![c]\!]^{\mathfrak{M}}$ for all definitions of propositions $c \equiv \ldots \in \Delta_n$.

The only non-trivial case in the induction is showing the third statement, but this is ensured by the instantiations that are added as definitions in the construction of Δ_{n+1}.   □

Example 6. Continuing Ex. 3, the reduction to a quantifier-free $\mathcal{T}_\mathcal{A}$ proceeds as follows. First, the definition of a_2 is "forgotten". The set of read indices used for instantiation is $P_{a_2} = \{k\}$ (from the definition $v_9 \equiv \mathsf{read}(a_3, k)$). Thus, the following definitions are added to the formula:

$$v_{a_2}^k \equiv \mathsf{read}(a_2, k) \qquad v_6^k \equiv \mathsf{read}(a_1, v_5^k) \qquad c_{a_2}^k \equiv v_{a_2}^k = s_2^k$$
$$c_2^k \equiv k \geq 1 \qquad v_7^k \equiv \mathsf{read}(a_1, k) \qquad c_4 \equiv c_3 \wedge c_{a_2}^k$$
$$v_5^k \equiv k - 1 \qquad s_2^k \equiv \mathsf{ITE}(c_2^k, v_6^k, v_7^k)$$

Here, definitions with superscript "k" are obtained from the definitions with the same name when constructing $s_2[j/k]$. The subsequent clean-up removes the definitions of s_2, v_7, v_6, v_5, and c_2. Finally, c_φ is updated to be c_4.

Next, the definition of a_1 is "forgotten". The set of read indices for a_1 is $P_{a_1} = \{v_5^k, k\}$ (from the definitions $v_6^k \equiv \mathsf{read}(a_1, v_5^k)$ and $v_7^k \equiv \mathsf{read}(a_1, k)$). Thus, the following definitions are added to the formula:

$$v_{a_1}^k \equiv \mathsf{read}(a_1, k)$$
$$c_1^k \equiv k \geq 0$$
$$v_2^k \equiv k + 1$$
$$v_3^k \equiv \mathsf{read}(a, v_2^k)$$
$$v_4^k \equiv \mathsf{read}(a, k)$$
$$s_1^k \equiv \mathsf{ITE}(c_1^k,\ v_3^k,\ v_4^k)$$

$$c_{a_1}^k \equiv v_{a_1}^k = s_1^k$$
$$c_5 \equiv c_4 \wedge c_{a_1}^k$$
$$v_{a_1}^{v_5^k} \equiv \mathsf{read}(a_1, v_5^k)$$
$$c_1^{v_5^k} \equiv v_5^k \geq 0$$
$$v_2^{v_5^k} \equiv v_5^k + 1$$

$$v_3^{v_5^k} \equiv \mathsf{read}(a, v_2^{v_5^k})$$
$$v_4^{v_5^k} \equiv \mathsf{read}(a, k)$$
$$s_1^{v_5^k} \equiv \mathsf{ITE}(c_1^{v_5^k},\ v_3^{v_5^k},\ v_4^{v_5^k})$$
$$c_{a_1}^{v_5^k} \equiv v_{a_1}^{v_5^k} = s_1^{v_5^k}$$
$$c_6 \equiv c_5 \wedge c_{a_1}^{v_5^k}$$

After performing a clean-up, the formula contains the definitions

$$v_1 \equiv \mathsf{read}(a, 0)$$
$$a_3 \equiv \mathsf{write}(a_2, 0, v_1)$$
$$v_8 \equiv \mathsf{read}(a, k)$$
$$v_9 \equiv \mathsf{read}(a_3, k)$$
$$c_3 \equiv v_8 \neq v_9$$
$$v_{a_2}^k \equiv \mathsf{read}(a_2, k)$$
$$c_2^k \equiv k \geq 1$$
$$v_5^k \equiv k - 1$$
$$v_6^k \equiv \mathsf{read}(a_1, v_5^k)$$
$$v_7^k \equiv \mathsf{read}(a_1, k)$$

$$s_2^k \equiv \mathsf{ITE}(c_2^k,\ v_6^k,\ v_7^k)$$
$$c_{a_2}^k \equiv v_{a_2}^k = s_2^k$$
$$c_4 \equiv c_3 \wedge c_{a_2}^k$$
$$v_{a_1}^k \equiv \mathsf{read}(a_1, k)$$
$$c_1^k \equiv k \geq 0$$
$$v_2^k \equiv k + 1$$
$$v_3^k \equiv \mathsf{read}(a, v_2^k)$$
$$v_4^k \equiv \mathsf{read}(a, k)$$
$$s_1^k \equiv \mathsf{ITE}(c_1^k,\ v_3^k,\ v_4^k)$$
$$c_{a_1}^k \equiv v_{a_1}^k = s_1^k$$

$$c_5 \equiv c_4 \wedge c_{a_1}^k$$
$$v_{a_1}^{v_5^k} \equiv \mathsf{read}(a_1, v_5^k)$$
$$c_1^{v_5^k} \equiv v_5^k \geq 0$$
$$v_2^{v_5^k} \equiv v_5^k + 1$$
$$v_3^{v_5^k} \equiv \mathsf{read}(a, v_2^{v_5^k})$$
$$v_4^{v_5^k} \equiv \mathsf{read}(a, k)$$
$$s_1^{v_5^k} \equiv \mathsf{ITE}(c_1^{v_5^k},\ v_3^{v_5^k},\ v_4^{v_5^k})$$
$$c_{a_1}^{v_5^k} \equiv v_{a_1}^{v_5^k} = s_1^{v_5^k}$$
$$c_6 \equiv c_5 \wedge c_{a_1}^{v_5^k}$$

and $c_\varphi = c_6$. Unsatisfiability of the formula can easily be shown using SMT solvers for $\mathcal{T_A}$. ◇

The following example shows why it is necessary to add instantiations for all $v_l \equiv \mathsf{read}(a_j, p_j)$ with $a_k \prec_{\mathcal{A}}^+ v_l$ instead of restricting attention to those $v_l \equiv \mathsf{read}(a_j, p_j)$ with $a_j = a_k$.

Example 7. Consider the $\mathcal{T_{\lambda A}}$ formula $(\Delta_\varphi, c_\varphi)$ with $\mathcal{T_I} = \mathcal{T_E} = \mathcal{T_{LIA}}$ where Δ_φ contains the definitions

$$a_1 \equiv \lambda i.\ 0$$
$$a_2 \equiv \mathsf{write}(a_1, 0, 1)$$

$$v_1 \equiv \mathsf{read}(a_2, k)$$
$$c_1 \equiv v_1 \neq 0$$

$$c_2 \equiv k \neq 0$$
$$c_3 \equiv c_1 \wedge c_2$$

and $c_\varphi = c_3$. Then this formula is clearly unsatisfiable.

If only definitions $v_l \equiv \mathsf{read}(a_j, p_j)$ with $a_j = a_k$ are considered when eliminating the definition of a_1, then no instantiations are added at all and

$$a_2 \equiv \mathsf{write}(a_1, 0, 1)$$
$$v_1 \equiv \mathsf{read}(a_2, k)$$

$$c_1 \equiv v_1 \neq 0$$
$$c_2 \equiv k \neq 0$$

$$c_3 \equiv c_1 \wedge c_2$$

remain. This formula is satisfiable (e.g., if a_1 contains 1 for all indices).

Using all $v_l \equiv \mathsf{read}(a_j, p_j)$ with $a_k \prec_{\mathcal{A}}^+ a_j$ as done in the proof of Thm. 3 adds an instantiation for k and the definitions

$$
\begin{aligned}
v_{a_1}^k &\equiv \mathsf{read}(a_1, k) & v_1 &\equiv \mathsf{read}(a_2, k) & c_3 &\equiv c_1 \wedge c_2 \\
c_{a_1}^k &\equiv v_{a_1}^k = 0 & c_1 &\equiv v_1 \neq 0 & c_4 &\equiv c_4 \wedge c_{a_1}^k \\
a_2 &\equiv \mathsf{write}(a_1, 0, 1) & c_2 &\equiv k \neq 0
\end{aligned}
$$

are obtained. Furthermore, c_φ is updated to c_4. As desired, the resulting formula is unsatisfiable. $\Diamond$

6   Implementation and Evaluation

We have conducted experiments with all reductions described in Sect. 5 for determining the satisfiability of quantifier-free $\mathcal{T}_{\lambda\mathcal{A}}$. Since our motivation was the application in the bounded model checking tool LLBMC [24], we have restricted attention to the case where $\mathcal{T}_{\mathcal{E}} = \mathcal{T}_{\mathcal{I}} = \mathcal{T}_{\mathcal{BV}}$ is the theory of bit-vectors.

6.1   Loop Summarization in LLBMC

The tool LLBMC is a bounded model checker for C and (to some extent) C++ programs. In order to support the complex and intricate syntax and semantics of these programming languages, LLBMC uses the LLVM compiler framework [21] in order to translate C and C++ programs into LLVM's intermediate representation (IR). This IR is then converted into a quantifier-free $\mathcal{T}_{\lambda\mathcal{A}}$ formula and simplified using an extensive set of rewrite rules. The simplified formula is finally passed to an SMT solver. Distinguishing features of LLBMC in comparison with related tools such as CBMC [9] and ESBMC [11] are its use of a flat, bit-precise memory model, its exhaustive set of built-in checks, and its performance (see [24]).

The use of the LLVM compiler framework proved itself very useful in implementing loop summarization in LLBMC, as LLVM provides passes for canonicalizing loops. Furthermore, information about a the start value, end value, and trip count of a loop's induction variable is available using LLVM' comprehensive scalar evolution analysis framework.

In our implementation, summarizable loops are transformed into λ-terms of the form $\lambda i.\ \mathsf{ITE}(g,\ s,\ r)$, where g is a guard indicating if a read at position i from the λ-term is in the summarized memory region or not, s is an encoding of the value stored in the summarized loop, and r is a read from position i of the memory state from before execution of the loop.

The implementation currently focuses on the most frequently found summarizable loops and is therefore restricted to loops with a single basic block[7], a single store instruction, and at most load instructions which are executed before the store instruction and access exactly the same memory location modified by the store instruction.

---

[7] This restriction can be easily relaxed in the future.

6.2   Evaluation

Within LLBMC, we have evaluated the following approaches for determining satisfiability of quantifier-free $\mathcal{T}_{\lambda\mathcal{A}}$ formulas:

1. The eager reduction to $\mathcal{T}_\mathcal{I} \oplus \mathcal{T}_\mathcal{E} \oplus \mathcal{T}_{\mathcal{E}\mathcal{U}\mathcal{F}}$ from Sect. 5.1 and the instantiation-based reduction to $\mathcal{T}_\mathcal{A}$ from Sect. 5.3 have been evaluated in combination with the SMT solvers STP [15] (SVN revision 1673), Boolector [4] (version 1.5.118), Z3 [26] (version 4.3.1), and CVC4 [2] (version 1.1). Here, the SMT solvers were executed using their C resp. C++ (CVC4) API.
2. The quantifier-based reduction to $\mathcal{T}_\mathcal{A}$ from Sect. 5.2 has been evaluated in combination with the SMT solvers Z3 and CVC4. Note that STP and Boolector do not support quantifiers. Since, according to its authors, the array solver in Z3 is optimized for quantifier-free problems [25], we have also evaluated an approach where arrays are encoded using uninterpreted functions and quantifiers (as suggested in [25]).
3. Loops that can be summarized using λ-terms can alternatively be treated like any other loop. Consequently, the boundedness restriction inherent to bounded model checking then applies. This approach was again evaluated in combination with STP, Boolector, Z3, and CVC4.

These approaches have been evaluated on a collection of 81 C and C++ programs. A total of 67 of these programs contain λ-terms corresponding to set or copy operations, where 55 programs were already used in the preliminary version of this work [14]. The set and copy operations in these programs may occur due to several reasons:

− The source code contains an explicit call to `memset` or `memcpy`.
− Library-specific implementation details included through header files may result in calls to `memset` or `memcpy`. This is in particular true for C++ programs that use the container classes of the STL.
− Default implementations of C++ constructors, especially the copy constructor, may make use of `memcpy` operations to initialize objects.

The remaining 14 programs contain loops that can be summarized using λ-terms as described in Sect. 4.1. Out of the 81 programs, 20 programs contain a bug and produce a satisfiable $\mathcal{T}_{\lambda\mathcal{A}}$ formula. The remaining 61 programs produce unsatisfiable $\mathcal{T}_{\lambda\mathcal{A}}$ formulas. The formulas that are produced for the different approaches are available in SMT-LIB v2 format at http://llbmc.org/.

The results of LLBMC on the collection of examples are summarized in Table 1. The reported times are in seconds and contain the time needed for the logical encoding into a $\mathcal{T}_{\lambda\mathcal{A}}$ formula, simplification of the formula, the time needed for the reductions, and the time needed by the SMT solver. A timeout of 60 seconds was imposed for each program and the experiments were performed on an Intel® Core™ 2 Duo 2.4GHz with 4GB of RAM.

The results indicate that the instantiation-based reduction achieves the best performance, regardless of the SMT solver that is used (but in particular in combination with STP). This can also be observed in the cactus plots displayed

Table 1. Times and success rates for the different approaches on 81 benchmark problems using a timeout of 60 seconds. "S" denotes the number of solved benchmark problems, "T" denotes the number of timeouts, "M" denotes the number of times the SMT solver ran out of memory, and "A" denotes the number of times the SMT solver aborted (i.e., gave up before reaching the timeout). Total times are in seconds and include timeouts, memory exhaustions, and solver aborts with their respective runtimes.

		Satisfiable					Unsatisfiable					All				
SMT solver	Approach	Total Time	S	T	M	A	Total Time	S	T	M	A	Total Time	S	T	M	A
STP	Instantiation	9.908	20	–	–	–	196.126	60	1	–	–	206.034	80	1	–	–
STP	Eager	182.084	17	3	–	–	597.460	53	8	–	–	779.544	70	11	–	–
STP	Loops	114.663	17	1	2	–	555.863	53	5	3	–	670.526	70	6	5	–
Boolector	Instantiation	112.886	19	1	–	–	705.896	52	9	–	–	818.782	71	10	–	–
Boolector	Eager	189.760	17	3	–	–	796.991	53	8	–	–	986.751	70	11	–	–
Boolector	Loops	203.644	16	2	2	–	935.839	45	13	3	–	1139.483	61	15	5	–
Z3	Instantiation	126.948	18	2	–	–	821.417	49	11	1	–	948.365	67	13	1	–
Z3	Eager	185.436	17	3	–	–	858.196	49	12	–	–	1043.632	66	15	–	–
Z3	Quantifiers	288.719	16	4	–	–	833.770	49	12	–	–	1122.489	65	16	–	–
Z3	Quantifiers+UF	147.033	18	2	–	–	1127.661	45	16	–	–	1274.694	63	18	–	–
Z3	Loops	364.796	13	5	2	–	1254.787	40	18	3	–	1619.583	53	23	5	–
CVC4	Instantiation	196.661	17	3	–	–	731.418	50	11	–	–	928.079	67	14	–	–
CVC4	Eager	244.884	17	3	–	–	874.864	48	13	–	–	1119.748	65	16	–	–
CVC4	Quantifiers	432.676	7	7	–	6	974.442	47	14	–	–	1407.118	54	21	–	6
CVC4	Quantifiers+UF	452.506	7	7	–	6	1136.908	45	16	–	–	1589.414	52	23	–	6
CVC4	Loops	430.052	12	6	2	–	1122.646	44	13	4	–	1552.698	56	19	6	–

in Fig. 1. Also note that all approaches using $\mathcal{T}_{\lambda A}$ perform better than the naïve implementation using loops, where the latter is furthermore incomplete in general due to the bounded number of loop iterations that can be considered.[8]

7   Related Work

Decidable extensions of the theory of arrays have been considered before. Suzuki and Jefferson [30] have studied the extension of $\mathcal{T}_A$ with a restricted use of a permutation predicate. Mateti [22] has described a theory of arrays where entries of an array can be exchanged. Jaffar [19] has investigated reading of array segments but does not discuss writing array segments. Ghilardi et al. [16] have considered the addition of axioms specifying the dimension of arrays, injectivity of arrays, arrays with domains, array prefixes, array iterators, and sorted arrays. All of these extensions are orthogonal to the theory $\mathcal{T}_{\lambda A}$ considered in this paper. A theory of arrays with constant-valued arrays has been proposed by Stump et al. [29]. These constant-valued arrays can easily be modelled in $\mathcal{T}_{\lambda A}$ using a simple λ-term of the form $\lambda i.\ k$ where k is the constant value. This theory has also been considered in [1]. De Moura and Bjørner [27] have introduced

---

[8] This incompleteness does not manifest itself in the evaluation since the number of loop iterations was chosen sufficiently large for each program. This causes LLBMC to run out of memory on some examples, though.

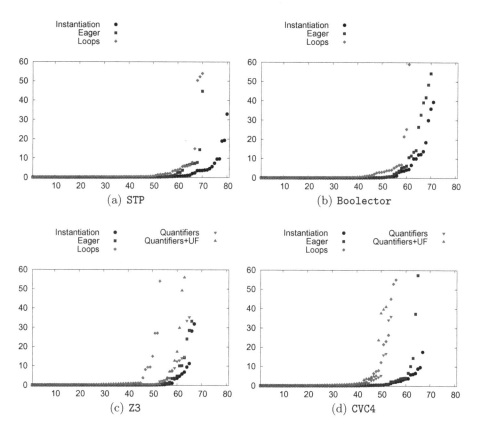

Fig. 1. Cactus plots for the 81 benchmark problems. The x-axis shows the number of solved problems and the y-axis shows the time limit for each problem in seconds. Thus, a curve that is closer to the bottom-right indicates a better performing approach.

combinatory array logic, which extends $\mathcal{T}_A$ by constant-valued arrays as in [29] and a map combinator.

The satisfiability problem for restricted classes of quantified formulas in the theory of arrays has been investigated as well. The work by Bradley *et al.* [3] identifies the *array property fragment*, where value constraints are restricted by index guards in universally quantified subformulas. Note that already the special case of the copy operation cannot be expressed in the array property fragment due to the "pointer arithmetic" $q + (r - p)$. The conceptually simpler set operation can be defined in the array property fragment, though. The array property fragment was later extended by Habermehl *et al.* [17,18], but the "pointer arithmetic" needed for copy is still not permitted. Finally, Zhou *et al.* [31] have investigated a theory of arrays where the elements are from a finite set.

A logic containing λ-terms has been considered by Bryant *et al.* [6], who also show that $\mathcal{T}_A$ can be simulated using λ-terms. The key distinction of the present work in comparison to [6] is that we *extend* $\mathcal{T}_A$ with λ-terms that denote anonymous arrays. This makes it possible to utilize powerful and efficient SMT solvers for $\mathcal{T}_{\mathcal{A}}$ in order to decide satisfiability of quantifier-free $\mathcal{T}_{\lambda\mathcal{A}}$ formulas using the reduction based on instantiating quantifiers (Sect. 5.3). In contrast, [6] has to apply β-reduction eagerly, which corresponds to our eager reduction (Sect. 5.1). As clearly shown in Sect. 6, the instantiation-based reduction from $\mathcal{T}_{\lambda\mathcal{A}}$ to $\mathcal{T}_{\mathcal{A}}$ performs much better than the eager reduction from $\mathcal{T}_{\lambda\mathcal{A}}$ to $\mathcal{T}_{\mathcal{I}} \oplus \mathcal{T}_{\mathcal{E}} \oplus \mathcal{T}_{\mathcal{EUF}}$.

8 Conclusions and Further Work

We have presented $\mathcal{T}_{\lambda\mathcal{A}}$, an extension of the theory of arrays with λ-terms. These λ-terms can be used in order to model library functions such as C's `memset` and `memcpy` in formal methods such as program analysis, (deductive) software verification, bounded model checking, or symbolic execution. Furthermore, we have shown how a class of loops can automatically be summarized using such λ-terms. We have presented three reductions from $\mathcal{T}_{\lambda\mathcal{A}}$ to theories that are supported by current SMT solvers and have reported on an evaluation in LLBMC [24].

For future work, we are particularly interested in adding "native" support for $\mathcal{T}_{\lambda\mathcal{A}}$ in SMT solvers such as STP [15], Boolector [4], Z3 [26], or CVC4 [2]. For this, it will be necessary to investigate lazy axiom instantiation or lemma-on-demand techniques for $\mathcal{T}_{\lambda\mathcal{A}}$ since these techniques have been fundamental for the performance gain that SMT solvers for $\mathcal{T}_{\mathcal{A}}$ have experienced in recent years. A first, simple idea is to add not all instantiations from Sect. 5.3 beforehand, but instead do this incrementally in a CEGAR-like loop guided by spurious models generated by the SMT solver for $\mathcal{T}_{\mathcal{A}}$. A further direction for future work is to widen the class of loops that can be summarized using λ-terms in the theory $\mathcal{T}_{\lambda\mathcal{A}}$. Finally, we are interested in adding an operation similar to `fold` as known from functional programming languages to the theory $\mathcal{T}_{\lambda\mathcal{A}}$.

References

1. Armando, A., Ranise, S., Rusinowitch, M.: A rewriting approach to satisfiability procedures. IC 183(2), 140–164 (2003)
2. Barrett, C., Conway, C.L., Deters, M., Hadarean, L., Jovanović, D., King, T., Reynolds, A., Tinelli, C.: CVC4. In: Gopalakrishnan, G., Qadeer, S. (eds.) CAV 2011. LNCS, vol. 6806, pp. 171–177. Springer, Heidelberg (2011)
3. Bradley, A.R., Manna, Z., Sipma, H.B.: What's decidable about arrays? In: Emerson, E.A., Namjoshi, K.S. (eds.) VMCAI 2006. LNCS, vol. 3855, pp. 427–442. Springer, Heidelberg (2006)
4. Brummayer, R., Biere, A.: Boolector: An efficient SMT solver for bit-vectors and arrays. In: Kowalewski, S., Philippou, A. (eds.) TACAS 2009. LNCS, vol. 5505, pp. 174–177. Springer, Heidelberg (2009)
5. Brummayer, R., Biere, A.: Lemmas on demand for the extensional theory of arrays. JSAT 6, 165–201 (2009)
6. Bryant, R.E., Lahiri, S.K., Seshia, S.A.: Modeling and verifying systems using a logic of counter arithmetic with lambda expressions and uninterpreted functions. In: Brinksma, E., Larsen, K.G. (eds.) CAV 2002. LNCS, vol. 2404, pp. 78–92. Springer, Heidelberg (2002)

7. Cadar, C., Dunbar, D., Engler, D.R.: KLEE: Unassisted and automatic generation of high-coverage tests for complex systems programs. In: OSDI 2008, pp. 209–224 (2008)
8. Cadar, C., Ganesh, V., Pawlowski, P.M., Dill, D.L., Engler, D.R.: EXE: Automatically generating inputs of death. TISSEC 12(2), 10:1–10:38 (2008)
9. Clarke, E., Kroning, D., Lerda, F.: A tool for checking ANSI-C programs. In: Jensen, K., Podelski, A. (eds.) TACAS 2004. LNCS, vol. 2988, pp. 168–176. Springer, Heidelberg (2004)
10. Cohen, E., Dahlweid, M., Hillebrand, M.A., Leinenbach, D., Moskal, M., Santen, T., Schulte, W., Tobies, S.: VCC: A practical system for verifying concurrent C. In: Berghofer, S., Nipkow, T., Urban, C., Wenzel, M. (eds.) TPHOLs 2009. LNCS, vol. 5674, pp. 23–42. Springer, Heidelberg (2009)
11. Cordeiro, L., Fischer, B., Marques-Silva, J.: SMT-based bounded model checking for embedded ANSI-C software. TSE 38(4), 957–974 (2012)
12. Cuoq, P., Kirchner, F., Kosmatov, N., Prevosto, V., Signoles, J., Yakobowski, B.: Frama-C: A software analysis perspective. In: Eleftherakis, G., Hinchey, M., Holcombe, M. (eds.) SEFM 2012. LNCS, vol. 7504, pp. 233–247. Springer, Heidelberg (2012)
13. Falke, S., Merz, F., Sinz, C.: A theory of C-style memory allocation. In: SMT 2011, pp. 71–80 (2011)
14. Falke, S., Sinz, C., Merz, F.: A theory of arrays with set and copy operations (extended abstract). In: SMT 2012, pp. 97–106 (2012)
15. Ganesh, V., Dill, D.L.: A decision procedure for bit-vectors and arrays. In: Damm, W., Hermanns, H. (eds.) CAV 2007. LNCS, vol. 4590, pp. 519–531. Springer, Heidelberg (2007)
16. Ghilardi, S., Nicolini, E., Ranise, S., Zucchelli, D.: Decision procedures for extensions of the theory of arrays. AMAI 50(3-4), 231–254 (2007)
17. Habermehl, P., Iosif, R., Vojnar, T.: A logic of singly indexed arrays. In: Cervesato, I., Veith, H., Voronkov, A. (eds.) LPAR 2008. LNCS (LNAI), vol. 5330, pp. 558–573. Springer, Heidelberg (2008)
18. Habermehl, P., Iosif, R., Vojnar, T.: What else is decidable about integer arrays? In: Amadio, R.M. (ed.) FOSSACS 2008. LNCS, vol. 4962, pp. 474–489. Springer, Heidelberg (2008)
19. Jaffar, J.: Presburger arithmetic with array segments. IPL 12(2), 79–82 (1981)
20. Kapur, D., Zarba, C.G.: The reduction approach to decision procedures. Tech. Rep. TR-CS-2005-44, Dept. of Computer Science, Univ. of New Mexico (2005)
21. Lattner, C., Adve, V.S.: LLVM: A compilation framework for lifelong program analysis & transformation. In: CGO 2004, pp. 75–88 (2004)
22. Mateti, P.: A decision procedure for the correctness of a class of programs. JACM 28(2), 215–232 (1981)
23. McCarthy, J.: Towards a mathematical science of computation. In: IFIP Congress 1962, pp. 21–28 (1962)
24. Merz, F., Falke, S., Sinz, C.: LLBMC: Bounded model checking of C and C++ programs using a compiler IR. In: Joshi, R., Müller, P., Podelski, A. (eds.) VSTTE 2012. LNCS, vol. 7152, pp. 146–161. Springer, Heidelberg (2012)
25. de Moura, L.: Answer to Support for AUFBV? on Stack Overflow, `http://stackoverflow.com/questions/7411995/support-for-aufbv` (2011)
26. de Moura, L., Bjørner, N.: Z3: An efficient SMT solver. In: Ramakrishnan, C.R., Rehof, J. (eds.) TACAS 2008. LNCS, vol. 4963, pp. 337–340. Springer, Heidelberg (2008)

27. de Moura, L., Bjørner, N.: Generalized, efficient array decision procedures. In: FMCAD 2009, pp. 45–52 (2009)
28. Sinz, C., Falke, S., Merz, F.: A precise memory model for low-level bounded model checking. In: SSV 2010 (2010)
29. Stump, A., Barrett, C.W., Dill, D.L., Levitt, J.R.: A decision procedure for an extensional theory of arrays. In: LICS 2001, pp. 29–37 (2001)
30. Suzuki, N., Jefferson, D.: Verification decidability of Presburger array programs. JACM 27(1), 191–205 (1980)
31. Zhou, M., He, F., Wang, B.Y., Gu, M.: On array theory of bounded elements. In: Touili, T., Cook, B., Jackson, P. (eds.) CAV 2010. LNCS, vol. 6174, pp. 570–584. Springer, Heidelberg (2010)

An Improved Unrolling-Based Decision Procedure for Algebraic Data Types

Tuan-Hung Pham and Michael W. Whalen

University of Minnesota

Abstract. Reasoning about algebraic data types and functions that operate over these data types is an important problem for a large variety of applications. In this paper, we present a decision procedure for reasoning about data types using abstractions that are provided by *catamorphisms*: fold functions that map instances of algebraic data types into values in a decidable domain. We show that the procedure is sound and complete for a class of *monotonic* catamorphisms.

Our work extends a previous decision procedure that solves formulas involving algebraic data types via successive unrollings of catamorphism functions. First, we propose the categories of *monotonic* catamorphisms and *associative-commutative* catamorphisms, which we argue provide a better formal foundation than previous categorizations of catamorphisms. We use monotonic catamorphisms to fix an incompleteness in the previous unrolling algorithm (and associated proof). We then use these notions to address two open problems from previous work: (1) we provide a bound on the number of unrollings necessary for completeness, showing that it is exponentially small with respect to formula size for associative-commutative catamorphisms, and (2) we demonstrate that associative-commutative catamorphisms can be combined within a formula whilst preserving completeness.

1 Introduction

Decision procedures have been a fertile area of research in recent years, with several advances in the breadth of theories that can be decided and the speed with which substantial problems can be solved. When coupled with SMT solvers, these procedures can be combined and used to solve complex formulas relevant to software and hardware verification. An important stream of research has focused on decision procedures for algebraic data types. Algebraic data types are important for a wide variety of problems: they provide a natural representation for tree-like structures such as abstract syntax trees and XML documents; in addition, they are the fundamental representation of recursive data for functional programming languages.

Algebraic data types provide a significant challenge for decision procedures since they are recursive and usually unbounded in size. Early approaches focused on equalities and disequalities over the structure of elements of data types [2,16]. While important, these structural properties are often not expressive enough

E. Cohen and A. Rybalchenko (Eds.): VSTTE 2013, LNCS 8164, pp. 129–148, 2014.
© Springer-Verlag Berlin Heidelberg 2014

to describe interesting properties involving the data stored in the data type. Instead, we often are interested in making statements both about the structure and contents of data within a data type. For example, one might want to express that all integers stored within a tree are positive or that the set of elements in a list does not contain a particular value.

In [23], Suter et al. described a parametric decision procedure for reasoning about algebraic data types using catamorphism (fold) functions. In the procedure, catamorphisms describe abstract views of the data type that can then be reasoned about in formulas. For example, suppose that we have a binary tree data type with functions to add and remove elements from the tree, as well as check whether an element was stored in the tree. Given a catamorphism *setOf* that computes the set of elements stored in the tree, we could describe a specification for an 'add' function as:

$$setOf(\text{add}(e, t)) = \{e\} \cup setOf(t)$$

where *setOf* can be defined in an ML-like language as:

```
fun setOf t = case t of Leaf ⇒ ∅ |
                        Node(l, e, r) ⇒ setOf(l) ∪ {e} ∪ setOf(r)
```

Formulas of this sort can be decided by the algorithm in [23]. In fact, the decision procedure in [23] allows a wide range of problems to be addressed, because it is parametric in several dimensions: (1) the structure of the data type, (2) the elements stored in the data type, (3) the collection type that is the codomain of the catamorphism, and (4) the behavior of the catamorphism itself. Thus, it is possible to solve a variety of interesting problems, including:

- reasoning about the contents of XML messages,
- determining correctness of functional implementations of data types, including queues, maps, binary trees, and red-black trees.
- reasoning about structure-manipulating functions for data types, such as sort and reverse.
- computing bound variables in abstract syntax trees to support reasoning over operational semantics and type systems, and
- reasoning about simplifications and transformations of propositional logic.

The first class of problems is especially important for *guards*, devices that mediate information sharing between security domains according to a specified policy. Typical guard operations include reading field values in a packet, changing fields in a packet, transforming a packet by adding new fields, dropping fields from a packet, constructing audit messages, and removing a packet from a stream. We have built automated reasoning tools (described in [9]) based on the decision procedure to support reasoning over guard applications.

The procedure was proved sound for all catamorphisms and complete for a class of catamorphisms called *sufficiently surjective* catamorphisms, which we will describe in more detail in the remainder of the paper. Unfortunately, the algorithm in [23] was quite expensive to compute and required a specialized predicate called M_p to be defined separately for each catamorphism and proved correct w.r.t. the catamorphism using either a hand-proof or a theorem prover.

In [24], a generalized algorithm for the decision procedure was proposed, based on unrolling the catamorphism. This algorithm had three significant advantages over the algorithm in [23]: it was much less expensive to compute, it did not require the definition of M_p, and it was claimed to be complete for all sufficiently surjective catamorphisms. Unfortunately, the algorithm in [24] is in fact not complete for all sufficiently surjective catamorphisms.

In this paper, we slightly modify the procedure of [24] to remove this incompleteness. We then address two open problems with the previous work [24]: (1) how many catamorphism unrollings are required in order to prove properties using the decision procedure? and (2) when is it possible to combine catamorphisms within a formula in a complete way? To address these issues, we introduce two further notions: *monotonic* catamorphisms, which describe an alternative formulation to the notion of *sufficiently surjective* catamorphisms for describing completeness, and *associative-commutative* (AC) catamorphisms, which can be combined within a formula while preserving completeness results. In addition, these catamorphisms have the property that they require a very small number of unrollings. This behavior explains some of the empirical success in applying catamorphism-based approaches on interesting examples from previous papers [24,9]. In short, the paper consists of the following contributions:

- We propose the notion of monotonic catamorphisms and show that all sufficiently surjective catamorphisms discussed in [23] are monotonic.
- We revise the unrolling-based decision procedure for algebraic data type [24] using monotonic catamorphisms and formally prove its completeness.
- We propose the notion of AC catamorphisms, a sub-class of monotonic catamorphisms, and show that decision procedure for algebraic data types with AC catamorphisms are *combinable* while the procedures for algebraic data types proposed by Suter et al. [23,24] only work with single catamorphisms.
- We solve the open problem of determining the maximum number of unrollings with both monotonic and AC catamorphisms.
- We show that AC catamorphisms can be automatically detected.
- We describe an implementation of the approach, called RADA [18], which accepts formulas in an extended version of the SMT-LIB2 syntax, and demonstrate it on a range of examples.

The rest of the paper is organized as follows. Section 2 presents some preliminaries about catamorphisms and the parametric logic in [23]. Section 3 discusses some properties of trees and shapes in the parametric logic. In Section 4, we propose an unrolling-based decision procedure for algebraic data types. The decision procedure works with monotonic catamorphisms, which are discussed in Section 5, and the correctness of the algorithm for these catamorphisms is shown in Section 6. Section 7 presents AC catamorphisms, and the relationship between different types of catamorphisms is discussed in Section 8. Experimental results for our approach are shown in Section 9. Section 10 presents related work. Finally, we conclude the paper with directions for future work in Section 11.

2   Preliminaries

We describe the parametric logic used in the decision procedures for algebraic data types proposed by Suter et al. [23,24], the definition of catamorphisms, and the idea of sufficient surjectivity, which describes situations in which the decision procedures [23,24] were claimed to be complete.

2.1   Parametric Logic

The input to the decision procedures is a formula ϕ of literals over elements of tree terms and abstractions produced by a catamorphism. The logic is *parametric* in the sense that we assume a data type τ to be reasoned about, an element theory $\mathcal{E}$ containing element types and operations, a catamorphism α that is used to abstract the data type, and a decidable theory $\mathcal{L}_C$ of values in a collection domain $\mathcal{C}$ containing terms C generated by the catamorphism function. Fig. 1 shows the syntax of the parametric logic instantiated for binary trees.

T	$::=$	$t \mid \mathsf{Leaf} \mid \mathsf{Node}(T, E, T) \mid \mathsf{left}(T) \mid \mathsf{right}(T)$	Tree terms
C	$::=$	$c \mid \alpha(T) \mid \mathcal{T}_C$	C-terms
E	$::=$	variables of type $\mathcal{E} \mid \mathsf{elem}(T) \mid \mathcal{T}_\mathcal{E}$	Expression
F_T	$::=$	$T = T \mid T \neq T$	Tree (in)equations
F_C	$::=$	$C = C \mid \mathcal{F}_C$	Formula of $\mathcal{L}_C$
F_E	$::=$	$E = E \mid \mathcal{F}_\mathcal{E}$	Formula of $\mathcal{L}_\mathcal{E}$
ϕ	$::=$	$\bigwedge F_T \wedge \bigwedge F_C \wedge \bigwedge F_E$	Conjunctions
ψ	$::=$	$\phi \mid \neg\phi \mid \phi \vee \phi \mid \phi \wedge \phi \mid \phi \Rightarrow \phi \mid \phi \Leftrightarrow \phi$	Formulas

Fig. 1. Syntax of the parametric logic. Its semantics can be found in [23].

The syntax of the logic ranges over data type terms T and C-terms of a decidable collection theory $\mathcal{L}_C$. $\mathcal{T}_C$ and $\mathcal{F}_C$ are arbitrary terms and formulas in $\mathcal{L}_C$, as are $\mathcal{T}_\mathcal{E}$ and $\mathcal{F}_\mathcal{E}$ in $\mathcal{L}_\mathcal{E}$. Tree formulas F_T describe equalities and disequalities over tree terms. Collection formulas F_C and element formulas E_C describe equalities over collection terms C and element terms E, as well as other operations ($\mathcal{F}_C$, $\mathcal{F}_\mathcal{E}$) allowed by the logic of collections $\mathcal{L}_C$ and elements $\mathcal{L}_\mathcal{E}$. E defines terms in the element types $\mathcal{E}$ contained within the branches of the data types. ϕ defines conjunctions of (restricted) formulas in the tree and collection theories. The ϕ terms are the ones solved by the decision procedures in [23]; these can be generalized to arbitrary propositional formulas (ψ) through the use of a DPLL solver [8] that manages the other operators within the formula. Although the logic and unrolling procedure is parametric with respect to data types, in the sequel we focus on binary trees to illustrate the concepts and proofs.

2.2   Catamorphisms

Given a tree in the parametric logic, we can map the tree into a value in $\mathcal{C}$ using a *catamorphism*, which is a fold function of the following format:

$$\alpha(t) = \begin{cases} \text{empty} & \text{if } t = \text{Leaf} \\ \text{combine}\big(\alpha(t_L), e, \alpha(t_R)\big) & \text{if } t = \text{Node}(t_L, e, t_R) \end{cases}$$

where empty is an element in $\mathcal{C}$ and combine $: (\mathcal{C}, \mathcal{E}, \mathcal{C}) \to \mathcal{C}$ is a function that combines a triple of two values in $\mathcal{C}$ and an element in $\mathcal{E}$ into a value in $\mathcal{C}$.

Table 1. Sufficiently surjective catamorphisms in [23]

Name	$\alpha(\text{Leaf})$	$\alpha(\text{Node}(t_L, e, t_R))$	Example
Set	$\emptyset$	$\alpha(t_L) \cup \{e\} \cup \alpha(t_R)$	$\{1, 2\}$
Multiset	$\emptyset$	$\alpha(t_L) \uplus \{e\} \uplus \alpha(t_R)$	$\{1, 2\}$
SizeI	0	$\alpha(t_L) + 1 + \alpha(t_R)$	2
Height	0	$1 + \max\{\alpha(t_L), \alpha(t_R)\}$	2
List	List()	$\alpha(t_L) \text{ @ List}(e) \text{ @ } \alpha(t_R)$ (in-order)	(1 2)
		$\text{List}(e) \text{ @ } \alpha(t_L) \text{ @ } \alpha(t_R)$ (pre-order)	(2 1)
		$\alpha(t_L) \text{ @ } \alpha(t_R) \text{ @ List}(e)$ (post-order)	(1 2)
Some	None	Some(e)	Some(2)
Min	None	$\min'\{\alpha(t_L), e, \alpha(t_R)\}$	1
Sortedness	(None, None, true)	(None, None, false) (if tree unsorted) (min element, max element, true) (if tree sorted)	(1, 2, true)

Catamorphisms from [23] are shown in Table 1. The first column contains catamorphism names[1]. The next two columns define $\alpha(t)$ when t is a Leaf and when it is a Node, respectively. The last column shows examples of the application of each catamorphism to $\text{Node}\big(\text{Node}(\text{Leaf}, 1, \text{Leaf}), 2, \text{Leaf}\big)$. In the *Min* catamorphism, min$'$ is the same as the usual min function except that min$'$ ignores None in the list of its arguments, which must contain at least one non-None value. The *Sortedness* catamorphism returns a triple containing the min and max element of the subtree, and true/false depending on whether it is sorted or not.

Tree shapes: The shape of a tree in the parametric logic is obtained by removing all element values in the tree.

Definition 1 (Tree shapes). *The shape of a tree is defined by constant SLeaf and constructor SNode(_, _) as follows:*

$$shape(t) = \begin{cases} \text{SLeaf} & \text{if } t = \text{Leaf} \\ \text{SNode}\big(shape(t_L), shape(t_R)\big) & \text{if } t = \text{Node}(t_L, \_, t_R) \end{cases}$$

Sufficiently surjective catamorphisms: The decision procedures proposed by Suter et al. [23,24] were claimed to be complete if the catamorphism used in the procedures is *sufficiently surjective* [23]. Intuitively, a catamorphism is sufficiently surjective if the inverse relation of the catamorphism has sufficiently large cardinality when tree shapes are larger than some finite bound.

---

[1] *SizeI*, which maps a tree into its number of *internal* nodes, was originally named *Size* in [23]. We rename the catamorphism to easily distinguish between itself and function *size*, which returns the total number of *all* vertices in a tree, in this paper.

Definition 2 (Sufficient surjectivity). α *is sufficiently surjective iff for each* $p \in \mathbb{N}^+$, *there exists, computable as a function of* p, *(1) a finite set of shapes* S_p *and (2) a closed formula* M_p *in the collection theory such that* $M_p(c)$ *implies* $|\alpha^{-1}(c)| > p$, *such that* $M_p(\alpha(t))$ *or* $shape(t) \in S_p$ *for every tree term* t.

Despite its name, sufficient surjectivity has no surjectivity requirement for the codomain of α. It only requires a "sufficiently large" number of trees for values satisfying the condition M_p. Table 1 describes all sufficiently surjective cata-morphisms in [23]. The only catamorphism in [23] not in Table 1 is the *Mirror* catamorphism; since the cardinality of the inversion function of the catamor-phism is always 1, the sufficiently surjective condition does not hold for this catamorphism.

3   Properties of Trees and Shapes in the Parametric Logic

We present some important properties of trees and shapes in the parametric logic which will play important roles in the subsequent sections of the paper.

3.1   Properties of Trees

Property 1 follows from the syntax of the parametric logic. Properties 2 and 3 are well-known properties of full binary trees [6,19] (i.e., binary trees in which every internal node has exactly two children).

Property 1 (Type of tree). Any tree in the parametric logic is a full binary tree.

Property 2 (Size). The number of vertices in any tree in the parametric logic is odd. Also, in a tree t of size $2k + 1$ ($k \in \mathbb{N}$), we have:

$$ni(t) = k \qquad\qquad nl(t) = k + 1$$

where $ni(t)$ and $nl(t)$ are the number of internal nodes and the number of leaves in t, respectively.

Property 3 (Size vs. Height). In the parametric logic, the size of a tree of height $h \in \mathbb{N}$ must be at least $2h + 1$.

3.2   Properties of Tree Shapes

In this section, we show a special relationship between tree shapes and the well-known Catalan numbers [22], which will be used to establish some properties of monotonic and AC catamorphisms in Sections 5 and 7.

Define the size of the shape of a tree to be the size of the tree. Let $\bar{\mathbb{N}}$ be the set of odd natural numbers. Because of Property 2, the size of a shape is in $\bar{\mathbb{N}}$. Let $ns(s)$ be the number of tree shapes of size $s \in \bar{\mathbb{N}}$ and let $\mathbb{C}_n$, where $n \in \mathbb{N}$, be the n-th Catalan number [22].

Lemma 1. *The number of shapes of size $s \in \bar{\mathbb{N}}$ is the $\frac{s-1}{2}$-th Catalan number:*

$$ns(s) = \mathbb{C}_{\frac{s-1}{2}}$$

Proof. Property 1 implies that tree shapes are also full binary trees. The lemma follows since the number of full binary trees of size $s \in \bar{\mathbb{N}}$ is $\mathbb{C}_{\frac{s-1}{2}}$ [22,13].   □

Using the expression $\mathbb{C}_n = \frac{1}{n+1}\binom{2n}{n}$ [22], we could easily compute the values that function $ns : \bar{\mathbb{N}} \to \mathbb{N}^+$ returns. This function satisfies the monotonic condition in Lemma 2.

Lemma 2. $1 = ns(1) = ns(3) < ns(5) < ns(7) < ns(9) < \ldots$

Proof. Provided in [17].   □

4   Unrolling-Based Decision Procedure Revisited

In this section, we restate the unrolling procedure proposed by Suter et al. [24] and propose a revised unrolling procedure, shown in Algorithms 1 and 2. The input of both algorithms is a formula ϕ written in the parametric logic and a program Π, which contains ϕ and the definitions of data type τ and catamorphism α. The decision procedure works on top of an SMT solver $\mathcal{S}$ that supports theories for $\tau, \mathcal{E}, \mathcal{C}$, and uninterpreted functions. Note that the only part of the parametric logic that is not inherently supported by $\mathcal{S}$ is the applications of the catamorphism. The main idea of the decision procedure is to approximate the behavior of the catamorphism by repeatedly unrolling it and treating the calls to the not-yet-unrolled catamorphism instances at the leaves as calls to an uninterpreted function. However, the uninterpreted function can return any values in its codomain; thus, the presence of these uninterpreted functions can make *SAT* results untrustworthy. To address this issue, each time the catamorphism is unrolled, a set of boolean control conditions B is created to determine whether the uninterpreted functions at the bottom level are necessary to the determination of satisfiability. That is, if all control conditions are true, no uninterpreted functions play a role in the satisfiability result.

Algorithm 1. Unrolling decision procedure in [24] with *sufficiently surjective catamorphisms*	**Algorithm 2.** Revised unrolling procedure with *monotonic catamorphisms*
1 $(\phi, B) \leftarrow unrollStep(\phi, \Pi, \emptyset)$ 2 **while** *true* **do** 3 **switch** $decide(\phi \wedge \bigwedge_{b \in B} b)$ **do** 4 **case** *SAT* 5 **return** *"SAT"* 6 **case** *UNSAT* 7 **switch** $decide(\phi)$ **do** 8 **case** *UNSAT* 9 **return** *"UNSAT"* 10 **case** *SAT* 11 $(\phi, B) \leftarrow unrollStep(\phi, \Pi, B)$	1 $(\phi, B) \leftarrow unrollStep(\phi, \Pi, \emptyset)$ 2 **while** *true* **do** 3 **switch** $decide(\phi \wedge \bigwedge_{b \in B} b)$ **do** 4 **case** *SAT* 5 **return** *"SAT"* 6 **case** *UNSAT* 7 **switch** $decide(\phi \wedge R_\alpha)$ **do** 8 **case** *UNSAT* 9 **return** *"UNSAT"* 10 **case** *SAT* 11 $(\phi, B) \leftarrow unrollStep(\phi, \Pi, B)$

The unrollings without control conditions represent an over-approximation of the formula with the semantics of the program with respect to the parametric logic, in that it accepts all models accepted by the parametric logic plus some others (due to the uninterpreted functions). The unrollings with control conditions represent an under-approximation: all models accepted by this model will be accepted by the parametric logic with the catamorphism.

The algorithm determines the satisfiability of ϕ through repeated unrolling α using the *unrollStep* function. Given a formula ϕ_i generated from the original ϕ after unrolling the catamorphism i times and the set of control conditions B_i of ϕ_i, function $unrollStep(\phi_i, \Pi, B_i)$ unrolls the catamorphim one more time and returns a pair (ϕ_{i+1}, B_{i+1}) containing the unrolled version ϕ_{i+1} of ϕ_i and a set of control conditions B_{i+1} for ϕ_{i+1}. Function $decide(\varphi)$ simply calls S to check the satisfiability of φ and returns $SAT/UNSAT$ accordingly. The algorithm either terminates when ϕ is proved to be satisfiable without the use of uninterpreted functions (line 5) or ϕ is proved to be unsatisfiable when assigning any values to uninterpreted functions still cannot make the problem satisfiable (line 9).

The central problem of Algorithm 1 is that its termination is not guaranteed. For example, non-termination can occur if the uninterpreted function U_α representing α can return values outside the range of α. Consider an unsatisfiable input problem: $SizeI(t) < 0$, for an uninterpreted tree t when $SizeI$ is defined over the integers in an SMT solver. Although $SizeI$ is sufficiently surjective, Algorithm 1 will not terminate since each uninterpreted function at the leaves of the unrolling can always choose an arbitrarily large negative number to assign as the value of the catamorphism, thereby creating a satisfying assignment when evaluating the input formula without control conditions. These negative values are outside the range of $SizeI$, and this termination problem can occur for any catamorphism that is not surjective. Unless an underlying solver supports predicate subtyping, such catamorphisms are easily constructed, and in fact $SizeI$ or *Height* catamorphisms are not surjective when defined against SMT-LIB 2.0 [3].

To address the non-termination issue, we need to constrain the assignments to uninterpreted functions $U_\alpha(t)$ representing $\alpha(t)$ to return only values inside the range of α. Let R_α be a condition that, together with $U_\alpha(t)$, represents the range of α. The collection of values that $U_\alpha(t)$ can return can be constrained by R_α. In Algorithm 2, the user-provided range R_α is included in the *decide* function to make sure that any values that $U_\alpha(t)$ returns could be mapped to some "real" tree $t' \in \tau$ such that $\alpha(t') = U_\alpha(t)$:

$$\forall c \in \mathcal{C} : \big(c = U_\alpha(t) \wedge R_\alpha(c)\big) \Rightarrow \big(\exists t' \in \tau : \alpha(t') = c\big) \tag{1}$$

Formula (1) defines a correctness condition for R_α. Unfortunately, it is difficult to prove this without the aid of a theorem prover. On the other hand, it is straightforward to determine whether R_α is a sound approximation of the range of R (that is, all values in the range of R are accepted by R_α) using induction and an SMT solver. To do so, we simply unroll α a single time over an uninterpreted tree t. We assume R_α is true for the uninterpreted functions in the unrolling but that R_α is false over the unrolling. If an SMT solver can prove that the formula is *UNSAT*, then R_α soundly approximates the range; this unrolling encodes both the base and inductive case.

5 Monotonic Catamorphisms

In the rest of the paper, we propose *monotonic* catamorphisms and prove that Algorithm 2 is complete for this class, provided that R_α accurately characterizes the range of α. We show that this class is a subset of sufficiently surjective catamorphisms, but general enough to include all catamorphisms described in [23,24] and all those that we have run into in industrial experience. Monotonic catamorphisms admit a termination argument in terms of the number of unrollings, which is an open problem in [24]. Moreover, a subclass of monotonic catamorphisms, *associative-commutative* (AC) catamorphisms can be combined while preserving completeness of the formula, addressing another open problem in [24].

5.1 Definition

Given a catamorphism α and a tree t, $\beta(t)$ is the size of the set of trees that map to $\alpha(t)$:

$$\beta(t) = |\alpha^{-1}(\alpha(t))|$$

Definition 3 (Monotonic catamorphism). *A catamorphism* $\alpha : \tau \to \mathcal{C}$ *is monotonic iff there exists* $h_\alpha \in \mathbb{N}^+$ *such that:*

$$\forall t \in \tau : height(t) \geq h_\alpha \Rightarrow \big(\beta(t) = \infty \ \vee$$
$$\exists t_0 \in \tau : height(t_0) = height(t) - 1 \wedge \beta(t_0) < \beta(t)\big)$$

Note that if α is monotonic with h_α, it is also monotonic with any $h'_\alpha \in \mathbb{N}^+$ bigger than h_α.

5.2 Examples of Monotonic Catamorphisms

This section proves that all sufficiently surjective catamorphims introduced by Suter et al. [23] are monotonic. These catamorphisms are listed in Table 1. Note that the *Sortedness* catamorphism can be defined to allow or not allow duplicate elements [23]; we define *Sortedness$_{dup}$* and *Sortedness$_{nodup}$* for the *Sortedness* catamorphism where duplications are allowed and disallowed, respectively.

The monotonicity of *Set*, *SizeI*, *Height*, *Some*, *Min*, and *Sortedness$_{dup}$* catamorphisms is easily proved by showing the relationship between infinitely surjective abstractions [23] and monotonic catamorphisms.

Lemma 3. *Infinitely surjective abstractions are monotonic.*

Proof. According to Suter et al. [23], α is infinitely surjective S-abstraction, where S is a set of trees, if and only if $\beta(t)$ is finite for $t \in S$ and infinite for $t \notin S$. Therefore, α is monotonic with $h_\alpha = \max\{height(t) \mid t \in S\} + 1$.   □

Theorem 1. *Set, SizeI, Height, Some, Min, and Sortedness$_{dup}$ are monotonic.*

Proof. [23] showed that *Set, SizeI, Height,* and *Sortedness$_{dup}$* are infinitely surjective abstractions. Also, *Some* and *Min* have the properties of infinitely surjective {Leaf}-abstractions. Therefore, the theorem follows from Lemma 3. □

It is more challenging to prove that *Multiset, List,* and *Sortedness$_{nodup}$* catamorphisms are monotonic since they are not infinitely surjective abstractions. First, we define the notion of strict subtrees and supertrees.

Definition 4 (Strict subtree). *Given two trees t_1 and t_2 in the tree domain τ, tree t_1 is a subtree of tree t_2, denoted by $t_1 \preceq t_2$, iff:*

$$t_1 = \mathsf{Leaf} \lor$$
$$t_1 = \mathsf{Node}(t_{1L}, e, t_{1R}) \land t_2 = \mathsf{Node}(t_{2L}, e, t_{2R}) \land t_{1L} \preceq t_{2L} \land t_{1R} \preceq t_{2R}$$

Tree t_1 is a strict subtree of tree t_2, denoted by $t_1 \precnsim t_2$, iff

$$t_1 \preceq t_2 \land size(t_1) < size(t_2)$$

Similarly, we define the notion $\succnsim$ of strict supertrees as the inverse of $\precnsim$. Next, we state Lemma 4 before proving that *Multiset, List,* and *Sortedness$_{nodup}$* catamorphisms are monotonic. The proof of Lemma 4 is omitted since it is obvious.

Lemma 4. *For all $h \in \mathbb{N}^+$, any tree of height h must be a strict supertree of at least one tree of height $h - 1$.*

Theorem 2. *List catamorphisms are monotonic.*

Proof. Let $h_\alpha = 2$. For any tree t such that $height(t) \geq h_\alpha$, there are exactly $ns(size(t))$ distinct trees that can map to $\alpha(t)$. Thus, $\beta(t) = ns(size(t))$. Due to Lemma 4, there exists t_0 such that $t_0 \precnsim t \land height(t_0) = height(t) - 1$, which leads to $size(t_0) < size(t)$. From Property 3, $height(t) \geq h_\alpha = 2$ implies $size(t) \geq 5$. From Lemma 2, $ns(size(t_0)) < ns(size(t))$, which means $\beta(t_0) < \beta(t)$. □

Theorem 3. *Multiset catamorphisms are monotonic.*

Proof. Provided in [17]. □

Theorem 4. *Sortedness$_{nodup}$ catamorphisms over integer trees are monotonic.*

Proof. Provided in [17]. □

6   Unrolling Decision Procedure - Proof of Correctness

We now prove the correctness of the unrolling decision procedure in Algorithm 2. We start with some properties of monotonic catamorphisms in Section 6.1 and then discuss the main proofs in Section 6.2. In this section, p stands for the number of disequalities between tree terms in the input formula.

6.1 Some Properties of Monotonic Catamorphisms

In the following α is assumed to be a monotonic catamorphism with h_α and β as defined earlier.

Definition 5 ($\mathcal{M}_\beta$). $\mathcal{M}_\beta(h)$ *is the minimum value of $\beta(t)$ of all trees t of height h:*

$$\forall h \in \mathbb{N} : \mathcal{M}_\beta(h) = \min\{\beta(t) \mid t \in \tau, height(t) = h\}$$

Corollary 1. $\mathcal{M}_\beta(h)$ *is always greater or equal to 1.*

Proof. $\forall h \in \mathbb{N} : \mathcal{M}_\beta(h) \geq 1$ since $\forall t \in \tau : \beta(t) = |\alpha^{-1}(\alpha(t))| \geq 1$.   □

Lemma 5 (Monotonic Property of $\mathcal{M}_\beta$). *Function $\mathcal{M}_\beta : \mathbb{N} \to \mathbb{N}$ satisfies the following monotonic property:*

$$\forall h \in \mathbb{N}, h \geq h_\alpha : \mathcal{M}_\beta(h) = \infty \Rightarrow \mathcal{M}_\beta(h+1) = \infty \qquad \vee$$
$$\mathcal{M}_\beta(h) < \infty \Rightarrow \mathcal{M}_\beta(h) < \mathcal{M}_\beta(h+1)$$

Proof. Provided in [17].   □

Corollary 2. *For any natural number $p > 0$, $\mathcal{M}_\beta(h_\alpha + p) > p$.*

Proof. By induction on h based on Lemma 5 and Corollary 1.   □

Theorem 5. *For every number $p \in \mathbb{N}^+$, there exists some height $h_p \geq h_\alpha$, computable as a function of p, such that for every height $h \geq h_p$ and for every tree t_h of height h, we have $\beta(t_h) > p$.*

Proof. Let $h_p = h_\alpha + p$. From Corollary 2, $\mathcal{M}_\beta(h_p) > p$. Based on Lemma 5, we could show by induction on h that $\forall h \geq h_p : \mathcal{M}_\beta(h) > p$. Hence, this theorem follows from Definition 5.   □

Lemma 6. *For all number $p \in \mathbb{N}^+$ and for all tree $t \in \tau$, we have:*

$$\beta(t) > p \Rightarrow \beta\big(Node(\_,\_,t)\big) > p \wedge \beta\big(Node(t,\_,\_)\big) > p$$

Proof. Consider tree $t' = Node(t_L, e, t)$. The value of $\alpha(t')$ is computed in terms of $\alpha(t_L)$, e, and $\alpha(t)$. There are $\beta(t)$ trees that can map to $\alpha(t)$ and we can substitute any of these trees for t in t' without changing the value of $\alpha(t')$. Hence, $\beta(t) > p$ implies $\beta(t') > p$. In other words, $\beta(t) > p \Rightarrow \beta\big(Node(\_,\_,t)\big) > p$. Similarly, we can show that $\beta(t) > p \Rightarrow \beta\big(Node(t,\_,\_)\big) > p$.   □

6.2 Proof of Correctness of the Unrolling-Based Decision Procedure

We claim that our unrolling-based decision procedure with monotonic catamorphisms is (1) sound for proofs, (2) sound for models, (3) terminating for satisfiable formulas, and (4) terminating for unsatisfiable formulas. Due to space limitations, we do not present the proofs for the first three properties, which can be adapted with minor changes from similar proofs in [24]. Rather, we focus on proving that Algorithm 2 is terminating for unsatisfiable formulas. As defined in Section 2.1, the logic is described over only conjunctions, but this can easily be generalized to arbitrary formulas using DPLL(T) [8]. The structure of the proof in this case is the same. The outline of the proof is as follows:

1. Given an input formula ϕ_{in}, without loss of generality, we perform purification and unification on ϕ_{in} to yield a formula ϕ_P. We then define a maximum unrolling depth $\mathfrak{D}$ and formula $\phi_{\mathfrak{D}}$, in which all catamorphism instances in $\phi_{\mathfrak{D}}$ are unrolled to depth $\mathfrak{D}$ as described in Algorithm 2. Note that the formulas differ only in the treatment of catamorphism terms.
2. Given an unrolling $\phi_{\mathfrak{D}}$, if all control conditions are true, then the catamorphism functions are completely determined. Therefore, any model for $\phi_{\mathfrak{D}}$ can be easily converted into a model for ϕ_{in}.
3. If at least one control condition for the unrolling is false, we may have a tree t where $\alpha_{\mathfrak{D}}(t)$ does not match $\alpha(t)$ since the computation of $\alpha_{\mathfrak{D}}(t)$ depends on an uninterpreted function. In this case, we show that it is always possible to replace t with a concrete tree t' that satisfies the other constraints of the formula and that yields the same catamorphism value.
4. To construct t', we first note that past a certain depth of unrolling $depth_{\phi_{in}}^{\max}+1$, the value chosen for any catamorphism applications will satisfy all constraints other than disequalities between tree terms. We then note that all tree disequality constraints can be satisfied if we continue to unroll the catamorphism h_p times.

Now, let ϕ_{in} be an input formula of Algorithm 2. Without loss of generality, we purify the formula ϕ_{in} (as in [23]) and then perform tree unification (as in [2]) on the resulting formula. If there is a clash during the unification process, ϕ_{in} must be unsatisfiable; otherwise, we obtain a substitution function $\sigma = \{t_{var}^1 \mapsto T_1, \ldots, t_{var}^m \mapsto T_m\}$ where each tree variable t_{var}^i, where $1 \leq i \leq m$, does not appear anywhere in tree terms $T_1, \ldots, T_m$. Following [23], the remaining variables (which unify only with themselves and occur only at the leaves of tree terms) we label *parametric variables*.

We substitute for tree variables and obtain a formula $\phi_P = \phi_t \wedge \phi_c \wedge \phi_e \wedge \phi_b$ that is equisatisfiable with ϕ_{in}, where ϕ_t contains disequalities over tree terms (tree equalities have been removed through unification), ϕ_c contains formulas in the collections theory, ϕ_e contains formulas in the element theory, and ϕ_b is a set of formulas of the form $c = \alpha(t)$, where c is a variable in the collections theory and t is a tree term. We observe that given σ and any model for ϕ_P, it is straightforward to create a model for ϕ_{in}.

Given ϕ_P, Algorithm 2 produces formulas $\phi_{\mathfrak{D}}$ which are the same as ϕ_P except that each term $c = \alpha(t)$ in ϕ_b is replaced by $c = \alpha_{\mathfrak{D}}(t)$, where $\alpha_{\mathfrak{D}}$ is the catamorphism unrolled $\mathfrak{D}$ times.

To prove the completeness result, we compute $depth_{\phi_{in}}^{\max}$, which is, intuitively, the maximum depth of any tree term in ϕ_P. Let $depth_{\phi_{in}}^{\max} = \max\{depth_{\phi_P}(t) \mid \text{tree term } t \in \phi_P\}$ where $depth_{\phi_P}(t)$ is defined as follows:

$$depth_{\phi_P}(t) = \begin{cases} 1 + \max\{depth_{\phi_P}(t_L), depth_{\phi_P}(t_R)\} & \text{if } t = \mathsf{Node}(t_L, \_, t_R) \\ 0 & \text{if } t = \mathsf{Leaf} \mid \text{tree variable} \end{cases}$$

We next define a lemma that states that assignments to catamorphisms are *compatible* with all formula constraints other than structural disequalities between trees. We define ϕ_P^* to be the formula obtained by removing all the tree disequality constraints ϕ_t in ϕ_P.

Lemma 7. *Given a formula ϕ_P^* with monotonic catamorphism α and correct range predicate R_α, after $\mathfrak{D} \geq depth_{\phi_{in}}^{max} + 1$ unrollings, if $\phi_{\mathfrak{D}}$ has a model, then ϕ_P^* also has a model.*

Proof. Provided in [17]. □

Theorem 6. *Given a formula ϕ_{in} with monotonic catamorphism α and correct range predicate R_α, after $\mathfrak{D} = depth_{\phi_{in}}^{max} + 1 + h_p$ unrollings, if $\phi_{\mathfrak{D}}$ has a model, then ϕ_{in} also has a model.*

Proof. Provided in [17]. □

Corollary 3. *Given a formula ϕ_{in} with monotonic catamorphism α and correct range predicate R_α, Algorithm 2 is terminating for unsatisfiable formulas.*

Proof. This is the immediate contrapositive of Theorem 6. Suppose ϕ_{in} does not have a model. In this case, $\phi_{\mathfrak{D}}$ also does not have a model and the SMT solver $\mathcal{S}$ will return *UNSAT*. □

This proof implies that Algorithm 2 terminates after no more than $depth_{\phi_{in}}^{max} + 1 + h_p$ number of unrollings for unsatisfiable formulas. If the number of unrollings exceeds $depth_{\phi_{in}}^{max} + 1 + h_p$, we conclude that ϕ_{in} is satisfiable; note that if we are interested in complete tree models, we still need to keep unrolling until we reach line 5 in Algorithm 2.

Corollary 4. *Monotonic catamorphisms are sufficiently surjective.*

Proof. Provided in [17]. □

7   Associative-Commutative (AC) Catamorphisms

This section presents associative-commutative (AC) catamorphisms, a sub-class of monotonic catamorphisms that have some important properties. They are detectable, combinable, and impose an exponentially small upper bound of the number of unrollings. The question whether these results extend to the full class of sufficiently surjective catamorphisms is still open.

7.1   Definition

Definition 6 (AC catamorphism). *Catamorphism $\alpha : \tau \to \mathcal{C}$ is AC if*

$$\alpha(t) = \begin{cases} id_\oplus & \text{if } t = Leaf \\ \alpha(t_L) \oplus \delta(e) \oplus \alpha(t_R) & \text{if } t = Node(t_L, e, t_R) \end{cases}$$

where $\oplus : (\mathcal{C}, \mathcal{C}) \to \mathcal{C}$ is an associative and commutative binary operator with an identity element $id_\oplus \in \mathcal{C}$ (i.e., $\forall x \in \mathcal{C} : x \oplus id_\oplus = id_\oplus \oplus x = x$) and $\delta : \mathcal{E} \to \mathcal{C}$ is a function that maps[2] an element value in $\mathcal{E}$ into a corresponding value in $\mathcal{C}$.

---

[2] For instance, if $\mathcal{E}$ is Int and $\mathcal{C}$ is IntSet, we can have $\delta(e) = \{e\}$.

Like catamorphisms defined in [23,24], AC catamorphisms are fold functions mapping the content of a tree in the parametric logic into a value in a collection domain where a decision procedure is assumed to be available. There are two main differences in the presentation between AC catamorphisms and those in [23,24]. First, the combine function is replaced by an associative, commutative operator $\oplus$ and function δ. Second, Leaf is mapped to the identity value of operator $\oplus$ instead of the empty value of $\mathcal{C}$ (though the two quantities are usually the same in practice).

Detection: Unlike sufficiently surjective catamorphisms, AC catamorphisms are detectable. A catamorphism, written in the format in Definition 6, is AC if the following conditions hold:

- $\oplus$ is an associative and commutative operator over $\mathcal{C}$.
- $id_\oplus$ is an identity element of $\oplus$.

These conditions can be easily proved by SMT solvers [1,5] or theorem provers such as ACL2 [11].

Signature: An AC catamorphism α is completely defined if we know its collection domain $\mathcal{C}$, element domain $\mathcal{E}$, AC operator $\oplus$, and function $\delta : \mathcal{E} \to \mathcal{C}$. In other words, the 4-tuple $\langle \mathcal{C}, \mathcal{E}, \oplus, \delta \rangle$ is the *signature* of α. It is unnecessary to include tree domain τ and identity element $id_\oplus$ in the signature since the former depends only on $\mathcal{E}$ and the latter must be specified in the definition of $\oplus$.

Definition 7 (Signature of AC catamorphisms). *The signature of an AC catamorphism α is defined as follows:*

$$sig(\alpha) = \langle \mathcal{C}, \mathcal{E}, \oplus, \delta \rangle$$

Values: Because of the associative and commutative operator $\oplus$, the value of an AC catamorphism for a tree has an important property: it is independent of the structure of the tree.

Corollary 5 (Values of AC catamorphisms). *The value of $\alpha(t)$, where α is an AC catamorphism, only depends on the values of elements in t. Furthermore, the value of $\alpha(t)$ does not depend on the relative positions of the element values.*

$$\alpha(t) = \begin{cases} id_\oplus & \text{if } t = \textsf{Leaf} \\ \delta(e_1) \ \oplus \ \delta(e_2) \ \oplus \ \ldots \ \oplus \ \delta(e_{ni(t)}) & \text{otherwise} \end{cases}$$

where $e_1, e_2, \ldots, e_{ni(t)}$ are all element values stored in $ni(t)$ internal nodes of t.

Examples: In Table 1, *Height*, *List*, *Some*, and *Sortedness* are not AC because their values depend on the positions of tree elements. This is also demonstrated by some concrete examples in [17].

Other catamorphisms in Table 1, including *Set*, *Multiset*, *SizeI*, and *Min* are AC. Furthermore, we could define other AC catamorphisms based on well-known associative and commutative operators such as $+, \cap, \max, \vee, \wedge$, etc. We could also use user-defined functions as the operators in AC catamorphisms; in this case, we will need the help of an additional analysis tool to verify that all conditions for AC catamorphims are met.

7.2   AC Catamorphisms are Monotonic

AC catamorphisms are not only automatically detectable but also monotonic. Thus, they can be used in Algorithm 2.

Lemma 8. *If α is an AC catamorphism then*

$$\forall t \in \tau : \beta(t) \geq ns\big(size(t)\big)$$

Proof. Provided in [17]. $\square$

Theorem 7. *AC catamorphisms are monotonic.*

Proof. Provided in [17]. $\square$

7.3   Exponentially Small Upper Bound of the Number of Unrollings

In the proof of Theorem 5, we use $h_p = h_\alpha + p$ to guarantee that the algorithm terminates after unrolling no more than $depth_{\phi_{in}}^{\max} + 1 + h_p$ times. The upper bound implies that the number of unrollings may be large when p is large, leading to a high complexity for the algorithm with monotonic catamorphisms.

In this section, we demonstrate that in the case of AC catamorphims, we could choose a different value for h_p such that not only the termination of the algorithm is guaranteed with h_p, but also the growth of h_p is *exponentially small* compared with that of p. Recall from the proof of Theorem 5 that as long as we can choose $h_p \geq h_\alpha$ such that $\mathcal{M}_\beta(h_p) > p$, Theorem 5 will follow. We will define such h_p after proving the following important lemma.

Lemma 9. *If α is AC then $\forall h \in \mathbb{N} : \mathcal{M}_\beta(h) \geq \mathbb{C}_h$.*

Proof. Let $t_h \in \tau$ be any tree of height h. We have $\beta(t_h) \geq ns\big(size(t_h)\big)$ from Lemma 8. Thus, $\beta(t_h) \geq ns(2h+1)$ due to Property 3 and Lemma 2. Therefore, $\beta(t_h) \geq \mathbb{C}_h$ by Lemma 1. As a result, $\mathcal{M}_\beta(h) \geq \mathbb{C}_h$ from Definition 5. $\square$

Let $h_p = \max\{h_\alpha, \min\{h \mid \mathbb{C}_h > p\}\}$. By construction, $h_p \geq h_\alpha$ and $\mathbb{C}_{h_p} > p$. From Lemma 9, $\mathcal{M}_\beta(h_p) \geq \mathbb{C}_{h_p} > p$. Thus, Theorem 5 follows.

The growth of $\mathbb{C}_n$ is exponential [7]. Thus, h_p is exponentially smaller than p since $\mathbb{C}_{h_p} > p$. For example, when $p = 10^4$, we can choose $h_p = 10$ since $\mathbb{C}_{10} > 10^4$. Similarly, when $p = 5 \times 10^4$, we can choose $h_p = 11$. In the example, we assume that $h_\alpha \leq 10$, which is true for all catamorphisms in this paper.

7.4   Combining AC Catamorphisms

Let $\alpha_1, \ldots, \alpha_m$ be m AC catamorphisms where the signature of the i-th catamor-phim $(1 \leq i \leq m)$ is $sig(\alpha_i) = \langle \mathcal{C}_i, \mathcal{E}, \oplus_i, \delta_i \rangle$. Catamorphism α with signature $sig(\alpha) = \langle \mathcal{C}, \mathcal{E}, \oplus, \delta \rangle$ is a combination of $\alpha_1, \ldots, \alpha_m$ if

- $\mathcal{C}$ is the domain of m-tuples, where the ith element of each tuple is in $\mathcal{C}_i$.
- $\oplus : (\mathcal{C}, \mathcal{C}) \rightarrow \mathcal{C}$ is defined as follows, given $\langle x_1, \ldots, x_m \rangle, \langle y_1, \ldots, y_m \rangle \in \mathcal{C}$:

$$id_\oplus = \langle id_{\oplus_1}, id_{\oplus_2}, \ldots, id_{\oplus_m} \rangle$$

$$\langle x_1, x_2, \ldots, x_m \rangle \oplus \langle y_1, y_2, \ldots, y_m \rangle = \langle x_1 \oplus_1 y_1, x_2 \oplus_2 y_2, \ldots, x_m \oplus_m y_m \rangle$$

- $\delta : \mathcal{E} \rightarrow \mathcal{C}$ is defined as follows: $\delta(e) = \langle \delta_1(e), \delta_2(e), \ldots, \delta_m(e) \rangle$
- α is defined as in Definition 6.

Theorem 8. *Every catamorphism obtained from the combination of AC cata-morphims is also AC.*

Proof. Provided in [17].   □

Note that while it is easy to combine AC catamorphims, it might be challeng-ing to compute R_α, where α is a combination of AC catamorphisms.

8   The Relationship between Abstractions

This section discusses the relationship between different types of catamorphisms, including sufficiently surjective, infinitely surjective, monotonic, and AC cata-morphisms. Their relationship is shown in Fig. 2.

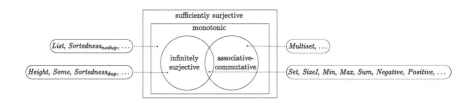

Fig. 2. Relationship between different types of catamorphisms

Monotonic and sufficiently surjective catamorphisms: Corollary 4 shows that all monotonic catamorphisms are sufficiently surjective. Theoretically, the set of sufficiently surjective catamorphisms is a super-set of that of monotonic cata-morphisms. In practice, however, we are not aware of any sufficiently surjective catamorphisms that are not monotonic.

Infinitely surjective and monotonic catamorphisms: All infinitely surjective cata-morphisms are monotonic, as proved in Lemma 3.

AC and monotonic catamorphisms: All AC catamorphisms are monotonic, as proved in Theorem 7.

Infinitely surjective and AC catamorphisms: The sets of the two types of catamorphisms are intersecting, as shown in Fig. 2.

9   Experimental Results

We have implemented our algorithm in RADA [18], a verification tool used in the Guardol system [9], and evaluated the tool with a collection of 38 benchmark guard examples listed in Table 2. The results are very promising: all of them were automatically verified in a very short amount of time.

Table 2. Experimental results

Benchmark	Result	# unrollings	Time (s)
sumtree(01|02|03|05|06|07|10|11|13)	sat	$1-4$	$0.52-1.02$
sumtree(04|08|09|12|14)	unsat	$0-2$	$0.52-0.98$
negative_positive(01|02)	unsat	$1-6$	$0.33-0.82$
min_max(01|02)	unsat	$1-6$	$0.74-1.44$
mut_rec1	sat	2	0.78
mut_rec(3|4)	unsat	$1-2$	$0.72-1.03$
Email_Guard_Correct_(01|...|17)	unsat	$1-2$	$0.72-0.99$

The collection of benchmarks is divided into four sets. The benchmarks in the first three sets were manually designed and those in the last set were automatically generated from Guardol [9]. The first set consists of examples related to *Sum*, an AC catamorphism that computes the sum of all element values in a tree. The second set contains combinations of AC catamorphisms that are used to verify some interesting properties such as (1) there does not exist a tree with at least one element value that is both positive and negative and (2) the minimum value in a tree can not be bigger than the maximum value in the tree. The definitions of the AC catamorphisms used in the first two sets of benchmarks can be found in [17].

To further evaluate the performance of our algorithm, we have conducted some experiments with non-monotonic catamorphisms in the last two sets of benchmarks. In particular, the third set contains simple mutually recursive catamorphisms. Each of the Guardol benchmarks in the last set has 8 mutually recursive data types, 6 catamorphisms, and complex verification conditions.

All benchmarks were run on a machine using an Intel Core I3 running at 2.13 GHz with 2GB RAM with Z3 [5] as the underlying solver ($\mathcal{S}$) in the experiments.

10   Related Work

We discuss some work that is closest to ours. Our approach extends the work by Suter et al. [23,24]. In [23], the authors propose a family of procedures for algebraic data types where catamorphisms are used to abstract tree terms. Their procedures are complete with sufficiently surjective catamorphisms, which are closely related to the notion of monotonic catamorphisms in this paper. We have shown that all monotonic catamorphisms are sufficiently surjective and all sufficiently surjective catamorphisms described in [23] are monotonic. Moreover, there are a number of advantages of using monotonic catamorphisms, as discussed in Sections 5 and 7. In the early phase of the Guardol project [9], we implemented the decision procedures [23] on top of OpenSMT [4] and found some flaws in the treatment of disequalities in the unification step of the procedures; fortunately, the flaws can be fixed using the techniques in [2].

Our unrolling-based decision procedure is based on the work by Suter et al. [24]. As pointed out in Section 4, their work has a non-terminating issue involving the use of uninterpreted functions. Also, their method works with sufficiently surjective catamorphisms while ours is designed for monotonic catamorphisms.

One work that is close to ours is that of Madhusudan et al. [15], where a sound, incomplete, and automated method is proposed to achieve recursive proofs for inductive tree data-structures while still maintaining a balance between expressiveness and decidability. The method is based on DRYAD, a recursive extension of the first-order logic. DRYAD has some limitations: the element values in DRYAD must be of type int and only four classes of abstractions are allowed in DRYAD. In addition to the sound procedure, [15] shows a decidable fragment of verification conditions that can be expressed in STRAND$_{dec}$ [14]. However, this decidable fragment does not allow us to reason about some important properties such as the height or size of a tree. However, the class of data structures that [15] can work with is richer than that of our approach.

Using abstractions to summarize recursively defined data structures is one of the popular ways to reason about algebraic data types. This idea is used in the Jahob system [25,26] and in some procedures for algebraic data types [21,24,10,15]. However, it is often challenging to directly reason about the abstractions. One approach to overcome the difficulty, which is used in [24,15], is to approximate the behaviors of the abstractions using uninterpreted functions and then send the functions to SMT solvers [5,1] that have built-in support for uninterpreted functions and recursive data types (although recursive data types are not officially defined in the SMT-LIB 2.0 format [3]).

Recently, Sato et al. [20] proposes a verification technique that has support for recursive data structures. The technique is based on higher-order model checking, predicate abstraction, and counterexample-guided abstraction refinements. Given a program with recursive data structures, we encode the structures as functions on lists, which are then encoded as functions on integers before sending the resulting program to the verification tool described in [12]. Their method can work with higher-order functions while ours cannot. On the other hand, their method cannot verify some properties of recursive data structures while ours can thanks to the use of catamorphisms. An example of such a property is as follows: after inserting an element to a binary tree, the set of all element values in the new tree must be a super set of that of the original tree.

11   Conclusion

We have proposed a revised unrolling decision procedure for algebraic data types with monotonic catamorphisms. Like sufficiently surjective catamorphisms, monotonic catamorphisms are fold functions that map abstract data types into values in a decidable domain. We have showed that all sufficiently surjective catamorphisms known in the literature to date [23] are actually monotonic. We have also established an upper bound of the number of unrollings with monotonic catamorphisms. Furthermore, we have pointed out a sub-class of monotonic catamorphisms, namely associative-commutative (AC) catamorphisms, which are proved to be detectable, combinable, and guarantee an exponentially small maximum number of unrollings thanks to their close relationship with Catalan numbers. Our combination results extend the set of problems that can easily be reasoned about using the catamorphism-based approach.

In the future, we would like to generalize the notion of catamorphisms to allow additional inputs related to either control conditions (e.g. *member*) or leaf values (e.g. *fold* functions), while preserving completeness guarantees. Also, we would like to generalize the completeness argument for mutually recursive data types involving multiple catamorphisms.

In addition, our decision procedure assumes a correct R_α value, and may diverge if this value is not correct. We believe that it is possible to check the R_α value during unrolling and to return *error* if the value is incorrect by examining the soundness of R_α after removing a value chosen for U_α within the problem (call this $R_{\alpha-U}$). If this is sound, then R is incorrect, and we should return *error*.

Acknowledgements. We thank David Hardin, Konrad Slind, Andrew Gacek, Sanjai Rayadurgam, and Mats Heimdahl for their feedback on early drafts of this paper. We thank Philippe Suter and Viktor Kuncak for discussions about their decision procedures [23,24]. This work was sponsored in part by NSF grant CNS-1035715 and by a subcontract from Rockwell Collins.

References

1. Barrett, C., Conway, C.L., Deters, M., Hadarean, L., Jovanović, D., King, T., Reynolds, A., Tinelli, C.: CVC4. In: Gopalakrishnan, G., Qadeer, S. (eds.) CAV 2011. LNCS, vol. 6806, pp. 171–177. Springer, Heidelberg (2011)
2. Barrett, C., Shikanian, I., Tinelli, C.: An Abstract Decision Procedure for Satisfiability in the Theory of Recursive Data Types. Electronic Notes in Theoretical Computer Science 174(8), 23–37 (2007)
3. Barrett, C., Stump, A., Tinelli, C.: The SMT-LIB Standard: Version 2.0. In: SMT (2010)
4. Bruttomesso, R., Pek, E., Sharygina, N., Tsitovich, A.: The OpenSMT solver. In: Esparza, J., Majumdar, R. (eds.) TACAS 2010. LNCS, vol. 6015, pp. 150–153. Springer, Heidelberg (2010)
5. De Moura, L., Bjørner, N.: Z3: An Efficient SMT Solver. In: Ramakrishnan, C.R., Rehof, J. (eds.) TACAS 2008. LNCS, vol. 4963, pp. 337–340. Springer, Heidelberg (2008)

6. Epp, S.S.: Discrete Mathematics with Applications, 4th edn. Brooks/Cole Publishing Co. (2010)
7. Flajolet, P., Sedgewick, R.: Analytic Combinatorics. Cambridge University Press (2009)
8. Ganzinger, H., Hagen, G., Nieuwenhuis, R., Oliveras, A., Tinelli, C.: DPLL(T): Fast Decision Procedures. In: Alur, R., Peled, D.A. (eds.) CAV 2004. LNCS, vol. 3114, pp. 175–188. Springer, Heidelberg (2004)
9. Hardin, D., Slind, K., Whalen, M., Pham, T.-H.: The Guardol Language and Verification System. In: Flanagan, C., König, B. (eds.) TACAS 2012. LNCS, vol. 7214, pp. 18–32. Springer, Heidelberg (2012)
10. Jacobs, S., Kuncak, V.: Towards Complete Reasoning about Axiomatic Specifications. In: Jhala, R., Schmidt, D. (eds.) VMCAI 2011. LNCS, vol. 6538, pp. 278–293. Springer, Heidelberg (2011)
11. Kaufmann, M., Manolios, P., Moore, J.: Computer-Aided Reasoning: ACL2 Case Studies. Springer (2000)
12. Kobayashi, N., Sato, R., Unno, H.: Predicate Abstraction and CEGAR for Higher-Order Model Checking. In: PLDI, pp. 222–233 (2011)
13. Koshy, T.: Catalan Numbers with Applications. Oxford University Press (2009)
14. Madhusudan, P., Parlato, G., Qiu, X.: Decidable Logics Combining Heap Structures and Data. In: POPL, pp. 611–622 (2011)
15. Madhusudan, P., Qiu, X., Stefanescu, A.: Recursive Proofs for Inductive Tree Data-Structures. In: POPL, pp. 123–136 (2012)
16. Oppen, D.C.: Reasoning About Recursively Defined Data Structures. J. ACM 27(3), 403–411 (1980)
17. Pham, T.-H., Whalen, M.W.: Abstractions in Decision Procedures for Algebraic Data Types. Technical Report 13-006, Department of Computer Science and Engineering, University of Minnesota (2013), http://www.msse.umn.edu/publications/tech-reports/13-006
18. Pham, T.-H., Whalen, M.W.: RADA: A Tool for Reasoning about Algebraic Data Types with Abstractions. In: ESEC/FSE (to appear, 2013)
19. Rosen, K.H.: Discrete Mathematics and Its Applications, 7th edn. McGraw-Hill Higher Education (2012)
20. Sato, R., Unno, H., Kobayashi, N.: Towards a Scalable Software Model Checker for Higher-Order Programs. In: PEPM, pp. 53–62 (2013)
21. Sofronie-Stokkermans, V.: Locality Results for Certain Extensions of Theories with Bridging Functions. In: Schmidt, R.A. (ed.) CADE-22. LNCS, vol. 5663, pp. 67–83. Springer, Heidelberg (2009)
22. Stanley, R.P.: Enumerative Combinatorics, vol. 2. Cambridge University Press (2001)
23. Suter, P., Dotta, M., Kuncak, V.: Decision Procedures for Algebraic Data Types with Abstractions. In: POPL, pp. 199–210 (2010)
24. Suter, P., Köksal, A.S., Kuncak, V.: Satisfiability Modulo Recursive Programs. In: Yahav, E. (ed.) SAS 2011. LNCS, vol. 6887, pp. 298–315. Springer, Heidelberg (2011)
25. Zee, K., Kuncak, V., Rinard, M.: Full Functional Verification of Linked Data Structures. In: PLDI, pp. 349–361 (2008)
26. Zee, K., Kuncak, V., Rinard, M.C.: An Integrated Proof Language for Imperative Programs. In: PLDI, pp. 338–351 (2009)

Program Checking with Less Hassle

Julian Tschannen[1], Carlo A. Furia[1], Martin Nordio[1], and Bertrand Meyer[1,2]

[1] Chair of Software Engineering, ETH Zurich, Switzerland
`firstname.lastname@inf.ethz.ch`
[2] ITMO National Research University, St. Petersburg, Russia

Abstract. The simple and often imprecise specifications that programmers may write are a significant limit to a wider application of rigorous program verification techniques. Part of the reason why non-specialists find writing good specification hard is that, when verification fails, they receive little guidance as to what the causes might be, such as implementation errors or inaccurate specifications. To address these limitations, this paper presents *two-step verification*, a technique that combines implicit specifications, inlining, and loop unrolling to provide improved user feedback when verification fails. Two-step verification performs two independent verification attempts for each program element: one using standard modular reasoning, and another one after inlining and unrolling; comparing the outcomes of the two steps suggests which elements should be improved. Two-step verification is implemented in AutoProof, our static verifier for Eiffel programs integrated in EVE (the Eiffel Verification Environment) and available online.

1 The Trouble with Specs

There was a time when formal verification required heroic efforts and was the exclusive domain of a small group of visionaries. That time is now over; but formal techniques still seem a long way from becoming commonplace. If formal verification techniques are to become a standard part of the software development process—and they are—we have to understand and remove the obstacles that still prevent non-specialists from using them.

A crucial issue is specification. Program correctness is a relative notion, in that a program is correct not in absolute terms but only relative to a given *specification* of its expected behavior; in other words, verified programs are only as good as their specification. Unfortunately, many programmers are averse to writing specifications, especially formal ones, for a variety of reasons that mostly boil down a benefit-to-effort ratio perceived as too low. Writing formal specifications may require specialized skills and experience; and the concrete benefits are dubious in environments that value productivity, assessed through simple quantitative measures, more than quality. Why should programmers subject themselves to the taxing exercise of writing specifications in addition to implementations, if there is not much in it for them other than duplicated work?

There are, however, ways to overcome these obstacles. First, not all program verification requires providing a specification because specifications can sometimes be *inferred* from the program text [8,24,18] or from observing common

E. Cohen and A. Rybalchenko (Eds.): VSTTE 2013, LNCS 8164, pp. 149–169, 2014.

usage patterns [14,37,36]. In particular, some useful specifications are *implicit* in the programming language semantics: types must be compatible; array accesses must be within bound; dereferenced pointers must be non-null; arithmetic operations must not overflow; and so on. Second, programmers are not incorrigibly disinclined to write specifications [7,15,31], provided it does not require subverting their standard programming practices, produces valuable feedback, and brings tangible benefits. Interesting challenges lie in reducing the remaining gap between the user experience most programmer are expecting and the state-of-the-art of formal verification techniques and tools.

In this paper, we combine a series of techniques to improve the applicability and usability of static program checkers such as Spec# [2], Dafny [27], or one of the incarnations of ESC/Java [17,11,20], which verify functional properties of sequential programs specified using contracts (preconditions, postconditions, and class invariants). To enable verification of code with little or no specification, we deploy implicit contracts, routine inlining, and loop unrolling. *Implicit contracts* (described in Section 3) are simple contracts that follow from the application of certain programming constructs; for example, every array access implicitly requires that the index be within bounds. Routine *inlining* (Section 4) replaces calls to routines with the routines' bodies, to obviate the need for a sufficiently expressive callee's specification when reasoning in the caller's context. Similarly, loop *unrolling* makes it possible to reason about loops with incomplete or missing invariants by directly considering the concrete loop bodies.

Implicit contracts, inlining, and unrolling—besides being directly useful to improve reasoning with scarce specification—are the ingredients of *two-step verification* (Section 5), a technique to improve the usability and effectiveness of static checking. Two-step verification performs two verification attempts for every routine: the first one is a standard static checking, using modular reasoning based on programmer-written contracts (whatever they are) plus possibly implicit contracts; the second one uses inlining and unrolling. Comparing the outcomes of the two verification steps provides valuable information about the state of the program and its specification, which is then used to improve the feedback given to users. Bugs violating implicit contracts make for early error detection, and may convince users to add some *explicit* contracts that avoid them. Discrepancies between the verification of calls with and without inlining may help understand whether failed verification attempts are due to errors in the implementation or in the specification, or simply a more accurate specification is required. For example, a call to some routine r that may violate r's user-written precondition but verifies correctly after inlining r's body signals that r's precondition may be unnecessarily strong. Two-step verification is applied completely automatically: users get the most complete feedback based on the integration of the results of the various verification steps—with and without inlining and similar techniques.

We implemented our techniques in AutoProof [34,35], a static verifier for Eiffel programs using Boogie [26] as back-end, and we used it to verify all the examples discussed in the paper. AutoProof is integrated in EVE [33], the research branch of the EiffelStudio development environment, and is freely available online:

http://se.inf.ethz.ch/research/eve/

The rest of the paper presents the verification techniques in detail, and illustrates them on non-trivial example programs taken from the VSTTE 2012 verification competition [16] and other software verification benchmarks [1]. Section 6 discusses other programs verified using our approach. We show how the basic techniques and their integration into two-step verification make for better feedback, early error detection, and successful verification even when very limited amounts of specification are available.

2 Overview and Illustrative Examples

Binary search is a widely-known algorithm and is considered a standard benchmark for software verification [1]. Most programmers have implemented it at least once in their life. According to Knuth [23, Vol. 3, Sec. 6.2.1], their implementations were often "wrong the first few times they tried".

```
1    binary_search (a: ARRAY [INTEGER]; x: INTEGER): INTEGER
2        require a ≠ Void
3        local middle: INTEGER
4        do
5            if a.count = 0 then
6                Result := −1
7            else
8                middle := (1 + a.count) / 2
9                if a[middle] = x then
10                   Result := middle
11               elseif a[middle] > x then
12                   Result := binary_search (a[1:middle − 1], x)
13               else
14                   assert a[middle] < x end
15                   Result := binary_search (a[middle + 1:a.count]), x)
16                   if Result ≠ −1 then  Result := Result + middle end
17               end
18           end
19       ensure Result = −1 or (1 ≤ Result and Result ≤ a.count)
```

Fig. 1. An implementation of binary search

To demonstrate, consider the binary search implementation in Figure 1,[1] which takes an integer array a and an integer value x and returns an integer

---

[1] All code examples are in Eiffel, with few occasional notational simplifications; even readers not familiar with the language should find the code easy to understand.

index (the value assigned to **Result**) pointing to an occurrence of x in a. Since we assume arrays numbered from one, if x is not found in a the routine by convention returns -1. The implementation in Figure 1 is indicative of what programmers typically write[30,15] when using a language supporting specifications in the form of contracts (pre- and postconditions, and intermediate assertions such as loop invariants and **assert** instructions): the implementation is "almost" correct (if you do not immediately see the error, read on), and the specification is obviously incomplete.

Part of the missing specification is implicit in the semantics of the programming language, which is probably why the programmer did not bother writing it down explicitly. In particular, arithmetic operations should not overflow for the program to have a well-defined semantics. The midpoint calculation on line 8 overflows when the array size $a.\ count$ has value equal to the largest representable machine integer, even if the value of $middle$ is within the bounds; this is indeed a common error in real implementations of binary search [4].

If we try to verify the program in Figure 1 using static verifiers such as Dafny, we do not find any error because integer variables are modeled using mathematical integers which do not overflow. In Section 3 we discuss our approach which automatically instantiates implicit specification elements that represent tacit assumptions about the programming language semantics. Such *implicit contracts* help early error detection of subtle errors not explicitly specified, such as the potential overflow just discussed. In addition, they are made available within a more general static verification mechanism, where they can complement programmer-written contracts to improve the efficiency of the overall verification process without sacrificing precision.

Not only do incomplete specifications limit the kinds of error that can be detected automatically during verification; they may also prevent verifying perfectly *correct* programs as we now illustrate with the example of Figure 2, taken from the VSTTE 2012 verification competition. Routine *two_way_sort* sorts an array a of Boolean values in linear time with a technique similar to the partitioning algorithm used in Quick Sort. Two pointers i and j scan the array from its opposite ends; whenever they point to an inversion (that is, a **False** in the right-hand side and a **True** in the left-hand side) they remove it by swapping the elements pointed. When the whole array is scanned, it is sorted.

The sorting algorithm calls an auxiliary routine *swap* that exchanges elements; *swap* does not have any specification—again, a situation representative of how programmers typically specify their programs. This is a problem because static verification uses specifications to reason *modularly* about routine calls: the effects of the call to *swap* on line 14 are limited to *swap*'s postcondition. Since it does not have any, the proof of *two_way_sort* does not go through; in particular, it cannot establish that the loop invariant at line 7 is inductive, which would then be the basis to establish the variant as well as any programmer-written postcondition.

In our approach, when modular verification fails the verifier makes another attempt after *inlining* routine bodies at their call sites. As we describe in Section 4, the application uses simple heuristics to avoid combinatorial explosion

```
1     two_way_sort (a: ARRAY [BOOLEAN])
2         require a.count > 0
3         local    i, j: INTEGER
4         do
5             i := 1 ; j := a.count
6             until   i ≥ j
7             invariant 1 ≤ i and i ≤ j + 1 and j ≤ a.count
8             loop
9                 if not a[i] then
10                    i := i + 1
11                elseif a[j] then
12                    j := j − 1
13                else
14                    swap (a, i, j)
15                    i := i + 1
16                    j := j − 1
17                end
18            variant j − i + 1   end
19         end
20
21    swap (b: ARRAY [BOOLEAN]; x, y: INTEGER)
22        local   t: BOOLEAN
23        do  t := b[x] ; b[x] := b[y] ; b[y] := t end
```

Fig. 2. An implementation of two-way sort of Boolean arrays

(for example, in the case of recursive calls). With inlining, we can prove that the invariant at line 7 is inductive without need for more specification.

Using inlining, we can also check interesting properties about *clients* of *two_way_sort*. For example, when calling the routine on an empty array, we compare a failed modular verification attempt (which reports a violation of *two_way_sort*'s precondition) to a successful verification with inlining (which only evaluates the routine's body); the discrepancy *suggests* that *two_way_sort*'s precondition is unnecessarily strong and can be relaxed to $a \neq$ **Void** without affecting the rest of the verification process. This kind of improved feedback, concocted from two different verification attempts, is the two-step verification we present in detail in Section 5.

3   Implicit Contracts

The first ingredients of our two-step verification approach are *implicit contracts*: simple specification elements that are implicit in the semantics of the programming language—Eiffel in our examples. Since they are implicit, programmers tend to reason informally about the program without writing them down as assertions. This limits the kinds of properties that can be proved automatically with a static verifier. With implicit contracts, the verifier transparently annotates the program under verification so that the feedback to users is more accurate and goes deeper than what would have been possible based on the explicitly written contract only. We currently support the following classes of implicit contracts.

3.1   Targets Non-Void

A qualified call $t.r_1(a_1).\ldots.r_n(a_n)$, with $n \geq 0$, is non-**Void** if $t \neq$ **Void** and, for $1 \leq k < n$, $t.r_1(a_1).\ldots.r_k(a_k)$ returns a non-**Void** reference. For every such qualified call appearing as instructions or in expressions, we introduce the corresponding implicit contract that asserts that the call is non-**Void**.

For example, *two_way_sort*'s precondition (Figure 2) is augmented with the implicit contract that $a \neq$ **Void** following from the qualified call $a.count$.

3.2   Routine Calls in Contracts

In programming languages supporting contracts there need not be a sharp distinction between functions used in the implementation and functions used in the specification. Routine *two_way_sort*, for example, uses the function call $a.count$—returning the length of array a—in its precondition and loop invariant, but also in the assignment instruction on line 5. Functions used in contracts may have preconditions too; programmers should make them explicit by replicating them whenever the function is mentioned, but they often neglect doing so because it is something that is implicit when those functions are used in normal instructions, whereas it is not checked when the same functions are used in contracts.

Consider, for instance, a function *is_sorted* with the obvious semantics, and suppose that its precondition requires that it is applied to non-empty lists. If *is_sorted* is called anywhere in the implementation, then it is the caller's responsibility to establish its precondition; the caller is aware of the obligation explicit in *is_sorted*'s contract. But if *is_sorted* is called, say, as precondition of *binary_search*, establishing *is_sorted*'s precondition is now the responsibility of callers to *binary_search*, who are, however, unaware of the non-emptiness requirement *implicit* in *binary_search*'s precondition. In fact, the requirement should explicitly feature as one of *binary_search*'s preconditions.

To handle such scenarios automatically, for every call to any function f appearing in contracts, we introduce the corresponding implicit contract that asserts that f's precondition holds right before f is evaluated in the contract. If f's precondition includes calls to other functions, we follow the transitive closure of the preconditions, also checking well-formedness (that is, no circularity occurs).

3.3   Array Accesses

For every array access of the form $a[exp]$ appearing in instructions or in expressions, we introduce the implicit contract $a.lower \leq exp$ **and** $exp \leq a.upper$ which asserts that the expression used as index is within the array's bounds.

In *binary_search*, for example, the accesses $a[middle]$ determine the implicit contract that *middle* is between 1 and $a.count$.

3.4   Arithmetic Expressions

The subexpressions $\mathsf{sub}(e)$ of an integer expression e are defined in the obvious way: if e is an integer constant or an integer variable then $\mathsf{sub}(e) = \{e\}$; if e is the application of a unary operator $\sim$, that is $e = \sim d$, then $\mathsf{sub}(e) = \{e\} \cup \mathsf{sub}(d)$; if e is the application of a binary operator $\oplus$, that is $e = c \oplus d$, then $\mathsf{sub}(e) = \{e\} \cup \mathsf{sub}(c) \cup \mathsf{sub}(d)$. For every integer expression e appearing in instructions or expressions, we introduce the implicit contract that asserts that no subexpression of e's may overflow:

$$\bigwedge_{x \in \mathsf{sub}(e)} \{INTEGER\}.min\_value \leq x \quad \textbf{and} \quad x \leq \{INTEGER\}.max\_value$$

For every subexpression of the form $c \oslash d$, where $\oslash$ is some form of integer division, we also introduce the implicit contract $d \neq 0$, which forbids division by zero.

The integer expression at line 8 in Figure 1, for example, determines the implicit contract $1 + a.count \leq \{INTEGER\}.max\_value$, which may not hold.

4   Inlining and Unrolling

Inlining and unrolling are routinely used by compilers to optimize the generated code for speed; they are also occasionally used for program checking, as we discuss in Section 7. The novelty of our approach is the automatic combination, in two-step verification, of inlining and unrolling with modular "specification-based" verification. Inlining and unrolling may succeed in situations where little programmer-written specification is available; in such cases, users get a summary feedback that combines the output of each individual technique and is aware of the potential unsoundness of inlining and unrolling. The combined feedback gives specific suggestions as to what should be improved. This section presents the definitions of inlining and unrolling; Section 5 discusses how they are combined in two-step verification.

4.1   Inlining

The standard approach to reasoning about routine calls is *modular* based on specifications: the effects of a call to some routine r within the callee are postulated to coincide with whatever r's specification is. More precisely, the callee should establish that r's precondition holds in the calling context; and can consequently assume that r's postcondition holds and that the call does not modify anything outside of r's declared frame.

The modular approach is necessary to scale verification to large pieces of code. At the same time, it places a considerable burden on programmers, since every shortcoming in the specifications they provide may seriously hinder what can be proved about their programs. This is a practical issue especially for helper functions that are not part of the public API: programmers may not feel compelled to provide accurate specifications—postconditions, in particular—for them because they need not be documented to clients; but they would still like to benefit from automated program checking. This is the case of routine *swap* in Figure 2, which is not specified but whose semantics is obvious to every competent programmer.

Inlining can help in these situations by replacing abstract reasoning based on specifications with concrete reasoning based on implementations whenever the former are insufficient or unsatisfactory. In particular, inlining is likely to be useful whenever the inlined routine has no postcondition, and hence its effects within the callee are undefined under modular reasoning. Of course, inlining has scalability limits; that is why we apply it in limited contexts and combine it with standard modular verification as we discuss in Section 5.

Definition of Inlining. Consider a routine r of class C with arguments a, which we represent as:

$$r\ (t:\ C\ ;\ a)\ \textbf{require}\ P_r\ \textbf{modify}\ F_r\ \textbf{do}\ B_r\ \textbf{ensure}\ Q_r\ \textbf{end}$$

For $n \geq 0$, the n-inlining inline(A, n) of calls to r in a piece of code A is defined as A with every call $u.r(b)$ on target u (possibly **Current**) with actual arguments b modified as follows:

$$\text{inline}(u.r(b), n) = \begin{cases} \textbf{assert}\ P_r[u, b]\ ;\ \textbf{havoc}\ F_r[u, b]\ ;\ \textbf{assume}\ Q_r[u, b] & \text{if } n = 0 \\ \text{inline}(B_r[u, b], n-1) & \text{if } n > 0 \end{cases}$$

Inlining works recursively on calls to routines other than r and recursive calls to r in B_r; non-call instructions are instead unchanged. 0-inlining coincides with the usual modular semantics of calls based on specifications. Otherwise, inlining replaces calls to r with $B_r[u, b]$ (r's body applied to the actual target u and arguments b of the calls), recursively for as many times as the recursion depth n.

Since inlining discards the inlined routine's precondition, it may produce under- or over-approximations of the calls under modular semantics, respectively if the declared precondition is weaker or stronger than the body's weakest precondition.

For any $n > 0$, the n-inlining of *swap* in *two_way_sort*'s body (Figure 2) consists of replacing the call to *swap* at line 14 with *swap*'s body instantiated in the correct context, that is $t := a[i]\ ;\ a[i] := a[j]\ ;\ a[j] := t$ with t a fresh local variable declared inside *two_way_sort*.

Inlining and Dynamic Dispatching. In programming languages with dynamic dispatching, the binding of routine bodies to routine calls occurs at runtime, based on the dynamic type of the call targets. This is not a problem for modular reasoning because it can rely on behavioral subtyping and the rule that routine redefinitions in descendants (overriding) may only weaken preconditions and strengthen postconditions. Inlining, instead, has to deal with dynamic dispatching explicitly: in general, verification using inlining of a routine r of class C is repeated for every overriding of r in C's descendants. This also requires to re-verify the system whenever new descendants of C are added, unless overriding

r is eventually forbidden (**frozen** in Eiffel, **final** or **private** in Java, or **sealed** in C#). These limitations are, however, not a problem in practice when we apply inlining not indiscriminately but only in limited contexts for small helper routines, and we combine its results with classic modular reasoning as we do in two-step verification.

4.2 Unrolling

The standard approach to modular reasoning also applies to loops based on their loop invariants: the effects of executing a loop on the state of the program after it are postulated to coincide with the loop invariant. The inductiveness of the invariant is established separately for a generic iteration of the loop, and so is the requirement that the invariant hold upon loop entry.

This reliance on expressive loop invariants is at odds with the aversion programmer typically have at writing them. This is not only a matter of habits, but also derives from the fact that loop invariants are often complex specification elements compared to pre- and postconditions [18]; and, unlike pre- and postconditions which constitute useful documentation for clients of the routine, loop invariants are considered merely a means to the end of proving a program correct. The loop of *two_way_sort* in Figure 2, for example, has a simple loop invariant that only bounds the values of the indexes i and j; this prevents proving any complex postcondition.

Unrolling can help in these situations by evaluating the effects of a loop in terms of its concrete body rather than its invariant. This may help prove the postcondition when the invariant is too weak, showing that a certain number of repetitions of the body are sufficient to establish the postcondition. Furthermore, in the cases where we have a way to establish a bound on the number of loop iterations, unrolling precisely renders the implementation semantics. We will generalize these observations when discussing how unrolling is applied automatically in the context of two-step verification (Section 5).

Definition of Unrolling. Consider a generic annotated loop L:

until *exit* **invariant** I **loop** B **variant** V **end**

which repeats the body B until the exit condition *exit* holds, and is annotated with invariant I and variant V. For $n \geq 0$, the n-unrolling $\mathsf{unroll}(L, n)$ of L is defined as:

$$\mathsf{unroll}(L, n) \;=\; (\textbf{if not } \textit{exit } \textbf{then } B \textbf{ end})^n$$

where the nth exponent denotes n repetitions. Since unrolling ignores the loop invariant, it may produce under- or over-approximations of the loop's modular semantics, respectively if the declared loop invariant is weaker or stronger than the body's weakest precondition.

5 Two-Step Verification

We have introduced all the elements used in two-step verification; we can finally show how they are combined to produce improved user feedback.

Implicit contracts are simply added whenever appropriate and used to have early detection of errors violating them. In AutoProof, which translates Eiffel to Boogie to perform static proofs, implicit contracts are not added to the Eiffel code but are silently injected into the Boogie translation, so that the input code does not become polluted by many small assertions; users familiar with Eiffel's semantics are aware of them without explicitly writing them down. Errors consisting of violations to implicit contracts reference back the original statements in Eiffel code from which they originated, so that the error report is understandable without looking at the Boogie translation.

Whenever the verifier checks a routine that contains routine calls, two-step verification applies inlining as described in Section 5.1. Whenever it checks a routine that contains loops, two-step verification applies unrolling as described in Section 5.2. The application of the two steps is completely automatic, and is combined for routines that includes both calls and loops; users only get a final improved error report in the form of suggestions that narrow down the possible causes of failed verification more precisely than in standard approaches. Section 5.4 briefly illustrates two-step verification on the running example of Section 2.

5.1   With Inlining

Consider a generic routine r with precondition P_r and postcondition Q_r, whose body B_r contains a call $t.s(a)$ to another routine s with precondition P_s, postcondition Q_s and body B_s (as shown in Figure 3). Two-step verification runs two verification attempts on r:

1. **Modular verification:** The first step of two-step verification for r follows the standard modular verification approach: it tries to verify that r is correct with respect to its specification, using s's specification only to reason about the call to s; and then it separately tries to verify s against its own specification.

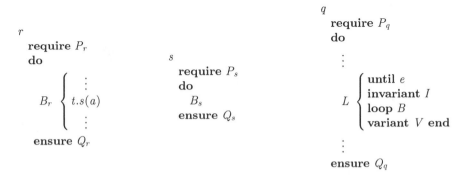

Fig. 3. A routine r calling another routine s; and a routine q with a loop

2. **Inlined verification:** The second step of two-step verification for r replaces the call to s in r with $\mathsf{inline}(t.s(a), n)$, for some $n > 0$ picked as explained in Section 5.3, and then verifies r with this inlining.

Table 1. Two-step verification with inlining: summary of suggestions

| step 1: modular | | step 2: inlined | |
VERIFY r	VERIFY s	VERIFY r	SUGGESTION
P_s fails	success	success	weaken P_s or use inlined s
Q_r fails	success	success	strengthen Q_s or use inlined s
success	Q_s fails	success	strengthen P_s or weaken Q_s

Each of the two steps may fail or succeed. According to the combined outcome, we report a different suggestion to users, as summarized in Table 1.

Precondition Fails. If modular verification (first step) fails to establish that s's precondition P_s holds right before the call, but both modular verification of s and inlined verification (second step) of r succeed, it means that s's precondition may be inadequate[2] while its implementation is correct with respect to its specification and to the usage made within r. In this case, there are two options: if s is a helper function used only in r or anyway in limited contexts, we may as well drop s's specification and just use it inlined wherever needed during verification. In more general cases, we should try to *weaken* P_s in a way that better characterizes the actual requirements of how s is used.

Postcondition Fails. If modular verification fails to establish that r's postcondition Q_r holds when B_r terminates, but both modular verification of s and inlined verification of r succeed, it means that s's postcondition fails to characterize r's requirements while s's implementation is correct with respect to its specification. As in the previous case, there are two options: we may drop s's specification and just use it inlined; or we should try to *strengthen* Q_s in a way that better characterizes the actual expectations of r on s. A similar scheme applies not just to failed postconditions Q_r but whenever modular verification fails to verify intermediate assertions occurring on paths after the call to s in r.

Local Proof Fails. If modular verification fails to establish that s's postcondition Q_s holds when B_s terminates, but both modular verification of r and inlined verification of r succeed, it means that s's specification cannot be proved consistent with its implementation, while the latter is correct with respect to the usage made within r. The suggestion is to change s specification in a way that still accommodates its usage within r and can be verified: strengthen the precondition P_s, weaken the postcondition P_s, or both. With this information, there is no way to decide if the problem is with the pre- or postcondition, but

---

[2] As with all failed static verification attempts, we cannot exclude that failure is simply due to limitations of the theorem prover.

we can always try to modify either one and run verification again to see if the suggestion changes.

In the remaining cases, two-step verification is inconclusive in the sense that it gives the same feedback as modular verification alone. In particular, when the second step fails it is of no help to determine whether the problem is in the specification or the implementation. If, for example, both modular and inlined verification of r fail to establish the postcondition Q_r, but modular verification of s succeeds, we cannot conclude that s's implementation is wrong because it does not achieve Q_r: it may as well be that r's implementation is wrong, or r's postcondition is unreasonable; which is exactly the information carried by a failed modular verification attempt.

Also notice that inlined verification cannot fail when modular verification fully succeeds: if s's implementation satisfies its specification, and that specification is sufficient to prove r correct, then the semantics of s within r is sufficient to prove the latter correct. Therefore, we need not run the second step when the first one is successful.[3]

5.2   With Unrolling

Consider a generic routine q with precondition P_q and postcondition Q_q, whose body B_q contains a loop L with exit condition e, invariant I, variant V, and body B (as shown in Figure 3). Two-step verification runs two verification attempts on r:

1. **Modular verification:** The first step of two-step verification for r follows the standard modular verification approach: it tries to verify that r is correct with respect to its specification, using the loop invariant I only to reason about the effect of L within r; and then it separately tries to verify that I is a correct inductive loop invariant (that is, it holds on entry and is maintained by iterations of the loop).
2. **Unrolled verification:** The second step of two-step verification for r replaces the loop L in r with unroll(L, n), for some $n > 0$ picked as explained in Section 5.3, and then verifies r with this unrolling and the additional assertion **assert** $V \leq n$, evaluated upon loop entry, that the loop executes at most n times.[4]

Each of the two steps may fail or succeed. According to the combined outcome, we report a different suggestion to users, as summarized in Table 2.

Postcondition Fails. Suppose that modular verification (first step) fails to establish that r's postcondition Q_q holds when B_q terminates, but unrolled

---

[3] Again, exceptions might occur due to shortcomings of the theorem prover used by the modular verifier, which might be able to prove a set of verification conditions but fail on a syntactically different but semantically equivalent set due to heuristics or limitations of the implementation. These are, however, orthogonal concerns.

[4] If a variant is not available or cannot be verified to be a valid variant, we proceed as if the assertion did not hold.

Table 2. Two-step verification with unrolling: summary of suggestions

step 1: modular	step 2: unrolled		
VERIFY r	assert $V \leq n$	VERIFY r	SUGGESTION
Q_q fails	success	success	use inlined L
Q_q fails	fail	success	strengthen I to generalize
I fails inductiveness	success	success	use inlined L
I fails inductiveness	fail	success	change I to generalize

verification (second step) of r succeeds. The suggestion in this case depends on whether the prover can also establish the intermediate assertion **assert** $V \leq n$. If it does, n is a finite upper bound on the number of loop iterations in every execution. Thus, the loop implementation is correct but the loop invariant I is inadequate to prove the postcondition; we may as well drop the invariant I and just use the exhaustively unrolled loop during verification. In the more general case where the assertion $V \leq n$ fails, the successful unrolled proof shows that the loop body works with a finite number of iterations, and hence it is likely correct; we may then try to strengthen (or otherwise change) the invariant I in a way that captures a generic number of loop iterations and is sufficiently strong to establish Q_q. A similar scheme applies not just to failed postconditions Q_q but whenever modular verification fails to verify intermediate assertions occurring on paths after the loop L in q.

Invariant Fails. Suppose that modular verification fails to establish that I is inductive, but unrolled verification of r succeeds. The suggestion depends on whether the prover can also establish the intermediate assertion **assert** $V \leq n$. If it does, the loop implementation is correct but the loop invariant I is inadequate; we may as well drop the invariant I and just use the exhaustively unrolled loop during verification. In the more general case where the assertion $V \leq n$ fails, the successful unrolled proof shows that the loop body works with a finite number of iterations, and hence it is likely correct; we may then try to change the invariant I in a way that captures a generic number of loop iterations and is sufficiently strong to establish Q_q. With this information, there is no way to decide if the invariant should be strengthened or weakened, but we can always try either one and run verification again.

In the remaining cases, two-step verification gives the same feedback as modular verification alone. And, as for inlining, we need not run the second step (unrolled verification) when modular verification is completely successful.

5.3   Bounds for Nesting and Loops

The application of inlining and unrolling requires a parameter n: the maximum depth of nested calls in the former case; and the number of explicit iterations of the loop in the latter. The choice of n is more subtle for unrolling—where it should represent a number of iterations sufficient to make the second step of verification succeed—than for inlining—where it becomes relevant only in the presence of nested calls or recursion.

In our implementation, we use simple heuristics to pick values for n that are "feasible", that is do not incur combinatorial explosion. In the case of inlining, we get a crude estimate of the size of the inlined program as follows. For a routine p, let π_p denote the total number of simple paths in p from entry to exit. If p has size $|p|$ (measured in number of instructions) and includes m calls to routines $r_1, \ldots, r_m$, we recursively define $\|p\|_n$ as: $|p|$ if $n = 0$, $|p| + \pi_p(\|r_1\|_{n-1} + \cdots + \|r_m\|_{n-1})$ if $n > 0$. Inlining in p uses an n such that $\|p\|_n \leq 10^4$.

In the case of unrolling a loop within routine q, our implementation does some simple static analysis to determine if the calling context of q or q's precondition suggest a finite bound of the loop (in practice, this is restricted to loops over arrays that are declared statically or with a constant upper bound in the precondition). In such cases, n is simply the inferred bound. Otherwise, we roughly estimate the size of an unrolled loop L as $n|L|$, where $|L|$ is the size of L in number of instructions; unrolling L uses an n such that $n|L| \leq 10^3$.

In many practical cases (in the absence of recursion or deeply nested calls), very small n's (such as $1 \leq n \leq 5$) are sufficient to produce a meaningful results in two-step verification.

5.4   Examples

Let us demonstrate how two-step verification works on the running examples introduced in Section 2. Figure 4 shows two clients of routine *two_way_sort* (Figure 2). Routine *client_1* calls *two_way_sort* on an empty array, which is forbidden by its precondition. Normally, this would be blamed on *client_1*; with two-step verification, however, the second verification attempt inlines *two_way_sort* within *client_1* and successfully verifies it. This suggests that *client_1* is not to blame, because *two_way_sort*'s precondition is unnecessarily strong (first case in Table 1), which is exactly what AutoProof will suggest in this case as shown in Figure 5. In fact, the sorting implementation also works on empty arrays, where it simply does not do anything.

```
1    client_1                          7    client_2
2        local   a: ARRAY              8        local   a: ARRAY [BOOLEAN]
              [BOOLEAN]                9        do
3        do                            10           a := [True, False, False,
4            a := [ ]  -- empty array             True]
5            two_way_sort (a)          11           two_way_sort (a)
6        end                           12           assert a[1] = False
                                       13       end
```

Fig. 4. Clients of *two_way_sort*

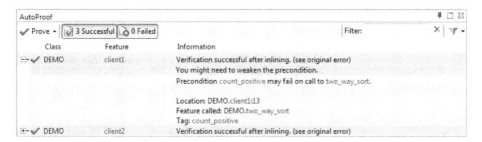

Fig. 5. AutoProof showing feedback of two-step verification

Routine *client_2* calls *two_way_sort* on a four-element array and checks that its first element is **False** after the call. Modular verification cannot prove this assertion: *two_way_sort* has no postcondition, and hence its effects within *client_2* are undefined. The second verification attempt inlines *two_way_sort* and unrolls the loop four times (since it notices that the call is on a four-element array); this proves that the first array element is **False** after the call (first line in Table 2). In all, *two_way_sort* is not to blame because its implementation works correctly for *client_2*. As summarized in the second line of Table 1, the user can either just be happy with the result or endeavor to write down a suitable postcondition for *two_way_sort* so that the correctness proof can be generalized to arrays of arbitrary length.

Suppose we provide a postcondition that specifies sortedness: using Eiffel's syntax, **across** $1..(a.count-1)$ **as** k **all** $(a[k] = a[k+1])$ **or** $(a[k] \neq a[k+1]$ **and** $a[k] = $ **False**). Modular verification of *two_way_sort* fails to prove this postcondition because the loop invariant at line 7 does not say anything about the array content. Two-step verification makes a second attempt where it unrolls the loop a finite number of times, say 5, and inlines *swap*. The situation is in the second entry of Table 2: we cannot verify that the arbitrary bound of five iterations generally holds (that is $j - i + 1 \leq 5$ holds before the loop), but the success of unrolling in this limited case suggests that *two_way_sort*'s implementation is correct. If we want to get to a general proof, we should improve the loop invariant, and this is precisely the suggestion that two-step verification brings forward.

6   Evaluation

The examples of the previous sections have demonstrated the kind of feedback two-step verification provides. This section contains a preliminary evaluation of the scalability of two-step verification.

Table 3 lists the example programs. The first labeled column after the program name contains the size of the implementation (not counting specification elements) in lines of code. The rest of the table is split in two parts: the first one contains data about two-step verification; the second one the same data about modular verification. The data reported includes: the amount of specification

Table 3. Comparison of two-step and modular verification on selected examples

	code	TWO-STEP P	Q	I	A	spec (Boogie)	Boogie	time	MODULAR P	Q	I	A	spec	Boogie	time
1. Maximum	32	1	3	0	0	4	1541	2.06	1	3	4	0	8	712	1.05
2. Sum and Max	32	3	1	0	0	4	1619	2.18	3	1	5	0	9	720	1.04
3. Two-way Sort	44	2	1	0	0	3	1803	2.35	2	1	5	0	8	742	1.06
4. Dutch Flag	45	2	1	0	0	3	1955	2.94	2	1	10	0	13	786	1.14
5. Longest common prefix	30	3	4	0	0	7	1585	2.10	3	4	7	0	14	730	1.05
6. Priority queue	119	0	0	0	7	7	2896	3.35	5	13	5	7	30	1088	1.56
7. Deque	127	0	0	0	11	11	1856	2.51	7	18	4	11	40	1230	1.59
8. Binary Search	48	0	0	0	1	1	2479	3.21	2	3	0	1	6	672	0.99
Total	*477*	*11*	*10*	*0*	*19*	*40*	*15734*	*20.70*	*25*	*44*	*40*	*19*	*128*	*6680*	*9.48*

necessary to successfully verify the example (number of annotations, split into preconditions P, postconditions Q, invariants I (loop invariants in examples 1–5; class invariants in examples 6–8), and intermediate assertions A); the size (in lines) of the Boogie code generated by AutoProof; and the time in seconds. Two-step verification includes modular verification as first step, but normally requires less specification to be successful; correspondingly, the Boogie code and the time in the first part of the table sum up both steps.

The examples include: (1) finding the maximum in an array, from the COST 2011 verification competition [6]; (2) computing maximum and sum of the elements in an array, from the VSTTE 2010 verification competition [22]; (3) the two-way sort algorithm of Section 2, from the VSTTE 2012 verification competition [16]; (4) Dikstra's Dutch national flag algorithm [13]; (5) computing the longest common prefix of two sequences, from the FM 2012 verification competition [19]; (6) a priority queue implementation, from Tinelli's verification course [32]; (7) a double-ended queue [23, Vol. 1, Sec. 2.2.1]; and (8) the binary search algorithm of Section 2, from the software verification benchmarks [1].

In the experiments with the algorithms 1–5, two-step verification succeeds with loop unrolling of depth $n = 6$, which corresponds to input arrays of the same length. The outcome suggests either to use the unrolled loop, for inputs of bounded length; or to write a suitable loop invariant. A correct loop invariant is necessary for modular verification alone to succeed, in which case the proof generalizes to arrays of arbitrary length. We prove the following postconditions: (1) the output is the array maximum; (2) the output sum is less than or equal to the output maximum times the array length; (3) sortedness of the output, as formalized in Section 5.4; (4) the output is partitioned in the three flag colors; (5) the output is the longest common prefix of the input array.

In the experiments 6–8 we verify *clients* of the queue, double-ended queue, and binary search, which call some routines and then formalize their expectations on the result with **asserts** after the call. The called routines have no specification (in particular, no postcondition); two-step verification verifies the clients using inlining of the callee, and suggests to add postconditions to generalize the proofs. The postconditions are necessary for modular verification alone to succeed.

The evaluation suggests that two-step verification can check the implementation even when little or no specification is given; its feedback may then help write the necessary specifications to generalize proofs for modular verification.

The runtime overhead of performing two verification steps instead of one is roughly linear in all examples; in fact, unrolling and inlining blow up mainly in the presence of recursion. To better assess how they scale, we have repeated two-step verification of examples 3 (using unrolling) and 6 (using inlining in the presence of recursion) for increasing value of the bound n. Table 4 shows the results in terms of size of the generated Boogie code (in lines) and time necessary to verify it (in seconds). Unrolling scales gracefully until about $n = 10$; afterward, the time taken by Boogie to verify increases very quickly, even if the size of the Boogie code does not blow up. Inlining is more sensitive to the bound, since the size of the inlined code grows exponentially due to the conditional branch in *binary_search*'s body; the time is acceptable until about $n = 7$. Notice that the heuristics for the choice of n discussed in Section 5.3 would generate running times in the order of tens of seconds, thus enforcing a reasonable responsiveness.

Table 4. Scalability of unrolling and inlining on examples 3 and 6 from Table 3

inlining/unrolling depth n	UNROLLING		INLINING	
	Boogie	time	Boogie	time
3	864	1.07	1201	1.44
4	937	1.13	1822	2.26
5	1010	1.21	3054	4.23
6	1083	1.32	5518	10.93
7	1156	1.52	10446	30.64
8	1229	2.03	20302	112.32
10	1375	4.26	–	–
13	1594	37.52	–	–
15	1667	253.30	–	–

7   Related Work

The steadily growing interest for techniques and tools that make verification more approachable indicates how some of the most glaring hurdles to the progress of formal methods lie in their applicability. Tools such as Dafny [27], Spec# [2], VCC [10], ESC/Java2 [11,20], and Why3 [5] define the state of the art in static program verification. Their approaches rely on accurate specifications, which are not easy to write and get right.

One way to ameliorate this situation is inferring specifications automatically using static [8,24,18] or dynamic [14,37,36] techniques. Specifications dynamically inferred are based on a finite number of executions, and hence may be unsound; this makes them unsuitable for use in the context of static verification. Static techniques can infer sound specifications from the program text; these are useful to document existing implementations, to discover auxiliary assertions (such as loop invariants), or for comparison with specifications independently written, but proving an implementation correct against a specification inferred from it is mostly a vacuous exercise.

The simple implicit contracts that we use in our approach express well-formedness properties of the input program, which are tacitly assumed by programmers reasoning informally about it; therefore, there is no risk of circularity. Some static verifiers use mathematical integers or assume purity of specification functions to have well-formedness by construction; a risk is that, when they are applied to real programming languages, the corresponding semantic gap may leave some errors go unnoticed. ESC/Java2, for example, does not check for overflows [21], nor if specification expressions are executable (for example, null-dereferencing could happen when evaluating a precondition). The Dafny verifier [27] checks well-formedness of pre- and postconditions, and may consequently require users to add explicit contracts to satisfy well-formedness. Our implicit contracts are instead added and checked automatically, without requiring users to explicitly write them. In this sense, they are similar to approaches such as VCC [10], which models the semantics of the C programming language as precisely as possible.

Besides inferring specifications, another approach to facilitate formal verification is combining complementary verification techniques. CEGAR model-checking [3], for example, uses model-checking exhaustive verification techniques on approximate program models, combined with a form of symbolic execution to determine whether the failed verification attempts are indicative of real implementation errors or only a figment of an imprecise abstraction. Tools such as DSD-Crasher [12] and our EVE [33] integrate testing and static checking to find when the errors reported by the latter are spurious. Collaborative verification [9] is also based on the combination of testing and static verification, and on the explicit formalization of the restrictions of each tool used in the combination. Two-step verification also integrates the results of different techniques, with the main purpose of improving error reporting and reducing the number of annotations needed, rather than complementing the limitations of specific techniques.

The Spec# system includes a verification debugger [25] to inspect error models when verification fails; more recently, an interpreter for Boogie programs [29] can help find the sources of failed verification attempts. Debuggers for verification can be quite useful in practice, but achieve a lesser degree of automation than two-step verification, since users need to manually inspect and understand the error models using the debugger.

Inlining and unrolling are standard techniques in compiler construction. The Boogie verifier [26] also supports inlining of procedures: through annotations, one can require to inline a procedure to a given depth using different sound or unsound definitions. Boogie also supports (unsound) loop unrolling on request. AutoProof's current implementation of inlining and unrolling works at source code level, rather than using Boogie's similar features, to have greater flexibility in how inlining and unrolling are defined and used. Methods specified using the Java Modeling Language (JML) with the "helper" modifier [11] are meant to be used privately; ESC/Java inlines calls to such methods [17]. ESC/Java also unrolls loops a fixed amount of times; users can choose between performing sound or unsound variants of the unrolling. In previous work [28], we used unrolling and inlining to check the type correctness of JavaScript programs. In two-step verification, we use inlining and unrolling completely automatically: users need not be aware of them to benefit from an improved feedback that narrows down the sources of failed verification attempts.

Acknowledgements. Work partially supported by the ERC grant CME/291389; by the SNF grants LSAT (200020-134974) and ASII (200021-134976); and by the Hasler foundation on related projects.

References

1. Weide, B.W., et al.: Incremental benchmarks for software verification tools and techniques. In: Shankar, N., Woodcock, J. (eds.) VSTTE 2008. LNCS, vol. 5295, pp. 84–98. Springer, Heidelberg (2008)
2. Barnett, M., Leino, K.R.M., Schulte, W.: The Spec# programming system: An overview. In: Barthe, G., Burdy, L., Huisman, M., Lanet, J.-L., Muntean, T. (eds.) CASSIS 2004. LNCS, vol. 3362, pp. 49–69. Springer, Heidelberg (2005)
3. Beyer, D., Henzinger, T.A., Jhala, R., Majumdar, R.: The software model checker Blast. STTT 9(5-6), 505–525 (2007)
4. Bloch, J.: (2006), http://goo.gl/sWLty
5. Bobot, F., Filliâtre, J.-C., Marché, C., Paskevich, A.: Why3: Shepherd your herd of provers. In: Boogie, pp. 53–64 (2011)
6. Bormer, T., et al.: The COST IC0701 verification competition. In: Beckert, B., Damiani, F., Gurov, D. (eds.) FoVeOOS 2011. LNCS, vol. 7421, pp. 3–21. Springer, Heidelberg (2012)
7. Chalin, P.: Are practitioners writing contracts? In: Butler, M., Jones, C.B., Romanovsky, A., Troubitsyna, E. (eds.) Fault-Tolerant Systems. LNCS, vol. 4157, pp. 100–113. Springer, Heidelberg (2006)
8. Chang, B.-Y.E., Leino, K.R.M.: Inferring object invariants. ENTCS 131, 63–74 (2005)
9. Christakis, M., Müller, P., Wüstholz, V.: Collaborative verification and testing with explicit assumptions. In: Giannakopoulou, D., Méry, D. (eds.) FM 2012. LNCS, vol. 7436, pp. 132–146. Springer, Heidelberg (2012)
10. Cohen, E., Dahlweid, M., Hillebrand, M.A., Leinenbach, D., Moskal, M., Santen, T., Schulte, W., Tobies, S.: VCC: A practical system for verifying concurrent C. In: Berghofer, S., Nipkow, T., Urban, C., Wenzel, M. (eds.) TPHOLs 2009. LNCS, vol. 5674, pp. 23–42. Springer, Heidelberg (2009)
11. Cok, D.R., Kiniry, J.: ESC/Java2: Uniting ESC/Java and JML. In: Barthe, G., Burdy, L., Huisman, M., Lanet, J.-L., Muntean, T. (eds.) CASSIS 2004. LNCS, vol. 3362, pp. 108–128. Springer, Heidelberg (2005)

12. Csallner, C., Smaragdakis, Y., Xie, T.: DSD-Crasher: A hybrid analysis tool for bug finding. ACM TOSEM 17(2), 8 (2008)
13. Dijkstra, E.W.: A Discipline of Programming. Prentice Hall (1976)
14. Ernst, M.D., Cockrell, J., Griswold, W.G., Notkin, D.: Dynamically discovering likely program invariants to support program evolution. IEEE TSE 27(2), 99–123 (2001)
15. Estler, H.-C., Furia, C.A., Nordio, M., Piccioni, M., Meyer, B.: The evolution of contracts (2012), http://arxiv.org/abs/1211.4775
16. Filliâtre, J.-C., Paskevich, A., Stump, A.: The 2nd verified software competition: Experience report. In: COMPARE, vol. 873, pp. 36–49 (2012)
17. Flanagan, C., Leino, K.R.M., Lillibridge, M., Nelson, G., Saxe, J.B., Stata, R.: Extended static checking for Java. In: PLDI, pp. 234–245. ACM (2002)
18. Furia, C.A., Meyer, B.: Inferring loop invariants using postconditions. In: Blass, A., Dershowitz, N., Reisig, W. (eds.) Fields of Logic and Computation. LNCS, vol. 6300, pp. 277–300. Springer, Heidelberg (2010)
19. Huisman, M., Klebanov, V., Monahan, R.: VerifyThis verification competition (2012), http://verifythis2012.cost-ic0701.org
20. James, P.R., Chalin, P.: Faster and more complete extended static checking for the Java Modeling Language. J. Autom. Reasoning 44(1-2), 145–174 (2010)
21. Kiniry, J.R., Morkan, A.E., Denby, B.: Soundness and completeness warnings in ESC/Java2. In: SAVCBS, pp. 19–24. ACM (2006)
22. Klebanov, V., et al.: The 1st verified software competition: Experience report. In: Butler, M., Schulte, W. (eds.) FM 2011. LNCS, vol. 6664, pp. 154–168. Springer, Heidelberg (2011)
23. Knuth, D.E.: The Art of Computer Programming. Addison-Wesley (2011)
24. Kovács, L., Voronkov, A.: Finding loop invariants for programs over arrays using a theorem prover. In: Chechik, M., Wirsing, M. (eds.) FASE 2009. LNCS, vol. 5503, pp. 470–485. Springer, Heidelberg (2009)
25. Le Goues, C., Leino, K.R.M., Moskal, M.: The Boogie verification debugger. In: Barthe, G., Pardo, A., Schneider, G. (eds.) SEFM 2011. LNCS, vol. 7041, pp. 407–414. Springer, Heidelberg (2011)
26. Leino, K.R.M.: This is Boogie 2. Technical report, Microsoft Research (2008)
27. Leino, K.R.M.: Dafny: an automatic program verifier for functional correctness. In: Clarke, E.M., Voronkov, A. (eds.) LPAR-16 2010. LNCS, vol. 6355, pp. 348–370. Springer, Heidelberg (2010)
28. Nordio, M., Calcagno, C., Furia, C.A.: Javanni: A verifier for JavaScript. In: Cortellessa, V., Varró, D. (eds.) FASE 2013. LNCS, vol. 7793, pp. 231–234. Springer, Heidelberg (2013)
29. Polikarpova, N.: Boogaloo (2012), http://goo.gl/YH9QT
30. Polikarpova, N., Ciupa, I., Meyer, B.: A comparative study of programmer-written and automatically inferred contracts. In: ISSTA, pp. 93–104 (2009)
31. Polikarpova, N., Furia, C.A., Pei, Y., Wei, Y., Meyer, B.: What good are strong specifications? In: ICSE, pp. 257–266. ACM (2013)
32. Tinelli, C.: Formal methods in software engineering (2011), http://www.divms.uiowa.edu/~tinelli/181/
33. Tschannen, J., Furia, C.A., Nordio, M., Meyer, B.: Usable verification of object-oriented programs by combining static and dynamic techniques. In: Barthe, G., Pardo, A., Schneider, G. (eds.) SEFM 2011. LNCS, vol. 7041, pp. 382–398. Springer, Heidelberg (2011)

34. Tschannen, J., Furia, C.A., Nordio, M., Meyer, B.: Verifying Eiffel programs with Boogie. In: BOOGIE Workshop (2011), http://arxiv.org/abs/1106.4700
35. Tschannen, J., Furia, C.A., Nordio, M., Meyer, B.: Automatic verification of advanced object-oriented features: The AutoProof approach. In: Meyer, B., Nordio, M. (eds.) LASER 2011. LNCS, vol. 7682, pp. 133–155. Springer, Heidelberg (2012)
36. Wasylkowski, A., Zeller, A.: Mining temporal specifications from object usage. Autom. Softw. Eng. 18(3-4), 263–292 (2011)
37. Wei, Y., Furia, C.A., Kazmin, N., Meyer, B.: Inferring better contracts. In: ICSE, pp. 191–200. ACM (2011)

Verified Calculations

K. Rustan M. Leino[1] and Nadia Polikarpova[2]

[1] Microsoft Research, Redmond, WA, USA
leino@microsoft.com
[2] ETH Zurich, Zurich, Switzerland
nadia.polikarpova@inf.ethz.ch

Abstract. Calculational proofs—proofs by stepwise formula manipulation—are praised for their rigor, readability, and elegance. It seems desirable to reuse this style, often employed on paper, in the context of mechanized reasoning, and in particular, program verification.

This work leverages the power of SMT solvers to machine-check calculational proofs at the level of detail they are usually written by hand. It builds the support for calculations into the programming language and auto-active program verifier Dafny. The paper demonstrates that calculations integrate smoothly with other language constructs, producing concise and readable proofs in a wide range of problem domains: from mathematical theorems to correctness of imperative programs. The examples show that calculational proofs in Dafny compare favorably, in terms of readability and conciseness, with arguments written in other styles and proof languages.

1 Introduction

There is no automatic way to decide, for any given statement, if it holds or not. Both in mathematics and in program verification, people construct proofs to convince themselves and others of the validity of statements, as well as to gain a better understanding of those statements and why they hold. Naturally, people strive to come up with a good notation for writing proofs: one that is easy to read and understand, and, if possible, guards against mistakes.

One such notation is the *calculational method* [4], whereby a theorem is established by a chain of formulas, each transformed in some way into the next. The relationship between successive formulas (for example, equality or implication) is notated, and so is a *hint* that justifies the transformation (see Fig. 4 in Sec. 2.2 for an example). The calculational method encourages making the transformation steps small in order to help the author avoid mistakes and to convince readers by fully explaining what is going on.

Even though calculational proofs are written in a strict format, they still tend to be informal. Manolios and Moore [25] discovered several errors in calculations written by Dijkstra (one of the biggest proponents of the style) and posed a challenge to mechanize calculational proofs, asking if "any attempt to render calculational proofs suitable for mechanical checking will result in ugly, hard to comprehend proofs" and if "the mechanized proof checker [will] necessarily be hard to learn and difficult to use".

E. Cohen and A. Rybalchenko (Eds.): VSTTE 2013, LNCS 8164, pp. 170–190, 2014.

Indeed, constructing proofs within *interactive proof assistants* (like Coq [8], Isabelle/HOL [26], or PVS [27]) has a reputation of being a demanding task[1]. The purpose of these tools is to give the user maximum control over the proof process, which is why they favor predictability over automation. Interaction with such an assistant consists of issuing low-level commands, called *tactics*, that guide the prover through the maze of proof states. This mode of interaction is biased towards expert users with a good knowledge of the tool's inner workings.

In contrast, *auto-active* program verifiers [24], like Dafny [22], VCC [13], or VeriFast [18], take a different approach to mechanised reasoning: they provide automation by default, supported by an underlying SMT solver. All the interaction with such a verifier happens at the level of the programming language, which has the advantage of being familiar to the programmer. So far, these tools have been used mostly for verifying functional correctness of programs, but their domain is gradually expanding towards general mathematical proofs.

It would be wonderful if we could just take a pen-and-paper calculational proof and get it machine-checked completely automatically. In this paper, we add support for proof calculations to the programming language and auto-active program verifier Dafny [22,21]. The extension, which we call *program-oriented calculations* (poC), is able to verify calculational proofs written with the same level of detail and the same degree of elegance as they would be on paper, thereby addressing the challenge of Manolios and Moore.

The main contributions of the present work are as follows. We integrate proof calculations as a statement in a programming language. The supporting syntax uses, for structuring proofs, constructs already familiar to programmers (such as conditionals and method calls). We develop tool support for machine-checking the proofs. Thanks to the underlying SMT solver, the resulting tool provides a high degree of automation. We provide a sound encoding of the new statement that tries to reduce the overhead of specifying that formulas are well defined (in the presence of partial expressions). We give a number of examples that use the proof format and provide a comparison with proof structuring in existing tools. And by adding this streamlined proof support to an auto-active program verifier, we are bringing SMT-based tools closer to what previously has been territory exclusive to interactive proof assistants.

2 Background and Motivation

This section reviews existing features for writing proofs in auto-active program verifiers and then argues in favor of adding support for calculations. While we use Dafny in our examples, other auto-active verifiers have a similar range of features.

2.1 Proofs in an Auto-Active Program Verifier

Automatic verification attempts may fail for several reasons. One reason is that the program correctness may depend on mathematical properties that the program verifier is unable to figure out by itself. In such cases, the user of an auto-active verifier may

---

[1] A popular quote from an old version of the PVS website states that it takes six months to become a moderately skilled user [33].

```
datatype List⟨T⟩ = Nil | Cons(T, List⟨T⟩)

function length(xs: List): nat {
  match xs
  case Nil ⇒ 0
  case Cons(x, xrest) ⇒ 1 + length(xrest)
}
```

Fig. 1. Definition of a generic datatype List ⟨T⟩ and a function that returns the length of a list. We omit the type parameter of List where Dafny can infer it automatically, as for function length here.

```
ghost method LemmaLength(n: int)
  requires n ≥ 0;
  ensures ∃ xs • length(xs) = n;
{
  if n = 0 {
    // trivial
  } else {
    LemmaLength(n - 1); // invoke induction hypothesis
    var xs :| length(xs) = n - 1;
    assert length(Cons(496, xs)) = n;
} }
```

Fig. 2. The ghost method states a theorem and its body gives the proof. More precisely, the body of the method provides some code that convinces the program verifier that all control-flow paths terminate in a state where the postcondition holds.

augment the program text with *lemmas*, which will give the verifier clues about how to proceed.

The simplest form of a lemma is an **assert** statement. It directs the verifier's focus by adding a proof obligation that subsequently can be used as an assumption. As an example, consider an algebraic List datatype with a length function in Fig. 1. Suppose we want to prove that there exists a list of length one:

$$∃ \ xs • length(xs) = 1$$

The proof of such an existential property requires supplying the witness manually, and we can do so by inserting the following assert statement:

assert length(Cons(496, Nil)) = 1;

In more complex cases, an **assert** statement is not enough, perhaps because we want to reuse a multiple-step proof, or, in case of an inductive argument, because we want to apply the same proof recursively. For example, suppose we want to generalize our previous statement and assert that there exists a list of any non-negative length:

$$∀ \ n • 0 ≤ n ⟹ ∃ \ xs • length(xs) = n$$

Since this property may be useful in several places, we would like to state and prove it once as a theorem and later be able to refer to it by name.

To state a theorem in the programming language, we declare a method (see Fig. 2) whose postcondition is the conclusion of the theorem, whose precondition is the assumption made by the theorem, and whose in-parameters show how the theorem can be parameterized. Since we intend this method only for the program verifier, we declare it to be *ghost*, which means that the compiler will not generate any code for it.

To use a lemma stated in this way, the program then simply calls the method, upon return of which the caller gets to assume the postcondition (as usual in program verification). Given a method declaration, the program verifier will, as usual, set out to prove that the method body is terminating and that it terminates with the given postcondition. Thus, the method body essentially gives the proof of the theorem.

In Fig. 2, the method body introduces two cases, n = 0 and n ≠ 0. In the first case, the verifier can automatically come up with the witness using the definition of length, and therefore no further code needs to be given in the **then** branch. The **else** branch performs a method call, so the verifier checks that the callee's precondition holds. Furthermore, since the call is recursive, the verifier needs to check termination, which it does (in the standard program-verification way) by checking that some variant function decreases in some well-founded ordering. In this example, the default variant function— the argument n—is good enough, but in general the variant function may need to be supplied by the user. Upon return from the call, the verifier assumes the postcondition of the call: ∃ xs • length(xs) = n - 1. With this fact at hand, we use the Dafny :| ("assign such that") operator to save an arbitrary list of length n - 1 in a local variable xs. From that list, we construct one of length n, whereby convincing the verifier that the enclosing postcondition holds. The body of method LemmaLength is essentially a proof by induction, where the recursive call denotes the appeal to the induction hypothesis.

The example above illustrates how auto-active program verifiers exploit the analogy between programs and proofs to reuse programming constructs for proof structuring: **if** (and **match/case**) statements for case splits, procedures for stating and reusing lemmas, recursion for inductive arguments. This spares programmers the effort of learning a new language and, more importantly, a new paradigm.

To convince the verifier of some non-trivial fact, one may need to appeal to multiple lemmas (either **assert** statements or method calls), and the discovery of which lemmas are useful is non-trivial. One way to discover what is needed is to start writing a detailed proof, proceeding in small steps and trying to figure out in which step the verifier gets stuck. It is for writing such detailed proofs that poC provides helpful features. Once a detailed proof has been constructed, one often finds that the tool would have been satisfied with some smaller set of lemmas; the user then has the choice of either deleting the steps that are not needed or keeping the proof steps, which may facilitate better readability and maintainability.

2.2 Calculational Proofs

Having reviewed how manual proofs are supplied in an auto-active program verifier, let us now turn our attention to some properties that require a somewhat larger manual effort.

```
function reverse(xs: List): List {
  match xs
  case Nil ⇒ Nil
  case Cons(x, xrest) ⇒ append(reverse(xrest), Cons(x, Nil))
}
function append(xs: List, ys: List): List {
  match xs
  case Nil ⇒ ys
  case Cons(x, xrest) ⇒ Cons(x, append(xrest, ys))
}
```

Fig. 3. Definition of a function reverse that reverses the order of elements in a list and its helper function append that concatenates two lists

$$
\begin{aligned}
&reverse(reverse(x :: xs)) \\
={}& \quad \{ \text{ def. } reverse \ \} \\
&reverse(reverse(xs) \mathbin{+\!\!+} [x]) \\
={}& \quad \{ \text{ lemma } \forall xs, ys \bullet reverse(xs \mathbin{+\!\!+} ys) = reverse(ys) \mathbin{+\!\!+} reverse(xs) \ \} \\
&reverse([x]) \mathbin{+\!\!+} reverse(reverse(xs)) \\
={}& \quad \{ \text{ induction hypothesis } \} \\
&reverse([x]) \mathbin{+\!\!+} xs \\
={}& \quad \{ \text{ def. } reverse, \ append \ \} \\
&[x] \mathbin{+\!\!+} xs \\
={}& \quad \{ \text{ def. } append \text{ twice } \} \\
&x :: xs
\end{aligned}
$$

Fig. 4. Hand proof of $reverse(reverse(x :: xs)) = x :: xs$ written in calculational style. The proof uses Coq-style notation with $x :: xs$ for Cons(x, xs), $[x]$ for Cons(x, Nil), and $xs \mathbin{+\!\!+} ys$ for append(xs, xy).

As a motivating example, we consider proving that reversing a list is an involution:

$$\forall \ \text{xs} \ \bullet \ \text{reverse(reverse(xs))} = \text{xs}$$

There are systems for automatic induction that can prove this property automatically (*e.g.* [20,12,30]), but it requires some manual effort in Dafny. The relevant definitions are found in Fig. 3[2], along with the definition of List from Fig. 1.

Here is how one would prove this fact by hand. Because the definition of reverse is inductive, it is natural that the proof should proceed by induction on xs. The base case $reverse(reverse(Nil)) = Nil$ holds trivially by definition of reverse. For the step case, we can write a little calculation shown in Fig. 4. This calculation consists of five *steps*, each stating an equality between two consecutive *lines* and accompanied by a *hint*, which explains why the equality holds. Typically, hints reference definitions or well-known properties of used operations, invoke auxiliary lemmas, or appeal to the

---

[2] We use a naive definition of reverse for this example; our case study (Sec. 5.1) also contains an efficient tail-recursive definition, and a proof that the two are equivalent.

induction hypothesis. The *conclusion* of this calculation is $reverse(reverse(x : xs)) = x : xs$ (the first line is equal to the last line), which holds due to transitivity of equality.

In Fig. 5, we show the same proof written in Dafny, in a "classical" style with each step represented by an **assert** statement. This proof is harder to read than the one in Fig. 4: it is less structured and more verbose (each inner line appears twice). In the next section, we show how poC improves the situation.

3 Calculations in Dafny

Using poC, we can write the proof of LemmaReverseTwice as shown in Fig. 6. The calculation is introduced using the **calc** statement, which adheres to the following grammar:

$$
\begin{aligned}
CalcStatement &::= \text{“\textbf{calc}”} \; Op^? \; \text{“\{”} \; CalcBody^? \; \text{“\}”} \\
CalcBody &::= Line \; (Op^? \; Hint \; Line)^* \\
Line &::= Expression \; \text{“;”} \\
Hint &::= (BlockStatement \mid CalcStatement)^* \\
Op &::= \text{“=”} \mid \text{“≤”} \mid \text{“<”} \mid \text{“≥”} \mid \text{“>”} \mid \text{“⟹”} \mid \text{“⟸”} \mid \text{“⟺”} \mid \text{“≠”}
\end{aligned}
$$

Non-syntactic rules further restrict hints to only ghost and side-effect free statements, as well as impose a constraint that only *chain-compatible* operators can be used together in a calculation.

The notion of chain-compatibility is quite intuitive for the operators supported by poC; for example, it is clear that $<$ and $>$ cannot be used within the same calculation, as there would be no relation to conclude between the first and the last line. We treat this issue more formally in Sec. 4. Note that we allow a single occurrence of the intransitive operator $\neq$ to appear in a chain of equalities (that is, $\neq$ is chain-compatible with equality but not with any other operator, including itself).

Calculations with fewer than two lines are allowed, but have no effect. If a step operator is omitted, it defaults to the calculation-wide operator, defined after the **calc** keyword. If that operator if omitted, it defaults to equality. Hints are optional in our syntax; we find it useful, however, to still supply a comment for human readers when Dafny requires no hint (for examples, in the first step of Fig. 6).

In the following, we review more features and usage patterns of poC. Most of them we get for free, simply reusing language constructs already present in Dafny. This indicates that calculations integrate well with the rest of the language.

3.1 Contextual Information

It is often desirable to embed a calculation in some context (for example, when proving an implication, the context of the antecedent). Dijkstra gives an example [15] of how choosing an appropriate context can significantly simplify a calculational proof.

Inside a Dafny method, a proof is always embedded in the context of the method's precondition; however, whenever additional context is required, this is easily achieved with a conventional **if** statement.

```
ghost method LemmaReverseTwice(xs: List)
  ensures reverse(reverse(xs)) = xs;
{
  match xs {
    case Nil ⇒
    case Cons(x, xrest) ⇒
      // by def. reverse, we have:
      assert reverse(reverse(xs))
        = reverse(append(reverse(xrest), Cons(x, Nil)));
      LemmaReverseAppendDistrib(reverse(xrest), Cons(x, Nil));
      assert reverse(append(reverse(xrest), Cons(x, Nil)))
        = append(reverse(Cons(x, Nil)), reverse(reverse(xrest)));
      LemmaReverseTwice(xrest); // induction hypothesis
      assert append(reverse(Cons(x, Nil)), reverse(reverse(xrest)))
        = append(reverse(Cons(x, Nil)), xrest);
      // by def. reverse and append:
      assert append(reverse(Cons(x, Nil)), xrest)
        = append(Cons(x, Nil), xrest);
      // by def. append applied twice:
      assert append(Cons(x, Nil), xrest)
        = xs;
} }

ghost method LemmaReverseAppendDistrib(xs: List)
  ensures reverse(append(xs, ys)) = append(reverse(ys), reverse(xs));
```

Fig. 5. Theorem that reverse is involutive stated and proven in Dafny without poC. The proof shown here makes use of an auxiliary lemma LemmaReverseAppendDistrib, which shows how reverse distributes over append (and whose proof we have omitted for brevity). The proof can be improved with poC.

Fig. 7 gives an example of the same result being proven in two different ways: with and without additional context. Theorem Monotonicity states that for a function f of a natural argument, the "single step" characterization of monotonicity, *i.e.* $\forall$ n • f(n) ≤ f(n + 1) is as good as the more common characterization with two quantified variables: $\forall$ a, b • a ≤ b ⟹ f(a) ≤ f(b). Because it has been embedded in a richer context, the calculation in the second proof in Fig. 7 has fewer steps and manipulates simpler terms than the one in the first proof.

3.2 Structuring Calculations

Since hints are statements, they can themselves contain calculations. This gives rise to nested calculations, akin to *structured calculational proofs* [2] and *window inference* [34]. In fact, since this is a common case, a hint that consists solely of a calculation need not be enclosed in curly braces. The example in Fig. 8 uses a nested calculation to manipulate a sub-formula of the original line, in order to avoid dragging along the unchanged part of the formula and focus the reader's attention on the essentials.

```
ghost method LemmaReverseTwice(xs: List)
  ensures reverse(reverse(xs)) = xs;
{
  match xs {
    case Nil ⇒
    case Cons(x, xrest) ⇒
      calc {
        reverse(reverse(xs));
      = // def. reverse
        reverse(append(reverse(xrest), Cons(x, Nil)));
      = { LemmaReverseAppendDistrib(reverse(xrest), Cons(x, Nil)); }
        append(reverse(Cons(x, Nil)), reverse(reverse(xrest)));
      = { LemmaReverseTwice(xrest); } // induction hypothesis
        append(reverse(Cons(x, Nil)), xrest);
      = // def. reverse, append
        append(Cons(x, Nil), xrest);
      = // def. append (x2)
        xs;
} }   }
```

Fig. 6. Proof that reverse is involutive using Dafny's **calc** statement

As demonstrated by Back *et al.* [2], nesting is a powerful mechanism for structuring calculational proofs, especially if a subderivation can be carried out in its own context. For example, the following structured calculation (where s0 and s1 are sets and ⌀ says that two sets are disjoint) succinctly proves an implication by manipulating subterms of the consequent under the assumption of the antecedent:

```
calc {
  s0 ⌀ s1 ⟹ f((s0 ∪ s1) ∩ s0) = f(s0);
  { if s0 ⌀ s1 {
      calc {
        (s0 ∪ s1) ∩ s0;
        (s0 ∩ s0) ∪ (s1 ∩ s0);
        // s0 ⌀ s1
        s0;
} } }
  s0 ⌀ s1 ⟹ f(s0) = f(s0);
  true;
}
```

Another way of adding context is parametrization: Dafny's **forall** statement (which in programming is used to perform aggregate operations) makes it possible in proofs to introduce arbitrary values to be manipulated within a subderivation, whose conclusion is then universally generalized. Fig. 9 gives an example. It shows one missing step of the extensionality proof of Fig. 8, namely the one that establishes the precondition for the invocation of the induction hypothesis:

```
function f(n: nat): nat

ghost method Monotonicity(a: nat, b : nat)
  requires ∀ n: nat • f(n) ≤ f(n + 1);
  ensures a ≤ b ⟹ f(a) ≤ f(b);
  decreases b - a; // variant function
{
  // The first proof:                    // The second proof:
  calc ⟹ {                               if a < b {
    a < b;                                  calc ≤ {
    a + 1 ≤ b;                                f(a);
    { Monotonicity(a + 1, b); }               // precondition
    f(a + 1) ≤ f(b);                          f(a + 1);
    // precondition                           { Monotonicity(a + 1, b); }
    f(a) ≤ f(a + 1) ≤ f(b);                   f(b);
    f(a) ≤ f(b);                            }
  }                                       }
}
```

Fig. 7. Theorem that connects different ways of expressing monotonicity and two proofs thereof. Both proofs establish a < b ⟹ f(a) ≤ f(b), which is sufficient since the a = b case is trivial. The difference is that the second proof uses a < b as a context for the calculation, which simplifies it significantly.

$$\forall\ i \bullet\ 0 \le i < length(xrest) \implies ith(xrest, i) = ith(yrest, i)$$

The **forall** statement in the figure introduces a local immutable variable i, whose values range over $[0, length(xrest))$. This block will automatically *export* (*i.e.* make available to the following statements) the conclusion of the nested calculation, quantified over the range of i, which amounts precisely to the missing precondition in Fig. 8.

4   Encoding

Since calculation statements are an incremental addition to Dafny, largely reusing existing constructs such as expressions and statements, the poC implementation required relatively little effort. This means that a similar feature can easily be added to other auto-active verifiers, especially ones based on verification engines like Boogie [6] or Why3 [9].

We explain the encoding of calculation statements in terms of their desugaring into **assert** and **assume** statements. The simplest approach would be to treat a **calc** statement merely as syntactic sugar for asserting all of its steps, which is how one would write such a proof in the absence of support for calculations (see Fig. 5). This approach is trivially sound (since it does not introduce any **assume**s), but it has some practical disadvantages. First, with this encoding, the SMT solver will accumulate all the facts it learns from each calculation step and try to apply them while proving the next step;

```
ghost method Extensionality(xs: List, ys: List)
  requires length(xs) = length(ys); // (0)
  requires ∀ i • 0 ≤ i < length(xs) ⟹ ith(xs, i) = ith(ys, i); // (1)
  ensures xs = ys;
{
  match xs {
    case Nil ⟹
    case Cons(x, xrest) ⟹
      match ys { case Cons(y, yrest) ⟹
        calc {
          xs;
          Cons(x, xrest);
          calc { // nested calculation
            x;
            ith(xs, 0);
            // (1) with i := 0
            ith(ys, 0);
            y;
          }
          Cons(y, xrest);
          { /* Show (1) for xrest, yrest -- omitted in this figure */
            Extensionality(xrest, yrest); }
          Cons(y, yrest);
          ys;
} }    } }
```

Fig. 8. Extract from a proof of extensionality of lists. A nested calculation is used to transform a subterm of a line. The omitted step is fleshed out in Fig. 9.

thus in a large proof, the solver is more likely to get "confused" or "bogged down". Second, the conclusion of the calculation is not stated explicitly, so it might not be readily available after the proof.

Instead, we would like to make use of the fact that steps in a calculational proof are conceptually independent. Our goal is to ask the SMT solver to verify each step in isolation, and then simply postulate the conclusion of the calculation, without wasting the solver's time on putting the steps together and reasoning about transitivity. To this end, we introduce the encoding in Fig. 10. The construct **if** (∗) denotes nondeterministic choice, and the conclusion relation $C\langle N\rangle$ is computed from the sequence $S\langle 0\rangle, \ldots, S\langle N-1\rangle$ of the step operators. Ending each branch of the conditional with **assume false** prevents the control flow from exiting it, effectively telling the SMT solver to forget everything it has learned from the branch.

To determine the conclusion relation $C\langle N\rangle$, following the Isabelle/Isar approach [7], we define a set of *transitivity rules* of the form $R \circ S \subseteq T$ (in the terminology of Sec. 3, this makes R and S chain-compatible). One example of such a rule is $a = b \wedge b < c \Rightarrow a < c$. Fig. 11 summarizes the transitivity rules used in poC.

We define C_i to be the conclusion relation after the first i steps: C_0 is equality, and transitivity rules are used to compute C_{i+1} from the previous conclusion relation

```
calc {
  xs;
  Cons(x, xrest);
  //...
  Cons(y, xrest);
  { forall (i: nat | i < length(xrest)) {
      calc {
        ith(xrest, i);
        ith(xs, i + 1);
        // enclosing precondition
        ith(ys, i + 1);
        ith(yrest, i);
      } }
    Extensionality(xrest, yrest);
  }
  Cons(y, yrest);
  ys;
}
```

Fig. 9. Expanding the omitted step in the outer calculation of Fig. 8. We use Dafny's **forall** statement to introduce a variable i in the nested calculation and then generalize its conclusion.

C_i and the step operator S_i. It is easy to see that if the rules are sound (which is trivial to show for all chain-compatible operators in poC), and the individual steps of a calculation are valid, then each intermediate conclusion $line_0$ C_i $line_i$, and thus the final conclusion, is also valid.

The above argument comes with two caveats for users of traditional proof assistants. First, Dafny is an imperative language and its expressions can depend on mutable state. Obviously, verifying calculation steps in one state and postulating its conclusion in another state can cause trouble. We require that all hints be side-effect free, enforced by a simple syntactic check that disallows assignments and calls to impure methods (that is, methods with a nonempty **modifies** clause). Thus the state is preserved throughout the calculation statement, which implies that the encoding in Fig. 10 is sound. Second, unlike most proof languages, functions in Dafny (including some useful built-in functions like sequence indexing) can be partial (*i.e.* they can have preconditions). Thus, we have to make sure not only that the conclusion of the calculation holds, but also that it is well-defined. This is discussed in the next section.

4.1   Partial Lines

Each Dafny expression e has an associated *well-formedness* condition wf[e], and each Dafny statement is responsible for checking well-formedness of all its sub-expressions (in case of the **calc** statement, all the lines). We modify the encoding in Fig. 10 to assert wf[line$\langle 0 \rangle$] before the first branch, and for every step i assert wf[line$\langle i+1 \rangle$] after Hint$\langle i \rangle$, since the hint might be useful in verifying well-formedness.

```
calc {                              if (*) {
  line⟨0⟩;                            Hint⟨0⟩
S⟨0⟩ { Hint⟨0⟩ }                      assert line⟨0⟩ S⟨0⟩ line⟨1⟩;
  line⟨1⟩;                            assume false;
                                    } else if (*) {

  ...                                 ...

                                    } else if (*) {
  line⟨N-1⟩;                          Hint⟨N-1⟩
S⟨N-1⟩ { Hint⟨N-1⟩ }                  assert line⟨N-1⟩ S⟨N-1⟩ line⟨N⟩;
  line⟨N⟩;                            assume false;
                                    }
}                                   assume line⟨0⟩ C⟨N⟩ line⟨N⟩;
```

Fig. 10. A **calc** statement (on the left) and its **assert/assume** desugaring (on the right), where C⟨N⟩ denotes the conclusion relation for the full N steps

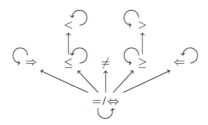

Fig. 11. Graphical representation of the transitivity rules for poC operators: For any two operators R and S such that S is reachable from R, add two rules: $R \circ S \subseteq S$ and $S \circ R \subseteq S$

It gets more interesting with lines of type **bool**, because in Dafny some boolean operators, in particular implication, have short-circuiting (aka conditional) semantics, which is reflected in their well-formedness conditions:

$$wf[P \Rightarrow Q] \equiv wf[P] \wedge (P \Rightarrow wf[Q])$$

This allows one to write expressions like P(x) $\Longrightarrow$ Q(f(x)), where P is the precondition of function f.

It seems natural that implications should have the same effect in calculations. For example, the following calculation should be considered well-formed:

```
calc {
  P(x);
⟹ { /* Hint with a precondition P(x) */ }
  Q(f(x));
⟺
  R(f(x));
}
```

```
// Step "line⟨i⟩ ⟹ line⟨i+1⟩"      // Step "line⟨i⟩ S⟨i⟩ line⟨i+1⟩"
assume wf[line⟨i⟩];                assume wf[line⟨i⟩];
assume line⟨i⟩;                    Hint⟨i⟩
Hint⟨i⟩                            assert wf[line⟨i+1⟩];
assert wf[line⟨i+1⟩];              assert line⟨i⟩ S⟨i⟩ line⟨i+1⟩;
assert line⟨i+1⟩;                  assume false;
assume false;
```

Fig. 12. Encoding of an implication-step (left) and any other step (right) that supports short-circuiting semantics. In addition, the **assert** wf[line0]; is performed to check the well-formedness of line0.

The translation as defined so far will not accept this example. Moreover, the condition that each line be well-formed in the enclosing context is too strong in this case. Instead, we propose the following definition: a calculation is well-formed if each of its intermediate conclusions is well-formed.

The final version of our encoding, which allows the example to go through, is given in Fig. 12. It differentiates between $\Longrightarrow$[3] and other step operators, which are not short-circuiting in Dafny. We can show that this encoding implements our definition of well-formed calculations. For example, in a calculation with only implication steps, the intermediate conclusion is $wf[line_0] \wedge (wf[line_0] \wedge line_0 \Rightarrow wf[line_i] \wedge line_i)$, which is well-formed according to Dafny rules.

5 Experiments and Discussion

5.1 Case Studies

To confirm the usefulness of poC, we tried it on five examples from various domains[4]:

- Identity, SingleFixpoint and KnasterTarski are mathematical theorems. The former two state properties of functions over natural numbers and the combination of function iteration and fixpoints, respectively; the latter is one part of the Knaster-Tarski fixpoint theorem.
- List is a set of properties of inductively defined lists, such as ReverseTwice and Extensionality discussed above. This case study is representative of reasoning about functional programs.
- MajorityVote is an algorithm, due to Boyer and Moore, that finds the majority choice among a sequence of votes. This example is representative of verifying imperative programs.

In total, our case studies comprise about 650 lines of Dafny.

To evaluate the benefits of calculations, we developed a second version of each example, where all proofs are at the same level of detail, but using the traditional approach

---

[3] $\Longleftarrow$ Is handled by reversing the calculation and replacing it with $\Longrightarrow$.

[4] The examples are available online as http://se.inf.ethz.ch/people/polikarpova/poc/

	Methods	Traditional		Calculational		
		Tokens	Time(s)	Calculations	Tokens	Time(s)
Identity	5	527	2.0	4	460	2.0
SingleFixpoint	3	444	2.0	4	396	2.0
KnasterTarski	1	472	13.1	2	486	4.9
List	14	2445	27.4	15	1967	3.0
MajorityVote	4	1003	2.1	5	931	2.1
Total	27	4891	46.6	30	4240	14.0

Fig. 13. Case studies and results

```
Lemma rev_involutive : forall l:list A, rev (rev l) = l.
  Proof.
    induction l as [| a l IHl].
    simpl; auto.

    simpl.
    rewrite (rev_unit (rev l) a).
    rewrite IHl; auto.
  Qed.
```

Fig. 14. Proof that list reversal is an involution written as a Coq tactic script. The example is taken from the standard library.

with **assert** statements instead of calculations, along the lines of Fig. 5. Fig. 13 gives the comparison between the two versions of each example in terms of verbosity (expressed as the number of code tokens) and verification times (measured on a 2.7GHz i7 CPU, using a single core). We observe that calculations provide more concise proofs, reducing the number of tokens by around 10% on average. The effect of the more efficient encoding on verification times does not show consistently, but it is significant in a few larger proofs.

5.2   Comparison with Other Proof Notations

In this section, we provide a detailed comparison of poC with the proof formats used in two prominent interactive proof assistants: Coq and Isabelle/HOL. Other tools that support calculational proofs are briefly reviewed in related work (Sec. 6).

Proof languages are commonly divided into *procedural* (or imperative) and *declarative* (see *e.g.* [14]). In procedural languages, the proof—also called a *tactic script*—consists of commands, which make the assistant modify the proof state. Declarative languages, which aim at human-readable proofs, are instead oriented toward writing down the intermediate proof states, and letting the tool figure out the commands automatically whenever possible. In the following, we show the same lemma proven first in a procedural, and then in a declarative (more precisely, calculational) style.

Consider our motivational example from Sec. 2.2—list reversal is an involution—written as a Coq tactic script in Fig. 14. The commands induction, simpl, auto, and

```
lemma rev_rev_ident: "rev (rev xs) = xs"
proof (induct xs)
   show "rev (rev []) = []" by simp
next
  fix x xs
  assume IH: "rev (rev xs) = xs"
  show "rev (rev (x # xs)) = x # xs"
  proof -
    have "rev (rev (x # xs)) = rev (rev xs @ [x])" by simp
    also have "... = rev [x] @ rev (rev xs)" by (rule rev_append)
    also have "... = rev [x] @ xs" by (simp, rule IH)
    also have "... = [x] @ xs" by simp
    also have "... = x # xs" by simp
    finally show ?thesis .
  qed
qed
```

Fig. 15. Proof that list reversal is an involution written in Isar in a calculational style. In Isabelle, Cons is written as # and append as @.

rewrite tell the proof assistant which tactics to apply, while rev_unit refers to a lemma (a special case of our ReverseAppendDistrib where one of the arguments is a singleton list). This script does not tell much to a non-expert user, except that it is a proof by induction and that it makes use of the lemma rev_unit.

In the Isabelle standard library, the same lemma looks as follows:

```
lemma rev_rev_ident [simp]: "rev (rev xs) = xs"
by (induct xs) auto
```

The perceived full automation is somewhat misleading: the secret is that all required auxiliary lemmas (in particular the counterpart of ReverseAppendDistrib) have been stated in the same theory and equipped with the [simp] attribute, which instructs the simplifier to automatically apply them as rules. In general, users have to be careful with this attribute, because some combinations of rewrite rules might cause the simplifier to go into an infinite loop. Moreover, this approach, though very concise, damages readability even more: the above script does not even contain the information about the required lemmas.

Now let us turn to declarative proofs. Both Isabelle and Coq have a built-in declarative language. The former one is called Isar ("Intelligible semi-automated reasoning") [35] and is well-established in the Isabelle community. The latter, named simply the Mathematical Proof Language [14], is more recent and not widely used. Both of them support some form of calculations.

Fig. 15 shows a proof of the same lemma in Isar, written in a calculational style. Isar supports calculations through a set of shortcuts [7]: ... refers to the right-hand side of the most recently stated fact; **also** applies transitivity rules to the current intermediate conclusion and the new step to obtain the new conclusion; **finally** is like **also**, expect that it instructs the prover to use the new conclusion in proving what follows (in this case ?thesis, which refers to the goal of the enclosing **proof** block).

The **by** clauses play the role of hints: they tell the prover which tactics and facts to use in establishing the step. For this example, we removed the magic [simp] attributes from the supporting lemmas, so we have to specify the lemma rev_append explicitly at the second step. We can use the lemma-rule to justify this calculation step because the step matches its statement *exactly*; otherwise, we would need additional, more sophisticated tactics to massage the formula into the right shape first (like in the third step, which appeals to the induction hypothesis).

The tactics used in this example are quite simple. Isabelle users also have more powerful tactics, such as auto or metaprover Sledgehammer [10], at their disposal, so in practice Isar proofs can be written without excessive detail. However, using this powerful automation still requires deep understanding of how the tool works. In particular, the **by** clauses include elements of the procedural proof language, such as the names of tactics[5], while poC hints are stated entirely in the language of the problem domain.

The support for calculations in Isar is very flexible: the step relations are not hard-coded, and are easily customizable through the addition of new transitivity rules. This comes at a price that sometimes Isabelle does not know which transitivity rule to apply, and you have to specify this explicitly.

Finally, we believe that the possibility to introduce custom syntax, such as infix operators for list functions above, increases proof readability and it would be nice to have it in Dafny as well.

In conclusion, Isar and Dafny in general (and their respective support for calculations in particular) have different target audiences: Isar is focused on flexibility and maximum control, oriented towards experts with a strong background in formal methods, while Dafny takes the "automation by default" approach, which provides for a lower entrance barrier.

Calculational proofs in Coq's declarative language are not as flexible, in particular equality is the only supported step relation. Fig. 16 shows our running example. This notation is entirely declarative (and thus closer to poC): note that there is no mention of tactics inside the calculation and the trivial steps do not require justification. The downside is that the default justification tactic, though sufficient for this example, does not provide the same level of automation as SMT solvers.

5.3   Irrelevant Hints and Bogus Steps

One benefit of rule-based proof assistants, like Isabelle, is their ability to determine if the justification of a proof step does not make sense: they will either fail to apply a rule or the rule application will fail to reach the desired proof state.

This is not always the case in poC: one can provide hints that do not justify the step, as well as construct *bogus* steps, which just happen to be true by chance. Although these issues do not pose any threat to soundness, they are detrimental to readability, and thus important nevertheless. We have not implemented any solution to this problem, but we discuss some possibilities in this section.

---

[5] Even what looks like punctuation (dash and dot) actually denotes tactics!

```
Lemma rev_involutive {A: Type} (l:list A) : rev (rev l) = l.
proof.
  per induction on l.
    suppose it is nil.
      thus thesis.
    suppose it is (x :: xs) and IH:thesis for xs.
      have (rev (rev (x :: xs)) = rev (rev xs ++ [x])).
                          ~= (rev [x] ++ rev (rev xs))
                            by (rev_unit (rev xs) x).
                          ~= (rev [x] ++ xs)
                            by (IH).
                          ~= ([x] ++ xs).
                    thus ~= (x :: xs).
  end induction.
end proof.
Qed.
```

Fig. 16. Proof that list reversal is an involution written in Coq's Mathematical Proof Language in a calculational style. In Coq, Cons is written as :: and append as ++.

To check if a hint is required to justify a calculation step, the tool might try to remove it and check if the program still verifies (within the given timeout). Unfortunately, this does not cover the cases when Dafny can do without the hint, but it would still be useful for a human reader: for example, since Dafny has an automatic induction heuristic, invoking the induction hypothesis will be considered irrelevant most of the time. Perhaps such a mode would be still useful; this remains a part of future work.

One might hope that most irrelevant hints are filtered out just because they are either not applicable in the current context (*i.e.* their precondition does not hold) or they fail to make the step go through. This highlights another benefit of stating the assumptions a lemma makes in its precondition, as opposed to adding them as antecedents to the postcondition: in the latter case, a useless lemma would simply be ignored.

Bogus steps are most likely to occur in calculations with boolean lines, where the truth value of some or all the lines is fixed[6]. Here is an example inspired by an actual error in an old version of one of our case studies. Recall the Monotonicity lemma from Fig. 7, whose postcondition is an implication $a \leq b \implies f(a) \leq f(b)$. When trying to prove this postcondition with a calculation, for the case of $a < b$, one might write:

```
if a < b {
  calc {
    a ≤ b;
    f(a) ≤ f(a + 1);
    ...
    ⟹ f(a) ≤ f(b);
  }
}
```

---

[6] In other cases, the probability that the values of the lines are related by pure chance is low.

The first step of this calculation looks suspicious to say the least, but it holds because a $\leq$ b follows from the case split, and f(a) $\leq$ f(a + 1) is implied by the method's precondition, thus the step reduces to **true** $\Longleftrightarrow$ **true**. This calculation is logically valid, but it does not serve to explain the proof to a human reader, if anything, it only confuses them.

In this example, one can avoid the risk of bogus lines by choosing a weaker context (see the proof in Fig. 7). In general, it is a useful methodological rule to always perform a calculation in the weakest context required for it to go through.

Unfortunately, it is not always possible to avoid lines with fixed truth values: it is a common pattern to establish validity of a boolean formula by transforming it into the literal **true** by a chain of $\Longleftrightarrow$ or $\Longleftarrow$. Such calculations are dangerous: as soon as the formula is simple enough for Dafny to prove it, all subsequent steps (which might still be useful for a human reader) are potentially bogus. One approach could be to verify such steps out of (some parts of) their context, so that the validity of the lines cannot be established anymore, while the relation between the lines is still verifiable.

6   Related Work

It is hard to say who invented calculational proofs, but Dijkstra (who credits W. H. J. Feijen) definitely played an important role in popularizing them [16].

There are numerous dialects and extensions of this proof format. Back, Grundy and von Wright propose nested calculations [2], combining "the readability of calculational proof with the structuring facilities of natural deduction". They show how common proof paradigms (such as proof by contradiction, case split, induction) can be expressed using nested calculations, with the ultimate goal to make it possible to write a large proof as a single calculation, without the need to "escape" into natural language. A follow-up to this work is structured derivations [3]. Window inference [28,34] is a related paradigm focusing on managing context during the transformation of subterms. As we showed in Sec. 3.2, poC naturally supports such structuring paradigms.

Attempts to mechanize calculational proofs go back to the Mizar system developed in the early 1990s [29], which supports iterated equality reasoning. There exists a number of implementations of window inference within various proof systems (*e.g.* [17]). The capabilities of those tools are constrained (for example, Mizar only supports equalities), and the level of automation is quite low.

The structured proof language Isar for the Isabelle proof assistant provides a very general support for calculations [7]. However, it is not purely declarative, and one still has to explicitly issue commands that modify the proof state.

At the other end of the spectrum is Math∫pad [5], where one can write proofs in common mathematical notation, not restricted to a particular formal language. It is a document preparation system oriented towards calculational construction of programs. Verhoeven and Backhouse [33] present an attempt to combine it with PVS in order to machine-check the proofs, however, a fully automatic translation of the informal components of the notation is, of course, not possible. Other early systems for writing and manipulating calculations in a similar way are Chisholm's editor [11] and Proxac [31].

"Programs as proofs" is a paradigm commonly used in auto-active program verifiers (see *e.g.* [19]), which allows the reuse of common programming language constructs familiar to programmers for structuring proofs. Pushing auto-active verification into areas previously exclusive to interactive proof assistants is currently an active research topic, with recent advances in automatic induction [23] and even co-induction.

Programs can be derived using an extension of the calculational format [32]. The extension essentially consists in allowing hints to include state transformations, *i.e.*, side effects. This would be interesting to explore in Dafny, since Dafny already deals with imperative programs.

7   Conclusions and Future Work

We have presented a tool for verifying calculational proofs, which stands out due to the combination of a high degree of automation and a programmer-friendly proof language oriented towards to the problem domain rather than the mechanics of the prover.

We believe that poC is not just a useful feature in a program verifier, but also an important step towards a full-fledged auto-active proof assistant. We envision such a tool to be very close to Dafny; in particular, reusing the programs-as-proofs paradigm, but perhaps putting more emphasis on proof concepts rather than on, say, method declarations. Towards this goal, we would need to extend Dafny with support for more general mathematical constructs, such as infinite sets. In order to provide soundness guarantees for an SMT-based proof assistant, a promising approach is generating proof certificates [1] that can be checked by a system with a small trusted core, such as Coq. This seems to be a fertile opportunity for combining the automation found in poC with the rigor inherent in Coq.

Acknowledgments. We thank Carlo A. Furia, Ioannis T. Kassios, and Scott West for comments on a draft of this paper, as well as Valentin Wüstholz for suggesting one of our case studies.

References

1. Armand, M., Faure, G., Grégoire, B., Keller, C., Théry, L., Werner, B.: A modular integration of SAT/SMT solvers to Coq through proof witnesses. In: Jouannaud, J.-P., Shao, Z. (eds.) CPP 2011. LNCS, vol. 7086, pp. 135–150. Springer, Heidelberg (2011)
2. Back, R., Grundy, J., von Wright, J.: Structured calculational proof. Formal Aspects of Computing 9(5-6), 469–483 (1997)
3. Back, R.-J.: Structured derivations: a unified proof style for teaching mathematics. Formal Aspects of Computing 22(5), 629–661 (2010)
4. Backhouse, R.: Special issue on the calculational method. Information Processing Letters 53(3), 121–172 (1995)
5. Backhouse, R., Verhoeven, R., Weber, O.: Mathʃpad: A system for on-line preparation of mathematical documents. Software — Concepts and Tools 18(2), 80 (1997)
6. Barnett, M., Chang, B.-Y.E., DeLine, R., Jacobs, B., Leino, K.R.M.: Boogie: A modular reusable verifier for object-oriented programs. In: de Boer, F.S., Bonsangue, M.M., Graf, S., de Roever, W.-P. (eds.) FMCO 2005. LNCS, vol. 4111, pp. 364–387. Springer, Heidelberg (2006)

7. Bauer, G., Wenzel, M.T.: Calculational reasoning revisited: an Isabelle/Isar experience. In: Boulton, R.J., Jackson, P.B. (eds.) TPHOLs 2001. LNCS, vol. 2152, pp. 75–90. Springer, Heidelberg (2001)

8. Bertot, Y., Castéran, P.: Interactive Theorem Proving and Program Development — Coq'Art: The Calculus of Inductive Constructions. Springer (2004)

9. Bobot, F., Filliâtre, J.-C., Marché, C., Paskevich, A.: Why3: Shepherd your herd of provers. In: BOOGIE 2011: Workshop on Intermediate Verification Languages, pp. 53–64 (2011)

10. Böhme, S., Nipkow, T.: Sledgehammer: Judgement day. In: Giesl, J., Hähnle, R. (eds.) IJCAR 2010. LNCS, vol. 6173, pp. 107–121. Springer, Heidelberg (2010)

11. Chisholm, P.: Calculation by computer. In: Third International Workshop on Software Engineering and its Applications, Toulouse, France, pp. 713–728 (December 1990)

12. Claessen, K., Johansson, M., Rosén, D., Smallbone, N.: Automating inductive proofs using theory exploration. In: Bonacina, M.P. (ed.) CADE 2013. LNCS, vol. 7898, pp. 392–406. Springer, Heidelberg (2013)

13. Cohen, E., Dahlweid, M., Hillebrand, M.A., Leinenbach, D., Moskal, M., Santen, T., Schulte, W., Tobies, S.: VCC: A practical system for verifying concurrent C. In: Berghofer, S., Nipkow, T., Urban, C., Wenzel, M. (eds.) TPHOLs 2009. LNCS, vol. 5674, pp. 23–42. Springer, Heidelberg (2009)

14. Corbineau, P.: A declarative language for the Coq proof assistant. In: Miculan, M., Scagnetto, I., Honsell, F. (eds.) TYPES 2007. LNCS, vol. 4941, pp. 69–84. Springer, Heidelberg (2008)

15. Dijkstra, E.W.: EWD1300: The notational conventions I adopted, and why. Formal Asp. Comput. 14(2), 99–107 (2002)

16. Dijkstra, E.W., Scholten, C.S.: Predicate calculus and program semantics. Texts and monographs in computer science. Springer (1990)

17. Grundy, J.: Transformational hierarchical reasoning. Comput. J. 39(4), 291–302 (1996)

18. Jacobs, B., Piessens, F.: The VeriFast program verifier. Technical Report CW-520, Department of Computer Science, Katholieke Universiteit Leuven (2008)

19. Jacobs, B., Smans, J., Piessens, F.: VeriFast: Imperative programs as proofs. In: VS-Tools workshop at VSTTE 2010 (2010)

20. Kaufmann, M., Manolios, P., Moore, J.S.: Computer-Aided Reasoning: An Approach. Kluwer Academic Publishers (2000)

21. Koenig, J., Leino, K.R.M.: Getting started with Dafny: A guide. In: Software Safety and Security: Tools for Analysis and Verification, pp. 152–181. IOS Press (2012)

22. Leino, K.R.M.: Dafny: An automatic program verifier for functional correctness. In: Clarke, E.M., Voronkov, A. (eds.) LPAR-16 2010. LNCS, vol. 6355, pp. 348–370. Springer, Heidelberg (2010)

23. Leino, K.R.M.: Automating induction with an SMT solver. In: Kuncak, V., Rybalchenko, A. (eds.) VMCAI 2012. LNCS, vol. 7148, pp. 315–331. Springer, Heidelberg (2012)

24. Leino, K.R.M., Moskal, M.: Usable auto-active verification. In: Ball, T., Zuck, L., Shankar, N. (eds.) Usable Verification Workshop (2010), http://fm.csl.sri.com/UV10/

25. Manolios, P., Moore, J.S.: On the desirability of mechanizing calculational proofs. Inf. Process. Lett. 77(2-4), 173–179 (2001)

26. Nipkow, T.: Programming and Proving in Isabelle/HOL (2012), http://isabelle.informatik.tu-muenchen.de/

27. Owre, S., Rushby, J.M., Shankar, N.: PVS: A prototype verification system. In: Kapur, D. (ed.) CADE 1992. LNCS, vol. 607, pp. 748–752. Springer, Heidelberg (1992)

28. Robinson, P.J., Staples, J.: Formalizing a hierarchical structure of practical mathematical reasoning. J. Log. Comput. 3(1), 47–61 (1993)

29. Rudnicki, P.: An overview of the MIZAR project. In: University of Technology, Bastad, pp. 311–332 (1992)

30. Sonnex, W., Drossopoulou, S., Eisenbach, S.: Zeno: An automated prover for properties of recursive data structures. In: Flanagan, C., König, B. (eds.) TACAS 2012. LNCS, vol. 7214, pp. 407–421. Springer, Heidelberg (2012)
31. van de Snepscheut, J.L.A.: Proxac: an editor for program transformation. Technical Report CS-TR-93-33, Caltech (1993)
32. van Gasteren, A.J.M., Bijlsma, A.: An extension of the program derivation format. In: PRO-COMET 1998, pp. 167–185. IFIP Conference Proceedings (1998)
33. Verhoeven, R., Backhouse, R.: Interfacing program construction and verification. In: World Congress on Formal Methods, pp. 1128–1146 (1999)
34. von Wright, J.: Extending window inference. In: Grundy, J., Newey, M. (eds.) TPHOLs 1998. LNCS, vol. 1479, pp. 17–32. Springer, Heidelberg (1998)
35. Wenzel, M.: Isabelle/Isar — a versatile environment for human-readable formal proof documents. PhD thesis, Institut für Informatik, Technische Universität München (2002)

Preserving User Proofs
across Specification Changes[*]

François Bobot[3], Jean-Christophe Filliâtre[1,2], Claude Marché[2,1],
Guillaume Melquiond[2,1], and Andrei Paskevich[1,2]

[1] Lab. de Recherche en Informatique, Univ. Paris-Sud, CNRS, Orsay, F-91405
[2] INRIA Saclay – Île-de-France, Orsay, F-91893
[3] CEA, LIST, Software Reliability Laboratory, PC 174, 91191 Gif-sur-Yvette France

Abstract. In the context of deductive program verification, both the specification and the code evolve as the verification process carries on. For instance, a loop invariant gets strengthened when additional properties are added to the specification. This causes all the related proof obligations to change; thus previous user verifications become invalid. Yet it is often the case that most of previous proof attempts (goal transformations, calls to interactive or automated provers) are still directly applicable or are easy to adjust. In this paper, we describe a technique to maintain a proof session against modification of verification conditions. This technique is implemented in the Why3 platform. It was successfully used in developing more than a hundred verified programs and in keeping them up to date along the evolution of Why3 and its standard library. It also helps out with changes in the environment, *e.g.* prover upgrades.

1 Introduction

The work presented in this paper arose as a part of ongoing development and use of the Why3 system. Though we believe that our methods are applicable and useful in diverse settings of automated deduction, it would be most natural to introduce them in the context of our own project.

Why3 is a platform for deductive program verification. It provides a rich language, called WhyML, to write programs [9] and their logical specifications [4,8], and it relies on external theorem provers, automated and interactive, to discharge verification conditions. Why3 is based on first-order logic with rank-1 polymorphic types, algebraic data types, inductive predicates, and several other extensions. When a proof obligation is dispatched to a prover that does not support some language features, Why3 applies a series of encoding transformations in order to eliminate, for example, pattern matching or polymorphic types [5]. Other transformations, such as goal splitting or insertion of an induction hypothesis, can be manually invoked by a user upon individual subgoals.

---

[*] This work is partly supported by the Bware (ANR-12-INSE-0010, http://bware.lri.fr/) project of the French national research organization (ANR), and the Hi-lite project (http://www.open-do.org/projects/hi-lite/) of the System@tic ICT cluster of Paris-Région Île-de-France.

E. Cohen and A. Rybalchenko (Eds.): VSTTE 2013, LNCS 8164, pp. 191–201, 2014.

To keep track of verification progress and to ensure that a once attained proof can be rechecked later, Why3 records applied transformations and proof attempts (calls to interactive and automated theorem provers). Maintaining this record against changes in proof obligations (that may ensue from changes in specification, program, or VC generation algorithm) is a difficult task, which, fortunately, can be automated to a certain degree. This paper deals with mechanisms of such automation.

Let us consider a typical user workflow in Why3. The user, an enlightened programmer named Alice, desires to formally verify an intricate algorithm. She starts by writing down the program code, fixes one or two simple mistakes (readily spotted by static typing), and, before annotating the program with any pre- or postconditions, runs the interactive verifier to perform the safety checks against out-of-bounds array accesses, arithmetic overflows, division by zero, etc. Why3 presents the whole verification condition for a given function as a single goal, and thus the first step is to split it down to a number of simple proof obligations and then to launch the provers, say, Alt-Ergo [3], CVC4 [1], or Z3 [7] on each of them. Let each safety condition be satisfied, except for one, which requires an integer parameter to be positive. Alice writes a suitable precondition, effectively putting the whole VC under an implication. It is now the verifier's job to detect that the once proved goals changed their shape and have to be reproved. Besides, since Alice's algorithm is recursive, a new proof obligation appears at each recursive call.

Alice continues to work on the specification; she adds the desired functional properties and regularly runs the verifier. The program's VC grows and, in addition to the first split, other interactive interventions are required: more splits, an occasional definition expansion, a call to an SMT solver with ten times the default time limit, a call to an interactive proof assistant to prove an auxiliary lemma by triple induction. The verified program now carries a complex proof script, which we call a *session*: a tree of goal transformations and a history of individual proof attempts at the leaves of that tree.

Almost every modification in the code or in the specification changes (even if slightly) almost every verification condition, requiring the proofs to be redone. Keeping the automated provers running on almost the same goals is only part of the bother. What could quickly make the verification process unmanageable is reconstructing, manually and every time, the proof session: finding those particular subgoals that required an increased time limit, a definition expansion, a Coq proof. Subgoals do not have persistent names, they may appear and vanish, and their respective order may change. Thus the only way to rebuild a proof is to look for similarities between the new goals and the old ones in order to find out where to re-apply the transformations and to re-launch the provers. This is a task where computer assistance would be highly appreciated.

Meanwhile, Alice finishes her program and puts it—code, specification, and proof—on her web page, so that it can be read and rechecked by other enlightened programmers. Three weeks later, a new version of an SMT solver used in the session is released, and the session file must be updated. Five weeks later, a new release of Why3 comes out: it features an improved VC generator as well as numerous additions and corrections in the standard library. The latter affects the premises of proof obligations, the former, conclusions, so that the proof session has to be updated again.

Just like Alice, we prefer to be busy developing and proving new programs. Therefore, we have devised and implemented in Why3 a set of algorithms that maintain proof sessions, keep them up to date across prover upgrades and, most importantly, across changes in verification conditions. In the best course of events, Why3 is able to rebuild the proof session fully automatically, leaving to the user just the new subgoals (for which no previous proof attempts were made) or the ones that cannot be reproved without user intervention (typically when a Coq proof script requires modifications). These algorithms are the subject of the current paper.

In Section 2, we give a formal description of a Why3 proof session. Section 3 contains the algorithm of goal pairing that is used to rebuild proof sessions. In Section 4, we discuss additional measures to maintain proof scripts for interactive proof assistants like Coq or PVS. In Section 5, we explain how to configure and use Why3 in an environment of multiple automated and interactive provers.

2   Proof Sessions: Static Model

Transformations and proof attempts applied to proof obligations are stored in a tree-like structure, called *proof session*. We describe it in this section.

Proof Attempts. A prover is characterized by a name, a version number, and a string field that is used to discriminate different ways to call the same prover.

$$prover ::= \langle name, version, options \rangle$$

A proof attempt describes a call to an external prover.

$$proof\_attempt ::= \langle prover, timelimit, memlimit, result \rangle$$
$$result ::= \langle time, status \rangle$$
$$status ::= \texttt{valid} \mid \texttt{invalid} \mid \texttt{unknown} \mid$$
$$\texttt{timeout} \mid \texttt{outofmemory} \mid \texttt{failure}$$

Information is the prover, the maximal amount of CPU time and memory given to the prover, and the result of that call. A result is a pair: the time of the execution of the external process, and the prover outcome (*status*). Such a status is obtained by matching the prover output using regular expressions or by looking at its exit code. A status has six possible values: one for a successful proof attempt (`valid`), and five unsuccessful ones. Status `invalid` means that the prover declared the goal to be invalid; `unknown` means an inconclusive outcome (neither `valid` nor `invalid`) before the time limit is reached; `timeout` (resp. `outofmemory`) means the prover had been stopped because it exhausted the given resources; and `failure` means any other reason for an unsuccessful execution. This is similar to the SZS *no-success* ontology [14].

Proofs and Transformations. The entities for proof tasks (*proof_task*) and transformations (*transf*) have the following structure:

$$proof\_task ::= \langle name, expl, goal, proof\_attempt*, transf*, verified \rangle$$
$$transf ::= \langle name, proof\_task*, verified \rangle$$
$$verified ::= \texttt{true} \mid \texttt{false}$$

A proof task is characterized by a name, an explanation (a text describing its origin *e.g.* "loop invariant preservation"), and a goal. A proof task contains a collection of proof attempts, as well as a collection of transformations. There is no contradiction in having a proof task with both proof attempts and transformations. A transformation has a name (as registered in Why3 kernel) and a collection of sub-tasks. A proof task has status *verified* if and only if there is at least one proof attempt with status `valid` or one transformation with status *verified*. A transformation has status *verified* if and only if all its sub-tasks have status *verified*.

Theories, Files, and Sessions. A theory has a name and a collection of proof tasks. A file has a pathname (relative to the session file) and a collection of theories. A proof session is a set of files:

$$theory ::= \langle name, proof\_task*, verified \rangle$$
$$file ::= \langle pathname, theory*, verified \rangle$$
$$proof\_session ::= file*$$

A theory has status *verified* if and only if all its tasks are verified. A file has status *verified* if and only if all its theories are verified.

Example. In Fig. 1, we show an example of a simple session. It consists of one file, `f_puzzle.why`, which contains one theory, `Puzzle`. This theory, whose WhyML source is shown in the bottom right corner, introduces an uninterpreted function symbol f and two axioms:

```
function f int: int
axiom H1: forall n: int. 0 <= n → 0 <= f n
axiom H2: forall n: int. 0 <= n → f (f n) < f (n+1)
```

Our final goal consists in revealing that f is the identity on natural numbers:

```
goal G: forall n: int. 0 <= n → f n = n
```

To that purpose, we use four simple lemmas and two instances of the induction scheme on natural numbers, provided by the Why3 standard library. We also apply a transformation called `split_goal_wp` to split a conjunction into two separate subgoals (see lemma L3 on Fig. 1). Each subgoal is successfully verified due to the combined effort of three automated provers.

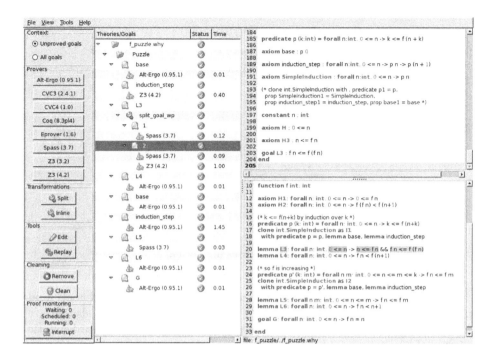

Fig. 1. An example of Why3 session

3 Session Updates

The problem we address in this section is to update a proof session when the set of goals changes. There are many possible reasons for such a change: a user modification of a goal statement, a modification of a goal context (*e.g.* the introduction of additional hypotheses), a modification of a program and/or its specifications resulting in a different VC, etc. Wherever the change comes from, the problem boils down to matching an old proof session (typically stored on disk during a previous verification process) with a new collection of files, theories, and goals. Such a matching is performed on a file and theory-basis, where files and theories are simply identified by names.[1]

This matching process is performed recursively over the tree structure of a session. Given the collection of (old) proof tasks and a collection of new goals, we match each new goal g either to an old task t or to a freshly created task with no proof attempt and no transformation. In the former case, each transformation Tr of the old task t is applied to the new goal g, resulting into a collection of new goals. Then we proceed recursively, matching these new goals with the sub-tasks of Tr.

---

[1] We could provide refactoring tools to rename files and/or theories, but this is not what is discussed in this paper.

$$\overline{n} = {}'\mathtt{c}' + n$$
$$\overline{x} = {}'\mathtt{v}' + unique(x) \quad \text{if } x \text{ is a local variable}$$
$$= {}'\mathtt{v}' + x \quad \text{otherwise}$$
$$\overline{\mathtt{true}} = {}'\mathtt{t}'$$
$$\overline{\mathtt{false}} = {}'\mathtt{f}'$$
$$\overline{f(t_1, \ldots, t_n)} = {}'\mathtt{a}' + f + \overline{t_1} + \ldots + \overline{t_n}$$
$$\overline{\forall x : \tau . t} = \overline{t} + {}'\mathtt{F}'$$
$$\overline{t_1 \Rightarrow t_2} = \overline{t_2} + {}'\mathtt{I}' + \overline{t_1}$$
$$\overline{\neg\, t} = {}'\mathtt{N}' + \overline{t}$$
$$\overline{\mathtt{let}\ x = t_1\ \mathtt{in}\ t_2} = \overline{t_2} + {}'\mathtt{L}' + \overline{t_1}$$
$$\overline{\mathtt{if}\ t_1\ \mathtt{then}\ t_2\ \mathtt{else}\ t_3} = {}'\mathtt{i}' + \overline{t_3} + \overline{t_2} + \overline{t_1}$$

Fig. 2. Shapes of terms and formulas

We are now left with the sub-problem of pairing a collection of old goals (and their associated tasks) and a collection of new goals. We first pair goals that are exactly the same.[2] In a second step, we pair remaining goals using a heuristic measure of similarity based on a notion of goal *shape*.

3.1 Goal Shape

The shape of a goal is a character string. The similarity between two goals is defined as the length of the common prefix of their shapes. To match our intuition of logical similarity, we adopt the following principles for computing shapes:

- shapes should take explanations into account, so that only goals with same explanations are paired;
- shapes are invariant by renaming of bound variables;
- conclusion is more important than hypotheses, *e.g.* the shape of an implication $A \Rightarrow B$ is built from the shape of B first, and then the shape of A.

Declarations, definitions, and axioms are disregarded when computing shapes. There are two reasons: first, it keeps shapes reasonably small; second, it is unlikely that two goals differ only in their contexts. The shape of a term or formula t, written $\overline{t}$, is recursively defined over the structure of t, as given in Fig. 2. The shape computation is not injective: two formulas may have the same shape. It is not an issue for us, as we only use shapes as an heuristic for pairing.

Let us consider the goal

```
forall x: int. f x = x
```

Its shape is the string a=afVOVOF. If we modify it into the following goal

---

[2] Technically, since the old goal is not stored on disk, we detect identical goals using MD5 checksums.

```
forall n: int. 0 <= n → f n = n
```

then its shape becomes the string `a=afVOVOIa<=cOVOF`. These two shapes share a common prefix of length 8, that is `a=afVOVO`. As illustrated on this example, bound variables are mapped to unique integers, numbered from zero for a given goal.

3.2   Matching Algorithm

We are given a collection of N "old" shapes and a collection of M "new" shapes. This section describes an algorithm that tries to map each new shape to an old one. We note $lcp(u, v)$ the length of the longest common prefix of strings u and v, *i.e.* the largest k such that $u_i = v_i$ for all $0 \leq i < k$. We choose the following greedy algorithm, which repeatedly picks up the pair that maximizes the length of the common prefix.

> $new \leftarrow$ new shapes
> $old \leftarrow$ old shapes
> **while** $new \neq \emptyset$ **and** $old \neq \emptyset$
>   find o in old and n in new such that $lcp(o, n)$ is maximal
>   pair o and n
> $old \leftarrow old - \{o\}$
> $new \leftarrow new - \{n\}$

Notice that goal o is removed from set old as soon as it is paired with a new goal. We could have chosen to keep it, in order to pair it later with another new goal. However, the purpose of our algorithm is to reassign former successful proofs to new goals, and not to discover new proofs.

Given as such, this algorithm is inefficient. Let shapes have maximal length L. Assuming $N = M$, the algorithm has complexity $O(LN^3)$, since finding the pair that maximizes lcp is $O(LN^2)$. One can turn this into a more efficient algorithm, by making a list of all shapes (be they old or new) and then sorting it in lexicographic order. In that case, the pair (o, n) that maximizes $lcp(o, n)$ is necessarily composed of two shapes n and o that are consecutive in the list. So finding the pair becomes linear and the overall complexity is now $O(LN^2)$. It is even possible to reduce this complexity using a priority queue containing all pairs (o, n) of consecutive shapes (either old/new or new/old), ordered according to $lcp(o, n)$. As long as the priority queue is not empty, we extract its maximal element (o, n), we pair the corresponding shapes whenever both o and n are not yet already paired to another shape, and we (possibly) insert a new pair in the priority queue. The cost of sorting is $O(LN \log N)$ and, assuming a priority queue with logarithmic insertion and extraction, the cost of repeated extractions and insertions is also $O(N(L+\log N))$ (there is at most one insertion for each extraction, and thus the priority queue never contains more than $2N - 1$ elements). Whenever $N \neq M$, the cost of sorting is dominating and thus we have a total cost $O(L(N + M) \log(N + M))$.

A property of the algorithm above is that, whenever there is at least as many new shapes as old ones, each old shape gets paired with a new one. Said otherwise, no former proof task is lost. When there are less new shapes, however, some shapes cannot be paired and, subsequently, former proof tasks are lost.[3]

4   Script Updates for Interactive Provers

Updating sessions is sufficient for handling transformations and calls to automated provers, since their inputs are just Why3 goals which are parts of sessions. For interactive proof assistants, the situation is slightly different. Indeed, an interactive proof script is the mix of a skeleton generated from a goal and an actual proof written by the user. Currently, Why3 supports two proof assistants: Coq and PVS. Yet the ideas presented in this section apply to any interactive proof assistant that supports a textual input.

In a nutshell, Why3 outputs a theorem statement, together with definitions and axioms corresponding to the Why3 context for that goal. Then the user writes commands for guiding the proof assistant towards a proof of that statement. The user may introduce auxiliary lemmas and definitions for proving the main theorem.

In Coq, proof commands are part of the same file as the definitions and theorem statements, while in PVS, they are usually stored in a separate file. Still, in both cases, user statements and Why3-generated statements are intermingled in the proof script. When a session is updated, the context and the statement of the main theorem might change, so the proof script needs to be regenerated. There are two main issues though, which are not present for automated provers. First, it is important not to lose any part of the script the user might have painstakingly written. Second, while preserving user parts, it is important to discard parts previously generated by Why3, since they are now obsolete.

As far as Why3 is concerned, a proof script is simply a sequence of definitions and facts, each of them possibly followed by its proof (that is, a sequence of commands). Why3 makes the following assumptions: axioms were generated by Why3 itself, while proof commands, if any, were written by the user. For definitions and theorem statements, there is an ambiguity, so Why3 annotates them with a comment when they are generated. These comments have a low impact on readability, since most entries do not need any disambiguation. The following Coq script is the one generated for the running example; all the `Axiom` and `Parameter` statements are generated by Why3; this is also the case for the theorem statement, and it is prefixed by an annotation so that it is not mistaken for some user content; finally, proof commands such as `intros` are written by the user.

```
Parameter f: Z -> Z.
Axiom H1 : forall (n:Z), 0 <= n -> 0 <= f n.
```

---

[3] We could devise some kind of `lost+found` pool of abandoned proofs, to be used in subsequent rounds of the matching algorithm or to be manually selected by the user.

```
Axiom H2 : forall (n:Z), 0 <= n -> f (f n) < f (n + 1).
... (* other Why3 statements *)

(* Why3 goal *)
Theorem G : forall (n:Z), 0 <= n -> f n = n.
intros n h1.
... (* other user commands *)
Qed.
```

Regarding script regeneration, Why3 takes the following approach. Whenever it needs to output a statement, if a statement with the same name is already present in the old script, it first outputs any user content that was preceding it. If the user had attached commands to that statement, they are output. This seemingly simple process is actually quite effective in practice.

Note that, while this mechanism is currently applied only to interactive proof assistants, it might also make sense for automated provers. Indeed, some of them accept user hints for guiding proof search. For instance, an SMT solver may require some facts to be removed from the context, or some triggers to be modified. Alt-Ergo supports such user hints. Another example is Gappa, which only performs branch-and-bound when instructed, so the user should have a chance of modifying the Gappa script beforehand to add this kind of hint.

5 Environment Changes

The environment is composed by the installed version of Why3 and the installed provers. This environment changes when users upgrade Why3 or one of the provers.

For the first case, Why3's developers try to keep backward compatibility in every aspect of Why3. Unsurprisingly, that encompasses backward compatibility of the application programming interface, but also backward compatibility of the session on-disk format. More indirectly, modifications of the weakest precondition calculus, of the simplifications, and of the transformations, are done so as to keep provability whenever possible. This is checked during the nightly regression test which verifies that all the program examples from the Why3 gallery are still proved. Moreover, this test suite also exercises the mechanism of session update, since pairing breakage would cause some goals to become unproved.

For the second case, Why3 offers a tool for auto-detection of provers, called why3config. According to the name and version of the prover, it selects the configuration file, called *driver*, that specifies the built-in functions and the transformations to apply before sending a goal to the prover. When a new version of the prover is released, a new version of the driver is created. Old drivers are kept, so that older versions can still be used. If the user upgrades a prover and runs why3config --detect, then Why3 asks, when old sessions are open, whether to copy or move proof attempts to the newer version of the prover.

In order to compare the results of different provers or in order to update proofs incrementally, a user can install different versions of the same prover at the same time. The `why3session` command-line tool allows to copy/move proof attempts done with one prover to another prover or to compare results of different provers.

6   Conclusions, Related Work, and Perspectives

We described in this paper the way we designed a proof session system in Why3. The technical choices were guided by the general need of maintaining proofs across specification changes. The same technique is also useful in case of changes in the system itself: upgrade of Why3's kernel, upgrade of the standard library, upgrade of external provers. Our session system allowed us to maintain, for more than 2 years now, a gallery of verified programs (`http://toccata.lri.fr/gallery/index.en.html`) containing more than 100 examples. Several versions of Why3 and of external provers were released during this period. Moreover, session files are available on that website, so that anyone should be able to replay the proofs.

The contributions of this paper are mainly technical, not much scientific in the noble sense. Nevertheless we believe that our design of proof sessions are worth publicizing, hoping that some ideas can be useful to others. Indeed, writing this paper allowed us to discover a few subtle bugs in our implementation.

We found few related works in the literature. An early work by Reif and Stenzel in 1993 [12] aimed at managing changes in the context of the KIV verification system. Some ideas were reused by V. Klebanov in 2009 [10] for managing changes in proof scripts made inside the KeY system [2]. They both introduce a notion of similarity of goals, although different from ours. Indeed, their aim was to manage changes in interactive proof scripts, which is only a part of our own aim. It is not really meaningful to compare these works with our own approach, since in their case, they have a whole proof object at hand, performed by a single prover, in which they can search for example if a lemma is used or not. We are instead dealing with small pieces of proof made by different provers.

Note that some deductive verification systems rely on a single automated prover and express proof skeletons at the source level only (*e.g.* lemmas, ghost code, but no Why3-like transformations). Thus they do not have a need for proof management, as all the proof obligations will be handled the same way. This is the case for VCC, Dafny, Verifast, and so on.

We also found some attempts at designing large shared databases for bookkeeping proofs. The *Evidential Tool Bus* is a first step towards this idea by J. Rushby in 2005 [13]. Recently, Cruanes, Hamon, Owre, and Shankar [6] presented a formal setting on how several independent tools can cooperate and exchange proofs on such a tool bus. A similar effort is the goal of D. Miller's ProofCert project[4], where a general framework for a common proof format is proposed [11]. As far as we understand, the issue of maintaining proofs across specification changes is not yet addressed in these settings. We hope that our techniques could be useful in these contexts.

---

[4] `http://www.lix.polytechnique.fr/Labo/Dale.Miller/ProofCert.html`

Acknowledgments. We would like to thank Rustan Leino for suggesting the example of this paper. We also thank the anonymous reviewers for their useful comments and suggestions.

References

1. Barrett, C., Conway, C.L., Deters, M., Hadarean, L., Jovanović, D., King, T., Reynolds, A., Tinelli, C.: CVC4. In: Gopalakrishnan, G., Qadeer, S. (eds.) CAV 2011. LNCS, vol. 6806, pp. 171–177. Springer, Heidelberg (2011)
2. Beckert, B., Hähnle, R., Schmitt, P.H. (eds.): Verification of Object-Oriented Software: The KeY Approach. LNCS (LNAI), vol. 4334. Springer, Heidelberg (2007)
3. Bobot, F., Conchon, S., Contejean, E., Iguernelala, M., Lescuyer, S., Mebsout, A.: The Alt-Ergo automated theorem prover (2008), http://alt-ergo.lri.fr/
4. Bobot, F., Filliâtre, J.-C., Marché, C., Paskevich, A.: Why3: Shepherd your herd of provers. In: Boogie 2011: First International Workshop on Intermediate Verification Languages, Wrocław, Poland, pp. 53–64 (August 2011)
5. Bobot, F., Paskevich, A.: Expressing Polymorphic Types in a Many-Sorted Language. In: Tinelli, C., Sofronie-Stokkermans, V. (eds.) FroCoS 2011. LNCS, vol. 6989, pp. 87–102. Springer, Heidelberg (2011)
6. Cruanes, S., Hamon, G., Owre, S., Shankar, N.: Tool integration with the evidential tool bus. In: Giacobazzi, R., Berdine, J., Mastroeni, I. (eds.) VMCAI 2013. LNCS, vol. 7737, pp. 275–294. Springer, Heidelberg (2013)
7. de Moura, L., Bjørner, N.S.: Z3: An efficient SMT solver. In: Ramakrishnan, C.R., Rehof, J. (eds.) TACAS 2008. LNCS, vol. 4963, pp. 337–340. Springer, Heidelberg (2008)
8. Filliâtre, J.-C.: Combining Interactive and Automated Theorem Proving in Why3 (invited talk). In: Heljanko, K., Herbelin, H. (eds.) Automation in Proof Assistants 2012, Tallinn, Estonia (April 2012)
9. Filliâtre, J.-C., Paskevich, A.: Why3 — where programs meet provers. In: Felleisen, M., Gardner, P. (eds.) Programming Languages and Systems. LNCS, vol. 7792, pp. 125–128. Springer, Heidelberg (2013)
10. Klebanov, V.: Extending the Reach and Power of Deductive Program Verification. PhD thesis, Universität Koblenz-Landau (2009), http://formal.iti.kit.edu/~klebanov/pubs/vstte09.pdf
11. Miller, D., Pimentel, E.: A formal framework for specifying sequent calculus proof systems. In: Theoretical Computer Science, pp. 98–116 (2013)
12. Reif, W., Stenzel, K.: Reuse of proofs in software verification. In: Shyamasundar, R.K. (ed.) FSTTCS 1993. LNCS, vol. 761, pp. 284–293. Springer, Heidelberg (1993)
13. Rushby, J.: An evidential tool bus. In: Lau, K.-K., Banach, R. (eds.) ICFEM 2005. LNCS, vol. 3785, p. 36. Springer, Heidelberg (2005)
14. Sutcliffe, G.: The SZS ontologies for automated reasoning software. In: Rudnicki, P., Sutcliffe, G., Konev, B., Schmidt, R.A., Schulz, S. (eds.) Proceedings of the LPAR 2008 Workshops, Knowledge Exchange: Automated Provers and Proof Assistants, and the 7th International Workshop on the Implementation of Logics, vol. 418. CEUR Workshop Proceedings, pp. 38–49 (2008)

An Automatic Encoding from VeriFast Predicates into Implicit Dynamic Frames

Daniel Jost and Alexander J. Summers

ETH Zurich, Switzerland
dajost@ethz.ch, alexander.summers@inf.ethz.ch

Abstract. VeriFast is a symbolic-execution-based verifier, based on separation logic specifications. Chalice is a verifier based on verification condition generation, which employs specifications in implicit dynamic frames. Recently, theoretical work has shown how the cores of these two verification logics can be formally related. However, the mechanisms for abstraction in the two tools are not obviously comparable; VeriFast employs parameterised recursive predicates in specifications, while Chalice employs recursive predicates without parameters, along with heap-dependent abstraction functions.

In this paper, we show how to relate a subset of VeriFast, including many common uses of separation logic recursive predicates, to the implicit dynamic frames approach. In particular, we present a prototype tool which can translate a class of VeriFast examples into Chalice examples. Our tool performs several semantic analyses of predicate definitions, and determines which of a selection of novel techniques can be applied to infer appropriate predicate and function definitions, as well as corresponding code instrumentation in a generated program. The tool is automatic, and produces programs which can themselves be directly handled by the automatic Boogie/Z3-based Chalice verifier.

1 Introduction

Separation logic [3,8] is a well-established approach for the verification of heap-based imperative programs; many verifiers have been built using separation logic as their specification language. VeriFast [5,4] is a mature verification tool for C and Java programs, which handles separation logic specifications by internally maintaining a representation of the current program state (symbolic execution), while passing queries off to an SMT solver about arithmetical problems and other theories. The key primitive features of separation logic are the *points-to assertions* $x.f \mapsto v$, which provide the only means of dereferencing heap locations in assertions, and the *separating conjunction* $*$, whose semantics can be used to divide ownership of heap locations between assertions. The ability to specify unbounded heap structures is provided by recursive *abstract predicates* [9].

Implicit dynamic frames [12] is a more-recently-introduced specification logic, which is designed to facilitate implementations based not only on symbolic execution but also on verification condition generation (i.e., encoding the entire

E. Cohen and A. Rybalchenko (Eds.): VSTTE 2013, LNCS 8164, pp. 202–221, 2014.

verification problem, including heap information, to an SMT solver). It separates the notion of having permission to access a heap location from the means of actually referring to the location's value. The key primitives here are *accessibility predicates* $\mathbf{acc}(x.f)$, which represent permission to access a heap location, and a conjunction (also written $*$ in this paper) which acts multiplicatively on accessibility predicates (i.e., sums the permissions from the two conjuncts), while not enforcing a strict separation between the heap locations actually dereferenced in expressions. Instead, a concept of *self-framing* assertions is imposed on those assertions used in pre/post-conditions etc., which essentially requires that the assertion only reads from heap locations for which it also requires permission via accessibility predicates. For example, $x.f = 5$ is an implicit dynamic frames assertion, but is not self-framing, while $\mathbf{acc}(x.f) * x.f = 5$ is.

Chalice [6,7] is a verifier which handles a small object-oriented language (with many concurrency-related primitives) annotated with implicit dynamic frames specifications. It works by verification condition generation; as such, certain design decisions in the language have been made in order to facilitate the encoding to SMT. In particular, although recursively-defined predicates are available in the specification logic, in contrast to VeriFast (and most similar tools), such predicates cannot take parameters (other than the implicit this receiver). Compared with VeriFast predicates, Chalice predicates by themselves are therefore significantly less expressive. However, Chalice specifications *can* include (parameterised) recursive *functions*, whose evaluations can depend on the heap, in contrast to separation logic based tools. Thus, the mechanisms in the two tools for handling recursion in specifications are not directly comparable.

It has been recently shown that separation logic and implicit dynamic frames can be formally related, and that it is possible to encode from separation logic specifications into equivalent specifications in implicit dynamic frames [10,11]. Using the relationship defined, the IDF assertion $\mathbf{acc}(x.f) * x.f = 5$ is shown to be equivalent to the separation logic assertion $x.f \mapsto 5$; indeed, is it shown that a large fragment of separation logic can be encoded into IDF. This hints at the possibility of encoding programs annotated for, say, VeriFast, into programs annotated instead for Chalice. However, the cited work only applied to the "core" fragments of the two logics; in particular, recursive predicates/functions were not treated in those papers. Since almost all interesting separation logic examples employ predicates in some form or other, this limitation is a serious obstacle to relating the two approaches in practice.

In this paper, we tackle the problem of making this relationship practical. In particular, we present a novel technique for translating VeriFast programs which include parameterised predicate definitions, into Chalice programs (which cannot). Our work helps with understanding the two approaches and their relationships/differences, and potentially provides a platform for future comparative studies on issues such as performance and annotation overhead.

Our approach involves the introduction of heap-dependent functions and ghost state/annotations, and relies crucially on a custom-made assertion analyser, which is used to extract simple semantic information about predicate definitions, without the need to invoke a background prover. While our techniques cannot handle all possible predicate definitions, they are fully automatic, and produce code which can be handled by the Chalice tool without modifications. Our preliminary experiments indicate that non-trivial examples can be handled by our techniques, and we have many ideas for extending their applicability. To our knowledge, this also presents the first method for verifying separation-logic-annotated code solely via verification condition generation to a first-order SMT solver (Z3 [2]). Our approach is implemented, and available to download [1].

2   Background

In this section, we give a swift introduction to the important aspects of VeriFast and Chalice. For more details, we refer the reader to the papers [5,4,6,7]

2.1   VeriFast Predicates, in and Out Parameters

VeriFast source files can declare *predicate definitions*; a predicate has a name, a sequence of formal parameters, and a body, which is a VeriFast assertion. Predicate definitions may occur outside of class definitions (*static predicates*), or inside a class definition (*instance predicates*), in which case they also have an implicit this parameter. For example, an instance predicate describing (non-empty) linked lists, can be defined as follows:

```
1   predicate linkedlist(list<int> elems) =
2     this.value |-> ?v &*& this.next |-> ?n &*&
3     (n == null ? elems = cons(v,nil) :
4       n.linkedlist(?rest) &*& elems = cons(v,rest))
```

The &*& syntax denotes the separating conjunction (∗) of separation logic. The ?v syntax indicates a binding of a (logical) variable to a value (which must be uniquely determined by the context); occurrences of the same variable name afterwards refer to this value. The same syntax can be used with predicate instances in, e.g., method specifications:

```
1   void add(int x)
2   //@ requires this.linkedList(?xs);
3   //@ ensures this.linkedList(cons(x,xs));
4   { ... }
```

When handling a call to such a method, the verifier matches the variable xs with the actual parameter to the currently-held predicate instance. Such a matching is only guaranteed to be deterministic because the elems parameter is uniquely determined by the predicate body, in any given state. Such a parameter is called an *out parameter* of the predicate, in VeriFast. Conversely, some predicate parameters are used to *determine* the meaning of the predicate body; for example, the parameter end in the famous list segment predicate (a static predicate, here):

```
5  predicate lseg(LinkedList start, LinkedList end ;) =
6    ((start == null || start == end) ? true :
7      (start.value |-> _ &*& start.next |-> ?n &*& lseg(n,end)))
     ;
8  }
```

The _ syntax here, represents a wildcard value - essentially, the particular value is anonymously existentially quantified. In this predicate, both start and end parameters must be known before the meaning of the predicate body can be determined. VeriFast calls these *in parameters*. For in parameters, it is not possible to use the ? binding (as in the add declaration above); the values of the parameters are not determined by holding a predicate instance.

In both Verifast and Chalice, ghost unfold and fold statements are used to direct the verifier to replace a predicate instance with its defined body, and vice versa. For example, an instance of the above predicate could be obtained via a VeriFast source statement fold lseg(null,null). When a predicate instance is held, the permissions (points-to assertions) and other constraints given by its definition are not directly available to the verifier; an unfold statement makes them available. This guidance tames the problem of reasoning statically about unbounded recursive definitions; and isorecursive semantics is used [13].

2.2   Chalice Predicates and Functions

Chalice allows a restricted form of predicate definitions, compared with VeriFast. Predicates can only be instance predicates, and cannot take parameters (other than the implicit this receiver). Predicate definitions can still be recursive: for example, the following predicate definition includes the same permissions as the analogous VeriFast example in the previous subsection (the analogous connective to separating conjunction is written &&, in the Chalice tool):

```
1  predicate linkedlist {
2    acc(this.value) && acc(this.next) &&
3    (this.next != null ==> this.next.linkedlist)
4  }
```

The reason for the above restrictions is to simplify the bookkeeping of permissions held by the current thread, for the verification condition generation. Nonetheless, Chalice includes an additional mechanism for abstraction/recursion: the ability to define heap-dependent *functions*. These play a role analogous with pure methods, as often used in contract languages; they can be used to abstract over values represented by the underlying heap data structure. A Chalice function definition includes a *pre-condition*, which must require permissions to (at least) the heap locations on which the function's evaluation depends. Function invocations in assertions do not themselves represent these permissions, but must occur within an assertion in which the permissions are required. For example, the following declaration defines a function which extracts the elements from a linked list structure:

```
1  function elems() : list<int>
2    requires this.linkedlist
3    {
4      unfolding this.linkedlist in
5      (next == null ? [value] : [value] ++ next.elems())
6    }
```

The unfolding expression in Chalice permits the definition of expressions which access heap locations whose permissions are currently folded inside a predicate instance; they do not affect the expression's value, but help the verifier to check that appropriate permissions are held. The notion of *self-framing* assertions is extended to check function pre-conditions. For example, this.elems() == [4] is not a self-framing assertion (it does not contain sufficient permissions to satisfy the function's pre-condition), but this.linkedlist && this.elems() == [4] is.

2.3   Running Example

In this paper, we will use as a running example an adapted list segment predicate, in which the list elements are also exposed as a predicate parameter. Our predicate is not quite analogous to the typical lseg; we only model non-empty list segments, with this definition. Our tool can actually handle a more general definition (in which non-empty list segments can also be represented), but we explain the relevant limitations (and how we plan to lift them) in Section 6. The VeriFast definition for our running example is:

```
1  predicate listSeg(List start, List end, list<int> elems) =
2    start != null &*& start.value |-> ?x &*& start.next |-> ?n
       &*&
3    (n != end ? listSeg(n, end, ?nextElems) &*&
4                elems == cons(x, nextElems)
5              : elems == cons(x, nil));
```

3   Approach

We base our approach around two main ideas: replacing out parameters with abstraction functions, and replacing in parameters with ghost fields; these are detailed in the next two subsections. Note that we do not stick to the VeriFast notions of in/out parameters, but instead try to infer that as many parameters as possible can be treated as out parameters. In the following, we will first outline those two main ideas in detail. Second, we will show how those abstract ideas are used when translating VeriFast predicates (and programs) to Chalice; for concreteness, we show how they apply to our running example (from Section 2.3). Finally, we will motivate the analysis presented in Section 4.

3.1   From out Parameters to Abstraction Functions

The observation that out parameters can be determined by the underlying heap (along with the in parameters of a predicate definition) led us to an encoding in which such out parameters can be replaced by abstraction functions. The constraints determining the value of the predicate parameter can be re-encoded as a function which computes the value itself. Uses of the predicate parameter can, in general, then be replaced by invocations of the function. For example, the elems parameter of our linkedlist predicate can be replaced by an elems() function, providing the same abstraction of the underlying data structure.

Abstraction functions introduced in this way take the (translated version of the) original predicate as a pre-condition; this provides the appropriate permissions to the heap locations on which the function's evaluation depends. An instance of the original predicate can then be replaced by an occurrence of the new predicate, conjoined with a fact relating the abstraction function's value to the original parameter value. For example an instance this.linkedlist(l) of the parameterised list predicate, is replaced by this.linkedlist * this.elems()=l.

Where the original predicate is recursive, the body of the predicate will usually relate the parameters of the original and recursive predicate instance via some constraint; this results in a recursive definition of the extracted abstraction function. For example, in the body of the parameterised predicate linkedlist, we find that, if this.next = null holds, then elems=nil is required, while if this.next != null then we have that elems = v:rest is required, where rest is the corresponding parameter of the *recursive* linkedlist predicate instance. This gives rise to a natural function definition, as shown at the end of Section 3.4, in which rest corresponds to a recursive call to the function.

3.2   From in Parameters to Ghost State

While out parameters can be naturally handled as abstraction functions, it is clear that the same trick cannot be applied to all predicate parameters. In particular, if the value of a parameter cannot be uniquely determined from the predicate body, but is instead used to *decide* the meaning of the predicate body (for example, the end parameter of the lseg predicate), then it must necessarily be provided for each predicate instance. We handle this situation by introducing additional *ghost fields* to represent the values of the in parameters of a currently-held predicate instance. In particular, a *fold* of the original parameterised predicate definition is handled by instead first writing to the ghost field(s) (with the values that were originally provided for the in parameters), and then folding the translated predicate definition. When the resulting predicate instance is unfolded, the ghost fields can be used in place of any occurrences of the original parameters. For instance, when folding a linked list segment predicate taking the start as receiver and the end as parameter, fold(start.lseg(end)) gets replaced by start.end = end; fold(start.lseg).

This handling of in parameters using ghost state comes with a clear limitation: since a (ghost) field can only have a single value at any one time, it is only possible for us to encode uses of predicates for which it is never required to hold multiple instances of the same predicate, for the same receiver but for different values of the other parameters. This problematic situation could arise in two (related) ways. Firstly, it could really be that the in parameter is used to select between two different views of the same data structure. For example, while it is not possible to hold lseg(this,x) * lseg(this,y) in a scenario where this, x and y are all distinct references (since this would require too much permission to e.g., the field this.next), it *is* possible to hold these two predicate instances if, e.g., x=this holds. In this case, the first instance of the predicate holds no permissions at all, but is still a valid instance. In this particular case, it is possible for our tool to often provide a further workaround, as described in Section 6. In the presence of list segments involving *fractional permissions* (denoted for the fraction p in VeriFast by $[p]e.x\mapsto y$ or $[p]pred$ for predicates, and in Chalice by $\mathbf{acc}(e.x, p)$), this problematic case can even arise in the former scenario. If it is possible to express list segments which require partial permissions, such as [1/2]lseg(this,x) * [1/2]lseg(this,y) for different x and y; essentially, this allows for two overlapping (and read-only) "views" on different portions of the same list. Our ghost-state-based approach is not able to handle this case, which nonetheless has not yet arisen in the examples we have looked at so far.

Since our ghost field approach involves writing to the ghost fields before a fold statement, we need write permission to the ghost-fields at these points. In addition, we need to put at least some permission to this field inside the predicate body, so that we can refer to its value. However, how to distribute the permission throughout arbitrary code, is less obvious. Our solution is to attempt to determine a field to which a predicate definition always requires full permission; we then *mirror* the permissions to that field throughout the entire program; whereever some permission to the mirrored field occurs, we conjoin the same amount of permission to the ghost field. In particular, this guarantees that whenever the predicate is foldable we also have full permission to the ghost-field (and so, may write to it).

3.3   Initial Translation

In the following subsections we will describe the steps performed by our tool to translate VeriFast programs to Chalice. Note that this translation consists of multiple steps, each of which can potentially fail, aborting the translation; our tool cannot handle every VeriFast program.

We begin with the body (assertion) of a predicate definition, and firstly apply the following translation recursively throughout: every points-to assertion $[p]x.f\mapsto v$ (in which v is neither bound using ?y, nor the wildcard _ expression), is replaced by the assertion $x \neq null * \mathbf{acc}(x.f, p) * x.f == v$. The first conjunct reflects the implicit non-nullity guarantee that VeriFast bakes into points-to assertions, while the latter two reflect the basic encoding from separation logic into implicit dynamic frames [11]. In the case of a bound variable or a wildcard, we translate $[p]x.f\mapsto_-$ as $x \neq null * \mathbf{acc}(x.f, p)$; for a bound variable ?v, subsequent occurrences of v get replaced by $x.f$. The non-nullity conjunct $x \neq null$ is also omitted for the special this reference (since this $\neq null$ is implicit in Chalice predicate definitions, as in VeriFast).

Turning our attention to our running example from Section 2.3, we note that this VeriFast predicate is static; Chalice, in contrast, only supports instance predicates. In order to turn this static predicate into an instance predicate we need to pick one of the reference parameters and make it the new receiver[1]. This only works if the parameter is guaranteed to be non-null: in our running example the predicate body includes the assertion start $\neq$ null, indicating that start would be a valid choice. Our tool must be able to make this selection automatically; this is the first of several use-cases for an analysis of predicate definitions, capable of extracting (dis)equalities of interest. The technical details of this analysis will be provided in Section 4. In fact, our tool makes further use of our analysis to deal with a wider range of static predicates, for which the new receiver cannot necessarily proven to be non-null; we will outline this idea in Section 6.

By the end of a successful translation of a VeriFast program, each recursive predicate instance will correspond to an instance of the corresponding Chalice predicate in our translated program. Furthermore, as we will detail in the next two subsections, both of our techniques for replacing predicate parameters (described informally in the previous two subsections) result in the introduction of a Chalice function, which retrieves the corresponding value. Therefore, for a predicate p with formal parameters $y_1, y_2, \ldots$, we replace each predicate instance $x.p(t_1, t_2, \ldots)$ with an assertion $p * x.y_1() == t_1 * x.y_2() == t_2 \ldots$ in which $y_1(), y_2()$ etc. are now *function applications*[2]. The following two subsections describe how we find the definitions for the functions. Having applied the steps detailed in *this* subsection, the predicate definition of our running example looks as follows:

```
1   predicate listseg(LinkedList end, list<int> elems) =
2       this != null
3       &*& acc(this.value)
4       &*& acc(this.next)
5       &*& (this.next != end
6               ? this.next.listseg &*& this.next.end() == end &*&
                  elems == cons(this.value, this.next.elems())
7               : elems == cons(this.value, nil));
```

3.4   Inferring Abstraction Functions

After the initial translation steps described in the previous subsection, we attempt to identify predicate arguments to be replaced by abstraction functions (cf. Section 3.1). In order to come up with abstraction functions, we *extract equality facts* about the predicate body; this is another motivation for the underlying analysis we designed, presented in the next section). Applied to our running example, our analysis is able to extract just a single equality fact:

---

[1] We considered an encoding with a "dummy" receiver object. However, representing that this receiver is the same for all occurring instances of the predicate is difficult.

[2] In fact, we only conjoin equalities for those predicate parameters which we concretely specified in the original predicate instance; those which were bound with ?y or _ syntax are omitted in the resulting assertion.

elems = (next≠end?cons(value, next.elems()):cons(value, nil)). This fact is deduced by combining information from the branches of the conditional expression. Note that no such fact is generated concerning end; this is because information about the value of end is not present in both branches.

Having extracted those equality facts, the approach is quite simple: for each predicate parameter v, we search for an equality fact $v = e$ for some arbitrary expression e (or the symmetric case). In order to make this strategy more robust, we have also implemented a very simple equation solver which is able to solve (some) equalities for v rather than relying on v being already one side of the equation. Furthermore, solving an equation for v can also introduce a side-condition, such as preventing zero division. In case a suitable expression e was found, we can now generate a new function definition for the parameter in question; in case we have extracted more than one equality for v, we pick an arbitrary one. The function takes the original predicate, as well as the side-condition a, as pre-condition, and the body of the function is **unfolding** this.p in e where p is the predicate under analysis.

In our running example, we cannot extract any equality for the parameter end, but we have one for elems. Thus, we generate the following new function definition:

```
1  function elems(): list<int>
2     requires acc(this.listseg) {
3     unfolding acc(this.listseg) in
4        this.next != end ? cons(this.value, this.next.elems())
5                         : cons(this.value, nil)
6  }
```

We then substitute the function's *body* for occurrences of the original parameter in the predicate body[3]. This can typically introduce trivial equalities, and so we simplify the resulting assertion yielding an updated predicate definition:

```
1  predicate listseg(LinkedList end) =
2     acc(this.value);
3     &*& acc(this.next);
4     &*& (this.next != end
5              ? this.next.listseg
6                  &*& this.next.end() == end()
7              : true;
8     };
```

Note that, in general, we have to take some extra steps to avoid introducing cyclic function definitions, here. For example, given the (non-sensical) example of a predicate defined by: $p(x, y) \stackrel{def}{=} (x == y)$, a naïve approach might be to define a function for each parameter, each calling the other function directly in

---

[3] Note that we cannot substitute a call to the function itself, since the function requires the predicate under analysis as a pre-condition, and these occurrences are inside the predicate body.

its body. Our tool detects and breaks such cycles; this means that at most one parameter will be replaced with a function, in this example.

3.5 Introducing Ghost Fields

Any remaining predicate parameters are handled by introducing extra ghost fields (one per parameter). As described in Section 3.2, this requires us to identify a suitable field in the original program to which full permission is guaranteed to be held whenever the predicate itself is held. Therefore, we require another analysis of the predicate body, able to extract information about the *permissions* held by the predicate. Applied to our running example this results in the knowledge that the predicate body holds full permission on this.value and this.next. In our running example, the predicate parameter end remains to be dealt with and from our learnt knowledge about the permissions it is clear that either field value or field next will suffice. Therefore, picking the first, we will have the permissions to the newly-introduced ghost field end mirror those to value in our output code. In particular, these permissions are included in the assertion under analysis.

We also provide a Chalice function to access the ghost field's value when the predicate is folded. This means that all predicate parameters, whether backed by abstraction functions (as described in the previous subsection) or by ghost fields, can be accessed uniformly (cf. Section 3.3). For our running example, this results in a final set of definitions as follows:

```
1   ghost LinkedList end;
2
3   predicate listseg =
4     acc(this.value) &*& acc(this.end) &*& acc(this.next)
5     &*& (this.next != this.end ? this.next.listseg
6            &*& this.next.end() == this.end
7          : true; };
8
9   function end(): LinkedList
10     requires acc(listseg) {
11       unfolding acc(listseg) in this.end;
12   }
13
14  function elems(): list<int>
15     requires acc(this.listseg) {
16       unfolding acc(this.listseg) in
17         this.next != end ? cons(this.value, this.next.elems())
18                     : cons(this.value, nil)
19  }
```

3.6 Translating Programs

While the above sections explain the details of our analysis of predicates, we explain here how we adapt our approach to translating entire programs.

The initial translation described in Section 3.3 above is applied also to the rest of the program specifications; this results in the elimination of points-to assertions, and every predicate instance being replaced by the unparameterised predicate, plus appropriate equalities with function invocations.

The translation from Section 3.4 and 3.5 is then applied to each predicate definition in the program; if both of them fail for any definition, then the overall translation fails. For each additional ghost field introduced, the field which was found for "mirroring" is also recorded. The mirroring of permissions is then applied throughout the program text; in our running example, any accessibility predicate of the form $\mathbf{acc}(e.value, p)$ is replaced by a conjunction $\mathbf{acc}(e.value, p)$ && $\mathbf{acc}(e.end, p)$.

Furthermore, when encoding method signatures, if a predicate parameter value is bound inside the pre-condition of a method (e.g. ?xs as shown in Section 2.1), then, in the original code, that variable may be referred in both the method body and the post-condition. Occurrences in the post-condition are replaced by the appropriate function call wrapped inside an old expression (referring to the state of the pre-condition). If the variable is used in the method body, an additional ghost-variable capturing the value is introduced in the beginning of the method body, and used in place of the original occurrences.

Every fold statement of the original program which concerns a predicate for which ghost fields have been introduced, is translated into a sequence of field updates to the ghost fields, followed by a fold of the new predicate. For example, fold this.listseg(x, xs) could be translated to this.end := x; fold this.listseg. However, we should also reflect explicitly-provided values for parameters which have been replaced by abstraction functions in our translation. Where values are *not* concretely provided (i.e. with ?xs or _ syntax) in the input program, we do nothing extra. However, if a concrete expression *is* provided in the original program, we can reflect the correct semantics by adding an assert statement to check that the supplied parameter matches the value of the corresponding abstraction function. Thus, our translation of fold this.listseg(x, xs) actually produces this.end := x; fold this.listseg; assert this.elems() == xs.

Many small syntactic differences between VeriFast and Chalice syntax are trivially handled by the Chalice pretty-printer of our internal AST; we do not detail these syntactic differences here.

3.7   Usage of Predicate Analysis

We have now presented the main ideas behind our translation from VeriFast predicates to Chalice predicates and functions. As remarked throughout, in order to automate the translation, we require an analysis of predicate bodies, able to infer equalities and disequalities (as in Section 3.4 and for handling static predicates) and permissions guaranteed by the predicate body (cf. Section 3.5). Finally, the ability to simplify assertions/expressions during translation helps to keep our output code readable (and also permits our analysis to work more simply). In the next section, we present the semantic analysis of predicate bodies that we developed to tackle all of these problems.

4   Core Analysis

4.1   Our Core Analysis

The semantic analysis of predicates is the main component of our tool and is used in various places as outlined in Section 3. It is designed to follow the reasoning we performed by hand when extracting information from an assertion. In this section we will present the technical details of the so-far informal concepts of extracting (dis)equality facts, subsequently called *value facts*, and extracting *permission facts*, which approximate the permissions making up the footprint of an assertion; both of the two kinds collectively referred to as *analysis facts*.

Our analysis aims to attack questions of the form: what do we know about an assertion/expression under a certain set of assumed facts? Our approach reasons in terms of limited semantic information about assertions, but does not involve external interactions with any kind of theorem prover/SMT solver; we employ a somewhat limited but simple and efficient set of procedures in our tool for accumulating and making use of information extracted from the input program. The use of simplifications/rewriting throughout our analysis is partly to aid code readability, but also limits the impact of our simple representation of facts. We present our algorithms for a representative subsyntax of the assertions which our implementation handles, as follows:

Definition 1 (Assertions and Boolean Expressions for Analysis). *We assume a set of (unspecified, here) unanalysed expressions, ranged over by e. We assume the syntax of e to (at least) include Chalice function applications. Our analysis handles the following syntax of boolean expressions, ranged over by b, and assertions, ranged over by a (in which p represents a permission amount):*

$$b ::= \mathit{true} \mid \mathit{false} \mid e_1 = e_2 \mid e_1 \neq e_2 \mid \neg b \mid b_1 \wedge b_2 \mid b_1 \vee b_2 \mid (b?b_1:b_2)$$
$$a ::= b \mid \mathbf{acc}(e.f, p) \mid a_1 * a_2 \mid (b?a_1:a_2) \mid e_1.P$$

Note that this syntax does not include VeriFast-specific assertions; in particular, no points-to assertions or parameterised predicate instances. These will be handled in our tool before invoking our main analysis, as explained in Section 3.3.

4.2   Value Facts

To represent heap information described by assertions, our analysis works with equalities and disequalities of expressions, which we call *value facts*. We extract sets of value facts by syntactically traversing an input assertion/expression. The extracted set is constructed to satisfy the property that *if* the input assertion/boolean expression is true in a state, *then* the conjunction of the set of value facts is also guaranteed to be true. In some cases, it can be useful to know if the reverse implication also holds; this depends on whether the set of value facts is sufficiently rich to precisely characterise when the input assertion holds. When the reverse implication is also guaranteed, we call the set of value facts *invertible*, and track this status with a boolean flag on each set.

Definition 2 (Value Facts and Contexts). Value facts, *ranged over by v,* *are the subset of boolean expressions generated by the following grammar:* $v ::=$ $(e_1=e_2) \mid (e_1 \neq e_2)$. *Value facts are always treated modulo symmetry; i.e., we implicitly identify* $(e_1=e_2)$ *with* $(e_2=e_1)$ *when considering them as value facts.* *Value fact sets, ranged over by* V, *are sets of value facts, i.e.,* $V ::= \{\vec{v_i}\}$ *for some value facts* $\vec{v_i}$. *We write* $\emptyset$ *for the empty value fact set.*

Value fact contexts, ranged over by Γ, *consist of a value fact set along with a boolean constant, i.e.,* $\Gamma ::= V^B$ *for* $B ::= true \mid false$. *When* $B = true$, Γ *is called* invertible.

The use of implicit symmetries for value facts simplifies several of the following definitions. For example, when we write $(e_1=e_2) \in V$, this criterion is insensitive to the order of the two expressions. Similarly, $\{(e_1=e_2)\} \cap \{(e_2=e_1)\} \neq \emptyset$, with this interpretation; this can avoid discarding such equalities unnecessarily.

Note that value fact contexts are always interpreted via conjunction; we have no way to directly represent disjunctions of sets of value facts. This makes our analysis much simpler, and partly reflects its use cases; as we have seen in Section 3.4, we are typically interested in extracting a single equality fact from our value sets, which can be used as the basis for a new definition. Generalisations are certainly possible, but so far we have not found this to be a serious limitation in our examples. Note that, while we do not directly represent disjunctions, we can still employ conditional expressions as operands to value facts; this can in some cases replace a disjunction between facts, and is useful when analysing conditionals from within a predicate body.

We next define a number of operations on our value fact contexts, that are used in our analysis. The conditional merge is used in the analysis of conditionals, to combine facts about the branches; the other operations are more familiar.

Definition 3 (Value Fact Context Operators). *The* union *of two value fact contexts is defined (where* & *denotes the boolean conjunction function on two boolean constants) by:* $V_1^{B_1} \cup V_2^{B_2} = (V_1 \cup V_2)^{B_1 \& B_2}$ *The* intersection *of two value fact contexts is defined as follows:*

$$\Gamma \cap \Gamma = \Gamma$$
$$V_1^{B_1} \cap V_2^{B_2} = (V_1 \cap V_2)^{false} \quad (otherwise)$$

The negation *of a value fact context is defined as follows:*

$$(neg \ \{(e_1=e_2)\}^{true}) = \{e_1 \neq e_2\}^{true}$$
$$(neg \ \{(e_1 \neq e_2)\}^{true}) = \{e_1=e_2\}^{true}$$
$$(neg \ \Gamma) = \emptyset^{false} \quad (otherwise)$$

The conditional merge *of two value fact contexts (over a boolean expression b) is defined by:*

$$V_1^{B_1} \overset{b}{\wedge} V_2^{B_2} = \{(e_0=(b?e_1:e_2)) \mid (e_0=e_1) \in V_1 \ and \ (e_0=e_2) \in V_2\}^{false}$$

These operations treat "invertibility" status of contexts very conservatively. Intersection of value fact contexts never results in an invertible value fact context,

unless the original contexts are identical, while merging two contexts never returns an invertible context. Furthermore, even when we have an invertible value
fact context, we only actually define the negation of the context in a meaningful
way for singleton sets of value facts; this results from our choice not to represent
disjunctions explicitly in our value facts. It is clear that these operations could
be made much more general with a richer treatment of value facts; nonetheless,
the above definitions have been sufficiently expressive for our experiments so far.

4.3   Analysis of Boolean Expressions

Having presented our notions of value facts, we can define the analysis we perform
on boolean expressions. We define a function *analyseE* which takes as parameters
a boolean expression, and a value fact context (representing information that is
currently *assumed* in our analysis), and returns a similar pair; the resulting
expression is equivalent to the input expression, and the resulting value context
contains information about the facts learned in the analysis.

Definition 4 (Analysis of Boolean Expressions)

$$
\begin{aligned}
analyseE\ v\ \Gamma\ \ &=\ ((tryEval\ v\ \Gamma\ ), \{v\}^{true}) \\
analyseE\ \neg b\ \Gamma\ \ &=\ (\neg b', (neg\ \Gamma'\ )) \\
\textit{where}\quad (b', \Gamma')\ &=\ analyseE\ b\ \Gamma \\
analyseE\ b_1 \wedge b_2\ \Gamma\ \ &=\ (b_1' \wedge b_2', \Gamma_1 \cup \Gamma_2) \\
\textit{where}\quad (b_1', \Gamma_1)\ &=\ analyseE\ b_1\ \Gamma \\
(b_2', \Gamma_2)\ &=\ analyseE\ b_2\ \Gamma \cup \Gamma_1 \\
analyseE\ b_1 \vee b_2\ \Gamma\ \ &=\ (b_1' \vee b_2', \Gamma_1 \cap \Gamma_2) \\
\textit{where}\quad (b_1', \Gamma_1')\ &=\ analyseE\ b_1\ \Gamma \\
(b_2', \Gamma_2')\ &=\ analyseE\ b_2\ \Gamma
\end{aligned}
$$

$$
\begin{aligned}
analyseE\ (b_0 ? b_1 : b_2)\ \Gamma\ =\ \ & \\
\textit{if}\ b_0' = true : & (b_1', \Gamma_0 \cup \Gamma_1) \\
\textit{else if}\ b_0' = false : & (b_2', (neg\ \Gamma_0\ ) \cup \Gamma_2) \\
\textit{else if}\ b_1' = false : & ((b_0' ? b_1' : b_2'), (\{b_0 == false\}^{true} \cup (neg\ \Gamma_0\ ) \cup \Gamma_2)) \\
\textit{else if}\ b_2' = false : & ((b_0' ? b_1' : b_2'), (\{b_0 == true\}^{true} \cup (neg\ \Gamma_0\ ) \cup \Gamma_1)) \\
& \overset{b_0'}{} \\
\textit{else} : & ((b_0' ? b_1' : b_2'), (\Gamma_1 \wedge\!\!\wedge \Gamma_2)) \\
\textit{where}\quad (b_0', \Gamma_0)\ &=\ analyseE\ b_0\ \Gamma \\
(b_1', \Gamma_1)\ &=\ analyseE\ b_1\ \Gamma \cup \Gamma_0 \\
(b_2', \Gamma_2)\ &=\ analyseE\ b_2\ \Gamma \cup (neg\ \Gamma_0\ )
\end{aligned}
$$

The definition above is designed such that if *analyseE b Γ* = (b', Γ'), then, in
any state in which the conjunction of the value facts in Γ holds, the following
properties are also guaranteed. Firstly, $b' \Leftrightarrow b$. Secondly, in any state in which b
is true, the conjunction of the value facts in Γ' is true. Thirdly, *if Γ' is invertible,*
then in any state in which b is false, the conjunction of the value facts in Γ' is
also false. The function *tryEval v Γ* implements a simple (conservative) attempt
to determine whether the inequality v is guaranteed to be either true or false,

assuming the value facts in Γ. If either can be shown, then *true* or *false* are returned, otherwise v is returned unchanged.

The ability to simplify conditional expressions in four cases above gives more precise information about the assertion; only in the case that neither can the condition b_0 be simplified, nor can either of the two assertions a_1 and a_2 be rewritten to *false*, does the $⋏$ operator have to be applied (typically losing information). Note that the if-conditionals in the analysis of conditional expressions compare for *syntactic* equality of boolean expressions. These conditionals also propagate simplifications throughout the structure of expressions, where possible.

4.4   Permission Facts

In the case of analysing assertions (rather than just boolean expressions), we also require information about the *permissions* required by a particular assertion. We do not require very precise permission accounting (which would be difficult in the presence of aliasing questions), since ultimately we are only concerned with two particular outcomes - whether or not an assertion is known to guarantee *no* permissions (e.g., a simple boolean expression), and whether or not it guarantees *full* permission to some field location. As we have seen, knowing that a predicate body holds full permission to at least one field is crucial when trying to replace in-parameters; knowing that a predicate body holds no permissions at all is beneficial when applying some tricks to deal with static predicates. Guided by these goals, we choose a simple representation of permission facts for our analysis.

Definition 5 (Permission Facts and Operations). *Permission facts, ranged over by* Π, *are defined by* $\Pi ::= \psi \mid \pi$, *where the symbol* ψ *is called the* unknown permission fact *(written* ψ*), and where* π *is a* known permission fact set*: a (possibly empty) set of tuples of the form* (e, f, p), *satisfying the constraint that no pair of* e, f *occurs in more than one tuple.*
Addition *of permission facts is defined as follows:*

$$\psi + \psi = \psi \qquad \psi + \emptyset = \emptyset + \psi = \psi$$
$$\pi_1 + \pi_2 = \pi_1 \uplus \pi_2 \qquad \psi + \pi = \pi + \psi = \pi \quad otherwise$$

where $\uplus$ *takes the union of the two sets, except that when the same* e, f *occur in a tuple of each set, the resulting set has a tuple with the* sum *of the two permission amounts: e.g.,* $\{(x, f, p_1), (y, f, p_2)\} \uplus \{x, f, p_3\} = \{(x, f, p_1 + p_3), (y, f, p_2)\}$
Intersection *of permission facts is defined by:*

$$\psi \cap \Pi = \Pi \cap \psi = \psi \qquad \pi_1 \cap \pi_2 = \{(e, f, min(p_1, p_2)) \mid (e, f, p_1) \in \pi_1 \ and \ (e, f, p_2) \in \pi_2\}$$

The unknown permission fact is employed in our analysis whenever we are forced to be approximate conservatively, either because an exact fractional permission is not know, or because an assertion contained a further predicate instance (we do not unfold predicate definitions recursively, and this would in general not terminate).

We are now ready to define our analysis of assertions: we define a function *analyse*, which takes an assertion and value fact context (assumed knowledge) as input, and produces a triple of (possibly simplified) assertion, value fact context, and permission fact, as output.

Definition 6 (Analysis of Assertions)

$$
\begin{aligned}
analyse\ e\ \Gamma \quad &= (e', \Gamma', \emptyset) \\
\text{where} \quad (e', \Gamma') &= analyseE\ e\ \Gamma \\
analyse\ a_1 * a_2\ \Gamma \quad &= (a_1' * a_2', \Gamma_1 \cup \Gamma_2, \Pi_1 + \Pi_2) \\
\text{where} \quad (a_1', \Gamma_1, \Pi_1) &= analyse\ a_1\ \Gamma \\
(a_2', \Gamma_2, \Pi_2) &= analyse\ b_2\ \Gamma \cup \Gamma_1 \\
analyse\ \mathbf{acc}(e.f, p)\ \Gamma \quad &= (\mathbf{acc}(e.f, p), \emptyset^{false}, \{(e, f, p)\})
\end{aligned}
$$

$$
\begin{aligned}
analyse\ (b_0?a_1{:}a_2)\ \Gamma \quad &= \\
&\quad \text{if}\ b_0' = true : (b_1', \Gamma_0 \cup \Gamma_1, \Pi_1) \\
&\quad \text{else if}\ b_0' = false : (b_2', ((neg\ \Gamma_0\ ) \cup \Gamma_2), \Pi_2) \\
&\quad \text{else if}\ b_1' = false : ((b_0'?b_1'{:}b_2'), (\{b_0 == false\}^{true} \cup (neg\ \Gamma_0\ ) \cup \Gamma_2), \Pi_2) \\
&\quad \text{else if}\ b_2' = false : ((b_0'?b_1'{:}b_2'), (\{b_0 == true\}^{true} \cup (neg\ \Gamma_0\ ) \cup \Gamma_1), \Pi_1) \\
&\quad \text{else} : ((b_0'?b_1'{:}b_2'), (\Gamma_1 \overset{b_0'}{\cap} \Gamma_2), \Pi_1 \cap \Pi_2) \\
\text{where} \quad (b_0', \Gamma_0) &= analyseE\ b_0\ \Gamma \\
(a_1', \Gamma_1, \Pi_1) &= analyse\ a_1\ \Gamma \cup \Gamma_0 \\
(a_2', \Gamma_2, \Pi_2) &= analyse\ a_2\ \Gamma \cup (neg\ \Gamma_0\ )
\end{aligned}
$$

Note that, as in Definition 4, the cases for conditional expressions allow us to retain more-precise information and simpler assertions, where possible. In particular, the $\cap$ and $\overset{}{\cap}$ operators are not applied if an earlier case applies.

The analysis rules above are defined to guarantee similar properties to those for Definition 4. Specifically, if $analyse\ a\ \Gamma = (a', \Gamma', \Pi)$, then, in any state in which the conjunction of Γ holds:

1. a and a' are equivalent assertions (typically, a' is syntactically simpler).
2. Whenever a is true, the conjunction of the value facts in Γ' is true.
3. If Γ' is invertible and a is false, the conjunction of Γ' is false.
4. If $\Pi = \pi$ for some known permission fact set π, then a logically entails the iterated conjunction of all recorded permissions: $*\{\mathbf{acc}(e.f, p) \mid (e, f, p) \in \pi\}$

We make use of the above analysis at every stage of our translation: in particular, to discover equalities suitable for generating function definitions (as detailed further in the next subsection), and identify suitable fields and parameters for the handling of ghost field permissions and static predicates, as discussed in Section 3. We also constantly simplify the assertions we are working with, as a side-effect of our algorithm above.

4.5   Equation Solver

In addition to the main analysis described above, we have defined a simple equation solver, with the aim of rewriting equalities into the form $x = e$ for some chosen variable x. This is needed, for example, when we wish to extract new function definitions (to replace predicate parameters), or when dealing eliminating bound variables from VeriFast expressions. Our solver takes the left-hand and the right-hand sides of an equation, and a variable to solve for. It either fails (indicated by a special $\bot$ return value), or returns a result expression and an additional side-condition (assertion), expressing for instance that no zero-division occurs when solving an equation containing multiplications.

Definition 7 (Equation Solver). *We write* $occs(x, e)$ *for the number of occurrences of the variable* x *in expression* e. *We define an operation solve* e e' x , *which is only defined when* $occs(x, e) = 1 \wedge occs(x, e') = 0$, *by the rules below. Rules using the meta-variable* e_1 *have a side-condition: that* $occs(x, e_1) = 1$ *(i.e., the rule only applies if* x *occurs in this sub-expression).*

$$solve \; x \; e_3 \; x \quad\quad = (e_3, true)$$
$$solve \; e_1 + e_2 \; e_3 \; x = solve \; e_1 \; e_3 - e_2 \; x$$
$$solve \; e_2 + e_1 \; e_3 \; x = solve \; e_1 \; e_3 - e_2 \; x$$
$$solve \; e_1 - e_2 \; e_3 \; x = solve \; e_1 \; e_3 + e_2 \; x$$
$$solve \; e_2 - e_1 \; e_3 \; x = solve \; e_1 \; e_2 - e_3 \; x$$
$$solve \; e_1 * e_2 \; e_3 \; x = (e', e_2 \neq 0 \wedge c')$$
$$where \quad (e', c') = solve \; e_1 \; e_3 / e_2 \; x$$

$$solve \; e_2 * e_1 \; e_3 \; x = (e', e_2 \neq 0 \wedge c')$$
$$where \quad (e', c') = solve \; e_1 \; e_3 / e_2 \; x$$
$$solve \; e_1 / e_2 \; e_3 \; x = solve \; e_1 \; e_3 * e_2 \; x$$
$$solve \; e_2 / e_1 \; e_3 \; x = (e', e_3 \neq 0 \wedge c')$$
$$where \quad (e', c') = solve \; e_1 \; e_2 / e_3 \; x$$
$$solve \; e_1 \; e_3 \; x \quad\quad = (\bot, false)$$
$$otherwise$$

Note that the last case can match arbitrary expression syntax; for example, if x occurs as the parameter to a function application. The aim of our solver is not to apply deep reasoning to resolve such scenarios, but just to apply simple rewrites where possible.

Based on the *solve* function, we can then define *findExpressionFor* , which takes a value fact context and a variable name, and returns a set of expressions e' known to be equivalent to x, paired with corresponding side-conditions c. Furthermore, the function takes a set of "forbidden" variables vs that are not allowed to occur in the identified expressions. This expression e' along with the potential side-condition c can then directly be used to build the new abstraction function as outlined in Section 3.4.

$$findExpressionFor \; V \; x \; vs \; = \{(e', c) \mid (e', c) \in s \wedge e' \neq \bot \wedge vars(e') \cap vs = \emptyset\}$$
$$where$$
$$s = \{(solve \; e_1 \; e_2 \; x \;) \mid (e_1 == e_2) \in V \; and \; occs(x, e_1) = 1 \; and \; occs(x, e_2) = 0\}$$

5   Results and Evaluation

We have performed some preliminary experiments to gain some insight about the feasibility of our approach. Rather than as a full evaluation, it should be understood more as a starting point for further investigation and work. Furthermore, we were also interested in how well Chalice does on the translated examples and whether some general observations can be made when comparing Chalice to VeriFast.

Our experiments indicate so far that practical predicates can be handled by our analysis. From the (Java) examples provided with VeriFast, not a single one failed due to an untranslatable predicate; however only a handful of the test cases can actually be translated by our tool and the others failed due to a number of features not supported by Chalice at the time the tool was written, such as subtyping, general abstract data types, and unsupported language features. Nonetheless, the following examples from VeriFast could be translated: *Spouse*, *Spouse2*, *SpouseFinal*, *AmortizedQueue*, and *Stack*; they can be found together with the translated Chalice code in our examples [1]. We also included two of our own hand-written examples: *LinkedList*, *LinkedListSeg_simple*, and the full running-example (*LinkedListSeg*). While those are only few examples, several contain non-trivial recursive predicates, with both in and out parameters.

All the examples above translated without any modification, except for *Stack* which needed a single modification (as commented) in the original file[4]. Furthermore, they all verify in Chalice except for *AmortizedQueue* which needed an additional tweak (due a somewhat prototypical current support for static functions in Chalice) unrelated to the handling of the predicates. Notice that some of the examples will produce warnings from Chalice regarding termination checks for recursive functions which operate purely on abstract data types; this is due to a lack of support for general termination measures.

The only predicate that our approach could not handle is in *LinkedListSeg*, due to the predicate not being unique for a given receiver as the empty segment can be fold arbitrary often on any receiver. However, we will outline in section 6 some ideas of how we could extend our analysis to handle such cases.

In addition, our experiments indicate that Chalice can sometimes manage with fewer ghost annotations than VeriFast needs. In particular, several VeriFast examples contained consecutive unfold / fold pairs on exactly the same predicate instance; often they serve only for the purpose of binding the arguments to a variable, and in this case we can just call the corresponding getter function without having to unfold the predicate in Chalice. Interestingly, removing those superfluous unfold / fold pairs seems to speed up the verification in Chalice significantly for harder examples; we intend further investigation to disclose the underlying reason for this. Furthermore, many of the built in lemma methods of VeriFast (especially for lists) are not required in Chalice; while adding an equivalent assertion helps in terms of verification speed (probably by pointing the verifier into the right direction), the verification still succeeds without them.

6   Conclusions and Future Work

In this paper, we have presented the first implemented encoding from a subset of separation logic to a verifier based on first-order-verification-condition-generation (Chalice). To achieve this for interesting examples, we have presented a number of novel ideas for eliminating predicate parameters, and employing alternative verification features available. In particular, we have presented a

---

[4] VeriFast permits the wildcard _ to be used even for in parameters; in this case, the symbolic heap is searched for any appropriate predicate instance. We provided the (obviously unique, in this example) value explicitly.

simple but flexible automatic analysis of predicate definitions, which enables us to rewrite such definitions without user intervention.

Our analysis is currently limited in several ways, largely as an engineering trade-off between simplicity and expressiveness. However, our approach is easily extensible in many ways which do not affect the overall approach. Firstly, our value facts could be easily extended to capture more precise information about the entailment between the assertion and our knowledge; the same holds also for our permission facts. One can construct predicates in which reasoning in terms of *inequalities* is desirable. In addition, disjunctions could be added to value-fact contexts, making the negation of a context more often expressible. Both extensions would enable more examples in general, but also make the analysis itself, and particularly the entailment checking (built into *tryEval* of Section 4.3) much more complex; indeed, it is likely that a prover would be required for serious reasoning about inequalities. The *tryEval* function, as well as our equality solver (Section 4.5) could be made arbitrarily more sophisticated; at present, not even transitivity of equalities is taken into account, but in principle complex theories could be incorporated, with the aid of suitable prover support.

The main limitation of our current approach is that whenever a predicate has an in parameter, predicate instances must be unique per receiver; many separation logic predicates (such as the classical lseg definition) do not satisfy that restriction. On the other hand, the cases for which a predicate describing a recursive data structure can be held for the same receiver in many different ways, often coincide with the predicate instance not holding any permissions. In such cases, the predicate "degenerates" to a boolean expression referring only to the parameter values; for example, the base case of the lseg predicate in Section 2. Our tool currently has the ability to deal with a specific kind of these predicates: if the designated receiver r of a static predicate is potentially null, we check whether the predicate does not hold any permissions when $r = null$. If, in addition, all other predicate parameters can be uniquely determined in this case, we can drop the problematic predicate instances (in these cases) in our output code, by replacing all the occurrences of the predicate with e.g., $r \neq null \Rightarrow r.p$) and replacing all calls to getter functions (which would not make sense on a null receiver) with constant expressions: e.g., $r \neq null\,?\,r.f()$: const_val. This limited trick is already implemented, but in future work, we would like to generalise the technique to deal with cases where the condition for not needing to hold the predicate might be arbitrary (but still determinable from the in parameters). The classical list segment predicate would need start $\neq$ end as the condition; we wish to deduce this automatically and then apply a similar approach.

In trying our tool out on several VeriFast examples, we have established the feasibility of an encoding, in which separation logic examples are handled entirely by an SMT solver. This has also provided us with several new and interesting test cases for the Chalice verifier, and the ability to experiment with comparisons between the two approaches. While Chalice is generally able to handle the output code efficiently, one example (the translation of the AmortizedQueue.java VeriFast example) takes many minutes to verify (while VeriFast handles all examples in a few seconds). Interestingly, we found that we can delete many of the resulting fold/unfold statements in this example by hand: the verification still succeeds, and faster (presumably because the SMT encoding involves representing fewer states). We also found that we can delete several assertions which correspond to calls to lemma methods in the original code: these are also not required for the Chalice verifier to succeed, although do seem to speed up the verification. We would like to investigate these issues further, and believe that our tool opens up new and interesting possibilities for comparing the two approaches.

Acknowledgements. We are very grateful to Bart Jacobs for many useful and detailed discussions of predicates in VeriFast, and providing us with his source code to study. We would also like to thank the anonymous reviewers, whose feedback significantly improved the presentation of our work.

References

1. Verifast2chalice,
   http://www.pm.inf.ethz.ch/research/chalice/verifast2chalice.zip
2. de Moura, L., Bjørner, N.S.: Z3: an efficient SMT solver. In: Ramakrishnan, C.R., Rehof, J. (eds.) TACAS 2008. LNCS, vol. 4963, pp. 337–340. Springer, Heidelberg (2008)
3. Ishtiaq, S.S., O'Hearn, P.W.: BI as an assertion language for mutable data structures. In: POPL, pp. 14–26. ACM Press (2001)
4. Jacobs, B., Piessens, F.: The VeriFast program verifier. Technical report, Katholieke Universiteit Leuven (August 2008)
5. Jacobs, B., Smans, J., Philippaerts, P., Vogels, F., Penninckx, W., Piessens, F.: VeriFast: A Powerful, Sound, Predictable, Fast Verifier for C and Java. In: Bobaru, M., Havelund, K., Holzmann, G.J., Joshi, R. (eds.) NFM 2011. LNCS, vol. 6617, pp. 41–55. Springer, Heidelberg (2011)
6. Leino, K.R.M., Müller, P.: A basis for verifying multi-threaded programs. In: Castagna, G. (ed.) ESOP 2009. LNCS, vol. 5502, pp. 378–393. Springer, Heidelberg (2009)
7. Leino, K.R.M., Müller, P., Smans, J.: Deadlock-free channels and locks. In: Gordon, A.D. (ed.) ESOP 2010. LNCS, vol. 6012, pp. 407–426. Springer, Heidelberg (2010)
8. O'Hearn, P.W., Reynolds, J.C., Yang, H.: Local reasoning about programs that alter data structures. In: Fribourg, L. (ed.) CSL 2001. LNCS, vol. 2142, pp. 1–19. Springer, Heidelberg (2001)
9. Parkinson, M., Bierman, G.: Separation logic and abstraction. In: POPL, pp. 247–258. ACM Press (2005)
10. Parkinson, M.J., Summers, A.J.: The relationship between separation logic and implicit dynamic frames. In: Barthe, G. (ed.) ESOP 2011. LNCS, vol. 6602, pp. 439–458. Springer, Heidelberg (2011)
11. Parkinson, M.J., Summers, A.J.: The relationship between separation logic and implicit dynamic frames. Logical Methods in Computer Science 8(3:01), 1–54 (2012)
12. Smans, J., Jacobs, B., Piessens, F.: Implicit dynamic frames: Combining dynamic frames and separation logic. In: Drossopoulou, S. (ed.) ECOOP 2009. LNCS, vol. 5653, pp. 148–172. Springer, Heidelberg (2009)
13. Summers, A.J., Drossopoulou, S.: A formal semantics for isorecursive and equirecursive state abstractions. In: Castagna, G. (ed.) ECOOP 2013. LNCS, vol. 7920, pp. 129–153. Springer, Heidelberg (2013)

Automated Code Proofs on a Formal Model of the X86

Shilpi Goel and Warren A. Hunt, Jr.

Department of Computer Science, University of Texas at Austin
{shigoel,hunt}@cs.utexas.edu

Abstract. Analysis of binary programs is important to ensure correct execution of corresponding higher-level programs, especially because it accounts for bugs introduced by compilers. Moreover, source code may not always be available for correctness analysis. Proving correctness of binaries often involves significant user expertise and time-consuming manual effort. We describe an approach to automatically verify some X86 binary programs using symbolic execution on an executable formal model of the X86 instruction set architecture. Our approach can reduce the time and effort involved in the proof development process for complex programs.

1 Introduction

In support of our program verification efforts, we have developed an executable formal model of a significant subset of the X86 instruction set architecture (ISA) in the ACL2 [1] programming language. Our ISA model can run X86 binary programs, and we can reason about them using the ACL2 theorem proving system. In this paper, we describe an approach to verify some binary programs fully automatically using a symbolic execution technique. Formal verification of binary programs is important because it is often the only means available to ensure correctness of higher-level programs. Verification based purely on analysis of high-level code does not detect bugs introduced by compilers, thereby decreasing confidence that the program will behave as expected during run-time. Moreover, source code is not available for analysis when software is distributed as binaries.

Our model of the X86 ISA has been developed using an interpreter approach to operational semantics [2]; the model takes a step by taking a processor state as input and producing the next state as output. Our evolving ISA model currently supports the 64-bit mode of Intel's X86 IA32e architecture, including IA32e paging. We have specified all the addressing modes of the architecture and formalized all the integer instructions (both one and two byte opcodes) of the X86 instruction set. To increase confidence in the accuracy of our model, we have and will continue to run extensive co-simulations against physical X86 processors. X86 binaries, for example, obtained as an output of compiling higher level programs using the GCC/LLVM compiler, can be executed on our formal model.

We use the ACL2 system to analyze X86 binaries. There are well-established methods in ACL2 for reasoning about programs for an operational model, including clock functions and inductive invariants [3]. Sometimes, these approaches can involve significant user effort. We describe a method of reasoning about some user-level X86 binary

E. Cohen and A. Rybalchenko (Eds.): VSTTE 2013, LNCS 8164, pp. 222–241, 2014.
© Springer-Verlag Berlin Heidelberg 2014

programs that is fully automatic, in the sense that the user is not required to provide any lemmas to prove the program's correctness. We use the ACL2 GL package [4] to achieve this automation; GL is a framework for proving ACL2 theorems about finite ACL2 objects by symbolic execution. In order to run the GL package efficiently, we use an extension of ACL2, called ACL2(h) [5], that supports function memoization and applicative hash tables. In the remainder of the paper, we refer to ACL2(h) as ACL2 for the sake of simplicity.

The rest of the paper is organized as follows. We present our motivation in Section 2 and then provide a brief introduction to ACL2 in Section 3. In Section 4, we describe our formal X86 ISA model written in ACL2 in some detail. We then describe the automated verification of an example X86 binary, a population bit-count program, in Section 5. This program counts the number of non-zero bits in the binary representation of an integer input in an optimized and non-obvious manner. We conclude with a discussion of how automated correctness proofs of programs in an interactive theorem proving environment can benefit verification efforts, and we present our plans for future work. We also provide a brief description of the ACL2 syntax and some ACL2 function definitions in our formal model in the Appendix.

2   Motivation

Many verification projects in the theorem proving community use a formal model of a processor ISA — such a model is useful for the formalization and verification of programs, operating systems, and translators (compilers, assemblers). Such models are also used as target specifications for the verification of microprocessor designs [6–9]. Building accurate models of processor ISAs, let alone reasoning about programs running on them, is a challenging task. Recently, there have been investigations into developing domain-specific languages [10, 11] to facilitate clear and precise specification of ISAs.

Machine-code verification on formal models of processors has a long history. Bevier's work on operating system kernel verification [12] using the NQTHM [13] theorem prover entailed proving machine code correct for a von Neumannn machine. Boyer and Yu [14] also used NQTHM to formalize most of the user-mode instruction set of a commercial Motorola MC68020 microprocessor and then verify the binary code produced by compiling the Berkeley String library using GCC. However, these code proofs required significant user guidance.

Matthews et al. [15] mechanized assertional reasoning for machine code by implementing a Verification Condition Generator (VCG) in ACL2 [1]. This technique requires the user to annotate the binary program to be verified and deploy ACL2 to discharge verification conditions obtained from the annotations.

Sewell et al. have developed formal models in HOL [16] for subsets of the ISAs of X86 [17], Power and ARM [18]. The focus of their work is the study of relaxed-memory concurrency; for example, these formalizations of processor ISAs were used to prove that the behaviors of some data-race free programs are sequentially consistent.

Feng et al. [19] use the Coq proof assistant [20] to prove the functional correctness of machine code on a simplified formal model of the X86. Hoare-style logics (domain-specific logics, separation logic, etc) are used to prove program modules correct; these proofs are then composed to get the correctness proof of the entire software.

Myreen's "decompilation into logic" technique [21], developed in HOL, takes machine code as input and outputs logic functions capturing the functional behavior of the machine code and a theorem that relates the binary code to these functions. The problem of machine code verification is then reduced to the problem of reasoning about these simpler logic functions, but some user guidance is still required for this purpose.

Our contribution concerns both the accuracy of our X86 ISA model and our automated mechanism of verifying some X86 binary programs. All techniques mentioned just above required manual effort to some degree. Work similar to ours has been done by using bit-blasting [22] as a proof procedure in order to lend automation to an interactive verification system, for example, in the Jitawa project [23]. However, such tools have been used only to prove small but complicated lemmas purely about bit-vectors.

We present an approach using symbolic execution to verify non-trivial user-level X86 binary programs fully automatically in an interactive theorem proving environment using our formalization of a significant subset of the X86 ISA. Unlike the typical use of interactive theorem provers, users are not required to prove tedious lemmas about their formalizations. Moreover, unlike assertional reasoning methods, there is no need to annotate programs to discharge verification conditions. Neither an external (un)trusted tool nor significant user expertise is needed to carry out proofs using this technique. Our technique can be combined with the traditional methods of interactive theorem proving (rewriting, induction, etc) to reduce the time and effort involved to verify binary programs.

3   ACL2: A Brief Introduction

Our work involves extensive use of the ACL2 system for specification, programming, and reasoning. ACL2 stands for *A Computational Logic for Applicative Common Lisp*. It is both a mathematical logic based on an applicative subset of Common Lisp and a mechanical theorem prover used to prove theorems in that logic. Because ACL2 is based on Common Lisp, it offers the execution efficiency provided by the underlying Common Lisp compilers. This gives us the ability to build efficient executable formal models in ACL2.

The ACL2 logic is a first-order logic of recursive functions. The logic provides syntax to represent terms using constants, variables, and function symbols, and some axioms to describe the properties of Common Lisp primitives. More information about the ACL2 syntax can be found in Appendix A.1. Terms in ACL2 can be thought of as formulas; if a term P is proved to be non-nil, then P is a theorem. The ACL2 logic includes some rules of inference like instantiation, a well-founded induction principle, and extension principles. The extension principles extend the current ACL2 first-order theory by allowing addition of new definitions if they satisfy the admissibility requirements.

The ACL2 theorem prover has proof strategies built into it; the application of a proof strategy breaks down the goal formula into zero or more subgoals. The formula is a theorem if all the subgoals, if any, have been proved. Users can extend the prover by adding their own proof strategies known as *clause processors*. In this paper, we use a symbolic execution framework called GL [4], a verified ACL2 clause processor, as a proof procedure.

ACL2 is a freely available system and includes 2100+ pages of documentation [24]. ACL2 libraries are also freely available and are called *community books* [25]. These books have been developed by ACL2 users over many years; they can be *certified* by ACL2 before use to ensure their soundness. Books can be included in an ACL2 project to take advantage of existing definitions and theorems.

4   Executable Formal Model of the X86 ISA

The X86 ISA is a large and complicated architecture, and deciding what subset of it to specify formally is a challenge. Our focus is on the 64-bit mode of Intel's IA32e architecture [26]. Our current formal specification includes all addressing modes, the user-level integer instructions (one and two-byte opcodes), and some system features like paging.

Our model of the X86 ISA has been written in the ACL2 language; this model can be used for execution as well as formal analysis. Our modeling strategy for the X86 ISA is to optimize the definitions for execution but at the same time, to keep them as simple as possible for reasoning. We want our definitions to correspond exactly to the X86 architectural definition, and we are using two methods to help assure its accuracy: code reviews and co-simulation with a physical X86 processor.

Our current X86 model simulates the user-level ISA at about ~3.3 million instructions per second with paging disabled; otherwise, it runs at ~330,000 instructions per second. Our model is around 40,000 lines of code, which includes functions that specify the X86 and theorems about their properties. Given the size of our model, our co-simulation speed allows us to run programs to gain confidence in its accuracy. For the sake of simplicity in the remainder of this paper, we talk only about the programmer's view of the model, i.e., the model where paging is disabled.

We now describe our formalization of the X86 ISA, which uses an interpreter-style, operational semantics. Several relevant ACL2 function definitions can be found in Appendix A.2.

The state of our X86 ISA model contains fields that describe the components of the processor. It is defined using ACL2 structured objects called (concrete) STOBJs [27] and abstract STOBJs [28]. Concrete STOBJs are mutable objects with applicative semantics in ACL2; hence, they provide us with high performance by allowing destructive assignments while providing copy-on-write semantics for reasoning. Abstract STOBJs may provide a simple interface to a concrete STOBJ to enable effective reasoning. More details about modeling processor state using abstract STOBJs can be found elsewhere [29].

All components in the state of our model are listed in Table 1. We specify the complete 2^{52}-byte physical memory (the maximum supported by contemporary commercial processors) by implementing a space-efficient memory model [30], where memory is allocated on demand instead of all at once. The X86 memory is implemented as an array of 16MB blocks. The field `mem-table` stores the pointers to the blocks, `mem-array-next-addr` stores the pointer to the block to be allocated next, and `mem-array` stores the actual bytes. Thus, our memory model breaks a byte address into two parts — a pointer to the 16MB block and an offset within that block.

Our definition of the state contains a field called the `ms` (model state), which is an artifact of our model. The `ms` field is used to indicate situations unsupported by our model as well as to indicate problems in a processor execution step. The processor state is expected to be correct if the model state is `NIL` (empty); otherwise, this field indicates the possible problem and processor execution is halted.

Table 1. Components of the X86 State

Component	Description
rgf	16 general-purpose registers
rip	instruction pointer
flg	64-bit status/rflags register
seg	6 segment registers
str	system-table registers (GDTR and IDTR)
ssr	segment-table registers
ctr	control registers
dbg	debug registers
msr	model-specific registers
mem-array	the X86 memory
mem-table	memory-access table (not a part of the real X86 state, but used by our model to efficiently implement the 2^{52}-byte memory)
mem-array-next-addr	next block address used by mem-table
ms	state of our X86 model (not a part of the real X86 state, but used to specify erroneous model conditions)

The X86 *run* function specifies our X86 model. It takes the initial state and the number of instructions to be executed as input. This *run* function operates by calling the *step* function repeatedly. The *step* function fetches a single instruction from the memory, decodes it, and executes it by dispatching control to the appropriate *instruction semantic function*. Every instruction in the model has its own semantic function, which describes the effects of executing that instruction. A semantic function takes the X86 state as input (among other inputs that are obtained from the instruction decoding process), and outputs the next state, which is modified as per the effects of the instruction.

Initializing our model for execution of an X86 binary is straightforward. Then, the bytes in the X86 binary are written to the memory of the formal model at the appropriate addresses. Other updates, like setting the instruction pointer to the start address and initializing the registers and memory, are also made to the state of the model. The *run* function is then called with the initial state and the appropriate number of instructions to be executed. Execution stops when either the program runs to completion (i.e., a halt instruction is encountered), or an error occurs. The resulting state can then be examined for further analysis.

The development of our X86 formal specification has proceeded through several iterations, each one involving months of effort. Given time, we believe that it is certainly possible to formalize the user-level X86 ISA completely. However, the supervisor model (with features like virtualization) continues to evolve and it may be difficult to catch up with the industry. In addition, as the model grows, the engineering required to manage such a large model is similar to that required to manage a large software system.

5   Reasoning about X86 Binaries

There are many techniques for reasoning about programs on an operational formal model. We describe our use of one such technique — symbolic execution — to perform automated verification of programs in ACL2's interactive theorem proving environment. The GL package [4,31] (freely available as an ACL2 community book) provides us with a framework for proving ACL2 theorems involving finite objects using either an ACL2-verified BDD utility or an external SAT solver; we adopt the BDD approach for the proof described here. GL is a verified clause processor in ACL2, and therefore, enjoys the same trust as the ACL2 system itself. Providing the specification is the primary user requirement in order to prove theorems using GL. If a conjecture fails, GL can compute counterexamples.

GL encodes finite objects into boolean expressions representing symbolic objects [31]. The conversion from finite to symbolic objects has been proven correct and is handled automatically by GL. Computations involving symbolic objects can be done using verified BDD operations; for example, the bitwise XOR of two symbolic objects representing 32-bit integers produces another symbolic object representing a 32-bit integer that encapsulates all the possible resultant values. Thus, GL provides the capability for performing symbolic execution. Such a symbolic execution technique can be used to prove theorems if two requirements are met: all the free variables in the theorem (which must be finite-sized objects such as 32-bit numbers) have been assigned a symbolic object, and the symbolic objects account for all the cases necessary for the proof of the theorem.

`Def-gl-thm` is the main command provided by the GL package; it allows the user to state a conjecture's hypotheses (keyword `:hyp`), conclusion (keyword `:concl`), and bindings of finite free variables to symbolic objects (keyword `:g-bindings`). The bindings also encode the BDD variable ordering for representing the symbolic objects, and as such, affect the symbolic execution performance. When a `def-gl-thm` is processed by ACL2, GL symbolically executes the goal formula. If the symbolic execution results in an expression that represents the value `nil`, GL can produce counterexamples, which can either be symbolic or concrete. Otherwise, the conjecture is proven. To ensure that this symbolic execution accounts for the entire domain of free variables in the theorem, GL also proves coverage with respect to these symbolic objects. In short, a def-gl-thm theorem is proved if and only if the symbolic simulation results in an expression that represents a non-NIL value and coverage is proven.

To demonstrate our approach of using GL to do code proofs, we will reason about a population bit-count program. The specification of the following C function popcount_32 [32], despite appearances, is simple: given a 32 bit unsigned integer as input, popcount_32 computes the number of non-zero bits in its binary representation.

```
int popcount_32 (unsigned int v) {
    v = v - ((v >> 1) & 0x55555555);
    v = (v & 0x33333333) + ((v >> 2) & 0x33333333);
    v = ((v + (v >> 4) & 0xF0F0F0F) * 0x1010101) >> 24;
    return(v);
}
```

We can use the function popcount_32 to compute the population count of larger inputs, for example, we can call popcount_32 once on the upper 32 bits and once on the lower 32 bits of a 64-bit unsigned number and add the results to get the population count of the 64-bit number. This may seem to suggest that proving the correctness of popcount_32 is key to reasoning about such programs.

We obtain the X86 binary corresponding to popcount_32 using GCC/LLVM and using some simple scripts, convert it into a Lisp/ACL2-readable format. The result is then written into the memory of our X86 model. The following GL theorem x86-popcount-32-correct establishes the correctness of popcount_32.

```
(def-gl-thm x86-popcount-32-correct
    ;; Hypothesis: n is a 32-bit unsigned integer
    :hyp (and (natp n) (< n (expt 2 32)))
    ;; Conclusion:
    :concl (let* ((start-address #x4005c0)
            (halt-address #x4005f6)
            (x86 (setup-for-popcount-run
                    nil start-address halt-address
                    ;; The register RDI holds input n to
                    ;; function popcount_32
                    (acons *rdi* n nil)
                    ;; Loading binary into model's memory
                    0 *popcount-binary*))
            ;; Setting the stack pointer to 2$^45$
            (x86 (!rgfi *rsp* *2^45* x86))
            ;; numIns: num. of instructions to execute
            (numIns 300)
            ;; Running the binary on the X86 model
            (x86 (x86-run numIns x86)))
        (and (equal (rgfi *rax* x86)
                    (logcount n))   ;; built-in ACL2 function
            (equal (rip x86) (+ 1 halt-address))))
    :g-bindings `((n     (:g-number ,(gl-int 0 1 33)))))
```

We did not need to build any reasoning infrastructure (i.e. supporting lemmas) to prove the above theorem — it is proved fully automatically in ~60s on a machine with Intel Xeon E31280 CPU @ 3.50GHz.

The theorem states that at the end of execution of popcount_32 binary program, spanning from memory address #x4005c0 to #x4005f6, the register RAX will contain the population count of the input n and the instruction pointer will point to the address following the last instruction. The g-bindings field specifies n as a numeric symbolic object with 33 boolean variables, 32 for the number of bits in n and one-bit for the (positive) sign. Note that the value 300 for numIns is just a number that is large enough to allow the program to run to completion. If a halt instruction is encountered before numIns becomes zero, the symbolic execution of x86-run stops and returns an appropriate X86 state.

We use the ACL2 built-in function logcount to specify popcount_32. The function logcount counts the number of non-zero bits in a positive integer input using a straightforward recursion. (See Appendix A.3 for the ACL2 definition.) The algorithm used to specify logcount is completely different from the algorithm for popcount_32. This proof demonstrates that, unlike classical theorem proving approaches like induction and rewriting, we can prove formulas stating the equivalence of specification functions and implementation functions fully automatically (i.e., without using intermediate lemmas) using GL's symbolic execution even if the specification functions and implementation functions are defined using different algorithms.

We now reason about two functions, popcount_64 and popcount_128, that call popcount_32. To make matters more interesting, we introduce a bug in the program. When the popcount_64 function is run in a "bug-free" mode, it computes the popcount of its 64-bit unsigned integer input v by calling popcount_32 twice, on the upper and lower 32-bits of v. However, popcount_64 does not compute the popcount of v if its input intro_bug is non-zero and if v is equal to 100; in this case, popcount_64 returns 8. The function popcount_128 is simple — if popcount_64 has no bug, it returns the sum of the popcounts of its 64-bit unsigned integer inputs v1 and v2.

```
int popcount_64 (long unsigned int v, int intro_bug) {
  if ((intro_bug != 0) && (v == 100))
    // Introduce a bug!
    return (8);
  else {
    // Bug-free program
    long unsigned int v1, v2;
    v1 = (v & 0xFFFFFFFF); // v1: lower 32 bits of v
    v2 = (v >> 32);        // v2: upper 32 bits of v
    return (popcount_32(v1) + popcount_32(v2));
}}

int popcount_128 (long unsigned int v1, long unsigned int v2,
                  int intro_bug) {
  return (popcount_64(v1, intro_bug) +
          popcount_64(v2, intro_bug));
}
```

Inspection of the binary of the above functions shows that popcount_32, essentially the most complex function in our program, is never called in the other functions; GCC's optimizations result in inlining two copies of the code for popcount_32 in the binary for the function popcount_64. Such commonplace compiler optimizations make code proofs harder — the theorem popcount-32-correct can not be used directly to prove the correctness of popcount_128 compositionally because of differences in memory addresses, registers, etc.

Like popcount_32, we can reason about popcount_128 as well using our symbolic execution framework. Again, there is no need of any supporting lemmas to prove x86-popcount-128-correct; it is proved fully automatically in ~80s on a machine with Intel Xeon E31280 CPU @ 3.50GHz.

The theorem x86-popcount-128-correct states that at the end of execution of our binary, where address #x400768 represents a call from the main program, if intro_bug is 0, the register RAX will contain the sum of the popcounts of the inputs v1 and v2, and the instruction pointer will point to the address following the initial call instruction. v1 and v2 are specified as numeric symbolic objects representing 64-bit integers. The variable intro_bug has been specified as a 32-bit integer because it has been declared as an int in the C program. Note that the symbolic objects corresponding to v1, v2, and intro_bug have interleaved bits — this provides an efficient BDD ordering, resulting in a compact BDD representation for the symbolic objects. We omit comments in x86-popcount-128-correct because it is syntactically similar to x86-popcount-32-correct.

```
(def-gl-thm x86-popcount-128-correct
  :hyp (and (natp v1)
            (< v1 (expt 2 64))
            (natp v2)
            (< v2 (expt 2 64))
            (equal intro_bug 0))
  :concl (let* ((start-address #x400768)
                (halt-address #x40076d)
                (x86 (setup-for-popcount-run
                       nil start-address halt-address
                       0 *popcount-binary*))
                (x86 (!rgfi *rdi* v1 x86))
                (x86 (!rgfi *rsi* v2 x86))
                (x86 (!rgfi *rdx* intro_bug x86))
                (x86 (!rgfi *rsp* *2^45* x86))
                (numIns 300)
                (x86 (x86-run numIns x86)))
           (and (equal (rgfi *rax* x86)
                       (+ (logcount v1) (logcount v2)))
                (equal (rip x86) (+ 1 halt-address))))
  :g-bindings
  `((v1       (:g-number ,(gl-int 0 3 65)))
    (v2       (:g-number ,(gl-int 1 3 65)))
    (intro_bug (:g-number ,(gl-int 2 3 33))))))
```

If, instead of the hypothesis (equal intro_bug 0) in x86-popcount-128-correct, we had the hypothesis that intro_bug is a 32-bit unsigned integer, GL would fail to prove the theorem, producing helpful counterexamples (three, by default) in the process. These counterexamples can help the user debug failed proofs and formulate the correct theorem. The following counterexamples produced by GL clearly indicate that v2 being unequal to 100 should be a pre-condition for the goal formula to be a theorem.

```
Example 1, generated by assigning 0/NIL to all possible bits:
Assignment:
((V1 0) (V2 100) (INTRO_BUG 2147483648))

Example 2, generated by assigning 1/T to all possible bits:
Assignment:
((V1 18446744073709551615) (V2 100) (INTRO_BUG 4294967295))

Example 3, generated randomly:
Assignment:
((V1 10212762264297238869) (V2 100) (INTRO_BUG 2055358792))
...
   GL::GLCP: Counterexamples found in main theorem; aborting
...
```

With the modified def-gl-thm (i.e., after adding (not (equal v2 100)) to the hypotheses), we again get three counterexamples, this time indicating that v1 should not be 100. This allows us to formulate and successfully prove the theorem with the same goal formula as x86-popcount-128-correct, but with the following hypotheses.

- v1 and v2 are 64-bit unsigned integers
- intro_bug is a 32-bit unsigned integer
- v1 and v2 should not be equal to 100.

We show this theorem, called x86-popcount-128-correct-debugging-attempt, in Appendix A.3. This approach of debugging failed proofs using counterexamples not only helps the user find obscure bugs in programs, but also allows the discovery of different conditions under which the stated formula is a theorem.

Such automated proofs of non-trivial programs in an interactive theorem proving environment are possible because of two important reasons:

- *Capacity of GL's Symbolic Engine*: GL is an automatic procedure and there is a limit to the capacity of its symbolic engine. However, this limit is generally much higher as compared to the capacity of exhaustive testing. Though theorems like x86-popcount-128-correct may look straightforward, many large and complicated logical definitions (see Appendix A.2) had to be executed with symbolic data during their proofs. GL is able to perform such proofs because of its fast BDD operations and efficient symbolic execution strategy. For example, GL can perform "actual" execution instead of symbolic execution if concrete data is available in the statement of possible theorems.

- *Efficient Data Structures*: The choice of data structures needed to represent state in a formal model influences the symbolic execution performance. For example, all the elements of state in our previous X86 formal model [33] were logically represented as linear lists. Given our very large memory model, the X86 state was a structure that included an enormous list to represent the memory, and every read or write operation involving the state required linear traversals of these lists. Hence, it was impractical to use the GL framework to do code proofs on that model. Our re-formalization of the state using abstract STOBJs [28] and efficient logical data structures called records [34] enabled use of symbolic execution as an automated proof procedure.

6   Conclusion and Future Work

We described our executable formal model of a significant subset of the X86 ISA and demonstrated a method of automatically verifying some X86 binary programs. Our work involves the verification of "real" X86 binaries; for example, the binaries produced by compiling higher-level programs using the GCC/LLVM compiler. A notable point of our work is that our formal model accurately represents a significant subset of the X86 ISA, i.e., we do not simplify the semantics of the X86 instructions.

We use GL, an ACL2-based symbolic execution framework, to prove some binary programs correct automatically. No lemma construction is needed in order to guide the GL framework to perform these proofs. Also, apart from not requiring any significant user expertise in constructing mathematical proofs, the benefit of being able to use GL for proofs of interesting programs, like our example popcount program, is that we can verify non-trivial pieces of X86 binary code oautomatically. Though we have used GL to verify recursive programs like factorial and fibonacci, verification of straight line code (with conditionals and procedure calls) is GL's forte. Reasoning about general programs with loops will require some intervention — a specification of the loop needs to be provided. However, we can easily imagine using GL to verify subroutines of a program that implements, for example, an encryption algorithm. Proof of correctness of that entire encryption program can then be obtained compositionally by using traditional theorem proving techniques.

We use our symbolic execution framework to reason directly about the semantics of binary programs; i.e., we use GL to reason about binary code that is embedded within our ACL2-based X86 ISA model. The scope of our symbolic execution framework is large; no manual intervention was needed to reason about our example popcount program. The binary of the popcount program has 99 assembly instructions (around 400 bytes of binary code). Also, long and complicated logical definitions, like the step function of our formal model, were symbolically executed in order to reason about this program. This is in contrast to other bit-blasting techniques that have a lower capacity; they are usually employed to prove the correctness of small subgoals generated by verification tools. In addition to the reduction of effort involved in code proofs, having such an automated verification procedure included within an interactive theorem prover speeds up the proof development process. Moreover, our method of using symbolic execution as a proof procedure for code proofs is independent of the ISA being modeled.

We will continue to develop a more complete X86 ISA model (more instructions and modes of operation). We aim to verify "real" programs used in the industry (like security protocols), and to use satisfiability techniques along with BDDs for symbolic execution. We will explore mechanisms for speeding up and increasing the scope of our framework for doing automated code proofs as well as to investigate ways of easily deriving proofs of larger programs compositionally.

Acknowledgements. This material is based upon work supported by DARPA under contract number N66001-10-2-4087. We thank Matt Kaufmann and Robert Krug for their contributions to our evolving X86 model and feedback on this paper. We also thank Marijn Heule, David Rager, Ben Selfridge, and Nathan Wetzler for their feedback on our paper. Finally, we thank the reviewers for their useful and thorough reviews.

References

1. Kaufmann, M., Moore, J.S.: ACL2 home page,
   http://www.cs.utexas.edu/users/moore/acl2
2. Moore, J.S.: Mechanized Operational Semantics,
   http://www.cs.utexas.edu/users/moore/
   publications/talks/marktoberdorf-08/index.html
3. Ray, S., Moore, J.S.: Proof Styles in Operational Semantics. In: Hu, A.J., Martin, A.K. (eds.) FMCAD 2004. LNCS, vol. 3312, pp. 67–81. Springer, Heidelberg (2004)
4. Swords, S.: A Verified Framework for Symbolic Execution in the ACL2 Theorem Prover. PhD thesis, Department of Computer Sciences, The University of Texas at Austin (2010)
5. Boyer, R.S., Hunt Jr., W.A.: Function memoization and unique object representation for ACL2 functions. In: Proceedings of the Sixth International Workshop on the ACL2 Theorem Prover and its Applications, pp. 81–89. ACM (2006)
6. Hunt Jr., W.A.: FM8501: A Verified Microprocessor. LNCS, vol. 795. Springer, Heidelberg (1994)
7. Sawada, J., Hunt Jr., W.A.: Verification of FM9801: An Out-of-Order Microprocessor Model with Speculative Execution, Exceptions, and Program-Modifying Capability. Formal Methods in Systems Design 20(2), 187–222 (2002)
8. Hunt, J. W.A.: Microprocessor design verification. Journal of Automated Reasoning 5, 429–460 (1989)
9. Hunt Jr., W.A., Swords, S., Davis, J., Slobodova, A.: Use of Formal Verification at Centaur Technology. In: Hardin, D.S. (ed.) Design and Verification of Microprocessor Systems for High-Assurance Applications, pp. 65–88. Springer (2010)
10. Fox, A.: Directions in ISA specification. Interactive Theorem Proving, 338–344 (2012)
11. Degenbaev, U.: Formal specification of the x86 instruction set architecture (2012)
12. Bevier, W.R.: A Verified Operating System Kernel. PhD thesis, Department of Computer Sciences, The University of Texas at Austin (1987)
13. Boyer, R.S., Kaufmann, M., Moore, J.S.: The Boyer-Moore theorem prover and its interactive enhancement. Computers & Mathematics with Applications 29(2), 27–62 (1995)
14. Boyer, R.S., Yu, Y.: Automated Proofs of Object Code for a Widely Used Microprocessor. Journal of the ACM 43(1), 166–192 (1996)

15. Matthews, J., Moore, J.S., Ray, S., Vroon, D.: Verification condition generation via theorem proving. In: Hermann, M., Voronkov, A. (eds.) LPAR 2006. LNCS (LNAI), vol. 4246, pp. 362–376. Springer, Heidelberg (2006)

16. Gordon, M.J.C., Melham, T.F. (eds.): Introduction to HOL: A Theorem-Proving Environment for Higher-Order Logic. Cambridge University Press (1993)

17. Sewell, P., Sarkar, S., Owens, S., Nardelli, F.Z., Myreen, M.O.: x86-tso: a rigorous and usable programmer's model for x86 multiprocessors. Communications of the ACM 53(7), 89–97 (2010)

18. Alglave, J., Fox, A., Ishtiaq, S., Myreen, M.O., Sarkar, S., Sewell, P., Nardelli, F.Z.: The semantics of power and arm multiprocessor machine code. In: Proceedings of the 4th Workshop on Declarative Aspects of Multicore Programming, pp. 13–24. ACM (2009)

19. Feng, X., Shao, Z., Guo, Y., Dong, Y.: Certifying low-level programs with hardware interrupts and preemptive threads. Journal of Automated Reasoning 42(2), 301–347 (2009)

20. Dowek, G., Felty, A., Huet, G., Paulin, C., Werner, B.: The Coq Proof Assistant User Guide Version 5.6. Technical Report TR 134, INRIA (December 1991)

21. Myreen, M.O., Gordon, M.J.C., Slind, K.: Decompilation Into Logic - Improved. In: Formal Methods in Computer-Aided Design (FMCAD), pp. 78–81 (2012)

22. Fox, A.C.J.: LCF-style bit-blasting in HOL4. In: van Eekelen, M., Geuvers, H., Schmaltz, J., Wiedijk, F. (eds.) ITP 2011. LNCS, vol. 6898, pp. 357–362. Springer, Heidelberg (2011)

23. Myreen, M., Davis, J.: A verified runtime for a verified theorem prover. In: Interactive Theorem Proving, pp. 265–280 (2011)

24. Kaufmann, M., Moore, J.S.: ACL2 documentation,
    `http://www.cs.utexas.edu/users/moore/acl2/acl2-doc.html`

25. Google Code: ACL2 Books Repository,
    `http://code.google.com/p/acl2-books/`

26. Intel: Intel 64 and IA-32 Architectures Software Developer's Manual (January 2013),
    `http://download.intel.com/products/`
    `processor/manual/325462.pdf`

27. Boyer, R.S., Moore, J.S.: Single-threaded Objects in ACL2. In: Adsul, B., Ramakrishnan, C.R. (eds.) PADL 2002. LNCS, vol. 2257, pp. 9–27. Springer, Heidelberg (2002)

28. ACL2 Documentation: Abstract Stobjs,
    `http://www.cs.utexas.edu/users/moore/`
    `acl2/current/DEFABSSTOBJ.html`

29. Goel, S., Hunt, W., Kaufmann, M.: Abstract Stobjs and Their Application to ISA Modeling. In: Gamboa, R., Davis, J. (eds.) Eleventh International Workshop on the ACL2 Theorem Prover and Its Applications (ACL2 2013) (2013)

30. Hunt Jr., W.A., Kaufmann, M.: A formal model of a large memory that supports efficient execution. In: Cabodi, G., Singh, S. (eds.) Proceedings of the 12th International Conference on Formal Methods in Computer-Aided Design (FMCAD 2012), Cambrige, UK, October 22-25 (2012)

31. Swords, S., Davis, J.: Bit-blasting ACL2 theorems. In: Hardin, D., Schmaltz, J. (eds.) Proceeding 10th International Workshop on the ACL2 Theorem Prover and its Applications. EPTCS, vol. 70, pp. 84–102 (2011)

32. Anderson, S.: Bit Twiddling Hacks,
    `http://graphics.stanford.edu/~seander/bithacks.html`

33. Kaufmann, M., Hunt Jr., W.A.: Towards a formal model of the x86 ISA. Technical Report TR-12-07, Department of Computer Sciences, University of Texas at Austin (May 2012)

34. Kaufmann, M., Sumners, R.: Efficient Rewriting of Data Structures in ACL2. In: 3rd ACL2 Workshop (2002)

A Appendix

A.1 ACL2 Syntax

In this section, we provide a very brief introduction to the ACL2 syntax to enable the reader to go over the definitions listed in Appendix A.2 and A.3.

The ACL2 syntax is the same as Lisp syntax. Terms are written in the prefix notation. For example, `(- 4 3)` represents the term 4 - 3. The keyword `defun` is used to introduce a new function. The following is the ACL2 definition of the factorial function. The `fact` function has one formal argument n and its body contains an `if` expression. The "true" branch of the `if` expression produces 1 as the result and the "false" branch is the product of n and a recursive call to `fact` with n-1 as its argument.

```
(defun fact (n)
  (if (zp n)
      1
    (* n (fact (- n 1))))))
```

The macro `let*` is used for binding lexically scoped (local) variables. In the following example, the variable x is bound to 4 and y is bound to the product of x and 2, resulting in 12 as output.

```
(let* ((x (+ 2 2))
       (y (* x 2)))
  (+ x y))
```

The macro `b*`, used later in the functions listed in this appendix, is a generalization of `let*`. This macro `b*` is defined in the community book `books/tools/bstar.lisp`.

There is extensive documentation [24] for the ACL2 system, and there are 1000s of examples of ACL2 definitions and theorems in the ACL2 community books.

A.2 ACL2 Definitions of X86 ISA Model

X86 State. We use the ACL2 STOBJ mechanism to create a data structure to represent the state of our X86 model. As can be seen by reading the definition (see below), we have modeled the X86 state with a number of components. For example, the first component listed, **rgf**, is an array of 16, 64-bit signed integers. The second component is the instruction pointer, **rip**, is limited to 48 bits for current X86 implementations. The **flg** component is a 64-bit value that models the various state flags (rflags) as defined by the X86 architecture. The **seg**, **str**, **ssr**, **ctr**, **dbg**, **cpl**, and the **msr** represent various parts of the X86 architecture that have to do with memory management, debugging, privilege level, and the model-state registers. The **ms** field allows our X86 model to represent erroneous events, such as illegal instructions. The final three fields are used to implement a complete 52-bit, byte-addressable memory; this model allocates 16 MByte pages on an as needed basis, and will keep allocating pages as long as the host system can provide memory.

```
(defstobj x86
  (rgf :type (array (signed-byte 64)
                    (*64-bit-general-purpose-registers-len*))
       :initially 0 :resizable nil)
  (rip :type (signed-byte 48)
       :initially 0)
  (flg :type (unsigned-byte 64)
       :initially 2)
  (seg :type (array (unsigned-byte 16)
                    (*segment-register-names-len*))
       :initially 0 :resizable nil)
  (str :type (array (unsigned-byte 80)
                    (*gdtr-idtr-names-len*))
       :initially 0 :resizable nil)
  (ssr :type (array (unsigned-byte 16)
                    (*ldtr-tr-names-len*))
       :initially 0 :resizable nil)
  (ctr :type (array (unsigned-byte 64)
                    (*control-register-names-len*))
       :initially 0 :resizable nil)
  (dbg :type (array (unsigned-byte 64)
                    (*debug-register-names-len*))
       :initially 0 :resizable nil)
  (cpl :type (integer 0 3) :initially 0)
  (msr :type (array (unsigned-byte 64)
                      (*model-specific-register-names-len*))
       :initially 0 :resizable nil)
  (ms :type t :initially nil)
  (fault :type t :initially nil)
  (mem-table :type (array (unsigned-byte 26)
                          (*mem-table-size*))
             :initially 1 :resizable nil)
  (mem-array :type (array (unsigned-byte 8)
                          (*initial-mem-array-length*))
             :initially 0 :resizable t)
  (mem-array-next-addr :type (integer 0 33554432)
                       :initially 0))
```

X86 Run Function. Our X86 top-level specification is a simple recursive function that recurs when simulation time ($n > 0$) remains and there is no modeling error (the **ms** field is empty).

```
(defun x86-run (n x86)
  (if (or (zp n) (ms x86))
      x86
    (let ((x86 (x86-fetch-decode-execute x86)))
      (x86-run (1- n) x86))))
```

X86 Step Function. To decode and simulate any X86 instruction is a multi-step process. Below, our x86-fetch-decode-execute function shows the steps our X86 specification uses to fetch an instruction. A X86 instruction can include up to four prefix bytes; these bytes can modify the intent of a X86 instruction. Once the prefix bytes are read (if any), then the X86 opcode is read. Depending on the opcode, additional modifier (ModRM and SIB) bytes are collected. Finally, immediate data, if present, is collected. Once all of this information is gathered, the function opcode-execute is called to dispatch to the appropriate sub-routine to execute the instruction that was fetched.

```
(defun x86-fetch-decode-execute (x86)
  (b*
    ((ctx 'x86-fetch-decode-execute)

     ;; We start each function (just above) by saving its name;
     ;; this is used for returning errors.  Next, we fetch the
     ;; (first part) of the instruction, processing any prefixes.

     (start-rip (the (signed-byte 48) (rip x86)))
     ((when (<= *2^47* (+ 5 start-rip)))
      (!!ms-fresh :start-rip-too-large start-rip))
     ((mv flg0 (the (unsigned-byte 59) prefixes) x86)
      (get-prefixes start-rip 0 5 x86))
     ((when flg0)
      (!!ms-fresh :memory-error-in-reading-prefixes flg0))
     ((the (unsigned-byte 8) opcode/rex/escape-byte)
      (prefixes-slice :next-byte prefixes))

     ;; We determine the number (and length) of the prefixes.

     (prefix-length (prefixes-slice :num-bytes prefixes))
     ((the (signed-byte 49) temp-rip)
      (if (= 0 prefix-length)
          (+ 1 start-rip)
        (+ prefix-length start-rip 1)))

     ;; If rex-byte is present, collect it and get next byte.

     ((the (unsigned-byte 8) rex-byte)
      (if (= (ash opcode/rex/escape-byte -4) 4)
       opcode/rex/escape-byte
        0))

     ;; Collect the first byte of instruction; at this point
     ;; all prefix bytes have been processed.

     ((mv flg1 (the (unsigned-byte 8) opcode/escape-byte) x86)
      (if (int= 0 rex-byte)
          (mv nil opcode/rex/escape-byte x86)
```

```
    (rm08 temp-rip :x x86)))
((when flg1)
 (!!ms-fresh :opcode/escape-byte-read-error flg1))

((the (signed-byte 49) temp-rip)
 (if (int= rex-byte 0) temp-rip (1+ temp-rip)))

;; If present, process the ModRM byte.

(modr/m? (x86-one-byte-opcode-ModR/M-p opcode/escape-byte))
((mv flg2 modr/m x86)
 (if modr/m? (rm08 temp-rip :x x86) (mv nil 0 x86)))
((when flg2)
 (!!ms-fresh :modr/m-byte-read-error flg2))

((the (signed-byte 49) temp-rip)
 (if modr/m? (1+ temp-rip) temp-rip))

((when (not (i48p temp-rip)))
 (!!ms-fresh :temp-rip-too-large temp-rip))

;; If present, process the SIB byte.

(sib? (and modr/m? (x86-decode-SIB-p modr/m)))
((mv flg3 sib x86)
 (if sib? (rm08 temp-rip :x x86) (mv nil 0 x86)))
((when flg3)
 (!!ms-fresh :sib-byte-read-error flg3))

((the (signed-byte 49) temp-rip)
 (if sib? (1+ temp-rip) temp-rip))
((when (not (valid-vm-rip-p temp-rip)))
 (!!ms-fresh :virtual-address-error temp-rip)))

;; opcode-execute dispatches to an appropriate
;; instruction semantic function.

   (opcode-execute start-rip temp-rip prefixes rex-byte
                   opcode/escape-byte modr/m sib x86)))
```

An X86 Semantic Function: CMPXCHG. We present the semantic function of the X86 CMPXCHG instruction (covering two-byte opcodes OF B0 and OF B1); this is one of the simplest X86-instruction semantic functions in our model. CMPXCHG compares the value in the accumulator registers (AL, AX, EAX, or RAX) with the destination operand. If the two values are equal, the source operand is loaded into the destination operand. Otherwise, the destination operand is loaded into the accumulator registers.

Note that there are hundreds of X86 instructions, and therefore, there are a quite a number of other functions like this that are used to specify other X86 instructions.

```
(defun x86-cmpxchg
  (start-rip temp-rip prefixes rex-byte opcode modr/m sib x86)

  ;; Opcode:  0F B0: CMPXCHG r/m8, r8
  ;; Opcode:  0F B1: CMPXCHG r/m16/32/64, r16/32/64

  (b*
   ((ctx 'x86-cmpxchg)
    (lock (= *lock* (prefixes-slice :group-1-prefix prefixes)))
    (r/m (mrm-r/m modr/m))
    (mod (mrm-mod modr/m))
    (reg (mrm-reg modr/m))

    ;; If the lock prefix is present and the destination is
    ;; not a memory operand, then cause the #UD exception.

    ((when (and lock (= mod #b11)))
     (!!ms-fresh
      :lock-prefix-but-destination-not-a-memory-operand
      prefixes))

    (p4 (= *addr-size-override*
           (prefixes-slice :group-4-prefix prefixes)))

    (select-byte-operand (= opcode #xB0))
    (reg/mem-size (select-operand-size select-byte-operand
                                       rex-byte nil prefixes))
    (rAX (rgfi-size reg/mem-size *rax* rex-byte x86))

    ;; Fetch the first (destination) operand:

    ((mv flg0 reg/mem increment-RIP-by v-addr x86)
     (x86-operand-from-modr/m-and-sib-bytes
      reg/mem-size p4 temp-rip rex-byte r/m mod sib x86))
    ((when flg0)
     (!!ms-fresh :x86-operand-from-modr/m-and-sib-bytes flg0))

    (temp-rip (+ temp-rip increment-RIP-by))
    ((when (not (valid-vm-rip-p temp-rip)))
     (!!ms-fresh :virtual-memory-error temp-rip))

    ;; Computing the flags and the result.  The higher
    ;; 32-bits of the eflags register are RAZ (Read As Zero).

    (eflags (flg x86))
    ((the (unsigned-byte 32) eflags)
     (if (<= *2^32* eflags) (logand #xffffffff eflags) eflags))
```

```
(raw-result (- reg/mem rAX))
(result (n-size reg/mem-size (- reg/mem rAX)))
(eflags
 (the (unsigned-byte 32)
   (eflags-for-x86-add/or/adc/sbb/and/sub/xor/cmp/test
     reg/mem-size *OP-CMPXCHG* raw-result result
     reg/mem rAX eflags))))

;; Update the x86 state:

((mv flg1 x86)
 (if (= result 0) ;; rAX == reg/mem
   ;; Fetch the second operand and put it in the
   ;; destination operand.
   (let ((register (rgfi-size reg/mem-size
                    (reg-index reg rex-byte *r*)
                    rex-byte x86)))
   (x86-operand-to-reg/mem reg/mem-size register v-addr
                   rex-byte r/m mod x86))
   ;; rAX != reg/mem
   ;; Put the destination operand into the accumulator.
   (let ((x86 (!rgfi-size reg/mem-size *rax*
                   reg/mem rex-byte x86)))
    (mv nil x86))))

;; If flg1 is non-nil, we exit with no X86 state changes.

((when flg1)
 (!!ms-fresh :x86-operand-to-reg/mem-error flg1))

(x86 (!flg eflags x86))
(x86 (!rip temp-rip x86)))
x86))
```

A.3   ACL2 Theorems of the Example Popcount Program

ACL2 Definition: Logcount

Below is the ACL2 definition for the `logcount` function. This function counts the number of 1 bits in an integer. It first decides if the integer in question is positive or negative; in the case of an negative integer, its input is first negated. This function operates recursively, incrementing a count each time the current value isn't even. Finally, when the input is zero, it stops.

```
(defun logcount (x)
  (cond ((zip x) 0)
    ((< x 0) (logcount (lognot x)))
    ((evenp x)
     (logcount (nonnegative-integer-quotient x 2)))
    (t (1+ (logcount (nonnegative-integer-quotient x 2)))))))
```

Popcount Theorem: Obtained from Debugging Failed Proofs

The following theorem was obtained by debugging failed proofs using counterexamples produced by GL.

```
(def-gl-thm x86-popcount-128-correct-debugging-attempt
  :hyp (and (natp v1)
            (< v1 (expt 2 64))
            (natp v2)
            (< v2 (expt 2 64))
            (natp intro_bug)
            (< intro_bug (expt 2 32))
            (not (equal v1 100))
            (not (equal v2 100)))
  :concl (let* ((start-address #x400768)
                (halt-address #x40076d)
                (x86 (setup-for-popcount-run
                       nil start-address halt-address
                       0 *popcount-binary*))
                (x86 (!rgfi *rdi* v1 x86))
                (x86 (!rgfi *rsi* v2 x86))
                (x86 (!rgfi *rdx* intro_bug x86))
                (x86 (!rgfi *rsp* *2^45* x86))
                (numIns 300)
                (x86 (x86-run numIns x86)))
         (and (equal (rgfi *rax* x86)
                     (+ (logcount v1) (logcount v2)))
              (equal (rip x86) (+ 1 halt-address))))
  :g-bindings
  `((v1       (:g-number ,(gl-int 0 3 65)))
    (v2       (:g-number ,(gl-int 1 3 65)))
    (intro_bug (:g-number ,(gl-int 2 3 33)))))
```

Verification of a Virtual Filesystem Switch

Gidon Ernst, Gerhard Schellhorn, Dominik Haneberg,
Jörg Pfähler, and Wolfgang Reif

Institute for Software and Systems Engineering
University of Augsburg, Germany
{ernst,schellhorn,haneberg,joerg.pfaehler,reif}
@informatik.uni-augsburg.de

Abstract. This work presents part of our verification effort to construct a correct file system for Flash memory. As a blueprint we use UBIFS, which is part of Linux. As all file systems in Linux, UBIFS implements the Virtual Filesystem Switch (VFS) interface. VFS in turn implements top-level POSIX operations. This paper bridges the gap between an abstract specification of POSIX and a realistic model of VFS by ASM refinement. The models and proofs are mechanized in the interactive theorem prover KIV. Algebraic directory trees are mapped to the pointer structures of VFS using Separation Logic. We consider hard-links, file handles and the partitioning of file content into pages.

Keywords: Flash File System, Verification, Refinement, POSIX, VFS, Separation Logic, KIV.

1 Introduction

The popularity of Flash memory as a storage technology has been increasing constantly over the last years. It offers a couple of advantages compared to magnetic storage: It is less susceptible to mechanical shock, consumes less energy and read access is much faster. However, it does not support overwriting data in-place. This limitation leads to significant complexity in the software accessing Flash memory. One solution is a Flash translation layer (FTL) built into the hardware, which emulates the behavior of magnetic storage. Embedded systems, however, often contain "raw Flash", which requires specific Flash file systems (FFS for short) that deal with the memory's write characteristics. A state-of-the-art example is *UBIFS* [15], which is part of the Linux kernel.

The use of Flash memory in safety-critical applications leads to high costs of failures and correspondingly to a demand for high reliability of the FFS implementation. As an example, an error in the software access to the Flash store of the Mars Exploration Rover "Spirit" nearly ruined the mission [22]. In response, Joshi and Holzmann [16] from the NASA JPL proposed in 2007 the verification of an FFS as a pilot project of Hoare's Verification Grand Challenge [14].

We are developing such a verified FFS as an implementation of the POSIX file system interface [29], using UBIFS as a blueprint. The project is structured

E. Cohen and A. Rybalchenko (Eds.): VSTTE 2013, LNCS 8164, pp. 242–261, 2014.

into layers, as (partially) visualized in Fig. 1. These correspond to the various logical parts of the file system, and to different levels of abstraction.

The top level is an abstract formal model of the file system interface as defined by the POSIX standard. It serves as the specification of the functional requirements, i.e., what it means to create/remove a file/directory and how the contents of files are accessed. The POSIX interface addresses files and directories by paths and views files as a linear sequence of bytes. File system objects are structured hierarchically as a tree. Directories correspond to the inner nodes of the tree, whereas files are found at the leaf nodes.

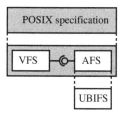

Fig. 1. Upper layers

The first contribution of this work is a formal POSIX model that supports all essential file system operations.

Such high-level concepts are mapped to an efficient pointer-based data representation in the file system. In Linux as well as in our approach this mapping is realized by a *Virtual Filesystem Switch* (VFS). The analogous component in Windows is named Installable File System (IFS). This layer implements generic operations that are common to all file systems, e.g., mapping of file content to a sparse array of pages, permission checks and management of open file handles. VFS delegates lower-level operations to concrete file systems, such as UBIFS.

We have recently published a formal VFS model [6]. It contains an abstract sub-specification AFS of the expected behavior of concrete file systems. The idea is that AFS can be replaced by a concrete implementation as long as the latter behaves as specified by AFS. The VFS model calls AFS through an internal interface, visualized by the symbol —⦶—in Fig. 1. A benefit of this approach is that AFS is independent of the characteristics of Flash memory and may serve as specification for traditional file systems as well, e.g., Ext2-4, ReiserFS or FAT.

Functional correctness is established by nested *refinements* (visualized as dashed lines in Fig. 1). For instance, a proof of the topmost refinement implies that the VFS model realizes the POSIX specification, and in particular that input-/output behavior is preserved.

We describe such a proof in this paper, which is the second contribution.

This refinement is conceptually challenging because of subtle requirements of the POSIX standard, and technically challenging because of the pointer structures and partitioning of file content into pages found in VFS. Models and proofs are mechanized in the interactive theorem prover KIV [23] and can be found on our website [7]. We also provide executable simulations (written manually in Scala) that integrate into Linux via FUSE [28]. As a consequence of the verification we can focus on the Flash File system's internals in the future, namely to refine AFS without further considering VFS. Formally, we refine AFS to UBIFS (in several steps), which then automatically guarantees correctness of VFS+UBIFS with respect to POSIX.

The text continues with a description of the approach in Sec. 2. Sections 3 and 4 describe the POSIX and VFS+AFS models; Sec. 5 formalizes the abstraction from VFS data structures to POSIX, Sec. 6 describes the proofs. We compare to related work in each of these three sections individually. Finally, Sec. 7 draws conclusions and points out ongoing and future work.

2   Scope and Approach

The purpose of this section is to give a high-level description of the approach. We consider the following structural POSIX system-level operations: `create`, `mkdir`, `rmdir`, `link`, `unlink`, and `rename`. File content can be accessed by the operations `open`, `close`, `read`, `write`, and `truncate`. Finally, directory listings and (abstract) metadata can be accessed by `readdir`, `readmeta` (= `stat`), and `writemeta` (subsuming `chmod`/`chown` etc).

These operations and the data types occurring in parameters constitute the signature of the system interface. Functionality is realized abstractly in the POSIX model and "concretely" by the VFS, which delegates low-level modifications to some concrete file system abstracted by AFS. POSIX and VFS share a common signature but have their own representation of the file system's state. By convention, we prefix operations with `posix_` resp. `vfs_`/`afs_` to distinguish between the different layers.

2.1   Formalism

Our specification language is based on *Abstract State Machines* [3] (ASMs). We use algebraic specifications to axiomatize data types, and a weakest-precondition calculus to verify properties.

We frequently use freely generated data types. For example, paths are defined by two constructors: the constant ϵ denoting the empty path, and an infix operator / that adds a leading component.[1] The corresponding selectors `first` and `rest` retrieve the constructor's arguments.

  data $Path = \epsilon \mid$ `_/_`(`first` : $String$, `rest` : $Path$)

We overload the symbol / to add a trailing path component p/s resp. to concatenate two paths p/p'.

Besides free types, we use partial functions types $\tau_1 \nrightarrow \tau_2$ in this work. All partial functions in this paper have a finite domain by construction as a non-free data type from the function with empty domain $\emptyset$ and function update $\_[\_ \mapsto \_]$. Partial function application $f[a]$ uses square brackets. Removing a from the domain of f is denoted by $f - a$. We use the abbreviation $a \in f$ for $a \in \mathrm{dom}(f)$.

ASMs maintain a state as a vector of logical variables that store algebraically defined data structures. The language features programming constructs such as

---

[1] Paths are actually defined as an instance of algebraic lists $Path := List\langle String \rangle$ plus some renaming. This paper deviates from the KIV specifications in minor details to aid readability. Such differences are noted on the web presentation.

parallel (function) assignments (where $f[a] := b$ abbreviates $f := f[a \mapsto b]$), conditionals, loops, recursive procedures, and also nondeterministic choice. ASMs are executable, provided that the nondeterminism is resolved somehow and the algebraic operations on data types are executable.

An ASM $M = ((\mathtt{OP}_i)_{i \in I}, State, \mathtt{INIT})$ consists of operations $\mathtt{OP}_i(in; st, out)$ that take an input in and the current state $st : State$, and produce an output out and a modified state st'. The semicolon in the parameter list separates input parameters from reference parameters: assignments to the latter inside an operation are visible to the caller. Predicate $\mathtt{INIT} \subseteq State$ specifies a set of initial states. A run of an ASM starts in an initial state and repeatedly executes operations.

A "concrete" machine $C = ((\mathtt{COP}_i)_{i \in I}, CState, \mathtt{CINIT})$ *refines* an "abstract" machine $A = ((\mathtt{AOP}_i)_{i \in I}, AState, \mathtt{AINIT})$ if for each run of C there is a matching run of A with the same inputs and outputs. Refinement can be proven by forward simulation with a simulation relation $\mathtt{R} \subseteq AState \times CState$.

The calculus is based on sequents $\Gamma \vdash \Delta \equiv \forall \underline{x}. \bigwedge \Gamma \to \bigvee \Delta$ for a list of assumptions Γ, potential conclusions Δ and free variables of the sequent $\underline{x}$. We prove properties about ASM operations using the weakest precondition calculus implemented by KIV. It offers three modalities: the weakest precondition $\langle\!| p |\!\rangle \varphi$ of p with respect to φ (total correctness, all runs of p starting in the current state terminate in a state satisfying φ); the weakest liberal precondition $[p]\varphi$ (partial correctness); and $\langle p \rangle \varphi \equiv \neg [p] \neg \varphi$ that asserts the existence of some terminating run of p with a final state satisfying φ. For deterministic programs, $\langle\!| \_ |\!\rangle_-$ and $\langle \_ \rangle_-$ are equivalent. The calculus symbolically executes programs in modalities, reducing goals to predicate logic formulas.

The logic can express relationships between multiple programs, such as program inclusion or equivalence. In particular, proof obligations for data refinement [13] (as an instance of ASM refinement) can be formalized. Concretely, in this work we prove

   initialization: (1)

$$\mathtt{CINIT}(cs) \vdash \exists as. \; \mathtt{AINIT}(as) \wedge \mathtt{R}(as, cs)$$

   correctness: (2)

$$\mathtt{R}(as, cs) \vdash \langle\!| \mathtt{COP}_i(in; cs, out_1) |\!\rangle \langle \mathtt{AOP}_i(in; as, out_2) \rangle \; (\mathtt{R}(as, cs) \wedge out_1 = out_2)$$

for $A = $ POSIX and $C = $ VFS+AFS. These assertions establish a forward simulation from commuting 1:1 diagrams. Intuitively, "correctness" asserts that for each run of the concrete operation there is a matching abstract run with the same output, i.e., that the behavior of the concrete machine is covered by the specification/abstract machine. The predicate $\mathtt{R}$ relates a concrete state $cs : CState$ to an abstract state $as : AState$. It is composed of the invariants of the two machines and an abstraction relation

$$\mathtt{R}(as, cs) \; \leftrightarrow \; \mathtt{CINV}(cs) \wedge \mathtt{AINV}(as) \wedge \mathtt{ABS}(as, cs)$$

Background about ASM refinement and its relation to other refinement approaches can be found in [2,25].

2.2   Separation Logic

Separation Logic [24] is a logic designed to reason about pointer structures and destructive updates. It is particularly well-suited for structures with limited aliasing, such as the representation of the directory tree in VFS/AFS (Sec. 4).

Formulas in the logic are assertions $\varphi : Heap \to \mathbb{B}$ about the shape of heaps, which are mappings from locations to values, $Heap := (Loc \nrightarrow Val)$. Heap assertions are built from the constant $\mathtt{emp} = (\lambda h.h = \emptyset)$, the maplet $l \mapsto v$ describing singleton heaps, and the separating conjunction $\varphi_1 * \varphi_2$ that asserts that the heap can be split into two disjoint parts satisfying φ_1 resp. φ_2.

Ordinary formulas, connectives and quantifiers are lifted over heaps, so that they can be used in separation logic assertions.

We have formalized separation logic as a straight-forward shallow embedding into higher-order logic, similar to [21,30]. For this work, we instantiate the sorts *Loc* and *Val* to the pointer structures used in VFS.

In our approach, the heap h is explicitly given as an ordinary program variable. This has the consequence that the frame rule for heap-modular reasoning is not generally valid. A counterexample is the non-local assignment $h := \emptyset$. Interestingly, this does not pose a problem in practice, as one can generalize contracts by a fresh placeholder variable f for the context, i.e., proving the frame rule for a particular contract for program p as $(\varphi * f)(h) \vdash \langle p \rangle (\psi * f)(h)$. By the semantics of sequents, f is universally quantified and can be instantiated arbitrarily.

3   POSIX Specification

This section defines the state, operations and invariants of the POSIX ASM.

3.1   Data Structures

The file system state consists of a directory tree t, a file store fs, and a registry of open file handles oh. Files are referenced by file identifiers of the abstract sort *Fid*. Open files are referenced by natural numbers ("file descriptors" in Unix).

> **state vars** $t : Tree,$ $fs : Fid \nrightarrow FData,$ $oh : \mathbb{N} \nrightarrow Handle$

The directory tree is specified as an algebraic data type *Tree* with two constructors: File nodes (**fnode**) form the leaves and store the identifier of the corresponding file. Directory nodes (**dnode**) make up the internal nodes and store the directory entries as a mapping from names to the respective subtrees.

> **data** *Tree* = **fnode**(**fid** : *Fid*)
> | **dnode**(**meta** : *Meta*, **entries** : *String* $\nrightarrow$ *Tree*)

The test $t.\mathtt{isdir}$ yields whether tree t is a **dnode**. The abstract sort *Meta* is a placeholder for any further associated information. We postulate some selectors for $md : Meta$, to retrieve for example read, write and execute permissions

$pr(u, md), pw(u, md), px(u, md)$ for some unspecified user $u : User$. This formalization of permissions has been taken from [12].

Files are given by the data type *FData* that stores the content as a list of bytes, and—analogously to directories—some associated metadata.

$$\textbf{data } FData \; = \; \texttt{fdata}(\texttt{meta} : Meta, \texttt{content} : List\langle Byte \rangle)$$

File handles store a file identifier $\texttt{fid}$, and keep track of the current read/write offset $\texttt{pos}$ in bytes, and a mode, which can be read-only, write-only or read-write.

$$\textbf{data } Handle \; = \; \texttt{handle}(\texttt{fid} : Fid, \texttt{pos} : \mathbb{N}, \texttt{mode} : Mode)$$
$$\textbf{data } \quad Mode \; = \; \texttt{r} \mid \texttt{w} \mid \texttt{rw}$$

The initial state is given by an empty root directory and no files:

$$\textbf{initial state} \quad t = \texttt{dnode}(md, \emptyset) \wedge fs = \emptyset \wedge oh = \emptyset \tag{3}$$

A path p is valid in a directory tree t, denoted by $p \in t$, if starting from the root t the path can be followed recursively such that each component is mapped by the respective subdirectory. Validity is defined by structural recursion over the path, where ϵ denotes the empty path, s/p denotes a path starting with component $s : String$ and remainder p, and $\epsilon \in t$ always holds.

$$s/p \in \texttt{fnode}(fid) \; \leftrightarrow \; \texttt{false}$$
$$s/p \in \texttt{dnode}(md, st) \; \leftrightarrow \; (s \in st \wedge p \in st[s])$$

Lookup of a valid path p retrieves the respective subtree of t, denoted by $t[p]$. It is defined similarly to validity of paths:

$$t[\epsilon] = t \qquad \text{and} \qquad \texttt{dnode}(md, st)[s/p] = st[s][p] \quad \text{if } s \in st$$

It follows that validity of paths is prefix-closed, i.e., if $p/p' \in t$ then $p \in t$, furthermore $t[p]$ is a directory node if $p' \neq \epsilon$.

The expression $t[p/s \leadsto t']$ denotes the tree t with an additional subtree t' at path p/s. It is only specified for $p \in t$, i.e., it only adds the last component of the path to the tree. A converse function $t - p$ denotes the tree t without the whole subtree at path p. It is only specified for $p \in t$. Note that both modifications are non-destructive and construct new trees. Let the assignment $t[p] := t'$ abbreviate $t := t[p \leadsto t']$, analogously to function update.

Validity, lookup, insertion and deletion of paths compose with $\_/\_$, e.g.:

$$p/p' \in t \quad \leftrightarrow \quad (t \in p \wedge p' \in t[p]) \qquad \text{and} \qquad t[p/p'] = t[p][p'] \quad \text{if } p \in t$$

3.2 Operations and Error Handling

Operations realize the POSIX specification by using the algebraic functions on trees. Additionally, they perform extensive *error checks* to guard the file system against unintended or malicious calls to operations. Specifically, all operations are total (defined for all possible values of input parameters). Nevertheless, we use the term "precondition" to characterize valid inputs such that an operation succeeds. Violation of preconditions leads to an error *without* modifying the internal state. The POSIX model is presented in Fig. 4—omitting some generic error handling code at the beginning of each operation, which we explain by means of the create operation fully shown in Fig. 2.

Error handling is nondeterministic. It is possible that two errors conditions occur simultaneously, e.g., the whole path does not exist, or permissions to traverse an existing prefix are violated. The POSIX model does not restrict the order in which different conjuncts of preconditions are checked. Preconditions are defined as predicates **pre-*op***(in, err) that specify possible error codes for an input in given to the operation op. An implementation just has to satisfy the constraints imposed by these predicates.

Technically, an appropriate error code err' is nondeterministically chosen and assigned to the output variable err. If the operation is determined to succeed (implying a valid input) the body of `posix_create` picks a fresh file identifier fid for the new file, updates the directory tree with the corresponding file node and extends the file store by an empty file with the given initial metadata md. The operation is visualized in Fig. 3. The grey subtree corresponds to the parent directory $t[\mathtt{parent}(p)]$; the newly created file node and associated data are denoted by the dashed triangle and box respectively.

Precondition-predicates contribute a significant part of the specification. They are defined by case distinction on possible error codes, as shown below. Certain errors, such as hardware failure or memory allocation (denoted by EIO, . . .) are not restricted, i.e. they may occur anytime. Note that an implementation must thus recover from such situations to the previous abstract state.

$\mathtt{pre\text{-}create}(p, md, t, fs, e)$

$$\leftrightarrow \begin{cases} p \notin t \land \mathtt{parent}(p) \in t \land t[\mathtt{parent}(p)].\mathtt{isdir}, & \text{if } e = \text{ESUCCESS} \\ p \in t, & \text{if } e = \text{EEXIST} \\ \text{true}, & \text{if } e \in \{\text{EIO}, \ldots\} \\ \ldots & \end{cases}$$

The ASM code relies on several helpers that operate on lists: $\mathtt{resize}(len; l)$ adjusts the size of list l to len, possibly padding l with zeroes at the end; `copy` and `splice` copy len elements of the source list src starting from offset $spos$ into list dst at offset $dpos$. The latter operation corresponds exactly to the semantics of the POSIX write operation, i.e., it may extend dst at the end as shown below. The length of a list l is denoted by $\# l$.

```
splice(src, spos, dpos, len; dst)
   if len ≠ 0 then
      if dpos + len < # dst then resize(dpos + len; dst)
      copy(src, spos, dpos, len; dst)
```

As a further twist the operations `posix_read` and `posix_write` may actually process less than *len* bytes and still succeed, either because the concrete implementation runs out of disk-space during the write, or due to an intermediate low-level error. This is modeled by `choose` n `with` $n < len$ `in` $len := n$.

Handles may refer to files that are not referenced by the tree any more, subsequently called *orphans*. This facility is actually exploited by applications to hide temporary files (e.g, MySQL caches, Apache locks) and during system/package updates.

3.3   Invariants

The POSIX state t, fs, *oh* has two explicit invariants. The easy one is simply that the root must be a directory (t.`isdir`). The second invariant states that the set of file identifiers referenced by t or *oh* is equal to $\text{dom}(fs)$. It guarantees that for any *fid* in use, the associated file data in *fs* is available, and that *fs* contains no garbage. Given an overloaded function

$$\texttt{fids} : \textit{Tree} \rightarrow \textit{Multiset}\langle \textit{Fid} \rangle \qquad \texttt{fids} : (\mathbb{N} \nrightarrow \textit{Handle}) \rightarrow \textit{Set}\langle \textit{Fid} \rangle$$

the invariant can be defined formally:

$$\textbf{invariant} \quad \text{dom}(fs) = \underbrace{\{\textit{fid} \mid \textit{fid} \in \texttt{fids}(t)\} \cup \texttt{fids}(\textit{oh})}_{\texttt{fids}(t, \textit{oh})} \tag{4}$$

with $\texttt{fids}(\textit{oh}) = \{\textit{oh}[n].\texttt{fid} \mid n \in \textit{oh}\}$ and

$$\texttt{fids}(\texttt{fnode}(\textit{fid})) = \{\textit{fid}\} \qquad \texttt{fids}(\texttt{dnode}(\textit{md}, \textit{st})) = \biguplus_{s \in \textit{st}} \texttt{fids}(\textit{st}[s])$$

where $\uplus$ denotes multiset sum. Multisets are preferred over ordinary sets for the file identifiers in the tree for two reasons. On one hand, the number of occurrences of *fid* in the set $\texttt{fids}(t)$ correlates to the number of hard links to a file. On the other hand, the effect of insertion or removal of a subtree on $\texttt{fids}$ directly maps to $\uplus$ respectively $\setminus$. The proofs for invariant (4) are straightforward. The critical operations are `unlink`, `rename`, and `close`, that need to check whether the last link was removed and delete the file content if so.

3.4   Related Work

There exist several file system models with different scope and data structures, with a degree of abstraction similar to our POSIX model. These approaches typically make strong simplifications.

The approach to formalize a POSIX file system with an algebraic tree has been used previously only by Heisel [11] to evaluate specification languages and specification reuse.

Two other approaches occur in related models. In [19,12,8] the file system is specified as a mapping from paths to directories and files. This comes at the

posix_create$(p, md; err)$
  choose err'
  with pre-create(p, md, t, fs, err')
  in $err := err'$

  if $err = $ ESUCCESS then
    choose fid with $fid \notin fs$
    in $t[p]$:= fnode(fid)
       $fs[fid]$:= fdata$(md, \langle \rangle)$

Fig. 2. POSIX create operation

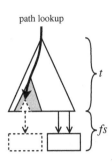

Fig. 3. FS tree

posix_mkdir$(p, md; err)$
  $t[p]$:= dnode$(md, \emptyset)$

posix_rmdir$(p; err)$
  $t := t - p$

posix_link$(p_1, p_2; err)$
  let $fid = t[p_1].$fid
  in $t[p_2]$:= fnode(fid)

posix_unlink$(p; err)$
  let $fid = t[p].$fid
  in $t := t - p$
     if $fid \notin$ fids(t, oh)
     then $fs := fs - fid$

posix_rename$(p_1, p_2; err)$
  let $t_1 = t[p_1], \ t_2 = t[p_2]$
     $ex = p_2 \in t$
  in $t := t - p_2$
     $t[p_2]$:= t_1
     if $ex \wedge \neg t_2.$isdir
        $\wedge t_2.$fid $\notin$ fids(t, oh)
     then $fs := fs - t_2.$fid

posix_truncate$(p, len; err)$
  let $fid = t[p].$fid
  in resize$(len; fs[fid].$content$)$

posix_readdir$(p; names, err)$
  $names :=$ dom$(t[p].$entries$)$

posix_open$(p, mode; fd, err)$
  let $fid = t[p].$fid
  in choose n with $n \notin oh$
  in fd := n
     $oh[fd]$:= handle$(fid, 0, mode)$

posix_close$(fd; err)$
  let $fid = oh[fd].$fid
  in $oh := oh - fd$
     if $fid \notin$ fids(t, oh)
     then $fs := fs - fid$

posix_read$(fd; buf, len, err)$
  let $fid = oh[fd].$fid
     $pos = oh[fd].$pos
  in choose n with $n \le len$
     in $len := n$
     copy$(fs[fid].$content$, pos, 0, len; buf)$
     $oh[fd].$pos := $pos + len$

posix_write$(fd, buf; len, err)$
  let $fid = oh[fd].$fid
     $pos = oh[fd].$pos
  in choose n with $n \le len$
     in $len := n$
     splice$(buf, 0, pos, len; fs[fid].$content$)$
     $oh[fd].$pos := $pos + len$

Fig. 4. POSIX operations

cost of an extra invariant that path validity is prefix-closed, which holds by construction in our model. However, only Hesselink and Lali [12] actually verify that it is preserved by operations.

Of these three models, only the one of Morgan and Sufrin [19] supports hard-links, using file identifiers as we do. In [12], equivalence classes of paths are suggested as an alternative solution. We are not aware of an attempt to realize this idea, though it would be interesting.

Damchoom et al. [5], in contrast, formalize the hierarchical structure by parent pointers with an acyclicity invariant. Hard links are inherently not supported by this design. We think that this approach is too different from the intuitive understanding of a file system to serve as top-level specification.

Morgan and Sufrin's work [19] contains a minor error (also found in [17,9]): they do not specify an equivalent of the test $len \neq 0$ in splice (Sec. 3.2), which may result in overly large files. The corresponding requirement in the POSIX standard [29] states that *[..] if nbytes [=len] is zero [..] the write() function shall return zero and have no other results.*

Open file handles have not been mechanized before, although these are specified on paper in [19], including the possibility of orphaned files.

Preconditions are treated similarly to [12], i.e., operations must not modify the state on errors. Ferreira et al [8] also have a comprehensive error specification in their POSIX-style specification, however, they fix the order of checks and allow arbitrary behavior on errors in their refinement proof obligations. To our knowledge, underspecified hardware failures are not admitted in related work.

4   VFS and AFS Models

We give a short overview over the interplay between VFS and AFS and how generic file system aspects are separated from FS specific concerns. For details not covered here the reader is referred to [6] and the web presentation [7].

4.1   Interplay

The task of the VFS layer is to break down high-level POSIX operations to several calls of AFS operations. Fig. 5 visualizes a typical sequence for structural operations like vfs_create. In this case, it relies on three operations provided by the file system implementation, namely

1) lookup of the target of a single edge in the graph (afs_lookup),
2) retrieve the access permissions at each encountered node (afs_iget),
3) and finally the creation of the file.

Since many operations rely on *path lookup*, it is implemented as a subroutine vfs_walk that repeatedly performs steps 1) and 2). Figure 6 visualizes the representation of the file system state and effect of the operation. Analogously to Fig. 3, the parent directory is shaded in grey and the new parts are indicated by dashed lines. The cloud-shaped symbol summarizes the remaining directories and files.

The interface between VFS and AFS (resp. the concrete file system) is defined in terms of three communication data structures. *Inodes* ("Index Nodes") correspond to files and directories. They are identified by inode numbers *ino* : *Ino* and store some metadata such as permissions but also size information and the number of hard-links. *Dentries* ("Directory Entries") correspond to the link between a parent directory and the inode of an entry. They contain the target inode number and a file/directory name. The content of files is partitioned into uniformly sized *pages*, which are sequences of bytes. A concrete implementation, as well as AFS, maps these to some internal state and on-disk structures. This approach decouples VFS from the file system, which is essential for modularity.

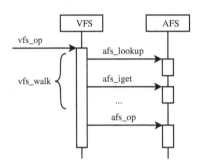

Fig. 5. VFS/AFS interplay

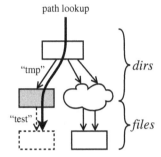

Fig. 6. FS as pointer structure

4.2 State

Although the VFS code is independent of the AFS state, its behavior is not. To define the abstraction relation (Sec. 5) and to prove the refinement (Sec. 6), we need to look into the AFS state, which is a pointer based acyclic graph with forward links. AFS keeps directories and files in two stores (partial functions) with disjoint domains, mapping inode numbers to the respective objects:

state vars $dirs : Ino \nrightarrow Dir$, $files : Ino \nrightarrow File$ where $Ino \simeq \mathbb{N}$

The separation is motivated by the distinction into structural and content modifications: the former will affect mainly *dirs* while the latter will affect only *files*.

Directory entries are contained in the parent directory, likewise, pages are contained in the file object they belong to:

data Dir = dir(meta : *Meta*, entries : *String* $\nrightarrow$ *Ino*)
data $File$ = file(meta : *Meta*, size : $\mathbb{N}$, pages : $\mathbb{N} \nrightarrow Page$)   where
type $Page = List_{\text{PAGE\_SIZE}}\langle Byte \rangle$

Inode numbers $ino \in dirs$ or $ino \in files$ are called *allocated*, they refer to valid directories resp. files. The pages of a file need not to be contiguous, there may be holes in a file that implicitly contain zeroes. A function $\text{links}(ino, dirs)$ returns a set of pairs $(p\_ino, name)$ such that $dirs[p\_ino].\text{entries}[name] = ino$

The VFS state consists of open file handles that are equivalent to the ones in POSIX:

state var $oh : \mathbb{N} \nrightarrow Handle,$ where

data $Handle = \text{handle}(ino : Ino, \text{pos} : \mathbb{N}, \text{mode} : Mode)$

The initial state is given by an empty root directory with a fixed inode number ROOT_INO and no files:

$$\textbf{initial state} \quad dirs = [\text{ROOT\_INO} \mapsto \text{dir}(md, \emptyset)] \wedge fs = \emptyset \wedge oh = \emptyset \tag{5}$$

4.3 Operations

For each POSIX operation there is a corresponding VFS operation with the same signature, implementing the desired functionality, e.g. $\text{vfs\_create}(p, md; err)$. Subroutine vfs_walk is shown in Fig. 7, as well as afs_create. Calls to afs_iget occur during the permission-check in vfs_maylookup. On success, vfs_walk establishes validity of a path q ($= \text{parent}(p)$ for vfs_create), expressed as

$$\text{vfs\_walk post:} \quad err = \text{ESUCCESS} \rightarrow \text{path}(q, p\_ino, ino, dirs, files)$$

The predicate **path** defined recursively on the path by the axioms

$$\text{path}(\epsilon, p\_ino, ino, dirs, files) \leftrightarrow \quad p\_ino = ino \wedge ino \in (dirs \cup files)$$
$$\text{path}(s/p, p\_ino, ino, dirs, files) \leftrightarrow \quad p\_ino \in dirs \wedge s \in si$$
$$\wedge \, \text{path}(p, si[s], ino, dirs, files)$$

where si abbreviates $dirs[p\_ino].\text{entries}$.
An overloaded version $\text{path}(p, p\_ino, dirs, files)$ hides ino by existential quantification.

```
vfs_walk(q; ino, err)                      afs_create(p_ino, md; dent, err)
   err := ESUCCESS                            if   p_ino ∈ dirs
   while q ≠ ε ∧ err = ESUCCESS do                 ∧ dent.isnegdentry
      vfs_maylookup(ino; err)                      ∧ dent.name ∉ dirs[p_ino].entries
      if err = ESUCCESS then                  then choose ino
         let dent = negdentry(q.first)        with ino ∉ dirs ∧ ino ∉ files ∧ ino ≠ 0
         in  afs_lookup(ino; dent, err)       in  dirs[p_ino].entries[dent.name] := ino
             if err = ESUCCESS then               files[ino]  := file(md, 0, ∅)
                ino := dent.name                   dent        := dentry(dent.name, ino)
                q   := q.rest                      err         := ESUCCESS
```

Fig. 7. VFS create operation and path walk

The VFS read and write operations break file access down to a number of individual page reads resp. writes in a loop (Fig. 8). It writes at most $end - start$ bytes of *buf* to the file specified by *inode*.ino, beginning at file offset *start* (in bytes); *total* counts the number of bytes already written.

The body of the write loop, vfs_write_block (Fig. 9), unifies partial writes to the first and last page alongside writes of entire pages, in order to avoid code for these special cases and intermediate assertions in the verification. The operation afs_readpage returns page number *pageno* of the file inode numbered *inode*.ino if that page is stored. Otherwise, an empty page is returned. The relevant part of *buf* is copied into the page and the page is written back.

Note that less than $end - start$ bytes may be written overall, since the loop is aborted as soon as an error is returned by AFS. Such an error is recovered by the test for $total \neq 0$ in Fig. 8, and—if necessary—the file size is adjusted to the number of bytes actually written.

```
. . .
let start = oh[fid].pos,  end = start + len,  total = 0,  done = false in
while ¬ done ∧ err = ESUCCESS do
  vfs_write_block(start, end, inode; done, buf, total, err)
if total ≠ 0 then err := ESUCCESS
if err = ESUCCESS ∧ inode.size < start + total then
  afs_truncate(inode.ino, start + total; err)
```

Fig. 8. VFS write operation (omitting error handling)

```
vfs_write_block(start, end, inode, buf, dirs; total, done, files, err)
  let pageno = (start + total)  /  PAGE_SIZE        // integer division
      offset = (start + total)  %  PAGE_SIZE        // and      modulo
      page   = emptypage
  in      // bytes to write in this iteration
      let n = min(end       – (start + total),      // write size     boundary
                  PAGE_SIZE – offset) in            // current page boundary
      if n ≠ 0 then
          afs_readpage(inode.ino, pageno, dirs, files; page, err)
          if err = ESUCCESS then
              copy(buf, total, offset, n; page)
              afs_writepage(inode.ino, pageno, page, dirs; files, err)
              total := total + n
      else done := true
```

Fig. 9. VFS code to write a partial page

4.4   Related Work

Galloway et al. [10] abstract the existing Linux VFS code to a SPIN model to check correct usage of locks and reference counters. Work with similar focus that directly checks the C source code is [20,31]. However, these approaches limit themselves to specific properties that are weaker than functional correctness (e.g., memory safety) or cover concepts orthogonal to this work (e.g., correct usage of locks).

Reading and writing files at byte-level has been addressed in [1,17]. We compare to this work in more detail in Sec. 6.3.

To our knowledge, our model [6] is the first one separating common functionality (VFS) and file system specific parts (AFS) with the goal of full functional verification.

5   Abstraction Relation

The abstraction relation ABS is defined as

$$\text{ABS}(t, \mathit{fs}, oh_1, \mathit{dirs}, \mathit{files}, oh_2)$$
$$\leftrightarrow \quad \mathit{fs} = \text{fs}(\mathit{files}) \land \text{tree}(t, \text{ROOT\_INO})(\mathit{dirs}) \land oh_1 = oh_2$$

where $\text{fs} : (Ino \twoheadrightarrow File) \to (Fid \twoheadrightarrow File)$ specifies the abstract file store fs and $\text{tree} : Tree \times Ino \to ((Ino \twoheadrightarrow Dir) \to \mathbb{B})$ abstracts the pointer structure with root ROOT_INO to the directory tree t using Separation Logic. By defining $Fid := Ino$, open file handles can be mapped by identity. This section formally defines tree and fs and states several key lemmas connecting the abstract and concrete states.

5.1   Directory Abstraction

The directory tree is mapped to the store of directories dirs, instantiating the separation logic theory from Sec. 2.2 with $Loc := Ino$ and $Val := Dir$. We define the predicate $\text{tree}(t, ino)$ by structural recursion on the tree. The idea is that whenever $\text{tree}(t, ino)(\mathit{dirs})$ holds, ino is the number of the root inode of a file system tree in dirs that corresponds to t.

$$\text{tree}(\text{fnode}(\mathit{fid}), ino) = (\text{emp} \land ino = \mathit{fid}) \tag{6}$$
$$\text{tree}(\text{dnode}(md, st), ino) = \tag{7}$$
$$\exists \, si. \, \text{dom}(si) = \text{dom}(st) \land ino \mapsto \text{dir}(md, si) \, * \, \underset{s \in st}{\circledast} \, \text{tree}(st[s], si[s])$$

Assertion (6) for file nodes requires that the inode number corresponds to the fid of the node and that the remaining part of the heap is empty.

Assertion (7) for directory nodes requires a corresponding directory in dirs that has the same metadata and corresponding directory entries si. The iterated separating conjunction $\circledast$ recursively asserts the abstraction relation for all subtrees $st[s]$ to children $si[s]$ in pairwise $\mathit{disjoints}$ parts of dirs.

One can show by induction on p that $\text{tree}(t, ino)(\mathit{dirs})$ implies

$$\text{path}(p, ino, \mathit{dirs}, \mathit{files}) \, \leftrightarrow \, p \in t$$

We furthermore define the assertion $\mathtt{tree}|_p(t, ino_1, ino_2)(dirs)$ that cuts out the subtree with root ino_2 at path p. Equality (8) encodes one main reasoning step for the proofs. It allows us to unfold the directory that is modified by an operation, given postcondition $\mathtt{path}(p, ino_1, ino_2, dirs, files)$ of $\mathtt{vfs\_walk}$

$$\mathtt{tree}(t, ino_1)(dirs) \;\leftrightarrow\; (\mathtt{tree}|_p(t, ino_1, ino_2) * \mathtt{tree}(t[p], ino_2))(dirs) \qquad (8)$$

Another critical lemma discards algebraic tree modifications if p is a (not necessarily strict) prefix of q:

$$q = p/p' \;\rightarrow\; \mathtt{tree}|_p(t[q \rightsquigarrow t'], ino_1, ino_2) = \mathtt{tree}|_p(t, ino_1, ino_2) \qquad (9)$$

Finally, the abstraction implies the following equivalence, which ensures correct deletion of file content in $\mathtt{close}$, $\mathtt{unlink}$ and $\mathtt{rename}$:

$$fid \notin \mathtt{fids}(t) \;\leftrightarrow\; \mathtt{links}(ino, dirs) = \emptyset \quad \text{for } ino = fid$$

5.2   File Abstraction

The abstract file store is defined for each $fid \in files$, $fid = ino$ with $files[ino] = \mathtt{file}(md, size, pages)$ by the extensional equation

$$\mathtt{fs}(files)[fid] = \mathtt{fdata}(md, \mathtt{content}(pages) \text{ to } size)$$

where $\mathtt{content} : (\mathbb{N} \nrightarrow Page) \to Stream\langle Byte \rangle$ assembles a stream of bytes from the pages of a file. The abstract file must store the finite prefix of length $size$ of that stream. Streams $\sigma : Stream\langle\alpha\rangle$ can either be finite (a list) or infinite (a total function from natural numbers to values)

$$\textbf{type } Stream\langle\alpha\rangle = List\langle\alpha\rangle + (\mathbb{N} \to \alpha)$$

with a function $\#\sigma : \mathbb{N} + \{\infty\}$ to retrieve the length of a stream σ, prefix and postfix selectors σ $\mathtt{to}$ n resp. σ $\mathtt{from}$ n (defined for $n \leq \#\sigma$), and concatenation $\sigma_1 \;\text{+}\!\!\text{+}\; \sigma_2$.

The abstraction to streams eliminates a lot of reasoning about list bounds and many case distinctions that would otherwise be necessary in definitions and proofs. In particular it simplifies the invariants of the loops in operations $\mathtt{vfs\_read}$ and $\mathtt{vfs\_write}$, see Sec. 6.2.

We define the content of a file as an infinite stream with trailing zeroes beyond the end of the file:

$$\mathtt{content}(pages) = \lambda n.\, \mathtt{getpage}(pages, n/\mathtt{PAGE\_SIZE})[n\%\mathtt{PAGE\_SIZE}]$$
$$\mathtt{getpage}(pages, m) = \text{if } m \in pages \text{ then } pages[m] \text{ else } \langle 0, \ldots \rangle$$

6   Proofs

Proof obligation "initialization" (1) is trivial: (5) implies (3) for the same metadata md of the root directory and all invariants hold.

Proof obligation "correctness" (2) is established by symbolic execution of the VFS operation, which yields a state $dirs', files', oh_1', out_1$, followed by symbolic execution of the POSIX operation to construct a matching witness run with a final state t', fs', oh_2', out_2.

During symbolic execution, whenever the VFS chooses some value by the left rule for $\langle\_|\rangle\_$ in (10), the POSIX is free to choose the *same* value by the existential quantifier in the right rule for $\langle\_\rangle\_$ in (10).

$$\frac{\vdash \forall x.\varphi(x) \to \langle p \rangle \psi \quad \vdash \exists x.\varphi(x)}{\vdash \langle\!\langle \text{choose } x \text{ with } \varphi(x) \text{ in } p \rangle\!\rangle \psi} \qquad \frac{\vdash \exists x.\varphi(x) \wedge \langle p \rangle \psi}{\vdash \langle \text{choose } x \text{ with } \varphi(x) \text{ in } p \rangle \psi} \tag{10}$$

The error code err' selected by POSIX is determined this way, as well as e.g. the fid in in the operation $\texttt{create}$ in Fig. 2 corresponding to the new inode number ino picked in Fig. 7.

The predicate logic goals resulting from symbolic execution have the form

$$\Gamma \vdash \text{R}(t', fs', oh_1', dirs', files', oh_2') \wedge out_1 = out_2$$

where $\Gamma = \text{R}(t, fs, oh_1, dirs, files, oh_2), \ldots$ contains the initial instance of the simulation relation, as well as preconditions and other information that has been gathered during symbolic execution (e.g., results of the tests in conditionals and subroutine postconditions). The goals reduce to two core proof obligations:

directories: $\quad \texttt{tree}(t, \texttt{ROOT\_INO})(dirs), \Gamma \vdash \texttt{tree}(t', \texttt{ROOT\_INO})(dirs')$

files: $\qquad\qquad\quad fs = \texttt{fs}(files), \Gamma \vdash fs' = \texttt{fs}(files')$

6.1   Proof Strategy for Directories

Two types of modifications to the directory tree occur: insertions $t' = t[p \rightsquigarrow \ldots]$ and deletions $t' = t - p$ at a path p. These correspond to a local modification of some directory $dirs' = dirs[ino \mapsto \texttt{dir}(md', si')]$ (for some new metadata md' and directory entries si') resp. $dirs' = dirs - ino$, where ino is found at $\texttt{parent}(p)$.

The proof strategy is determined by the symbolic execution rules for assignment and deallocation. The notation $\psi_h^{h'}$ denotes renaming of the heap h to a fresh variable h' representing the updated heap in the remaining program modality resp. postcondition ψ.

$$\frac{(l \mapsto v * \varphi)(h') \vdash \psi_h^{h'}}{(l \mapsto \_ * \varphi)(h) \vdash \langle h[l] := v \rangle \psi} \text{ assign-h} \qquad \frac{(\varphi)(h') \vdash \psi_h^{h'}}{(l \mapsto \_ * \varphi)(h) \vdash \langle h := h - l \rangle \psi} \text{ dealloc}$$

The first step is to unfold the tree by (8) and (7) so that the maplet for ino is explicit and the assignment can be applied, propagating the assertion to the new directory store $dirs'$. The $\texttt{dnode}$ predicate for ino is restored wrt. the new subdirectories si', e.g., by introducing an additional $\texttt{fnode}$ assertion in the proof for $\texttt{create}$. The context $\texttt{tree}|_p$ is rewritten to t' as well by (9) (applied from right to left), so that the whole abstraction can be folded by reverse-applying (8). Most of these steps are automated by rewrite rules.

6.2   Proof Strategy for Files

For $ino = fid$ and given $\sigma = \text{content}(pages)$ the following two top-level equalities promote the concrete modification through the abstraction fs:

$$\text{fs}(files[ino \mapsto \text{file}(size, md, pages)]) = \text{fs}(files)[fid \mapsto \text{fdata}(md, \sigma \text{ to } size)]$$
$$\text{fs}(files - ino) = \text{fs}(files) - fid$$

It remains to establish that σ to $size$ matches the abstract operation, which is trivial for create (σ to $0 = \langle\rangle$) and difficult for write because of the loop in VFS, see Fig. 9.

The loop invariant for writing states that the file content can be decomposed into parts of the initial file $\text{content}(pages_0)$ at the beginning and at the end, with data from the buffer in between:

$$\text{write inv:}\quad \text{content}(pages) = \quad \text{content}(pages_0) \text{ to } start \tag{11}$$
$$+\!\!+ \quad buf \text{ to } total$$
$$+\!\!+ \quad \text{content}(pages_0) \text{ from } (start + total)$$

The key idea behind the proofs to propagate the invariant through the loop is to normalize all terms of type stream to a representation with $+\!\!+$. For example, the effect of afs_writepage is captured by the equality

$$\text{content}(pages[pageno \mapsto page])$$
$$= \quad \text{content}(pages) \text{ to } (pageno * \text{PAGE\_SIZE})$$
$$+\!\!+ \quad page$$
$$+\!\!+ \quad \text{content}(pages) \text{ from } (pageno * (\text{PAGE\_SIZE} + 1))$$

A similar theorem exists for $\text{copy}(buf, total, offset, n; page)$. Equation (11) is then restored by distribution lemmas such as $(\sigma_1 +\!\!+ \sigma_2)$ from $n = \sigma_2$ from $(n - \#\sigma_1)$ if $n \geq \#\sigma_1$, and by cancellation of leading stream components of both sides of the equation $(\sigma +\!\!+ \sigma_1 = \sigma +\!\!+ \sigma_2) \leftrightarrow \sigma_1 = \sigma_2$ for finite σ. Finally, the loop invariant is mapped to the respective abstract POSIX operation.

Compared to the canonical alternative—a formulation of the loop invariants with splice (resp. copy for reading)—our approach is considerably more elegant: Invariant (11) does not need to mention the "current" size of the file, which would lead to case distinctions whether the file needs to grow. Such case distinctions (also found in max) produce a quadratic number of cases in the proof as one needs to consider the previous *and* the new version of the invariant.

6.3   Related Work

Hesselink and Lali [12] refine the mapping from paths to files to a pointer-based tree that is structurally similar to our AFS model. Their abstraction function is a point-wise comparison on path lookup. Our verification bridges a wider conceptual gap, since we start with a more abstract data structure (algebraic tree) and our VFS model is closer to a real implementation (e.g., uses a while-loop for path lookup, separates AFS). We have specified and verified additional operations, namely, access to files via file handles and the operations `read`, `write` and `truncate`.

Damchoom et al. [5] introduce several concepts such as the distinction between files and directories and permissions by small refinement steps. These aspects are covered by our POSIX model, except that their model is more detailed wrt. metadata (file owners, timestamps). Furthermore, in [4] the same authors decompose file write into parallel atomic updates of single pages, though not down to bytes.

Arkoudas et al. [1] address reading and writing of files in isolation (without file handles). Their model of file content is similar to ours (i.e., non-atomic pages). They prove correctness of read and write with respect to an abstract POSIX-style specification. However, their file system interface allows only to access *single bytes* at a time, which is a considerable simplification.

The work of Kang and Jackson [17] is closest to our work with respect to read and write—it provides the same interface (buffer, offset, length). However, their model only deals with file content but not with directory trees or file handles. They check correctness with respect to an abstract specification for small bounded models. In comparison, their read and write algorithm is less practical than ours, because it relies on an explicit representation of a list of blocks that needs to be modified during an operation.

The VeriFast tool[2], which is based on Separation Logic, ships with some examples for binary trees, in particular, a solution to the VerifyThis competition[3] that specifies an equivalent to $tree|_p$ for binary trees. Finally, [18] is a nice application of Separation Logic to the verification of B^+ trees in the Coq prover.

7   Discussion and Conclusions

We have presented a formal specification of the POSIX file system interface, and a verified refinement to a formal model of a Virtual Filesystem Switch as a major step in the construction of a verified file system for Flash memory. As a consequence we can focus on the flash specific aspects in the future.

The different models have been developed more or less simultaneously in order to clarify the requirements for VFS, and to ensure that refinements will work out (the one presented in this paper as well as future ones).

We estimate that the net-effort put into this work was about six person-months: Understanding the POSIX requirements as well as the design of the Linux VFS and its source code took roughly one month. The remaining time was spent for design and specification of the models (about three months) and verification of invariants and refinement (two months). As a reference, we think that the verification was about three times as complex as the original Mondex challenge [27]. The size of the models is roughly as follows. The state machines

---

[2] `www.cs.kuleuven.be/~bartj/verifast/`
[3] `http://fm2012.verifythis.org`

consist of 50 lines in the POSIX model, 500 for VFS and 100 for AFS. Additionally, there are around 450 of lines algebraic specification for POSIX and 200 for VFS+AFS on top of the KIV libraries.

For this particular verification, state invariants were fairly easy to prove, while the simulation proofs were challenging. Paying attention to details (short read-/write, orphans, errors) introduced additional complexity. We experienced that choosing the right data structures simplified both specification and verification (fids as multisets, file abstraction to streams).

Several orthogonal aspects remain for future work. Concurrency in VFS has been intentionally left out so far. Caching of inodes, dentries and pages in VFS could be realized without changing the AFS code. Fault tolerance against power loss is of great interest and we are currently proving that the models can deal with unexpected power loss anytime during the run of an operation, using the temporal program logic of KIV [26]. Translation of the models to C code is still an open issue.

References

1. Arkoudas, K., Zee, K., Kuncak, V., Rinard, M.: Verifying a file system implementation. In: Davies, J., Schulte, W., Barnett, M. (eds.) ICFEM 2004. LNCS, vol. 3308, pp. 373–390. Springer, Heidelberg (2004)
2. Börger, E.: The ASM Refinement Method. Formal Aspects of Computing 15(1-2), 237–257 (2003)
3. Börger, E., Stärk, R.F.: Abstract State Machines—A Method for High-Level System Design and Analysis. Springer (2003)
4. Damchoom, K., Butler, M.: Applying Event and Machine Decomposition to a Flash-Based Filestore in Event-B. In: Oliveira, M.V.M., Woodcock, J. (eds.) SBMF 2009. LNCS, vol. 5902, pp. 134–152. Springer, Heidelberg (2009)
5. Damchoom, K., Butler, M., Abrial, J.-R.: Modelling and proof of a tree-structured file system in Event-B and Rodin. In: Liu, S., Araki, K. (eds.) ICFEM 2008. LNCS, vol. 5256, pp. 25–44. Springer, Heidelberg (2008)
6. Ernst, G., Schellhorn, G., Haneberg, D., Pfähler, J., Reif, W.: A Formal Model of a Virtual Filesystem Switch. In: Proc. of SSV, pp. 33–45 (2012)
7. Ernst, G., Schellhorn, G., Haneberg, D., Pfähler, J., Reif, W.: KIV models and proofs of VFS and AFS (2012),
http://www.informatik.uni-augsburg.de/swt/projects/flash.html
8. Ferreira, M.A., Silva, S.S., Oliveira, J.N.: Verifying Intel flash file system core specification. In: Modelling and Analysis in VDM: Proc. of the fourth VDM/Overture Workshop, pp. 54–71. School of Computing Science, Newcastle University. Technical Report CS-TR-1099 (2008)
9. Freitas, L., Woodcock, J., Fu, Z.: Posix file store in Z/Eves: An experiment in the verified software repository. Sci. of Comp. Programming 74(4), 238–257 (2009)
10. Galloway, A., Lüttgen, G., Mühlberg, J.T., Siminiceanu, R.I.: Model-checking the linux virtual file system. In: Jones, N.D., Müller-Olm, M. (eds.) VMCAI 2009. LNCS, vol. 5403, pp. 74–88. Springer, Heidelberg (2009)
11. Heisel, M.: Specification of the Unix File System: A Comparative Case Study. In: Alagar, V.S., Nivat, M. (eds.) AMAST 1995. LNCS, vol. 936, pp. 475–488. Springer, Heidelberg (1995)

12. Hesselink, W.H., Lali, M.I.: Formalizing a hierarchical file system. Formal Aspects of Computing 24(1), 27–44 (2012)
13. Hoare, C.A.R.: Proof of correctness of data representation. Acta Informatica 1, 271–281 (1972)
14. Hoare, C.A.R.: The verifying compiler: A grand challenge for computing research. Journal of the ACM 50(1), 63–69 (2003)
15. Hunter, A.: A brief introduction to the design of UBIFS (2008), http://www.linux-mtd.infradead.org/doc/ubifs_whitepaper.pdf
16. Joshi, R., Holzmann, G.J.: A mini challenge: build a verifiable filesystem. Formal Aspects of Computing 19(2) (June 2007)
17. Kang, E., Jackson, D.: Formal Modelling and Analysis of a Flash Filesystem in Alloy. In: Börger, E., Butler, M., Bowen, J.P., Boca, P. (eds.) ABZ 2008. LNCS, vol. 5238, pp. 294–308. Springer, Heidelberg (2008)
18. Malecha, G., Morrisett, G., Shinnar, A., Wisnesky, R.: Toward a verified relational database management system. In: Proc. of POPL, pp. 237–248. ACM (2010)
19. Morgan, C., Sufrin, B.: Specification of the unix filing system. In: Specification Case Studies, pp. 91–140. Prentice Hall Ltd., Hertfordshire (1987)
20. Mühlberg, J.T., Lüttgen, G.: Verifying compiled file system code. Formal Aspecpts of Computing 24(3), 375–391 (2012)
21. Nanevski, A., Vafeiadis, V., Berdine, J.: Structuring the verification of heap-manipulating programs. In: Proc. of POPL, pp. 261–274. ACM (2010)
22. Reeves, G., Neilson, T.: The Mars Rover Spirit FLASH anomaly. In: Aerospace Conference, pp. 4186–4199. IEEE Computer Society (2005)
23. Reif, W., Schellhorn, G., Stenzel, K., Balser, M.: Structured specifications and interactive proofs with KIV. In: Bibel, W., Schmitt, P. (eds.) Automated Deduction—A Basis for Applications, vol. II, pp. 13–39. Kluwer, Dordrecht (1998)
24. Reynolds, J.C.: Separation logic: A logic for shared mutable data structures. In: Proc. of LICS, pp. 55–74. IEEE Computer Society (2002)
25. Schellhorn, G.: ASM Refinement and Generalizations of Forward Simulation in Data Refinement: A Comparison. Journal of Theoretical Computer Science 336(2-3), 403–435 (2005)
26. Schellhorn, G., Tofan, B., Ernst, G., Reif, W.: Interleaved programs and rely-guarantee reasoning with ITL. In: Proc. of TIME, pp. 99–106. IEEE Computer Society (2011)
27. Stepney, S., Cooper, D., Woodcock, J.: An Electronic Purse Specification, Refinement, and Proof. Technical monograph PRG-126, Oxford University Computing Laboratory (2000)
28. Szeredi, M.: File system in user space, http://fuse.sourceforge.net
29. The Open Group. The Open Group Base Specifications Issue 7, IEEE Std 1003.1, 2008 Edition (2008), http://www.unix.org/version3/online.html (login required)
30. Tuch, H., Klein, G., Norrish, M.: Types, bytes, and separation logic. In: Proc. of POPL, pp. 97–108. ACM (2007)
31. Yang, J., Twohey, P., Engler, D., Musuvathi, M.: Using Model Checking to Find Serious File System Errors. In: Proc. of OSDI, pp. 273–288. USENIX (2004)

Verifying Chinese Train Control System under a Combined Scenario by Theorem Proving

Liang Zou[1], Jidong Lv[2], Shuling Wang[1], Naijun Zhan[1],
Tao Tang[2], Lei Yuan[2], and Yu Liu[2]

[1] State Key Lab. of Comput. Sci., Institute of Software, Chinese Academy of Sciences
[2] State Key Lab. of Rail Traffic Control and Safety, Beijing Jiaotong University

Abstract. In this paper, we investigate how to formalize and verify the System Requirements Specification (SRS) of Chinese Train Control System Level 3 (CTCS-3), which includes a set of basic operational scenarios that cooperate with each other to achieve the desired behavior of trains. It is absolutely necessary to prove that the cooperation of basic scenarios indeed completes the required behavior. As a case study, a combined scenario with several basic scenarios integrated is studied in this paper. We model each scenario as a Hybrid CSP (HCSP) process, and specify its properties using Hybrid Hoare Logic (HHL). Given such an annotated HCSP model, the deductive verification of conformance of the model to the properties is then carried out. For the purpose, we implement a theorem prover of HHL in Isabelle/HOL, with which the process including modelling and verification of annotated HCSP models can be mechanized. In particular, we provide a machine-checked proof for the combined scenario, with the result indicating a design error in SRS of CTCS-3.

Keywords: Chinese Train Control System, Hybrid System, Specification and Verification, Theorem Proving.

1 Introduction

The System Requirements Specification (SRS) of Chinese Train Control System Level 3 (CTCS-3) [16] is a standard specification for supervising train movements to ensure the high reliability, safety and efficiency of high-speed trains in China. CTCS-3 includes 14 basic operational scenarios, each of which with different system components involved, and the cooperations among these scenarios to achieve the desired behavior of trains. One important problem in this area is to formalise and verify the specifications for the scenarios of CTCS-3, both separately and integrally, to guarantee the correctness.

Due to continuous character of train movement and discrete interactions between different system components, we model each scenario of CTCS-3 as a hybrid system. Hybrid system seamlessly combines the models for discrete controllers and for dynamic systems represented by differential or algebraic equations. In this paper, we adopt Hybrid CSP (HCSP) [2,20] as the formal modelling

E. Cohen and A. Rybalchenko (Eds.): VSTTE 2013, LNCS 8164, pp. 262–280, 2014.

language for hybrid systems. As an extension of CSP, HCSP introduces real-time constructs and differential equations for continuous evolution; and being a process algebra, it provides standard means for constructing complex systems out of simpler ones, which facilitates compositionality.

By using HCSP, each basic scenario of CTCS-3 is formalized as an HCSP process, which is usually a parallel composition of sub-processes corresponding to different components involved in this scenario. A combined scenario integrates several basic scenarios that occur in a same situation, and the HCSP process for it can be constructed from the processes corresponding to each separate scenario. However, the combination of scenarios may not preserve correctness because of complex interactions between these scenarios, thus as a remedy, to verify correctness of combined scenarios is very necessary.

In this paper, we consider one combined scenario that integrates several basic scenarios including *movement authority*, *level transition* and *mode transition*. We model the combined scenario using HCSP, and then formulate the property to be proved using Hybrid Hoare logic (HHL) proposed in [6]. HHL is defined especially for reasoning about HCSP processes, including first-order logic to specify pre/post-conditions which describe the properties related to discrete jumps, and duration calculus (DC) [18,17] to record execution history that specifies continuous properties of systems, and a set of axioms and inference rules to axiomatize each construct of HCSP. Finally, we prove the negation of the property that a train eventually passes through the location at which a level transition and a mode transition take place simultaneously. This result reflects some design error in SRS of CTCS-3.

In order to provide a machine-checked proof for the negation of the property, we implement a theorem prover for HHL in proof assistant Isabelle/HOL. The implementation includes the encodings of HCSP language and HHL proof system, including both syntax and semantics (or inference rules for HHL instead). It is built from scratch, i.e., defining the datatype for expressions from the bottom most, in the style of deep embedding. Therefore, we can make full use of inductive structure of assertions and thus reduce the size of verification conditions generated.

1.1 Related Work

There have been a number of abstract models and specification languages proposed for formalizing and verifying hybrid systems. The most popular is hybrid automata [1,8,4], with real-time temporal logics [8,9] interpreted on their behaviors as specification languages. However, analogous to state machines, hybrid automata provides little support for structured description and composition. The approach most closely related to ours is the work by Platzer [11], where hybrid programs and the related differential dynamic logic for the deductive verification of hybrid systems are proposed. As a case study of the approach, the safety and liveness of movement authority scenario of European Train Control System was proved [12]. However, hybrid programs do not support parallelism and communication.

For mechanization of HCSP verification, the encodings of the assertion languages of HHL especially DC are most essential. The first attempt at encoding DC in a theorem prover was done in PVS [14], where shallow embedding is adopted thus reasoning is done directly in high-order meta-logic of PVS. Later, the work in both [3] and [13] considers the encoding of DC in Isabelle/HOL in deep embedding style, and our encoding combines their approaches.

For formal modelling and verification of scenarios of train control systems, most of existing work only consider single scenario so far, e.g. in [12,5], some separate scenarios of European Train Control System are considered.

1.2   Structure of the Paper

We give a brief introduction of HCSP and HHL in Sec. 2, and then introduce a combined scenario of CTCS-3 and its formal model in HCSP in Sec. 3. We present the mechanization of HCSP specifications in Isabelle/HOL in Sec. 4, based on which verify the combined scenario via interactive theorem proving in Sec. 5. Finally, the paper concludes and discusses the future work.

2   Preliminaries

This section introduces briefly the modelling language and specification language for hybrid systems that we adopt in the paper.

2.1   Hybrid CSP Language

HCSP [2,20] is a formal language for describing hybrid systems, which is an extension of CSP by introducing timing constructs, interrupts, and differential equations for representing continuous evolution. Exchanging data among processes are described solely by communications, and no shared variable is allowed between processes in parallel, so each program variable is local to the respective sequential component. The syntax of HCSP is given as follows:

$$P ::= \text{skip} \mid x := e \mid ch?x \mid ch!e \mid P; Q \mid B \rightarrow P \mid P \sqcup Q \mid P^*$$
$$\mid \langle \mathcal{F}(\dot{s}, s) = 0 \& B \rangle \mid \langle \mathcal{F}(\dot{s}, s) = 0 \& B \rangle \trianglerighteq [\![_{i \in I}(io_i \rightarrow Q_i)$$
$$S ::= P \mid S \| S$$

Here P, Q, Q_i, S are HCSP processes, x and s stand for process variables, ch for channel name, io_i for a communication event (either $ch?x$ or $ch!e$), B and e for boolean and arithmetic expressions, and d for a non-negative real constant, respectively.

The intended meaning of the individual constructs is explained as follows:

- skip terminates immediately having no effect on variables; and $x := e$ assigns the value of expression e to x and then terminates.
- $ch?x$ receives a value along channel ch and assigns it to x, and $ch!e$ sends the value of e along ch. A communication takes place as soon as both the sending and the receiving parties are ready, and may cause one side to wait.

- The sequential composition $P; Q$ behaves as P first, and if it terminates, as Q afterwards.
- The conditional $B \to P$ behaves as P if B is true, otherwise it terminates immediately.
- The internal choice $P \sqcup Q$ behaves as either P or Q, and the choice is made randomly by the system.
- The repetition P^* executes P for some finite number of times.
- $\langle \mathcal{F}(\dot{s}, s) = 0\&B \rangle$ is the continuous evolution statement (hereafter shortly *continuous*). It forces the vector s of real variables to evolve continuously according to the differential equations $\mathcal{F}$ as long as the boolean expression B, which defines the *domain of s*, holds, and terminates when B turns false.
- $\langle \mathcal{F}(\dot{s}, s) = 0\&B \rangle \trianglerighteq []_{i \in I}(io_i \to Q_i)$ behaves like the continuous $\langle \mathcal{F}(\dot{s}, s) = 0\&B \rangle$, except that it is preempted as soon as one of the communications io_i takes place. That is followed by the respective Q_i. Notice that, if the continuous terminates before a communication from among $\{io_i\}_{i \in I}$ occurs, then the process terminates immediately without waiting for communication.
- $S_1 \| S_2$ behaves as if S_1 and S_2 run independently except that all communications along the common channels connecting S_1 and S_2 are to be synchronized. S_1 and S_2 in parallel can neither share variables, nor input nor output channels.

The basic constructs of HCSP are expressive enough to define a number of constructs known in process calculi. For instances, the **stop** and *external choice* in timed CSP can be respectively defined as

$$\textbf{stop} \; \widehat{=} \; \langle \dot{t} = 1\&\text{True} \rangle, \text{ and}$$
$$[]_{i \in I}(io_i \to Q_i) \; \widehat{=} \; \textbf{stop} \trianglerighteq []_{i \in I}(io_i \to Q_i);$$

and especially, the timeout $\langle \mathcal{F}(\dot{s}, s) = 0\&B \rangle \trianglerighteq_d Q$ can be defined by

$$t := 0; \langle F(\dot{s}, s) = 0 \wedge \dot{t} = 1\&t < d \wedge B \rangle; t \geq d \to Q,$$

which behaves like the continuous $\langle \mathcal{F}(\dot{s}, s) = 0\&B \rangle$, if the continuous terminates before d time units, otherwise, after d time units of evolution according to $\mathcal{F}$, it moves on to execute Q. Based on timeout, the wait statement can be defined as wait $d \; \widehat{=} \; \langle \dot{t} = 1 \rangle \trianglerighteq_d \text{skip}$.

Super-Dense Computation. For HCSP, we adopt the notion of super-dense computation [8] to assume that digital control does not consume time compared to continuous evolution of environment. Discrete processes such as skip, assignment, as well as the evaluation of boolean expressions in $B \to P$, take no time to complete. Thus at a time point, multiple discrete processes may occur. Because of synchronization, the input or output process may cause to wait for the compatible party being available, but as soon as both parties become ready, a communication will occur and complete immediately.

2.2   Hybrid Hoare Logic

HHL [6] is an extension of Hoare logic for specifying and reasoning about HCSP processes. In HHL, each specification for a sequential process P takes the form $\{Pre\}P\{Post; HF\}$, where $Pre, Post$ represent pre-/post-conditions, expressed by first-order logic, to specify discrete properties of variables held at starting and termination of the execution of P; and HF history formula, expressed by DC [18,17], to record the execution history of P, including real-time and continuous properties. The effect of discrete processes will be specified by the pre-/post-conditions, but not be recorded in the history. The specification for a parallel process is then defined by assigning to each sequential component of it the respective pre-/post-conditions and history formula, that is

$$\{Pre_1, Pre_2\}P_1\|P_2\{Post_1, Post_2; HF_1, HF_2\}$$

In HHL, each of HCSP constructs is axiomatized by a set of axioms and inferences rules, which constitute a basis for implementing the verification condition generator for reasoning about HCSP specifications in Sec. 4. The full explanation of HHL can be found in [6].

DC is a real extension of Interval Temporal Logic (ITL) [10] for specifying and reasoning about real-time systems. Like ITL, the only modality in DC is the chop $\frown$ to divide a considered interval into two consecutive sub-intervals such that its first operand is satisfied on the first sub-interval, while the second operand is satisfied on the second sub-interval. Besides, DC extends ITL by introducing durations of state expressions $\int S$, and the temporal variable ℓ to denote the length of the considered interval, i.e. $\int 1$. Here, we will adopt the notion of point formula introduced in [19], denoted by $\lceil S \rceil^0$, to mean that S holds at the considered point interval. Then the formula $\lceil S \rceil$ is defined as $\neg(\ell > 0 \frown \lceil \neg S \rceil^0 \frown \ell > 0)$, meaning that the state expression S holds at each point of the considered reference interval.

3   A Combined Scenario of CTCS-3 and Its HCSP Model

A train at CTCS-3 applies for movement authorities (MAs) from Radio Block Center via GSM-Railway and is guaranteed to move safely in high speed within its MA. CTCS-2 is a backup system of CTCS-3, under which a train applies for MAs from Train Control Center via train circuit and balise instead. There are 9 main operating modes in CTCS-3, among which the Full Supervision and Calling On modes will be involved in the combined scenario studied in this paper. During Full Supervision mode, a train needs to know the complete information including its MA, line data, train data and so on; while during Calling On mode, the on-board equipment of the train cannot confirm cleared routes, thus a train is required to move under constant speed 40km/h.

The operating behavior of CTCS-3 is specified by 14 basic scenarios, all of which cooperate with each other to constitute normal functionality of train control system. The combined scenario considered here integrates the Movement

Authority and Level Transition scenarios of CTCS-3, plus a special Mode Transition scenario.

For modeling a scenario, we model each component involved in it as an HCSP process and then combine different parts by parallel composition to form the model of the scenario. In particular, the train participates in each scenario, and the HCSP model corresponding to the train under different scenarios has a very unified structure. Let s be trajectory, v velocity, a acceleration, t clock time of a train respectively, then we have the following general model for the train:

$$Train \; \widehat{=} \; \left(\frac{\langle \dot{s} = v, \dot{v} = a, \dot{t} = 1 \& \, B \rangle \trianglerighteq [\![]_{i \in I}(io_i \to P_{comp_i});}{Q_{comp}} \right)^{*}$$

where P_{comp_i} and Q_{comp} are discrete computation that takes no time to complete. The train process proceeds as follows: at first the train moves continuously at velocity v and acceleration a, as soon as domain B is violated, or a communication among $\{io_i\}_{i \in I}$ between the train and another component of CTCS-3 takes place, then the train movement is interrupted and shifted to Q_{comp}, or P_{comp_i} respectively; after the discrete computation is done, the train repeats the above process, indicated by $*$ in the model. For each specific scenario, the domain B, communications io_i, and computation P_{comp_i} and Q_{comp} can be instantiated correspondingly. We assume the acceleration a is always in the range $[-b, A]$.

In the rest of this section, we will first model three basic scenarios separately, and then construct a combined scenario from them.

3.1   Movement Authority Scenario

Among all the scenarios, MA is the most basic one and crucial to prohibit trains from colliding with each other. Before moving, the train applies for MA from Radio Block Center (RBC, in CTCS-3) or Train Control Center (in CTCS-2), and if it succeeds, it gets the permission to move but only within the MA it owns. An MA is composed of a sequence of segments. Each segment is represented as a tuple $(v_1, v_2, e, mode)$, where v_1 and v_2 represent the speed limits of emergency brake pattern and normal brake pattern by which the train must implement emergency brake and normal brake (thus v_1 is always greater than v_2), e the end point of the segment, and $mode$ the operating mode of the train in the segment. We introduce some operations on MAs and segments. Given a nonempty MA α, we define $hd(\alpha)$ to return the first segment of α, and $tl(\alpha)$ the rest sequence after removing the first segment; and given a segment seg, we define $seg.v_1$ to access the element v_1 of seg, and similarly to other elements.

Given an MA, we can calculate its static speed profile and dynamic speed profile respectively. As an illustration, Fig. 1 presents an MA with three segments, separated by points s_1, s_2, and s_3. In the particular case, we assume s_3 the end of the MA, thus the train is required to fully stop at s_3 if the MA is not extended. The static speed profile corresponds to two step functions formed by the two speed limits (i.e. v_1 and v_2) of each segment; and for any segment seg, the dynamic speed profile is calculated down to the higher speed limit of next

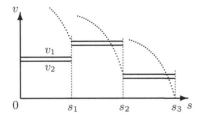

Fig. 1. Static and dynamic speed profiles

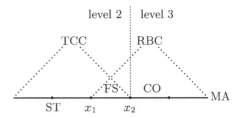

Fig. 2. Level and mode transition

segment taking into account the train's maximum deceleration (i.e. constant b), and corresponds to the inequation $v^2 + 2b\,s < next(seg).v_1^2 + 2b\,seg.e$, where $next(seg)$ represents the next segment following seg in the considered MA. The train will never be allowed to run beyond the static and dynamic speed profiles.

By instantiation to the general model, we get the model for a train under MA scenario. Let B_0 represent the general restriction that the train always moves forward, i.e. $v \geq 0$, or otherwise, the train has already stopped deceleration (denoted by $a \geq 0$). If B_0 fails to hold, the acceleration a needs to be set by a non-negative value in $[0, A]$. Notice that we add T_{delay} to clock t to guarantee that the interrupt B_0 can at most occur once every T_{delay} time units, to avoid Zeno behavior. This is in accordance with the real system to check the condition periodically. We adopt this approach several times.

Let B_1 denote the case when the speed is less than the lower limit v_2, or otherwise the train has already started to decelerate; and B_2 the case when the speed is less than the higher limit v_1 and not exceeding the dynamic speed profile, or otherwise the train has already started an emergency brake, respectively. When B_1 or B_2 is violated, the acceleration a will be assigned to be negative or maximum deceleration b respectively, as shown in $Q1_{comp}$ below. For future use, we denote the formula for specifying dynamic speed profile, i.e. $\forall seg : MA\,.\,v^2 + 2b\,s < next(seg).v_1^2 + 2b\,seg.e$, by DSP_Form.

Let B_7 represent that the train moves within the first segment of current MA. Whenever it is violated, i.e. $s > hd(MA).e$, the train will apply for extension of MA from TCC and RBC respectively. Define $rMA2$ and $rMA3$ to represent the MAs allocated by TCC and RBC respectively, then normally the MA of train will be defined as the minimum of the two. As defined in $Q1_{comp}$, the application procedure behaves as follows: the train first sends the value of $\neg B_7$ to both TCC and RBC; if $\neg B_7$ is true, it sends the end of authorities (defined by $getEoA$) of $rMA2$ and $rMA3$ to TCC and RBC, and then receives the new extended authorities (defined by $setMA2$, $setMA3$) for $rMA2$ and $rMA3$ from TCC and RBC respectively; and finally the MA will be updated correspondingly (defined by $comb$).

$$B_0 \;\; \widehat{=} \;\; (v \geq 0 \vee a \geq 0 \vee t < Temp + T_{delay})$$
$$B_1 \;\; \widehat{=} \;\; (\forall seg : MA . v < seg.v_2) \vee a < 0 \vee t < Temp' + T_{delay}$$
$$B_2 \;\; \widehat{=} \;\; (\forall seg : MA . v < seg.v_1 \wedge v^2 + 2b\,s < next(seg).v_1^2 + 2b\,seg.e) \vee a = -b$$
$$B_7 \;\; \widehat{=} \;\; (s <= hd(MA).e)$$
$$Q1_{comp} \;\; \widehat{=} \;\; \neg B_0 \rightarrow (Temp := t; \sqcup_{\{0<=c<=A\}} a := c);$$
$$\neg B_1 \rightarrow (Temp' := t; \sqcup_{\{-b<=c<0\}} a := c);$$
$$\neg B_2 \rightarrow a := -b;$$
$$CH_{b2}!\neg B_7; CH_{b3}!\neg B_7;$$
$$\neg B_7 \rightarrow (CH_{eoa2}!getEoA(rMA2); ch_{ma2}?rMA2;$$
$$CH_{eoa3}!getEoA(rMA3); ch_{ma3}?rMA3;$$
$$MA := comb(rMA2, rMA3))$$
$$TCC \;\; \widehat{=} \;\; CH_{b2}?b2; b2 \rightarrow (CH_{eoa2}?eoa2; ch_{ma2}!setMA2(eoa2))$$
$$RBC_{ma} \;\; \widehat{=} \;\; CH_{b3}?b3; b3 \rightarrow (CH_{eoa3}?eoa3; ch_{ma3}!setMA3(eoa3))$$

3.2   Level Transition

When a train moves under CTCS-2, then whenever passing a balise, which is assumed to be equally distributed every δ meters along the track, the train can apply for upgrade to CTCS-3 when necessary. Let B_3 represent the negative of the case when the train is at level 2 and passing a balise. When B_3 is violated, then as specified in $Q2_{comp}$, the following computation will take place: first, the train sends a level upgrade application signal to RBC; as soon as RBC receives the application, it sends back the package (b, x_1, x_2) to the train, where b represents whether RBC approves the application, x_1 the location for starting level upgrade, and x_2 the location for completing level upgrade; if RBC approves the level upgrade (i.e. b is true), the train enters level 2.5 and meanwhile passes the balise. Notice that level 2.5 does not actually exist, but is used only for modelling the middle stage between level 2 and level 3, during which the train will be supervised by both CTCS-2 and CTCS-3. Finally, as soon as the train at level 2.5 reaches location x_2 (the negative denoted by B_4), the level will be set to 3, specified in $Q3_{comp}$. RBC_{lu} defines the process for RBC under the level transition scenario. Notice that the locations x_1 and x_2 are constants, and should be determined before the transition is performed.

$$B_3 \;\; \widehat{=} \;\; level \neq 2 \; \vee \; s \neq n * \delta$$
$$B_4 \;\; \widehat{=} \;\; level \neq 2.5 \; \vee \; s \leq LU.x_2$$
$$Q2_{comp} \;\; \widehat{=} \;\; \neg B_3 \rightarrow (CH_{LUA}!; CH_{LU}?LU; LU.b \rightarrow level = 2.5; n = n + 1);$$
$$Q3_{comp} \;\; \widehat{=} \;\; \neg B_4 \rightarrow level := 3$$
$$RBC_{lu} \;\; \widehat{=} \;\; CH_{LUA}?; \sqcup_{b_{LU}\in\{true,false\}} CH_{LU}!(b, x_1, x_2)$$

3.3 Mode Transition

When a train moves under CTCS-2, it will always check whether its operating mode is equal to the mode of current segment, i.e. $hd(MA).mode$. We denote this condition by B_5, and as soon as it is violated, the train will update its mode to be consistent with $mode$ of the segment, specified in $Q4_{comp}$.

$$B_5 \quad \hat{=} \ mode = hd(MA).mode$$
$$Q4_{comp} \ \hat{=} \ \neg B_5 \rightarrow mode := hd(MA).mode$$

We consider the mode transition from Full Supervision (FS) to Calling On (CO) under CTCS-3, which is a little complicated. In the MA application stage, RBC can only grant the train the MAs before the CO segment. The train needs to ask the permission of the driver before moving into a CO segment at level 3. To reflect this situation in modelling, we initialize both the speed limits for CO segments to be 0, and as a result, if the train fails to get the permission from the driver, it must stop before the CO segment; but if the train gets the driver's permission, the speed limits of the CO segments will be reset to be positive.

Let B_6 denote the negation of the case when the train is at level 3, and it moves to 300 meters far from the end of current segment, and the mode of next segment is CO. As soon as B_6 is violated, then as specified in $Q5_{comp}$, the following computation will take place: first, the train will report the status to the driver and ask for permission to enter next CO segment via communications; if the driver sends true, the speed limits of next CO segment will be reset to be $40km/h$ and $50km/h$ respectively (abstracted away by function $coma(MA)$). As a consequence, the train is able to enter next CO segment at a positive speed successfully. $Driver_{mc}$ defines the process for the driver under the mode transition scenario.

$$B_6 \quad \hat{=} \ level \neq 3 \vee CO \neq hd(tl(MA)).mode \vee hd(MA).e - s > 300$$
$$\qquad\qquad \vee t < Temp + T_{delay}$$
$$Q5_{comp} \ \hat{=} \ CH_{win}!\neg B_6; \neg B_6 \rightarrow Temp := t; CH_{DC}?b_{rConf}; b_{rConf} \rightarrow coma(MA)$$
$$Driver_{mc} \ \hat{=} \ CH_{win}?b_{win}; b_{win} \rightarrow \sqcup_{b_sConf \in \{true, false\}} CH_{DC}!b_{sConf}$$

3.4 Combined Scenario and Model

We combine the scenarios introduced above, but with the following assumptions for the occurring context:

- The train moves inside an MA it owns;
- There are two adjacent segments in the MA, divided by point x_2. The train is supervised by CTCS-2 to the left of x_2 and by CTCS-3 to the right, and meanwhile, it is operated by mode FS to the left of x_2 and by mode CO to the right. Thus the locations for mode transition and for level transition are coincident. As the starting point of a CO segment, both speed limits for location x_2 are initialized to 0 by RBC;

– The train has already got the permission for level transition from RBC which sends $(true, x_1, x_2)$.

Please see Fig. 2 for an illustration.

The model of the combined scenario can then be constructed from the models of all the basic scenarios contained in it. The construction takes the following steps: firstly, decompose the process for each basic scenario to a set of sub-processes corresponding to different system components that are involved in the scenario (usually by removing parallel composition on top); secondly, as a component may participate in different basic scenarios, re-construct the process for it based on the sub-processes corresponding to it under these scenarios (usually by conjunction of continuous domain constraints and sequential composition of discrete computation actions); lastly, combine the new obtained processes for all the components via parallel composition. According to this construction process, we get the following HCSP model for the combined scenario:

$$
\begin{aligned}
System &\;\hat{=}\; Train^* \;\|\; Driver^*_{mc} \;\|\; RBC^*_{lu} \;\|\; RBC^*_{ma} \;\|\; TCC^* \\
Train &\;\hat{=}\; \langle \dot{s} = v, \dot{v} = a, \dot{t} = 1\,\&\; B_0 \wedge B_1 \wedge B_2 \wedge B_3 \wedge B_4 \wedge B_5 \wedge B_6 \wedge B_7 \rangle; P_{train} \\
P_{train} &\;\hat{=}\; Q1_{comp}; Q2_{comp}; Q3_{comp}; Q4_{comp}; Q5_{comp}
\end{aligned}
$$

According to SRS of CTCS-3, we hope to prove that the combined scenario satisfies a liveness property, i.e., the train can eventually pass through the location for level transition and mode transition. Our work applies deductive verification method for verifying HCSP models. First, the requirements to be proved are specified using HHL assertions as annotations in HCSP model, and then based on the proof system of HHL, the annotated HCSP model is reduced to a set of logical formulas whose validity implies the conformance of the model with respect to the requirements. This process can be mechanized in proof assistant, which will be the main content of the rest.

4   Isabelle Implementation

In this section, we aim to check if an HCSP process is correct with respect to a specification written in HHL, by providing a machine-checkable proof in Isabelle/HOL. For this purpose, we need to encode HCSP including both its syntax and semantics, and moreover, the axioms and inference rules of HHL. We adopt the deep embedding approach [15] here, which represents the abstract syntax for both HCSP and assertions by new datatypes, and then defines the semantic functions that assign meanings to each construct of the datatypes. It allows us to quantify over the syntactic structures of processes and assertions, and furthermore, make full use of deductive systems for reasoning about assertions written in FOL and DC.

The full repository including all the mechanization code related to Sec. 4 and Sec. 5 can be found at **https://github.com/liangdezou/HHL_prover**, and we present part of them here. We start from encoding the bottom construct, i.e. expressions, that are represented as a datatype **exp**:

datatype exp = RVar *string* | SVar *string* | BVar *string* | Real *real*
       | String *string* | Bool *bool* | exp + exp | exp − exp | exp ∗ exp

An expression can be a variable, that can be of three types, `RVar x` for real variable, `SVar x` and `BVar x` for string and boolean variables; a constant, that can be also of the three types, e.g. `Real 1.0`, `String ''CO''` and `Bool True`; an arithmetic expression constructed from operators +, −, ∗. Based on expressions, we can define the assertion languages and the process language HCSP respectively.

4.1   Assertion Language

There are two assertion logics in HHL: FOL and DC, where the former is used for specifying the pre-/post-conditions and the latter for the execution history of a process respectively. The encodings for both logics consist of two parts: syntax and deductive systems. We will encode the deductive systems in Gentzen's sequent calculus style, which applies backward search to conduct proofs and thus is more widely used in interactive and automated reasoning. A sequent is written as $\Gamma \vdash \Delta$, where both Γ and Δ are sequences of logical formulas, meaning that when all the formulas in Γ are true, then at least one formula in Δ will be true. We will implement a sequent as a truth proposition. The sequent calculus deductive system of a logic is composed of a set of sequent rules, each of which is a relation between a (possibly empty) sequence of sequents and a single sequent. In what follows, we consider to encode FOL and DC respectively.

First-Order Logic. The FOL formulas are constructed from expressions by using relational operators from the very beginning, and can be represented by the following datatype `fform`:

datatype fform = [True] | [False] | exp [=] exp | exp [<] exp
       | [¬] fform | fform [∨] fform | [∀] *string* fform

The other logical connectives including [∧], [→], and [∃] can be derived as normal. For quantified formula [∀]*string* `fform`, the name represented by a string corresponds to a real variable occurring in `fform`. We only consider the quantification over real variables here, but it can be extended to variables of other types (e.g. string and bool) without any essential difficulty. Notice that we add brackets to wrap up the logical constructors in order to avoid the name conflicts between `fform` and the FOL system of Isabelle library. But in sequel, we will remove brackets for readability when there is no confusion in context; and moreover, in order to distinguish between FOL formulas and Isabelle meta-logic formulas, we will use ⇒, & and | to represent implication, conjunction and disjunction in Isabelle meta-logic.

Now we need to define the sequent calculus style deductive system for `fform`. The Isabelle library includes an implementation of the sequent calculus of classical FOL with equation, based upon system LK that was originally introduced by Gentzen. Our encoding of the sequent calculus for `fform` is built from it directly, but with an extension for dealing with the atomic arithmetic formulas that are defined in fform. We define an equivalent relation between the validity of formulas of fform and of *bool*, the built-in type of Isabelle logical formulas, represented as follows:

formT (f :: fform) $\Leftrightarrow$ ⊢ f

where the function formT transforms a formula of type fform to a corresponding formula of *bool*. This approach enables us to prove atomic formulas f of fform by applying the built-in arithmetic solvers of Isabelle and proving formT (f) instead.

Duration Calculus. Encoding DC into different proof assistants has been studied, such as [14] in PVS, and [3,13] in Isabelle/HOL. DC can be considered as an extension of Interval Temporal Logic (ITL) by introducing state durations (here point formulas instead), while ITL an extension of FOL with the introducing of temporal variables and chop modality by regarding intervals instead of points as worlds. Therefore, both [3] and [13] apply an incremental approach to encode ITL on top of an FOL sequent calculus system, and then DC on top of ITL. We will follow a different approach here, to represent DC formulas as a datatype, as a result, the proving of DC formulas can be done by inductive reasoning on the structures of the formulas.

The datatype dform encodes the history formulas *HF*:

datatype dform = [[True]] | [[False]] | dexp[[=]]dexp | dexp[[<]]dexp
    | [[¬]]dform | dform[[∨]]dform |[[∀]] *string* dform | pf fform | dform⌢dform

We will get rid of double brackets for readability if without confusion in context. The datatype dexp defines expressions that are dependent on intervals. As seen from *HF*, it includes the only temporal variable ℓ for representing the length of the interval, and real constants. Given a state formula S of type fform, pf S encodes the point formula $\lceil S \rceil^0$, and furthermore, the following high S encodes formula $\lceil S \rceil$:

high :: fform $\Rightarrow$ dform
high S $\equiv$ ¬ (True ⌢pf (¬S)⌢ ℓ > Real 0)

The chop modality ⌢ can be encoded as well.

To establish the sequent calculus style deductive system for dform, we first define the deductive system for the first-order logic constructors of dform, which can be taken directly from the one built for fform above, and then define the deductive system related to the new added modalities for DC, i.e. ℓ, ⌢ and pf.

For ℓ and ⌢, we encode the deductive system of ITL from [17], which is presented in Hilbert style. Thus, we need to transform the deductive system to sequent calculus style, and it is not so natural to do. We borrow the idea from [13] that for each modality, define both the left and right introducing rules, e.g., the following implementation

LI : \$H, P ⊢ \$E $\Rightarrow$ \$H, P⌢(ℓ = Real 0) ⊢ \$E
RI : \$H ⊢ P, \$E $\Rightarrow$ \$H ⊢ P⌢(ℓ = Real 0), \$E

where \$H, \$E represent arbitrary sequences of logical formulas of type dform, encodes the axiom of ITL: $P \leftrightarrow P^\frown(\ell = 0)$. In the same way, for point formula pf, we encode the deductive system of DC defined in [17] in sequent calculus style, e.g., the following implementation

PFRI : \$H ⊢ (pf S_1⌃pf S_2), \$E ⟹ \$H ⊢ pf ($S_1 \wedge S_2$), \$E

encodes the axiom of DC: $\lceil S_1 \rceil^{0\frown} \lceil S_2 \rceil^0 \to \lceil S_1 \wedge S_2 \rceil^0$.

4.2   HCSP Syntax

We represent HCSP processes as a datatype proc, and each construct of HCSP can be encoded as a construct in datatype proc correspondingly. Most of the encoding is directly a syntactic translation, but with the following exceptions:

- In the deductive verification of HCSP process, the role of differential equation is reflected by an differential invariant with respect to the property to be verified. Inv is a differential invariant of $\langle \mathcal{F}(\dot{s}, s) = 0 \& B \rangle$ with respect to initial state s_0, if Inv holds for s_0, and furthermore, holds for all the reachable states according to the equation within domain B. In [7], a complete method for generating differential invariants for polynomial differential equations with respect to given domain and initial values of continuous variables is proposed.

   In proc, instead of differential equation, we use differential invariant to describe the underlying continuous, and for aiding verification, we also add execution time range of the continuous. Thus, we encode continuous of form $\langle \mathcal{F}(\dot{s}, s) = 0 \& B \rangle$ as <Inv&B> : Rg, where Inv represents the differential invariant of the continuous, B the domain constraint, and Rg the range of execution time, of the continuous respectively; and Inv, B are implemented as formulas of type fform, while Rg of type dform.
- For sequential composition, we encode $P; Q$ as P; mid; Q, where P and Q represent the encodings of P and Q respectively, and mid is added to represent the intermediate assertions between P and Q. This is requisite for reducing proof of sequential composition to the ones of its components, and commonly used in theorem proving.
- For parallel composition, we remove the syntax restriction that it can only occur in the outmost scope, thus it is encoded with the same datatype proc as other constructs.

4.3   Verification Condition

Based on the inference rules of HHL, we implement the verification condition generator for reasoning about HCSP specifications. The inference rules encoded here are slightly different from those presented in [6], in the sense that we remove the point formulas for specifying discrete changes in history formulas and use $\ell = 0$ instead. This will not affect the expressiveness and soundness of HHL.

In deep embedding, the effects of assignments are expressed at the level of formulas by substitution. We implement a map as a list of pairs (exp * exp) list, and then given a map σ and a formula p of type fform, we define function substF(σ, p) to substitute expressions occurring in p according to the map σ. Based on this definition, we have the following axiom for assignment e:=f:

axioms Assignment :
$\vdash$ (p $\rightarrow$ substF ([(e, f)] , q)) $\land$ (ℓ = Real 0 $\rightarrow$G) $\Rightarrow$ {p} (e :=f) {q; G}

According to the rule of assignment, the weakest precondition of e := f with respect to postcondition q is substF ([(e, f)], q), and on the other hand, the strongest history formula for assignment is ℓ= Real 0, indicating that as a discrete action, assignment takes no time. Therefore, {p} (e :=f) {q; G} holds, if p implies the weakest precondition, and moreover, G is implied by the strongest history formula.

For continuous <Inv & B> : Rg, we assume that the precondition can be separated into two conjunctive parts: Init referring to initial state of continuous variables, and p referring to other distinct variables that keep unchanged during continuous evolution. With respect to precondition Init$\land$p, according to the rule of continuous, when it terminates (i.e. B is violated), the precondition p not relative to initial state, the closures of Inv and of $\neg$B hold in postcondition; moreover, there are two cases for the history formula: the continuous terminates immediately, represented by ℓ= Real 0, or otherwise, throughout the continuous evolution, p, Inv and B hold everywhere except for the endpoint, represented by high (Inv$\land$p$\land$B), where both cases satisfy Rg.

axioms Continuous : $\vdash$(Init $\rightarrow$ Inv) $\land$ ((p $\land$ close(Inv) $\land$ close($\neg$B)) $\rightarrow$q)
$\land$ ((((ℓ = Real 0) $\lor$ (high (Inv $\land$ p $\land$ B))) $\land$ Rg) $\rightarrow$ G)
$\Rightarrow$ {Init $\land$ p} <Inv & B> : Rg {q; G}

where function close returns closure of corresponding formulas. The above axiom says that {Init$\land$p} <Inv & B> : Rg {q;G} holds, if the initial state satisfies invariant Inv, and furthermore, both q and G are implied by the postcondition and the history formula of the continuous with respect to Init$\land$p respectively.

For sequential composition, the intermediate assertions need to be annotated (i.e., (m, H) below) to refer to the postcondition and the history formula of the first component. Therefore, the specification {p} P; (m, H);Q {q; H$\neg$G} holds, if both {p} P {m;H} and {m} Q {q;G} hold, as indicated by the following axiom.

axioms Sequence : {p} P {m; H}; {m} Q {q; G} $\Rightarrow${p} P; (m, H); Q {q; H$\neg$G}

The following axiom deals with communication P1; ch!e || P2;ch?x, where P1 and P2 stand for sequential processes. Let p1 and p2 be the preconditions for the sequential components respectively, and (q1, H1), (q2, H2) the intermediate assertions specifying the postconditions and history formulas for P1 and P2 respectively. r1 and G1 represent the postcondition and history formula for the left sequential component ended with ch!e, while r2 and G2 for the right component ended with ch?x. Rg stands for the execution time range of the whole parallel composition.

axioms Communication :

$\{p1, p2\}$ P1 $\|$ P2 $\{q1, q2;$ H1, H2$\}$;
$\vdash$ $(q1 \to r1) \wedge (q2 \to \text{substF} ([(x, e)], r2))$;
$\vdash$ $(H1 \frown \text{high} (q1)) \to G1) \wedge (H2 \frown \text{high} (q2)) \to G2)$;
$\vdash$ $(((H1 \frown \text{high} (q1)) \wedge H2) \vee ((H2 \frown \text{high} (q2)) \wedge H1)) \to Rg$;
$\Rightarrow \{p1, p2\} ((P1; (q1, H1); \text{ch} ! e) \| (P2; (q2, H2); \text{ch} ? x))$
$\{r1, r2; G1 \wedge Rg, G2 \wedge Rg\}$

As shown above, to prove the final specification, the following steps need to be checked: first, the corresponding specification with intermediate assertions as postconditions and history formulas holds for P1 $\|$ P2; second, after the communication is done, for the sending party, q1 is preserved, while for the receiving party, x is assigned to be e. Thus, r1 must be implied by q1, and q2 implies the weakest precondition of the communicating assignment with respect to r2, i.e. substF $([(x, e)], r2)$; third, for the communication to take place, one party may need to wait for the other party to be ready, in case that P1 and P2 do not terminate simultaneously. The left sequential component will result in history formula H1$\frown$**high** (q1), in which **high** (q1) indicates that during waiting time, the postcondition of P1 is preserved, and similarly for the right component. Thus, G1 and G2 must be implied by them respectively; and finally, for both cases when one party is waiting for the other, the conjunction of their history formulas must satisfy the execution time Rg.

For repetition, we have the following implementation:

axioms Repetition :

$\{p1, p2\}$ P $\|$ Q $\{p1, p2;$ H1, H2$\}$; $\vdash (H1 \frown H1 \to H1) \wedge (H2 \frown H2 \to H2)$
$\Rightarrow \{p1, p2\}$ P* $\|$ Q* $\{p1, p2;$ H1 $\vee (\ell = \text{Real } 0)$, H2 $\vee (\ell = \text{Real } 0)\}$

The above axiom says that the final specification for P$^*\|$ Q* holds, if the same specification holds for one round of execution, i.e. P $\|$ Q, and moreover, H is idempotent with respect to chop modality. The formula $\ell =$ **Real** 0 indicates that the repetition iterates zero time.

4.4 Soundness

First, we define the operational semantics of HCSP by function **evalP** (only the case for sequential processes is presented here):

consts evalP :: proc $\Rightarrow$ cstate $\Rightarrow$ *real* $\Rightarrow$ proc $*$ cstate $*$ *real*

where **cstate** is of the form *real* $\Rightarrow$ **state list**. Each state of type **state** assigns respective values to process variables; and each element of type **cstate**, called by a *behavior*, associates a sequence of states to each time point. A behavior defines the execution history of a process, and is able to reflect super-dense computation by recording all the discrete changes in the sequence of states respectively at a time point. Given a process P, an initial behavior f, an initial time a, the transition evalP (P, f, a) = (P', f', b) represents that executing from behavior f at time a, P evolves to P' and ends at behavior f' and time b.

Second, the history formulas of DC are interpreted over behaviors and timed intervals. Given a behaviour `f` of type `cstate` and a timed interval `[c, d]`, `ievalE(f,ℓ, c, d)` returns the value of ℓ, that is `d-c`, under the behavior `f` and the timed interval `[c, d]`. Given a behavior `f` of type `cstate`, a DC formula `ip`, and a timed interval `[c, d]`, `ievalF(f, ip, c, d)` evaluates the truth value of `ip` under the behavior `f` and the timed interval `[c, d]`. In particular, the point formula and chop can be defined as follows:

pf_eval : ievalF (f, pf (P), c, d) = (c=d & evalF (f, P, c))
chop_eval: ievalF (f, P⌢Q, c, d) = ∃ k. c<=k & k<=d & ievalF (f, P, c, k)
                                   & ievalF (f, Q, k, d)

Thus, `pf(P)` holds, iff the interval is a point interval, and `P` holds at the last state of the state list `f(c)`.

We then define the validity of a specification `{p} P {q;H}` with respect to the operational semantics, as follows:

definition Valid :: fform ⇒ proc ⇒ fform ⇒ fform ⇒ *bool*
where Valid (p, P, q, H) = ∀ f d f' d'. evalP (P, f, d) = (Skip, f', d') ⇒
              evalF (f, p, d) ⇒ (evalF (f', q, d') & ievalF (f', H, d, d'))

which says that, given a process `P`, for any initial behavior `f` and initial time `d`, if `P` terminates at behavior `f'` and time `d'`, and if the precondition `p` holds under the initial state, i.e. the last element in state list `f(d)` (represented by `evalF (f, p, d)`), then the postcondition `q` will hold under the final state, i.e. the last element in state list `f'(d')` (represented by `evalF (f', q, d')`), and the history formula will hold under `f'` between `d` and `d'` (represented by `ievalF (f', H, d, d')`).

Based on the above definitions, we have proved the soundness of the proof system in Isabelle/HOL, i.e. all the inference rules of the proof system are valid.

5   Proof of the Combined Scenario

Under the given assumptions in Section 3.4, we need to check whether the combined scenario (i.e. model *System*) satisfies a liveness property, i.e., the train will eventually move beyond location x_2 for both level transition and mode transition. In this section, instead of proving the liveness property directly, we provide a machine-checked proof for negation of the livness, which says, after moving for any arbitrary time, the train will always stay before location x_2. We start from encoding the model *System* and the negation property first.

According to HCSP syntax implemented by `proc`, most encoding of model *System* is a direct translation, except for continuous and sequential composition. Firstly, the continuous of *System* needs to be represented in the form of differential invariants. According to the differential invariant generation method proposed in [7], the differential invariant $(a = -b) \rightarrow DSP\_Form$ is calculated for the continuous, indicating that when the train brakes with maximum deceleration b, it will never exceed the dynamic speed profile. Obviously it is a complement to the domain constraint B_2, saying that the train will never exceed the dynamic speed profile except for the case of emergency brake. We adopt the conjunction of these two formulas, that results in DSP_Form, as the final invariant for the continuous. Thus we represent the continuous as `<Inv&B>` : `Rg`, where `Inv` and `B` correspond to encodings of DSP_Form and the domain constraints respectively, and `Rg` is `True`, specifying the executing time of the continuous; Secondly, the intermediate formulas for all sequential composition are added. We finally get the encoding of $System$, represented by `System` below.

Now it is turn to encode the negation property, specified by pre/post-conditions, and history formula. The precondition is separated into two parts depending on whether it is relative to initial values, shown by `Init` and `Pre` below:

definition Init :: form **where** Init $\equiv$ (x2 $-$ s $>$ Real 300)
definition Pre :: form **where**
Pre $\equiv$ (level $=$ Real 2.5) $\wedge$ (fst (snd (snd (hd (MA))))) $=$ x2)
        $\wedge$ (snd (snd (snd (hd (MA))))) $=$ String "FS")
        $\wedge$ (snd (snd (snd (hd (tl (MA)))))) $=$ String "CO")
        $\wedge$ (fst (hd (MA)) $=$ Real 0) $\wedge$ (fst (snd (hd (MA))) $=$ Real 0)

The `Init` represents that the initial position of the train (i.e. `s`) is more than 300 meters away from `x2`. The `Pre` indicates the following aspects: the train moves at level `2.5`, i.e. in process of level transition from CTCS-2 to CTCS-3; the end of current segment is `x2`; the mode of the train in current segment is ''`FS`''; the mode of the train in next segment is ''`CO`''; and at the end of current segment, both speed limits are initialized to be 0. Notice that for any segment seg, $seg.v_1$ is implemented as `fst (seg)`, and $seg.v_2$ as `fst (snd (seg))`, and so on.

We then get a specification corresponding to the negation property, with the postcondition and history formula for the train to indicate that the train will never pass through location x_2:

theorem System_proof : {Init $\wedge$ Pre, True, True, True, True} System
        {Pre $\wedge$ s $<=$ x2, True, True, True, True;
        (ℓ $=$ Real 0) $\vee$ (high (Pre $\wedge$ s $<=$ x2)), True, True, True, True}

In Isabelle/HOL, we have proved this specification as a theorem. From this fact, we know that the model `System` for level transition and mode transition fails to conform to the liveness property. This reflects some design flaw for the specifications of related scenarios in CTCS-3.

6   Conclusion and Future Work

In this paper, we have studied the formalization and verification of the scenarios defined in SRS of CTCS-3, by using HCSP and HHL as the modelling and specification languages respectively. We consider a combination of several basic scenarios, which is expected to conform to a liveness property according to SRS of CTCS. Especially, we have shown in the case study how to construct the model for the combined scenario from the separate ones corresponding to basic scenarios involved in it. The modelling technique can be applied to train control systems in general, especially for other combined scenarios of CTCS-3. For tool support, we have implemented a theorem prover in Isabelle/HOL for verifying HCSP models annotated with HHL assertions, within which we have proved the violation of the combined scenario with respect to the liveness property.

Future Work. First of all, the case study in this paper is only a first step towards the formal checking of the correctness of SRS of CTCS-3, and we will study the whole SRS of CTCS-3 in forthcoming research. Second, the automation of the theorem proving implementation of HCSP in Isabelle/HOL is not considered currently, which needs the incorporation of existing tools (e.g. automatic SMT solvers) for arithmetic and the decision procedure implementation for subset of DC (i.e. one assertion language included in HHL). Finally, because of non-compositionality of HHL proposed in [6], the proof system is incomplete to prove all HCSP processes. These three aspects constitute our main future research.

Acknowledgements. The work has been supported mainly by projects NSFC-91118007, NSFC-6110006, and National Science and Technology Major Project of China (Grant No. 2012ZX01039-004).

References

1. Alur, R., Courcoubetis, C., Henzinger, T.A., Ho, P.: Hybrid automata: An algorithmic approach to the specification and verification of hybrid systems. In: Grossman, R.L., Ravn, A.P., Rischel, H., Nerode, A. (eds.) HS 1991 and HS 1992. LNCS, vol. 736, pp. 209–229. Springer, Heidelberg (1993)
2. He, J.: From CSP to hybrid systems. In: A Classical Mind, Essays in Honour of C.A.R. Hoare, pp. 171–189. Prentice Hall International (UK) Ltd. (1994)
3. Heilmann, S.T.: Proof Support for Duration Calculus. PhD thesis, Technical University of Denmark (1999)
4. Henzinger, T.A.: The theory of hybrid automata. In: LICS 1996, pp. 278–292. IEEE Computer Society (1996)
5. Hoenicke, J., Olderog, E.: CSP-OZ-DC: A combination of specification techniques for processes, data and time. Nord. J. Comput. 9(4), 301–334 (2002)
6. Liu, J., Lv, J., Quan, Z., Zhan, N., Zhao, H., Zhou, C., Zou, L.: A calculus for hybrid CSP. In: Ueda, K. (ed.) APLAS 2010. LNCS, vol. 6461, pp. 1–15. Springer, Heidelberg (2010)
7. Liu, J., Zhan, N., Zhao, H.: Computing semi-algebraic invariants for polynomial dynamical systems. In: EMSOFT 2011, pp. 97–106. ACM (2011)
8. Manna, Z., Pnueli, A.: Verifying hybrid systems. In: Grossman, R.L., Ravn, A.P., Rischel, H., Nerode, A. (eds.) HS 1991 and HS 1992. LNCS, vol. 736, pp. 4–35. Springer, Heidelberg (1993)
9. Manna, Z., Sipma, H.: Deductive verification of hybrid systems using STeP. In: Henzinger, T.A., Sastry, S.S. (eds.) HSCC 1998. LNCS, vol. 1386, pp. 305–318. Springer, Heidelberg (1998)
10. Moszkowski, B.C., Manna, Z.: Reasoning in interval temporal logic. In: Clarke, E., Kozen, D. (eds.) Logic of Programs, vol. 164, pp. 371–382. Springer, Heidelberg (1983)
11. Platzer, A.: Differential dynamic logic for hybrid systems. Journal of Automated Reasoning 41(2), 143–189 (2008)

12. Platzer, A., Quesel, J.: European train control system: A case study in formal verification. In: Breitman, K., Cavalcanti, A. (eds.) ICFEM 2009. LNCS, vol. 5885, pp. 246–265. Springer, Heidelberg (2009)
13. Rasmussen, T.M.: Interval Logic - Proof Theory and Theorem Proving. PhD thesis, Technical University of Denmark (2002)
14. Skakkebaek, J.U., Shankar, N.: Towards a duration calculus proof assistant in PVS. In: Langmaack, H., de Roever, W.-P., Vytopil, J. (eds.) FTRTFT 1994 and ProCoS 1994. LNCS, vol. 863, pp. 660–679. Springer, Heidelberg (1994)
15. Wildmoser, M., Nipkow, T.: Certifying machine code safety: Shallow versus deep embedding. In: Slind, K., Bunker, A., Gopalakrishnan, G.C. (eds.) TPHOLs 2004. LNCS, vol. 3223, pp. 305–320. Springer, Heidelberg (2004)
16. Zhang, S.: CTCS-3 Technology Specification. China Railway Publishing House (2008)
17. Zhou, C., Hansen, M.R.: Duration Calculus: A Formal Approach to Real-Time Systems. Series: Monographs in Theoretical Computer Science. An EATCS Series. Springer (2004)
18. Zhou, C., Hoare, C.A.R., Ravn, A.P.: A calculus of durations. Information Processing Letters 40(5), 269–276 (1991)
19. Zhou, C., Li, X.: A mean-value duration calculus. In: A Classical Mind, Essays in Honour of C.A.R. Hoare, pp. 432–451. Prentice-Hall International (1994)
20. Zhou, C., Wang, J., Ravn, A.P.: A formal description of hybrid systems. In: Alur, R., Sontag, E.D., Henzinger, T.A. (eds.) HS 1995. LNCS, vol. 1066, pp. 511–530. Springer, Heidelberg (1996)

Formal Verification of Loop Bound Estimation for WCET Analysis[*]

Sandrine Blazy[1], André Maroneze[1], and David Pichardie[2]

[1] IRISA - Université Rennes 1
[2] Harvard University / INRIA

Abstract. Worst-case execution time (WCET) estimation tools are complex pieces of software performing tasks such as computation on control flow graphs (CFGs) and bound calculation. In this paper, we present a formal verification (in Coq) of a loop bound estimation. It relies on program slicing and bound calculation.

The work has been integrated into the CompCert verified C compiler. Our verified analyses directly operate on non-structured CFGs. We extend the CompCert RTL intermediate language with a notion of loop nesting (a.k.a. weak topological ordering on CFGs) that is useful for reasoning on CFGs. The automatic extraction of our loop bound estimation into OCaml yields a program with competitive results, obtained from experiments on a reference benchmark for WCET bound estimation tools.

1 Introduction

Avionics embedded software is developed according to international regulations. Among them is the DO-178C, that has been published in 2012, thirty years after its previous version DO-178B [19]. The DO-178C promotes the use of formal methods for developing real-time safety-critical software rigorously. Airplane manufacturers also follow their own development standards, and formal methods were already used by the Airbus airplane manufacturer for developing safety-critical software during DO-178B.

In this context, Airbus conducted experiments (see [5]) in order to compile in a realistic environment an up-to-date flight control software with CompCert, a formally verified compiler [16]. The CompCert compiler is a formally verified optimizing compiler for the C language that has been specified, implemented and proved using the Coq proof assistant. The compiler is exempt from miscompilation issues: it is equipped with a proof of semantic preservation. This proof is done once for all in Coq; it states that every compiled program behaves as prescribed by the semantics of its source program.

Even if formal methods are promoted by avionics standards, adopting a formally verified compiler is not self-evident in an industrial context. The quality of

---

[*] This work was supported by Agence Nationale de la Recherche, grant number ANR-11-INSE-003 Verasco.

E. Cohen and A. Rybalchenko (Eds.): VSTTE 2013, LNCS 8164, pp. 281–303, 2014.

the code generated by the compiler is as important as the formal guarantees. For real-time safety-critical software, a common practice is to measure this quality by counting the size of the compiled code and by estimating its worst-case execution time (WCET) [5]. Estimating WCET is a crucial step when developing real-time software. It ensures that no run of a program will exceed its allowed execution time. Computing the exact WCET of any program is not always possible and simulations or static analyses are required to estimate it.

WCET estimation tools are complex pieces of software performing three main tasks related to 1) control flow facts, 2) hardware features (e.g. cache misses) and 3) estimate calculation; see [23] for a survey of techniques and tools. Sound estimate calculation computes an upper bound of all execution times of a whole program (i.e. a global bound) from the flow and timing information obtained by the first two tasks (i.e. from local bounds). This paper focuses on the first and third tasks: control flow facts that are useful for estimating loop bounds. A loop bound is a static over-approximation of the number of times a loop is executed during any execution of a given program. Estimating the execution time of instructions on a given hardware is still an active field of research in the WCET community and is out of the scope of this paper.

There are many studies on loop bound estimation in the literature. The techniques range from pattern-matching (for identifying simple loop patterns), modeling computations using affine equalities and inequalities (that are solved by a decision procedure for Presburger arithmetic), data flow analysis, symbolic execution to abstract interpretation. Basic techniques handle only simple loops; advanced techniques handle various forms of nested loops. Some of these static analysis techniques are well understood for several years now but their implementations in a real toolchain are still error prone, because these implementations operate directly on unstructured CFGs originating from C programs. We focus here on the SWEET loop bound analysis technique [9] that demonstrated a good precision in the context of WCET analysis.

Compiling Airbus flight control software with CompCert has shown that the quality of the compiled code is better than the quality of the compiler currently used at Airbus [5]. The next step towards an industrial use of CompCert is to qualify it according to DO-178C, and to strengthen the confidence in the results of tools such as WCET estimation tools. In that perspective, combining the CompCert verified compiler with a formal verification of a loop bound analysis estimation for WCET analysis is valuable.

Our work is significant for many reasons.

- It constitutes the first machine-checked proof of a nontrivial loop bound estimation algorithm operating over an intermediate language having the same expressiveness as C. This proof combines two proof techniques, whole formal verification using the Coq proof assistant and formal verification of untrusted checkers.
- It provides a reference implementation of a tool combining independent techniques: loop reconstruction in an unstructured CFG, program slicing and loop bound calculation. Program slicing is required to improve the precision

of the analysis, by removing irrelevant variables that do not impact on the number of iterations of a loop.
- A tool has been generated automatically from our formalization. Its performances are close to those of reference tools for estimating loop bounds. In this paper, we compare our tool with a reference tool called SWEET that also relies on program slicing [13]. Our tool has been integrated into the CompCert compiler, thus enabling the transmission of loop bound annotations to other WCET tools.

All results presented in this paper have been mechanically verified using the Coq proof assistant. The complete Coq development is available online at the following URL: `http://www.irisa.fr/celtique/ext/loopbound`. Consequently, the paper only sketches the proofs of some of its results; the reader is referred to the Coq development for the full proofs.

The remainder of this paper is organized as follows. First, Section 2 introduces our loop bound estimation. Then, Section 3 defines an abstract notion of loop nesting. Section 4 explains the formal verification of program slicing. Section 5 is devoted to the formal verification of the loop bound calculation. Section 6 describes the experimental evaluation of our implementation. Related work is discussed in Section 7, followed by concluding remarks.

2   A Loop Bound Estimation for WCET Analysis

First, this section gives an overview of our loop bound estimation and explains informally its key features. The loop bound estimation operates over a language that is introduced in the second part of this section. Then, the main theorems stating the soundness of our loop bound estimation are explained.

2.1   Overview

Fig. 1 shows the user's view of our analysis. The CompCert compiler consists in many intermediate languages and passes. It provides a general mechanism to attach annotations to program points. Annotations are transported throughout compilation, all the way to the generated assembly code [16]. Our loop bound analysis computes bounds on the RTL intermediate representation and attaches them to these annotations. Moreover, thanks to the semantic preservation of the CompCert compiler, we obtain semantic guarantees about these bounds in terms of the semantics of the assembly code generated by the compiler: each annotation in the assembly code is attached with a provably correct bound.

Classically, bounding a loop consists in estimating by static analysis how many times at most the loop will be executed. In our setting, the estimation of the loop bound is calculated by approximating the variation of the sizes of the domains of some selected variables (we call them *interesting* variables), that influence the loop bound estimation. If the loop is not nested into another loop, the estimation of the loop bound is the product of all the sizes of the domains

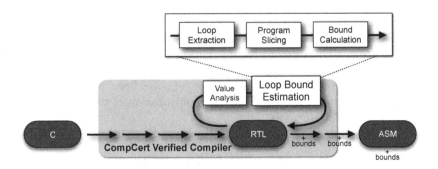

Fig. 1. Main architecture of our loop bound analysis

related to interesting variables. If all variables are considered as interesting, then we may obtain a bad over-approximation of the loop bound. If some interesting variables are forgotten, then we obtain an incorrect approximation. When the loop is nested, the local bounds of all the loop bounds involved in the nesting are estimated separately as if there was no nesting, and the global estimation of the innermost loop combines in a product the estimations of local bounds.

There are several challenges for estimating a loop bound.

1. The loop structure of the program must be reconstructed from the unstructured graph representation of the program. Efficient loop extraction algorithms have been developed for graphs but directly reasoning on them in a semantic proof is challenging.
2. An analysis is required to select the interesting variables. It is performed in two steps: program slicing and computation of locally modified variables in loop bodies. First, the program is sliced w.r.t. each loop condition, as described in [9]. There are as many slices as loops and each slice is an executable program. Secondly, interesting variables are selected among the variables belonging to the slice. Due to nested loops, a computation is performed to select the interesting variables of the current nested loop. Given such a loop L, the interesting variables of L are live variables at the entry of L that may be both modified and used in the body of L. This computation is simpler than program slicing, but complementary to program slicing. It can be seen as a slicing of the program restricted to one of its nested loops.
3. A final calculation is required to take into account nested loops and collect all the local estimations of bounds involved in nestings.

A last challenge is related to the value analysis that is required to estimate at any program point the valuation of all program variables. A value analysis is usually based on abstract interpretation and uses widening and narrowing operators to speed up fixpoint resolution. The formal verification of a value analysis based on abstract interpretation and operating over a real-world language raises many challenging verification problems that are detailed in [7].

For the purpose of illustrating our approach, a succinct example program P is presented in Fig. 2, extracted from a LU decomposition algorithm. In P, there are 2 annotations, written as 2 calls to a specific built-in function and used here to mark loop entries.[1] They are attached to program points 4 and 6 and will be transported throughout compilation. The CompCert compiler will place the comment "loop1" (resp. "loop2") at the exact program point corresponding to the program point 4 (resp. 6) in the assembly code. The right part of the figure shows the CFG of the program and its loop nestings that will be presented in Section 3. First, the program P at the left of the figure is sliced twice as there are two loops in P. The third (resp. fourth) column shows the slice w.r.t. the first (resp. second) loop of P.

The first slice consists of the statements that contribute to the number of executions reaching program point 4. It includes the variables used in the loop exit condition (i.e. at program point 15). Intuitively, we slice w.r.t. a loop condition, but we could also slice w.r.t. any other program point of the slice. To facilitate our proofs (i.e. the reasoning on graphs), we choose to slice w.r.t. loop headers (i.e. loop entries, see Section 3) and show that this amounts to slicing w.r.t. loop conditions. It is then easy to bound the loop of the first slice. At program point 4, the value analysis states that the values of n and i belong to respectively $[5; 5]$ (size 1) and $[0; 5]$ (size 6). Thus, the condition of this loop is evaluated $1 * 6 = 6$ times and the bound of this loop is estimated to 6. This result is written as a comment in the corresponding loop, for illustration purposes.

The second slice of Fig. 2 is related to the loop entry at program point 6 (i.e. the second loop of P) and includes variables j and n used in the loop exit condition at program point 12. Because j is defined at program point 5, in the slice, the second loop is still nested in the first one. Among the variables in the second slice, only j is an interesting variable (only j is modified in the loop body). The local bound of the second loop is 6, that is estimated from the second slice as the size of the domain of j (that is the size of $[0; 5]$, the interval estimated by the value analysis). Note that if the value of i was modified in the second loop, then the local bound would have been estimated as the product between 6 and the size of the domain of i.

The last step is the calculation of the global bound of the innermost loop, from the local bounds. The most widely used technique consists in translating the CFG (and some extra information about the control flow) into an ILP (i.e. integer linear program) [23]. The goal function of the ILP solver expresses the total execution time to be maximized. Here, we do not rely on an ILP solver but we simply compute the product of both previous local bounds which may over-approximate the exact bound in some cases. In Fig. 2, the global bound is estimated to the exact bound $6 * 6 = 36$.

This example shows that program slicing is complementary to the computation of modified variables. For instance, only the program slicing can eliminate all statements related to w, since w would have been considered as an interesting variable if it had not been sliced. Moreover, the computation of modified

---

[1] Annotations can be written manually by the user or generated by an untrusted tool.

	Program P	Slice of P w.r.t. 1st loop (at 4)	Slice of P w.r.t. 2nd loop (at 6)	
1	n = 5;	n = 5;	n = 5;	
2	i = 0;	i = 0;	i = 0;	
3	w = 0.0;			
4	do { _annot("loop1");	do { _annot("loop1");	do { _annot("loop1");	
5	j = 0;	/* bound=6 */	j = 0;	
6	do { _annot("loop2");		do { _annot("loop2");	
7	a[i][j] = i+1+j+1;		/* bound=6 */	
8	if (i == j)			
9	a[i][j] *= 5.0;			
10	w += a[i][j];			
11	j++;		j++;	
12	} while (j <= n);		} while (j <= n);	
13	b[i] = w;			
14	i++;	i++;	i++;	
15	} while (i <= n);	} while (i <= n);	} while (i <= n);	

Fig. 2. An example program, its computed slices and its loop nestings

variables eliminates non-interesting variables belonging to a slice (e.g. the variable i) that would make the bound estimation less precise.

2.2   RTL Semantics with Counters

Instead of reasoning at the assembly level, our loop bound estimation operates on the RTL intermediate language, mainly because RTL programs are represented by their control flow graph (CFG), with explicit program points. RTL stands for "Register Transfer Language". Among the intermediate languages of CompCert, RTL is the most adapted for representing gotos and CFGs. Moreover, the compiler optimizations are also performed at the RTL level and we can benefit from them (e.g. common subexpression elimination). Thus, our loop bound estimation operates at the RTL level and extends the RTL representation of programs with a notion of loop nesting [10]. RTL is just an intermediate representation in our tool: our final theorem is related to assembly code thanks to the correctness of the CompCert compiler, that states that any RTL program behaves as its corresponding assembly program.

Real-time systems only use a restricted form of programming, where each program consists in a main reacting loop triggering tasks that always terminate and where recursion is not allowed [23]. Hence, in our theorems, we consider only finite executions of programs, even if the CompCert semantics model diverging executions. In the same way, functions are inlined before bounding loops. This is how WCET estimation tools proceed to perform interprocedural analyses.

The semantic preservation theorem of the CompCert compiler requires the definition of formal semantics for all the languages of the compiler. Each of these operational semantics is defined in small-step style as a transition relation between execution states. We use σ to denote execution states in the RTL semantics. Among the components of a tuple σ are the current program point l (i.e. a CFG vertex) and an environment E mapping program variables to values. We have instrumented the RTL semantics by counting the number of times each program point is reached. We have thus added counters (i.e. mapping program points to natural numbers) in execution states. We need two kinds of counters: a global counter c_{glob} such that $c_{glob}(l)$ is incremented each time the program point l is reached during program execution, and a local counter c_{loc} modeling the execution of nested loops. We slice n nested loops into n separate loops, and we need local counters to count for each sliced loop how many times each vertex of the loop is reached. Thus, local counters are incremented as global counters, except at loop exits where they are reset to zero. Loop exits depend on loop nestings and are defined in Section 3.

We use $\sigma.l$, $\sigma.E$, $\sigma.c_{glob}$ and $\sigma.c_{loc}$ to denote label, environment and counters of a program state σ, respectively. We use $\mathrm{dom}(\sigma.E)$ to denote the domain of the environment $\sigma.E$ (i.e. the set of its variables). We write $P \Downarrow c_{glob}$ to express that the execution of program P terminates with the final counters c_{glob}. In this paper, we omit the value returned by the main function of the program, even if it is part of the program behavior in our development. We use $\mathrm{reach}(P)$ to denote the set of states belonging to the execution trace of P.

2.3   Soundness of Loop Bound Estimation

We prove two soundness theorems for our analysis. The first main theorem states the soundness of the loop bound estimation at the RTL level. For any RTL program P and any program point l of P, the bound estimation at l is a correct estimation of the counter computed by the instrumented semantics at l.

Theorem 1 (Main theorem). *Let P be a RTL program such that $P \Downarrow c_{glob}$ and l a program point of P. Then, we have $c_{glob}(l) \leq \mathrm{bound}(P)(l)$.*

[COQ PROOF] [2]

Note that this theorem (and the following one) only gives estimations on finite executions. This limitation is inherited from the SWEET methodology we formalize here. A termination analysis (e.g. see [8]) may be required here but formally verifying it is out of the scope of this paper.

The second main theorem states the start-to-end (i.e. from C to assembly) property of our enhanced compiler, that generates an executable code as well as a table of bounds for every program point where an annotation is attached. The CompCert semantics emit a special event each time such a point is reached during program execution. Then, we characterize bounds as an over-approximation of the number of occurrences of such an event in the execution trace of assembly

---

[2] This is a direct link to the web page showing the corresponding Coq theorem.

programs. In other words, this theorem states that the number of executions we estimate for a given program point at the RTL level is still true at the assembly level.

Theorem 2 (Start-to-end correctness). *Let P_C be a source C program, free of runtime errors. Let P_{Asm} and* bound_table *be the result of the compilation of P_C. Then, for any finite execution P_{Asm} that produces a trace of events* tr *and any annotation label* al, *we have* $\#tr_{\downarrow al} \le$ bound_table[al], *where* $\#tr_{\downarrow al}$ *represents the number of occurrences of the event attached to* al *in* tr.

[Coq Proof]

This theorem is a consequence of the main theorem and the CompCert theorems about preservation of annotation events trough compilation. As our loop bound estimation relies on three main tasks (loop reconstruction, program slicing and local bound calculation), the proof of the first main theorem follows from the proof of each of these tasks, that are detailed in the three following sections.

Example 1. In program P of Fig. 2, our enhanced compiler will generate a table that associates the string "loop1" (resp. "loop2") to the bound 6 (resp. 36).

Our proofs follow the methodology chosen to formally verify the CompCert compiler [16]. Most of the compiler passes are written and proved in Coq. Other passes of the compiler (e.g. the register allocation and some optimizations such as software pipelining) are not written in Coq but validated *a posteriori*. We have implemented efficiently in OCaml some algorithms and we have formally verified (in Coq) a checker that validates *a posteriori* the untrusted results of the OCaml program. More precisely, we have validated *a posteriori* two algorithms, an efficient algorithm for computing loop nestings from a CFG, and the control and data dependence analysis of the slicer.

3   Loop Nestings

Reasoning about loops on a CFG may require complex proofs in graph theory. The 3 tasks of our tool manipulate CFGs that are equipped with *loop nestings*. Loop nestings represent a hierarchical view of the CFG loops. First, this section specifies loop nestings. Then, it explains how they are built. In Section 2.1, we mentioned that the user provides marks (e.g. see the program P in Fig. 2) to indicate the program points that are annotated in the final assembly program. The information we compute in Section 3 does not use these marks at all.

3.1   Axiomatization of Loop Nestings

Our axiomatization of loop nestings (that we call nestings in the sequel of this paper) is given in Fig. 3, where the abstract type for nestings is called t. The right part of the previous example given in Fig. 2 shows the three nested nestings associated with program P. Given a nesting s, vertices(s) denotes the list of its vertices. A vertex v belongs to a nesting s (notation $v \in s$) if it belongs to the list of its vertices. In the same way, we define an inclusion relation $\subseteq$ between nestings as a set inclusion between the sets of vertices of the nestings.

Each RTL function f must be equipped with a *family* of nestings. The type called family(f) describes in a Coq record the elements of such a family. It contains four functions nesting, header, parent and elements and eleven properties about these functions. The record type is itself parameterized by the function f because some properties directly mention it.

Each vertex v of the CFG belongs to its nesting nesting(v) (P_1) that is the least nesting containing v (P_2). Each nesting s is given a header vertex header(s) in f (P_3) such that its nesting is s itself (P_4). It implies that header(s) $\in$ s. The header of a nesting represents the loop entry. For instance, in Fig. 2, header(11) $=$ 6. The hierarchy of nestings is described by a map called parent returning the parent nesting of a nesting. The parent nesting parent(s) of a nesting s contains s itself (P_5) and is included in any (strict) sub-nesting of s (P_6).[3] At last, the family contains a list called elements of all its nestings (P_7).

Only three properties relate nestings and CFG edges. (P_8) ensures that header (s) is the unique entry of s and that the only incoming edges start from parent(s). (P_9) ensures that each CFG cycle is cut by a header, except for loops starting at headers which are either totally included in their nesting or that are cut by the header of the parent nesting (P_{10}).

The last property (P_{11}) describes the specific role of the CFG entry point.

In our semantics, local counters are reset at loop exits. We use nestings to define precisely loop exits in the semantics. Exiting the loop of a vertex n_0 means traversing an edge $n \mapsto n'$ such that $n \in$ nesting(n_0) but $n' \notin$ nesting(n_0).

3.2   Computation of Loop Nestings

Various algorithms exist in the literature to compute nestings. We follow the Bourdoncle algorithm [10], a variation of the famous Tarjan algorithm for computing strongly connected components. We chose this algorithm because it is also useful for our value analysis. The worst-case complexity of this algorithm is $D \times E$ where D is the maximum depth of the graph vertices and E is the number of edges. The algorithm gives a weak topological ordering of the CFG.

We have implemented in OCaml our algorithm, and we have formally verified a checker that validates a *posteriori* the untrusted results of the algorithm. We use the nesting ordering to efficiently check the properties (P_9) and (P_{10}) about cycles. Our verified checker takes as input a nesting of the following type.

Inductive nesting := I(v : vertex) | L(h : vertex)(l : list nesting)

An element of type nesting is either a single vertex (I v) that directly belongs to the current nesting or a new nesting (L h l) with h a header vertex and l a list of sub-elements. The verified checker outputs a record of type (family f) or aborts if the verification fails. Let us note that our checker could also validate any other algorithm (e.g. [17]) for computing loop nestings.

---

[3] The functions header, nesting and parent will be used in the lemmas of Section 5.

Parameter t : **Type**
Parameter vertices : $t \to$ list node
Notation $v \in s := v \in_{list}$ vertices(s)
Notation $s_1 \subseteq s_2 :=$ vertices$(s_1) \subseteq_{set}$ vertices(s_2)
Record family$(f : $ function$) := \{$
(f_1) nesting : vertex $\to t$
(f_2) header : $t \to$ vertex
(f_3) parent : $t \to t$
(f_4) elements : list t
(P_1) in_nesting : $\forall v, $ f_In$(v, f) \Rightarrow v \in$ nesting(v)
(P_2) nesting_least : $\forall s \in_{list}$ elements, $\forall v \in s,$ nesting$(v) \subseteq s$
(P_3) header_f_In : $\forall s \in_{list}$ elements, f_In$($header$(s), f)$
(P_4) nesting_header : $\forall s \in_{list}$ elements, nesting$($header$(s)) = s$
(P_5) incl_in_parent : $\forall s \in_{list}$ elements, $s \subseteq$ parent(s)
(P_6) parent_least : $\forall s\, s' \in_{list}$ elements, $s \subseteq s' \Rightarrow s = s' \lor$ parent$(s) \subseteq s'$
(P_7) nesting_in_elements : $\forall v,$ nesting$(v) \in_{list}$ elements
(P_8) enter_in_nesting_at_header_only : $\forall v\, v',$ is_succ_vertex$(f, v, v') \Rightarrow$
          $v \notin$ nesting$(v') \Rightarrow v' =$ header$($nesting$(v')) \land$ parent$($nesting$(v')) =$ nesting(v)
(P_9) cycle_at_not_header : $\forall l \neq nil, \forall v, v \neq$ header$($nesting$(v)) \Rightarrow$
          path$(f, v, l, v) \Rightarrow$ header$($nesting$(v)) \in_{list} l$
(P_{10}) cycle_at_header : $\forall l \neq nil, \forall v, v =$ header$($nesting$(v)) \Rightarrow$ path$(f, v, l, v) \Rightarrow$
          header$($parent$($nesting$(v))) \in_{list} l \lor (\forall v' \in_{list} l, v' \in$ nesting$(v))$
(P_{11}) in_nesting_root : $\forall s \in_{list}$ elements, fn_entrypoint$(f) \in s \Rightarrow$
          fn_entrypoint$(f) =$ header$(s)\}$.

Fig. 3. Axiomatization of loop nestings

4   Program Slicing

As shown previously in Fig.2, each local bound is estimated from a slice of the program. Precise slicing is an important step in this methodology because it reduces the number of variables we have to consider when estimating the sizes of the domains of the variables that are used in a loop. First, this section presents the two soundness theorems we proved on our program slicer. Secondly, it describes the *a posteriori* validation of our program slicing. Then, it explains the matching we define between execution states in order to prove the soundness.

4.1   Soundness Theorems

Given a program point l_s of a program P, slicing P w.r.t. the slicing criterion l_s means slicing P w.r.t. all the variables that are used at l_s. Two theorems state the soundness of program slicing. The first one is the soundness of program slicing w.r.t. the local counters[4]. It states that for any terminating program P and slicing criterion l_s, a bound of the local counter at l_s of a sliced program P'

---

[4] As explained in Section 2, only local counters are considered in theorems related to sliced programs.

is also a bound of the local counter at l_s of the original program P. As we will show in Section 5, this is the key property we use to estimate local bounds on P' instead of P.

Theorem 3. *Let P be a program and l_s a program point of P. Let P' be the sliced program w.r.t. the slicing criterion l_s. If M is a bound of every reachable local counter at l_s in P': $\forall \sigma \in \text{reach}(P')$, $\sigma.c_{loc}(l_s) \leq M$ then M is also a bound of every reachable local counter at l_s in P: $\forall \sigma \in \text{reach}(P)$, $\sigma.c_{loc}(l_s) \leq M$.*

[COQ PROOF]

The second theorem states that if a program P terminates, then its sliced program P' also terminates. This theorem is needed to prove our main theorem related to bound calculation (see Section 5.3). Let us note that this property is not obvious. There are slicing algorithms [20] that transform terminating programs into diverging programs, thus program slicing does not always preserve the termination of programs.

Theorem 4. *Let P be a program and l_s a program point of P. Let P' be the sliced program w.r.t. the slicing criterion l_s. If P terminates, then P' terminates.*

[COQ PROOF]

The standard approach to prove both theorems is to formalize each component of the slicer: data dependencies, control dependencies and post-dominators. Moreover, we need an executable program slicer relying on efficient data structures such as postdominator trees and program dependence graphs. In order to facilitate the proof and avoid intensive reasoning on these data structures, we formally verify a checker that validates *a posteriori* the untrusted results of a slicer written in OCaml. Another advantage of this approach is that our checker can be reused to verify other program slicers.

4.2 *A Posteriori* **Validation of Program Slicing**

We implement an untrusted program slicer that, given a program P and a slicing criterion l_s yields a slice $\text{SL}(l_s)$ giving the set of vertices preserved by the slicing of P w.r.t. l_s. For any vertex outside this set we transform[5] the corresponding statement (resp. condition) into a skip statement (resp. a constant condition).

Alone, this set $\text{SL}(l_s)$ is not enough for an efficient *a posteriori* validation. Because we need to find information that can guide the validator, we reuse the notion of relevant variables and next observable vertices that are used in paper-and-pencil proofs of program slicing [18]. A set $\text{RV}(l)$ of relevant variables at program point l contains the variables whose values are preserved by the slicing and influence the computation in $\text{SL}(l_s)$. Given a vertex l in $\text{SL}(l_s)$, $\text{NObs}(l)$ is defined as the closest vertex (i.e. when following a path of CFG edges) to l belonging to $\text{SL}(l_s)$; $\text{DObs}(l)$ is the distance (i.e. the number of edges of the

---

[5] Slicing is often described as a program transformation that removes statements, but for the purpose of our soundness proof we need to preserve the CFG structure.

SL	Program P (sliced at 6)	Relevant Variables (RV)	Next Observable (NObs)	Distance to Next Observable (DObs)
1	n = 5;	∅	1	0
2	i = 0;	{n}	2	0
3	skip;	{n, i}	4	1
4	do { __annot("Loop1");	{n, i}	4	0
5	j = 0;	{n, i}	5	0
6	do { __annot("Loop2");	{n, i, j}	6	0
7	skip;	{n, i, j}	11	3
8	if (false)	{n, i, j}	11	2
9	skip;	{n, i, j}	11	2
10	skip;	{n, i, j}	11	1
11	j++;	{n, i, j}	11	0
12	} while (j <= n);	{n, i, j}	12	0
13	skip;	{n, i}	14	1
14	i++;	{n, i}	14	0
15	} while (i <= n);	{n, i}	15	0

Fig. 4. Relevant variables and next observable vertices for the program P in Fig. 2, sliced at vertex 6, shown with skip statements and constant conditions at sliced vertices

shortest path) from l to $\mathtt{NObs}(l)$. This distance is used in the proof we detail in Appendix A. It is used to follow the shortest path in the sliced program, and thus select the next statement to execute while avoiding possibly infinite loops.

Fig. 4 shows these sets for each program point of the second slice of the example program of Fig. 2. This slice is written in grey; it is defined as the set $\mathtt{SL}(6) = \{1; 2; 4; 5; 6; 11; 12; 14; 15\}$ consisting of the program points without skip statement or constant condition. As the variable j is initialized at program point 5, and its last use is at program point 12, j is relevant in program points 6 to 12. Vertices 7 and 8 do not belong to the slice; $\mathtt{NObs}(7)$ (resp. $\mathtt{NObs}(8)$) gives the closest vertex of 7 (resp. 8) that belongs to $\mathtt{SL}(6)$. Thus, $\mathtt{NObs}(7) = \mathtt{NObs}(8) = 11$. $\mathtt{DObs}(7)$ is 3, the length of the shortest path from 7 to 11; $\mathtt{DObs}(8)$ is 2.

We implement a checker taking as input the results of an untrusted slicer and performing some coherence checks to ensure mainly the properties that are described in Fig. 5. They axiomatize the notions of slice, relevant variables and observable vertices. They are checked all at once. The figure shows only the main properties; similar properties taking into account memory accesses are ensured in our Coq development. In Fig. 5, l_s denotes a vertex that is a slicing criterion. We use $n \mapsto s$ to denote a vertex n and its successor s. We use $\mathtt{def}(n)$ (resp. $\mathtt{use}(n)$) to denote the set of defined (resp. used) variables for a program point n. Property (C_1) states that a slice criterion belongs to its slice.

Fig. 5 shows that $\mathtt{RV}(l)$ and $\mathtt{SL}(l_s)$ are mutually dependent sets: $\mathtt{RV}(l)$ contains the variables that are defined in $\mathtt{SL}(l_s)$ and whose value may affect the execution of the statements in $\mathtt{SL}(l_s)$, while $\mathtt{SL}(l_s)$ contains every statement assigning variables in $\mathtt{RV}(l)$. This is expressed by properties (C_2) to (C_4) that characterize a backward data-flow algorithm. Property (C_2) states that any variable that is

(C_1) $l_s \in \mathtt{SL}(l_s)$
(C_2) If $n \in \mathtt{SL}(l_s)$, then $\mathtt{use}(n) \subseteq \mathtt{RV}(n)$
(C_3) If $n \mapsto s$, then $\mathtt{RV}(s)\backslash\mathtt{def}(n) \subseteq \mathtt{RV}(n)$
(C_4) If $\mathtt{def}(n) \cap \mathtt{RV}(n) \neq \emptyset$, then $n \in \mathtt{SL}(l_s)$
(C_5) $n \in \mathtt{SL}(l_s) \iff \mathtt{NObs}(n) = n$
(C_6) If $n \notin \mathtt{SL}(l_s) \wedge \mathtt{NObs}(n) = o$, then $\forall s, n \mapsto s \Rightarrow \mathtt{NObs}(s) = o$
(C_7) If $n \notin \mathtt{dom}(\mathtt{NObs}) \wedge n \mapsto s$, then $s \notin \mathtt{dom}(\mathtt{NObs})$
(C_8) If $n \notin \mathtt{SL}(l_s) \wedge \mathtt{DObs}(n) = d$, then $\forall s, n \mapsto s \Rightarrow \mathtt{DObs}(s) \geq d - 1$
(C_9) If $n \notin \mathtt{SL}(l_s) \wedge \mathtt{DObs}(n) = d$, then $\exists s, n \mapsto s \wedge \mathtt{DObs}(s) = d - 1$

Fig. 5. Main formally verified properties related to slices, relevant variables, next observable vertices and distances

used in a slice must be a relevant variable. Property (C_3) expresses the backward propagation from s to n of relevant variables that are not defined at n. The backward propagation ends at vertices where variables are defined. (C_4) states that any vertex n defining a relevant variable belongs to the slice.

The following properties axiomatize next observable vertices and their distance. Property (C_5) states that any vertex of a slice is its own observable vertex. Property (C_6) states that the observable vertex o of a vertex n that is not in the slice is the same for all successors of n. The companion property (C_7) is related to vertices having no next observable vertex: none of their successors has a next observable vertex. Properties (C_8) and (C_9) are related to the distance of next observable vertices. Given a vertex n that is not in the slice such that $\mathtt{DObs}(n) = d$, they state that at least one of the successors of n has a distance equal to $d - 1$; some successors may have a greater distance.

Our checker is efficient and verifies the whole properties in a single CFG traversal. Indeed, while [18] introduce relevant variables and sets of observable vertices for the purpose of their paper-and-pencil proof, they are not concerned with computation on this information and state them in terms of paths in the CFG. We have adapted these properties by rewriting them into local properties enabling an efficient checker. Our local properties can be checked just by looking at each vertex and its immediate successors. Moreover, our checker is complete: Ranganath et al. [18] show that standard slicing algorithms based on control and data dependencies always satisfy constraints (C_1) to (C_9).

4.3   Proof by Simulation

To prove the soundness of program slicing, the major difficulty is to relate states occurring during the execution of an initial program P and that of each of its slices P'. To account for these differences between the initial program and each of its slices, we define a matching relation between execution states, written $\sigma \sim \sigma'$ and defined in Fig. 6. To simplify the figure, execution states are considered as triples (program point l, environment E, counters c)[6]; other state components are omitted. Given a program point l, we use $\simeq_{RV(l)}$ to denote the equivalence

---
[6] c denotes either a local or a global counter.

$$\frac{l \in SL(l_s) \quad E \simeq_{RV(l)} E' \quad c(l_s) = c'(l_s)}{(l, E, c) \sim (l, E', c')} \ (R_1)$$

$$\frac{l \notin SL(l_s) \quad l' \notin SL(l_s) \quad \mathtt{NObs}(l) = \mathtt{NObs}(l') \quad E \simeq_{RV(l)} E' \quad c(l_s) = c'(l_s)}{(l, E, c) \sim (l', E', c')} \ (R_2)$$

$$\frac{l \notin dom(NObs) \quad c(l_s) = c'(l_s)}{(l, E, c) \sim (l_{\text{exit}}, E', c')} \ (R_3)$$

Fig. 6. Matching between execution states of a program and one of its slices $SL(l_s)$

relation between two environments restricted to relevant variables at l. We use l_{exit} to denote the (unique) exit vertex of the program.

All the rules express that the counters at the slicing criterion must be the same. More constraints on the states are expressed in the rules. The first rule matches intuitively an execution state of the initial program with an execution state of the sliced program when the program point l is the same in both states and it belongs to the slice $SL(l_s)$: both states match when the relevant variables have the same values in both environments E and E'.

The second rule matches two states such that neither of their program points l and l' belong to the slice $SL(l_s)$, but some of their successors belong to $SL(l_s)$. These successors are precisely identified using next observable vertices. Both states match when the next observable vertex at l and l' is the same and, as in the first rule, the relevant variables have the same values in both environments E and E'. The third rule is required to ensure the termination of the sliced program. It matches any state of the initial program such that its program point l exited from the slice (i.e. there is no next observable at l) with the state of the sliced program at program point l_{exit}.

These rules allow us to prove Lemma 1, which states that assuming the constraints of Fig. 5, the sliced program executes in ways that simulate the execution of the corresponding initial program. The proof by simulation of this lemma is detailed in Appendix A. We use $\rightarrow$ to denote a single execution step, and $\rightarrow^*$ to denote the reflexive transitive closure of $\rightarrow$.

Lemma 1. *Let P be a program, l_s a program point of P, and let the result of slicing P w.r.t. l_s be $(P', \mathtt{SL}(l_s), \mathtt{RV}, \mathtt{NObs}, \mathtt{DObs})$. Assume $(\mathtt{SL}(l_s), \mathtt{RV}, \mathtt{NObs}, \mathtt{DObs})$ satisfy the constraints (C_1) to (C_9). $\forall \sigma_1, \sigma_2 \in \mathtt{reach}(P), \sigma_1' \in \mathtt{reach}(P')$, if $\sigma_1 \rightarrow \sigma_2$ and $\sigma_1 \sim \sigma_1'$, there exists σ_2' such that $\sigma_1' \rightarrow^* \sigma_2'$ and $\sigma_2 \sim \sigma_2'$.*

[COQ PROOF]

5   Bound Calculation

This section explains how we combine program slicing, value analysis and loop nestings to build a safe over-approximation of program counters. This calculation called **bound** is based on the 3 steps we described previously. Each step is proved by a lemma that is explained in this section. Each proof of a lemma requires to strengthen the lemma into a non-trivial inductive property. We give in Appendix B an account of the formal arguments we have machine-checked.

5.1 The Header Counter Dominates the Other Counters in the Nesting

The nesting header plays an important role for bound calculation since its counter dominates the counters of the other program points in the nesting (i.e. every path from the start to these program points must go through the nesting header). This property is expressed by the following lemma.

Lemma 2. *For any reachable state* $\sigma \in$ reach(P) *and any vertex* l *of* P, *we have:* $\sigma.c_{glob}(l) \leq \sigma.c_{glob}(\text{header}(\text{nesting}(l)))$.   [COQ PROOF]

We have proved a similar property for the local counter c_{loc}. Thanks to this lemma, the bounds of a vertex l can be computed by simply computing a bound for its header: bound$(P)(l) =$ bound$(P)(\text{header}(\text{nesting}(l)))$.

5.2 Relating Global and Local Counters

To compute a bound for the global counter of a nesting header l_h, we need two bounds: a global bound of the global counter of the parent nesting and a local bound of the local counter of the current header. The following lemma states how the local and global counters at l_h are related. We assume the current header differs from the entry point of the program. The latter is executed only once (after a normalization of RTL control flow graphs).

Lemma 3. *Let* l_h *be a nesting header and* l_p *the header of its parent nesting, i.e.* $l_p =$ header$(\text{parent}(\text{nesting}(l_h)))$. *Let* M *be a bound for the local counter of* l_h: $\forall \sigma \in$ reach$(P), \sigma.c_{loc}(l_h) \leq M$. *Then, we have:* $\forall \sigma \in$ reach$(P), \sigma.c_{glob}(l_h) \leq M \times \sigma.c_{glob}(l_p)$

[COQ PROOF]

This lemma allows us to program the bound computation of l_h by a recursive call to the bound of its parent followed by a multiplication by the estimation of the local counter in l_h. This local counter is called loc_bound(P, l_h) and defined in the next subsection.

$$\text{bound}(P)(l_h) = \text{bound}(P)(\text{header}(\text{parent}(\text{nesting}(l_h)))) \times \text{loc\_bound}(P, l_h)$$

5.3 Bounding Local Counters

Our value analysis (called value) computes, at each program point of a program, an over-approximation of the domain size of each variable, i.e. the estimated values (represented by an interval) of the program variables. Thus, given a program P and a vertex l, value$(P)(l)$ yields a map such that for any variable x, value$(P)(l)(x)$ is an interval $[a, b]$ representing a conservative range of the possible values of x at l. We use $|[a, b]| = b - a + 1$ to denote the size of the interval $[a, b]$. Our formally verified value analysis is detailed in [7].

The value analysis could be used directly to estimate local bounds. We could compute the size of each interval and estimate a local bound as the product of all the sizes that were computed at the loop header. Since we assume that programs terminate, a value in this domain is never reached twice. Thus, we have: $\text{loc\_bound}(P, l_h) \leq \prod_{x \in \text{vars}(P)} |\text{value}(P)(l_h)(x)|$, where $\text{vars}(P)$ is the set of all program variables. While intuitive, this inequality requires a good amount of formal details to be proved in a proof assistant (see Appendix B).

Example 2. In the following program, our value analysis will infer the loop invariant $i \in [0, 9] \wedge j \in [0, 1]$. As a consequence, we bound the local counter of the loop header by $2 \times 10 = 20$.

$$j = 0; \ i = 0; \ \textbf{while} \ (i < 9) \ \{ \ j = 1 - j; \ \textbf{if} \ (j) \ i + +; \ \}$$

In order to increase the precision of the local bound estimation, it is important to restrict the set of variables involved in this product. This set is modified as follows. First, we slice P w.r.t. program point l_h and only compute the local bound of l_h on P: $\text{loc\_bound}(P, l_h) = \text{loc\_bound\_after\_slice}(\text{slicing}(P, l_h), l_h)$. Second, in the sliced program $P' = \text{slicing}(P, l_h)$, we only consider the interesting variables that are live at l_h and used in a statement belonging to the nesting S of l_h (thus $S = \text{nesting}(l_h)$) and also defined in any (possibly different) statement of S.

$$\text{loc\_bound\_after\_slice}(P', l_h) = \prod_{x \in \text{live}(l_h) \cap \text{use}(S) \cap \text{def}(S)} |\text{value}(P')(l_h)(x)|$$

This last part of the bound computation is proved correct using the following lemma stating that the previous computation over-estimates the local counters.

Lemma 4. *For any reachable state* $\sigma \in \text{reach}(P')$, *we have*

$$\sigma.c_{loc}(l_h) \leq \prod_{x \in \text{live}(l_h) \cap \text{use}(\text{nesting}(l_h)) \cap \text{def}(\text{nesting}(l_h))} |\text{value}(P')(l_h)(x)|$$

[COQ PROOF]

By combining lemmas 4, 3 and 2 we obtain the proof of our main Theorem 1.

6 Experimental Evaluation

We have integrated our loop bound estimation in the CompCert 1.11 compiler. Our formal development comprises about 15,000 lines of Coq code (consisting of 8,000 lines of Coq functions and definitions and 7,000 lines of Coq statements and proof scripts) and 1,000 lines of OCaml. Our formalization has been translated into an executable OCaml code using Coq's extraction facility.

Our implementation has been compared to the SWEET reference tool [13] against the Mälardalen WCET benchmark [12], a reference benchmark for WCET

Program	#L	Our tool		SWEET			Our tool		SWEET	
		#LE	%LE	#LE	%LE		#GB	%GB	#GB	%GB
1 adpcm	27	13	48%	22	81%		16	59%	18	67%
2 cnt	4	4	100%	4	100%		4	100%	4	100%
3 cover	3	3	100%	3	100%		3	100%	3	100%
4 crc	6	4	67%	6	100%		6	100%	6	100%
5 edn	12	9	75%	11	92%		12	100%	12	100%
6 expint	2	2	100%	2	100%		2	100%	2	100%
7 fdct	2	2	100%	2	100%		2	100%	2	100%
8 fft1	29	3	10%	6	21%		7	24%	7	24%
9 fibcall	1	1	100%	1	100%		1	100%	1	100%
10 fir	2	1	50%	1	50%		1	50%	2	100%
11 insertsort	2	1	50%	1	50%		1	50%	1	50%
12 jfdctint	3	3	100%	3	100%		3	100%	3	100%
13 lcdnum	1	1	100%	1	100%		1	100%	1	100%
14 ludcmp	11	6	55%	6	55%		6	55%	6	55%
15 matmult	7	7	100%	7	100%		7	100%	7	100%
16 ndes	12	12	100%	12	100%		12	100%	12	100%
17 ns	4	4	100%	4	100%		4	100%	4	100%
18 qurt	3	2	67%	3	100%		3	100%	3	100%
19 ud	11	11	100%	11	100%		11	100%	11	100%
Geometric mean			73%		82%			81%		85%

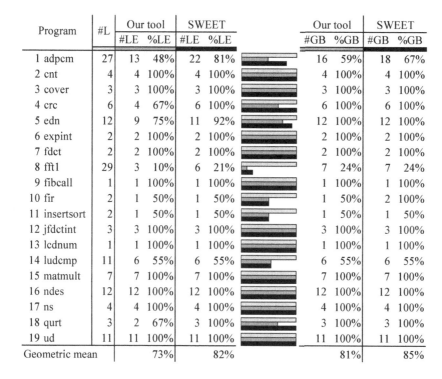

Fig. 7. Exact local bounds and meaningful global bounds of the benchmark. The numbers of loop bounds are given relative to the total number of loops.

estimation tools. This benchmark provides a set of programs with representative loops, mainly used by WCET tools but also by static analyzers [14]. Its focus on flow analysis makes it a reference on WCET-related loop bound estimations. It is especially suited for interval-based analyses, currently the state-of-the-art on industrial WCET tools. Results for both methods are given in Fig. 7. The programs considered are those analyzed in [9] for which SWEET could estimate at least one bound, excluding 2 of them that CompCert cannot compile (i.e. one program with a longjmp statement and another one with an unstructured switch statement such as in Duff's device).

The number #L of loops of each program is given in the second column of Fig. 7. The third column of Fig. 7 shows the accuracy of our estimation of local bounds: it gives the number #LE of estimations of local loop bounds (and their percentage) that are exact bounds. Unfortunately, this column is not given in [9], but we have estimated it from the results of our tool and our manual analysis to infer which loops are estimated by SWEET.

Our results are close to those obtained by SWEET. On average, 73% of the loops are exactly estimated by our method, while 82% of the loops are exactly bounded by SWEET. The histogram in Fig. 7 shows for each program, the number of exact local bounds for our tool (in dark grey) and for SWEET (in black) relatively to the total number of loops (baseline in light grey). Differences in precision come from our value analysis, that is slightly less precise than SWEET's. As our value analysis does neither handle floating-point values nor global variables, nor performs a pointer analysis, 17 loops are bounded by SWEET and not by our method.

The last two columns of Fig. 7 give the number #GB of meaningful estimations (i.e. realistic estimations, that differ from MAX_INT for instance) of global loop bounds (and their percentages). On average, our tool estimates almost as many global bounds as SWEET. Indeed, 81% of global bounds are estimated by our tool, and 85% of global loops are estimated by SWEET.

Concerning the analysis time, hardware differences make it difficult to compare them with SWEET's. Nevertheless, we could verify that the use of checkers does not incur a significant overhead in our analysis. Benchmarking the programs in Fig. 7 using a current personal computer takes less than a minute.

7   Related Work

Ranganath, Amtoft et al. [18,20] developed paper-and-pencil proofs of program slicing, introducing the notion of observable vertices. Their main concern is to deal with generalized programs, having several or no end nodes. Ranganath et al. prove slicing soundness by weak bisimulation, dealing with infinite behaviors. Amtoft extends the proof, obtaining a smaller slice by using a weak simulation at the cost of not preserving termination. Based on their work, a formal verification of program slicing in Isabelle is given in [22], where program slicing is used for detecting non-interference of information flow. This formalization of program slicing is relational and generic; it has been instantiated on Java programs in the Jinja framework but it is not executable, contrary to our work.

To the best of our knowledge, the only work related to formal verification of loop bound calculation is [3], where the formal verification consists in using Hoare logic to verify that a program satisfies its specification including a cost annotation (expressed by an equality of the form *global cost = constant value*). A Frama-C plugin has been developed in order to experiment the approach on simple programs without nested loops. Contrary to this work where loops are handled syntactically, our work relies on an abstract interpreter with widening capabilities that has been formally verified in Coq. As far as we know, their Hoare logic is neither formalized nor proved sound.

Many papers have been published on resource analysis [1,2] and loop bound is just one example of resource. The associated algorithms generally target more difficult loop bounds that WCET tools like SWEET or our own tool. It is unclear if they provide significant precision gains on representative WCET benchmarks. Resource analysis tools are not formally verified using a proof assistant. One exception is [2] where a shallow embedding of a separation logic in Coq is mentioned. The only mechanized proof is the soundness of the core logic presented in the research paper. This should not be confused with the kind of formalization effort we provide in order to formally verify a tool for C programs. Advanced ressource analyses such as [11,24] are able to infer symbolic loop bounds that are out of reach for WCET tools like SWEET. This kind of static analysis relies on SMT solvers, hence their formal verification would require the *a priori* verification of a SMT solver.

Checkers are powerful tools for verifying the soundness of program transformations. Several formally verified checkers have been developed for compiler passes of CompCert (e.g. [21,4]). Even if all these checkers are specific tools devoted to a specific compiler pass, previous work and ours has shown that this alternative formal verification technique is worthwhile when the formalization requires to reason on sophisticated imperative data structures and algorithms.

Our long-term goal is to complement the CompCert compiler with WCET guarantees about the code it generates. The formally verified operating system kernel seL4 [15] is faced to similar challenges. Blackham et al. [6] apply traditional WCET estimation techniques on the seL4 kernel and provide conservative upper bounds about its worst-case interrupt response time. Their WCET tool is neither verified nor formalized.

8 Conclusion

We have presented, formalized and implemented a loop bound estimation for WCET analysis. Its design follows closely the techniques used by the reference tool SWEET and our experiments show that it is competitive with it in terms of precision of the estimated bounds. The work strengthens the CompCert framework. It provides bound estimations on the assembly programs generated by the compiler and it increases the CompCert toolchain with non trivial components that could be reused in different contexts, e.g. for developing new optimizations of the compiler: a loop reconstruction for RTL and a program slicer. Moreover, the bound calculation theorem makes an important formal link between the estimated loop bounds and the size of variable ranges.

Our loop bound estimation can be improved in several directions. One is to improve the bound calculation by formalizing ILP solvers to relate precisely local and global bounds. These solvers contain probably too much highly engineered heuristics to be directly formalized and we would like to develop efficient validation checkers for them. Another direction is to increase CompCert with a precise hardware cost model and link abstract counters and realistic costs.

References

1. Albert, E., Bubel, R., Genaim, S., Hähnle, R.: al. Verified resource guarantees using COSTA and KeY. In: PEPM 2011, pp. 73–76. ACM (2011)
2. Atkey, R.: Amortised resource analysis with separation logic. Logical Methods in Computer Science 7(2) (2011)
3. Ayache, N., Amadio, R.M., Régis-Gianas, Y.: Certifying and reasoning on cost annotations in C programs. In: Stoelinga, M., Pinger, R. (eds.) FMICS 2012. LNCS, vol. 7437, pp. 32–46. Springer, Heidelberg (2012)

4. Barthe, G., Demange, D., Pichardie, D.: A formally verified SSA-based middle-end - Static Single Assignment meets CompCert. In: Seidl, H. (ed.) Programming Languages and Systems. LNCS, vol. 7211, pp. 47–66. Springer, Heidelberg (2012)
5. Bedin França, R., Blazy, S., Favre-Felix, D., Leroy, X., et al.: Formally verified optimizing compilation in ACG-based flight control software. In: ERTS (2012)
6. Blackham, B., Shi, Y., Heiser, G.: Improving interrupt response time in a verifiable protected microkernel. In: Proc. of EuroSys, pp. 323–336. ACM (2012)
7. Blazy, S., Laporte, V., Maroneze, A., Pichardie, D.: Formal verification of a C value analysis based on abstract interpretation. In: Logozzo, F., Fähndrich, M. (eds.) SAS 2013. LNCS, vol. 7935, pp. 324–344. Springer, Heidelberg (2013)
8. Cook, B., Podelski, A., Rybalchenko, A.: Termination proofs for systems code. In: PLDI 2006, pp. 415–426. ACM Press (2006)
9. Ermedahl, A., Sandberg, C., Gustafsson, J., Bygde, S., Lisper, B.: Loop bound analysis based on a combination of program slicing, abstract interpretation, and invariant analysis. In: Workshop on WCET Analysis (2007)
10. Bourdoncle, F.: Efficient chaotic iteration strategies with widenings. In: Pottosin, I.V., Bjorner, D., Broy, M. (eds.) FMP&TA 1993. LNCS, vol. 735, pp. 128–141. Springer, Heidelberg (1993)
11. Gulwani, S.: SPEED: Symbolic complexity bound analysis. In: Bouajjani, A., Maler, O. (eds.) CAV 2009. LNCS, vol. 5643, pp. 51–62. Springer, Heidelberg (2009)
12. Gustafsson, J., Betts, A., Ermedahl, A., Lisper, B.: The Mälardalen WCET benchmarks: Past, present and future. In: Proc. WCET 2010, pp. 137–147 (2010)
13. Gustafsson, J., Ermedahl, A.: Automatic derivation of path and loop annotations in object-oriented real-time programs. Scalable Computing: Practice and Experience 1(2) (1998)
14. Halbwachs, N., Henry, J.: When the decreasing sequence fails. In: Miné, A., Schmidt, D. (eds.) SAS 2012. LNCS, vol. 7460, pp. 198–213. Springer, Heidelberg (2012)
15. Heiser, G., Murray, T.C., Klein, G.: It's time for trustworthy systems. IEEE Security & Privacy 10(2), 67–70 (2012)
16. Leroy, X.: Formal verification of a realistic compiler. CACM 52(7), 107–115 (2009)
17. Ramalingam, G.: On loops, dominators, and dominance frontiers. ACM TOPLAS 24(5), 455–490 (2002)
18. Ranganath, V.P., Amtoft, T., Banerjee, A., Hatcliff, J., et al.: A new foundation for control dependence and slicing for modern program structures. ACM TOPLAS 29(5) (2007)
19. RTCA. DO-178C: Software considerations in airborne systems and equipment certification. Radio Technical Commission for Aeronautics Std. (2012)
20. Amtoft, T.: Slicing for modern program structures: a theory for eliminating irrelevant loops. Inf. Process. Lett. 106(2), 45–51 (2008)
21. Tristan, J.-B., Leroy, X.: A simple, verified validator for software pipelining. In: Proc. of POPL, pp. 83–92. ACM Press (2010)
22. Wasserrab, D., Lochbihler, A.: Formalizing a framework for dynamic slicing of program dependence graphs in Isabelle/HOL. In: Mohamed, O.A., Muñoz, C., Tahar, S. (eds.) TPHOLs 2008. LNCS, vol. 5170, pp. 294–309. Springer, Heidelberg (2008)
23. Wilhelm, R., Engblom, J., Ermedahl, A., Holsti, N., Thesing, S.: al. The worst-case execution-time problem — overview of methods and survey of tools. ACM Trans. Embed. Comput. Syst. 7, 36:1–36:53 (2008)
24. Zuleger, F., Gulwani, S., Sinn, M., Veith, H.: Bound analysis of imperative programs with the size-change abstraction. In: Yahav, E. (ed.) Static Analysis. LNCS, vol. 6887, pp. 280–297. Springer, Heidelberg (2011)

A   Detailed Simulation Proof for the Program Slicing

The simulation between states used in the soundness proof of program slicing is a *weak simulation*, i.e. it does not preserve infinite executions. In particular, a program P may not terminate while a sliced program P' may terminate (some infinite loops may be sliced away).

We consider two matching states, $\sigma_1 \in \mathtt{reach}(P)$ and $\sigma_1' \in \mathtt{reach}(P')$: $\sigma_1 \sim \sigma_1'$. An execution step $\sigma_1 \to \sigma_2$ is *observable* if $\sigma_1.l \in \mathtt{SL}(l_s)$, and *silent* otherwise. A silent step corresponds to an execution step from a `skip` statement in the sliced program.

Assume the program P satisfies the constraints (C_1) to (C_9). Its entry point is always in the slice, so at the beginning of the execution, the rule (R_1) holds. If $\sigma_1 \to \sigma_2$, then P' follows in lock-step $(\sigma_1' \to \sigma_2')$ to the same vertex l_2, which corresponds to the intuitive idea that a statement in the slice is executed in both programs. If $l_2 \in \mathtt{SL}(l_s)$, then rule (R_1) still holds. Otherwise, either l_2 has a next observable vertex (and rule (R_2) holds), or it doesn't $(l_2 \notin dom(\mathtt{NObs}))$ and rule (R_3) holds.

The crux of the simulation happens when the original and sliced programs are desynchronized: rule (R_2) holds and the states have different program points. In this case, whenever $\sigma_1 \to \sigma_2$, there is no corresponding step in the sliced program, until σ_2 is reaching a vertex belonging to the slice. Properties (C_2) to (C_4) ensure that no relevant variable will be modified in P, so the matching relation still holds.

When the execution returns in the slice $(\sigma_2 \in \mathtt{SL}(l_s))$, we need to resynchronize the programs. In this case, the sliced program performs one or several (silent) steps $(\sigma_1' \to^+ \sigma_2')$ until it reaches $\sigma2'.l = \sigma2.l$, where $\sigma2.l$ (resp. $\sigma2'.l$) is the next observable vertex of $\sigma_1.l$ (resp. $\sigma_1'.l$). This is where the *next observable distance* comes into play: it exhibits a finite number of steps that are required for the resynchronization to happen. After resynchronization, both states match again and rule (R_1) holds.

This alternation between vertices inside and outside the slice can happen several times, until either P reaches the exit node (if it is in the slice) and the simulation ends, or until P reaches a vertex that is after the slice $(\sigma_2.l \notin dom(\mathtt{NObs}))$. In this case, property (C_7) ensures that we cannot return to the slice anymore. P' then performs an arbitrary number of steps until it reaches the (unique) end vertex l_{exit}. By using an *exit distance* similar to the next observable distance, we know that l_{exit} can always be reached in a finite number of steps. This ensures termination of P'.

Afterwards, states match by rule (R_3), for any further steps performed by P. We do not need to match match relevant variables anymore.

B   Detailed Proofs for the Bound Calculation

Proof (of Lemma 2). We establish this property by proving, by induction on finite execution traces, that for any vertex l, distinct from its header $l_h = \text{header}(\text{nesting}(l))$, and any partial finite execution trace $\xi = \sigma, \sigma_1, ...\sigma_n$, one of three following conditions holds:

- either the expected inequality holds strictly: $\sigma.c_{glob}(l) < \sigma.c_{glob}(l_h)$,
- or l has not been reached yet: $\sigma.c_{glob}(l) = 0$,
- or $\sigma.c_{glob}(l) = \sigma.c_{glob}(l_h)$ but there exists $k \in [0, n-1]$ such that σ_k is at the program point l and all states $\sigma_{k+1}, \dots, \sigma_{n-1}$ did not reach the header l_h.

The last condition implies that we cannot reach vertex l in σ_n: it would build a cycle from l to l that does not contain l_h and this is forbidden by the property cycle_at_not_header (Section 3).

Proof (of Lemma 3). We first consider execution traces of the form $\xi = \xi_0 \cdot \sigma_p \cdot \xi_1 \cdot \sigma$ such that σ_p is a state at point l_p and all states in trace ξ_1 did not reach l_p again. On such traces we show that $\sigma.c_{glob}(l_h) - \sigma_p.c_{glob}(l_h) \le M$ holds. Unfortunately, this property is not inductive. We strengthen it into a disjunction where:

- either $\sigma.c_{glob}(l_h) = \sigma_p.c_{glob}(l_h)$ and no state in ξ_1 did reach l_h yet,
- or $\sigma.c_{glob}(l_h) = \sigma_p.c_{glob}(l_h) + \sigma.c_{loc}(l_h)$ and the state σ is currently in the nesting of l_h,
- or σ is currently out of the nesting of l_h, $\sigma.c_{glob}(l_h) - \sigma_p.c_{glob}(l_h) \le M$ and l_h has been reached during ξ_1.

We prove this disjunction by induction on the execution trace ξ_1.

To conclude this proof, we consider an arbitrary trace $\xi = \sigma_0 \cdots \sigma$ and we divide it into $K + 1 = 1 + \sigma.c_{glob}(l_p)$ subtraces $\xi = \xi_0 \cdot \xi_1 \cdots \xi_K$ such that $\forall i \in [1, K], \xi_i$ starts with a state σ_i at point l_p and then never reaches it again. We note $\sigma_{K+1} = \sigma$. We then express $\sigma.c_{glob}(l_h)$ as

$$\sigma.c_{glob}(l_h) = \sigma_0.c_{glob}(l_h) + \sum_{k=0}^{K-1} (\sigma_{k+1}.c_{glob}(l_h) - \sigma_k.c_{glob}(l_h))$$

In the initial state σ_0, every counter is null and each element in the sum is bounded by M. Thus, we conclude that $\sigma.c_{loc}(l_h) \le K \times M$ and finish the proof since $K = \sigma.c_{glob}(l_p)$.

Proof (of Lemma 4). Given a vertex l, we use $I(l)$ to denote the set $\text{live}(l) \cap \text{use}(\text{nesting}(l_h)) \cap \text{def}(\text{nesting}(l_h))$ of interesting variables at l. We first prove that, if there exists an execution trace $\xi = \xi_1 \cdot \sigma_1 \cdot \xi_2 \cdot \sigma_2$ such that $\sigma_1.l = \sigma_2.l$ and both states σ_1 and σ_2 match pointwise on each variable of $I(l)$, then we can build a valid execution trace of arbitrary large size $\xi_1 \cdot \sigma_1 \cdot (\xi_2 \cdot \sigma_2)^N$. Since we assume that P terminates, we obtain a contradiction.

Now, any execution trace ξ reaching l_h at least once can be divided into $\xi = \xi_1 \cdot \sigma_1 . \xi_2 . \sigma_2$ where σ_1 is the last state in the execution that enters in the nesting of l_h. The counter $\sigma_2.c_{loc}(l_h)$ is equal to the length of the sub-trace ξ^h

that we obtain by projecting $\sigma_1.\xi_2.\sigma_2$ on the states that are at vertex l_h. Each state in ξ^h can be turned into a n-tuple, where $n = |I(l_h)|$ contains the value of each variable of $I(l_h)$ in this state. Mapping this transformation on ξ^h, we obtain a list of size $\sigma_2.c_{loc}(l_h)$. This list contains distinct n-tuples thanks to the *Reductio ad absurdum* we made early in this proof. By soundness of the value analysis, each n-tuple belongs to the direct product of the interval $\texttt{value}(P')(l_h)$. We prove that there exists a list of size $\prod_{x \in I} |\texttt{value}(P')(l_h)(x)|$ containing all the possible n-uples of this direct product and conclude our proof by a pigeon hole argument.

Result Certification of Static Program Analysers with Automated Theorem Provers*

Frédéric Besson, Pierre-Emmanuel Cornilleau, and Thomas Jensen

Inria Rennes – Bretagne Atlantique
Campus de Beaulieu, 35042, Rennes Cedex, France
firstname.lastname@inria.fr

Abstract. The automation of the deductive approach to program verification crucially depends on the ability to efficiently infer and discharge program invariants. In an ideal world, user-provided invariants would be strengthened by incorporating the result of static analysers as untrusted annotations and discharged by automated theorem provers. However, the results of object-oriented analyses are heavily quantified and cannot be discharged, within reasonable time limits, by state-of-the-art automated theorem provers. In the present work, we investigate an original approach for verifying automatically and efficiently the result of certain classes of object-oriented static analyses using off-the-shelf automated theorem provers. We propose to generate verification conditions that are generic enough to capture, not a single, but a *family* of analyses which encompasses Java bytecode verification and Fähndrich and Leino type-system for checking null pointers. For those analyses, we show how to generate tractable verification conditions that are still quantified but fall in a decidable logic fragment that is reducible to the Effectively Propositional logic. Our experiments confirm that such verification conditions are efficiently discharged by off-the-shelf automated theorem provers.

1 Introduction

In recent years, the automation of deductive program verification frameworks (*e.g.*, [5,15,26,10]) has made impressive progress. Proving the functional correctness of real programs can now be done with reasonable effort. A major automation breakthrough is due to the improvements of automated theorem provers (ATPs) (notably Satisfiability Modulo Theory (SMT) solvers [18,12,6]) that allow to routinely and efficiently discharge first-order verification conditions. At the same time, static analysers have also made significant progress. They can infer automatically sophisticated invariants that would strengthen user-provided invariants and therefore automate further the verification process. Yet, this potential for further automation has not fully materialised yet. Indeed, there are still obstacles hindering the systematic integration of static analysis results into deductive program verification frameworks.

---

* This work was partly funded by the ANR DeCert and FNRAE ASCERT projects.

E. Cohen and A. Rybalchenko (Eds.): VSTTE 2013, LNCS 8164, pp. 304–325, 2014.
© Springer-Verlag Berlin Heidelberg 2014

There are two main approaches for integrating automatically generated invariants into deductive program verification frameworks depending on whether static analyses results are *trusted* or *untrusted*. Static analyses that are trusted are usually built into the verification methodology. For instance, SPEC♯ [5] is using @NonNull type information [20] to generate Boogie [4] intermediate code and the Why3 platform [10] is using an effect system to tame aliasing. In this scenario, those static analyses are part of the Trusted Computing Base (TCB). Hence, the addition of a novel analysis is potentially jeopardising the soundness of whole verification methodology. In another approach, static analyses results are untrusted and are treated as candidate invariants which, following the verification process, are transformed into verification conditions that are eventually discharged by automated theorem provers. For instance, candidate invariants generated by HOUDINI [21] are validated by ESC/JAVA [22]. This integration scheme has the advantage that static analyses are not part of the TCB and therefore an error in the static analysis, or a misinterpretation of the static analysis result, cannot compromise the soundness of the verification methodology.

This latter approach comes with both theoretical and practical challenges. If the static analysis and the verification methodology are grounded on semantics that are too far apart, filling the semantic gap may prove unfeasible or be responsible for an unbearable encoding overhead. Semantic discrepancies can show up in multiple places. A typical example is the modelling of machine integers in case of overflows: is it an error or a normal behaviour? More serious is the question of the memory models that can be incompatible, especially if the verification methodology enforces a hardwired alias control mechanism or object ownership. In the propitious case that the analysis result can be encoded in logical form with reasonable overhead, there is absolutely no guarantee that the verification conditions will be automatically discharged by automated theorem provers. Because static analyses operate over a program logic that is essentially computable, the loss of decidability comes from the logic encoding of the static analysis result. This absence of (relative) completeness of ATPs *w.r.t.* a particular static analysis makes this approach for validating static analyses fragile and unpredictable.

This paper aims at ensuring that proof obligations originating from static analysis results can be discharged with *certainty* by automated theorem provers. The result certification of static analyses has been studied for its own sake. However, existing works propose *ad hoc* solutions that are specific to a single analysis *e.g.*, for polyhedral program analyses [9] and register allocation in the CompCert C compiler [29]. A universal solution, working for arbitrary analyses, is very likely impossible. We propose an intermediate solution which leverages the deductive power of automated provers and covers a relevant *family* of static analyses for object-oriented languages. For this family, we show how to generate tractable verification conditions that are reducible to the Effectively Propositional (EPR) fragment of first-order logic. This fragment is decidable and in practise state-of-the-art automated provers are able of discharge the proof obligations.

We shall consider static analyses that have been defined using the theory of abstract interpretation. The first step in the result verification consists of translating the elements of the analyser's abstract domain into a logical formalism in which the semantic correctness of the analysis can be expressed. Our translation is defined using the concretisation function γ of the abstract interpretation which maps abstract domain elements to properties of the concrete semantic domain. More precisely, it translates abstract domain elements associated to program points into pre- and post-conditions, expressed in Many Sorted First Order Logic (MSFOL). Running a Verification Condition Generator (VCGen) on such an annotated program results in a set of proof obligations expressed in first-order logic. These Verification Conditions (VCs) are then given to be proved by ATPs. As already mentioned, this is no formal guarantee that ATPs will be able to discharge those proof obligations. For object-oriented analyses, the formulae make extensive use of quantifiers and are therefore challenging for ATPs. This very work is motivated by the experimental observation that state-of-the-art ATPs are in practise incapable of discharging those formulae. An important part of this paper is therefore concerned with identifying a logical fragment for expressing pre-, post-conditions and VCs, and to present a method for transforming these VCs into VCs that can be discharged efficiently.

1.1 Overview

Our approach to get tractable verification conditions is to restrict our attention to a family of object-oriented static analyses. Each static analysis in the family is equipped with a specific *base* abstract domain and is thus equipped with a specific concretisation function. Yet, the lifting of this analysis specific concretisation function to the program heap is generic and shared by all the analyses in the family. We exploit these similarities to generate specialised verification conditions that are reducible to EPR. To demonstrate the approach, we have developed result certifiers for two different object-oriented static analyses belonging to the family: a bytecode verifier (BCV) [28] for Java and Fähndrich and Leino type-system [20] for checking null pointers.

We restrict ourselves to static analyses based on the theory of abstract interpretation [17]. In this framework static analyses are defined *w.r.t.* a *collecting semantics* which extracts the properties of interest from the program concrete semantics. For formalisation purposes, we give a core object-oriented bytecode language (see Section 2) a mostly small-step operational semantics $\cdot \rightarrow \cdot \subseteq \mathit{State} \times \mathit{State}$, *i.e.*, a small-step semantics with big-step reduction for method calls. A program state $(e, h, p) \in \mathit{Env} \times \mathit{Heap} \times \mathit{PP}$ is a triple where e is a local environment mapping variables to locations; h is a mapping from locations to objects representing the heap and p is the current program point. The semantics is fairly standard except for a generic instrumentation of instance fields. This instrumentation is expressed using a dedicated IF domain with a specific element *inull* and an operation *ifield* that models field update.

$$\mathit{inull} : \mathit{IF} \qquad \mathit{ifield} : \mathit{IF} \rightarrow \mathit{IF}$$

Fields of a newly created object are tagged by *inull* and the *ifield* function is called whenever a field is updated. Using the terminology of deductive verification, for each field, we add a ghost field that is updated together with the concrete field. By construction, the instrumentation is transparent *i.e.*, erasing the instrumentation has no impact on the semantics.

Each static analysis is defined by a particular instrumentation (IF, *inull*, *ifield*) and by an abstract domain *Abs* equipped with a concretisation function:

$$\gamma : \mathit{Abs} \to \mathcal{P}(\mathit{State})$$

As collecting semantics we consider the set of reachable *instrumented* states Reach of the program semantics. A correct (over-)approximation of Reach is an abstract element $b^\sharp \in \mathit{Abs}$ whose concretisation is such that $\mathit{Reach} \subseteq \gamma(b^\sharp)$. As a result, verifying the static analysis result amounts to proving the following proof obligation:

$$s \in \gamma(b^\sharp) \wedge s \to s' \Rightarrow s' \in \gamma(b^\sharp)$$

Providing the concretisation function and the program semantics can be axiomatised in first-order logic, the proof obligation can be sent to ATPs such as SMT solvers or first-order provers. In our case, the logic embedding does not incur a particular encoding overhead as it is demonstrated by our modelling of the semantics [7] using the Why platform.

This approach has demonstrated its effectiveness to certify the result of numerical analyses [16]. However, for object-oriented analyses, ATPs fail to discharge the proof obligation because the formulae quantify over infinite domains such as the set of memory locations. An obvious optimisation that simplifies the task of the prover consists in splitting the proof obligation into program point specific verification conditions. In our experiments, off-the-shelf ATPs still fail to reliably and consistently discharge all the proof obligations. This absence of (relative) completeness of ATPs *w.r.t.* a particular static analysis makes this approach for validating static analyses fragile and unpredictable.

To alleviate the problem, provers could be tuned on a *per* analysis basis. However, this solution is fragile and comes without any formal guarantee: what about its robustness *w.r.t.* slight modifications of the static analysis? Here, we explore another solution that is robust and does not require any modification of the provers. We propose to tame static analyses so that, by construction, proof obligations fall in fragments that are well-understood by the prover and are therefore discharged reliably. The *family* of static analyses we have identified can be characterised almost syntactically by the definition of concretisation function. As a result, the static analysis designer can have the guarantee that the proof obligations will be discharged without any knowledge of the internals of the provers. The proof obligations we generate are easily reducible to Effectively Propositional logic. This logic is still quantified but decidable and, as the ATP System Competition shows, existing provers are already tuned for this logic.

Our family of analyses is parametrised by a base abstract domain $\mathit{Val}^\sharp$ for abstracting values (see Section 3). This abstract domain is automatically lifted to the program abstraction *Abs*.

$$\mathcal{H}eap^{\sharp} = \mathcal{F} \to \mathcal{V}al^{\sharp} \times \mathcal{V}al^{\sharp} \qquad \mathcal{E}nv^{\sharp} = \mathcal{V}ar \to \mathcal{V}al^{\sharp} \qquad Abs = \mathcal{H}eap^{\sharp} \times (\mathcal{PP} \to \mathcal{E}nv^{\sharp})$$

This abstraction corresponds to static analyses that are flow-sensitive (the abstraction of local variables is program specific) and heap-insensitive (the abstraction of the heap is shared by every program-point). The abstraction of fields is relational: a field f is abstracted by a pair $(v_1, v_2) \in \mathcal{V}al^{\sharp} \times \mathcal{V}al^{\sharp}$ such that v_2 is the abstraction of x.f providing v_1 is the abstraction of x. This family of analyses encompasses well-known static analyses such as Java bytecode verification [28] and Fähndrich and Leino type-system for checking null pointers [20].

For this family of analyses, we show how to generate verification conditions of the following shape (see Section 4.1):

$$\forall \bar{c} \in \mathcal{C}lass, \bar{f} \in \mathcal{F}, \bar{i} \in \mathcal{IF}, \bar{v} \in \mathcal{V}ar.\phi$$

where $\bar{c}, \bar{f}, \bar{i}, \bar{v}$ are vectors of universally quantified variables and ϕ is a quantifier-free propositional formula built over the following atomic propositions

$$p ::= v^{\sharp} \in \gamma_{null} \mid (c, f, i) \in \gamma_L(v^{\sharp}) \mid c \preceq c \mid f \in c.$$

In this definition, γ_{null} and γ_L are used to specify the concretisation of the base domain $\mathcal{V}al^{\sharp}$, $\preceq$ is a subclass test and $f \in c$ checks whether a field belongs to a class. As soon as the domain $\mathcal{IF}$ is finite, quantifications are only over finite domains. Thus, the formulae are Effectively propositional providing that γ_L can be expressed in this fragment.

Using our approach, the designer of the analysis can verify at the analysis level the logic fragment the verification conditions will fall into. This is a formal guarantee that makes this technique for verifying the analyses results very robust. In practise, even if the formulae are decidable, the provers might not be complete. Our experiments show that for EPR the provers are really efficient at discharging our verification conditions.

1.2   Organisation

In Section 2 we present a small object-oriented language with its operational semantics. Section defines the family of analyses we consider and presents the encoding of Java bytecode verification and Fähndrich and Leino type-system for checking null pointers [20]. For this specific class of analyses, Section 4 shows how to generate verification conditions in the EPR fragment. A prototype implementation in Why3 is described in Section 5. Section 6 reviews related work and Section 7 concludes.

2   Language, Syntax and Semantics

In the formalisation, we consider a core object-oriented language. Let $\mathcal{PP}$, $\mathcal{V}ar$, $\mathcal{C}lass$, $\mathcal{M}ethod$ and $\mathcal{F}$ be finite sets of program points, variable names, classes, method names and field names. The set Var contains distinguished elements for the this pointer, the parameters p_0 and p_1 and the method result res.

$$Var \ni x ::= \text{this} \mid p_0 \mid p_1 \mid \text{res} \mid \ldots$$
$$Stmt \ni s ::= x := \text{null} \mid x := y \mid x := y.f \mid x := \text{new } C \mid x := y.c.m(x, y)$$
$$\mid x.f := y \mid \text{Ifnull}(x, pc) \mid \text{skip}$$

Programs: In our model, a method $(c, m) \in Class \times Method$ is identified by its defining class c and its name m. Its entry point (written $(c.m)_0$) and its exit point (written $(c.m)_\infty$) are given by the mapping $\text{sig} \in Class \times Method \to (PP \times PP)_\perp$. The code is described via two functions: $\text{get\_stmt} \in PP \to Stmt$ returns the statement at program point; the normal successor of a program point p is written p^+. For a conditional statement $\text{Ifnull}(e, p')$, if e is null, the successor is p', otherwise it is p^+. The class hierarchy is represented by a relation extends relating a class and its direct super-class. The subclass relation $\preceq$ is defined as the reflexive, transitive closure of **extends**. Each class defines a set of fields. We write $f \in c$ for a field that is either defined or inherited by c, *i.e.*, recursively defined by a super-class of c. The lookup function models virtual method dispatch and is defined if a matching method is found by walking-up the class hierarchy. We identify a method signature by a defining class and a method name.

$$\text{lookup} : Class \to (Class \times Method) \to Class_\perp$$

Semantics: The semantic domains are built upon an infinite set of locations $\mathcal{L}$, and parametrised by an unspecified domain $I\!F$ of field annotations. At object creation, field annotations are tagged by $inull \in I\!F$ and updated at field updates by the $ifield : I\!F \to I\!F$ function. Values are either a location or the constant $null$; an environment is a mapping from variables to values; an object is a pair made of a class and a mapping from fields to values and annotations of fields; the heap is a partial mapping from locations to objects. A state is a tuple of $Env \times Heap \times PP$. Given a state s, we have $s = (s.env, s.hp, s.cpp)$. We add a set of error states Err for null pointer dereferencing and calls to undefined methods or lookup failure.

$$Val = \mathcal{L} \cup \{null\} \qquad Env = Var \to Val \qquad Obj = Class \times (\mathcal{F} \to Val \times I\!F)$$
$$Heap = \mathcal{L} \to Obj_\perp \quad State = Env \times Heap \times PP \quad Err = \{NullPointer, LookupFail\}$$

The semantics rules are given in Fig. 2 of Appendix A. We use a *mostly small-step* presentation of the semantics, defining inductively a relation $\to$ between successive states in the same method and modelling method calls by the transitive closure $\to^*$. The rules for modelling method calls are given below

$$\text{SCall} \frac{
\begin{array}{c}
s.env[y] = l \quad s.hp[l] = (c, o) \quad s.env[a_0] = v_0 \quad s.env[a_1] = v_1 \\
\text{lookup}(c)(c_0, m) = c' \qquad \text{sig}(c', m) = (p_{beg}, p_{end}) \\
env' = (\lambda x.null)[\text{this} \leftarrow l][p_0 \leftarrow v_0][p_1 \leftarrow v_1]
\end{array}
}{
s \triangleright_{c_0, m} ((env', s.hp, p_{beg}), p_{end})
}$$

$$\text{Call} \frac{
\begin{array}{c}
\text{get\_stmt}(s.cpp) = x := y.c_0.m(a_0, a_1) \quad x \text{ is assignable} \\
s \triangleright_{c_0, m} (init, p_{end}) \quad init \longrightarrow^* end \quad end.cpp = p_{end}
\end{array}
}{
s \longrightarrow (s.env[x \leftarrow end.env[\text{res}]], end.hp, s.cpp^+)
}$$

The side-condition x *is assignable* means that $x \notin \{\text{this}, p_0, p_1\}$ and ensures that those variables are not mutable. The rule [SCall] is responsible for initialising the environment of a called method and retrieving the method exit point. The rule [Call] models method invocation.

Figure 3 of Appendix A. describes the semantics of programs "which go wrong". The semantics is blocking with respect to ill-formed programs (assignment to the variables this, p_0 and p_1), but programs leading to null pointer dereferencing or *method not found* lead to special error states (*NullPointer* and *LookupFail*).

The *set of reachable states* are obtained by the reflexive, transitive closure of the relation $\twoheadrightarrow$ which enriches the semantic relation $\rightarrow$ with states reachable from sub-calls.

$$\frac{s \rightarrow s'}{s \twoheadrightarrow s'} \qquad \frac{\text{get\_stmt}(s.cpp) = \text{x} := \text{y.c}_0.\text{m}(\text{a}_0, \text{a}_1) \quad x \text{ is assignable}}{s \twoheadrightarrow s'}$$

The set of reachable states for an initial set S_0 of initial states is then defined as

$$\mathcal{R}each = \{s \mid s_0 \in S_0 \wedge s_0 \twoheadrightarrow^* s\}.$$

The role of static analyses presented in the next section is to compute an abstract over-approximation *Abs* of the set of reachable states ($\mathcal{R}each \subseteq \gamma(Abs)$) that can rule out the run-time errors *NullPointer* and *LookupFail*.

3 Defining a Family of Analyses

To obtain a more parsimonious embedding of abstract domains into pre- and post-conditions, we restrict ourselves to a particular class of analyses. This class is defined by a parametrisation of the operational semantics and of the concretisation of the analyses it contains.

3.1 Parametrised Analyses

We restrict our attention to analyses parametrised by a particular instrumentation of the semantics ($I\mathcal{F}$, *ifield*, *inull*) and an abstract domain $\mathcal{V}al^{\sharp}$. A variable x is abstracted in a flow-sensitive manner by an element $v \in \mathcal{V}al^{\sharp}$; a field f is abstracted in a flow-insensitive manner by a pair $(v_1, v_2) \in \mathcal{V}al^{\sharp} \times \mathcal{V}al^{\sharp}$ such that v_2 is the abstraction of x.f providing v_1 is the abstraction of x. The form of the abstract domain is defined by

$$\mathcal{H}eap^{\sharp} = \mathcal{F} \rightarrow \mathcal{V}al^{\sharp} \times \mathcal{V}al^{\sharp} \qquad \mathcal{E}nv^{\sharp} = \mathcal{V}ar \rightarrow \mathcal{V}al^{\sharp} \qquad Abs = \mathcal{H}eap^{\sharp} \times (\mathcal{PP} \rightarrow \mathcal{E}nv^{\sharp})$$

The concretisation function $\gamma : Abs \rightarrow \mathcal{P}(\mathcal{S}tate)$ is parametrised by γ_{null} and γ_L that are used to build the concretisation $\gamma_{\mathcal{V}al}$ of values. In the semantics, a value is either the constant *null* or a location l. The constant *null* can be abstracted by any abstract value v part of $\gamma_{null} \subseteq Val^{\sharp}$. As locations are abstraction of memory addresses in the semantics, a concretisation function $\gamma_L : Val^{\sharp} \to \mathcal{P}(L)$ would make little sense. The purpose of $\gamma_L : Val^{\sharp} \to \mathcal{P}(Class \times \mathcal{F} \times I\mathcal{F})$ is to relate in the heap the class of the location and the instrumentation of the fields. As a result γ_{Val} is parametrised by a heap h and is defined as follows:

$$\frac{v^{\sharp} \in \gamma_{null}}{null \in \gamma^h_{Val}(v^{\sharp})} \qquad \frac{h(l) = (c,o) \qquad \forall f \in c.(c,f,o(f)_2) \in \gamma_L(v^{\sharp})}{l \in \gamma^h_{Val}(v^{\sharp})}$$

The abstraction of environments is defined component-wise, *i.e.*, the abstraction of each variable is non-relational.

$$\frac{\forall x, e(x) \in \gamma^h_{Val}(e^{\sharp}(x))}{e \in \gamma^h_{Env}(e^{\sharp})}$$

The abstraction of the heap is also non-relational and each field is abstracted by a pair of abstract values.

$$\frac{\forall l,c,o.h(l) = (c,o) \Rightarrow (\forall f \in c.(c,f,o(f)_2) \in \gamma_L(h^{\sharp}(f)_1) \Rightarrow o(f)_1 \in \gamma^h_{Val}(h^{\sharp}(f)_2))}{h \in \gamma_{Heap}(h^{\sharp})}$$

Finally, the abstract domain *Abs* is a set of pairs of an abstract heap $h^{\sharp}$ and a flow-sensitive abstract environment $e^{\sharp}_{fs} : PP \to Env^{\sharp}$.

$$\frac{e \in \gamma^h_{Env}\left(e^{\sharp}_{fs}(p)\right) \qquad h \in \gamma_{Heap}\left(h^{\sharp}\right)}{(e,h,p) \in \gamma\left(h^{\sharp}, e^{\sharp}_{fs}\right)}$$

In the rest of this section, we model well-known analyses: Java byte-code verification [30] and a null-pointer analysis *à la* Fähndrich and Leino [20].

3.2 Bytecode Verification

For our core language, the purpose of byte-code verification consists in ensuring the absence of *LookupFail* errors. This error cannot be triggered if for every call instruction $x := y.c_0.m(a_1, a_2)$ the class of y is a subclass of c_0. To rule out this error, byte-code verification would compute as abstraction for y a class c that is a subclass of c_0. Byte-code verification does not require any instrumentation of the semantics. An abstract value $v \in Val^{\sharp} = Class_{\perp}$ is either a class c which represents either *null* or any object of class $c' \preceq c$, or $\perp$ which represents *null*.

$$I\mathcal{F} = \{\perp\} \quad inull = \perp \quad ifield(i) = \perp \quad \gamma_{null} = Val^{\sharp} \quad \gamma_L(c) = \{(c',f,i) \mid c' \preceq c\}$$

3.3 Null Pointer Analysis

Our parametrised concretisation can also model more sophisticated analyses similar to the null-pointer analysis of Fähndrich and Leino [20]. A key insight of

the analysis is the notion of *raw* type: an object of type $raw(c)$ is such that all the fields of c (or inherited from super-classes) are initialised. The crux is that the flow-insensitive abstraction of the heap is only valid for initialised fields. Hubert *et al.*, have formalised Fähndrich and Leino's type system in the context of abstract interpretation [25]. In order to track down the initialisation state of fields, they are using an instrumented semantics which annotates field with the status *def* (defined) as soon as their are initialised. With our semantics, this behaviour is modelled by the following instrumentation:
$IF = \{def, undef\}$ $inull = undef$ $ifield(i) = def$.

For precision, the analysis requires **this** to be given a more precise abstraction than other variables. Instead of a *raw* type, **this** is abstracted by an explicit mapping $f \in \mathcal{F} \to \{Def, UnDef\}$ where *Def* means *definitively defined* and *UnDef* means *may be defined*. In our framework, all the variables are treated in an homogeneous way and doing a special case for **this** is not possible. As a result, in our abstraction, all the variables are treated like **this**. This is a generalisation as a raw type $raw(c)$ is just a compact representation for $\lambda f.$ if $f \in c$ then *Def* else *UnDef*.

Another deviation from Fähndrich and Leino or Hubert *et al.*, is that our **new** statement is just allocating memory but does not calls a constructor. To precisely track down the state of a newly created object of class c, we introduce the type $\hat{c}$ which represents a totally uninitialised object of class exactly c.

$$IF^{\sharp} = \{Def, UnDef\} \qquad Val^{\sharp} = \{MaybeNull, NotNull\} \cup \widehat{Class} \cup (\mathcal{F} \to IF^{\sharp})$$

The type *MaybeNull* represents an arbitrary value and *NotNull* represents a non-null object with all its fields initialised. The type $\hat{c}$ represents an uninitialised object of class (exactly) c and a mapping $F \in \mathcal{F} \to IF^{\sharp}$ represents an object such that the initialisation state of a field f is given by $F(f)$.

$$\gamma_{IF}(Def) = \{def\} \qquad \gamma_{IF}(UnDef) = IF \qquad \gamma_{null} = \{MaybeNull\}$$

$$\gamma_L(MaybeNull) = Class \times \mathcal{F} \times IF \quad \gamma_L(NotNull) = \{(c, f, v) \mid f \in c \Rightarrow v = def\}$$

$$\gamma_L(\hat{c}) = \{c\} \times \mathcal{F} \times IF \qquad \gamma_L(F) = \{(c, f, v) \mid f \in c \Rightarrow v \in \gamma_{IF}(F(f))\}$$

A feature of this analysis is that the abstraction of the heap is only valid for initialised field. This property is obtained as soon as an abstract heap $h^{\sharp} \in Heap^{\sharp}$ is such that $h^{\sharp}(f)_1(f) = def$.

4 Generating Tractable Verification Conditions

The verification conditions generated for our restricted class of analyses are not automatically discharged by off-the-shelf provers. A significant difficulty is that the formulae quantify over the (infinite) set of memory locations and do not fall into known decidable fragments. To tackle this problem, our approach consists in generating abstract verification conditions that are geared towards the family of parametrised analyses presented in Section 3.1.

4.1   Almost Effectively Propositional Logic

The EPR logic, also known as the Bernays-Schönfinkel-Ramsey (BSR) class, is a decidable fragment of first-order logic where formulae are of the form

$$\exists^* \forall^* . \phi$$

where ϕ is a quantifier-free formula without function symbols. Piskac *et al.* [35] have shown how to decide EPR formulae extended with equality using the SMT solver Z3. Fontaine [23] has shown that the BSR class can be combined with decidable theories under mild assumptions (more relaxed than the standard Nelson-Oppen combination scheme). This makes this logic a good target for our verification conditions.

After transformation, our optimised verification conditions are of the form

$$\forall \bar{c} \in \mathit{Class}, \bar{f} \in \mathcal{F}, \bar{i} \in \mathit{IF}, \bar{v} \in \mathit{Var} . \phi$$

where $\bar{c}, \bar{f}, \bar{i}, \bar{v}$ are vectors of universally quantified variables and ϕ is a quantifier-free propositional formula built over the following atomic propositions

$$p ::= v^{\sharp} \in \gamma_{null} \mid (c, f, i) \in \gamma_L(v^{\sharp}) \mid c \preceq c \mid f \in c.$$

Here, $v^{\sharp}$ is a constant of the abstract domain $\mathit{Val}^{\sharp}$; c is either a constant class name or a class variable bound in $\bar{c}$; f is either a constant field or a field variable bound in $\bar{f}$; i is an annotation of the form $ifield^n(i)$ where i is either a constant annotation or an annotation variable bound in $\bar{i}$; x is a variable.

In those formulae, constants play the role of existential variables. Observe that ground formulae $c \preceq c'$ and $f \in c$ are syntactic properties of programs that can be evaluated. The subclass predicate $\preceq$ is defined as the reflexive transitive closure of the **extends** relation. Fixpoints, even in the restricted form of transitive closure, are not expressible in first-order logic and are therefore outside the EPR fragment. We sidestep the difficulty by tabulating the relation subclass. We also tabulate the fact that a field f belongs to a class c. The translation is quadratic in the worst case. However, in practise, class hierarchies are never very deep [37]. The remaining atoms are static analysis dependent. Therefore, the reducibility to EPR is a property of the static analysis that can be decided by just looking at the definitions of γ_{null} and γ_L.

The byte-code verification logic is trivially reducible to EPR: The atomic formula $v^{\sharp} \in \gamma_{null}$ always holds because *null* belongs to any abstract element $v^{\sharp}$. Moreover, $(c, f, i) \in \gamma_L(v^{\sharp})$ reduces to $c \preceq v^{\sharp}$.

The null-pointer logic is also reducible to EPR. The atomic formula $v^{\sharp} \in \gamma_{null}$ can always be evaluated; it holds if and only if $v^{\sharp} = MaybeNull$. Atomic formulae of the form $(c, f, i) \in \gamma_L(v^{\sharp})$ can be encoded in EPR extended with the theory of equality and a F interpreted function.

$$
\begin{aligned}
(c, f, i) \in \gamma_L(MaybeNull) \quad &\text{iff} \quad True \\
(c, f, i) \in \gamma_L(NotNull) \quad &\text{iff} \quad f \in c \Rightarrow v = def \\
(c, f, i) \in \gamma_L(\hat{c}') \quad &\text{iff} \quad c' = c \\
(c, f, i) \in \gamma_L(F) \quad &\text{iff} \quad f \in c \Rightarrow F(f) = Def \Rightarrow i = def
\end{aligned}
$$

The theory of equality can be reduced to EPR [35] and is not a problem. In this specific case, the interpreted function F is known and defined over a finite domain. For a given F, the formula $F(f) = Def$ can therefore be expanded into a (finite) disjunction $\bigwedge_{F(f')=Def} f' = f$. The obtained formula lies within the required fragment.

For these restrictions to be of interest we must show that our verification conditions can be expressed in this fragment. This is far from evident and is proved in Section 4.2

4.2   Abstract Verification Conditions

We show how to obtain sound abstract verification conditions The essential property of the VCs is that they fall in the logic fragment identified in Section 4.1. The reduction has been formally proved in Coq and is available [7].

Our verification conditions require the instrumentation to be monotonic *w.r.t.* to the abstraction of location.

$$\forall v^\sharp, c, f, i.(c, f, i) \in \gamma_L(v^\sharp) \Rightarrow (c, f, ifield(i)) \in \gamma_L(v^\sharp)$$

This property has already been identified as being instrumental for coping with multi-threading [20]. In a sequential setting, it could be relaxed at the cost of introducing an additional quantification modelling the fact that, for instance, during a method call the instrumentation can be updated an arbitrary number of times.

The VCs given in Fig. 1 use the following short-hands.

$$v_1^\sharp \stackrel{\bullet}{\sqsubseteq} v_2^\sharp \stackrel{\Delta}{=} \bigwedge \begin{array}{l} v_1^\sharp \in \gamma_{null} \Rightarrow v_2^\sharp \in \gamma_{null} \\ \forall c, i, f \in c.(c, f, i) \in \gamma_L(v_1^\sharp) \Rightarrow (c, f, i) \in \gamma_L(v_2^\sharp) \end{array}$$

$$v_1^\sharp \stackrel{\bullet}{\sqcap} v_2^\sharp \stackrel{\bullet}{\sqsubseteq} v_3^\sharp \stackrel{\Delta}{=} \bigwedge \begin{array}{l} v_1^\sharp \in \gamma_{null} \wedge v_2^\sharp \in \gamma_{null} \Rightarrow v_3^\sharp \in \gamma_{null} \\ \forall c, i, f \in c. \\ (c, f, i) \in \gamma_L(v_1^\sharp) \wedge (c, f, i) \in \gamma_L(v_2^\sharp) \Rightarrow (c, f, i) \in \gamma_L(v_3^\sharp) \end{array}$$

Given an abstraction $(H, E) \in \mathcal{H}eap^\sharp \times (\mathcal{PP} \to \mathcal{E}nv^\sharp)$ of the program, we generate for each program point p a verification condition $VC^{\sharp(H,E)}_p$ for the statement $s \in Stmt$ such that $\mathtt{get\_stmt}(p) = s$. For each method signature $m' \in Class \times Method$ which overrides a method $m \in Class \times Method$ in a sub-class, we also generate abstract verification conditions $VC^{\sharp(H,E)}(m', m)$ modelling the usual variance/co-variance rules for method redefinitions. The comprehensive VCs are given in Fig. 1. In all rules, the terms of the statement on which the VC is produced are capital letters in a True-Type font (*e.g.*, x) and the two parts of the abstraction are written in italic capital letters. We do not indicate the sorts of the quantified variables to keep the formulae readable, but all v are variables in Var, c are classes in $Class$, f are fields in $\mathcal{F}$, i are instrumentations of fields in $I\mathcal{F}$, except in the VC for call instructions, where it is specified $\forall i \in \{0, 1\}$ to avoid repeating the condition.

$$VC^\sharp(\mathbf{skip})_{cpp}^{(H,E)} \quad = \forall v.E(cpp)(v) \overset{\bullet}{\sqsubseteq} E(cpp^+)(v)$$

$$\overset{12}{VC^\sharp}(\mathbf{x} := \mathbf{null})_{cpp}^{(H,E)} \quad = \begin{cases} \forall v \neq \mathbf{x}.E(cpp)(v) \overset{\bullet}{\sqsubseteq} E(cpp^+)(v) \\ \wedge E(cpp^+)(\mathbf{x}) \in \gamma_{null} \end{cases}$$

$$VC^\sharp(\mathbf{x} := \mathbf{x}')_{cpp}^{(H,E)} \quad = \begin{cases} \forall v \neq \mathbf{x}.E(cpp)(v) \overset{\bullet}{\sqsubseteq} E(cpp^+)(v) \\ \wedge E(cpp)(\mathbf{x}') \overset{\bullet}{\sqsubseteq} E(cpp^+)(\mathbf{x}) \end{cases}$$

$$VC^\sharp(\mathbf{x} := \mathbf{y.f})_{cpp}^{(H,E)} \quad = \begin{cases} \forall v \neq \mathbf{x}.E(cpp)(v) \overset{\bullet}{\sqsubseteq} E(cpp^+)(v) \\ \wedge \forall c, i. \\ \quad \mathbf{f} \in c \Rightarrow \\ \quad (c, \mathbf{f}, i) \in \gamma_L(E(cpp)(\mathbf{y})) \Rightarrow \\ \quad ((c, \mathbf{f}, i) \in \gamma_L(H(\mathbf{f})_1) \Rightarrow H(\mathbf{f})_2 \in \gamma_{null}) \Rightarrow \\ \quad E(cpp^+)(\mathbf{x}) \in \gamma_{null} \\ \wedge \forall c, c', f', i, i'. \\ \quad \mathbf{f} \in c \Rightarrow \\ \quad (c, \mathbf{f}, i) \in \gamma_L(E(cpp)(\mathbf{y})) \Rightarrow \\ \quad ((c, \mathbf{f}, i) \in \gamma_L(H(\mathbf{f})_1) \Rightarrow (c', f', i') \in \gamma_L(H(\mathbf{f})_2)) \Rightarrow \\ \quad (c', f', i') \in \gamma_L(E(cpp^+)(\mathbf{x})) \end{cases}$$

$$VC^\sharp(\mathbf{x} := \mathbf{new}\ \mathbf{c})_{cpp}^{(H,E)} \quad = \begin{cases} \forall v \neq \mathbf{x}.E(cpp)(v) \overset{\bullet}{\sqsubseteq} E(cpp^+)(v) \\ \wedge \forall f \in \mathbf{c}.(\mathbf{c}, f, inull) \in \gamma_L(E(cpp^+)(x)) \\ \wedge \forall c', f \in c'.(c', f, inull) \in \gamma_L(H(f)_1) \Rightarrow H(f)_2 \in \gamma_{null} \end{cases}$$

$$VC^\sharp(\mathbf{x.f} := \mathbf{y})_{cpp}^{(H,E)} \quad = \begin{cases} \forall c, i. \\ \quad \mathbf{f} \in c \Rightarrow \\ \quad (c, \mathbf{f}, i) \in E(cpp)(x) \Rightarrow \\ \quad (c, \mathbf{f}, ifield(i)) \in E(cpp^+)(x) \\ \wedge \forall v \neq \mathbf{x}.E(cpp)(v) \overset{\bullet}{\sqsubseteq} E(cpp^+)(v) \\ \wedge \forall i, c, f' \neq \mathbf{f}. \\ \quad \mathbf{f} \in c \Rightarrow \\ \quad (c, f', i) \in \gamma_L(E(cpp)(\mathbf{x})) \\ \quad (c, f', i) \in \gamma_L(E(cpp^+)(\mathbf{x})) \\ \wedge E(cpp)(\mathbf{y}) \overset{\bullet}{\sqsubseteq} H(\mathbf{f})_2 \\ \wedge \forall c, f', i. \\ \quad (c, \mathbf{f}, i) \in \gamma_L(E(cpp)(x)) \Rightarrow (c, \mathbf{f}, ifield(i)) \in \gamma_L(H(f')_2) \end{cases}$$

$$VC^\sharp(\mathbf{x} := \mathbf{y.c.m}(\mathbf{v_0, v_1}))_{cpp}^{(H,E)} = \begin{cases} \forall i, f, c' \preccurlyeq \mathbf{c}.(c', f, i) \in \gamma_L(E(cpp)(\mathbf{y})) \Rightarrow (c', f, v) \in \gamma_L(E((\mathbf{c, m})_0)(\mathbf{this})) \\ \wedge \forall i \in \{0, 1\}.E(cpp)(v_i) \overset{\bullet}{\sqsubseteq} E((\mathbf{c, m})_0)(p_i) \\ \wedge E((\mathbf{c, m})_\infty)(\mathbf{res}) \overset{\bullet}{\sqsubseteq} E(cpp^+)(x) \\ \wedge \forall v \notin \{\mathbf{x, y}, \mathbf{v_0, v_1}\}.E(cpp)(v) \overset{\bullet}{\sqsubseteq} E(cpp^+)(v) \\ \wedge E((\mathbf{c, m})_\infty)(\mathbf{this}) \overset{\bullet}{\sqcap} E(cpp)(y) \overset{\bullet}{\sqsubseteq} E(cpp^+)(y) \\ \forall i \in \{0, 1\}.E((\mathbf{c, m})_\infty)(p_i) \overset{\bullet}{\sqcap} E(cpp)(\mathbf{v_i}) \overset{\bullet}{\sqsubseteq} E(cpp^+)(\mathbf{v_i}) \end{cases}$$

$$VC^\sharp(\mathbf{Jnull}(\mathbf{x}, p'))_{cpp}^{(H,E)} \quad = \begin{cases} E(cpp)(\mathbf{x}) \in \gamma_{null} \Rightarrow E(cpp^+(x)) \in \gamma_{null} \\ \wedge \forall v \neq \mathbf{x}.E(cpp)(\mathbf{x}) \in \gamma_{null} \Rightarrow E(cpp)(v) \overset{\bullet}{\sqsubseteq} E(cpp^+)(v) \\ \wedge \forall c, i, f \in \mathbf{c}.(c, f, i) \in \gamma_L(E(cpp)(\mathbf{x})) \Rightarrow (c, f, i) \in \gamma_L(E(cpp^+)(\mathbf{x})) \\ \wedge \forall c, i, f, v \neq \mathbf{x}.(f \in c \Rightarrow (c, f, i) \in \gamma_L(E(cpp)(\mathbf{x}))) \Rightarrow E(cpp)(v) \overset{\bullet}{\sqsubseteq} E(p')(v) \end{cases}$$

$$VC^{\sharp(H,E)}(m', m) = \begin{cases} E(m'_\infty)(\mathbf{res}) \overset{\bullet}{\sqsubseteq} E(m_\infty)(\mathbf{res}) \\ \wedge \forall c \preccurlyeq class(m'), f, i.(c, f, i) \in \gamma_L(E(m_0)(\mathbf{this})) \Rightarrow (c, f, i) \in \gamma_L(E(m'_0)(\mathbf{this})) \\ \wedge \forall i \in \{0, 1\}.E(m_0)(p_i) \overset{\bullet}{\sqsubseteq} E(m'_0)(p_i) \\ \wedge \forall v \notin \{\mathbf{this}, p_0, p_1\}.E(m_0)(v) \in \gamma_{null} \end{cases}$$

Fig. 1. Optimised verification conditions

Assignments. We produce different VCs for assignments $x := e$ depending on the expression e. If e is simply `null`, then the VC simply propagates the information on all variables different from x and checks that the abstract value for x at the next program point can represent a null value.

$$VC^{\sharp}(x := \texttt{null})_p^{(H,E)} = \begin{cases} \forall v \neq x.\ E(p)(v) \stackrel{\bullet}{\sqsubseteq} E(p^+)(v) \\ \wedge E(p^+)(x) \in \gamma_{null} \end{cases}$$

The other VC for assignment deals with instructions of the form $x := x'$, and checks that the information on x' are propagated to the information on x at the next program point, replacing the condition $E(p^+)(x) \in \gamma_{null}$ by $E(p)(x') \stackrel{\bullet}{\sqsubseteq} E(p^+)(x)$.

Method Calls. Along the same lines, most of the conditions of the VC for call statements $x := y.\texttt{C.M}(V_0, V_1)$ simply check that the correct information is propagated. First, the information on all local variables that are not concerned by the call—variables that are neither x, y, V_0 nor V_1—must be propagated to the next program point.

$$\forall v \notin \{x, y, V_0, V_1\}.\ E(p)(v) \stackrel{\bullet}{\sqsubseteq} E(p^+)(v)$$

Then, the VC must check that the pre-condition of the method called is enforced, *i.e.*, it must check that the information on the argument of the call y, V_0 and V_1 implies the information on the parameter $\texttt{this}, p_0$ and p_1 at the entry point of the method. We take the entry point of the implementation of the method in the highest possible class $(C, M)_0$. A different VC checks that all implementations respect the usual variance/co-variance rule for method redefinitions.

$$\forall i, f, c' \preccurlyeq C.\ (c', f, i) \in \gamma_L(E(p)(y)) \Rightarrow (c', f, v) \in \gamma_L(E((C, M)_0)(\texttt{this}))$$
$$\forall i \in \{0, 1\}.\ E(p)(V_i) \stackrel{\bullet}{\sqsubseteq} E((C, M)_0)(p_i)$$

The constraint concerning the parameter `this` is a bit relaxed: we know that the object y is not null and at most of class C. A different VC is in charge of checking that the lookup never fails. The VC checks that the information on y at the call point *up to* C is propagated to the information on `this` at the entry point.

Finally, the VC checks that the information at the exit point $(C, M)_\infty$—*i.e.*, the post-condition of the method—is propagated.

$$E((C, M)_\infty)(\texttt{res}) \stackrel{\bullet}{\sqsubseteq} E(p^+)(x)$$
$$E((C, M)_\infty)(\texttt{this}) \stackrel{\bullet}{\sqcap} E(p)(y) \stackrel{\bullet}{\sqsubseteq} E(p^+)(y)$$
$$\forall i \in \{0, 1\}.\ E((C, M)_\infty)(p_i) \stackrel{\bullet}{\sqcap} E(p)(V_i) \stackrel{\bullet}{\sqsubseteq} E(p^+)(V_i)$$

Note that even if the semantics specify that the value—*i.e.*, the location—of the variables y, V_0 and V_1 is not touched by the call, the object they point to may have been modified by the call, *e.g.*, more fields could be initiated. Therefore, the information at the next program point on these variables is actually the intersection of the information at the call point—*i.e.*, $E(p)(\bullet)$—and of the information on the parameters—this for y, p_0 for V_0 and p_1 for V_1—at the exit point of the method $E((\mathtt{C},\mathtt{M})_\infty)(\bullet)$, hence the use of the shorthand $v_1^\sharp \stackrel{\bullet}{\sqcap} v_2^\sharp \stackrel{\bullet}{\sqsubseteq} v_3^\sharp$.

Conditional Tests. A program point p annotated with a branching statement $\mathtt{Jnull}(x, p')$ generates one VC, with conditions related to the two branches. If the information on x at program point p indicates that the variable can be null, *i.e.*, $E(p)(x) \in \gamma_{null}$, then the jump may occur, therefore the information on x at p' must signal that x may be null, and the information on all other variables must be propagated from p to p'.

$$E(p)(x) \in \gamma_{null} \Rightarrow E(p')(x) \in \gamma_{null}$$
$$\forall v \neq x.\ E(p)(x) \in \gamma_{null} \Rightarrow E(p)(v) \stackrel{\bullet}{\sqsubseteq} E(p')(v)$$

As soon as the information on x at p indicates that the variable can be not-null, *i.e.*, if $(c, f, i) \in \gamma_L(E(p)(x))$ is true, then some executions may continue to p^+ and the information must be propagated accordingly.

$$\forall c, i, f \in c.\ (c, f, i) \in \gamma_L(E(p)(x)) \Rightarrow (c, f, i) \in \gamma_L(E(p^+)(x))$$
$$\forall v \neq x, \forall c, i, f \in c.\ (c, f, i) \in \gamma_L(E(p)(x)) \Rightarrow E(p)(v) \stackrel{\bullet}{\sqsubseteq} E(p^+)(v)$$

Note that the information that x may be null at p is not propagated to p^+, we use a constraint a bit more relaxed than a simple $E(p)(x) \stackrel{\bullet}{\sqsubseteq} E(p^+)(x)$, and can therefore certify *guard-sensitive* analyses *i.e.*, exploit guards to refine analysis results.

Object Allocation. The VC for the x := new C statement is straightforward. It only has to check—besides the fact that variables other than x are unchanged—that the information on x at the next program point can account for the fact that all the fields of the object stored in x have a *inull* annotation and have a null value.

$$\forall f \in \mathtt{C}.\ (\mathtt{C}, f, inull) \in \gamma_L(E(p^+)(x))$$
$$\forall f \in \mathtt{C}.\ (\mathtt{C}, f, inull) \in \gamma_L(H(f)_1) \Rightarrow H(f)_2 \in \gamma_{null}$$

Accesses in the Heap. The VC for a program point p annotated with an access in the heap x := y.f states that the information on f in the flow-insensitive abstraction of the heap, *i.e.*, $H(\mathtt{f})_2$, should be propagated to the information on x at the next program point. Nonetheless, recall that the abstraction of the heap may distinguish between the possible annotations of f. Therefore, the information from H must be propagated to $E(p^+)(x)$ depending on what the information on y at p can say about the flag on y.f.

$$\forall c, i.$$
$$\mathbf{f} \in c \Rightarrow$$
$$(c, \mathbf{f}, i) \in \gamma_L(E(p)(\mathbf{y})) \Rightarrow$$
$$\left((c, \mathbf{f}, i) \in \gamma_L(H(\mathbf{f})_1) \Rightarrow H(\mathbf{f})_2 \in \gamma_{null} \right) \Rightarrow$$
$$E(p^+)(\mathbf{x}) \in \gamma_{null}$$

$$\forall c, c', f', i, i'.$$
$$\mathbf{f} \in c \Rightarrow$$
$$(c, \mathbf{f}, i) \in \gamma_L(E(p)(\mathbf{y})) \Rightarrow$$
$$\left((c, \mathbf{f}, i) \in \gamma_L(H(\mathbf{f})_1) \Rightarrow (c', f', i') \in \gamma_L(H(\mathbf{f})_2) \right) \Rightarrow$$
$$(c', f', i') \in \gamma_L(E(p^+)(\mathbf{x}))$$

There are two kinds of information to propagate: f may be null, *i.e.*, $H(\mathbf{f})_2 \in \gamma_{null}$, and the set of objects the abstraction of f may correspond to, hence the two conditions. Remark that the parentheses does not allows the use of the shorthand $H(\mathbf{f})_2 \stackrel{\bullet}{\sqsubseteq} E(p^+)(\mathbf{x})$.

Updates in the Heap. The VC for a program point p annotated with an update in the heap $\mathbf{x}.\mathbf{f} := \mathbf{y}$ checks that the information on $\mathbf{y}$ is propagated in the heap

$$E(p)(\mathbf{y}) \stackrel{\bullet}{\sqsubseteq} H(\mathbf{f})_2$$

but must also checks that the abstraction accounts for the update on the flag attached to the field. It must be accounted for in the abstraction of the environment, for all objects in which $\mathbf{f}$ is defined, but only for the field $\mathbf{f}$

$$\forall c, i.$$
$$\mathbf{f} \in c \Rightarrow$$
$$(c, \mathbf{f}, i) \in E(p)(x) \Rightarrow$$
$$(c, \mathbf{f}, ifield(i)) \in E(p^+)(x)$$
$$\forall i, c, f' \neq \mathbf{f}.$$
$$\mathbf{f} \in c \Rightarrow$$
$$(c, f', i) \in \gamma_L(E(p)(\mathbf{x})) \Rightarrow$$
$$(c, f', i) \in \gamma_L(E(p^+)(\mathbf{x}))$$

and it must be accounted for in the heap.

$$\forall c, f', i. \quad (c, \mathbf{f}, i) \in \gamma_L(E(p)(x)) \Rightarrow (c, \mathbf{f}, ifield(i)) \in \gamma_L(H(f')_2)$$

Theorem 1. *Let P be a program and (H, E) be the untrusted result of an analysis such that the instrumentation is monotonic. If the abstract VCs hold for all the statements ($\forall p \in \mathcal{PP}, s \in Stmt.get\_stmt(p) = s \Rightarrow VC_p^{\#(H,E)}(s)$) and the abstract VCs hold for method redefinitions ($\forall m, m'.override(m', m) \Rightarrow VC^{\#(H,E)}(m', m)$) then the concrete VCs hold and as a consequence the analysis result is sound ($\mathcal{Reach} \subseteq \gamma(H, E)$).*

This theorem is proved correct in our Coq development [7].

For each statement $s \in Stmt$ at program point p which can potentially be responsible for an error $e \in Err$ we generate an abstract verification condition $Chk^\sharp(s)_p^{(H,E)}$ ruling out this error.

$$Chk^\sharp(\text{x} := \text{y.f})_p^{(H,E)} = \neg(E(p)(\text{y}) \in \gamma_{null})$$
$$Chk^\sharp(\text{x.f} := \text{y})_p^{(H,E)} = \neg(E(p)(\text{x}) \in \gamma_{null})$$
$$Chk^\sharp(\text{x} := \text{y.c.m}(\text{v}_0, \text{v}_1))_p^{(H,E)} = \begin{cases} \neg(E(p)(\text{y}) \in \gamma_{null}) \\ \wedge \forall c', f, i.(c', f, i) \in E(p)(\text{y}) \Rightarrow c' \preceq \text{c} \end{cases}$$

Theorem 2. *Let P be a program and (H, E) be a sound analysis (Reach $\subseteq \gamma(H, E)$). If the abstract VCs hold for all the statements*

$$\forall p \in PP, s \in Stmt.\texttt{get\_stmt}(p) = s \Rightarrow Chk^{\sharp(H,E)}_p(s)$$

then the absence of errors is guaranteed by the static analysis result ($\forall s, e.s \in$ Reach $\Rightarrow s \not\rightarrow e$).

5 Experiments

For our experiments, we consider the null pointer analysis presented in Section 3.3. To get type annotations, we have ported the NIT implementation [25] to the SAWJA platform [24] thus benefiting from a Bytecode Intermediate Language [19] that is closed to the idealised language of Section 2. For the time being, we do not generate VCs for BIR instructions that do not have a direct counterpart in our idealised language. In particular, we ignore instructions manipulating primitive types, static fields and static methods (with the notable exception of constructors). Following Fähndrich and Leino [20], a constructor implicitly defines all the fields of the current class. We emulate this behaviour by adapting our VC for method returns. For a constructor, we add in the hypotheses that the fields of the current class are necessarily defined.

For other instructions, we generate VCs according to Figure 1. At generation time, verification conditions are partially evaluated with respect to the analysis result. In particular, this is the case for terms of the form $\gamma_L(E(\text{p})(\text{v}), (c, f, i))$ where E, p and v are constant or of the form $\gamma_L(E(p)(v), (c, f, i))$ where only E and p are constant. The generated VCs are then processed by Why3 and sent to different ATPs.

Results: All experiments [7] were done on a laptop running Linux with 4GB memory and Intel Core 2 Duo cpu at 2.93GHz. We used Why3 0.80 version and tested the ability of different provers to discharge the VCs. We limited our choice to provers to which Why3 could interface to *off-the-shelf*, and not, for instance, the latest winners of the EPR category of the CASC competition [36]. We generated VCs for a limited set of small Java programs, testing the different cases of the analysis. All VCs were discharged in less than 0.2 seconds, most in less than 0.05 seconds, times hardly significant. Some provers were not able to discharge all VCs, TPTP provers in particular did not managed to discharge most VCs. Among SMT provers, only CVC3 was able to discharge all VCs, altergo failing very quickly in some cases, and Z3 reaching timeout (5 seconds). This differences could be due to the encoding we used, and more experiment would be needed to understand why some provers performed better.

Nevertheless, our experiments showed that the VC calculus presented in Section 4.2 produced VCs consistently discharged by multiple provers, therefore demonstrating the relevance of the EPR fragment presented in Section 4.1 as a framework for efficient result certification of object-oriented properties. The only limiting factor to scalability appears to be the encoding of the class hierarchy $c' \preccurlyeq c$ and the relation $f \in c$. Analysing programs that use the standard Java library may involve hundreds of classes and thousands of fields, and describing an efficient encoding for relation on such large domains is a problem in its own right.

6   Related Work

Static program analysis is a core technology for verifying software. Most static analysers are complex pieces of software that are not without errors. Hence, we have witnessed a growing interest in *certified static analysis.*

Certified static analysis has been pioneered by Necula in his seminal work on Proof-Carrying Code (PCC) [32]. Necula insists on the fact that proof generation should be automatic and therefore invariant generation should be based on static analysis. The back-end of a PCC architecture is a proof generating theorem prover able to discharge the verification conditions. In a PCC setting, the Touchstone theorem prover [33] generates LF proof terms for a quantifier-free fragment of first-order logic enhanced with a specific theory for modeling types and typing rules. For the family of static analyses we consider, a traditional VC-Gen would not generate verification conditions in the scope of Touchstone. The Open Verifier [14] aims at providing a generic Proof-Carrying architecture for proving memory safety. For each analysis, a new type checker is an untrusted module which, using a scripting language, instructs the kernel of a proof strategy for discharging the verification conditions. In our work, the verification conditions are compiled for our family of analyses and the verification conditions are discharged using trusted solvers.

Foundational Proof-Carrying Code [2] proposes to reduce the TCB to a proof-checker and the definition of the program semantics. A foundational proof of safety for a static analyser can be obtained by certifying the analyser inside a proof-checker. Klein and Nipkow have formalised the Java bytecode verifier in Isabelle [27]. Pichardie *et al.* [13,34] formalised the abstract interpretation framework [17] in Coq and used it to prove the soundness of several program analysers. This approach requires to develop and prove in Coq the whole analyser which is a formidable effort of certification and raises efficiency concerns, Coq being a pure lambda-calculus language. Another way to obtain a foundational proof of safety is to certify, inside the proof-checker, a verifier of analysis result rather than the analyser. Besson *et al.* [9] applied this *result certification methodology* [38] to a polyhedral analysis, developing an analyser together with a dedicated checker whose soundness is proved inside Coq. These works target a single analysis but aim at a minimal TCB. Our approach is more automatic and capture a family of analyses at the cost of integrating provers in the TCB. However, generating foundational proofs for provers is also an active research area [11,8,3]. These works pave the way for foundational proofs of family of static analysis results.

Albert *et al.* [1] who have shown how results of the state-of-the-art static analysis system COSTA can be checked using the verification tool Key. COSTA produces guarantees on how resources are used in programs. Resource guarantees are expressed as upper bounds on number of iterations and worst-case estimation of resource usage, and injected into Key as JML annotations. The derived proof obligations are proved automatically using the prover of Key.

7   Conclusion and Further Work

Result verification of abstract interpretation-based static analysers can be implemented using ATP, by injecting the static analysis results into a program verification tool, and generating the corresponding verification conditions. A straightforward generation from the operational semantics will generate VCs that are likely to be too complex for current provers. For this approach to work, the verification conditions must be generated with care. We show how to generate VCs optimised for a class of analyses (here including byte code verification and null pointer analysis) and which fall in a logical fragment that is amenable to automatic proving. We have conducted a machine-checked proof (in Coq) that these VCs are sound with respect to the standard VCs for the semantics. This approach has been validated through an implementation with the Why3 tool which is capable of verifying analysis results in a few seconds using off-the-shelf solvers.

Further work includes larger experiments for assessing the scalability of our approach. We are confident that our EPR VCs are *easy* instances (quantifications can be bounded by exploiting the class hierarchy) that will be discharged without problem by off-the-shelf provers. However, this needs to be validated experimentally. We also intend to widen the family of analyses in the scope of our approach and study how to extend the class studied in the present paper with relational numeric analyses. We expect the VCs to fall in a combination of EPR with arithmetic. A longer-term research goal consists in automating the generation of provably sound tractable VCs. Recently, Marché and Tafat have shown how to prove a *classic* WP calculus in Why3 [31]. We will investigate how to adapt this approach for custom Verification Condition Generators specialised for classes of static analyses.

Acknowledgments. Thanks are due to P. Vittet for porting the Null Inference Tool (NIT) to SAWJA and helping with the experiments.

References

1. Albert, E., Bubel, R., Genaim, S., Hähnle, R., Puebla, G., Román-Díez, G.: Verified resource guarantees using COSTA and KeY. In: PEPM 2011, SIGPLAN, pp. 73–76. ACM (2011)
2. Appel, A.W.: Foundational proof-carrying code. In: LICS 2001, pp. 247–256. IEEE Computer Society (2001)
3. Armand, M., Faure, G., Grégoire, B., Keller, C., Théry, L., Werner, B.: A modular integration of SAT/SMT solvers to Coq through proof witnesses. In: Jouannaud, J.-P., Shao, Z. (eds.) CPP 2011. LNCS, vol. 7086, pp. 135–150. Springer, Heidelberg (2011)
4. Barnett, M., Chang, B.-Y.E., DeLine, R., Jacobs, B., Leino, K.R.M.: Boogie: A modular reusable verifier for object-oriented programs. In: de Boer, F.S., Bonsangue, M.M., Graf, S., de Roever, W.-P. (eds.) FMCO 2005. LNCS, vol. 4111, pp. 364–387. Springer, Heidelberg (2006)
5. Barnett, M., Leino, K.R.M., Schulte, W.: The Spec# programming system: An overview. In: Barthe, G., Burdy, L., Huisman, M., Lanet, J.-L., Muntean, T. (eds.) CASSIS 2004. LNCS, vol. 3362, pp. 49–69. Springer, Heidelberg (2005)
6. Barrett, C., Tinelli, C.: Cvc3. In: Damm, W., Hermanns, H. (eds.) CAV 2007. LNCS, vol. 4590, pp. 298–302. Springer, Heidelberg (2007)
7. Besson, F., Cornilleau, P.-E., Jensen, T.: Why3 and Coq source of the development (2012), http://www.irisa.fr/celtique/ext/chk-sa
8. Besson, F., Cornilleau, P.-E., Pichardie, D.: Modular SMT proofs for fast reflexive checking inside Coq. In: Jouannaud, J.-P., Shao, Z. (eds.) CPP 2011. LNCS, vol. 7086, pp. 151–166. Springer, Heidelberg (2011)
9. Besson, F., Jensen, T., Pichardie, D., Turpin, T.: Certified result checking for polyhedral analysis of bytecode programs. In: Wirsing, M., Hofmann, M., Rauschmayer, A. (eds.) TGC 2010, LNCS, vol. 6084, pp. 253–267. Springer, Heidelberg (2010)
10. Bobot, F., Filliâtre, J.-C., Marché, C., Paskevich, A.: Why3: Shepherd your herd of provers. In: Boogie 2011, pp. 53–64 (2011)
11. Böhme, S., Nipkow, T.: Sledgehammer: Judgement day. In: Giesl, J., Hähnle, R. (eds.) IJCAR 2010. LNCS, vol. 6173, pp. 107–121. Springer, Heidelberg (2010)
12. Bouton, T., de Oliveira, D.C.B., Déharbe, D., Fontaine, P.: VeriT: an open, trustable and efficient SMT-solver. In: Schmidt, R.A. (ed.) CADE-22. LNCS, vol. 5663, pp. 151–156. Springer, Heidelberg (2009)
13. Cachera, D., Jensen, T., Pichardie, D., Rusu, V.: Extracting a data flow analyser in constructive logic. Theoretical Computer Science 342(1), 56–78 (2005)
14. Chang, B.-Y.E., Chlipala, A., Necula, G.C., Schneck, R.R.: The Open Verifier framework for foundational verifiers. In: TLDI 2005, pp. 1–12. ACM (2005)
15. Cohen, E., Dahlweid, M., Hillebrand, M., Leinenbach, D., Moskal, M., Santen, T., Schulte, W., Tobies, S.: VCC: A practical system for verifying concurrent C. In: Berghofer, S., Nipkow, T., Urban, C., Wenzel, M. (eds.) TPHOLs 2009. LNCS, vol. 5674, pp. 23–42. Springer, Heidelberg (2009)
16. Cornilleau, P.-E.: Prototyping static analysis certification using Why3. In: Boogie 2012 (2012)
17. Cousot, P., Cousot, R.: Abstract interpretation: A unified lattice model for static analysis of programs by construction or approximation of fixpoints. In: POPL 1977, pp. 238–252. ACM (1977)
18. de Moura, L.M., Bjørner, N.: Z3: An efficient SMT solver. In: Ramakrishnan, C.R., Rehof, J. (eds.) TACAS 2008. LNCS, vol. 4963, pp. 337–340. Springer, Heidelberg (2008)

19. Demange, D., Jensen, T.P., Pichardie, D.: A provably correct stackless intermediate representation for java bytecode. In: Ueda, K. (ed.) APLAS 2010. LNCS, vol. 6461, pp. 97–113. Springer, Heidelberg (2010)

20. Fähndrich, M., Leino, K.R.M.: Declaring and checking non-null types in an object-oriented language. In: OOPSLA 2003, pp. 302–312 (2003)

21. Flanagan, C., Leino, K.R.M.: Houdini, an annotation assistant for esc/java. In: Oliveira, J.N., Zave, P. (eds.) FME 2001. LNCS, vol. 2021, pp. 500–517. Springer, Heidelberg (2001)

22. Flanagan, C., Leino, K.R.M., Lillibridge, M., Nelson, G., Saxe, J.B., Stata, R.: Extended static checking for Java. In: PLDI 2002, pp. 234–245. ACM (2002)

23. Fontaine, P.: Combinations of Theories and the Bernays-Schönfinkel-Ramsey Class. In: VERIFY. CEUR Workshop Proceedings, vol. 259. CEUR-WS.org (2007)

24. Hubert, L., Barré, N., Besson, F., Demange, D., Jensen, T.P., Monfort, V., Pichardie, D., Turpin, T.: Sawja: Static analysis workshop for java. In: Beckert, B., Marché, C. (eds.) FoVeOOS 2010. LNCS, vol. 6528, pp. 92–106. Springer, Heidelberg (2011)

25. Hubert, L., Jensen, T., Pichardie, D.: Semantic foundations and inference of non-null annotations. In: Barthe, G., de Boer, F.S. (eds.) FMOODS 2008. LNCS, vol. 5051, pp. 132–149. Springer, Heidelberg (2008)

26. Jacobs, B., Smans, J., Philippaerts, P., Vogels, F., Penninckx, W., Piessens, F.: VeriFast: a powerful, sound, predictable, fast verifier for C and Java. In: Bobaru, M., Havelund, K., Holzmann, G.J., Joshi, R. (eds.) NFM 2011. LNCS, vol. 6617, pp. 41–55. Springer, Heidelberg (2011)

27. Klein, G., Nipkow, T.: Verified bytecode verifiers. Theoretical Computer Science 298(3), 583–626 (2003)

28. Leroy, X.: Java bytecode verification: Algorithms and formalizations. Journal of Automated Reasoning 30(3-4), 235–269 (2003)

29. Leroy, X.: Formal certification of a compiler back-end or: programming a compiler with a proof assistant. In: POPL 2006, pp. 42–54. ACM (2006)

30. Lindholm, T., Yellin, F.: Java Virtual Machine Specification, 2nd edn. Addison-Wesley Longman Publishing Co., Inc. (1999)

31. Marché, C., Tafat, A.: Weakest Precondition Calculus, Revisited using Why3. Research report RR-8185, INRIA (December 2012)

32. Necula, G.C.: Proof-carrying code. In: POPL 1997, pp. 106–119. ACM (1997)

33. Necula, G.C., Lee, P.: Proof generation in the Touchstone theorem prover. In: McAllester, D. (ed.) CADE 2000. LNCS, vol. 1831, pp. 25–44. Springer, Heidelberg (2000)

34. Pichardie, D.: Interprétation abstraite en logique intuitionniste: extraction d'analyseurs Java certifiés. PhD thesis, Université Rennes 1 (2005) (in French)

35. Piskac, R., de Moura, L.M., Bjørner, N.: Deciding Effectively Propositional Logic Using DPLL and Substitution Sets. J. Autom. Reasoning 44(4), 401–424 (2010)

36. Sutcliffe, G.: The 5th IJCAR Automated Theorem Proving System Competition - CASC-J5. AI Communications 24(1), 75–89 (2011)

37. Tempero, E., Boyland, J., Melton, H.: How do java programs use inheritance? an empirical study of inheritance in java software. In: Vitek, J. (ed.) ECOOP 2008. LNCS, vol. 5142, pp. 667–691. Springer, Heidelberg (2008)

38. Wasserman, H., Blum, M.: Software reliability via run-time result-checking. Journal of the ACM 44(6), 826–849 (1997)

A   Operational Semantics

The semantic rules can be found in Fig. 2 and Fig. 3.

$$\text{Skip} \frac{\texttt{get\_stmt}(s.cpp) = \texttt{skip}}{s \longrightarrow (s.env, s.hp, s.cpp^+)}$$

$$\text{Assign} \frac{\texttt{get\_stmt}(s.cpp) = \texttt{x := e} \quad x \text{ is assignable} \quad (s.env, e) \Rightarrow v}{s \longrightarrow (s.env[x \leftarrow v] , s.hp , s.cpp^+)}$$

$$\text{JumpNull} \frac{\texttt{get\_stmt}(s.cpp) = \texttt{Ifnull}(\texttt{t}, \texttt{p}') \quad (s.env, t) \Rightarrow null}{s \longrightarrow (s.env , s.hp , s.cpp^+)}$$

$$\text{JumpLoc} \frac{\texttt{get\_stmt}(s.cpp) = \texttt{Ifnull}(\texttt{t}, \texttt{p}') \quad (s.env, t) \Rightarrow l}{s \longrightarrow (s.env , s.hp , p')}$$

$$\text{New} \frac{\texttt{get\_stmt}(s.cpp) = \texttt{x := new c} \quad x \text{ is assignable} \quad s.hp[l] = \bot \quad o = \lambda f.(null, inull)}{s \longrightarrow (s.env[x \leftarrow l] , s.hp[l \leftarrow (c,o)] , s.cpp^+)}$$

$$\text{Getfield} \frac{\texttt{get\_stmt}(s.cpp) = \texttt{x := y.f} \quad x \text{ is assignable} \quad s.env[y] = l \quad s.hp[l] = (c, o) \quad o[f] = (v, i)}{s \longrightarrow (s.env[x \leftarrow v] , s.hp , s.cpp^+)}$$

$$\text{Putfield} \frac{\texttt{get\_stmt}(s.cpp) = \texttt{x.f := y} \quad s.env[x] = l \quad s.hp[l] = (c, o) \quad v' = s.env[y] \quad (v, i) = o[f] \quad i' = ifield(i) \quad o' = o[f \leftarrow (v', i')]}{s \longrightarrow (s.env , s.hp[l \leftarrow (c, o')] , s.cpp^+)}$$

$$\text{Call} \frac{\texttt{get\_stmt}(s.cpp) = \texttt{x := y.c}_0\texttt{.m(a}_0, \texttt{a}_1\texttt{)} \quad x \text{ is assignable} \quad s \triangleright_{c_0, m} (init, p_{end}) \quad init \longrightarrow^* end \quad end.cpp = p_{end}}{s \longrightarrow (s.env[x \leftarrow end.env[\texttt{res}]] , end.hp , s.cpp^+)}$$

$$\text{SCall} \frac{s.env[y] = l \quad s.hp[l] = (c, o) \quad (s.env, a_0) \Rightarrow v_0 \quad (s.env, a_1) \Rightarrow v_1 \quad \texttt{lookup}(c)(c_0, m) = c' \quad \texttt{sig}(c', m) = (p_{beg}, p_{end}) \quad env' = (\lambda x.null)[\texttt{this} \leftarrow l][\texttt{p}_0 \leftarrow v_0][\texttt{p}_1 \leftarrow v_1]}{s \triangleright_{c_0, m} ((env' , s.hp , p_{beg}), p_{end})}$$

Fig. 2. Semantics

$$\text{GetfieldNullP} \frac{\texttt{get\_stmt}(s.cpp) = \texttt{x} := \texttt{y.f} \quad x \text{ is assignable} \quad s.env[y] = null}{s \leadsto NullPointer}$$

$$\text{PutfieldNullP} \frac{\texttt{get\_stmt}(s.cpp) = \texttt{x.f} := \texttt{y} \quad x \text{ is assignable} \quad s.env[x] = null}{s \leadsto NullPointer}$$

$$\text{CallNullP} \frac{\texttt{get\_stmt}(s.cpp) = \texttt{x} := \texttt{y.c}_0\texttt{.m}(\texttt{a}_0, \texttt{a}_1) \quad x \text{ is assignable} \quad s.env[y] = null}{s \leadsto NullPointer}$$

$$\text{LookupFail} \frac{\texttt{get\_stmt}(s.cpp) = \texttt{x} := \texttt{y.c}_0\texttt{.m}(\texttt{a}_0, \texttt{a}_1) \quad x \text{ is assignable} \quad s.env[y] = l \quad s.hp[l] = (c, o) \quad \texttt{lookup}(c)(c_0, m) = \bot}{s \leadsto LookupFail}$$

Fig. 3. Error conditions

A Formally Verified Generic Branching Algorithm for Global Optimization

Anthony Narkawicz and César Muñoz

NASA Langley Research Center, Hampton VA 23681, USA
{anthony.narkawicz,cesar.a.munoz}@nasa.gov

Abstract. This paper presents a formalization in higher-order logic of a generic algorithm that is used in automated strategies for solving global optimization problems. It is a generalization of numerical branch and bound algorithms that compute the minimum of a function on a given domain by recursively dividing the domain and computing estimates for the range of the function on each sub-domain. The correctness statement of the algorithm has been proved in the Prototype Verification System (PVS) theorem prover. This algorithm can be instantiated with specific functions for performing particular global optimization methods. The correctness of the instantiated algorithms is guaranteed by simple properties that need to be verified on the specific input functions. The use of the generic algorithm is illustrated with an instantiation that yields an automated strategy in PVS for estimating the maximum and minimum values of real-valued functions.

1 Introduction

Formal verification of safety-critical cyber-physical systems often requires proving formulas involving multivariate polynomials and other real-valued functions. For example, the following function appears in the formal proof of correctness of an alerting algorithm for parallel landing [9] in the Prototype Verification System (PVS) [12].

$$\psi(v, \phi) \equiv \frac{180\, g}{\pi v\, 0.514} \tan(\frac{\pi \phi}{180}), \tag{1}$$

where $g = 9.8$ (gravitational acceleration in meters per second squared). This formula computes the turn rate (in degrees per second) of an aircraft flying at a ground speed v (in knots) with a bank angle ϕ (in degrees). In [9], propositions involving ψ, e.g., $3 \leq \psi(250, 35) \leq 3.1$, were first checked using computer algebra tools. The mechanical, but non-automated, proof in PVS of the statement $3 \leq \psi(250, 35) \leq 3.1$ is about one page long and requires the use of several trigonometric properties.

Problems involving nonlinear real-valued functions also appear in the safety analysis of control systems. For instance, the safe domain $\mathcal{S}$ for a certain control system described in [2] is defined as follows.

E. Cohen and A. Rybalchenko (Eds.): VSTTE 2013, LNCS 8164, pp. 326–343, 2014.
© Springer-Verlag Berlin Heidelberg 2014

$$S \equiv \{(x, y) \in \mathbb{R}^2 \mid g_1(x, y) < 0 \text{ and } g_2(x, y) < 0\}, \text{where} \qquad (2)$$

$$g_1(x, y) \equiv x^2 y^4 + x^4 y^2 - 3x^2 y^2 - xy + \frac{x^6 + y^6}{200} - \frac{7}{100}, \qquad (3)$$

$$g_2(x, y) \equiv -x^2 y^4 - x^4 y^2 + 3x^3 y^3 + \frac{x^5 y^3}{10} - \frac{9}{10}. \qquad (4)$$

If S is the safe domain of a safety-critical system, the formal verification of such a system may require deciding whether or not a set of points of interest $\mathcal{I}$ is included in S. Analytical formulas that decide these kinds of inclusions do not exist in general.

Formal modeling of biological systems can also yield non-trivial problems involving real-valued functions. Consider the polynomial

$$H \equiv -x_1 x_6^3 + 3x_1 x_6 x_7^2 - x_3 x_7^3 + 3x_3 x_7 x_6^2 - x_2 x_5^3 + 3x_2 x_5 x_8^2 - x_4 x_8^3 + \\ 3x_4 x_8 x_5^2 - 0.9563453, \qquad (5)$$

where $x_1 \in [-0.1, 0.4]$, $x_2 \in [0.4, 1]$, $x_3 \in [-0.7, -0.4]$, $x_4 \in [-0.7, 0.4]$, $x_5 \in [0.1, 0.2]$, $x_6 \in [-0.1, 0.2]$, $x_7 \in [-0.3, 1.1]$, and $x_8 \in [-1.1, -0.3]$. This multivariate polynomial appears in the electrolytic determination of the resultant dipole moment in the heart. Finding an enclosure to the minimum value of the polynomial in the variables' range is a challenge problem for global optimization methods [13].

The problems above, which are challenging for formal verification tools, can be solved using numerical global optimization methods [11]. One of these methods is called *branch and bound*. Branch and bound is a method to compute an enclosure to the range of a real-valued function on a given domain by recursively computing enclosures to the range of the function on subdomains. The method requires a bounding function that returns a crude, but correct, enclosure of the range of the real-valued function on any domain. The bounding function has the property of providing more accurate enclosures on smaller domains. Hence, the range of a function can be approximated to any given accuracy by splitting the original domain into two subdomains and recursively computing enclosures of the range of the function on each subdomain. This recursion continues until an appropriate enclosure is determined or until a maximum recursion depth is reached. In general, when a given domain is subdivided into two subdomains, it is possible that one of those subdomains will need further subdivision, while the other subdomain will not. That is, the recursion tree in a branch and bound algorithm is not, in general, symmetric.

Usually, in branch and bound problems, the domain of a real-valued function on n-variables is an n-dimensional hyper-rectangle, called a *box*. A box is represented as a list of closed intervals, where each interval is the range of an input variable of the function. Figure 1, which shows one possible recursion tree for a problem solved with a branch and bound algorithm. In this case, the recursion first splits the large box into left/right halves, then splits the left subbox

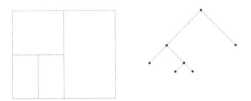

Fig. 1. Branch and Bound Recursion on a Box

into top/bottom halves, and finally splits the bottom half of this subbox into left/right halves again.

The fact that a branch and bound algorithm requires a bounding function to compute a crude estimate of a function's range on a box does not hinder the usefulness of the approach, since there are multiple ways to define such a function. One way to compute such an estimate, which works for a large class of functions, is known as *interval arithmetic* [3,7,8], which in many cases provides a worst case, naive estimate of the range of the given function. For instance, for $x \in [0, 1]$, it is easy to see that the function $f(x) = x - x^2$ always takes values in $[-1, 1]$, since each of the two monomials in this polynomial takes values in $[0, 1]$. This estimate can be mechanically computed using interval arithmetic. This is clearly a very crude estimate of the range, since the actual range of f in $[-1, 1]$ is $[0, \frac{1}{4}]$. Interval arithmetic extends to multiple variables and from polynomials to trigonometric functions, logarithms, etc. using, for example, Taylor series approximations. PVS strategies for solving simply quantified inequalities, such as those involving function ψ given by Formula (1), are presented in [3]. Those strategies are based on a branch and bound algorithm using interval arithmetic.

For polynomial functions a more accurate estimation method is available through Bernstein polynomials [5]. Any polynomial $p(x)$ of degree at most n can be written in the form of a Bernstein polynomial: $p(x) = \sum_{i=0}^{n} b_i \binom{n}{i} x^i (1-x)^{n-i}$. The coefficients b_i are called *Bernstein coefficients* and are computed directly from the coefficients of p in the power basis. Once a polynomial is written in a Bernstein polynomial form, the Bernstein coefficients yield an estimate for the range of the polynomial p for $x \in [0, 1]$: $\min_{i \le n} b_i \le p(x) \le \max_{i \le n} b_i$. Furthermore, $p(0) = b_0$ and $p(1) = b_n$. This result is generally applicable to variables in an arbitrary range $[A, B]$ since any polynomial p can be translated into another polynomial q such that $q(y)$, with $y \in [0, 1]$, attains the same values as $p(x)$, with $x \in [A, B]$. The case where the range of x is unbounded has been discussed in [10].

There are many types of problems that can be approached using branch and bound algorithms. Lower and upper bounds of a function on a box that are accurate to a given precision can often be computed in this way. This can be accomplished through interval arithmetic or, if the function is a polynomial, by using Bernstein polynomials. Another problem that can be solved using a branch and bound algorithm is determining whether a given polynomial is always positive, negative, nonnegative, or nonpositive on a box. In a previous work [10], the authors presented an automated solution to this problem. That tool can be used to *automatically* and *formally* prove polynomial inequalities such as $H \geq -1.7435$, where H is the multivariate polynomial given by Formula (5). The tool itself is a collection of strategies that are implemented in PVS and are based on a branch and bound algorithm for Bernstein Polynomials [5].

Another problem that can be solved with a branch and bound algorithm is the problem of solving Boolean expressions involving more than one polynomial. This problem seems to be more common in engineering than problems with only a single polynomial. For instance, to ensure that the simply connected disk of radius 0.4 around the origin is contained in the set S given by Formula (2), it suffices to prove that for all $x, y \in [-1, 1]$,

$$x^2 + y^2 < 0.4^2 \text{ implies } (g_1(x, y) < 0 \text{ and } g_2(x, y) < 0).$$

This problem can be solved using a branch and bound method. A branch and bound approach can also be used to prove that the disk of radius 0.41 around the origin is not contained in S and to find counterexamples such as

$$(x, y) \equiv (-\frac{89186267828861}{281474976710656}, \frac{146479537812029}{562949953421312}).$$

Another global optimization problem that can be solved with a branch and bound algorithm is the problem of computing an approximation, by a list of boxes, to a set defined by a Boolean expression of polynomial inequalities. Given such a Boolean expression, three sets of subboxes of the domain can be computed: those where the property holds, those where it does not hold, and "unknown" boxes where the algorithm terminated before deciding on the truth of the expression. This problem is known as *paving*. Figure 2 shows a paving computed for the region S, where $|x| \leq 2$ and $|y| \leq 2$, using a branch and bound algorithm [2]. The union of the green rectangles is an under-approximation of S, the red rectangles are not in S, and the union of the green and white rectangles is an over-approximation of S.

This paper presents a formalization of a generic branch and bound algorithm in the higher order logic of PVS. In contrast to the branch and bound algorithms in [2, 3, 10], which use specific bounding methods and solve specific type of problems, the algorithm presented in this paper is generic with respect to the bounding function, the type of input problems, and the type of output computed by the algorithm. Since the correctness of the algorithm is formally verified in PVS, it can be used to produce strategies for automatically and formally solving a variety of global optimization problems. The use of the generic algorithm is illustrated with an instantiation that yields an automated strategy for computing estimates of the minimum and maximum value of real-valued function via interval arithmetic. The formal development presented in this paper is electronically available as part of the NASA PVS Library at http://shemesh.larc.nasa.gov/fm/ftp/larc/PVS-library.

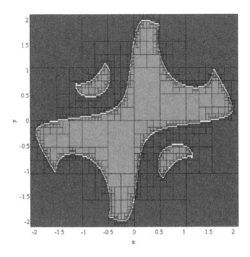

Fig. 2. Paving of a Polynomial Region

2   Generic Branch and Bound Algorithm

The motivating principle of a branch and bound algorithm is that some properties of a given function are easier to decide on small sets than on large sets. Thus, by breaking up a large domain into smaller subdomains, one can often determine whether a property holds, whereas it can not be decided easily by simply considering the large domain alone.

The rest of this section is organized as follows. The generic types used by the algorithm are described in Section 2.1. The inputs of the algorithm are given in Section 2.2. A complete description of the algorithm is presented in Section 2.3.

2.1   Generic Types

The generic branch and bound algorithm presented here depends on four generic types:

- ObjType: A type consisting of objects to analyze, such as Bernstein polynomials, functions admitting interval arithmetic operations, Boolean expressions of polynomial inequalities, etc.
- AnsType: The intended output type of the branch and bound algorithm, such as intervals containing the minimum and maximum values of a function, a Boolean value representing whether an inequality holds, a list of boxes describing an approximation to a polynomial-defined set, etc.
- DomainType: A type specifying exactly how (or where) elements of ObjType should be analyzed, such as the domain where a polynomial inequality is to be determined, or where a function is to be minimized. This may contain

not just the bounds of the interval where the polynomial is defined, but also whether it is open or closed at the boundary.

- VarType: A type representing variables of the objects to be analyzed. For instance, in the case of polynomials, VarType is a type representing the polynomial variables such as $\mathbb{N}$, where 0, 1, 2 might correspond to x_0, x_1, x_2, etc.

Specific types to substitute for these generic types are provided by the user, who chooses them with a specific application in mind. While AnsType is the intended output type of the branch and bound algorithm, this type is wrapped up in a larger record type that is called Output, which has one field consisting of an element from AnsType, and three other fields that give information about the execution of the function.

$$\text{Output} \equiv \text{ans}:\text{AnsType} \times \text{exit}:\text{boolean} \times \text{depth}:\mathbb{N} \times \text{splits}:\mathbb{N}.$$

Upon exit, the exit field will be set to true if the algorithm is forced to globally exit from the recursion, e.g., when the recursion reaches a maximum depth or a maximum number of subdivisions. As explained later, the precise conditions under which the recursion globally exits are specified by the user. The depth field counts the maximum recursion depth that the algorithm reaches along any branch during its execution. The splits field counts the total number of times that the algorithm subdivides a larger problem into two smaller problems, such as splitting a large box into two subboxes. The function mk_out takes as parameters an element of type AnsType, a Boolean value, and two naturals numbers, and builds a record of type Output.

The generic algorithm itself has functions for inputs, some of which depend on elements of the tuple type DirVar $\equiv$ boolean $\times$ VarType. During the recursion of a branch and bound algorithm, the domain often must be split in two. When this happens, a variable and a direction, i.e., VarType and a direction represented by a Boolean value, respectively, are selected for splitting the domain. The two halves of the original domain can be referred to by the two pairs (true, j) and (false, j), where j is the element of VarType referring to the variable chosen for subdivision. In the type DirVar, true refers to the left subdivision and false refers to the right subdivision.

Another type that is important for the execution of the generic algorithm is the type DirVarStack $\equiv$ stack[DirVar], which represents a stack of elements of type DirVar. The branch and bound algorithm presented in this paper implements a depth-first recursion approach. An object called dirvars of type DirVar is maintained by the algoritm, and it reflects the sequence of subdivisions, i.e., variables and directions, at any moment during the recursion.

2.2   Inputs to the Algorithm

The inputs to the generic branch and bound algorithm are listed in the table below, each with its type next to it. The element obj of type ObjType is the

Table 1. Inputs to branch_and_bound

Input	Type
simplify	[ObjType → ObjType]
evaluate	[DomainType, ObjType → AnsType]
branch	[VarType, ObjType → [ObjType, ObjType]]
subdivide	[VarType, DomainType → [DomainType, DomainType]]
denorm	[[boolean, VarType], AnsType → AnsType]
combine	[VarType, AnsType, AnsType → AnsType]
prune	[DirVarStack, AnsType, AnsType → boolean]
lex	[AnsType → boolean]
gex	[DirVarStack, AnsType, AnsType → boolean]
select	[DirVarStack, AnsType, DomainType, ObjType → [boolean, VarType]]
accumulate	[AnsType, AnsType → AnsType]
maxd	ℕ
obj	ObjType
dom	DomainType
acc	$Maybe[\text{AnsType}]$
dirvars	DirVarStack

concrete expression, e.g., a polynomial or interval expression, that the algorithm is analyzing. The element dom is the specific element of DomainType with regard to which information about obj is to be calculated. For example, if ObjType consists of polynomials, DomainType may consist of boxes that constraint the range of the polynomial variables.

The function simplify rewrites obj to make it easier to manipulate before carrying out the next recursive calculations. In many cases this function is just the identity function. However, in some cases, a canonical form of obj may yield more efficient computations.

The function evaluate gives a crude estimate of an element of AnsType that would describe obj for a particular element of DomainType. For instance, if obj is a function and the algorithm is being used to give a precise estimate for the range of the function over a box, evaluate may use interval arithmetic to give a crude estimate of the range on a specific domain without splitting this domain in two.

The function branch, for a specific element of VarType, takes an element of ObjType and gives two more elements of ObjType that correspond to splitting the problem in two. For instance, if VarType corresponds to the possible variables of a function, and if ObjType consists of polynomials written in Bernstein form, then given a specific variable x_j, the function branch will take a polynomial and turn it into two polynomials. Each of these polynomials represents the original polynomial on half of the original unit box, which has been split along the variable x_j. The two polynomials themselves are translated from each of these half boxes back to the unit box by changing the variable x_j linearly. These polynomials each represent the original polynomial on half of the original box after a linear translation in x_j.

As explained before, the input `dirvars` reflects the subdivision that have occurred up to the current recursive call. The value of this parameter at every recursive step is maintained by the algorithm. The initial value, provided by the user, is expected to be an empty stack. The value of `dirvars` can be used by several other input functions to choose the variable for subdivision at the current step, determine whether to prune the recursion tree, or decide to exit globally from the recursion.

The function `subdivide` takes an element of `DomainType` and divides it into two new elements of `DomainType`, where the exact division is specified by an element of `VarType`. For instance, `DomainType` may consist of boxes and `VarType` to variables, in which case `subdivide` may split a box in the middle along a given variable.

The function `denorm` translates an element of `AnsType`, which gives information about the object on one half of an element of `DomainType`, after that element has been split using `subdivide`, back to level of the original, non-subdivided object in the recursion. For instance, if the algorithm is designed to find a counterexample to a polynomial inequality and a box is split into two subboxes, then a counterexample found by the algorithm on one of these subboxes is also a counterexample on the larger box. In this example, the function `denorm` would translate the point where the counterexample was found to a point in the original box. The first parameter of this function, which has the type `VarType`, would represent the variable along which the original box was split, and the Boolean value would represent whether this particular subbox was the right half or the left half of the original.

The function `combine` takes two elements of type `AnsType`, each giving information about the object in question on half of the original box, and combines them into one element of `AnsType` that gives information about the object on the larger box. It depends on an element of type `VarType`, which may, for example, represent the variable along which the original box was split to give the two subboxes in question.

The function `prune` decides whether to locally exit the recursion at the current step and continue the recursion at the next step without subdividing the problem further on the current branch. It takes an accumulated value of type `AnsType` from previous steps in the recursion, namely the element `acc`, which gives information about the object in question at locations other than the current location in the domain, and uses this to decide whether it is beneficial to continue down the current branch in the recursion. For example, consider an algorithm finding an interval that is guaranteed to contain the minimum value attained by the a function. Suppose that in a branch of the recursion, this interval was reduced to $[0.9, 1.0]$, which will be stored in the `acc` element of `AnsType`. If on the current branch, the `evaluate` function gives $[1.2, 1.3]$ as as a crude estimate of the minimum on a small subset of the larger domain, then the recursion can often be stopped from further continuing down the current branch, since the minimum will not be found on the current branch.

The accumulated value `acc` that is passed as a parameter to **prune** is computed by the function **accumulate**. This function combines all of the information from previous recursive steps, along with the information gained at the current step, in the element `acc` for use further down the current branch and in other branches still unexplored. Depending on the problem that the branch and bound algorithm is trying to solve, there are cases where previous information cannot be reused in a different branch. This possibility is handled by the return type `Maybe[AnsType]` of the function **accumulate**. This type represents an undefined value, represented by `None`, or an actual value v of type `AnsType`, represented by `Some(v)`. The functions `none?` and `some?` check if an element of type `Maybe` is either `None` or `Some(v)` for some v, respectively. In the latter case, the value v can be accessed with the function `val`.

The `lex` function, which stands for *local exit*, determines when the function has locally succeeded and therefore does not need to subdivide on the current branch anymore. It considers an element of type `AnsType` given by the output of `evaluate`, and uses this information to determine success. For example, if the algorithm is proving that a function is always nonnegative, and if the function `evaluate` indicates that it is true on the small subbox represented at this point in the recursion tree, then the algorithm has proved the result on this local subbox and does not need to divide the subbox further. It then moves on with the recursion elsewhere.

The function `gex`, which stands for *global exit*, determines whether, at the current recursion step, the algorithm should exit completely from the recursion without computing anything else. This is desirable when the recursion has reached a depth that is larger than the user wants, and it is also desirable when the algorithm has found a satisfactory answer at the current recursive step and no longer needs to continue the recursion. One example of a condition that warrants a global exit is when the algorithm is searching for a counterexample to the positivity of a function and it finds such a counterexample at the current step.

The function `select` determines where the next subdivision will occur. For example, if `DomainType` consists of boxes in n variables, then any subdivision of a box will occur along a particular variable. In this context, the `select` function will determine the variable along which to subdivide and a Boolean value representing whether the recursion should first compute either the left subdivision or the right one. An additional parameter to this function is `dirvars`, which gives information about the other variables that have been chosen for subdivision at previous steps in the current branch. This allows `select` to be defined in a way that is fair, meaning that in every possible infinite branch of the infinite recursion tree, every variable occurs an infinite number of times.

The input `maxd` represents a maximum recursion depth and removes the possibility of a non-terminating algorithm. When the current depth reaches `maxd`, the algorithm forces a local exit as opposed to a global one. Depending on the problem that the branch and bound algorithm is solving, an output can still be sound even if some branches have reached the maximum depth. Hence, even though the algorithm always terminates, it may take a very long time to do so. If the user wants to specify a global exit when the maximum depth maxd is reached, this has to be done through the input function gex.

2.3   The Branching Algorithm

The algorithm branch_and_bound is defined in Figure 3. Lines 1-12 define the bounding and pruning aspects of the branch and bound algorithm. These lines concern the computation of a crude estimate for the object obj in the domain dom (Line 5). It is noted that the estimate, namely thisans, is actually computed for the object thisobj, which is intended to be a simplified version of obj (Line 4). The accumulated value thisacc is computed from the previous value acc and the computed answer thisans (Line 6). The function gex uses the information on thisacc, thisans, and the stack dirvars to determine if the algorithm should stop (Line 8). This information is propagated to the remaining recursive calls through the field exit in thisans. If the answer value thisans is good enough, which is determined by the functions lex and prune, or if the maximum depth maxd is reached, the current recursive call ends (Lines 11-12). In this case, the output consists of the answer thisans, the Boolean value computed by the function gex, a value of depth that is equivalent to the length of the stack dirvars, and 0, which represents the number of splits. The function mk_out builds such a record of type Output (Line 9).

The branching aspect of the algorithm is defined in Lines 14-39. First, a direction dir and a variable v are selected for subdivision (Line 14). Subdivided objects obj_l, obj_r, and subdivided domains dom_l, dom_r are computed accordingly (Line 15-18). Then, the first recursive call, in the direction determined by dir, is made (Lines 19-21). When the recursion returns, it may be the case that a global exit was signaled during the previous recursive call (Line 24). In this case, an answer is computed from the value returned by the recursive call and the current answer thisans (Lines 24-25). In order to combine these values, the answer from the subdivided domain dom_1 has to be translated to the whole domain dom. This is performed by the function denorm (Line 24). The values of the fields depth and splits in the output record are computed appropriately (Line 25).

The second recursive call is specified in Lines 27-35. In this case, the answers returned by the two calls, for each one of the subdivisions, are combined into an answer for the whole domain (Line 32). The output record consists of this combined answer and appropriate values for the fields exit, depth, and splits (Lines 34-35).

3   Correctness of the Algorithm

The output of the function branch_and_bound in Figure 3 has type Output. In order for the algorithm to be useful for solving problems in global optimization, the element of Output returned by the algorithm must satisfy a correctness property. Not only does the algorithm branch_and_bound take a generic set of

```
01 : branch_and_bound(simplify, evaluate, branch, subdivide, denorm, combine, prune,
02 :         lex, gex, select, accumulate, maxd, obj, dom, acc, dirvars) : Output ≡
03 :   let
04 :     thisobj = simplify(obj),
05 :     thisans = evaluate(dom, thisobj),
06 :     thisacc = if none?(acc) then thisans
07 :                   else accumulate(val(acc), thisans) endif,
08 :     thisexit = gex(dirvars, thisacc, thisans),
09 :     thisout = mk_out(thisans, thisexit, length(dirvars), 0)
10 :   in
11 :     if length(dirvars) = maxd or lex(thisans) or thisexit or
12 :         prune(dirvars, thisacc, thisans) then thisout
13 :     else let
14 :         (dir, v) = select(dirvars, thisacc, dom, thisobj),
15 :         (obj_l, obj_r) = branch(v, thisobj),
16 :         (obj_1, obj_2) = if dir then (obj_l, obj_r) else (obj_r, obj_l) endif,
17 :         (dom_l, dom_r) = subdivide(v, dom),
18 :         (dom_1, dom_2) = if dir then (dom_l, dom_r) else (dom_r, dom_l) endif,
19 :         out_1 = branch_and_bound(simplify, evaluate, branch, subdivide, denorm,
20 :                         combine, prune, lex, gex, select, accumulate, maxd,
21 :                         obj_1, dom_1, thisacc, push((dir, v), dirvars))
22 :       in
23 :         if out_1.exit then
24 :           mk_out(combine(v, denorm((dir, v), out_1.ans), thisans), true,
25 :                     out_1.depth, out_1.splits + 1)
26 :         else let
27 :             newacc = accumulate(thisacc, out_1.ans),
28 :             out_2 = branch_and_bound(simplify, evaluate, branch, subdivide, denorm,
29 :                             combine, lex, gex, select, accumulate, maxd,
30 :                             obj_2, dom_2, newacc, push((¬dir, v), dirvars))
31 :             (out_l, out_r) = if dir then (out_1, out_2) else (out_2, out_1) endif,
32 :             ans = combine(v, denorm((true, v), out_l.ans), denorm((false, v), out_r.ans))
33 :           in
34 :             mk_out(ans, out_2.exit, max(out_1.depth, out_2.depth),
35 :                     out_1.splits + out_2.splits + 1)
36 :         endif
37 :     endif
```

Fig. 3. The function branch_and_bound

inputs with numerous possible instantiations, but its correctness property is generic as well. This correctness property is represented by the abstract predicate *sound?*, which has the type indicated below.

$$sound? : [\texttt{DomainType}, \texttt{ObjType}, \texttt{AnsType} \rightarrow \texttt{boolean}]$$

The strength of a generic branching algorithm such as branch_and_bound relies on the fact that it reduces the correctness proof of a particular instantiation to proving simpler statements about the compatible behavior of the input functions evaluate, simplify, subdivide, branch, denorm, and combine. The correctness property depends *only* on these input function parameters. In particular, the generic algorithm has been proved to be *sound* for any particular instantiation of the functions lex, gex, prune, and select. Those functions are usually the most technically involved since they deal with heuristics that improve the efficiency of the algorithm. All of these concerns are abstracted away in the correctness stament of the algorithm.

The main correctness result is stated as follows.

Theorem 1. *For all inputs that satisfy*

- *accommodates?(sound?, evaluate),*
- *simplify_invariant?(sound?, simplify),*
- *evaluate_simplify?(evaluate, simplify),*
- *branch_simplify?(branch, simplify),*
- *subdiv_presound?(sound?, subdivide, branch, denorm, combine), and*
- *subdiv_sound?(sound?, subdivide, branch, denorm, combine),*

sound?(dom, obj, bnb.ans) is true, *where* bnb *is equal to*

$$branch\_and\_bound(simplify, evaluate, branch, subdivide, denorm, combine,$$
$$prune, lex, gex, select, accumulate, maxd, obj, dom, None, empty\_stack).$$

The proof of this theorem, which has been mechanically verified in PVS, proceeds by induction on maxd − length(dirvars). The predicates *accommodates?*, *simplify_invariant?*, *evaluate_simplify?*, *branch_simplify?*, *subdiv_presound?* and *subdiv_sound?* are defined as follows.

The predicate *accommodates?* states that the function evaluate computes a valid estimate for the object obj on the domain dom.

$$accommodates?(sound?, \texttt{evaluate}) \equiv$$
$$\forall\,(\texttt{dom}, \texttt{obj}) : sound?(\texttt{dom}, \texttt{obj}, \texttt{evaluate}(\texttt{dom}, \texttt{obj})).$$

The predicate *simplify_invariant?* states the function simplify preserves soundness.

$$simplify\_invariant?(sound?, \texttt{simplify}) \equiv \forall\,(\texttt{dom}, \texttt{obj}, \texttt{ans}) :$$
$$sound?(\texttt{dom}, \texttt{obj}, \texttt{ans}) \iff sound?(\texttt{dom}, \texttt{simplify}(\texttt{obj}), \texttt{ans}).$$

The predicate *evaluate_simplify?* states that simplified objects evaluate to the same value.

$$evaluate\_simplify?(\texttt{evaluate}, \texttt{simplify}) \equiv \forall\, (\texttt{dom}, \texttt{obj}):$$
$$\texttt{evaluate}(\texttt{dom}, \texttt{obj}) = \texttt{evaluate}(\texttt{dom}, \texttt{simplify}(\texttt{obj})).$$

The predicate *branch_simplify?* states that the function simplify and branch commute.

$$branch\_simplify?(\texttt{branch}, \texttt{simplify}) \equiv \forall (v, \texttt{obj}):$$
$$\texttt{let}\ (\texttt{obj}_l, \texttt{obj}_r) = \texttt{branch}(v, \texttt{obj})\ \texttt{in}$$
$$\texttt{branch}(v, \texttt{simplify}(\texttt{obj})) = (\texttt{simplify}(\texttt{obj}_l), \texttt{simplify}(\texttt{obj}_r)).$$

The last two predicates specify the core behavior of the functions subdivide, branch, denorm, and combine. They express that the soundness of the output on the whole domain can be deduced from the soundness of the outputs on the subdivided domains. The former predicate refers to the case where only one branch is recursively explored. The latter predicate refers to the case where both left and right branches are recursively explored.

$$subdiv\_presound?(sound?, \texttt{subdivide}, \texttt{branch}, \texttt{denorm}, \texttt{combine}) \equiv$$
$$\forall\, (v, \texttt{dom}, \texttt{obj}, \texttt{dir}, \texttt{ans}_1, \texttt{ans}_2):$$
$$\texttt{let}\ (\texttt{dom}_l, \texttt{dom}_r) = \texttt{subdivide}(v, \texttt{dom}),$$
$$(\texttt{obj}_l, \texttt{obj}_r) = \texttt{branch}(v, \texttt{obj})$$
$$\texttt{in}\ sound?(\texttt{dom}, \texttt{obj}, \texttt{ans}_1)\ \texttt{and}$$
$$(\texttt{dir} \implies sound?(\texttt{dom}_l, \texttt{obj}_l, \texttt{ans}_2))\ \texttt{and}$$
$$(\neg\texttt{dir} \implies sound?(\texttt{dom}_r, \texttt{obj}_r, \texttt{ans}_2))$$
$$\implies sound?(\texttt{dom}, \texttt{obj}, \texttt{combine}(v, \texttt{denorm}((\texttt{dir}, v), \texttt{ans}_2, \texttt{ans}_1))).$$

$$subdiv\_sound?(sound?, \texttt{subdivide}, \texttt{branch}, \texttt{denorm}, \texttt{combine}) \equiv$$
$$\forall\, (v, \texttt{dom}, \texttt{obj}, \texttt{dir}, \texttt{ans}_1, \texttt{ans}_2):$$
$$\texttt{let}\ (\texttt{dom}_l, \texttt{dom}_r) = \texttt{subdivide}(v, \texttt{dom}),$$
$$(\texttt{obj}_l, \texttt{obj}_r) = \texttt{branch}(v, \texttt{obj})$$
$$\texttt{in}\ sound?(\texttt{dom}_l, \texttt{obj}_l, \texttt{ans}_1)\ \texttt{and}\ sound?(\texttt{dom}_r, \texttt{obj}_r, \texttt{ans}_2)$$
$$\implies sound?(\texttt{dom}, \texttt{obj}, \texttt{combine}(v, \texttt{denorm}((\texttt{true}, v), \texttt{ans}_1),$$
$$\texttt{denorm}((\texttt{false}, v), \texttt{ans}_2))).$$

Theorem 1 is significantly simpler when the function simplify is the identity. The next corollary considers this case.

Corollary 1. *Let I be the identity function on the type ObjType. For all inputs that satisfy*

- *accommodates?*(*sound?*, `evaluate`),
- *subdiv_presound?*(*sound?*, `subdivide, branch, denorm, combine`), *and*
- *subdiv_sound?*(*sound?*, `subdivide, branch, denorm, combine`),

sound?(`dom, obj, bnb.ans`) *is* `true`, *where* **bnb** *is equal to*

$$branch\_and\_bound(I, \mathtt{evaluate, branch, subdivide, denorm, combine, prune,}$$
$$\mathtt{lex, gex, select, accumulate, maxd, obj, dom, None, empty\_stack}).$$

4 Branch and Bound Algorithm for Interval Expressions

This section presents an instantiation of the function `branch_and_bound` in Figure 3 that yields a strategy in PVS for computing estimates of the minimum and maximum values of a multivariate real-valued functions. These estimates are found using interval arithmetic.

In order to define this instantiation, it is necessary to provide a deep embedding of arithmetic expressions. Such an embedding has been developed and is available as part of the interval arithmetic development in the NASA PVS Library.[1] The abstract data type `IntervalExpr`, which is part of the library, represents arithmetic expressions constructed from basic operations, power, absolute value, square root, trigonometric functions, the irrational constants π and e, the exponential and logarithm functions, numerical constants, and variables that range over closed intervals. Henceforth, elements of type `IntervalExpr` are called *expressions*. The following types and functions are also available.

- `Interval`: A tuple of two elements that represents the upper and lower bounds of a closed, non-empty, interval. Elements of this type are called *intervals*.
- `Box`: A list of elements of type `Interval`. Elements of this type are called *boxes*.
- `Env`: A list of real numbers representing an evaluation environment for the variables in a given expression. Elements of this type are called *environments*.
- `well_typed?`: A predicate that has as parameters a box B and an expression E. The predicate holds when E is well-defined in B. This predicate is used to avoid the case of division by zero.
- `eval`: A function that has as parameters an expression E and an environment Γ. The function returns a real value that corresponds to the evaluation of E in Γ.
- `Eval`: A function that has as parameters an expression E and a box B. The function returns an interval value that correspond to the interval arithmetic evaluation of E in B.

The following two key theorems of interval arithmetic are mechanically proved in PVS.

---

[1] http://shemesh.larc.nasa.gov/people/cam/Interval

Theorem 2 (Inclusion Theorem). *For all B, E, and Γ,*

$$well\_typed?(B, E) \text{ and } \Gamma \in B \text{ implies } eval(E, \Gamma) \in Eval(E, B).$$

Theorem 3 (Fundamental Theorem). *For all $B_1 \subseteq B_2$ and E,*

$$well\_typed?(B_2, E) \text{ implies } Eval(E, B_1) \subseteq Eval(E, B_2).$$

A simple of instantiation of the generic branch and bound algorithm is obtained as follows. The parameter types `ObjType`, `AnsType`, and `DomainType` are instantiated with the concrete types `IntervalExpr`, `Interval`, and `Box`. The parameter type `VarType`, representing variables in `IntervalExpr`, is instantiated with the concrete type `nat`. Furthermore,

- the function `evaluate` is defined as $evaluate(B, E) \equiv Eval(E, B)$,
- the function `branch` is defined as $branch(n, E) \equiv (E, E)$,
- the function `subdivide` is defined as $subdivide(n, B) \equiv split(n, B)$ that returns two boxes that are equal to B except in their n-th interval, where the original interval is divided into mid-left and mid-right intervals,
- the functions `combine` and `accumulate` are both defined as the union of two intervals,
- the functions `simplify` and `denorm` are defined as identity functions on the types `IntervalExpr` and `Interval`, respectively.

Since the soundness theorem of the generic branch and bound algorithm does not depend on the predicates `gex`, `lex`, or `prune`, they can be arbitrarily instantiated. In particular, they are instantiated such that they always return `false`. This means that the instantiated branch and bound algorithm, called `simple_interval`, completely explores the recursion tree up to the maximum depth. The direction and variable selection function `select` is simply defined using a round-robin approach.

$$simple\_interval(\text{maxd}, E, B) : \text{Output} \equiv$$
$$branch\_and\_bound(\text{simplify, evaluate, branch, subdivide, denorm,}$$
$$\text{combine, prune, lex, gex, select, accumulate, maxd, } E, B).$$

The intended soundness property of the function `simple_interval` is expressed by the following predicate.

$$sound?(B, E, \text{ans}) \equiv \text{well\_typed?}(B, E) \Longrightarrow \forall (\Gamma \in B) : eval(E, \Gamma) \in \text{ans}.$$

The following theorem has been proved in PVS. It follows from Corollary 1. The fact that the predicate *accommodates?* holds follows directly from the Inclusion Theorem (Theorem 2). The properties concerning *subdiv_presound?* and *subdiv_sound?* are consequences of the Fundamental Theorem (Theorem 3).

Theorem 4. *For any maximum depth* maxd, *expression* E, *and box* B, $sound?(B, E, simple\_interval(\text{maxd}, E, B).\text{ans})$ *holds.*

The function `simple_interval` and its correctness property (Theorem 4) are the basis of a computational reflection strategy in PVS for computing estimates of the minimum and maximum values of real expressions. The strategy, called `simple-numerical`, takes a PVS real expression, possibly involving variables, and reflects it in the type `IntervalExpr`. The key step in the strategy is the ground evaluation of the function `simple_interval`, which implements the instantiated branch and bound algorithm. Theorem 4 guarantees the soundness of the computation in the PVS logic. For instance, using `simple_interval`, it can be automatically proved the statement $|\psi(v, \phi)| \leq 3.825$, where ψ is defined as in Formula (1), $v \in [200, 250]$, and $|\phi| \leq 35$. This result, which is used in the correctness proof of an alerting algorithm for aircraft performing a parallel landing [9], states that for an aircraft flying at a ground speed between 200 and 250 knots, the maximum angular speed is less than 4 degrees (more precisely, less than 3.825 degrees), assuming a maximum bank angle of 35 degrees.

The development `interval_arith` in the NASA PVS Library includes more sophisticated instantiations of `branch_and_bound` and strategies based on these instantiations for computing estimates of the minimum and maximum values of real-valued functions up to a precision provided by the user and for proving real-valued inequalities. These instantiations make use of the input functions `select`, e.g., for implementing better heuristics to chose the direction of the branching and the variable to subdivide, of `lex`, e.g., for stopping the current branch when a given precision is reached, of `gex`, e.g., for stopping the recursion when a given inequality cannot be proved, and of `prune`, e.g., for pruning a branch when the recursion will not improve the accumulated value.

5   Conclusion

The generic branch and bound algorithm presented in this paper has been used in several contexts, e.g., computing the range of a function on a box using interval arithmetic, computing the range of a polynomial on a box using Bernstein polynomials, deciding whether a simply quantified polynomial inequality holds on a box, deciding whether a Boolean expression involving polynomial inequalities holds on a box, and paving a region defined by polynomial inequalities. For each of these instantiations, the correctness statement follows almost immediately from the correctness statement for the generic algorithm. In each case, this requires only proving certain properties about the input functions to the generic algorithm.

Strategies similar to the one described in Section 4, based on interval arithmetic and subdivision, are available in PVS [3], Coq [6], HOL Light [14], etc. The novelty of the work presented in this paper is not the development of interval arithmetic strategies, but the fact these strategies are implemented on top of a formally verified generic branching algorithm that can be instantiated with different domains. In addition to instances related to interval arithmetic and Bernstein polynomials, many other instances of the generic branch and bound algorithm are being considered including Taylor models and affine arithmetic.

The approach presented in this paper is similar, in spirit, to that of Carlier et al. [1] on the verification of a constraint solver, where the application domain is abstracted away. However, the emphasis here is to support the development of efficient automated strategies that execute the generic algorithm via computational reflection [4]. Indeed, even the simple interval arithmetic presented here, which fully explores the recursion tree, is significantly more efficient that the strategies presented in [3]. Furthermore, since the correctness statement of the algorithm does not depend on parameter functions for variable selection method and pruning, they can be freely instantiated for implementing advanced heuristics. In the case of Bernstein polynomials, this feature has allowed the authors to experiment with different pruning heuristics for the algorithm proposed in [10].

References

1. Carlier, M., Dubois, C., Gotlieb, A.: A certified constraint solver over finite domains. In: Giannakopoulou, D., Méry, D. (eds.) FM 2012. LNCS, vol. 7436, pp. 116–131. Springer, Heidelberg (2012)
2. Crespo, L.G., Muñoz, C.A., Narkawicz, A.J., Kenny, S.P., Giesy, D.P.: Uncertainty analysis via failure domain characterization: Polynomial requirement functions. In: Proceedings of European Safety and Reliability Conference, Troyes, France (September 2011)
3. Daumas, M., Lester, D., Muñoz, C.: Verified real number calculations: A library for interval arithmetic. IEEE Transactions on Computers 58(2), 1–12 (2009)
4. Harrison, J.: Metatheory and reflection in theorem proving: A survey and critique. Technical Report CRC-053, SRI Cambridge, Millers Yard, Cambridge, UK (1995), http://www.cl.cam.ac.uk/jrh13/papers/reflect.dvi.gz+
5. Lorentz, G.G.: Bernstein Polynomials, 2nd edn. Chelsea Publishing Company, New York (1986)
6. Melquiond, G.: Proving bounds on real-valued functions with computations. In: Armando, A., Baumgartner, P., Dowek, G. (eds.) IJCAR 2008. LNCS (LNAI), vol. 5195, pp. 2–17. Springer, Heidelberg (2008)
7. Moa, B.: Interval Methods for Global Optimization. PhD thesis, University of Victoria (2007)
8. Moore, R.E., Kearfott, R.B., Cloud, M.J.: Introduction to Interval Analysis. Cambridge University Press (2009)
9. Muñoz, C., Carreño, V., Dowek, G., Butler, R.: Formal verification of conflict detection algorithms. International Journal on Software Tools for Technology Transfer 4(3), 371–380 (2003)
10. Muñoz, C., Narkawicz, A.: Formalization of a Representation of Bernstein Polynomials and Applications to Global Optimization. Journal of Automated Reasoning 51(2), 151–196 (2013), http://dx.doi.org/10.1007/s10817-012-9256-3, doi:10.1007/s10817-012-9256-3
11. Neumaier, A.: Complete search in continuous global optimization and constraint satisfaction. Acta Numerica 13, 271–369

12. Owre, S., Rushby, J., Shankar, N.: PVS: A prototype verification system. In: Kapur, D. (ed.) CADE 1992. LNCS, vol. 607, pp. 748–752. Springer, Heidelberg (1992)
13. Ray, S., Nataraj, P.S.: An efficient algorithm for range computation of polynomials using the Bernstein form. Journal of Global Optimization 45, 403–426 (2009)
14. Solovyev, A., Hales, T.C.: Formal verification of nonlinear inequalities with Taylor interval approximations. In: Brat, G., Rungta, N., Venet, A. (eds.) NFM 2013. LNCS, vol. 7871, pp. 383–397. Springer, Heidelberg (2013)

Author Index